Expert Hadoop® Administration

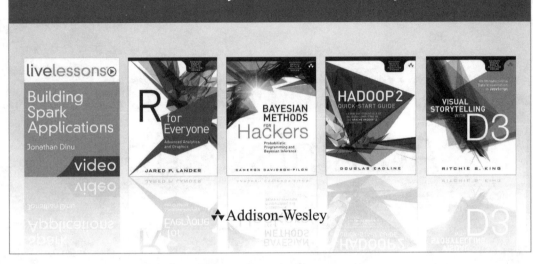

Expert Hadoop® Administration

Managing, Tuning, and Securing Spark, YARN, and HDFS

Sam R. Alapati

Addison-Wesley

Boston • Columbus • Indianapolis • New York • San Francisco • Amsterdam • Cape Town
Dubai • London • Madrid • Milan • Munich • Paris • Montreal • Toronto • Delhi • Mexico City
São Paulo • Sydney • Hong Kong • Seoul • Singapore • Taipei • Tokyo

For information about buying this title in bulk quantities, or for special sales opportunities (which may include electronic versions; custom cover designs; and content particular to your business, training goals, marketing focus, or branding interests), please contact our corporate sales department at corpsales@pearsoned.com or (800) 382-3419.

For government sales inquiries, please contact governmentsales@pearsoned.com.

For questions about sales outside the U.S., please contact intlcs@pearson.com.

Visit us on the Web: informit.com/aw

Library of Congress Control Number: 2016954056

ISBN-13: 978-0-13-459719-5
ISBN-10: 0-13-459719-2

1 16

To my cousin, Alapati Srinath, whom I consider my own brother. Thank you, Srinath, for your kindness, affection, and above all, graciousness, all of which have meant a lot to me over the years.

Contents

Foreword

Apache Hadoop 2 and the upcoming 3 were a major step forward in moving beyond the paradigm of MapReduce. At the core of this is the new YARN (Yet Another Resource Negotiator) processing framework for creating APIs and processing engines on top of Hadoop and HDFS, including the original MapReduce paradigm. Hadoop 2 is a significant upgrade to Hadoop 1, requiring updates to how a cluster is set up, managed and administered. This book provides everything a developer, operator or administrator would need to manage a production Hadoop 2 cluster of any size.

While Hadoop 2 and 3 at the core are HDFS and YARN, there are many other projects that are included in a typical production Hadoop cluster. For example, Hive, Pig, Spark, Flume and Kafka are often paired with the core Hadoop infrastructure to provide additional functionality and features. This book includes coverage of many of these complementary projects with introductory materials good for developers and administrators alike.

Sam Alapati is the principal Hadoop administrator at Sabre Holdings and has been working with production Hadoop clusters for the last six years. He's uniquely qualified to cover the administration of production clusters and has pulled everything together in this single resource. The depth of experience that Sam brings to this book has enabled him to write much more than a simple introduction to Hadoop and Spark. While it does provide that introductory material, it will be the go-to resource for administrators looking to spec, size, expand and secure their production Hadoop clusters.

—Paul Dix, Series Editor

Preface

Apache Hadoop is a popular open-source software framework for storing and processing large sets of data on a platform consisting of clusters of commodity hardware. The main idea behind Hadoop is to move computation to the data, instead of the traditional way of moving data to computation. Scalability lies at the heart of Hadoop, and one of the big reasons for its considerable popularity in the big data world we live in today is its extreme cost effectiveness owing to the use of commodity servers and open-source software.

I started working on this book in the fall of 2014. Hadoop 2 had come out a few months earlier, and there were numerous interesting changes in the Hadoop architecture in the new release. There was one very good book on administering generic (without the use of a third-party vendor's tools) Hadoop clusters (*Hadoop Operations* by Eric Sammer), but, over time, it became outdated in several areas (it was published in 2012). Tom White's book *Hadoop: The Definitive Guide* of course is wonderful, and it contains several useful discussions pertaining to Hadoop administration, but it's a book more geared toward developers and architects than cluster administrators. I decided to write this book to provide Hadoop users a comprehensive guide to administering, securing, and optimizing their Hadoop clusters.

As I progressed with the book, Spark became the most important processing framework for Hadoop. I therefore added four chapters to discuss the architecture of Spark, the nature of Spark applications and how to manage and optimize Spark jobs running in a Hadoop cluster.

In this book, I explain how to manage, optimize, and secure Hadoop environments by working directly with the Hadoop configuration files. You may wonder if you really need to learn how to administer Hadoop from the ground level up. Like many of the people that manage Hadoop environments, I use third-party Hadoop distributions such as Cloudera and Hortonworks. Of course, using a tool such as Cloudera Manager or Apache Ambari to manage a Hadoop cluster makes your life really easy. However, I realized that in order to master Hadoop environments, and to get the most out of your Hadoop cluster, you must understand what actually happens behind the scenes when you work with a management tool to administer your cluster. This is possible only if you learn how to build a cluster from scratch and learn how to configure it for various purposes—high availability, performance, security, encryption—as you go along.

Hadoop comes with a large number of configurable properties. In order to take advantage of Hadoop's powerful capabilities, you must understand the critical performance, security, high-availability and other configuration parameters and know how to tune them. To this end, I've explained all of the key administration-related Hadoop configuration properties in this book, along with plenty of examples, so you can configure, secure, and optimize your cluster with confidence.

Hadoop is an exciting area to work in, with its interactions with software that fall under the umbrella of the "Hadoop ecosphere." In this book, my main focus is on core Hadoop itself, specifically on HDFS, the Hadoop distributed file system, and YARN, the processing framework of Hadoop. I do discuss several members of the Hadoop—ecosphere, such as Apache Sqoop, Apache Flume and Apache Spark—but the emphasis is mostly on how to manage the Hadoop infrastructure itself. To this end, I spend quite a bit of time discussing the architecture of both HDFS and YARN in this book.

Who This Book Is For

I wrote this book with the Hadoop administrator in mind. However, you do not need to be a full-time Hadoop administrator to benefit from this book. If you're a big data architect, developer, or analyst, there are several things in this book that'll prove to be of use to you.

How This Book Is Structured and What It Covers

This book is divided into 5 parts, spread over 21 chapters. Following is a chapter-by-chapter summary of what this book covers.

Part I: Introduction to Hadoop—Architecture and Hadoop Clusters

- Chapter 1, "Introduction to Hadoop and Its Environment," introduces you to Hadoop and big data in general. You learn how Hadoop differs from traditional databases and about the concept of a data lake. You also learn where Hadoop fits in with big data and data science. It also introduces the concept of a Hadoop cluster.

  The chapter outlines the roles of the key Hadoop components and members of the Hadoop ecosphere, such as ZooKeeper, Apache Sqoop, Apache Flume and Apache Kafka.

  Although Hadoop 1 belongs to history now, it offers a convenient means of tracing the evolution of Hadoop to its current incarnation, especially how it separates processing and scheduling and allows multiple processing engines beyond just MapReduce. I therefore review the key differences between Hadoop 1 and Hadoop 2 to put things in perspective and to help you understand where Hadoop might be headed.

  This chapter provides a very brief introduction to MapReduce and Apache Spark, the two main computational frameworks for Hadoop, as well Pig and Hive. The chapter also describes popular Hadoop data ingestion frameworks such as Apache Flume and Apache Kafka. The chapter wraps up with a review of the main areas of focus for Hadoop administrators, such as resource allocation, job scheduling, performance tuning and security.

- Chapter 2, "An Introduction to the Architecture of Hadoop," introduces the architecture of Hadoop and explains how HDFS supports data storage and YARN, the other main component of Hadoop, provides the data processing capability.
- Chapter 3, "Creating and Configuring a Simple Hadoop Cluster," explains, step by step, how to create and configure a single node, pseudo-distributed cluster. While you can't do a whole lot of big data processing with a single node cluster, I do this so you learn the installation procedures without worrying about setting up multiple nodes right at the beginning. Everything you learn in this chapter carries over to the installation and configuring of a "real," multinode Hadoop cluster.
- Chapter 4, "Planning for and Creating a Fully Distributed Cluster," explains how to plan for a Hadoop cluster and how to size one. I show you the step-by-step procedures involved in creating a multinode Hadoop cluster.

  Once you learn how to create a Hadoop cluster, you need to know how to modify the default Hadoop configuration. Hadoop comes with a large number of configurable properties for all its capabilities, such as storage, processing, resource allocation and security.

  One of the key functions of a Hadoop administrator is to know how to configure, tune and optimize their cluster by setting the correct values for a large number of configuration properties. This chapter shows you how you get started with the configuration of Hadoop. You'll also learn about how to configure Hadoop services, its web interfaces and the various Hadoop ports.

Part II: Hadoop Application Frameworks

- Chapter 5, "Running Applications in a Cluster—The MapReduce Framework (and Hive and Pig)," explains the main concepts of MapReduce, which for many years was the only major processing framework available in Hadoop. With Hadoop 2, MapReduce isn't the only processing framework but is still used heavily in many Hadoop environments. The chapter shows the well-known WordCount program and how to run it in MapReduce.

  The chapter also introduces you to Apache Hive and Apache Pig, two popular data processing frameworks in many Hadoop shops.
- Chapter 6, "Running Applications in a Cluster—The Spark Framework," introduces Apache Spark, which is poised to take over from MapReduce as Hadoop's main processing framework. This chapter focuses on the architecture and installation of Spark, as well as how to load data into Spark from various sources.
- Chapter 7, "Running Spark Applications," explains what Spark resilient distributed datasets (RDDs) are and shows how to work with them. This chapter also shows

you how to run Spark jobs interactively, through the `spark-submit` command. You also learn the various ways to configure Spark applications and how to monitor Spark applications.

This chapter also introduces Spark Streaming, for handling streaming data, and Spark SQL, for handling structured data.

Part III: Managing and Protecting Hadoop Data and High Availability

- Chapter 8, "The Role of the NameNode and How HDFS Works," is a deep dive into how the NameNode and the DataNodes interact. You also learn how to configure rack awareness in your cluster.

  Data replication is the calling card of HDFS, and you'll learn about how HDFS organizes its data and how data replication works. You'll also learn how clients read data from HDFS and write data to HDFS. Finally, this chapter explains the HDFS recovery processes.

  Centralized cache management in HDFS offers key benefits, and this chapter explains the concepts of centralized cache management, as well as how to configure caching and manage it.
- Chapter 9, "HDFS Commands, HDFS Permissions and HDFS Storage," is about managing HDFS storage with HDFS shell commands. You'll also learn about the `dfsadmin` utility, a key ally in managing HDFS. The chapter also shows how to manage HDFS file permissions and create HDFS users.

  As a Hadoop administrator, one of your key tasks is to manage HDFS storage. The chapter shows how to check HDFS usage and how to allocate space quotas to HDFS users. The chapter also discusses when and how to rebalance HDFS data, as well as how you can reclaim HDFS space.
- Chapter 10, "Data Protection, File Formats and Accessing HDFS," focuses on safeguarding Hadoop data. In addition, the chapter discusses the compression of data and various Hadoop file formats. Finally, the chapter shows you how to access HDFS data through HTTP, using WebHDFS and HttpFS.
- Chapter 11, "NameNode Operations, High Availability and Federation," starts off with a detailed explanation of NameNode operations. You'll also learn about the checkpointing process and how to configure it. The chapter explains how the NameNode enters and leaves the safe mode of operations. You'll also learn how to back up the NameNode metadata, which is absolutely critical for the functioning of a Hadoop cluster.

  The chapter explains how to configure HDFS high availability through setting up a Standby NameNode.

Part IV: Moving Data, Allocating Resources, Scheduling Jobs and Security

- In Chapter 12, "Moving Data Into and Out of Hadoop," you'll learn how to move data through built-in HDFS file system commands, as well as through the DistCp utility, which enables you to move data between Hadoop clusters.

  The chapter shows you how to move data between a Hadoop cluster and a relational database through the Sqoop utility. You'll also learn how to ingest data from various external sources through Apache Flume and Apache Kafka.
- Chapter 13, "Resource Allocation in a Hadoop Cluster," explains the topic of resource allocation in a Hadoop cluster. You'll learn how to configure resource allocation among users and groups through the two main Hadoop built-in schedulers—the Capacity Scheduler and the Fair Scheduler.
- Chapter 14, "Working with Oozie and Hue to Manage Job Workflows," shows you how to use two very important components of a typical Hadoop environment—Apache Oozie and Apache Hue—to configure jobs and manage them, as well as to access HDFS, and to work with Hive, Pig, Impala and other processing frameworks.
- Chapter 15, "Securing Hadoop," is about securing Hadoop environments. The main thrust of this chapter is the setting up of authorization through Kerberos, an open-source security framework used widely in Hadoop environments. You'll also learn how to set up role-based authentication through Apache Sentry.

  This chapter also shows you how to audit Hadoop and YARN operations and how to secure Hadoop data through Hadoop's HDFS Transparent Encryption feature.

Part V: Monitoring, Optimization and Troubleshooting

- Chapter 16, "Managing Jobs, Using Hue and Performing Routine Tasks," shows you how to use the `yarn` command to monitor and manage jobs. The chapter explains how to perform various routine management tasks such as decommissioning and recommissioning nodes.

  The chapter also shows how to set up ResourceManager high availability.
- Chapter 17, "Monitoring, Metrics and Hadoop Logging," introduces Hadoop metrics and how to make the most of them. There's a brief review of how to use Ganglia to monitor Hadoop. The chapter discusses the basics of Linux system monitoring.

  The chapter reviews the most frequently used Hadoop web UIs to monitor your cluster. Hadoop logging is an important and complex topic, and the chapter shows you how to view various Hadoop-related logs and how to administer logging.
- Chapter 18, "Tuning the Cluster Resources, Optimizing MapReduce Jobs and Benchmarking," shows how to benchmark the performance of a Hadoop cluster with the TeraSort and the TestDFSIO testing tools.

The chapter's main focus is on configuring a cluster for optimal performance through setting memory and storage parameters in an efficient manner. The chapter shows how to tune the performance of MapReduce jobs, as well as offers pointers for optimizing Hive and Pig jobs.

- Chapter 19, "Configuring and Tuning Apache Spark on YARN," and the next chapter are dedicated to the configuration and tuning of Apache Spark running on YARN. The chapter also shows how to configure resources for Spark and how to monitor Spark applications.
- Chapter 20, "Optimizing Spark Applications," discusses the Spark execution model in detail. The chapter explains key aspects of Spark performance such as partitioning, parallelism, data serialization, compression and caching. You'll learn about shuffle operations and how to minimize them.
- Chapter 21, "Troubleshooting Hadoop—A Sampler," is a brief review of Hadoop troubleshooting. It discusses space- and memory-related issues, such as JVM garage collection strategies, and common failures that occur in a Hadoop cluster.

Hadoop is an exciting environment to work in, with new processing frameworks and tools coming on board continuously, keeping you on your toes all the time. It's, indeed, quite an exhilarating journey! I've thoroughly enjoyed writing this book, just as I do administering Hadoop clusters. I hope you enjoy reading and using the book as much as I've enjoyed writing it!

Register your copy of *Expert Hadoop® Administration* at informit.com for convenient access to downloads, updates, and corrections as they become available. To start the registration process, go to informit.com/register and log in or create an account. Enter the product ISBN (9780134597195) and click Submit. Once the process is complete, you will find any available bonus content under "Registered Products."

Acknowledgments

Writing a book is always the work of a team, of which the author is but one of the members. I'd like to acknowledge the immense help provided during the writing of this book by various people, starting with Debra Williams Cauley, executive editor at Addison-Wesley, who oversaw the writing and production of this book. Debra is probably the hardest working and most earnest editor I've worked with, and her dedication to the project and the sense of urgency with which she managed everything has had a huge influence on the way I approached this project, especially towards the later parts of the project.

I owe an immense debt to Chris Zahn for his astute editing of the book, while being enormously kind and graceful throughout the arduous process. Chris's encouragement and support has helped me immensely while writing this book, and the book has gained immeasurably from his skillful editing and his sharp eye for details, without losing the big picture. I've learned quite a few things about correct style and conventions from going over Chris's edits. It's quite unlikely that any major stylistic errors remain after Chris straightened things out, but if they do, you know who to blame!

I've been quite fortunate to have four great reviewers go through the chapters, all of them seasoned professionals from Hortonworks. Anubhav Awasthi, big data consultant, went through all the chapters, caught several errors, and made several important suggestions that helped me improve the book. Karthik Varakantham, system architect, reviewed the book, corrected several stylistic and technical points and made a number of highly useful suggestions. Kannappan Natarasan, senior consultant, reviewed several of the early chapters and provided an overview of how the chapters looked, as well as suggestions to improve the book. Ron Lee, platform engineering architect, made several great suggestions, especially regarding Chapter 15, as well as Chapters 16 through 21. Ron helped me improve the book considerably based on his detailed comments, stemming from his extensive in-the-trenches experience with Hadoop environments.

Earlier on, both Marina Stephens and John Guthrie reviewed and commented in great detail on several chapters in this book. I was able to improve the style as well as the technical content following these reviews. Thank you, Marina and John, for all of your painstaking work, for the many errors you caught, and for all your suggestions that have led me to improve the clarity of a number of topics!

I work as a big data administrator at Sabre, where I'm fortunate to work together with several amazing team members and great managers. I first of all thank Zeelani Shaik, my manager, for his unfailing courtesy, kindness, understanding and encouragement at work. Amjad Saeed was instrumental in bringing me to Sabre, and his cheerfulness, kindness and grace have always been a source of great pleasure to me. Zul Sidi, vice president for the Enterprise Data and Analytics (EDA) group, is a tremendous leader for the entire team, motivating us and setting a great example by the way he performs his own job. Zul's openness to suggestions for improving the way we do things and his constant encouragement and support has helped me and other members of the EDA team achieve numerous significant objectives for our customers during the short time he has been here.

I also owe a round of thanks to Sujoe Bose for his kindness and help, as well as to Senthil Selvaraj for his help when he worked with me at Sabre. I've learned a lot about Hadoop from Sadu Hegde, and I thank him for helping me get started at Sabre. Mallik Dontula has always been a source of wisdom regarding all matters concerning Hadoop and big data, and I've benefited from his valuable help and suggestions on several occasions. Chris Morris and Larry Pritchett have both been not only good friends, but also truly great professionals, and I've benefited immensely from working with them. I'd also like to thank Aaron Patenaude for his generosity, and his great help with anything I've ever asked of him. I would like to thank my friends Winfield Geng, for his unstinting help whenever I requested it, and Bob Newman, who is conscientious and keeps us on our toes, for his advice and help. I would like to thank both Mohammed Hossain and Andrew Ahmad for their friendship and help. I'd be remiss if I don't acknowledge the great support from my friend and colleague Vinay Shetty, who is not only amazingly good at his job, but also very helpful while working together. I certainly owe many thanks over the past two years to Linda Phipps, for all the things she helped me with, always with great cheer! Lance Tripp was the person who encouraged me to seek the position I currently hold at Sabre. Since I love my job, I must say a big thank you to Lance for his smart recruiting!

Writing a book always means you basically disappear from the home front, although the physical signs of your existence abound. I appreciate the love and kindness of my wife, Valerie, and the affection of my children, Nina, Nicholas and Shannon, who've always supported my writing and research endeavors. Thank you as well to Dale, Shawn and Keith, who always remain close to me. I also appreciate the affection and kindness of the Dixon family: Stephanie Dixon, as well as Clarence and Elaine, who have always been supportive of everything I've done. The kindness and affection of my brothers Hari and Bujji, my sisters-in-law Aruna and Vanaja, my nieces Aparna and Soumya, and my nephew Teja means everything to me, so thank you to all of you! Special thanks to my nephew Ashwin and his wife SreeVidya, whose kind hospitality during my stay in San Jose during a Hadoop conference helped me develop several key ideas I discuss in this book.

About the Author

Sam R. Alapati is a principal Hadoop administrator at Sabre, headquartered in Southlake, Texas, where he works with multiple Hadoop clusters on a daily basis. As part of his responsibilities as the point person for all Hadoop administration–related work for the Enterprise Data Analytics (EDA) group at Sabre, Sam manages and optimizes multiple critical data science and data analysis related Hadoop job flows. Sam is also an expert Oracle Database administrator, and his vast knowledge of relational databases and SQL contributes to his success in working with Hadoop-related projects. Sam's accomplishments in the database and middleware area include the publication of 18 well-received books over the past 14 years, mostly on Oracle Database administration and Oracle Weblogic Server. Sam is also the author of a forthcoming book titled *Modern Linux Administration* (O'Reilly, 2017). Sam's experience dealing with numerous configuration, architecture and performance-related Hadoop issues over the years led him to the realization that many working Hadoop administrators and developers would appreciate having a handy reference, such as this book, to turn to when creating, managing, securing and optimizing their Hadoop infrastructure.

I

Introduction to Hadoop—Architecture and Hadoop Clusters

1

Introduction to Hadoop and Its Environment

Welcome to the fascinating subject of managing Apache Hadoop! Hadoop is the leading platform for processing massive sets of data, usually referred to as *big data*. Hadoop, an open-source project, was introduced roughly around 2005, and over the past few years, Hadoop has become the de facto standard for processing big amounts of data using parallel processing algorithms and simple data processing models that underlie a highly efficient and reliable computing architecture. Hadoop is exciting and powerful, and it's a great time, indeed, to be a Hadoop administrator!

Hadoop has been clearly designed with the challenges of big data in mind. Companies desperately want to make sense out of the overwhelmingly large data flows generated by online clickstreams, server logs, social media, weather and other sensor data, email and cellphone data. Many organizations today use Hadoop to handle their big data needs.

In this first chapter, I

- Introduce the Hadoop framework
- Explain how Hadoop fits into the "big data" world
- Introduce cluster computing and Hadoop clusters
- Describe Hadoop components and the Hadoop "ecosphere"
- Explain the nature of the Hadoop administrator's work
- Explain distributed data processing with MapReduce and Spark
- Introduce data integration with Apache Sqoop, Apache Flume and Apache Kafka
- Introduce the key areas of Hadoop administration

As you can tell from the title of this book, our focus is entirely on administering Hadoop. The topics I discuss in the book benefit the folks who're tasked with administering Hadoop environments, as well as other groups such as Hadoop developers who may sometimes need to install and manage their own development environments. Linux administrators tasked with managing Hadoop systems will also find the contents of the book useful in their day-to-day work.

Hadoop environments mostly run on Linux (and UNIX) systems, although you can run them on Windows systems as well. They can be run both on premises and cloud, such as the Amazon Web Service's (AWS) Hadoop-based big data offering named Amazon EMR (Elastic MapReduce). This book deals with managing Hadoop on Linux-based systems. The basic principles of management, however, are the same regardless of the operating system.

While you can install the Apache Hadoop modules directly and set up your own fully functional Hadoop environment (as explained in Chapter 3, "Creating and Configuring a Simple Hadoop 2 Cluster," and Chapter 4, "Planning for and Creating a Fully Distributed Cluster"), it's more common for organizations to deploy a vendor-supported Hadoop distribution, such as Cloudera, HortonWorks, Pivotal or MapR. However, this book doesn't discuss the proprietary vendor-related products for a simple reason: This book's goal is to show you how to become a good Hadoop administrator, and I believe that the best way to do so is to learn Hadoop cluster administration from the ground up, by understanding how to work directly with the core Apache product set.

By learning things this way, you gain an enormous amount of understanding and confidence in your capability to troubleshoot, without having to merely click some buttons in a vendor-provided cluster manager without really knowing what is happening underneath. Having said this, I'm fully in support of using a vendor-provided Hadoop distribution, and I think all the leading vendors offer a good product. The best one for you is what works well for you in your environment.

Hadoop—An Introduction

Apache Hadoop (to be referred to simply as Hadoop in this text) is, in the words of its developers, "a project that develops open-source software for reliable, scalable, distributed computing." Distributed computing in this context involves the processing of data sets distributed over a large number of machines.

Hadoop has been explicitly architected to deal with very large sets of data, and it's helping transform the way organizations harness their data. A good example is the recent (2015) case of the national plebiscite held in Scotland to determine if the Scots should separate from the United Kingdom to become an independent entity. The proponents of Scottish independence relied on Hadoop-based data analysis to drive their efforts. Similarly, companies are using Hadoop to optimize websites that drive customer loyalty programs. Well-known marketing strategies such as product recommendations, customization and dynamic pricing (used heavily in the airline industry) can be effectively supported by Hadoop's capability to churn through massive amounts of data in a very short time.

Hadoop is both fascinating and very complex, due to the large number of products you work with in a Hadoop environment. Administering Hadoop requires you to understand not only the core Hadoop system, which involves data storage called HDFS (Hadoop distributed file system) and a processing framework called YARN (Yet Another Resource Negotiator), but also a dizzying array of components that work with the core Hadoop system. These components provide various services such as high availability, management of high volume data flows into and out of the Hadoop system, scheduling Hadoop jobs, providing security and others.

> **Note**
>
> As the Preface explains, this book deals with Hadoop 2. To be more specific, the book uses Hadoop 2, release 2.6.0. I occasionally explain some new features that are available only in the 2.7 release.

Unique Features of Hadoop

Following are the main ways in which Hadoop stands apart as a unique platform for big data analysis.

- Capability to handle large data sets: Hadoop is explicitly designed to handle large amounts of data, which can easily run into many petabytes and even exabytes. Hadoop file sizes are usually very large, ranging from gigabytes to terabytes, and large Hadoop clusters store millions of these files.
- Fault tolerance: Everything in Hadoop is based on the assumption that hardware fails. Hadoop depends on large numbers of servers so it can parallelize work across them. Server and storage failures are to be expected, and the system isn't affected by non-functioning storage units or even failed server. (As you'll learn soon, data is by default replicated three times in Hadoop systems.)

  Hadoop is highly fault reliant: Both YARN and HDFS will continue their processing unimpeded when one or more disks go bad, or even when one or more servers go down. This is the beauty of the built-in data replication capability of Hadoop.
- Streaming access to data: Traditional databases are geared mostly for fast access to data and not for batch processing. Hadoop was originally designed for batch processing such as the indexing of millions of web pages and provides streaming access to data sets. (Newer developments have enabled other processing paradigms such as interactive SQL, iterative processing, search and stream processing.)
- Simple data consistency model: Unlike traditional databases, Hadoop data files employ a write-once-read-many access model. Data consistency issues that may arise in an updatable database aren't an issue with Hadoop file systems, because only a single writer can write to a file at any time.

Big Data and Hadoop

Modern data types and new forms of data flows need a sophisticated data-processing system to harness them. Hadoop's modern data storage and processing framework stores large amounts of diverse types of data in a cost-effective fashion. More importantly, it'll also let you process the huge amounts of data it stores to help you derive business insights and make predictions, all of which would be beyond the capabilities offered by traditional types of data stores (such as relational databases, operational data marts and enterprise data warehouses) that businesses have counted on for years.

One of the key requirements in today's big data environment is to develop the ability to ask complex questions of this data to attain sharper business insights, thus making big data cost-effective and a source of competitive strength for your organization.

Hadoop has been clearly designed with the challenges of big data in mind. Using massive streams of data that are flowing into their systems to create more effective business strategies and thus gain completive advantage is, if not the most important challenge facing organizations, definitely near the top of the list. Companies desperately want to make sense out of the large data flows generated by online clickstreams, server logs, social media, weather and other sensor data, email and cellphone data, GPS data and so on.

Hadoop is typically used by organizations to handle large volumes of the following types of data:

- Clickstream data: This is data emanating from user clicks through their website visits. Companies analyze clickstream logs for customer segmentation, customer personalization, tracking customer activity and so on, in order to influence and modify customer decision-making.
- Call center data: These are the typed notes collected from call center operators.
- E-mail and instant messaging: E-mail and instant messaging repositories hold information critical to security and compliance.
- Server logs: This is the data relating to customer website login activity and plays a critical role in security.
- Sentiment data: This refers to the data from social media such as Twitter, which helps organizations garner crucial information regarding their customer behaviors and preferences.
- Sensor data: This is data captured from sensors embedded in machines, instruments and servers to predict and reduce failures and improve design.
- Unstructured data: This refers to data and pictures that help identify patterns and anticipate future activity such as criminal behavior, which can be forecast based on data relating to facial expressions (image classification).
- Geographic data: This category includes data from Global Positioning Systems (GPS) and radio-frequency identification (RID), which helps plan efficient routes for work such as designing highways and locating cell towers, as well as optimizing the layout of offices and commercial establishments.

The key to Hadoop's capability to process data so efficiently is the feature known as data locality, meaning Hadoop brings processing to where the data is stored, rather than doing things the old fashioned way, which involves moving data through the network. That tends to be far slower, due to the network/bandwidth bottleneck. Hadoop stores its data in a distributed file system called HDFS, and it moves computation such as MapReduce processing to the cluster's nodes using YARN, which is Hadoop's resource management system. As I explain later in this chapter, a distributed file system in this context means a file system that stores and manages data across a network of machines.

MapReduce is the most common processing framework used in Hadoop environments, although newer frameworks such as Spark are fast gaining ground, as I explain later in this chapter.

A Typical Scenario for Using Hadoop

Let's take one of the most popular uses of Hadoop—log data analysis—to show how Hadoop helps organizations that deal with large volumes of data that can't really be analyzed in any other way. Let's see how MapReduce helps process web clickstream data to derive useful conclusions about users' behavior on a company's website.

Typically, users access a company's website and look through the site, to see which items they may want to purchase. Once the users select an item they want to buy, they add the item to their shopping cart and pay for the purchase on the checkout page. However, users sometimes abandon their shopping carts before completing the purchase, and companies are naturally interested in finding out more about the nature of these abandoned purchases, since it is potential revenue they have lost.

MapReduce uses keys and values as the basis for sorting and aggregating data and, in this case, the key is the IP address and the value is the timestamp and URL. Using MapReduce processing, a company can gather detailed information about the abandoned shopping carts. MapReduce consists of two phases—map and reduce. During the map phase, the processing gets you the following information:

- The final pages visited by the users
- The contents of the abandoned shopping carts
- The user session's transaction state

The reduce phase then does the following:

- It gathers together all the data emitted by the map phase.
- It aggregates the data to figure out the total number of weekly (or monthly) abandoned carts and the total value of the items that were abandoned.
- It shows the most common final page visited by the users when they ended their website visit, abandoning their shopping carts.

This is a simple example that shows how companies use Hadoop and its processing frameworks such as MapReduce to derive useful conclusions from the vast amounts of data they own, such as the clickstream data in this example.

Traditional Database Systems

For a number of years now, businesses have relied on online transactional databases, data marts and data warehouses to store and analyze business data, which is also called structured data because it adheres to standard methods for organizing itself. All these traditional types of data stores are still immensely useful and will retain most of their functions even today when big data has become a pervasive phenomenon. However, several new developments over the past 10 to 15 years have made the need for a new data storage and processing framework imperative. I summarize these developments here:

- New types of data such as unstructured data and semi-structured data (e.g., Twitter feeds, server logs, video and audio) require a new way to store these types of data and to effectively make use of the information contained in the data.
- Increasingly large amounts of data flowing into organizations through websites and other sources overwhelm the storage and processing capabilities of traditional data warehouses.
- New computational paradigms use non-traditional NoSQL databases to rapidly mine and analyze very large data sets.
- There is an increasing cost of storing and analyzing the large amounts of data flowing into company systems.
- There is an increasing use of data analytics, which requires significant storage and processing capabilities.

A huge problem with traditional databases when it comes to dealing with big data is that traditional systems use a **scale up** architecture, which means that you add more CPU cores, RAM and disk storage to existing servers in order to process ever growing mounds of data. Scaling up with the help of ever more powerful computers is extremely expensive. With very high volumes, you also have to worry about the fact that moving the data from storage to the CPUs for processing becomes the bottleneck. Hadoop's HDFS file system lets you adopt a **scale out** architecture by letting you grow total storage capacity by continually adding more (small, commodity) servers as the data sizes grow.

> **Note**
>
> Two factors are behind Hadoop's capability to easily process large sets of data. The first is the framework's capability to harness a large number of computers, thereby making short work of processing humongous chunks of data that could extend to hundreds of petabytes. The second is the built-in fault tolerance.

Hadoop provides a way to solve all (or at least, most) of the problems posed by the new developments I listed above with respect to the usage of organizational data. Four key factors—cost effectiveness, easy scalability, high reliability and powerful processing capabilities—underlie Hadoop's success in harnessing enormous amounts of data. Here, briefly, is how Hadoop provides solutions to the problems I listed here:

- Hadoop can store and process traditional structured data as well as semi-structured and unstructured data.
- Hadoop can store virtually unlimited amounts of data and supports multiple processing frameworks that can analyze that data.

- Hadoop can handle SQL- and NoSQL-based computational frameworks and uses a computational strategy of parallel processing to efficiently process the large data sets it stores.
- Hadoop is extremely cost-effective, since it uses commodity servers and almost all of the components in the Hadoop environment are open-source software.
- Hadoop is tailor made for data analytics—it's designed for the storage and processing of vast data sets.

While we're on this topic, we might also want to note that while Hadoop (especially MapReduce) is ideal for analyzing large datasets and relational databases are optimized for speedy retrieval and updates, the differences between the two types of data stores are diminishing a bit. For example, Hive, which helps users impose a relational database–like abstraction over HDFS data, is adding features well known in the relational database world, such as indexes and transactions, although the transactions may be more limited than in relational databases (no support for Commit and Rollback, for example). However, Hadoop is inherently quite different from traditional databases and will remain so. Just to take one example, web server logs and other logs are popular Hadoop data sources. These logs are not normalized, and therefore they're ideal for use with Hadoop—whereas relational databases usually require you to normalize your data.

One of the biggest issues with traditional databases and data warehouses is scalability. Once your data reaches a few terabytes, queries take an extremely long time to finish. Scalability (and reliability) is Hadoop's calling card—the size of your data set is really irrelevant if you've the processing capacity. If you triple the number of nodes in a cluster, you can get the job done in a third of the time—simple as that!

Hadoop has been widely recognized as an established platform for handling big data. There are areas such as fraud detection that have been transformed due to the use of Hadoop, since you can now process entire data sets instead of having to sample portions of it, which helps with more accurate fraud modeling. More and more companies are not only adopting Hadoop but making it the centerpiece of their big data strategy. Hadoop makes it possible for you to not just query samples of large data sets but query all your data at once and reveal insights that were previously unattainable using traditional data-processing and analytical techniques. The natural outcome of this evolution is the concept of a data lake.

Data Lake

The concept of a **data lake** is relatively new and alludes to a central location to store all of an organization's data, irrespective of the source of the data as well as the analytical frameworks that utilize this data. The data lake serves as a data ingestion and analytical grid for the organization.

You can use the data lake as a landing place for all data arriving into a company's systems as well as to store data you wish to offload from data warehouses and other data stores. The key idea is that you maintain one big central repository for all your data—structured, semi-structured and unstructured—and use it in myriad ways for analysis.

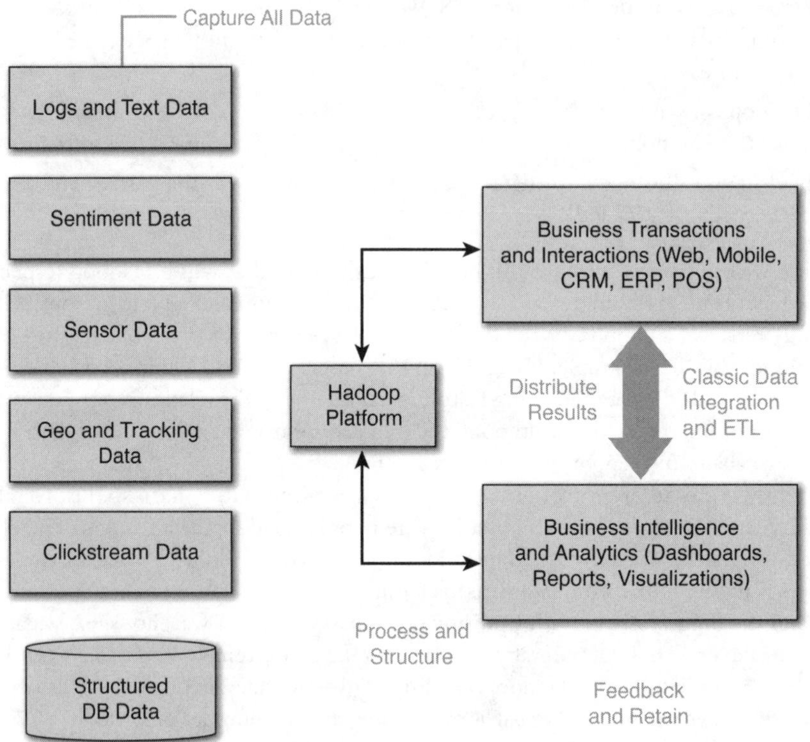

Figure 1.1 A Hadoop-based data lake architecture, with data from a variety of sources flowing into Hadoop, which processes the data and sends it to ETL and BI components

Figure 1.1 shows a typical data lake that gathers data from a variety of sources and feeds into Hadoop. The Hadoop platform is generally used to extract data that's sent to downstream ETL (extract, transform and load) tools or to BI (business intelligence) tools. Note that there may be a two-way interaction between the Hadoop platform and the BI and ETL components.

By its very design, a data lake lets you adapt to new types of data and lets you use a multitude of data-processing and analytical techniques to benefit from the vast troves of data stored therein.

Hadoop is at the center of a data lake, by providing a landing zone for all data flowing into an organization's systems. Hadoop is an excellent venue for the long-term retention of data and also serves as a powerful ETL platform. Due to its cost-effectiveness, it costs much less to store data in a Hadoop cluster than in traditional data warehouses. In addition to serving as a landing zone for data, Hadoop also stores the data so you can do the following:

- Query the data directly with tools such as Apache Hive and Apache Pig
- Preprocess and transform data before sending those data along to data warehouses for analysis

Big Data, Data Science and Hadoop

Data science involves the use of advanced statistical techniques and data mining (machine learning) algorithms to derive predictive and inferential insights using domain-specific data sets. While data science (usually in the form of old-fashioned statistical techniques such as regression, for example) has been around for a very long time, it's only in the past few years that data science at scale has become all the rage. Hadoop is the foundation for a lot of data science work, due to its ability to support the storage and analysis of humongous amounts of data in a reliable fashion, while using plain commodity servers.

Data products are the target of many data science projects. A data product in this context is the combination of data and statistical/data mining algorithms that lets you predict the future and make sound statistical inferences. Amazon's well-known product recommendations are a good example of a data product. As you know, this data product recommends books and other items to you based on your past purchases as well as the purchases made by users that have profiles similar to yours.

Data products are increasingly becoming a key part of various businesses and serve as the underpinning for many business decisions.

The typical analytical workflow for a data science project involves the following components, in the form of an interconnected data pipeline:

- Data ingestion
- Data wrangling
- Data modeling
- Visualization
- Reporting

Large Datasets and Hadoop

The vast outpouring of data over the past decade demanded a better approach to data analysis than the traditional statistical analysis strategies that relied on sampling large data sets.

Dealing with massive data sets generated by the avalanche of personal and shopping data generated non-stop by the Internet is out of the question for traditional data warehouses. It's Hadoop that's uniquely placed to handle these big data workflows. While Hadoop is certainly not the first distributed computing system, its arrival was perfectly timed: It came on the scene just as folks were casting around for a powerful platform for performing data analytics at scale.

Hadoop is unique in that not only does it offer cost-effective (cheap!) storage for large amounts of data but it also serves as a great platform for a whole set of ancillary tools that complement the storage and help provide various services such as integration with relational databases (Apache Sqoop), job scheduling (Apache Oozie) and others.

Why Hadoop Is Easy to Adopt

You don't have to be a behemoth of a company like Google or Facebook to use Hadoop as the foundation of your data science projects. Many companies begin with a small cluster, such as a 6 to 12 node cluster, and use it as a POC (proof of concept) and a starting point for growth. You can also jump onto the Hadoop bandwagon with minimal outlays, by simply using a cloud-computing model such as Amazon EC2 or the Google Compute Engine. The cloud-computing model especially makes Hadoop easily affordable and accessible for organizations with little money to spend and not many technical resources to lean on.

Cluster Computing and Hadoop Clusters

Hadoop is all about managing large-scale data processing over a large number of computing nodes, which together provide both efficient and fault-tolerant processing of large data sets. Let's quickly review what cluster computing involves in the following section.

Cluster Computing

Traditionally, when organizations sought to perform parallel processing, they used massive parallel computers with numerous processors and expensive specialized hardware. The flourishing of the Internet and web-based services has, however, resulted in companies using thousands of computing nodes that use commodity hardware. These massive systems provide the power of parallelism, while taking care of the reliability problems due to the spreading of the work among thousands of nodes, each of which is susceptible to failure but also avoids the problem of a single point of failure.

> **Note**
>
> The capability of big data infrastructures such as Hadoop to efficiently crunch through vast amounts of data is based on the application of what's called "embarrassingly parallel" computing algorithms that break up large workloads into small chunks that can be processed by an individual member of a cluster of machines.

The parallel computing architecture based on a large number of computing nodes is referred to as *cluster computing*. The commodity hardware is grouped into multiple **racks**, with each rack holding anywhere between 6 to 64 nodes on average. The nodes running in each rack are usually connected by Gigabit Ethernet (GbE), with multiple racks being connected to a network switch.

In a cluster-computing model, it's not uncommon at all to encounter server failures, which can result from the failure of a single node, or the failure of an entire rack of servers. Since the purpose of using this model of computing is to perform very large computations, it's not feasible to simply restart long-running jobs after each failure. The model uses two simple but highly effective strategies to guard against the loss of a single disk or an entire node. First, it makes use of redundant copies of the data blocks, making sure to store the copies on servers located in different racks. The data blocks divide a file into multiple chunks and replicate them (default Hadoop/HDFS replication factor is 3, but you can change it) across the cluster. Second, each large job is divided into **tasks**, and any failed task can easily be restarted independently from the other running tasks.

Cluster computing uses a distributed file system (DFS) that uses large files, ranging from hundreds of megabytes to terabytes. This is why you won't need Hadoop if you don't deal with large data sets. Further, to be amenable to the cluster-computing model, you must want to perform some type of analytical work with the data. This means that even though you have a very large data set in a database, you won't need Hadoop if all you want to do is perform simple lookups of data or perform insertions and deletions of data, as is the case in an online transaction processing (OLTP) system. The data model for cluster computing essentially deals with a write-once, read-often style of data processing. Mostly, data is written to the file system and is rarely updated after the initial write.

Hadoop Clusters

Throughout this chapter and the rest of the book, you'll often come across the term **Hadoop cluster**. A Hadoop cluster consists of a set of machines and the operating system daemons and software processes that run on those machines to store and process data. Hadoop clusters are easily scalable—all you have to do is add servers to increase both the storage and the processing capacities. A Hadoop 2 cluster can support over 10,000 servers.

A typical Hadoop cluster consists of the following entities:

- A set of master nodes (servers) where the daemons supporting key Hadoop frameworks run
- A set of worker nodes that host the storage (HDFS) and computing (YARN) work
- One or more **edge servers** (so called because they really don't run any Hadoop processes but can access the cluster), which are used for accessing the Hadoop cluster to launch applications
- One or more relational databases such as MySQL or PostGres for storing the metadata repositories for frameworks such as Hive, Sqoop, Oozie and Hue
- Dedicated servers for special frameworks such as Kafka and Storm

Figure 1.2 shows the basic architecture of a Hadoop cluster.

Although, technically speaking, Hadoop consists of just HDFS and YARN, it's very common to use a number of other frameworks and software such as Hive, Pig, Oozie, Spark and Flume in production Hadoop clusters. Therefore, your cluster, realistically speaking, will actually consist of the entire set of servers where the supporting cast of characters runs.

Mining of large sets of data is a primary goal for many large companies today. Ranking web pages and searching social-networking sites are two examples where you deal with pretty regular data flows, which makes it easy to mine them using data parallelism. In order to efficiently process these types of large data sets, a new programming paradigm using a

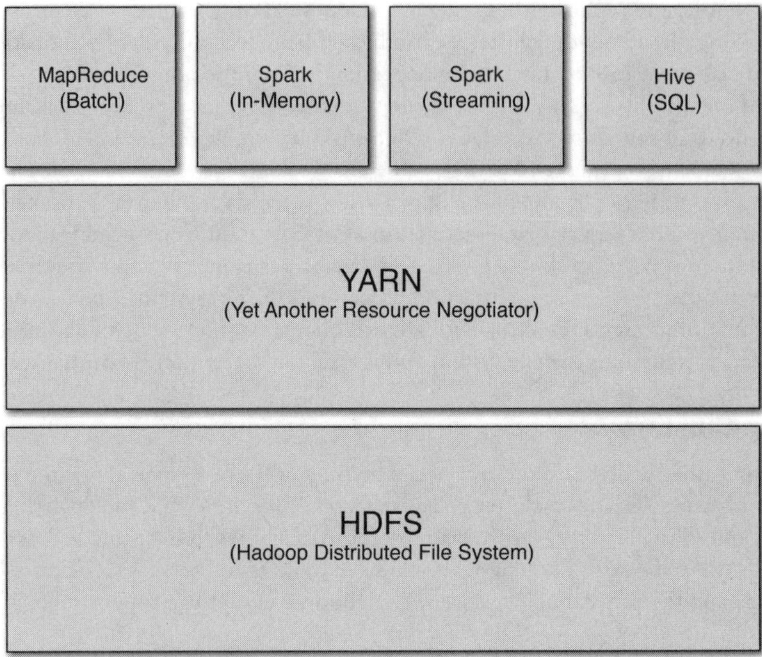

Figure 1.2 The basic architecture of a Hadoop cluster

different type of software stack has evolved. Whereas traditional data processing has focused on larger and larger computers, leading to the birth of supercomputers, this newer approach employs clusters of inexpensive computers connected by inexpensive switches or Ethernet cables.

The new software stack, as represented by Hadoop, has a distributed file system as its foundation. Unlike traditional databases, this file system typically uses very large data blocks in order to quickly process vast chunks of data. Another key feature is built-in redundancy of data, since the file system uses inexpensive computing nodes, each of which may fail at any time. The redundancy is provided by replicating all data across multiple servers, usually three in number.

While the distributed file system is the foundational layer designed for data storage, the new software stack started out providing the processing capability through a programming model called MapReduce. By combining the distributed file system with the MapReduce programming model, you can perform large-scale computations across a vast cluster, all the while being protected against intermittent hardware failures through the built-in data redundancy.

An important reason for the popularity of Hadoop is the fact that when you combine MapReduce with the Hadoop HDFS file system the economics of the combined system make sense to most organizations. You can use inexpensive servers, and you don't need to use storage area networks or fancy network configurations. If you don't want to set up your data center, you can always use a cloud-based Hadoop environment, such as Amazon's EC2 storage.

A big factor in the efficiency of Hadoop is avoiding the moving of data. You do the computing where the data is stored, instead of moving the data to a node where you perform the computations. You can schedule the MapReduce jobs on the same nodes where the HDFS data is stored, reducing the network load and limiting I/O to mostly local disks or within the same rack.

Hadoop Components and the Hadoop Ecosphere

Hadoop itself consists of several components and on top of that, you typically employ additional components such as Hive, Pig, Kafka and Sqoop, for example, to process the data you store in a Hadoop system and to integrate that data with other data stores.

New Hadoop users are somewhat bewildered by the large number of products they come across, including Hive, Pig, HBase, Spark, ZooKeeper and several other esoterically named products. Apache itself classifies the Hadoop framework simply as follows:

- Hadoop common: The base utilities that support the rest of the modules in the Hadoop environment, including:
  - Essential services for the Hadoop cluster, such as authentication of the operating system and its file system
  - Cluster startup scripts and the necessary Java files for those scripts
  - Documentation
  - Source code for the Hadoop Framework
- HDFS: A file system to provide high throughput access to data
- Hadoop YARN: A framework for scheduling jobs and managing resources
- Hadoop MapReduce: A framework for the parallel processing of large data sets

The best way to get a good handle on the vast Hadoop environment is to use the following informal classification to group the various Hadoop-related projects.

- Hadoop common: As mentioned above, these are the base utilities that support the rest of the modules in the Hadoop environment.
- Data storage: This is provided by HDFS. HBase provides structured data storage for large tables (see the Note on the next page).
- Operating system: The Hadoop "operating system," known as YARN, is Hadoop 2, which sits on the server operating system (such as Linux) and provides job scheduling and resource management capabilities.

- Data processing: This refers to distributed data processing of large data sets, offered by projects such as Hadoop's MapReduce, Apache Tez and the Apache Spark computing engine.
- Management tools and coordinator services: Ambari is Apache's Hadoop management and monitoring tool. ZooKeeper is the Apache component that coordinates the work of distributed applications.

Figure 1.3 shows a typical Hadoop ecosphere—just remember that the ecosphere is continually evolving, with newer and more efficient components supplanting or complementing existing components.

> **Note**
>
> Although this book doesn't go into its details, Hadoop does offer its own distributed, column-oriented database named HBase (Hadoop Database), which uses HDFS for its storage. HBase helps you perform batch-mode computations using MapReduce as well as random queries. HBase consists of an HBase Master that manages the cluster state and Region Servers, which run on all the nodes hosting HBase tables and are responsible for processing the I/O requests.

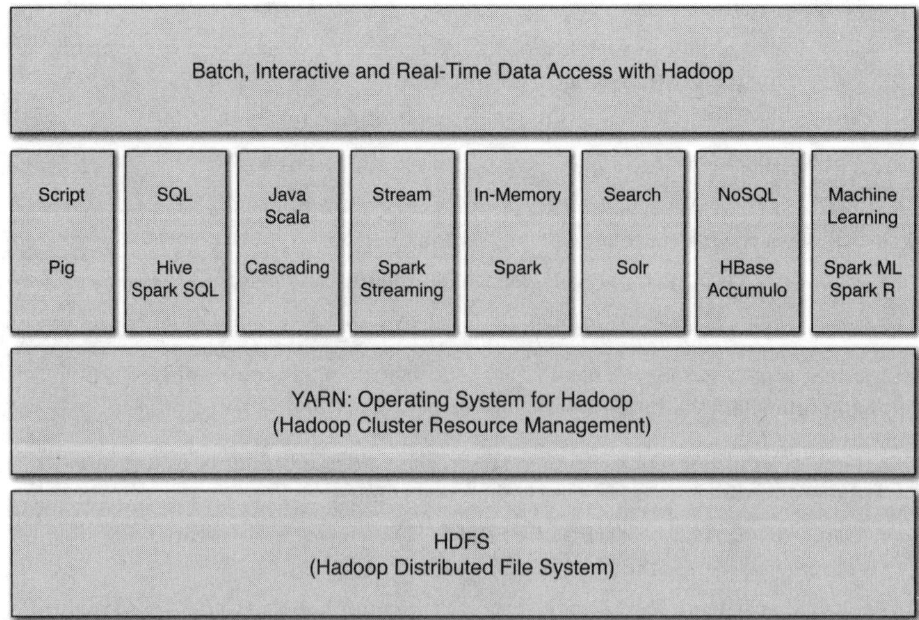

Figure 1.3 The Hadoop ecosphere, showing the Hadoop core components and commonly used tools

The Hadoop ecosystem consists of several related projects, which work very well together to sustain highly efficient and reliable large-scale distributed data processing. Most of these projects are supported by the Apache Software Foundation.

Table 1.1 lists the key Hadoop-related projects that constitute the Hadoop ecosystem—just remember that Hadoop and big data are fast-moving areas and new projects come online all the time!

As a Hadoop administrator, you most likely won't be expected to be an expert in all of these areas. Fortunately, there are other folks in a typical organization who architect and develop the data processing, data flows and data integration mechanisms in order to work with Hadoop. For example, data scientists are the experts in using Apache Mahout, which is Apache's machine learning tool.

As an administrator, your job is not so much to code MapReduce and Hive or Pig data extraction jobs, but to schedule jobs, load data and perform similar administrative tasks. To that end, this book explains how to work with the components that are most

Table 1.1 **The Hadoop Ecosphere**

Component	Description
Avro	Framework for transforming data into a compact binary format
Flume	Data-flow tool for moving streaming data into Hadoop
HBase	A columnar database that uses HDFS for its storage
HCatalog	A service that provides a relational view of data you store in HDFS
Hive	A distributed data warehouse for HDFS data that provides a SQL-like layer to this data
Hue	A user and administrative interface that lets you browse HDFS files, run Pig and Hive queries and schedule workflows through Oozie
Kafka	A message-queuing framework that handles large amounts of real-time data traffic
Mahout	A library of machine-learning algorithms implemented in MapReduce
Oozie	A job-scheduling tool
Pig	A framework for analyzing large data sets that let you create data pipelines
Sqoop	A data movement tool that moves data between HDFS and relational databases
Storm	An object-relational mapping library that supports real-time stream processing
Tez	A data-processing framework for batch processing that also provides interactive querying capabilities
ZooKeeper	A coordination service used by distributed applications such as Hadoop, HBase, Storm, Hive and Kafka

important for administrators, such as Apache Oozie, which you must master in order to efficiently schedule Hadoop-related jobs. Similarly, learning how to use Apache Sqoop lets you move data into and out of your cluster.

Just remember that even though Hadoop environments have a plethora of components, the only component that must be present is HDFS—the storage layer. You can select the components you need for your particular case from the set of available components.

What Do Hadoop Administrators Do?

Now that you have a bird's eye view of Hadoop and its role in big data environments, it's time to turn to the main focus of this book, which is the administering of Hadoop environments. So, what is Hadoop administration, and what do Hadoop administrators actually do? The functions of a Hadoop administrator are remarkably similar to those of a traditional database administrator in many ways. An Oracle or Microsoft SQL Server administrator will find the typical Hadoop administrator's responsibilities quite familiar. I worked as an Oracle database administrator for a long time before switching to Hadoop, and I found the transition easy, although there are significant differences between traditional database management and Hadoop-based systems.

One of the interesting aspects of Hadoop is the way the components in the Hadoop ecosystem are used with the base Hadoop framework of YARN and HDFS. As an administrator, you can't be expected to master the use of every one of these components—there are simply too many of them, and new ones keep springing up all the time! However, you need to know some of them, such as the ZooKeeper service that supports high availability, in great depth. As regards other components such as Pig and Hive, you need to know at least enough to understand how they work—your main responsibility is to support others that use these and other processing frameworks.

Let's quickly review the essential Hadoop administration functions in the following sections.

Hadoop Administration—A New Paradigm

A striking feature of Hadoop administration is that you're dealing with an inherently fault-tolerant system. Let me take a simple example of how this impacts management. If you're an Oracle (or any other relational database) administrator, you know that any space-related alerts could mean a potential issue on a production system. If you're getting alerts stating that tablespace or a file system is quickly filling up, you must quickly add space to that file system or to that tablespace ASAP. Otherwise, you're looking at a potential job failure because it will run out of space to write its data.

Of course, jobs will fail in a Hadoop environment if you don't have sufficient free storage space to accommodate new data. However, the failure of a single disk or even an entire server won't doom your job, because a task that fails due to the storage issues will automatically be restarted by Hadoop on a different node.

Since you're dealing with not one or two but potentially dozens and hundreds (even thousands) of data nodes in a cluster, it's good to know that you're not continually scurrying around attending to failed disks and downed servers. Of course, the failed entities must be revived, but there's no rush at all—you do so when you can.

Here's a short list of the most essential tasks performed by most Hadoop administrators, which I cover in the following sections:

- Installation and upgrades
- Assisting developers
- Performance tuning
- Monitoring and troubleshooting
- Backups and disaster recovery

Installation and Upgrades

Installing and configuring a Hadoop cluster is one of the basic tasks that a Hadoop administrator is expected to know well. Installing a single-node Hadoop environment, also called a **pseudo-distributed** system, is useful for initial forays into the Hadoop world and is pretty straightforward. Installing and configuring Hadoop across multiple computing nodes in a real cluster is definitely more complex and requires a comfort level with system administration.

In addition to installing Hadoop, you must also configure it for efficient and trouble-free performance. Typical databases such as Oracle have only a few configuration parameters that you need to set. Hadoop, as you'll soon find, has numerous "knobs" that you can tinker with. A Hadoop administrator will spend lots of time learning about and experimenting with numerous configuration parameters in order to fine tune the system.

Hadoop administration differs significantly from typical database administration, where your installation and configuration is really limited to just the database and a couple of additional tools. Hadoop environments utilize a large number of products, and an administrator is responsible for installing and configuring all of these products. Of course, as is the case with other types of system administrators, in addition to installing new Hadoop software, a Hadoop administrator spends a lot of time upgrading the various components, as and when necessary.

Assisting Developers

A typical Hadoop administrator will support multiple developers and analysts who work with data. The administrator sets up the identities for these users so they can work with Hadoop and ensures that the users have sufficient storage allocated for their HDFS directories. The administrator also usually helps the developers, analysts and other users overcome common issues such as connectivity, privileges and the troubleshooting of slow-running or failed jobs.

Performance Tuning

Performance tuning (or optimization) is a key responsibility of the Hadoop administrator. While developers are expected to understand and implement optimizations such as using combiners as part of their MapReduce programs and know the theory behind partitioning and parallelization of Spark jobs, there's much more to Hadoop performance tuning than writing more efficient MapReduce code. Other duties include the optimization of Pig (a data pipelining tool) and Hive (an abstraction over MapReduce that helps perform data warehousing—related analysis) jobs, which use the MapReduce execution engine underneath.

There are multiple areas that need the administrator's involvement. You must be adept at figuring out any server-level performance issues, including memory and CPU utilization. You must also know how to look for network-related issues in your cluster. Once you get past the server level and get to the actual Hadoop level, there are several areas you must focus on, in order to optimize the cluster's resources. These include the setting of appropriate values for several configuration parameters.

Monitoring and Troubleshooting

While Hadoop offers you several ways to monitor your system with its built-in interfaces, such as the **NameNode** and **ResourceManager** UIs, they can take you only so far in managing your cluster. Remember that the Hadoop cluster itself runs on the underlying operating system, typically a Linux-based system. Tools such as Nagios and Ganglia help you manage and monitor the entire cluster, including the operating system, storage and network.

Backups and Disaster Recovery

Unlike traditional databases, there's no concept of backing up the entire database in Hadoop, because, first of all, there's no one database in which all the data is stored. Rather, the data is stored in files in HDFS. Since Hadoop data is usually very large, backing up data isn't a very feasible or practical idea. In some cases, you can simply reproduce the data by going to the source. If you think some of the data is critical, you can certainly copy that data to a different cluster for protection. You can also use Hadoop's snapshot capability to protect key data, as explained in Chapter 12, "Moving Data Into and Out of Hadoop." In any case, know that you aren't really that vulnerable to the failure of a server or even an entire rack of servers. All bets are off, of course, if the whole data center is wiped out due to a natural calamity.

What You Need to Know to Administer Hadoop

One of the most common questions would-be Hadoop administrators ask is: "Do I need to know Java?" The simple answer is: No Java required. MapReduce, and for that matter HDFS and all Hadoop code, is written in Java. If you already know Java, that's great, but it's not a requirement by any means.

While you may get by without having even a basic understanding of Java, it sure helps to pick up some Java programming skills on the side while you're working with Hadoop. Any such Java knowledge you acquire is going to come in handy during troubleshooting and performance tuning. At the least, you should learn how to dig through Java stack traces. With Hadoop being written entirely in Java, you'll be digging through a lot of Java stack traces!

Apache Spark, which is becoming increasingly popular in Hadoop environments, can be programmed in Scala, Python or Java. However, Scala offers far more benefits and is quite popular. So, picking up a bit of Scala will come in handy when working with Spark applications, as well as for troubleshooting their performance in your cluster.

SQL knowledge is a different kettle of fish. If you are a Hadoop administrator, chances are you won't be spending your time solely on such issues as hardware maintenance and software upgrades. Whether you like it or not (I happen to enjoy it!), you'll most likely be called upon to help developers and analysts who run into various types of performance-related issues. These issues may range from things like users being unable to use the system at all due to some configuration issues to analyzing the reasons for poor performance of simple-looking queries.

Luckily for all involved, almost all your SQL skills acquired in a previous incarnation as a database (say, Oracle or MySQL) administrator are fully usable in a Hadoop environment. Remember that programming frameworks such as Hive use a SQL abstraction over MapReduce. So, you'll find yourself in situations where you can carry the day purely on the basis of your SQL background, despite not knowing a lick of Java!

The Hadoop Administrator's Toolset

Most Hadoop installations are being run on Linux systems. Thus, strong Linux administration skills are definitely very handy to have when administering Hadoop. It's also the case that in several organizations, the Hadoop environment is entirely managed by a Hadoop administrator with Linux skills or a Linux administrator who knows Hadoop.

It's a fair guess to say that the overwhelming majority of Hadoop environments use a third-party vendor-supported installation, such as Cloudera or Hortonworks or MapR. If your organization happens to be one of these companies, you'll be using management tools provided by the vendors, such as the highly popular Cloudera Manager or Ambari.

Using a vendor-supported distribution such as CDH (Cloudera) or HDP (Hortonworks) will undoubtedly make your life easy—these and other vendor distributions of Hadoop have proven themselves over the last few years in many organizations.

Key Differences between Hadoop 1 and Hadoop 2

Hadoop 2 was introduced in October 2013 to address the two main concerns with Hadoop 1 environments—scalability and availability. You may be curious about how Hadoop 2 is an advance over its predecessor, Hadoop 1. Also, by comparing the main features of the two releases, you gain an appreciation for how Hadoop has evolved over time, by providing new capabilities to meet new demands. For these reasons, I summarize the differences between the two architectures in the following sections.

The big difference between Hadoop 1 and Hadoop 2 is YARN. YARN is an abbreviation for the self-deprecating term "Yet Another Resource Negotiator." Hadoop 1 is merely a combination of HDFS and Java-based MapReduce programs. In Hadoop 2, as we've seen, YARN sits between the HDFS layer (which in turn rests on native server storage) and processing frameworks such as MapReduce and Spark. YARN is in charge of cluster resource management and scheduling. In Hadoop 1, MapReduce is really the only processing framework you could use and it interacted directly with HDFS. In Hadoop 2, MapReduce performs data processing in a fashion similar to that in Hadoop 1. So, which Hadoop component performed the cluster resource management and scheduling tasks in Hadoop 1? MapReduce performed the double duty of both data processing and cluster resource management.

Architectural Differences

Hadoop 1 used MRv1 and Hadoop 2 uses MRv2 (aka YARN). In Hadoop 2, there's a single global ResourceManager process that manages resources across the cluster, and it runs on a master node. The worker nodes will all have individual NodeManagers that perform data processing tasks.

In Hadoop 1, there was a single JobTracker process that managed jobs. Each worker node ran a node-specific TaskTracker process that actually executed the jobs. The JobTracker in Hadoop 1 performed both scheduling and task management functions. In Hadoop 2, the JobTracker functions have been broken into two—scheduling and resource management—with the ResourceManager handling the scheduling portion and the application-specific ApplicationMaster taking care of resource management.

The ResourceManager in Hadoop 2 manages several key functions previously performed by the JobTracker in Hadoop 1. To be more precise, the ResourceManager performs some of the old JobTracker's tasks and the new application-specific ApplicationMaster takes care of the rest of the JobTracker's duties. In Hadoop 1, the JobTracker was overwhelmed in a busy cluster, because of its heavy workload in managing both resource management and job scheduling. The separation of the twin key functionalities of the JobTracker—resource management and job scheduling/monitoring—lets dedicated daemons relieve this workload pressure.

The NodeManager in Hadoop 2 performs all the tasks previously taken care of by the TaskTrackers running on each node in a Hadoop 1 system. The NodeManager processes run on the worker nodes in a cluster and serves as an agent that monitors the processing performed on the nodes.

The ResourceManager is a pure scheduler in Hadoop 2 and there's no special linkage between it and MapReduce jobs, whereas in Hadoop 1, the JobTracker and MapReduce were tightly coupled.

High-Availability Features

Hadoop 2 has strong high-availability features and lets you run both a Standby NameNode as well as a Standby ResourceManager, both of which are critical to the functioning of a cluster.

In Hadoop 1, the NameNode was a single point of failure. If the NameNode server became unavailable, the whole cluster would become inoperable as all access to HDFS would be cut off.

Multiple Processing Engines

In Hadoop 1, you could use just MapReduce as the processing engine, regardless of whether you used Java-based MapReduce programs, Pig, Hive or a streaming model using Python, Ruby and so on. There simply was no alternative execution engine available. Hadoop 2 offers a wide variety of processing engines, such as MapReduce, Apache Spark, Apache Tez and others.

Instead of being able to support only batch processing, Hadoop 2 supports a wide variety of applications, as summarized here:

- Batch processing—MapReduce and Hive/Pig, Apache Tez
- Interactive SQL—Apache Tez
- Online database—HBase
- Streaming—Apache Storm, Apache Spark and Apache Samza
- In-memory (iterative applications)—Apache Spark
- Graph processing—Giraph and Spark GraphX
- HPC MPI—OpenMPI
- Scalable search—Apache Solr
- HBase on YARN—HOYA

MapReduce, while it performs several types of work admirably, isn't ideal for all types of big data use cases. One of the big complaints about MapReduce is the high latency of jobs. Hadoop 2 lets you choose an appropriate processing engine for specific types of use cases.

Hadoop 1 was limited by its batch-processing orientation, where time latency wasn't an issue and where you needed vast amounts of data to be processed. While Hadoop 1 was very good at processing large unstructured data sets containing even petabytes of information, it wasn't deemed to be very useful in the real-time analysis of live data sets. Hadoop 2 overcomes this batch-centric orientation of Hadoop 1.

Separation of Processing and Scheduling

YARN (MapReduce NextGen aka YARN aka MRv2) in Hadoop 2 marks a fundamental difference in how Hadoop performs its essential work. YARN is designed as a general-purpose, distributed application management framework and not as an all-in-one resource manager and performance engine as MapReduce was in Hadoop 1. In fact, quite frequently, YARN is referred to as the "operating system for Hadoop" because it performs functions such as the following:

- Maintaining a multitenant environment by running batch, interactive and real-time processing engines that can all simultaneously access the same HDFS data
- Managing and monitoring application workloads

Apache Hadoop MapReduce (aka MRv2) in Hadoop 2 retains its processing capabilities and becomes a pure distributed computation framework.

Resource Allocation in Hadoop 1 and Hadoop 2

Initially, Hadoop didn't have a very sophisticated way of allocating resources among the various jobs running simultaneously in a cluster. It used a first in, first out (FIFO) model of resource allocation by default, which meant that long running jobs, by hogging the cluster's resources, could potentially keep small but critical jobs from starting, even when the long-running jobs were non-critical in nature.

Hadoop in later versions has introduced much more sophisticated job schedulers, named the Fair Scheduler and the Capacity Scheduler. You'll learn about these two types of schedulers in Chapter 13, "Resource Allocation in a Hadoop Cluster."

Hadoop 1 uses slots to manage resource allocation, instead of using resource containers as Hadoop 2 does.

Finally, a key difference in terms of capability between a Hadoop 1 and a Hadoop 2 cluster is that while a Hadoop 1 cluster could scale "only" up to around 5,000 nodes, a Hadoop 2 cluster can scale up to around 10,000 nodes.

Distributed Data Processing: MapReduce and Spark, Hive and Pig

As a Hadoop administrator, you'll be responsible for managing several types of data-processing work in your Hadoop cluster. While MapReduce is the most common processing framework in many Hadoop clusters, Apache Spark is coming into being as a viable alternative to MapReduce. Hive and Pig are abstractions that use MapReduce as their underlying processing model. Understanding how these processing frameworks function is critical to your success as a Hadoop administrator. Let's briefly review the alternative Hadoop processing frameworks in the following sections.

MapReduce

MapReduce is a distributed processing framework that lets you write Java programs to process data you store in HDFS. The MapReduce framework simplifies the complex work involved in writing parallel distributed applications by taking care of all the processing logic except for the map and reduce functions. MapReduce is the most well-known of Hadoop's data-processing engines, and until the release of Hadoop 2, it was the only framework for processing data in a Hadoop system.

MapReduce has been a powerful presence in processing large data sets, by enabling you to write programs that a large cluster consisting of hundreds or even thousands of nodes can process in parallel. MapReduce offers a virtually linear level of scalability, because you can add more processing in the form of computing nodes as your data sets get larger. Since MapReduce breaks up huge processing tasks into smaller tasks, the model gracefully handles task failures.

MapReduce is named as it is because it consists of two primary phases—the map phase and the reduce phase. The map function's job is to map the input data to sets of key/value pairs. The reduce function then takes these key/value pairs and produces the output you seek by applying its own algorithms.

Developers don't have to deal with the problems of scheduling, resource management, failure handling and so on.

Alternatives to MapReduce

MapReduce is a batch processing system and hence not amenable for interactive analysis. However, YARN in Hadoop 2 lets you use alternative frameworks that offer you different processing paradigms. The following list isn't by any means exhaustive, but it gives you an idea of these alternative processing paradigms.

- Iterative computing: Apache Spark is great for performing iterative processing required by many machine learning programs
- Interactive SQL: Both Impala and Hive on Tez offer interactive SQL query capability
- Stream processing: Apache Storm, Apache Spark Streaming, Apache Samza and Apache Flink all let you run real-time distributed computations on streaming data
- Search: Apache Solr is a great search platform that can serve search queries on data stored in Hadoop clusters

---

Apache Spark

Apache Spark is a high-performance distributed computing framework that has evolved into the most active Apache project. Spark has received quite a bit of attention over the past couple of years, and some have wondered if it'll replace Hadoop. Well, Hadoop and Spark aren't alternatives to each other. Hadoop 2's YARN processing framework supports several processing frameworks, including Spark and MapReduce. Spark is becoming increasingly popular and is viewed as the eventual successor to MapReduce for data processing. Many companies still rely on MapReduce to process their workloads, but a lot of them are migrating their applications to Spark.

Unlike its predecessor Hadoop 1, Hadoop 2 isn't synonymous with MapReduce. As explained earlier, in Hadoop 2, MapReduce is now merely one more application framework and no more important than the other computing frameworks, all of which are supported by the underlying Hadoop processing entity, the YARN framework.

Spark enables you to process very large amounts of data, with high-level, easy-to-use APIs. High performance is Spark's calling card. Using Spark, you can write data transformation logic and machine learning algorithms in a parallelizable fashion, regardless of the underlying system. Hadoop, with its HDFS storage system, is uniquely qualified to run Spark jobs, and that's our focus in this book. Although you can run Spark on other computing frameworks, such as Mesos, I focus on how to work with Spark in a Hadoop cluster, with HDFS serving as the data storage and YARN as the computing framework. Often, organizations use several data sources to ingest data that become the source of most of their analytical work. By running Spark on Hadoop, you can use the same Hadoop cluster and the same data for running both MapReduce and Spark jobs.

MapReduce has well-known problems with processing iterative algorithms that require multiple passes over the same data. MapReduce is also not suitable for interactive computational work. Spark is designed to overcome both of these issues with MapReduce processing—it is designed for both fast interactive queries, as well as iterative algorithms. What's the nature of that design? Spark relies on an in-memory storage mode and efficient fault recovery.

Apache Hive

Apache Hive provides a SQL interface that enables you to use HDFS data without having to write programs using MapReduce. It's important to understand that unlike Apache HBase, Hive is not a database—it simply provides a mechanism to project a database structure on data you store in HDFS and lets you query that data using HiveQL, a SQL-like language. Hive uses a type of SQL that lets you query HDFS data in ways that are similar to how you query data stored in a relational database.

While Hive's SQL (HiveQL) doesn't have the full range of features available in SQL, it offers more than enough SQL capabilities for you to efficiently work with HDFS data. When you use a Hive query, Hive parses the SQL query and generates a MapReduce job to process the data to get you the query results.

It's important to understand that Hive, while it lets you use SQL type queries to process HDFS data, isn't a database itself, although it does use the concept of database tables. Hive simply maps HDFS directories to tables. If you've been using SQL to process data stored in relational databases, you can make a quick transition to Hive and start working with HDFS, without having to learn any MapReduce programming. Be forewarned that unlike the lightning quick results from SQL queries you may be used to, Hive is indeed quite plodding. Even for small queries, a Hive job needs to set the MapReduce engine in motion and the startup overhead takes some time.

When you write a query using HiveQL, internally, the Hive engine will transform the query into a MapReduce job. Hive offers several built-in functions to facilitate working with data warehouses, and users can also add their own user-defined functions (UDFs) in Java, to enhance Hive's functions. Hive's data types, tables and partitions are quite similar to what you deal with in the context of traditional relational databases.

Latency is usually an issue when dealing with test queries and small data sets. Hive is most definitely not practical for online transaction processing and real-time queries and updates.

Apache Pig

Pig is a high-level framework for data processing that enables you to use a scripting language called Pig Latin to process data using MapReduce on a Hadoop cluster. Pig thus works as a wrapper for MapReduce code. It's important to remember that, just as in the case of Hive, Pig doesn't provide functionality beyond that offered by MapReduce. It certainly makes it a lot easier to use various types of data operations though.

Unlike Hive, which is a SQL-like declarative language, Pig is a procedural language that's exceptionally suitable for data pipelining, by representing data analysis problems as data flows. You can create your own functions in Pig and also have Pig invoke code in different languages such as Java, JPython and JRuby. It's an ideal tool to use in typical ETL processing.

Data Integration: Apache Sqoop, Apache Flume and Apache Kafka

One of the most common use cases for Hadoop is the moving of data from a relational database into HDFS and vice versa. For example, a company may store its service call information in a relational database and would like to move the data to Hadoop to run Hive queries on the data. Apache Sqoop (short for "SQL to Hadoop") is the most well-known tool employed in Hadoop environments to move data back and forth from relational databases to HDFS.

Another common use case is the moving of large volumes of log data from entities such as web servers into HDFS. Web servers typically transmit large volumes of data, including user activity events such as logins, page visits, clicks and social networking activities such as likes and comments. Web servers also send a heavy amount of operational and system-related metric data.

Traditional logging mechanisms that use log aggregation can handle the high throughput of the web servers and send the logging data to Hadoop for offline analysis. Mining the logging data could lead to recommendations based on popularity or sentiment analysis and the appropriate targeting of advertising to the consumers. However, the large volume of logging data that's collected creates problems in the real-time processing of the data. Frameworks such as Apache Flume and Apache Kafka enable you to overcome this problem.

Apache Flume and Apache Kafka let a Hadoop cluster manage sporadic bursts of log data even though the cluster may not be able to handle the data flows on a continuous basis. By acting as a buffer between the data producers (say, web servers) and the data consumers (HDFS), these types of systems enable a steady flow of data into Hadoop.

Another problem when dealing with large amounts of log data is that the sources of the log data, such as various web servers, aren't near the Hadoop cluster. Flume and Kafka let you overcome this issue, by collecting and transmitting distributed log data from multiple sources. A brief description of Flume and Kafka follows:

- Apache Flume: Flume is a system for the collection, aggregation and moving of large amounts of streaming data from multiple sources to a data store such as HDFS. Although originally Flume was designed for aggregating log data, you can use it to move large amounts of event data or just about any type of data from any data source.
- Apache Kafka: Kafka, which started out at LinkedIn, is explicitly distributed and resembles a publish-subscribe system. Kafka lets you combine offline and online processing of streaming data by enabling parallel loading into the Hadoop system and the partitioning of real-time data consumption over the cluster. Architecturally, it's a system that's similar to well-known messaging systems such as ActiveMQ and RabbitMQ.

Besides Flume and Kafka, there are several other systems for log analysis. For example, the Elasticsearch/Logstash/Kibana (ELK) stack is useful for low latency log analytics as well as for search analysis. In addition to the open source log ingestion systems we've seen here (Flume and Kafka), there are also commercial systems such as Splunk, for example. The choice of which to use depends on the predominant type of use cases in your organization, types of data sources and the volume and velocity of data ingestion. Latency requirements are another key determining factor in the choice of the appropriate log ingestion tool.

Key Areas of Hadoop Administration

This book is all about administering Hadoop environments. I think it's a good idea to get a flavor of what the administration entails, by reviewing some of the key aspects of Hadoop administration that you'll be dealing with on a daily basis when managing Hadoop clusters.

In the following sections, I briefly explain

- Managing the cluster storage
- Allocating the cluster resources
- Scheduling Hadoop jobs
- Securing Hadoop data

Managing the Cluster Storage

Hadoop data is stored in HDFS. As an administrator, you'll be allocating space quotas to users of the cluster so they can store their Hadoop data. You'll also be performing tasks such as balancing the cluster data using Hadoop's balancer tool. To protect and secure (through encryption zones) the HDFS data, you'll most likely be creating HDFS snapshots.

As an administrator, it's your responsibility to add storage capacity to your cluster by adding more computing nodes to the cluster. In addition, you'll be taking care of any issues such as servers that are unreachable or get hit with software or hardware issues. You may need to decommission the bad nodes and recommission them after the server issues are resolved.

Allocating the Cluster Resources

The Fair Scheduler lets all applications get equal shares of resources over time. Memory is the key resource the Fair Scheduler uses to base its resource allocation decisions. However, a newer scheduling scheme, named Dominant Resource Fairness (DRF), goes beyond just the memory criterion, by using both memory and CPU as the resources to be allocated. If there's just a single application running in the cluster, it uses all the cluster's resources (or, to put it more precisely, it potentially *could* use all the resources). As new applications start running, resources freed up by the first application are assigned to the new applications, until each running application is allocated approximately the same amount of resources.

The idea behind the Fair Scheduler is to allow multiple jobs to run simultaneously. When the first job in a cluster, named Job 1, starts, the Fair Scheduler will let it consume all the resources available in the cluster. When new jobs such as Job 2 and Job 3 are submitted, the cluster won't keep them waiting behind Job 1. It allocates every new job some resources, while the first job, Job 1, runs with fewer resources. Fair scheduling essentially means that each job gets a "fair" or an even amount of resources.

The Fair Scheduler's resource allocation algorithm lets short-running applications finish quickly while not denying the long-running applications the resources they need. Fair scheduling also works with applications priorities, which are weights that determine what fraction of resources each application is allocated. Further, the scheduler also utilizes resource queues and shares resources among the queues. If you create a queue and assign an application to that queue, the request for the resources that the application needs is submitted to the queue. You can create a hierarchy of queues in order to divide the resources and configure the hierarchy with weights.

You can use the Fair Scheduler to assign guaranteed minimum shares to queues, thus letting users and applications always get the resources they need. When a queue doesn't need to use its allocated share of resources, those resources aren't tied up uselessly. Rather, the unused resources allocated to the queue are reassigned across all the running applications in the cluster.

The Capacity Scheduler is an alternative to the Fair Scheduler and was designed for managing a cluster's capacity by using job queues to enable systematic sharing of the cluster resources. Job queues are assigned both a guaranteed capacity and a maximum capacity, which is the upper limit on the resources the queues can utilize beyond their guaranteed capacity levels. The Capacity Scheduler optimizes cluster utilization by guaranteeing capacity levels for each of the job queues and using any unused capacity for queues that have bumped up against their capacity limits.

Scheduling Jobs

Scheduling Hadoop jobs (Spark, MapReduce, etc.) is a key part of any administrator's job. Oozie is a special workflow scheduler system designed to work with Hadoop, MapReduce and Pig. Oozie workflows are collections of Spark/MapReduce/Hive/Pig jobs arranged in a control dependency directed acyclic graph (DAG). The Oozie server starts the workflows and tracks the job status and attends to failures.

Organizations typically use MapReduce, Pig and Hive jobs to process the large amounts of data they store in HDFS. An interesting pattern here is that often, a single MapReduce, Pig or Hive job isn't sufficient to completely process the data to get what you need out of it. Often, you need to run a series of MapReduce, Pig or Hive jobs to get to the end result. That is, you must chain multiple jobs together, with the later jobs consuming the intermediate data produced by the earlier running jobs. This means that you need to coordinate the flow of execution of the chained jobs. This is where Oozie comes into the picture.

You may wonder why you can't schedule the series of Hadoop jobs one after the other, using traditional cron jobs. The problem with cronning the jobs is that, most of the time, Hadoop jobs are interdependent. Oozie offers an easy-to-use scheduling framework that lets you run interdependent Hadoop jobs and lets you recover easily when the jobs fail for any reason. Oozie is highly scalable and can handle thousands of jobs.

Securing Hadoop Data

Securing Hadoop and its environment is an important (and complex) topic for many administrators. Hadoop is inherently insecure, despite its built-in authorization features, which are quite strong. In the following sections, I'll quickly review Hadoop's security-related issues and how you're going to deal with them. Chapter 15, "Securing Hadoop," deals exclusively with securing Hadoop.

Default Security

Security was never a priority during Hadoop's evolution—rather, it was data processing that was the main concern. Hadoop assumes a trusted environment for the cluster, but as you know, this isn't appropriate for enterprise-level use, where you need true security for protecting sensitive business data. Unlike traditional client-server systems, in Hadoop there's no central server to authenticate users and there's no security gateway or authentication mechanism either. A user that's given access to the NameNode can, theoretically speaking, delete that data or impersonate other users and access data they aren't supposed to access. Hadoop doesn't contain any mechanism for assigning role-based or object-level access.

Since data is distributed across all DataNodes, you also have to worry about the potential for unauthorized users accessing these nodes and attacking your cluster. The default unencrypted and unsecured HTTP communications between web consoles and the NameNode and the DataNode let a user access the cluster metadata.

Kerberos

The primary security requirement is authentication, which determines that a user is legitimate before allowing that user access to the cluster. By default, Hadoop doesn't authenticate users. Kerberos, an open-source authentication mechanism, is the accepted way to secure Hadoop environments. When you implement Kerberos security, users attempting to log into a Hadoop cluster will query the Key Distribution Center (KDC) to validate their credentials. If the credentials are good, KDC will then provide the access requested by the user. Chapter 15, "Securing Hadoop," shows how to install and configure Kerberos authentication in a Hadoop cluster.

Apache Sentry

Authorization is the next important security area after authentication. Hadoop supports fine-grained authorization through the use of Access Control Lists (ACLs). You can also use Apache Sentry to configure granular authorization for users. You can define parts of your data as tables within a database and let Sentry configure permissions. Sentry uses the concept of user groups and lets you define rules and roles to develop a role-based authorization system.

Apache Ranger

Apache Ranger provides a comprehensive approach to securing Hadoop clusters, including components such as Apache Hive and HBase. Ranger provides centralized security policy administration pertaining to all aspects of enterprise security, such as authorization, accounting and data protection. Users can manage security policies through an administration console and can also enable audit tracking and policy analytics for controlling their environment.

Apache Knox

Apache Knox (Apache Knox Gateway) provides perimeter security so you can ensure that you're maintaining compliance with your security policies when enabling user access a Hadoop cluster. Knox integrates with centralized identity management systems and allows identities from those systems to be used for secure access to Hadoop clusters.

Summary

Here's what you learned in this chapter:

- Hadoop is the leading technology for efficiently processing vast amounts of data.
- Managing Hadoop environments is in many ways similar to how you manage relational databases, but you must also learn how to work with the common Hadoop-related processing frameworks and components.
- Hadoop 2 is architected quite differently from Hadoop 1, its predecessor.
- Hadoop consists of two major components—HDFS for storing data and YARN for processing it.
- Spark is increasingly becoming the main processing engine used in Hadoop environments.
- Key components in the Hadoop ecosphere include Pig, Hive, Sqoop and Oozie.

With this initial background behind us, let's move on to learning the basics of the architecture of a Hadoop cluster.

2

An Introduction to the Architecture of Hadoop

This chapter covers the following:

- The architecture of Hadoop
- Distributed clusters
- The architecture of HDFS
- The architecture of YARN

This chapter introduces you to the architecture of Hadoop. Before you can start learning how to administer Hadoop, it's a good idea to understand its basic architecture. The two foundational layers of Hadoop are its storage system, HDFS, and the processing framework, YARN.

This is a key chapter as it introduces several key terms, as well as the daemons and processes that work together to perform the storage and computational tasks in a Hadoop database.

Distributed Computing and Hadoop

As I explained in Chapter 1, "Introduction to Hadoop and Its Environment," Hadoop follows a distributed computation model—it distributes computations involving humongous chunks of data sets to a set of nodes, each of which works on a portion of the data set. Before I get into the nitty gritty of the Hadoop architecture itself, let me take a moment to explain the challenges posed by distributed computation and how Hadoop meets them.

At its core, distributed computing seeks to meet the following requirements:

- Scalability: Increasing the number of machines should result in a linear increase in processing capacity and storage.
- Fault tolerance: If one of the nodes in a distributed cluster fails, the main computational process itself shouldn't fail or be adversely affected.
- Recoverability: If a job or a part of it fails, you shouldn't lose any data.

Hadoop has been explicitly and carefully designed to meet these fundamental requirements of distributed computing. It meets the challenges of distributed computing through the following strategies and principles that underlie its architecture:

- Data is stored on all or most of the cluster's nodes. Bringing code to the data and not the other way around, Hadoop efficiently processes large amounts of data.
- Developers focus on the data and their algorithms, with Hadoop taking care of the low-level details of distributed programming.
- Jobs are highly tolerant of failures. If one or more nodes of a cluster fail or a component of a job (called a task) fails, the job itself will continue to completion.

Hadoop Architecture

In order to work well with Hadoop, it's important to understand its key components, HDFS, which is the storage component, and YARN, which is the processing component.

Ranking web pages and searching social networks and social-networking sites are two examples where you deal with pretty regular data flows, which makes it easy to mine the data through data parallelism. In order to efficiently process these types of large data sets, a new programming paradigm using a different type of software stack has evolved. Whereas traditional data processing has focused on larger and larger computers, leading to the birth of supercomputers, this newer approach employs clusters of interconnected inexpensive computers.

The new software stack, as represented by Hadoop, has a distributed file system as its foundation. Unlike traditional databases, this file system typically uses very large data blocks in order to quickly process vast chunks of data. Another key feature is built-in redundancy of data, since the file system uses inexpensive computing nodes, each of which may fail anytime. The redundancy is provided by replicating all data across multiple servers, usually three in number. Figure 2.1 shows Hadoop's distributed computational architecture.

In the following sections, we discuss the two main building blocks of Hadoop—data storage (HDFS) and the operating system (YARN). HDFS provides the underlying storage for all Hadoop operations. Data that you store in a Hadoop system is stored in HDFS, which happens to sit on the underlying Linux (or Windows) file system. YARN provides the processing framework for running not only MapReduce but also other frameworks such as Tez and Spark.

Before I plunge into a discussion of Hadoop in earnest, it's a good idea to clarify what a Hadoop cluster is, the different types of nodes in a cluster and the types of services that run in a cluster.

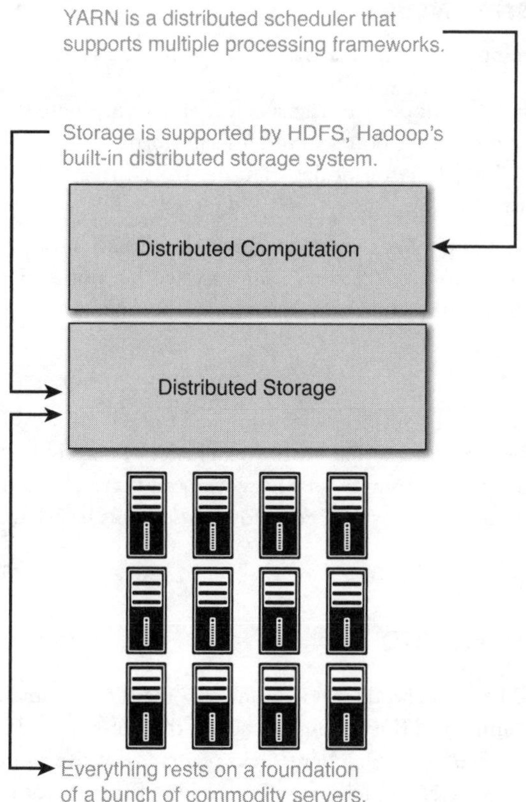

Figure 2.1 Hadoop and distributed computing, showing how computation and storage are distributed

A Hadoop Cluster

In Chapter 1, I explained what a Hadoop cluster means. To summarize, a Hadoop cluster is a collection of machines that uses the Hadoop software on the foundations of a distributed file system (HDFS) and a cluster resource manager (YARN). Anything more than a single machine will technically constitute a cluster. You can run small clusters with just a few nodes and there are very large clusters maintained by organizations such as Yahoo, whose largest Hadoop clusters range over 10,000 nodes. Regardless of its size, everything works the same in every Hadoop cluster.

In practical terms, Hadoop implements storage and processing through a set of daemon processes that run in the background. Users aren't concerned with these processes, as they perform input/output over the network without any intervention from users. On a Linux system, each of these daemons (processes) runs within a separate Java Virtual Machine (JVM).

Master and Worker Nodes

The nodes in a Hadoop cluster are classified into two basic types:

- Master nodes: These nodes run the services that coordinate the cluster's work. Clients contact the master nodes in order to perform computations. In each cluster, there are a handful of master nodes, ranging from three to six, depending on the size of the cluster.
- Worker nodes: These nodes perform under the direction of processes running on the master nodes. Most of a cluster's nodes are worker nodes. The worker nodes are where the data is stored and computations are performed.

Hadoop Services

There are several key Hadoop services that you need to be familiar with. These services, working together, perform the actual work in a cluster. There is a set of HDFS-related services that take care of the storage-related work, and there's a separate set of services dedicated to the computational tasks. The following sections briefly introduce the various Hadoop services.

HDFS Services

The HDFS services manage HDFS storage:

- NameNode: The NameNode service runs on a master node and maintains the metadata pertaining to HDFS storage, such as the file system directory tree and the locations of the files. When a client seeks to read or write to HDFS, it contacts the NameNode service, which provides the client information about the location of the files in HDFS.
- Secondary NameNode and Standby NameNode: You need to run one of these master services on each cluster. These services relieve the burden of the critical NameNode by performing tasks such as checkpointing (updating) the metadata file.
- DataNodes: These are worker nodes that store the HDFS data blocks on the Linux file system. The DataNodes keep in contact with the NameNode and update the latter with all the changes that occur in the file system.

YARN Services

As with HDFS, there are several services that run on both the master and worker nodes:

- ResourceManager: This is a single service for the entire cluster that runs on one of the master nodes and is responsible for allocating the cluster's resources and the scheduling of jobs on the worker nodes.
- ApplicationMaster: This is a master service, and there's one for each application you run in the cluster. The ApplicationMaster coordinates the execution of the application in the cluster and negotiates with the ResourceManager for resources for the application.

- NodeManager: There is one of these services running on each of the worker nodes. The NodeManager service runs and manages tasks (components of the application or job) on the worker nodes. They remain in touch with the ResourceManager and update it with their health, as well as the status of the tasks they're running.

With this initial exploration of a Hadoop cluster behind us, it's time to learn about the two pillars of Hadoop—HDFS and YARN. It is important to understand how the two entities work together to perform complex distributed computational tasks. I start with a discussion of HDFS.

Data Storage—The Hadoop Distributed File System

HDFS is a distributed file system that sits on the underlying server storage and has many similarities to the base storage system. A distributed storage system stores large amounts of data over a network of computers with built-in redundancy to protect data. HDFS is designed for fast, fault-tolerant processing, thus enabling the use of inexpensive storage hardware. Server storage, say on a Linux system, adheres to the POSIX requirements, some of which aren't met by HDFS. This is so by design, to enable streaming access to large chunks of data.

The MapReduce programming model was originally the only programming engine that Hadoop could use and is quite popular even now in Hadoop environments. MapReduce deals with large data volumes. It avoids slowdowns due to storage and network I/O that will be incurred if you use a storage system such as NFS. The large volume of data is spread out over the cluster's nodes, but MapReduce sees it as a single file system. So, each disk reads all of its data from local disks (HDFS, not the local file system), avoiding the need to transmit data through the network.

In a small Hadoop cluster, there may be just a handful of servers. Larger clusters have hundreds and even thousands of servers. Regardless of the size, Hadoop stores its data on all of the cluster's file system, with each of the cluster's nodes storing a small amount of the data.

HDFS Unique Features

HDFS has several unique features that make it ideal for large-scale distributed processing. In the following sections, I briefly review how HDFS supports the efficient processing of large data sets.

Handling Large Data Sets

Typically, non-Hadoop databases are small, with at most a few terabytes of data and a few data files. Hadoop deals with petabytes of data and thousands of data files.

Fault Tolerance

Hadoop depends on large numbers of servers so it can parallelize work across them. Server and storage failures are to be expected, and the system isn't affected by the non-functioning storage units—or even failed servers. Data is, by default, replicated thrice in Hadoop, meaning that each data block in HDFS is stored on three different nodes. You can decrease or increase the default "replication factor." You can also employ different replication levels for different sets of data, as replication is applied at the file level.

Streaming Access to Data

Traditional databases are geared mostly for fast access to data and not for batch processing. Hadoop was originally designed for batch processing (although newer developments have enabled other processing paradigms such as interactive SQL, iterative processing, search processing and stream processing) and provides streaming access to data sets.

Simple Data Consistency Model

Unlike traditional databases, Hadoop data files employ a write-once-read-many access model. Data consistency issues that may arise in an updateable database aren't an issue with Hadoop file systems because only a single writer can write to a file at any time.

HDFS Architecture

HDFS enables users to store data in files, which are split into multiple blocks. Since Hadoop is designed to work with massive amounts of data, HDFS block sizes are much larger than those used by typical relational databases. The default block size is 128MB, and you can configure the size to as high as 512MB.

> **Note**
>
> It's common to use the term *NameNode* to refer to both the NameNode daemon and the cluster node where the NameNode is configured to run. This is also the case with the term *DataNode*, which can refer alternatively to the DataNode daemon or the server on which the DataNode daemon runs.

Master Nodes and DataNodes

In a Hadoop cluster, which consists of multiple nodes, one or more of the nodes will act as *master nodes*. The master nodes run key Hadoop services such as the NameNode (manages the HDFS metadata among other things) and the ResourceManager (manages jobs and tasks). The rest of the servers in a Hadoop cluster are worker nodes, commonly referred to as *DataNodes*. It's these nodes that actually store the data blocks. Worker nodes also run NodeManagers (YARN). You don't need to run a NodeManager on every node, but you do most of the time. Figure 2.2 shows how the master and the worker nodes are connected together in a Hadoop cluster. The solid lines represent keyless SSH logins.

The worker nodes are where you actually store the cluster's data in the HDFS file system. The HDFS data is distributed among the cluster's nodes but appears to you as a single unified file system that you can access from any of the cluster's nodes. You can run a cluster with a single NameNode whose job is to maintain and store metadata pertaining to the HDFS file system. In production clusters, you'll usually use two NameNodes, one serving as the active NameNode and the other playing the role of a standby ready to take over as the active NameNode when the active NameNode fails for any reason.

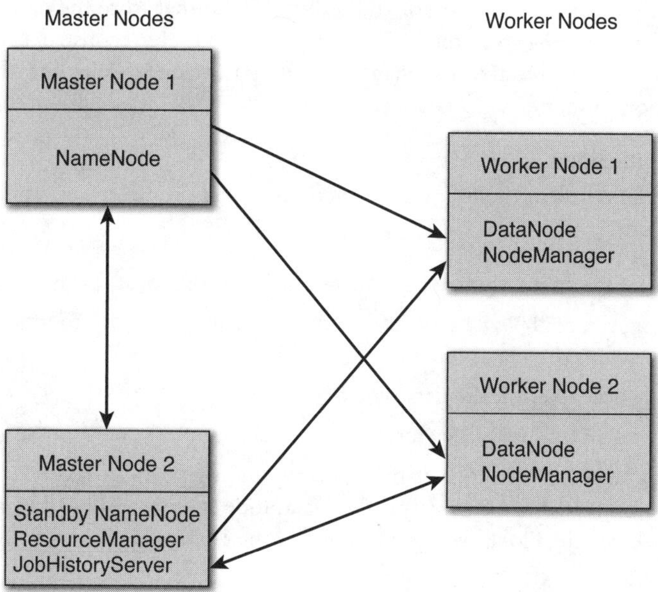

Figure 2.2 The relationship between the master nodes and the worker nodes

The NameNode and the DataNodes work in tandem to take care of all data writes and reads using HDFS, as summarized in the following sections.

NameNode Functions

The NameNode manages the file system namespace by performing the following tasks:

- Maintaining the metadata pertaining to the file system, such as the file hierarchy and the block locations for each file
- Managing user access to the data files
- Mapping the data blocks to the DataNodes in the cluster
- Performing file system operations such as opening and closing the files and directories
- Providing registration services for DataNode cluster membership and handling periodic heartbeats from the DataNodes
- Determining on which nodes data should be replicated, and deleting over replicated blocks
- Processing the block reports sent by the DataNodes and maintaining the location where data blocks live

While the NameNode is aware of all the DataNodes that store the data blocks for any HDFS file, it doesn't store the block locations—it simply reconstructs them from information sent by the DataNodes when you start up the cluster. Following this, it retains the information in memory for fast access to it.

DataNode Functions

The DataNodes perform the following functions, based on directives sent by the NameNode:

- Providing the block storage by storing blocks on the local file system.
- Fulfilling the read/write requests from the clients who want to work with the data stored on the DataNodes.
- Creating and deleting the data blocks.
- Replicating data across the cluster.
- Keeping in touch with the NameNode by sending periodic block reports and heartbeats. A heartbeat confirms the DataNode is alive and healthy, and a block report shows the blocks being managed by the DataNode.

> **Note**
>
> The key thing to understand is that at no point does actual HDFS data travel through the NameNode. Clients always access the file system (HDFS) that resides on the DataNodes. The NameNode facilitates and enables that data access. This is as it should be, because there's a single NameNode (there may be a Standby NameNode as well, but at any given point in time, only one NameNode is in operation), and that NameNode could be overwhelmed if it had to handle the enormous data transfers that occur in a Hadoop system. In addition, a key operational aspect of HDFS is data localization, wherein the client applications try to process on the nodes where the data is located, for operational efficiency.

The HDFS File System

Hadoop is all about the efficient processing of large chunks of data. It's therefore important to understand how Hadoop stores its data.

HDFS organizes its file system differently from the underlying file system such as the Linux ext3 or ext4 file system. HDFS employs a block-based file system, wherein files are broken up into blocks.

A file and a server in the cluster don't have a one-to-one relationship. This means that a file can consist of multiple blocks, all of which most likely won't be stored on the same machine.

A file's blocks are spread throughout the cluster on a random basis. This lets Hadoop support files that are larger than the size of a single disk drive. If you store a file's blocks across multiple servers, what happens when one of the machines is unavailable? You'll be fine, since Hadoop replicates each block three times by default.

Note

The key to understanding the logic behind the architecture of the Hadoop file system is to keep in mind that Hadoop wasn't designed to be a general purpose file system. Rather, it was designed for large batch jobs, where the jobs would typically sequentially read very large files, from start to finish. This is in contrast to seeking a specific value or range of values, which is common for most OLTP applications.

HDFS enables users to store data in files, which are split into multiple blocks. Since Hadoop is designed to work with massive amounts of data, HDFS block sizes are much larger than those used by a typical relational database.

Unlike blocks in a relational regular database, which are sized anywhere from 4MB to 16MB (typically), Hadoop uses a minimum block size of 64MB, and it's common to use a block size of 128MB or 256MB. Large block sizes provide the following benefits:

- The file system metadata is smaller when you use very large block sizes as opposed to small block sizes.
- Since large chunks of data can be read sequentially, fast streaming reads of data are easier to perform.

Larger and fewer blocks mean longer running tasks, which in turn may not gain maximum parallelism. The point here is that we don't want jobs with thousands of tasks, nor do we want too few, as that would keep us from completely utilizing our processing capacity.

Figure 2.3 shows how Hadoop breaks up a large file into multiple chunks. The size of each of the chunks is determined by the Hadoop block size, but it is 128MB by default.

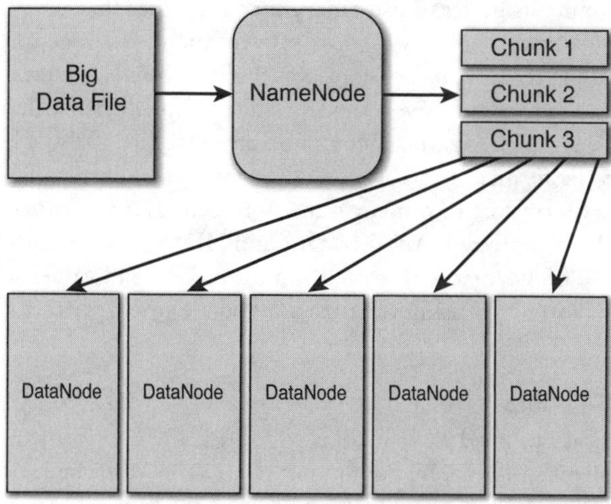

Figure 2.3 How Hadoop breaks up large files into smaller chunks to enable parallel processing of the data

Each of the 128MB (or larger) data chunks is replicated three times and distributed among the nodes. It's this ability to partition the data into easily digestible chunks that helps Hadoop process humongous data files in parallel using an array of nodes, each of which processes one of the chunks of data at a time.

I briefly review the key features of HDFS in the following sections.

File System Organization

The files in HDFS are organized in a fashion similar to files in a Linux or UNIX system, wherein there's a tree-based directory and file hierarchy. You can perform many common Linux/UNIX file system operations using analogous commands within HDFS.

Since HDFS employs a write-once-read-many access model, once you write a file to HDFS, you can't modify its contents. You also can't overwrite a file with an existing name. You can perform the following operations, since they're merely metadata operations and don't touch the contents of the file itself:

- Move a file
- Delete a file
- Rename a file

HDFS Data Formats

HDFS needs to work with massive amounts of data stored in very large files. When dealing with large HDFS files, MapReduce splits the files into multiple pieces at record boundaries, so it can read data from the large file simultaneously by starting multiple mapper processes. A splittable data format lets a file be correctly split into pieces at the record boundaries.

Hadoop environments prefer to use binary formats rather than text formats when dealing with HDFS, because binary formats prevent incomplete records being written to files, by catching and ignoring incorrect records that may be created due to data corruption or incompleteness. This type of issue can occur, for example, when a cluster accidentally runs out of space during a write. Data compression capability is also a key requirement for a good HDFS file format.

A popular binary format used by many is the Avro container file format, which is splittable and can also be compressed. Another common HDFS data format is a SequenceFile, which is a splittable file format represented as a list of keys and values. Users can also customize the data format by using serializers, which let them write data in any format they choose.

Writing to an HDFS File

When client applications need to write data to HDFS, they perform an initial write to a local file on the client machine, in a temporary file. When the client finishes the write and closes it, or when the temporary file's size crosses a block boundary, Hadoop will create a file and assign data blocks to the file. The temporary file's contents are then written to the new HDFS file, block by block. After the first block is written, two other replicas (based on the default replication factor of three) are written to two other DataNodes in the cluster, one after the other. The write operation will succeed only if Hadoop successfully places all data block replicas in all the target nodes.

Data Replication

Data replication is one of the pillars of Hadoop, since it provides fault tolerance. Since Hadoop maintains multiple copies of data, it's quite hard to lose data stored in a cluster.

> **Tip**
>
> HDFS automatically replicates any under-replicated data blocks. If you lose a disk or even a server, no need to lose sleep over it. Hadoop will automatically do what is needed!

Hadoop optimizes data reads by choosing to read the replica that's stored on the same node where the read request originates or at least on the same rack. It also prefers reading from a rack in a local data center to reading a replica from a remote rack.

Using Hadoop's native libraries, you can access data in HDFS. It's common for applications to want to access HDFS and move data in and out of the Hadoop cluster, using client-side native libraries instead of Hadoop's native libraries. WebHDFS helps in these situations by letting you use a HTTP REST API to access HDFS data. Using WebHDFS, you can access Hadoop through multiple languages without installing Hadoop. You can use tools such as curl and wget to download HDFS data as well, using WebHDFS. WebHDFS provides both read and write access and supports all HDFS operations. Chapter 10, "Data Protection, File Formats and Accessing HDFS," discusses WebHDFS in detail.

NameNode Operations

Each Hadoop cluster has a NameNode (as noted previously, there may be two of these in a high-availability environment—an active and a Standby NameNode). The NameNode holds all the metadata (such as the HDFS directory structure and file permissions) in memory for fast access but also persists the same information to disk. The following information is stored by the NameNode on disk in the fsimage file:

- The names of all the files in HDFS
- The HDFS directory structure
- The file permissions of all the files in HDFS

The namespace contains the directory and files listed in a hierarchical fashion. Each namespace has a unique namespace ID that's stored on all the cluster nodes, in order to prevent DataNodes with a different namespace ID from accidentally joining the wrong cluster.

Anytime there's a change in the metadata due to operations such as a file creation or deletion, it doesn't prompt the immediate revision of the fsimage file. Instead, the change information is recorded in the edits file on disk. By default, every hour, the Secondary NameNode merges the edits and fsimage files and writes the consolidated information as a fresh fsimage file. The NameNode truncates the old edits file at this point and starts writing new stuff to it.

Figure 2.4 shows how the NameNode relates to the DataNodes, as well as how HDFS clients communicate with the NameNode and the DataNodes. When HDFS clients

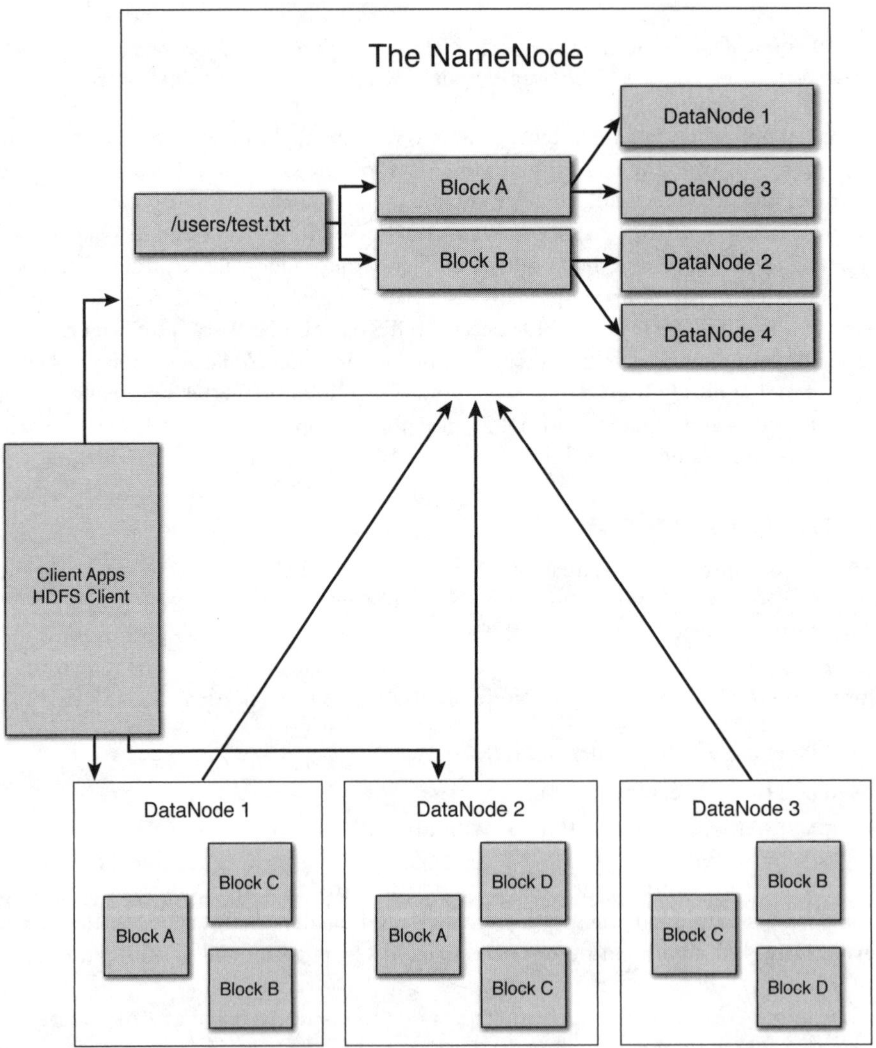

Figure 2.4 How HDFS clients communicate with the NameNode and DataNodes

want to read or write files stored on the DataNodes, they contact the NameNode, which has the file metadata. The NameNode uses the HDFS metadata to determine which DataNode is storing the data blocks for the HDFS file /users/test.txt.

The data files are made of blocks and data is replicated—by default there are three copies for each data block.

The only reason the NameNode keeps the HDFS metadata in RAM is for easily accessing that data when clients require access to HDFS data (reads and writes). A client can't access the DataNodes directly—clients don't have any idea which DataNode might be hosting the data that they need. Clients access the NameNode instead, which acts as the intermediary between the clients and the DataNodes. The NameNode passes along to the client information such as the file block numbers and data location (DataNode).

Initially, file metadata is stored in the fsimage file on disk. When the metadata changes due to actions such as file creation or deletion, the change information is written to a transaction log on disk named edits. It's the Secondary NameNode that periodically coalesces the fsimage and edits files, writing out a fresh fsimage file. The NameNode can delete the edits file after this.

When a client application writes data to an HDFS file, the NameNode updates the HDFS metadata in RAM, and the changes are also written simultaneously to the edits file. The reason the changes are written out to the edits file is to preserve the modifications to the namespace—if the NameNode crashes, the information stored in RAM is lost.

If your cluster's NameNode ceases functioning for any reason, HDFS becomes unavailable to you and the applications that are running. You must restore the NameNode in order to makes HDFS available to the users again. Of course, if you're using a Standby NameNode, the loss of the active NameNode will bring up the Standby NameNode automatically. In such a setup, losing the server on which the NameNode is running really won't affect anything, since the cluster will function uninterrupted in every way.

In order for a map process from a MapReduce job to read data from HDFS, it first contacts the NameNode. The NameNode will send the map client the block names and locations (DataNodes) for the first few blocks in the file.

Similarly, a reduce process that writes its results to HDFS will contact the NameNode, which will then supply the block names and the locations of the DataNodes where the reducer process should write its file.

It's thus the NameNode that determines where the client writes, by sending it a list of "approved" DataNodes to which the client should write. The NameNode itself never sees any of the data—it acts as the facilitator for the actual data access by the client on the DataNodes, where the data is stored. As you can see, both the read and write processes initiate their work by first touching base with the NameNode—hence, unavailability of the NameNode means that the cluster is basically unavailable.

While the Secondary NameNode performs housekeeping duties such as periodically checkpointing the fsimage file, it by no means can step in when the NameNode becomes unavailable. You need to set up a Standby NameNode (explained in Chapter 11, "NameNode Operations, High Availability and Federation") for that purpose.

The Secondary NameNode

NameNodes aren't supposed to be frequently restarted—when a NameNode isn't available, there is, in effect, a cluster outage, and, of course, you'd want to keep those types of outages to a bare minimum.

Without a NameNode, there's no way to know to which files the blocks stored on the DataNodes correspond to, and, in essence, all files in HDFS are lost. Also, the edits file (the transactions log for the NameNode metadata file, which is named the fsimage file) will grow to quite a large size over time. When you restart a NameNode with this large edits file, it'll take a very long time to start its operations.

In order to avoid this problem, Hadoop employs a Secondary NameNode. The Secondary NameNode performs a checkpoint of the fsimage file periodically—the checkpointing really means that the Secondary NameNode merges the fsimage and edits files. The Secondary NameNode is also called the checkpoint node because it performs checkpoint services for the NameNode. Since this NameNode also stores the file system namespace in memory and syncs it to the NameNode's namespace, it's also called a backup NameNode. However, it really doesn't provide any real backup functionality for the NameNode.

You can run a Hadoop cluster without a Secondary NameNode, but you don't want to do this! If you don't have a Secondary NameNode running, there's no way to perform a checkpoint. Let's say your cluster runs uninterrupted for six months and then the NameNode stops because it runs out of space for its logs. Restarting the cluster now will take you days, and your cluster is completely unavailable during this time.

When a client (such as a mapper process) needs to read a file on HDFS, it needs the block IDs that are part of that file. The client contacts the NameNode for those block IDs. The NameNode doesn't actually have to look up the fsimage file on disk for that information. It reads the block IDs from its memory (where it stores the fsimage file upon starting up) and sends that information over to the client.

Figure 2.5 shows how the Secondary NameNode performs the checkpointing of the fsimage file and sends it back to the NameNode so the NameNode doesn't have to worry about doing the checkpointing itself. The Secondary NameNode periodically queries the NameNode for edit logs. These logs record changes in the HDFS metadata. The Secondary NameNode updates its own fsimage with the edit logs from the NameNode. The Secondary NameNode copies the updated (checkpointed) fsimage to the NameNode.

When a data block is written to HDFS, it contains only data from the file. A file is split into multiple blocks before being written into HDFS. Each block consists of a portion of the data file, and the metadata file associated with the data block contains the checksum data confirming the block integrity when it's read. The DataNode itself has no idea as to what particular file a specific block is a part of—that information is part of the NameNode's metadata.

HDFS High Availability and the Standby NameNode

The NameNode, due to its responsibility for maintaining the file system name space and metadata, is indispensable for the cluster. Hadoop 2 overcomes a major drawback of Hadoop 1 by offering NameNode High Availability (HA). In Hadoop 2, you can create a

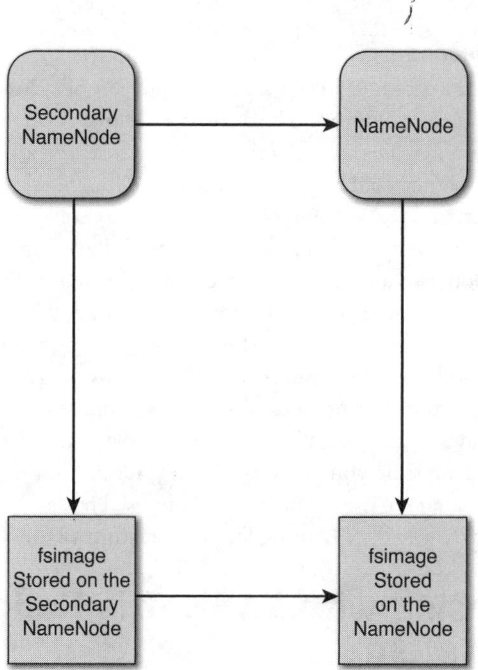

Figure 2.5 How the Secondary NameNode updates the fsimage file and sends it back to the NameNode

Standby NameNode to provide high availability. When using a Standby NameNode for high availability, you don't need to run the Secondary NameNode.

NameNode high availability permits the running of two NameNodes in a cluster, with one of them in the role of the active NameNode and the other a standby role. The dual NameNode setup keeps the all-important NameNode from being a single point of failure in your cluster. Using the standby capability means that your cluster remains operational when one of the NameNodes is down, either due to a machine crash or due to a planned maintenance event such as a software or hardware upgrade on the node hosting the NameNode.

Apache ZooKeeper

Apache ZooKeeper is a centralized service that provides distributed synchronization and group services for Hadoop's HDFS, which itself is distributed and highly reliable. For example, the NameNode HA feature relies on the ZooKeeper service. Besides HDFS, several components such as HBase require the ZooKeeper services to be running in the cluster. The point behind the deployment of the ZooKeeper service is to make it unnecessary for distributed applications to have to implement distributed and reliable consensus, group management and presence protocols.

Zookeeper is deployed as an ensemble of servers. An ensemble here means that the servers are in a cluster and as long as a majority of the members are up, the service is available.

Potential for Unbalanced Data

While HDFS spreads data around all DataNodes that are part of a cluster, the data spread isn't automatic. When you create a cluster and load data for the first time, or when you add new data to it, say on a daily basis, the incoming data (including the replicas) does get automatically spread out through the cluster, so that all DataNodes have roughly the same amount of data.

Over time, however, the data distribution may not and most likely won't remain balanced. Some nodes will end up with a higher percent of used space compared to others. Also, when you add new nodes to a cluster, HDFS doesn't automatically move some of the data onto the new node's storage disks. Those disks will get data written to them, but that'll be only for new data arriving into HDFS. If you don't do anything, the new disks will always continue to have a lower percentage of their storage system in use.

However, if continuous balancing of data is a concern, there's nothing to worry about here, as Hadoop provides a handy data balancing tool called the balancer. You can run the rebalancing command anytime you want, to make Hadoop move data around from the disks with a high percentage of use to the relatively unused nodes. You'll learn much more about the balancer in Chapter 4, "Planning for and Creating a Fully Distributed Cluster."

Data Processing with YARN, the Hadoop Operating System

HDFS is one of the two foundation stones of Hadoop. YARN is the other one. If HDFS is the *storage layer,* YARN is the *processing layer* of Hadoop. Simply put, YARN is a framework for managing distributed applications executed on multiple machines within a network). YARN manages all resources in a Hadoop cluster. Note that YARN supports other distributed processing frameworks such as Impala, Spark and Giraph, besides MapReduce v2. All applications running in a Hadoop environment, including MapReduce, Spark, Tez and the rest, use YARN to perform their work.

YARN is the Hadoop processing layer, and it contains a resource manager as well as a job scheduler. It's YARN that makes it possible for multiple processing frameworks to run on the same Hadoop cluster, such as

- Batch programs (such as Spark or MapReduce)
- Interactive SQL (such as Impala)
- Advanced analytics (Spark SQL, Spark ML, or Impala)
- Streaming (Spark Streaming)

Before we delve into the intricacies of YARN, first a clarification regarding the nomenclature—all the following are equivalent:

- MapReduce 2.0
- MRv2
- YARN
- Apache Hadoop NextGen MapReduce

Architecture of YARN

YARN depends on a cluster-wide ResourceManager, which is the authoritative arbitrator of resources among all the applications running in a Hadoop cluster. The ResourceManager works together with a NodeManager (NM) that runs on every worker node (DataNode) in the cluster. Together, the single ResourceManager and the per-node NodeManagers form the data computation framework.

Each of the applications that run on YARN has an ApplicationMaster (AM) associated with it. The ApplicationMaster's main purpose is to negotiate with the ResourceManager for resources and work with the NodeManagers to execute the tasks that are part of each application.

Before you dive into the architecture of YARN itself, it's helpful to understand the following terms:

- A **client** is the program that submits YARN jobs to the cluster. Sometimes a client also refers to the gateway machine on which the client program runs.
- A **job**, also called an application (for example, a MapReduce job will include mappers, optional reducers and the list of inputs they process), contains one or more tasks.
- When running a MapReduce job, a **task** can be either a **mapper** or a **reducer** task. There are some applications that use both mappers and reducers and some that just use mappers and no reducers.
- Each mapper and reducer task runs within its own container. The administrator configures the size of the containers. The job determines the number of mappers and reducers.

Figure 2.6 shows the high-level architecture of YARN and how its core components work together to process data. The ResourceManager, ApplicationMaster, and NodeManager

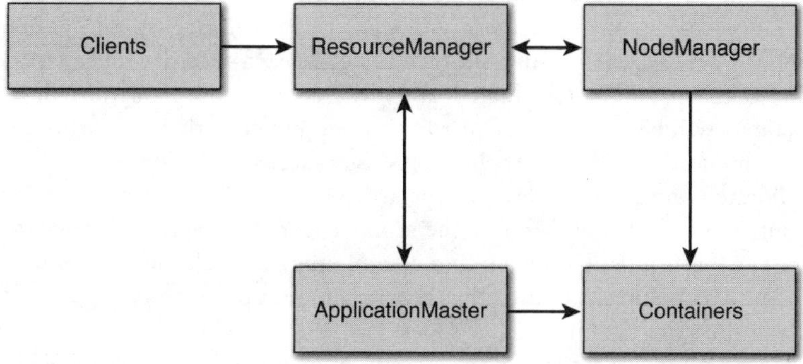

Figure 2.6 YARN clients, the ResourceManager and the NodeManager

are the key actors in performing the computational work. YARN clients create the apps and launch them. The RM is in charge of scheduling and managing resources. A NodeManager daemon runs on each DataNode and launches and manages containers. There's a single AM for each job. The AM is created by the RM and it makes all the requests for the containers needed to complete a job. Containers are abstractions that refer to resources such as RAM and CPU.

I look at the key components of YARN in more detail in the following sections.

YARN Containers—How YARN Allocates Resources

YARN uses **containers**, which are logical constructs that represent a specific amount of memory and other resources, such as the processing cores (CPU), to process its applications. For example, a container can represent 2GB memory and 2 processing cores. A container could be a set of physical resources such as memory, CPU, disk and network—right now only memory and CPU are used in sizing a container. All of your YARN application tasks run in containers. Each Hadoop job contains multiple tasks and each of the tasks runs in its own container. A container comes into being when the task starts. When the task completes, the container is killed and its resources allocated to other tasks.

You can configure the containers to suit your resource availability and processing needs. As with everything, Hadoop has default values for configuring the containers (such as 8GB RAM per container), and you can configure them to suit your resource availability and processing needs.

The ResourceManager allocates the containers for each application. The NodeManager manages the containers' lifecycles and the ResourceManager schedules the containers.

Each YARN application runs in one or more containers. By default, each container has a set amount of memory, and you can customize it. It's customary to use a size ranging from 1-4 GB for the map and reduce containers, but you can configure more memory if you need. As an administrator, you really can't specify or even predict where the individual containers for a job will run—that is managed entirely at the application layer.

If a job is allocated, let's say, 200 containers, each performing a task such as a map or reduce, it means that the containers will be distributed among the cluster nodes, with a bunch of containers running on each node. As each map or reduce task completes, the container will be terminated, and if there are pending map or reduce tasks, new containers will be started up to re-run the pending tasks that are part of the application. The application-specific ApplicationMaster launches the jobs in the containers that are allocated on various nodes for a specific job.

The number of tasks, and therefore the number of YARN applications you can run at any one time, is limited by the number of containers your cluster can spawn. The total number of containers is limited by the total amount of memory you allocated to YARN, as well as the total number of processors you assigned to YARN. Later in this chapter, I explain how to configure the amount of memory to allocate for YARN in your cluster.

The ResourceManager

There's one ResourceManager per cluster, and it does the following:

- Initiates the startup of all YARN applications
- Manages job scheduling and execution
- Allocates resources globally on all the DataNodes

The ResourceManager consists of two key components, the **Scheduler** and the **ApplicationsManager** (not to be confused with the per-application **ApplicationMaster**). The Scheduler allocates resources to running applications within the limits of capacities and queues. In order to allocate resources, the Scheduler uses resource containers. The ApplicationsManager accepts job requests submitted by clients and starts the first container for execution of a new ApplicationMaster. It also restarts an ApplicationMaster container upon its failure.

Following are the key functions of the ResourceManager:

- Creates the first container for an application. This is the container in which the ApplicationMaster for the application will run.
- Tracks the heartbeats from the NodeManagers to manage the DataNodes.
- Runs a Scheduler to determine resource allocation among the clusters.
- Manages cluster level security.
- Manages the resource requests from the ApplicationMasters.
- Monitors the status of the ApplicationMaster and restarts that container upon its failure.
- Deallocates the containers when the application completes or after they expire.

The scheduling algorithms that are part of the Scheduler component of the ResourceManager perform the following functions:

- Let users share a cluster in a predictable fashion, guided by a preset policy
- Support the implementation of multiple SLAs for which users are responsible
- Let short-running, small jobs run even when they're started after huge, resource-intensive, long-running jobs
- Reduce job latencies where you have different-sized jobs running together

The ResourceManager allocates cluster resources among the applications running in a cluster and in the process optimizes the cluster resource usage. The ResourceManager optimizes cluster utilization while following constraints imposed by capacity guarantees and SLAs, using a pluggable scheduler that incorporates capacity guarantees and fair scheduling features.

It's important to realize that that the ResourceManager is a pure scheduler—it doesn't care about the type of application or framework. It doesn't understand anything about

MapReduce or Spark per se—it simply assigns resources to applications that request them, regardless of the type of application or framework.

The NodeManager

Each DataNode in a Hadoop 2 cluster runs a NodeManager daemon for performing YARN functions (the DataNodes also run a DataNode daemon for performing HDFS functions). The per-node NodeManager agent performs the following functions:

- Communicates with the global ResourceManager through health heartbeats and container status notifications.
- Registers and starts the application processes.
- Launches both the ApplicationMaster and the rest of an application's resource containers (that is, the map and reduce tasks that run in the containers) on request from the ApplicationsManager.
- Oversees the lifecycle of the application containers.
- Monitors, manages and provides information regarding the resource consumption (CPU/memory) by the containers.
- Tracks the health of the DataNodes.
- Monitors container resource usage and kills runaway processes.
- Handles log management by aggregating the job logs and saving them to HDFS.
- Provides auxiliary services to YARN applications. Auxiliary services are applications that provide services to applications and are used by the MapReduce framework for its shuffle and sort operations.
- Maintains security at the node level.

Figure 2.7 shows how the NodeManager interacts with the ResourceManager to manage container resources. The NodeManager process coordinates the resource usage on the DataNodes where it runs and also reports the usage information to the ResourceManager. It starts and manages the application containers. The ResourceManager manages job scheduling and execution on the worker nodes.

The ApplicationMaster

There's a single, dedicated ApplicationMaster for each YARN application (same as a job). The ApplicationMaster's main functions are:

- Managing task scheduling and execution
- Allocating resources locally for the application's tasks

Unlike the ResourceManager and the NodeManager, the ApplicationMaster is specific to an application and serves the resource requirements of that application. While the ResourceManager and the NodeManager are always running, the ApplicationMaster is

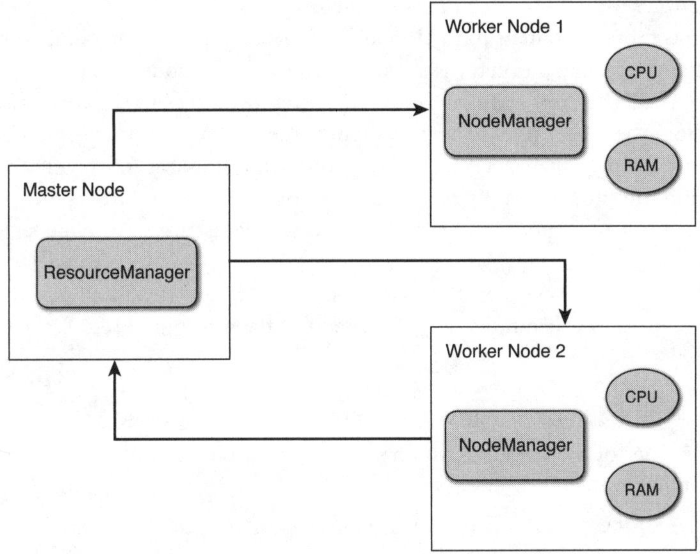

Figure 2.7 How the NodeManagers manage the resources on the nodes and interact with the ResourceManager to oversee application containers

only associated with running applications—if there are no currently running applications, there won't be an ApplicationMaster process running. It's important to remember that the ApplicationMaster tracks job progress for a specific application. Each time a new application starts, the ResourceManager deploys a container running the ApplicationMaster on one of the cluster's nodes.

> **Note**
>
> The ApplicationMaster isn't a continuously running daemon (unlike the ResourceManager and NodeManager daemons)—rather, it's application specific. Each application that runs in the cluster is associated with a single ApplicationMaster, which starts when the application is started and is terminated when that application completes. The ApplicationMaster is in charge of the entire lifecycle of an application, from requesting the necessary containers from the ResourceManager to submitting lease requests to NodeManagers for those containers.

How the ApplicationMaster Works with the ResourceManager to Allocate Resources

The ApplicationMaster, like all YARN processes, runs within a YARN container—in fact it runs inside the first container when an application starts. Once the Application-Master starts running in the application's very first container, it negotiates with the

ResourceManager for containers to process the mappers and reducers in the application. It then presents those containers to the NodeManagers running on each of the DataNodes where the ResourceManager has assigned resources for the containers.

The ApplicationMaster is in charge of requesting resources in the form of resource containers from the ResourceManager to support the application. It coordinates its work with that of the NodeManager service running on each DataNode to execute the resource containers and monitor how they're using the resources allocated to them.

One of the primary responsibilities of the ApplicationMaster is to provide fault tolerance for resources.

When the ApplicationMaster makes a resource request to the ResourceManager for running its map and reduce tasks, it's very specific. Each resource request specifies the following:

- The file blocks needed to process the job
- The amount of the resource, in terms of the number of containers to create for the application
- The size of the containers (for example, 1GB RAM and 1 Virtual Core)
- The location where the resources should be assigned (for example, 4 containers on Node 10, Rack 1 and 8 containers on Node 20, Rack 2) based on the information it gets from the NameNode as to the locations (nodes) where the data blocks are stored
- Priority of the resource request

If the resources requested by the ApplicationMaster are available, the ResourceManager grants the ApplicationMaster's resource requests. The ApplicationMaster will then allocate the map and reduce task containers to the NodeManagers running on the DataNodes.

> **Note**
>
> The ApplicationMaster is framework specific. For example, `MRAppMaster` is the name of the ApplicationMaster for MapReduce applications. For Spark, it's the `SparkAppMaster`.

The JobHistoryServer

There's a single JobHistoryServer for the entire cluster. The JobHistoryServer archives all YARN job metrics and their metadata and is exposed through the JobHistoryServer web UI. The cluster will run fine without the JobHistoryServer, but you won't be able to easily access the job logs and job history without it.

How YARN Components Work Together

The ResourceManager, NodeManager and ApplicationMaster work together to service application requests for resources. Figure 2.8 shows the basic YARN architecture and illustrates how they do so.

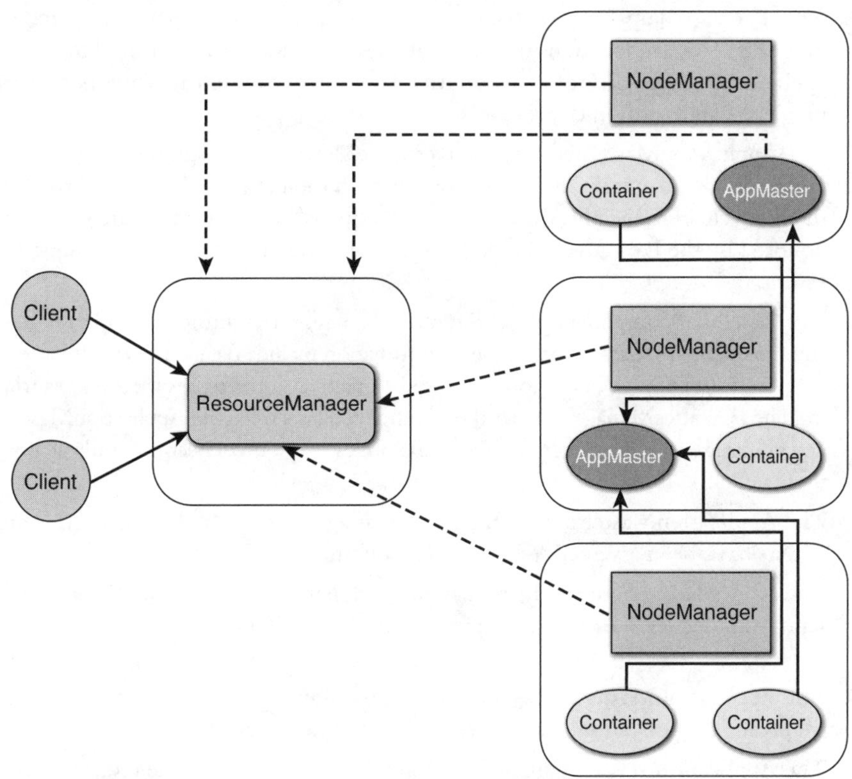

Figure 2.8 How YARN components work together

Following is the sequence of events that occurs when a MapReduce application is started in a YARN-based cluster.

1. Client submits the MapReduce v2 (MRv2) application request, such as the following, to the ResourceManager.

   ```
   $ hadoop jar wordcount.jar  WordCount  testdata output
   ```

2. The ApplicationManager component of the ResourceManager directs a NodeManager (there's one of these running on each worker node) to start a new ApplicationMaster instance for the application. This is Container 0 for that application. Containers created later on to run the mapper and reducer processes will be named 01, 02, 03 and so on.
3. The ApplicationMaster initializes itself by registering with the ResourceManager.
4. The ApplicationMaster calculates the processing resources necessary to complete the application. The ApplicationMaster determines the number of map tasks that

should be started up, based on the input splits. It calculates the input splits by requesting the names and locations of the input files and data blocks required by the application. Using this information, the ApplicationMaster calculates how many map tasks are required to process the input data.

5. The ApplicationMaster requests the ResourceManager to assign the necessary containers for the map tasks. It stays in contact with the ResourceManager throughout the lifecycle of the application, assuring that its list of required resources is being honored by the ResourceManager and also sending any necessary kill requests for killing tasks.
6. The Scheduler component of the ResourceManager determines on which nodes to run the map tasks. Key factors in the determination include data locality and available memory to support the new containers to be created on the nodes for the tasks to run in. The ResourceManager queues the resource requests from the ApplicationMaster and grants it leases for containers on specific nodes as resources become available on those nodes.
7. The ApplicationMaster directs the NodeManager, on the nodes where the containers have been assigned, to create the containers.
8. The NodeManager creates the requested containers and starts them. Containers send MapReduce status to the ApplicationMaster. (There's only one of these per job.)
9. The ApplicationMaster requests the ResourceManager for reducer tasks (if the MapReduce application contains reducers—some don't).
10. The ApplicationMaster requests the NodeManager to launch the reduce tasks on nodes where the ResourceManager allocates resources for the Reduce tasks.
11. The reduce tasks perform the shuffle and sort with the mapper's intermediate data and store the output in HDFS (outdir).
12. The NodeManager sends status and health reports to the ResourceManager. Once all tasks are completed, the ApplicationMaster sends the results to the client application. It also sends the job information and logs to the JobHistoryServer. Task containers clean up their state and the intermediate output is deleted from the local file system.
13. Once an application completes running, the ApplicationMaster informs the ResourceManager that the job has successfully completed and deregisters itself from the ResourceManager and shuts down.
14. The ResourceManager releases all the resources (containers) held by the application for reuse by the cluster.

As you'll see later in this book, MapReduce jobs typically involve a map and a reduce phase. If a map task on a node hangs while running a MapReduce job, the ApplicationMaster will eventually mark the map task attempt as failed and request the NodeManager to terminate the map task container.

Summary

Here's what you learned in this chapter:

- HDFS, the storage component, and YARN, the processing engine, work together to perform complex distributed computing tasks.
- HDFS uses the principle of redundancy to protect data.
- The NameNode manages HDFS and the DataNodes store the actual data.
- YARN is a general-purpose computing engine that contains both resource management and scheduling capabilities and supports diverse processing frameworks.
- YARN uses containers, which are logical entities, to allocate computing resources.

3

Creating and Configuring a Simple Hadoop Cluster

This chapter covers the following:

- Creating a simple pseudo-distributed (single node) Hadoop cluster
- Performing an initial Hadoop configuration
- Operating the new cluster
- Running a test program

Many people find the configuration of a well-running Hadoop cluster somewhat of a mystery, especially so because of the new architecture introduced by Hadoop 2. In this chapter, I show how to install and configure a pseudo-distributed Hadoop cluster, which is a Hadoop cluster that looks and functions the same as any real Hadoop cluster but uses just a single node. Understanding how to install and configure a Hadoop cluster properly helps a great deal in efficiently administering and optimizing your cluster.

There are a couple of important reasons why I chose to dedicate two separate chapters to installing a cluster—this chapter for a simple single-node cluster and the next chapter for a multinode, much more realistic cluster. First, setting up a full-fledged, production-grade Hadoop cluster involves a much more elaborate configuration when compared to that of a simple one-node pseudo-distributed cluster. I didn't want users to be overwhelmed at the outset with all the installation and configuration details involved in setting up a multinode cluster. The goal of this chapter is simply to get you familiar with a basic Hadoop cluster and how to install it on a single node. You take the baby steps first, learn a bit about HDFS and YARN, the two major components of Hadoop, and get yourself in a good place for dealing with the configuration of a real Hadoop cluster running on multiple nodes.

The other reason why I chose to start with a simple one-node cluster is that it enables you to get going with running Spark, MapReduce, Pig and Hive jobs in quick order, by simply using your laptop to download, install and configure Hadoop and its components. You're free to skip this chapter and move on to Chapter 4, "Planning for and Creating a Fully Distributed Cluster," if you're already familiar with Hadoop.

One of the key goals of this chapter is to help you master the configuration of Hadoop systems. Starting with configuring a parameter or two in each of Hadoop's key configuration files will let you get over any potential fear of "mucking with" configuration files—it's really straightforward to work with these files!

Hadoop Distributions and Installation Types

The only Hadoop product that's officially a release of Apache Hadoop is the distribution offered by the Apache Foundation (www.apache.org). Several companies and organizations release or sell Hadoop products that contain the official Apache Hadoop release files and tack on their own additions and other tools on top of it. Of course, support for these extended or modified Hadoop distributions is also provided by the respective companies that release those Hadoop products.

Hadoop Distributions

Here are some of the well-known products that Apache Hadoop Foundation lists on its website.

- Amazon Web Services: Amazon uses a version of Apache Hadoop based on their proprietary EC2 storage system.
- Apache Bigtop: This is a project for developing the packaging and testing of the Apache Hadoop ecosystem.
- Cloudera: This company distributes a Hadoop-based platform called Cloudera's Distribution Including Apache Hadoop (CDH).
- Hortonworks: Hortonworks provides a 100 percent open-source big data platform named Hortonworks Data Platform Powered by Apache (HDP). HDP is offered free of charge to users, with Hortonworks deriving most of its revenues from annual support subscriptions.
- IBM: IBM provides the BigInsights Enterprise Edition that builds on Apache Hadoop.
- MapR: MapR provides a MapReduce framework based on Apache Hadoop and offers higher performance due to its reengineering of several MapReduce components, including HDFS, the storage system for Hadoop.
- Pivotal HD: Pivotal offers Pivotal HD, geared toward advanced real-time analytics.
- VMware: VMware provides a product named Serengeti that enables the rapid deployment of a Hadoop cluster.
- WANdisco: WANdisco provides an advanced replication technology for Hadoop called Non-Stop Hadoop to provide continuous availability.

> **Note**
>
> One of the easiest ways to get started with a pseudo-distributed cluster is to install a virtual Hadoop distribution provided by a Hadoop vendor such as Cloudera's Quickstart VM, Hortonworks' sandbox or MapR's sandbox for Hadoop. However, I show how to install, configure and manage a Hadoop system that you create yourself—the goal is to learn how things work behind the scenes, so you can be a better administrator of Hadoop systems.

The list of Hadoop products is by no means exhaustive. This book uses the Hadoop distribution offered by Apache (www.apache.org). If you're using any of the aforementioned products, your administration procedures and tools may vary, but in every one of these products, Hadoop works exactly the same under the hood.

Hadoop Installation Types

You can install Hadoop 2 in the following three ways:

- Standalone: All Hadoop services run in a single JVM, and there are no daemons (a daemon is a UNIX or Linux long-running background process that answers requests for services). In this mode, Hadoop uses the local file system and not HDFS for storing its data, and MapReduce jobs run with a single mapper and a single reducer. This deployment model is best suited for developers to run their code.
- Pseudo-distributed: This is a simulation of a real multinode cluster. You configure all the services just as in the case of a fully distributed cluster, but all daemons (such as the DataNode, NameNode and ResourceManager processes) run on a single server. However, you can't use this in a real production environment—there's no way to configure data replication or high availability when all you've got is a single node!
- Fully distributed: This is the real deal. You configure Hadoop with data replication—and possibly high availability if you wish—because you'll install Hadoop over a set of servers and not on a single node. You have daemons for each process and the daemons run on multiple servers.

Figure 3.1 shows the three installation modes for Hadoop. The standalone method is quite simple to implement, but it really isn't useful for administrators since there are no daemons for the individual Hadoop services such as YARN and HDFS. This chapter shows you how to install and configure a single-node pseudo-distributed Hadoop system (the second of the three installation types I described). In Chapter 4, I describe how to install and configure a real-life, full-blown Hadoop cluster over multiple nodes, with all the bells and whistles.

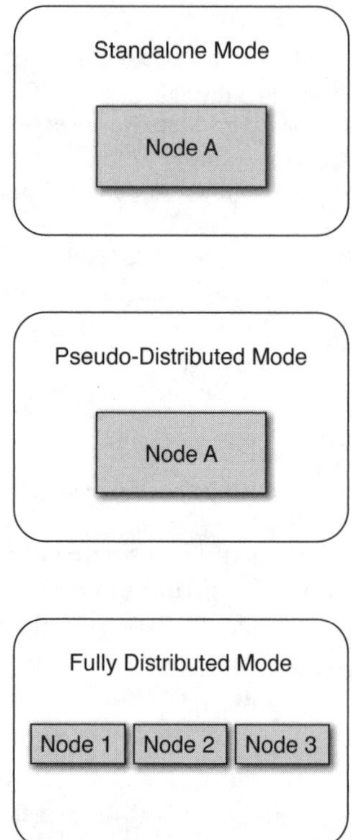

Figure 3.1 The standalone, pseudo-distributed and fully distributed modes of installation

Setting Up a Pseudo-Distributed Hadoop Cluster

A pseudo-distributed cluster is a fancy name for a cluster that has a single node. You won't have any data protection, since you can't replicate data. Similarly, you can't take advantage of the parallel processing capabilities of Hadoop.

Starting off a Hadoop installation with a pseudo-distributed cluster isn't a waste of time though. Many of the steps for installing the simple pseudo-distributed cluster are the same as those you'll need to perform when installing a distributed cluster. Doing it this way lets you test the waters yet not have to deal with a full-blown cluster until you learn how to work with the basic configuration files and so forth.

Note that when you complete installation of Hadoop as shown here, you'll have just HDFS and YARN. You can run any MapReduce application you want at this point. If you want to use Spark, Hive, Pig or any other component, you must install them separately. One of the big advantages of using a vendor-based (e.g., Cloudera, Hortonworks) installation setup is that you can quickly and effortlessly set up the entire Hadoop environment. However, manually installing each of those components isn't rocket science either!

In this chapter, I show how to install and configure Hadoop on a server running Oracle Linux (Release 6.5), which is fully compatible with Red Hat Linux. If you're using an alternative Linux distribution such as Ubuntu or something else, no need to panic, as the procedures are very similar and the differences really superficial.

Before you can actually install your pseudo-distributed Hadoop cluster, first you'll need to ensure that you meet all the Linux operating system prerequisites. Note that you must satisfy the same requirements as shown here when you install a real life multinode cluster, as well.

Meeting the Operating System Requirements

You can install Hadoop on various flavors of Linux such as Red Hat Enterprise Linux, CentOS 5/6 or SUSE Linux Enterprise Server 11, SP1. Make sure that you have the 64-bit version of the operating system.

Useful Utilities

It's good to check that you have the following utilities working in all your cluster servers. Later on, I do show how to install and use the `pdsh` utility, which is very handy for performing remote commands across the cluster.

- `yum` is the tool you use for getting, installing, deleting, querying and managing Red Hat Enterprise Linux RPM software packages from official Red Hat software repositories, as well as other third-party repositories. For other Linux distributions such as Ubuntu Linux, for example, the `apt-get` utility does the same things as the `yum` utility.
- `rpm` is a package manager for Red Hat, SUSE and Fedora Linux systems. You use `rpm` to build, install, query, verify, update and remove software packages. A package is an archive of files and package information such as the name and version.
- The `scp` command lets you securely copy files and directories between hosts without having to start an FTP session or logging into the remote system. Since `scp` uses SSH (secure shell) to transfer data, you need a password for authentication.
- `curl` is a command line tool that lets you send and get files using a URL syntax.
- `wget` is a non-interactive network utility that helps you retrieve files from the web using the popular HTTP and FTP protocols.
- `pdsh` is a parallel remote shell utility that lets you execute remote commands.

For my installation examples in this book, I use the `pdsh` tool to send files across the cluster nodes. Instead of `pdsh`, you can also use an automated deployment tool such as Red Hat's KickStart or Dell Crowbar.

Before you can install the Hadoop binaries, you must ensure that the Linux kernel has the appropriate settings for several parameters, as well as perform other actions such as disabling SELinux and IP tables. The following sections explain all the changes you need to make to the Linux system.

Modifying Kernel Parameters

It's fairly common for administrators to leave default Linux server kernel settings in place, but it's a bad mistake to do so, since it adversely affects your cluster's performance! Table 3.1 shows the recommended values for the Linux kernel parameters you should modify in a production Hadoop cluster.

Increasing the File Limits

In order to avoid any file descriptor errors in the cluster, increase the limits on the number of files a single user or process can have open at a time. The default is only 128. You can check the current limits with the following commands (the first one reveals the soft limits and the second, the hard limits):

```
[root@hadoop1 ~]# ulimit -Sn
1024
[root@hadoop1 ~]# ulimit -Hn
4096
[root@hadoop1 ~]#
```

You must raise the ulimits value to at least 4,096 (Hortonworks and others recommend 10,000, or even more). You can do this by editing the /etc/security/limits.conf file as shown here:

- Soft nofile 4096
- Hard nofile 4096

Once you change the kernel settings, you can dynamically load the new settings by executing the following command.

```
# sysctl -p
```

You can confirm the new kernel settings by issuing the following command.

```
# sysctl -a
```

Table 3.1 **The Modified Linux Kernel Parameters**

fs.file-mx=6815744	/* total number of file descriptors
fs.aio-max-nr=1048576	/* maximum number of concurrent I/O requests
net.core.rmem_default=262144	/* default OS receive buffer size
net.core.wmem_default=262144	/* default OS send buffer size
net.core.rmem_max=16777216	/* max OS receive buffer size
net.core.wmem_max=16777216	/* max OS send buffer size
net.ipv4.tcp_rmem=4096 262144 16777216	/* minimum, default and maximum receive window size
net.ipv4.tcp_wmem=4096 262144 16777216	/* minimum, default and maximum send window size

Setting noatime for Disks

Make sure that you mount all disks with **noatime** and all directories with **nodiratime**. By doing this, you avoid unnecessary write operations for each read access to a file or a directory in the Linux file system, thus improving the cluster performance.

Testing Disk I/O Speed

Test your disk speed with the `hdparm -t` command, as shown here:

```
$ hdparm -t /dev/sda1
```

If you don't see a speed of 70MB/second or higher, it's sign of a potential problem.

Check the Server BIOS Settings

Make sure the server BIOS settings are configured for optimal performance by making sure that features such as IDE emulation by the disk drives aren't enabled. Your storage and system administrators can take care of this for you.

> **Note**
>
> Change the file permissions on all Hadoop directories to 700 before mounting the disk drives, so any processes writing to these drives won't fill up the OS mount when you dismount the drives.

NIC Bonding

In order to increase throughput and resilience, it's a best practice to combine network interfaces by performing NIC bonding.

Enabling NTP

Ensure that the clocks of all cluster nodes are synchronized with each other. You must set up one of the cluster's servers as an NTP server if your cluster doesn't have access to the Internet. Synchronize the network time on all the cluster's nodes by enabling the NTP daemon by editing the /etc/sysconfig/ntpd file.

Synchronizing the network time on all cluster nodes is critical for applications such as ZooKeeper, Kerberos and HBase. It's also important to use a synchronized time across the cluster when going through log files to troubleshoot your cluster.

> **Note**
>
> Although not required, it's a best practice to dedicate a switching infrastructure for Hadoop using a separate virtual local area network (VLAN).

Checking DNS

Use hostnames and not IP addresses to identify the cluster nodes. Ideally, all nodes in your cluster must be configured for both DNS and reverse DNS. Make sure to set all hostnames to their fully qualified domain names (FQDNs). Here's an example:

```
# hostname --fqdn
hadoop1.localdomain
#
```

If you are unable to configure DNS for some reason, make sure to edit the /etc/hosts file on all nodes with the list of all the cluster's nodes. Each of the hosts must be able to perform both a forward lookup (of its hostname) and a reverse lookup (with its IP address). The host command helps you verify the forward and reverse lookups, as shown here:

```
# host hadoop1
hadoop1.localdomain has address 10.192.2.29
# host 10.192.2.29
29.2.192.10.in-addr.arpa domain name pointer hadoop1.localdomain.
#
```

Since Hadoop makes heavy use of network-based services such as DNS, it's a good idea to enable the name server cache daemon (nscd) to lower the name resolution delays.

Disabling Swap

Ideally, none of your servers should swap, especially the DataNodes. You can disable swap completely on these servers by issuing the following command.

```
# swapoff -a
```

You can check the status of swap on a server by issuing the following command.

```
# swapon -s
```

By default, most Linux operating systems come with a swappiness setting of 60. If swappiness is set to zero, Linux will avoid using the disk unless it runs out of memory, whereas a setting of 100 means that the OS will instantly swap programs to disk. As you can tell, a setting of 60 means that the OS will use the swap file on disk fairly often, starting from the time when the memory usage reaches around half the OS RAM allocation. If you turn swappiness down to 10, for example, the OS will use the swap file on disk only when the RAM usage is around 90 percent.

The Linux administrator can change the system swappiness value by adding the following to the /etc/sysctl.conf file:

```
vm.swappiness=10
```

The administrator must reboot the server for the new swappiness setting to take effect. There's no hard and fast rule on how low you must set the swappiness level. Cloudera experts recommend setting it to 1.

Disabling SELinux

Although this isn't an absolute requirement, SELinux is sometimes known to interfere with the installation of Hadoop, so it's a good idea to disable it before you start installing Hadoop. In addition, SELinux imposes a 7-10 percent performance penalty on your cluster. You can get the current SELinux status by executing the following command.

```
# getenforce
```

If the value for the current mode is **enforcing**, SELinux is enabled. Disable it by changing the status to **permissive**, as shown here:

```
# setenforce 0
```

Disabling IPv6

As you'll learn later in this chapter, you'll be setting the value 0.0.0.0 for some network-related Hadoop configuration parameters, with Hadoop binding to the server's IPv6 addresses as a result. If you aren't connected to an IPv6 network, you can simply disable IPv6 on the cluster nodes.

You can disable IPv6 by editing the /etc/sysctl.conf file and adding the following lines at the end of the file:

```
net.ipv6.conf.all.disable_ipv6  = 1
net.ipv6.conf.default.disable_ipv6 = 1
net.ipv6.conf.lo.disable_ipv6 = 1
```

You must reboot the server after making the changes to the sysctl.conf file. After the reboot, issue the following command to check that the change was made successfully:

```
$ cat /proc/sys/net/ipv6/conf/all/disable_ipv6
```

You should see an output of 1 if IPv6 is disabled and 0 otherwise.

You can alternatively disable IPv6 just for Hadoop by adding the following value for the environment variable `HADOOP_OPTS`. You add this line to your cluster's hadoop-env.sh file:

```
export HADOOP_OPTS=-Djava.net.preferIPv4Stack=true
```

Disabling the IP Tables

During the installation of Hadoop, it's a good idea to turn off the network firewall (and check it), as shown here:

```
# service iptables stop
# service iptables status
```

You can always re-enable IP tables once the installation is completed.

Setting the Ulimits

Limit the cluster resources that users can utilize by setting shell limits. You can do this by editing the /etc/security/limits.conf file, which dictates the limits on how users can use resources. The limits.conf file is used to configure "soft" and "hard" limits on important operating system properties such as file sizes, the stack size and the priority levels (niceness) of processes, as shown in Figure 3.2.

Add the following lines to your /etc/security/limits.conf file.

- soft nofile 32768
- hard nofile 32768
- soft nproc 32768
- soft nproc 32768

The **nofile** attribute limits the number of open file descriptors per user process and **nproc** specifies the maximum number of processes. The **soft** limit settings connote warnings and the **hard** limit settings are the actual resource limits.

```
#<type> can have the two values:
#        - "soft" for enforcing the soft limits
#        - "hard" for enforcing hard limits
#
#<item> can be one of the following:
#        - core - limits the core file size (KB)
#        - data - max data size (KB)
#        - fsize - maximum filesize (KB)
#        - memlock - max locked-in-memory address space (KB)
#        - nofile - max number of open file descriptors
#        - rss - max resident set size (KB)
#        - stack - max stack size (KB)
#        - cpu - max CPU time (MIN)
#        - nproc - max number of processes
#        - as - address space limit (KB)
#        - maxlogins - max number of logins for this user
#        - maxsyslogins - max number of logins on the system
#        - priority - the priority to run user process with
#        - locks - max number of file locks the user can hold
#        - sigpending - max number of pending signals
```

Figure 3.2 The limits.conf file showing the various operating system resources for which you can set soft and hard limits

Turning Off Transparent Huge Pages (THP) Compaction

According to Cloudera and Hortonworks experts, THP compaction can degrade Hadoop performance. So, it's a good practice to disable defragmenting as shown here (add this line to the /etc/rc.local file):

```
$ echo 'never'; defrag_file_pathname
```

Checking Connectivity

Check the passwordless connectivity among the nodes to make sure you've configured SSH correctly.

With the Linux operating system prerequisites out of our way, it's on to the actual installation of the Hadoop software. As mentioned earlier, I show you how to set up a one-node, pseudo-distributed cluster in this chapter. Chapter 4 shows how to create a full-fledged, multinode cluster.

Setting Up SSH

Before getting started with the Hadoop software installation, you'll first need to set up a passwordless connection (SSH) on the cluster. Although you have just a single node for now, the SSH daemon is required for using the Hadoop scripts that manage the Hadoop daemons.

Setting up SSH on the server is an optional step, as you may already have this configured. You can find out if SSH is enabled by attempting a passwordless login, through secure shell:

```
# ssh localhost
```

If this works, you have SSH and you're good to go. If not, perform the following steps to set up SSH:

```
$ ssh -keygen -t dsa -P '' -f ~/.ssh/id_dsa
$ cat ~/.ssh/id_dsa.pub >> ~/.ssh/authorized_keys
$ chmod 0600 ~/.ssh/authorized_keys
```

```
[root@hadoop12 ~]# ssh-keygen -t dsa -P '' -f ~/.ssh/id_dsa
Generating public/private dsa key pair.
Your identification has been saved in /root/.ssh/id_dsa.
Your public key has been saved in /root/.ssh/id_dsa.pub.
The key fingerprint is:
93:1a:d9:d9:c8:97:39:08:cd:dc:3b:6c:c3:f5:71:12 root@hadoop12.localdomain
The key's randomart image is:
+--[ DSA 1024]----+
|             E   |
|      + .      . |
|     . + . . o . |
|      = O = . +  |
|     o S &    .  |
|      o + +      |
|     .           |
|                 |
|                 |
+-----------------+
[root@hadoop12 ~]#
```

Figure 3.3 Generating the SSH key with the ssh-keygen utility so you can log in without a password

Figure 3.3 shows the generation of the SSH key with the help of the ssh-keygen utility.

Java Requirements

Hadoop 2 requires at least Oracle JDK 1.6 (Update 31). Here's how to install Java.

1. Check the current version of Java. Figure 3.4 shows how to check the Java version with the `java -version` command.

   ```
   # java -version
   ```

2. Remove any older versions of Java.

   ```
   # yum remove {java-1.*}
   ```

3. Download the latest Oracle 64-bit JDK.

   ```
   $ wget
   http://www.oracle.com/technetwork/java/javasebusiness/downloads/java-archive-downloads-javase6-419409.html#jdk-6u31-oth-JPR
   ```

4. Change the directory to the location on the server where you want to install the JDK.

   ```
   # cd /usr
   ```

5. Unpack the tarball and install the JDK.

   ```
   # tar -xvzf jdk-6u<version>-linux-x64.tar.gz
   ```

```
[root@hadoop1 etc]# java -version
java version "1.7.0_65"
OpenJDK Runtime Environment (rhel-2.5.1.2.0.1.el6_5-x86_64 u65-b17)
OpenJDK 64-Bit Server VM (build 24.65-b04, mixed mode)
[root@hadoop1 etc]#
```

Figure 3.4 Checking the Java version with the `java -version` command.

6. Test that you've correctly installed Java by issuing the following command:

```
# rpm -qa|grep jdk
java-1.6.0-openjdk-devel-1.6.0.0-1.62.1.11.11.90.el6_4.x86_64
java-1.6.0-openjdk-1.6.0.0-1.62.1.11.11.90.el6_4.x86_64
```

7. Create the necessary symbolic links.

```
# ln -s /usr/jdk1.6.0_31/jdk1.6.0_31 /usr/java/default
# ln -s /usr/java/default/bin/java /usr/bin/java
```

Once you install Java, you can set up the `JAVA_HOME` environment variable and include it in the /etc/profile.d directory, as shown here.

```
# echo "export JAVA_HOME=/usr/lib/jvm/java-1.6.0-openjdk-1.6.0.0.x86_64/" > /etc/
profile.d/java.sh
```

To avoid having to define the `JAVA_HOME` environment variable after every login, define the variable by sourcing the java.sh script as follows:

```
# source /etc/profile.d/java.sh
```

Installing the Hadoop Software

Installing Hadoop is remarkably easy. As mentioned earlier in this chapter, I use the Hadoop distribution provided by Apache, specifically the Hadoop 2.6.0 version. Follow these steps to install a pseudo-distributed Hadoop cluster.

1. Download the Hadoop distribution (Hadoop 2.6.0):

   ```
   http://apache.mirrors.tds.net/hadoop/common/
   $ cd /root
   # wget http://mirrors.ibiblio.org/apache/hadoop/common/hadoop-2.6.0/
   hadoop-2.6.0.tar.gz
   ```

   If you wish, you can make sure that the zip file is complete by running the following command:

   ```
   # md5sum .tmp/ hadoop-2.6.0.tar.gz
   ```

2. Unzip the downloaded Hadoop zip file into a directory as shown here:

   ```
   # mkdir -p /opt/yarn
   # cd /opt/yarn
   # tar -xvzf /root/hadoop-2.6.0.tar.gz
   ```

Once you install the Hadoop software, you need to create the necessary Hadoop users to run the Hadoop daemons, as well as create some required directories, as explained in the following sections.

Creating the Necessary Hadoop Users

Each of the key Hadoop daemons must run under a separate user. You'll need three Hadoop users to be set up:

- **yarn** for managing the ResourceManager
- **mapred** for managing MapReduce services
- **hdfs** for managing the HDFS file system

Place all three users in the same group, hadoop. First create this group and then add the three users, as shown here.

```
# groupadd hadoop
# useradd -g hadoop yarn # yarn owns the YARN related services
# useradd -g hadoop hdfs # hdfs owns the HDFS services
# useradd -g hadoop mapred # mapred owns the MapReduce Services
```

For now, these are all the service users you'll need. In a real-life cluster, you can also create other service users such hive, pig, hcatalog, hbase, zookeeper and oozie and place them all in the same group, hadoop.

Creating the Necessary Directories

Even though you're creating a basic single-server cluster, it's good to create appropriate data directories and log directories, so everything isn't created in a default directory by Hadoop.

The following commands will create directories for storing the NameNode (nn) and Standby NameNode (snn) data. It's in the /hdfs/nn (first line below) and /hdfs/snn (second line below) directories that the NameNode and the Standby NameNode will save their data. The Hadoop data you'll be using will be stored in the HDFS system and accessed by the DataNodes. The /hdfs/dn directory (third line) indicates where Hadoop should store the HDFS data.

```
# mkdir -p /var/data/hadoop/hdfs/nn
# mkdir -p /var/data/hadoop/hdfs/snn
# mkdir /var/data/hadoop/hdfs/dn
```

Make sure you change the ownership of the directories, as shown here:

```
# chown hdfs:hadoop /var/data/hadoop/hdfs
```

Individual users that run jobs in the cluster don't need to be granted access to these directories. It's enough to provide access to the user hadoop. Now that you've created the data directories for the NameNodes and the DataNode, it's time to create the YARN log directory:

```
# mkdir /var/log/hadoop-2.6.0/logs
```

Grant necessary permissions and change the ownership of the log directory:

```
# chmod 755 logs
# chown yarn:hadoop . -R
```

Now that the Hadoop software has been installed, it's time to configure Hadoop so you can start using it to analyze data.

Performing the Initial Hadoop Configuration

Hadoop uses a multitude of configuration files, and each of these configuration files will affect different aspects of a cluster's operation, such as HDFS operations, YARN operations and so on. Each of a cluster's nodes has its own copy of these configuration files, most of which are in the XML format. When the Hadoop daemons start up on each node, they read the appropriate configuration file for them. For example, when you start the DataNode daemon on a worker node, it looks up the `hdfs-site.xml` file for HDFS-related configuration settings.

> **Note**
>
> You need to restart the appropriate Hadoop daemon after modifying its configuration file. If you change some NameNode-related parameters, you don't restart the DataNodes, although they both use the same configuration file, hdfs-site.xml, for their configuration.

Hadoop has numerous configuration parameters. If you don't customize the Hadoop configuration, Hadoop uses default properties. As you progress through this book, I explain all the important configuration parameters in the appropriate setting—for example, the security chapter contains explanation of all the security-related configuration parameters. For now, let's set the basic configuration parameters in order to get going with the startup of our pseudo-distributed cluster, by editing the Hadoop configuration files.

There are several types of configuration files for a Hadoop cluster:

- Environment configuration files
- Default configuration files
- Site-specific configuration files.

Figure 3.5 shows the various types of Hadoop configuration files. The following sections describe how to configure these files.

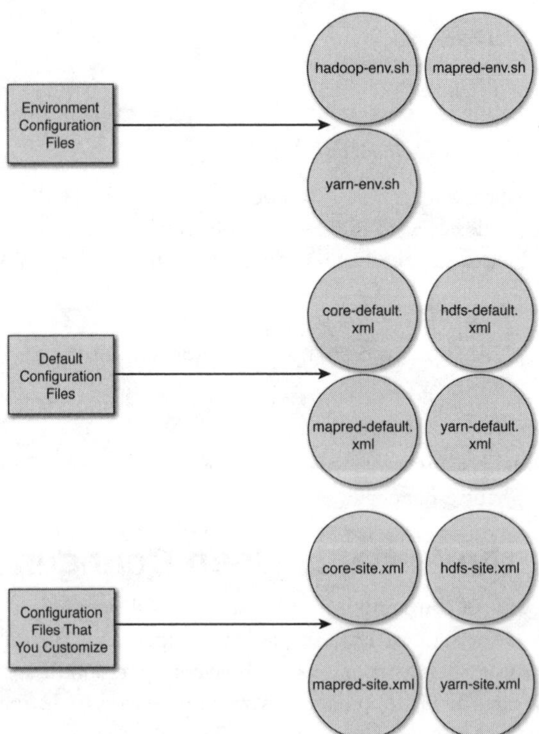

Figure 3.5 Hadoop Core, HDFS, Yarn and MapReduce configuration files

Environment Configuration Files

The environment configuration files help set up the environment in which various Hadoop daemons execute. Hadoop has several types of daemons that perform various services in the cluster:

- HDFS daemons: The NameNode, the Secondary NameNode and the DataNodes
- YARN daemons: The ResourceManager, the NodeManager and the JobHistoryServer

There's only one of each of the HDFS and YARN daemons, except the DataNode and the NodeManager—there's one of these two daemons running on every worker node.

Figure 3.6 shows the two main types of Hadoop daemons that run in a pseudo-distributed, as a well as a fully distributed, cluster.

The read-only default configuration files and the site-specific configuration files together help you configure the daemons themselves. Hadoop provides you several scripts (located in the $HADOOP_HOME/sbin directory) for starting and stopping the Hadoop 2 daemons. The environment files hadoop-env.sh, mapred-env.sh and yarn-env.sh enable you to control these Hadoop scripts. The hadoop-env.sh file, for example, sets up the environment for Hadoop to run and usually includes values for the following environment variables:

- `JAVA_HOME`
- `HADOOP_CLASSPATH`
- `HADOOP_HEAPSIZE`
- `HADOOP_LOG_DIR`
- `HADOOP_PID_DIR`

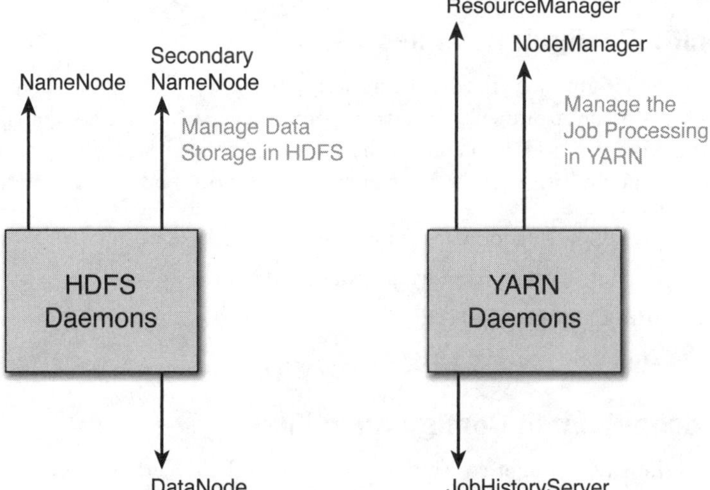

Figure 3.6 The two types of Hadoop daemons: HDFS daemons handle data storage and YARN daemons process the jobs.

You can source the values in the hadoop-env.sh file. Similarly, the yarn-env.sh file specifies values for the environment variables used by YARN and the mapred-env.sh file specifies values for environment files used by MapReduce.

Read-Only Default Configuration Files

The read-only default configuration files provide the default configuration for core Hadoop, YARN, HDFS and mapred. You can't edit these files—these files provide default configuration if you don't, for some reason, make the change in the corresponding site-specific configuration file. For example, don't modify the yarn-default.xml file if your goal is to configure YARN. Instead, use the yarn-site.xml file for this purpose. Here are the four default read-only Hadoop configuration files:

- core-default.xml: Core Hadoop settings, overridden by values you specify in the core-site.xml file.
- hdfs-default.xml: Default settings for HDFS related services. Override this file with settings in the hdfs-site.xml.
- yarn-default.xml: Default settings for YARN. Override the settings in this file with settings in the yarn-site.xml file.
- mapred-default.xml: MapReduce v2 default settings. Override this file with settings in the mapred-site.xml file.

All the xxxx-default.xml files serve the following two purposes:

- They document all available configuration parameters.
- They specify default values for the available configuration parameters.

Site-Specific Configuration Files

The site-specific configuration files are the most important set of configuration parameter files for any Hadoop environment, since they contain a large number of configurable parameters that you can modify to control the working of the cluster. Here are the names of the environment and site-specific configuration files you'll be working with:

- core-site.xml: Core Hadoop configuration
- mapred-site.xml: Configuring MapReduce
- hdfs-site.xml: Configuring HDFS
- yarn-site.xml: Configuring YARN

Other Hadoop-Related Configuration Files

In addition to the environment configuration files and the default and site-specific configuration files, it's common to use some or all of the following Hadoop-related configuration files:

- log4j.properties: For configuring logging
- hadoop-metric.properties (and hadoop-metric2.properties): For configuring Hadoop metrics
- allocations.xml: For configuring the Fair Scheduler
- capacity-scheduler.xml: For configuring the Capacity Scheduler
- include and exclude files: Used for specifying which hosts to include or exclude from a Hadoop cluster

Figure 3.7 shows the log4j.properties file, which you use to configure Hadoop logging. Chapter 17, "Monitoring, Metrics and Hadoop Logging," provides details about configuring Hadoop logging. Several of the Hadoop configuration files, especially the site-specific files, contain a large number of configuration parameters that you can set. For now, you only need to set one or two parameters to get your pseudo-distributed cluster going.

In the following sections, I review the nature of the configuration files you'll be working with. I make no attempt to list and explain all the Hadoop configuration parameters in this chapter—there are simply too many of them! But rest assured that as you proceed forward through the various chapters in this book, you'll encounter all the important configuration parameters you need to understand.

> **Tip**
>
> Properly configuring the Hadoop components such as HDFS and YARN is the single biggest factor that affects a cluster's performance and stability. Often, administrators leave the default settings on for various parameters, which results in poor performance and cluster instability.

Figure 3.7 The default log4j.properties file. Set properties in this file to configure Hadoop logging.

The following sections cover these topics:

- Precedence among the configuration files
- Configuring the Hadoop, MapReduce and YARN environment

Precedence among the Configuration Files

Files such as hdfs-site.xml and yarn-site.xml on the master nodes aren't the only way to configure HDFS and YARN. You can specify configuration settings in multiple ways. You can specify them when initializing a MapReduce job, for example, or by including them in the JobConf or Job object. You can also specify them in a file such as yarn-site.xml or hdfs-site.xml on either the DataNodes or the client node. Which one of these will a MapReduce job take into account at runtime? Here's the order of precedence among the configuration files, when configuring YARN settings:

1. The settings you specify in the JobConf or Job object take the highest precedence.
2. Next in precedence are the values you specify on the client, within a configuration file such as mapred-site.xml.
3. Next are any configuration parameter values you include in the configuration files on the DataNodes.
4. If you don't configure the value for a parameter in any of the aforementioned methods, the settings in the mapred-default.xml file will come into play.

The settings for HDFS and MapReduce work in a similar fashion. As an administrator, you can keep a program or the client from modifying certain configuration parameters by marking the parameters as final, as shown here:

```
<property>
  <name><attribute></name>
  <final>true</final>
</property>
```

For example, the following configuration marks the value you specify for the `dfs.hosts.include` parameter as final, thus ensuring that the parameter always points to the include file /etc/hadoop/conf/hosts.include.

```
<property>
   <name>dfs.hosts.include</name>
   <value>/etc/hadoop/conf/hosts.include</value>
   <final>true</final>
</property>
```

As an administrator, you may want to keep applications or client configurations from overriding some key configurations settings such as the HDFS block size, for example. The ability to mark those values as final gives you control over those system-wide settings.

Typically, administrators mark key parameters as final in the core-site.xml file, to keep applications or users from modifying them.

Let's say you've set the number of reducers per job to six in the mapred-site.xml file by setting the parameter `mapreduce.job.reduces` to 6. Let's assume that a developer runs a job and specifies the number of reducers in the MapReduce application driver by including `setNumReduceTasks(2)`. Finally, let's say a user runs a job with the command-line argument `-D mapreduce.job.reduces=8`. How does Hadoop determine how many reduce tasks to spawn for this job? Hadoop will start two reducer tasks because the value set by the developer in the code will override the number of reducers set through the other means. Of course, if you set the `mapreduce.job.reduces` parameter as final, then the number of reducers will be six. Once again, the order of precedence in job execution is the following:

1. Application code
2. Code from the command line (run-time command line options)
3. Client-side XML files (such as mapred-site.xml)
4. Node-side XML files (such as mapred-site.xml)
5. Default XML files

Figure 3.8 shows how the issue of configuration property precedence is resolved when in Hadoop. Note how the precedence of the configuration properties accords the properties in the client code the highest precedence.

Caution!

If you don't specify a value for a property the default values apply.

When you wish to change the configuration of all DataNodes in a cluster, you must first change the configuration files on the NameNode. The NameNode stores the master configuration files for all DataNodes in a cluster. Once you modify the configuration, restart all the DataNode daemons on the cluster in order to apply the changes to the DataNodes. Since you aren't changing the NameNode's configuration, there's no need to restart the NameNode.

When discussing the precedence of Hadoop's configuration files, it's important to understand that some configuration parameters are client-side parameters, and the value you set for these types of parameters on a specific server will trump any values you set for the same parameter in the server running the NameNode. For example, if you set the value of the `dfs.block.size` parameter to 64MB in the hdfs-site.xml file on a client machine and set it to 128MB on the server hosting the cluster's NameNode, Hadoop will use a block size of 128MB, not 64MB, when clients write files to HDFS on a server. This is true unless the client process writing the file to HDFS is running on the server hosting the NameNode.

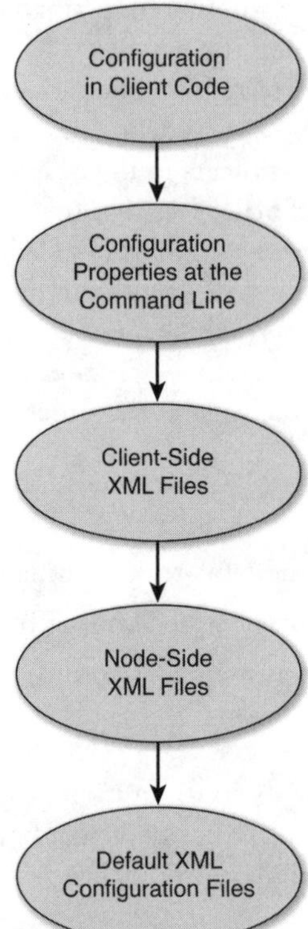

Figure 3.8 How Hadoop resolves the question of precedence when the same configuration property appears in different places

Variable Expansion and Configuration Parameters

Configuration parameter value strings are always first evaluated for variable expansion. For example, let's say I set the following property by including variables for the values and not the actual values.

```
<property>
  <name>basedir</name>
  <value>/user/${user.name}</value>
</property>

<property>
  <name>tempdir</name>
  <value>${basedir}/tmp</value>
</property>
```

The `${user.name}` variable will be resolved to the value of the system property with the same name. Let's say `{user.name}` evaluates to `sam`. Then the value of the configuration property `tempdir` is dynamically determined as `/user/sam/tmp`.

Now that you've learned about the various types of Hadoop configuration files, it's time to actually start configuring our pseudo-distributed Hadoop cluster. Configuring Hadoop involves configuring HDFS, YARN and MapReduce among other things.

The following sections explain how to configure HDFS, YARN and MapReduce.

Configuring the Hadoop Daemons Environment

The previous sections showed how to configure the Hadoop daemons such as YARN and HDFS. You can also customize the process environment for each of these key Hadoop daemons by configuring various environment variables in the following files.

- hadoop-env.sh
- mapred-env.sh
- yarn-env.sh

By default, these files are located in the $HADOOP_HOME/etc/hadoop directory. You can configure each of the Hadoop daemons with the `xxxx_xxx_OPTS` parameters as shown here:

```
YARN_RESOURCEMANAGER_OPTS           // ResourceManager daemon
HADOOP_NAMENODE_OPTS                   // NameNode daemon
HADOOP_DATANODE_OPTS                   // DataNode daemon
YARN_NODEMANAGER_OPTS                // NodeManager daemon
HADOOP_SECONDARYNAMENODE_OPTS    // SecondaryNameNode daemon
```

In order to individually configure a Hadoop daemon, you must set the appropriate property for a daemon in the correct configuration file. For example, to configure the NameNode, you must use the `HADOOP_NAMENODE_OPTS` parameter in the hdfs-site.xml file, as shown in the following example:

```
HADOOP_NAMENODE_OPTS="-XX:+UseParallelGC"
```

This example shows how to configure the NameNode to use parallel garbage collection for its JVM. Here's another example that shows how to set the memory size for each of the daemons:

```
YARN_RESOURCEMANAGER_OPTS = -Xmx4g          // ResourceManager daemon
HADOOP_NAMENODE_OPTS = -Xmx4g                  // NameNode daemon
HADOOP_DATANODE_OPTS = -Xmx4g                   // DataNode daemon
YARN_NODEMANAGER_OPTS = -Xmx1g                // NodeManager daemon
HADOOP_SECONDARYNAMENODE_OPTS = -Xmx4g   // SecondaryNameNode daemon
```

Although you can get by for now without configuring any of the Hadoop environment files (mapred-env.sh, hadoop-env.sh and yarn-env.sh), since our main goal here is to acclimatize to Hadoop configuration, let's go ahead and set values for the key environment variables in these files. If you don't edit any of these files, Hadoop will automatically assign values to the environment variables, thus setting default values for things such as the memory size for the daemons and the locations for the daemon log files.

You can set the values for the following in the Hadoop environment files:

- The Java home directory
- JVM options for the DataNode, NameNode, ResourceManager and other Hadoop daemons
- Locations of the various Hadoop log files

Let's learn how to edit the environment files for hadoop, yarn and mapred in order to set appropriate values for the environment variables used by the Hadoop, YARN and MapReduce daemons.

Configuring the Hadoop Environment

You must set the Hadoop-specific environment variables in the hadoop-env.sh file. At the least, you must specify the value for the `JAVA_HOME` environment variable (same in the mapred-env.sh and yarn-env.sh files as well). In addition, it's useful to set the following environment variables in the hadoop-env.sh file:

```
export HADOOP_HEAPSIZE=500
export HADOOP_LOG_DIR=/var/log/hadoop/hdfs
export HADOOP_CONF_DIR=/opt/yarn/hadoop-2.6.0
export HADOOP_LOG_DIR=/var/log/hadoop/hdfs
```

Configuring the YARN Environment

Hadoop 2 uses the parameter `YARN_HEAPSIZE` to determine the Java heap size for the YARN daemons. The default value of this parameter is 1,000MB. This heap size of 1GB applies to each of the YARN daemons, such as the ResourceManager and the NodeManager. The following two configuration parameters help you set the heap size of the ResourceManager and the NodeManager, respectively, within the yarn-env.sh file:

```
export JAVA_HOME=/usr/lib/jvm/java-1.6.0-openjdk-1.6.0.0.x86_64/
export YARN_HEAPSIZE=500
export YARN_RESOURCEMANAGER_HEAPSIZE=500
export YARN_NODEMANAGER_HEAPSIZE=500
export YARN_PID_DIR=/var/run/hadoop/yarn
export YARN_LOG_DIR=/var/log/hadoop/yarn
```

Configuring the MapReduce Environment

Edit the mapred-env.sh file as follows to set the environment for mapred:

```
export JAVA_HOME=/usr/lib/jvm/java-1.6.0-openjdk-1.6.0.0.x86_64/
export HADOOP_MAPRED_IDENT_STRING=mapred
export HADOOP_MAPRED_PID_DIR=/var/run/hadoop/mapred
export HADOOP_MAPRED_LOG_DIR==/var/log/hadoop/mapred
export HADOOP_JOB_HISTORYSERVER_HEAPSIZE=250
```

Adjusting the Heap Size for the Simple Cluster

When you're running a pseudo-cluster on a small server such as your laptop, it's a good idea to set the heap size for the individual daemons to a lower size, so the Hadoop,

YARN and MapReduce daemons can function properly. The default size for the heap size for the daemons is 1GB, which is fine in a real cluster. I'll lower this to 500MB so the cluster has enough memory to do its work. Here's how you configure the heap size separately for each individual daemon:

```
HADOOP_HEAPSIZE = 500                         // in the hadoop-env.sh file
YARN_HEAPSIZE = 500                          // in the yarn-env.sh file
HADOOP_JOB_HISTORYSERVER_HEAPSIZE= 250         // in the mapred-env.sh file
```

Configuring Core Hadoop Properties (with the core-site.xml File)

The core-site.xml file contains values for core Hadoop properties. You can use this file to override default parameter values stored in the core-default.xml file. Here's where a lot of configuration errors occur. You haven't explicitly set a parameter, and you're surprised to see that it has an outdated or a suboptimal value, and you wonder how that happened. Well, if you don't explicitly set a value for a configuration parameter, Hadoop doesn't complain—it just uses the default values in the core-default.xml file.

Override a default value by setting a new value within the `<configuration>` tags, in the following format:

```
<property>
  <name>property_name</name>
  <value>property value </value>
  <description> </description>    //optional tag
</property>
```

Setting the Basic HDFS Parameters

Start configuring the core Hadoop properties by editing the core-site.xml file, located in the /opt/yarn/hadoop-2.6.0/etc/hadoop directory. You'll find this to be an empty file when you open it. Set the following two parameters in this file:

- `fs.defaultFS` specifies the name of the default file system and the host and port information for the NameNode service.

  ```
  <property>
    <name>fs.defaultFS</name>
    <value>hdfs://hadoop1:8020</value>
  </property>
  ```

  The `fs.defaultFS` parameter specifies the name of the default file system for the cluster. Here, the value I specified is `hdfs`. The value is actually a URI whose schema and authority determine which file system is implemented.

- The parameter `hadoop.http.staticuser.user` specifies `hdfs` as the default user name

  ```
  <property>
    <name>hadoop.http.staticuser.user</name>
    <value>hdfs</value>
  </property>
  ```

  The default value for the `hadoop.http.staticuser.user` property is `dr.who`.

A Couple More Useful Parameters

While these two parameters will let you get going, it's probably a good idea to include the following two configuration parameters at this stage as well:

- The `fs.trash.interval` parameter specifies how long Hadoop should store a deleted HDFS file in the trash directory in HDFS. Since the default value for this parameter is 0, Hadoop will permanently remove all files you delete, without giving you a chance to reclaim files you or a user accidently deleted. In the following example, I specified 1,440 minutes (1 day) for this parameter. Once 24 hours elapse after deleting a file, Hadoop permanently removes it from HDFS storage.

```
<property>
  <name>fs.trash.interval</name>
  <value>1440</value>
</property>
```

- The `hadoop.tmp.dir` parameter specifies the base temporary directory both on the local file system and in HDFS. The default value for this parameter is `/tmp/hadoop-${user.name}`. Make sure you set it to a directory other than under /tmp, since some environments regularly run scripts to clean up everything under the /tmp directory!

  Hadoop uses the `hadoop.tmp.dir` parameter's value to derive the default values for many other Hadoop configuration parameters, such as `dfs.namenode.data.dir`. This parameter's default value is defined as follows in the hdfs-site.xml file:

```
file://${hadoop.tmp.dir} /
dfs/name
```

Configuring MapReduce (with the mapred-site.xml File)

You configure MapReduce by setting properties in the mapred-site.xml file. Figure 3.9 shows the location of the mapred-site.xml file, which is located under the /opt/yarn/hadoop-2.6.0/etc/hadoop directory in our case. Edit the mapred-site.xml file by adding YARN as the value for the `mapreduce.framework.name` configuration parameter. As you can probably tell, this parameter lets the cluster know that you want YARN as the framework for executing MapReduce.

You won't see a mapred-site.xml file initially when you install Hadoop 2. The cluster will use the mapred-default.xml file unless you create a mapred-site.xml file. Any values you specify in the mapred-site.xml file will override the values for the same parameters in the mapred-default.xml file. Create the mapred-site.xml from the file template provided by Hadoop, as shown here:

```
# cp mapred-site.xml.template mapred-site.xml
```

Once you have your mapred-site.xml file, edit it as follows.

```
<property>
  <name>mapreduce.framework.name</name>
  <value>yarn</value>
</property>
```

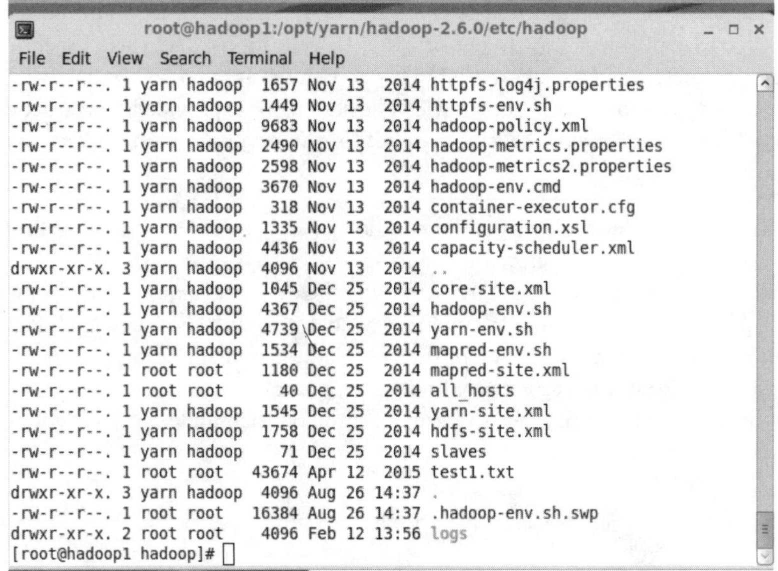

Figure 3.9 The file system locations where the mapred.xml file and other Hadoop configuration files are stored

The `mapreduce.framework.name` property sets the runtime framework for executing MapReduce jobs, and it can take one of three values: `local`, `classic` or `yarn`. The default value is `local`.

> **Note**
>
> All cluster nodes, including the client nodes, must have a copy of the configuration files.

Configuring YARN (with the yarn-site.xml File)

Next up is the configuring of YARN, which requires you to set configuration parameters in the yarn-site.xml file located in the /opt/yarn/hadoop-2.6.0/etc/hadoop directory. Add the following two parameters to this file:

- `yarn.nodemanager.aux-services`: Set this property to inform the NodeManager that it needs to implement the auxiliary service named `mapreduce.shuffle`. The property lets the NodeManager know that the MapReduce containers will need to perform a shuffle from the map tasks to the reduce tasks. Since this shuffle is an auxiliary service and not part of the NodeManager, you must explicitly set its value here. This property can include a list of multiple auxiliary services to support different application frameworks running under YARN. In this example, I specified `mapreduce.shuffle` as the value since I'm running only MapReduce-based jobs in the cluster.

- `yarn.nodemanager.aux-services.mapreduce.shuffle.class`: This parameter instructs MapReduce how to perform shuffle operations. The value I specified for this parameter, `org.apache.hadoop.mapredShulfflehandler`, instructs YARN to use this class to perform the shuffle. The class name is provided to instruct exactly how it must implement the value you set for the property `yarn.nodemanager.aux-services`.

To add the two parameters described here, edit the /opt/yarn/hadoop-2.6.0/etc/hadoop/yarn-site.xml file as shown in Figure 3.10.

Although at this point we can get by with using the default Hadoop values for memory usage, it's probably a good idea to start getting acquainted with some key YARN-related configuration parameters. One of the key Hadoop configuration parameters for a Hadoop administrator is `yarn.nodemanager.resource.memory-mb`. This parameter specifies the total memory that YARN can consume on each node. Let's say you set this parameter to 40,960MB, as shown here:

```
<property>
  <name>yarn.nodemanager.resource.memory-mb</name>
  <value>40960</value>
</property>
```

If you want YARN to launch a maximum of 10 containers per node, you can do so by specifying the `yarn.scheduler.minimum-allocation-mb` parameter, as shown here:

```
<property>
    <name>yarn.scheduler.minimum-allocation-mb</name>
    <value>4096</value>
</property>
```

Since you have a maximum of 40GB on this node for YARN, the fact that you've specified the minimum memory per container as 4,096MB (4GB) means that you've restricted this node to running no more than 10 containers at any given time. Each container runs a single map or reduce task, and as tasks finish, new containers may be started and assigned to new tasks—however, at any given point in time, no more than 10 containers or tasks can run on this node. Note that the administrator sets the default number of reducers for MapReduce v2 jobs by configuring the `mapreduce.job.reduces` property in the mapred-site.xml file. The developer can override this default value either by setting the number of reducers in the driver or on the command line at runtime.

```
<property>
   <name>yarn.nodemanager.aux-services</name>
   <value>mapreduce_shuffle</value>
</property>
<property>
   <name>yarn.nodemanager.aux-services.mapreduce.shuffle.class</name>
   <value>org.apache.hadoop.mapred.ShuffleHandler</value>
</property>
```

Figure 3.10 Editing the yarn-site.xml file to add the YARN auxiliary service parameters

Configure HDFS (with the hdfs-site.xml File)

The hdfs-site.xml file controls the behavior of all HDFS-related Hadoop components, such as the NameNode, Secondary NameNode and the DataNodes. You need to configure the following basic parameters to enable our single node cluster to function.

- `fs.default.name`: This attribute lets you specify the URI for the cluster's NameNode. DataNodes will use this URI to register with the NameNode, letting applications access the data stored on the DataNodes. Clients will also use this URI to retrieve the locations of the data blocks in HDFS. It's common to specify 9000 as the port, but you can use a different port if you wish.
- `dfs.replication`: By default, Hadoop replicates each data block three times when writing a file. Both the default value and the typically recommended value is 3. However, in our case, since you've only a single node, you must change the value of this parameter to 1.
- `dfs.datanode.data.dir`: This parameter determines exactly where on its local file system a DataNode stores its blocks. As you can see, you need to provide a normal Linux directory for storing HDFS data. Later, you'll format the NameNode, which converts this directory into something managed by HDFS and not the local Linux file system. Note the following about this parameter:
    - You can list the local file system directories in a comma-separated list. Make sure there aren't any spaces between a comma and the next directory path in the list.
    - You can specify different values for this parameter for each DataNode if you wish.
- `dfs.namenode.name.dir`: This parameter tells Hadoop where to store the NameNode's key metadata files, such as the fsimage and edits files. The value for this parameter points to a local file system, and only the NameNode service accesses it for reading and writing its metadata. In some ways, you can think of this parameter as the most important Hadoop configuration parameter of all, since losing the NameNode's HDFS metadata really means you've effectively lost all of your HDFS data. You surely will have all the data blocks in the cluster, but without the metadata that describes those blocks, you can't reconstruct the original files.
- `dfs.namenode.checkpoint.dir`: Specifies the directory where the Standby NameNode stores its versions of the metadata-related files. The secondary NameNode uses the values you specify for this parameter to store the fsimage and the edit log (journal for the fsimage file).

Edit the /opt/yarn/hadoop-2.6.0/etc/hadoop/hdfs-site.xml file to add the appropriate values for the parameters listed here, as shown in Figure 3.11.

At this point, you're all done with configuring Hadoop in a pseudo-distributed cluster. Just two steps remain for you to access HDFS and start running MapReduce applications in the shiny new Hadoop cluster! The next step is to format the newly created distributed file system (HDFS). The final step is to start up the Hadoop cluster.

```
<configuration>
 <property>
  <name>fs.default.name</name>
  <value>hdfs://hadoop1.localhost:9000</value>
 <property>
   <name>dfs.replication</name>
   <value>3</value>
 </property>
 <property>
   <name>dfs.namenode.name.dir</name>
   <value>file:/var/data/hadoop/hdfs/nn</value>
 </property>
 <property>
   <name>fs.checkpoint.dir</name>
   <value>file:/var/data/hadoop/hdfs/snn</value>
 </property>
 <property>
   <name>fs.checkpoint.edits.dir</name>
   <value>file:/var/data/hadoop/hdfs/snn</value>
 </property>
 <property>
   <name>dfs.datanode.data.dir</name>
   <value>file:/var/data/hadoop/hdfs/dn</value>
 </property>
```

Figure 3.11 Editing the hdfs-site.xml file to add HDFS-related configuration properties

Operating the New Hadoop Cluster

You've configured Hadoop services and also formatted the NameNode service. However, nothing is actually running in the cluster yet. In order to start the new Hadoop cluster, you must start the services that support the two primary components of Hadoop, which are the HDFS storage system and the YARN processing system.

Before you can start the cluster services up, there's one item of business you need to take care of—the formatting of HDFS.

Formatting the Distributed File System

Before you can start using HDFS for the very first time, you must format it. As you can probably guess, you do this only once.

> **Note**
>
> Formatting an existing HDFS file system essentially wipes all data on it and sets up a new HDFS file system! Formatting HDFS really means you're initializing where the NameNode stores its metadata.

As you may recall, the parameter `dfs.namenode.name.dir` in the hdfs-site.xml file specifies the location where the NameNode service stores its metadata. When you run the formatting command for the first time, it creates the necessary metadata files, and when you reformat it, it wipes out all the files in this directory. A real-life Hadoop administrator can't really format a production file system to get around a technical problem—one must persist and fix the problem!

In order to format HDFS, you must login not as the root user, which you've been doing until now, but as the user hdfs.

```
# cd /opt/yarn/hadoop-2.6.0/bin
$ su hdfs
$ ./hdfs namenode -format
INFO common.Storage: Storage directory /var/data/hadoop/hdfs/nn has been
successfully formatted.
$
```

Setting the Environment Variables

Before you issue the start and stop commands to control the Hadoop daemons, make sure you export the following environment variables:

```
export JAVA_HOME=/usr/lib/jvm/java-1.6.0-openjdk-1.6.0.0.x86_64/
export HADOOP_HOME=/opt/yarn/hadoop-2.6.0
export HADOOP_PREFIX=/opt/yarn/hadoop-2.6.0
export HADOOP_CONF_DIR=$HADOOP_HOME/etc/hadoop
```

You can also place these variables in the `/etc/profile.d` directory, within the `hadoop.sh` file, as shown here:

```
[root@hadoop1 hadoop]# cat /etc/profile.d/hadoop.sh
export JAVA_HOME=/usr/lib/jvm/java-1.6.0-openjdk-1.6.0.0.x86_64/
export HADOOP_HOME=/opt/yarn/hadoop-2.6.0/etc/hadoop
export HADOOP_PREFIX=/opt/yarn/hadoop-2.6.0/etc/hadoop
export HADOOP_CONF_DIR=$HADOOP_HOME/etc/hadoop
[root@hadoop1 hadoop]#
```

Now you're ready to fire up the cluster daemons so you can finally start working with your pseudo-distributed cluster!

Starting the HDFS and YARN Services

In order to work with a Hadoop cluster, you must start up the HDFS- and YARN HDFS-related services. HDFS services are the NameNode and DataNode services. YARN services include the ResourceManager (one per cluster), the NodeManager (one on each worker node) and the JobHistoryServer services.

The following sections explain how to start the HDFS and YARN services in the pseudo-distributed cluster.

Starting the Hadoop Services

In our simple pseudo-distributed cluster, there are three HDFS services:

- NameNode
- Secondary NameNode
- DataNode

> **Tip**
>
> If you configure a Standby NameNode, you don't need the Secondary NameNode.

By default, when you create a new Hadoop 2 cluster, you'll have a Secondary NameNode but not a Standby NameNode, which you'll need to explicitly configure. A Secondary NameNode doesn't help in failing over, so it can't offer high availability. In our present case, since we're dealing with a very simple cluster, we can use the default Secondary NameNode to perform the updates of the fsimage file. The recommended practice in a production Hadoop setup is to configure high availability for the NameNode by configuring a Standby NameNode. When you do this, you don't need to use the Secondary NameNode. In addition to the NameNode and the Secondary NameNode (or a Standby NameNode if you configure it), you'll also have multiple DataNodes, one for each node in your cluster (unless you choose not to run a DataNode on the master nodes where you run key Hadoop services such as the NameNode and ResourceManager).

Here are the steps to follow in order to start up all three of the HDFS services in our pseudo-distributed cluster:

```
$ su hdfs
$ cd /opt/yarn/hadoop2.6.0/sbin
$./hadoop-daemon.sh start namenode
starting namenode, logging to /opt/yarn/hadoop-2.6.0/logs/hadoop-hdfs-namenode-
limulus.out
[root@hadoop1 sbin]#

/*start this on the server where Secondary NameNode is configured to run
$ ./hadoop-daemon.sh start secondarynamenode
starting secondarynamenode, logging to /opt/yarn/hadoop-2.6.0/logs/hadoop-hdfs-
secondarynamenode-limulus.out
[root@hadoop1 sbin]#

[root@hadoop1 sbin]# ./hadoop-daemon.sh start datanode
starting datanode, logging to /var/log/hadoop/hdfs/hadoop-root-datanode-hadoop1
.localdomain.out
[root@hadoop1 sbin]#
```

If the NameNode or the DataNodes fail to start, it's easy to find out why. Just open the log file shown in the output (`hadoop-root-datanode-hadoop1.localdomain.out` shown for the DataNode) for the `start` command and check the reason. Usually it's because you haven't set the correct path for `HADOOP_HOME` or `HADOOP_PREFIX`. For example, to find out why the NameNode failed to start, view the file named `/opt/yarn/hadoop-2.6.0/logs/hadoop-hdfs-namenode-limulus.out`. As mentioned earlier, startup problems are usually quite easy to fix!

Now that you have all your HDFS services successfully started, it's time to start up the second Hadoop component, YARN.

Starting the YARN Services

Start the YARN services by logging in as the user yarn. There are three yarn services you must start:

- ResourceManager
- NodeManager
- JobHistoryServer

There's only one ResourceManager (later you'll learn how to set up a high-availability system with an active and a Standby ResourceManager) and a single JobHistoryServer per cluster, and the NodeManager service runs on every node where you run a DataNode in your cluster.

```
# su - yarn
$ cd /opt/yarn/hadoop-2.6.0/sbin
$ ./yarn-daemon.sh start resourcemanager
starting resourcemanager, logging to /opt/yarn/hadoop-2.6.0/logs/yarn-yarn-
resourcemanager-limulus.out
$ ./yarn-daemon.sh start nodemanager
starting nodemanager, logging to /opt/yarn/hadoop-2.6.0/logs/yarn-yarn-
nodemanager-limulus.out
$ ./mr-jobhistory-daemon.sh start historyserver
```

As with the HDFS services, if you're unable to start up one of the YARN services, go to the log directory shown in the output of the `start` command for the service. The log file will show you the reason why Hadoop was unable to start up the process. In a simple cluster like ours, mostly it's because one hasn't correctly configured something such as the home directory for Hadoop, for example.

Verifying the Service Startup

A quick and easy way to check whether all the HDFS and YARN services have started running is to run the `jps` (the Java Virtual Machine Process Status Tool) command as the root user. The `jps` command shows all running Java processes on your single server that hosts all the HDFS and YARN services.

```
[root@hadoop1 sbin]# jps
4180 NodeManager
9186 Jps
3833 NameNode
3940 DataNode
3772 SecondaryNameNode
4108 ResourceManager
[root@hadoop1 sbin]#
```

As you can tell, the `jps` command reveals that all the HDFS and YARN services, such as the ResourceManager and the NameNode that you've started earlier, are in fact running. You can alternatively use the `jps` command as shown here to find the process status for a specific Hadoop daemon:

```
$ /usr/jdk/latest/bin/jps | grep NameNode
3658 NameNode
$
```

You can also use normal Linux process commands to verify whether the Hadoop services are running, as shown here:

```
$ ps -ef|grep -i NameNode
$ ps -ef|grep DataNode
```

Once you've verified that all services are running as expected, you can check out the HDFS file system by issuing the following command:

```
$ hdfs dfs -ls /
```

This is a basic HDFS command that's quite similar to the Linux `ls` command and shows the directories under the HDFS root directory. As you'll see later, the directory under the /user directory in the HDFS hierarchy commonly serves as the "home directory" for services and users in your system. For example, Hive by default uses the /user/hive/warehouse directory for storing data in its tables.

```
[root@hadoop2 sbin]# hdfs dfs -ls /
Found 4 items
drwxr-xr-x   - hdfs supergroup          0 2014-12-26 17:08 /system
drwxr-xr-x   - hdfs supergroup          0 2015-01-25 16:05 /test
drwx-wx-wx   - hdfs supergroup          0 2014-12-26 14:39 /tmp
drwxr-xr-x   - hdfs supergroup          0 2014-12-26 14:39 /user
[root@hadoop2 sbin]#
```

Shutting Down the Services

Now that you've satisfied yourself that the new Hadoop pseudo-distributed cluster is working correctly, you may want to shut down your new cluster. Use the following set of commands to shut the cluster down.

```
$ su -hdfs

$ ./hadoop-daemon.sh stop datanode
$ ./hadoop-daemon.sh stop secondarynamenode
$ ./hadoop-daemon.sh stop namenode

# su - yarn
$ cd /opt/yarn/hadoop-2.6.0/sbin

$ /yarn-daemon.sh stop resourceManager
$ /yarn-daemon.sh stop nodemanager
$ /yarn-daemon.sh stop historyserver
```

Summary

Here's what you learned in this chapter:

- Installing a simple pseudo distributed cluster takes only a single server and you can get going in a couple of hours.
- Initial configuration of a simple cluster requires only a handful of parameters, so you can start running your applications very quickly.
- You use separate start and stop commands to control the various Hadoop daemons that are part of a cluster.

4

Planning for and Creating a Fully Distributed Cluster

This chapter covers the following:

- Planning your Hadoop cluster
- Sizing your cluster
- Installing a multinode, fully distributed Hadoop cluster
- Configuring HDFS and YARN for production

Chapter 3, "Creating and Configuring a Simple Hadoop Cluster," showed how to get going with Hadoop by creating a simple pseudo-distributed cluster that has essentially the same functionality as a full-fledged Hadoop cluster. This chapter takes things further by showing you how to create a multi-node cluster, as well as configure it for effective performance. Before I jump into the creation and configuration of a full-fledged, multinode Hadoop cluster, I'll discuss key factors in planning your cluster and how to size it.

Creating a simple one-node cluster is easy. However, most people want to know how to create their own working Hadoop cluster on a set of simple servers or even on a (powerful) laptop. Or, some of you may want guidance on setting up a real-life, multinode Hadoop cluster in a production environment. I therefore explain how to create a multinode Hadoop 2 cluster, using a virtual environment to keep things simple. More precisely, I show you how to create your own three-node Hadoop cluster using Oracle's VirtualBox to create multiple nodes on a single server. The book does include an appendix, Appendix A, "Installing VirtualBox and Linux and Cloning the Virtual Machines," that shows the actual VirtualBox installation and cloning steps.

Once you have a working multi-node cluster set up, you can follow the instructions in this book to create a Hadoop 2 cluster and configure it for operation. It's my firm belief that creating a full-fledged Hadoop cluster in this manner strengthens your understanding of the Hadoop architecture and gets you in the catbird seat for setting up a much larger real-life production cluster.

As you'll learn through this book, a large part of a Hadoop administrator's job is to master the various dials and knobs that make Hadoop run—the configuration parameters for HDFS, YARN and other components. Incorrect configuration settings, or configuration properties left at their default values, are at the heart of a vast majority of Hadoop-related performance issues. Installing a Hadoop cluster from scratch, as shown in this chapter, will make you aware of how the configuration parameters are used by Hadoop and help you learn how to optimize your cluster's operations.

Planning Your Hadoop Cluster

When planning a cluster, you must begin by understanding your company's data needs. You must also evaluate the type of data processing that'll occur in the cluster. Doing this will let you figure out the HDFS storage you'll need, as well as the throughput speed you must have in order to efficiently process the data.

The type of work to which you'll put the cluster has a huge bearing on how you configure a cluster's storage, network and CPU. If your expected workload is going to be CPU intensive, disk speed and network speed are less important. If your cluster is going to perform a large amount of heavy MapReduce processing, then network bandwidth becomes a significant factor. Maybe you'll need to get multiple NICs for each node in such a case.

Many organizations get their feet wet by starting with a very small cluster of about half a dozen nodes or so and add more nodes as the data volumes increase.

You can plan for the growth of the cluster in accordance with how your data grows. If your data is growing by 1TB daily, with Hadoop's default replication of 3, that's 90TB of additional storage required per month. If you allocate about 20-25 percent of the total storage to the local Linux file system (as you'll see, Hadoop also needs space on the local file system, in addition to space it needs for storing HDFS files), you'll need about 120TB of new storage per month. If you buy servers with 12 3TB size disks drives each, you'll need roughly 4 new servers a month on average.

General Cluster Planning Considerations

In a single node "cluster," also called a pseudo-distributed Hadoop installation, the single node will host all Hadoop services, such as the NameNode, the ResourceManager, the DataNode and the JobHistoryServer daemons. In a real-life production Hadoop cluster, the architecture will usually consist of one or more racks.

Each of the racks in a cluster will contain multiple server nodes within a cluster with a 1GbE switch. Each of the nodes is usually interconnected using a 1GbE switch. These rack-level switches are in turn connected to a set of larger (say, 10GbE) cluster-level switches, which may be connected to yet another level of switching infrastructure.

Figure 4.1 shows one way of architecting Hadoop, where all the key master services are located on dedicated master nodes. These are services such as the NameNode and ResourceManager, which are essential to the functioning of the cluster. However, in

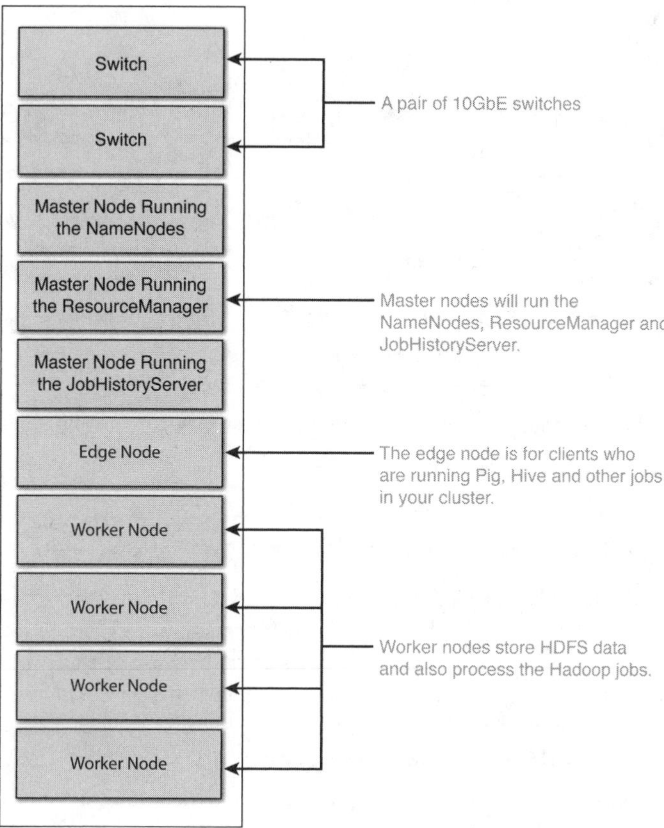

Figure 4.1 The basic components of a Hadoop cluster showing the master nodes and the DataNodes

many environments, it's common to have the master nodes share a node with other services such as the DataNodes.

Figure 4.2 shows the typical architecture for a small Hadoop cluster. You have a single rack of nodes in which you have all the master services running on nodes separate from the nodes where the DataNodes are running. A pair of 10GbE networks supports the cluster. On each master node in this single-rack configuration, you can deploy the master services as shown in Figure 4.2.

The master services are the NameNode (active and Standby), the ResourceManager (active and Standby), the JournalNodes and the JobHistoryServer. The JournalNodes are needed only in high-availability architectures. The lightweight ZooKeeper service needs to run on at least three nodes for quorum purposes and to support NameNode high availability, so we have it running on the three master nodes.

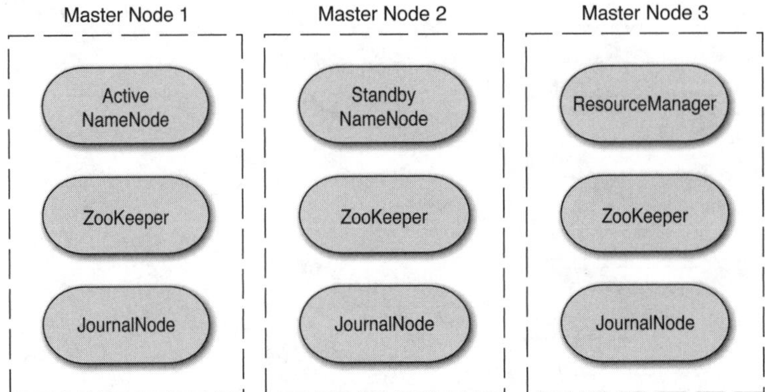

Figure 4.2 Multiple master nodes with various master services running on each node

Server Form Factors

You can choose between two different form factors for your cluster nodes:

- Blade servers are fitted inside blade enclosures, which provide storage, networking and power for the servers in the enclosures. A typical rack (72-inch floor rack) of servers can fit somewhere around 42 blade servers because of their small footprint (each server takes up 1 RU, which is short for "a rack unit"). However, blade servers aren't the best strategy for Hadoop installations, because they share resources with other servers and also have limited storage capacities.
- Rack servers are full-fledged, stand-alone servers, which don't share resources with other servers in a rack and also provide room for storage expansion. Rack servers have a larger footprint than blade servers, and usually about 18-20 of them will fit inside a standard server rack.

Criteria for Choosing the Nodes

While cost is definitely a key factor in choosing a specific type of server for your cluster, the initial cost of purchasing the servers is but one of the factors that determine the true long-term cost to an organization. In addition to the initial cost, you ought to consider other factors that add to the long-term total cost of managing your cluster, such as the power consumption and cooling factor of the servers, as well as the reliability and the maintenance costs for servicing the storage, CPUs and network.

It's not recommended that you use the most inexpensive desktop-class computers to build a Hadoop cluster. You should select a midrange Intel server, with a fairly large storage capacity—typically about 36-48TBs per server.

The term commodity server is commonly used to describe the class of servers a Hadoop cluster requires. A commodity server is usually an Intel server with some hard disk storage. A commodity server is considered an "average" level server, which means it is affordable but doesn't imply low quality by any means.

Going from a Single Rack to Multiple Racks

The architecture described thus far is for a small cluster and uses a single rack consisting of several nodes. Figure 2.2 from the previous chapter shows that the rack uses a pair of 10GbE switches. If you're dealing with a larger cluster that needs to go beyond a single rack, you simply add the racks to your cluster and still continue to use a 10GbE switch pair for each rack.

Figure 4.2 showed a single rack cluster with all the nodes—master and workers—running in the same rack. Let's say you've extended your single rack to a three-rack cluster. Now that you have three separate racks, you can take advantage of this to enhance high availability, by apportioning master nodes across the three racks—that is, you'll have a single master node running on each of the three racks. Figure 4.3 shows a cluster with multiple racks. Notice how the master nodes (three in this example) are distributed across

Figure 4.3 Multiple racks, each with a master node and several worker nodes—an architecture that provides more resiliency for a cluster

the three racks. This arrangement, with each rack with a master node and several worker nodes, is the most common architecture in practice.

As far as the configuration changes go when you move from a single rack to multiple racks, you simply change the appropriate parameters in your Hadoop configuration files to point to the new homes of the master services. The rest of the nodes in each rack will be just DataNodes.

Moving to a cluster using hundreds of nodes is fairly straightforward with this architecture—you simply add the nodes to your cluster configuration. For larger clusters, the network architecture could get pretty complex, and you may need to use a larger switch than the commonly used 10GbE-size switches.

Sizing a Hadoop Cluster

Sizing a Hadoop cluster involves sizing the storage, memory, network and other resources that are part of the cluster. Experience in various Hadoop environments suggests that a server with a 3TB disk size, 96GB RAM and 8-12 cores is common, but the disk storage size and the amount of RAM and the number of CPU cores vary widely across various environments, and there aren't any hard and fast rules concerning these.

Setting up a pilot cluster to get more insight into your potential data usage patterns is a good strategy before you actually start setting up a real production cluster. The pilot cluster will tell you if your data processing is going to be memory intensive or CPU or I/O bound.

General Principles Governing the Choice of CPU, Memory and Storage

Choosing the amount and type of CPUs, disks and RAM for the individual nodes in a cluster is a crucial decision. The key principles guiding your choices here are the following:

- Expected type of cluster workload: If you expect most of your workload to involve large amounts of data that require the sorting of data sets, you'll most likely need a large amount of disk storage. You'd also want to configure a cluster with more disks per node. Also, the disk size can be larger than the average disk size. If your workload tends toward a highly compute-intensive work pattern, you'll want to configure your cluster with smaller sized disks.

> **Note**
>
> Most Hadoop applications are disk and network I/O bound, and therefore you don't need to splurge on high-end CPUs.

- Expected amount of data storage: You may have to store certain types of data for specific periods of time for compliance purposes.
- Expected growth patterns: You need to estimate approximately how fast the data ingest will grow over a period of time.

Since extra performance on the DataNodes isn't really justifiable in terms of the cost involved, most of the time, you can manage with medium clock speed processors with less than two sockets. If you're configuring for a medium or large cluster, then the DataNodes ideally must use at least two quad-core or two six-core CPUs per server.

Following are the arguments against using virtualization and blade servers in a Hadoop environment:

- Although virtualization (using a virtual rather than a real set of servers, using VMWare, for example) is great for test and proof-of-concept clusters, network contention and the possibility of placing all replicas on the same physical host means that there could be a significant price to pay when you virtualize a Hadoop cluster.
- Blade servers are also not advisable, because several DataNodes will become unavailable when a blade chassis fails. Not only are there potential network bottlenecks in the network connections between the chassis and the top-of-rack switch, the disk capacity and RAM of blades is too low to support significant amounts of processing.

Now that we've learned something about the general principles that govern the choice of CPU, memory and storage, in the following sections I review how to approach the sizing of the cluster, including storage and memory.

Disk Sizing and Configuration

Since HDFS runs on the native file system of the server, you could theoretically work with nodes that have different file systems. For example, in a Linux system some nodes could have an ext3 and others an ext4 file system. Furthermore, all DataNodes don't have to have the same amount of storage.

Consider purchasing rack servers that are explicitly designed for Hadoop. These servers are designed to be more compact than traditional servers, and hence more of them will fit into a standard chassis (rack). Instead of the usual 18-20 servers, you may get close to 30 servers per rack with this design. In addition, since the servers are designed with Hadoop in mind, they also come with more disk drives than standard servers, offering greater density, which means your cluster will need less room.

As far as disk speed is concerned, you'll be fine with 7,200 RPM SATA drives, and there's no need to purchase the much more expensive 15,000 RPM disk drives. A key thing to remember here is that you're better off with many smaller disk drives than a few large disk drives, because in Hadoop environments, data is distributed and your application tasks will be seeking data spread out on multiple disks throughout the cluster.

> **Tip**
>
> Experience shows that if you allocate more than 36TB of data per DataNode, you might encounter network traffic issues when DataNodes die and Hadoop is forced to replicate data to other DataNodes in the cluster.

A key question is whether you can use disks configured in a JBOD (Just a Bunch of Disks) configuration or whether you must use RAID. Hadoop uses built-in data redundancy to protect against data loss. Hence, RAID is unnecessary—using RAID is overkill and reduces the storage available to HDFS.

For the all-important NameNode server, the recommendation is to use RAID. More specifically, you should use RAID-1 (mirroring) for the NameNode server, so it's highly available. In addition to the NameNode, you should use RAID-based storage for all your master machines, due to the critical nature of those machines.

Ideally, you should try to set up each of a cluster's nodes with about 12 disk drives, each with a 3TB disk. If you envisage your data storage needs growing at a high rate, you might be better served by purchasing disks with a larger capacity. Most commonly companies use 6-24 disk drives or more per DataNode.

As the number of disks per node increases, you're going to run a higher risk of a disk failure. Therefore, you must think of using two disk controllers per server to share the I/O load. Although SFF (small form factor) disks are in use in some environments, the recommendation here is to use either SATA or SAS interconnects.

Assuming that you're using the default replication factor of three, you'll be able to store data that's equal to roughly a third of the storage you assign to HDFS. For example, if your cluster has 12 nodes and 36TB of raw disk space per node (12 disk drives each with 3TB of storage), you'll be able to store 144TB of data in your Hadoop cluster (144 is two-thirds of 432, which is the total raw disk space across the cluster). From this, it's easy to figure out how many servers you need to add to your cluster over time to accommodate the data growth in your cluster. If the raw data that's being added to the cluster is growing at the rate of 150TB a month, you will need to plan on adding about 24 nodes every year.

Sizing the Memory

As with any server that crunches data, the amount of memory plays a significant role in the processing speed of queries based on data stored in a Hadoop system. As you'll learn soon, the amount of work you can perform on any node depends on the amount of total RAM allocated to that server.

Each Hadoop job spawns child tasks, each of which runs as part of a logical entity called a container. The size of the container is specified in terms of RAM. Therefore, the number of containers you can have Hadoop create and deploy on each node—and hence the amount of work a node performs—depends on two things: total RAM allocated to the server and the size of the containers. The more RAM you allocate to a DataNode, the more work you can perform simultaneously on that node.

It's common for most large-scale, busy Hadoop environments to size the RAM for the DataNodes at 48-96GB. I recommend going for 256GB RAM if you can, because real-time Hadoop processes are indeed memory hungry, and more memory will serve you better as your cluster load ramps up. In addition, frameworks such as Impala and Spark are much more memory intensive than MapReduce. In environments with memory-intensive processing, you can even use 512GB of RAM per DataNode.

Network Considerations

The most important thing you need to be aware of regarding the network requirements is that Hadoop workloads could place high stress on a network. It's important to ensure that the cluster nodes can communicate among themselves at good speeds. Typically, large Hadoop clusters use a dual 1GB link for all nodes in a rack (20 nodes). If your cluster stores a very large amount of data (multiple petabytes) and if your MapReduce jobs are expected to create large amounts of intermediate data, you'll need very high bandwidth, and therefore, you may seek 10GB/second connection speeds in such cases. The clusters also use a 2*10GB interconnect link per rack and could even have a pair of central switches.

Using a pair of bonded network connections helps you both improve throughput and gain redundancy at the same time.

Since the Hadoop cluster's network load is going to impact other users of a switch, it's optimal to dedicate a switch for the cluster rather than allocating a virtual circuit (VC) in another switch. When deciding on the type of switch, look for something that provides deep buffering, in preference to a low-latency switch.

Each rack in a cluster will be well served by a pair of top-of-rack (ToR) switches, which provide higher performance while ensuring redundancy. A 10GbE ToR switch is the recommended size in most cases. If you have more than two or three racks in your cluster, you also need to put in a pair of core switches to handle the high traffic, usually 40GbE switches.

Using jumbo frames across your cluster will ensure higher bandwidth in addition to providing packet integrity.

Special Treatment for the Master Nodes

The master nodes are highly important in a Hadoop cluster because, unlike the DataNodes, they run services such as the ResourceManager and the NameNode service that are critical to the functioning of the cluster. Therefore, accord the master nodes special treatment by doing the following:

- Invest in top-of-the-class hardware rather than commodity hardware.
- Use SAS drives rather than the cheaper SATA drives. SAS drives are highly reliable and much faster than SATA drives, although their storage capacity is usually smaller.
- Use hardware RAID or network storage.
- Use on-site disk replacement service options in your support contracts for the RAID disks on the master nodes, to keep outages to the minimum.
- Use a large number of CPU cores to handle the high amount of messaging traffic for the master nodes.
- Configure high amounts of RAM, ranging from 64GB to 128GB at the least. The NameNode and the Standby NameNode rely on RAM to store the HDFS metadata while the cluster is running. The larger the amount of data you store, the greater the need for memory for the NameNodes.

- Provision multiple network ports and high bandwidth (10GbE) to the switch.
- Use dual power supplies and bonded dual Ethernet cards to support failover.

Recommendations for Sizing the Servers

You can summarize the discussion in the previous sections to arrive at some broad recommendations for the various types of servers in a typical Hadoop environment.

- **Master nodes**
  - Processors: You need a single CPU with 6-8 cores.
  - Memory: You need 24-96GB RAM.
  - Storage: You only need 1-2TB local storage, as no HDFS data is stored on these nodes. You can use SAS disks with RAID-1 configuration.
- **DataNodes**
  - Processors: You need two CPUs with 4-8 cores each. If you'd like, you can have a single CPU with more cores, and you can add more cores later on. You must enable hyper-threading and quick-path interconnect (QPI).
  - Memory: You need 24-96GB per node. The more map and reduce processes you plan to run on each DataNode, the higher the memory requirement for each of your DataNodes in the cluster.
  - Storage: For storing HDFS data, use 6-12 disks with 2TB or 3TB disks. You can use 4TB disks as well if you anticipate large data volumes. SATA drives with a JBOD configuration are all you need—no RAID systems are necessary. The greater the number of disks, the higher the I/O bandwidth. You also need a pair of 2TB or 3TB disks for the operating system files and for storing Hadoop daemon logs. You can configure this pair of disks with RAID-1.
  - Network: Within each rack of servers, use a 1GbE or 10GbE network for connectivity within the rack.

Typically, a midrange configuration for a DataNode will look like the following:

- 12 X 3TB SATA II disk drives (non-RAID)
- 2 X 6-core 2.9 GHz CPUs
- 64GB RAM
- 2X1GbE

A more expensive configuration would look like this:

- 24 X 1TB Nearline/MDL SAS disk drives (non-RAID)
- 2 X 8-core 2.9 GHz CPUs
- 128GB RAM

As far as the operating system goes, there are no particular recommendations. Hadoop supports the mixing up of operating systems in the same cluster. In production systems, it's therefore common to see CentOS, Ubuntu and SuSE being widely used for DataNodes and Red Hat Linux for the master nodes.

Growing a Cluster

You can increase a cluster's size by adding more nodes or entire server racks to the cluster. Since it's sometimes difficult to anticipate future workloads, design your cluster in a somewhat loose fashion, by selecting hardware such as CPU and memory that is easily upgradeable over time.

If you're running low on free space in your Hadoop cluster, you can add more storage to existing DataNodes. The more common way to increase your storage capacity, however, is to extend your cluster by adding nodes (DataNodes).

Guidelines for Large Clusters

Apache Hadoop itself doesn't require a specific layout for the various services that are part of a cluster. However, a smart layout will take into consideration the unique requirements of each of the key services and design the placement of those services with a view to minimizing contention and enhancing efficiency. Following are some guidelines regarding the placement of key services in a medium to large cluster.

- ResourceManager: The ResourceManager is resource hungry! In the case of large clusters (over 50 nodes), you need to make sure you don't run the ResourceManager service on nodes where the ZooKeeper service is running. Except in the case of small clusters, run the ResourceManager service on a dedicated node.
- NameNode service: You should run this service on a dedicated node, for both performance and availability reasons. To enhance availability, as mentioned elsewhere in this chapter, it's a good practice to use RAID-1 storage for the server running the NameNode service.

> **Note**
>
> If you're setting up NameNode high availability, you should configure the servers hosting the active and Standby NameNodes identically.

- JournalNodes: You can run the JournalNodes on the same servers that are running the Hadoop master services such as the NameNode and the ResourceManager.
- JobHistoryServer: As with the JournalNodes, you can run the JobHistoryServer on one of the master nodes.
- DataNode and NodeManager services: The NodeManager runs on every DataNode. There are no special requirements for the NodeManager service location, except that you may want to minimize the amount of memory dedicated to it on servers

if you co-locate the NodeManager and the ZooKeeper services. The DataNode daemon, of course, runs on each of the DataNodes.

- MySQL database: The MySQL database is commonly used for storing the metadata for Hive, Oozie and other components in most medium to large clusters. There's no requirement that dictates that you must run the database on a cluster node. Since databases are usually resource hungry, consider setting up your MySQL database on a non-cluster node.
- ZooKeeper: You need an odd number of ZooKeeper services running to support NameNode high availability, with the minimum being three instances. Since these are quite lightweight instances, they can run on the same nodes as the master nodes.

> **Note**
>
> At a minimum, you'll need three ZooKeeper instances in a Hadoop cluster, one of which acts as the leader of the set of ZooKeeper instances. When a client issues a write request, a majority of the nodes, called a quorum, must respond successfully to the request in order for the write request to succeed. A quorum is reflected by a strict majority of the nodes. There's a good reason why you need at least three ZooKeeper instances: One node in the ZooKeeper ensemble doesn't provide high availability, and if you have two instances, both need to be up since one out of two nodes isn't a strict majority. If you configure three nodes in the ZooKeeper ensemble, even when one node goes down, you'll have a functioning service, since two out of three instances provides a strict majority.

Creating a Multinode Cluster

Some readers might be thinking by this point that learning how to create and use the simple pseudo-distributed cluster as shown in Chapter 3 is all well and fine, but the setting up of a fully distributed cluster must be a complex affair. Surely, this pseudo-distributed setup has got to be a Mickey Mouse affair, with no meaningful bearing on how you do things in the real world! In reality, however, creating a fully distributed Hadoop cluster isn't that different from creating a simple pseudo–distributed cluster.

One difference, of course, between a pseudo-distributed and a multinode cluster is that since it's a real cluster, HDFS data blocks can be replicated. Another difference you might find is that real-life clusters do need high availability in most cases, so that's something that'll be new.

How the Test Cluster Is Set Up

Our goal in this book is to learn how to administer a real-life Hadoop environment, and so we need to work with a multinode cluster, even if it's quite small. You can't learn how to work with replication if you only have a single node. You also can't learn how to work with Hadoop's high availability features, since a one-node pseudo-cluster doesn't permit any high availability!

I use a three-node cluster in this book, for the most part, to run the examples and demonstrate how various Hadoop components interact in a cluster. In this section, I show you how to quickly install and set up a three-node cluster using Oracle VM VirtualBox. You can do the same thing using VMware if you wish or even use three physical nodes for that matter. There's no real difference in how you set up the actual cluster.

Why three nodes? Well, you can use just two nodes, but that'll keep us from demonstrating how to use the ZooKeeper service for supporting HDFS high availability, which needs a quorum of an odd number of clusters. With three nodes being the smallest number to configure ZooKeeper, I chose to demonstrate the creation and setup of the three-node cluster. If you're creating this cluster on your laptop for testing purposes, just make sure you have enough RAM! A three-node cluster on virtual servers will run fine if you have at least 16GB of RAM.

Setting up a Hadoop cluster, whether using multiple physical servers or by using virtual servers using VMware or Oracle VM VirtualBox, is really an easy affair. How easy? You can complete the entire process—starting from the installation of Oracle VM VirtualBox to the starting up of the full three-node cluster—in just four hours!

Appendix A shows how to set up a three-node Hadoop cluster using Oracle VMBox and Oracle Linux (very similar to Red Hat Enterprise Linux). Following are the steps you must follow to complete the setup of the 3-node cluster.

1. Install Oracle VirtualBox (explained in the Appendix)
2. Install Oracle Enterprise Linux on an Oracle VM VirtualBox (explained in the Appendix)
3. Install Hadoop 2.6.0 on the virtual server (shown in Chapter 3)
4. Configure Hadoop 2.6.0 on the virtual server (shown in Chapters 3 and 4)
5. Clone the initial virtual server to create the other two virtual servers (explained in the Appendix)

Once you clone the initial Linux server, you'll have three nodes, all with Hadoop software already installed. If you followed all the steps presented in Appendix A, you'll have three Oracle Linux servers running in your Oracle VMBox. You're now ready to perform the tasks to get your multinode Hadoop 2 cluster going.

You use the same configuration files for setting up a multinode Hadoop cluster as you did earlier when setting up a pseudo-distributed cluster. However, now you have multiple servers, so you need to set up a few other things, such as passwordless SSH connectivity, and modify certain key important configuration parameters in various files, to enable a real Hadoop cluster.

In our three-node cluster, where the nodes are named hadoop1, hadoop2 and hadoop3, we use the first two nodes as our master nodes, and that's where we run the following services:

- Node 1 (hadoop1): NameNode, JobHistoryServer
- Node 2 (hadoop2): Standby NameNode, ResourceManager

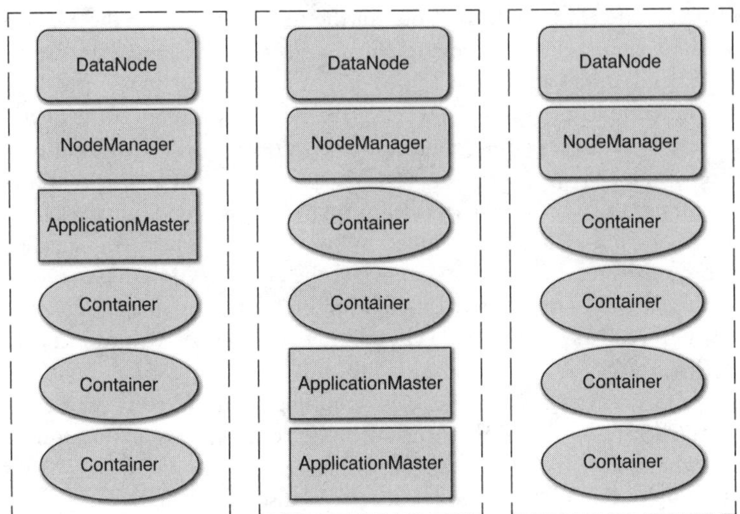

Figure 4.4 How the storage and processing services are typically deployed on the worker nodes

That leaves us only one node (hadoop3) as a pure worker node. However, I want to show you how to replicate your data, so I use the two "master nodes" (hadoop1 and hadoop2) for running the services that are usually run on worker nodes. Figure 4.4 shows the services that typically run on the worker nodes. Note that there is an ApplicationMaster for each YARN job. Also note that a worker node may not run any ApplicationMaster services since there is only one of those per job. There is a single DataNode (HDFS service) on each worker node. You also run a NodeManager service on each of the worker nodes (DataNodes).

The next sections cover the following topics:

- Installing `pdsh`
- Configuring passwordless SSH
- Editing the /etc/hosts file

Installing pdsh

You can make cluster administration easy by using `pdsh` to run commands on your entire cluster. The `pdsh` utility is a variant of the `rsh` command and is a high-performance parallel shell utility. Whereas `rsh` lets you run commands on a single remote host, `pdsh` lets you run commands on multiple remote servers simultaneously. So, if you need to issue the same command across all cluster nodes, you simply issue the command from a single server using `pdsh`, and that executes the command across the cluster.

You can use `pdsh` by issuing commands at the command line or by running the tool interactively. When run interactively, `pdsh` prompts you for commands and executes them when a carriage return occurs. You can also specify your commands in a file.

Note

The pdsh distribution also includes a parallel remote copy utility named pdsh, which copies files from a local host to a group of remote hosts in parallel.

You can install pdsh in the following manner:

```
# rpm -Uvh http://download.fedoraproject.org/pub/epel/6/i386/epel-release-6-8
.noarch.rpm
# yum install pdsh
```

You'll need to install the pdsh utility on all the cluster nodes. Using pdsh to perform remote operations is straightforward. Here's an example that shows you how to check the date on all nodes in a cluster with a single command from any node in your cluster.

```
# pdsh -w "all_nodes" date
```

The parameter all_nodes points to a file that lists all the nodes in the cluster. You can also exclude some servers when issuing a pdsh command if you wish.

Configuring Passwordless SSH among the Cluster Members

When you work with a multinode cluster, you need to configure a passwordless SSH connection among the cluster nodes. Setting up SSH enables you to run remote commands without being asked for a password. To set up the passwordless connection, you must first generate the public and private keys for a user. You can do this using the ssh-keygen commands shown here:

```
# ssh-keygen -t rsa
```

Just accept all the defaults and don't specify a passphrase, so you or any tool that executes remote commands in the cluster won't be prompted for a password when accessing the private key. Once you generate the keys, if your cluster consists of just a few nodes, as in our case, you can simply copy the public key to all the cluster nodes. However, in a large cluster, you can use the ssh-copy-id command to copy public keys to all hosts and add those hosts to the ssh_known_hosts file. Here's an example:

```
# ssh-copy-id -i /root/.ssh/id_rsa.pub <fqdn>
```

Editing the /etc/hosts File

On each of the three virtual nodes, edit the/etc/hosts file so they show the hostnames and IP addresses for all the nodes. The three nodes are named hadoop1, hadoop2 and hadoop3, and I used hadoop1 as the master node. When you're done, the /etc/hosts file in each server should look like the following:

```
10.1.3.66      hadoop1
10.1.3.67      hadoop2
10.1.3.68      hadoop3
```

Figure 4.5 presents the /etc/hosts file, showing that all three nodes in our cluster are listed in this file on each of the nodes.

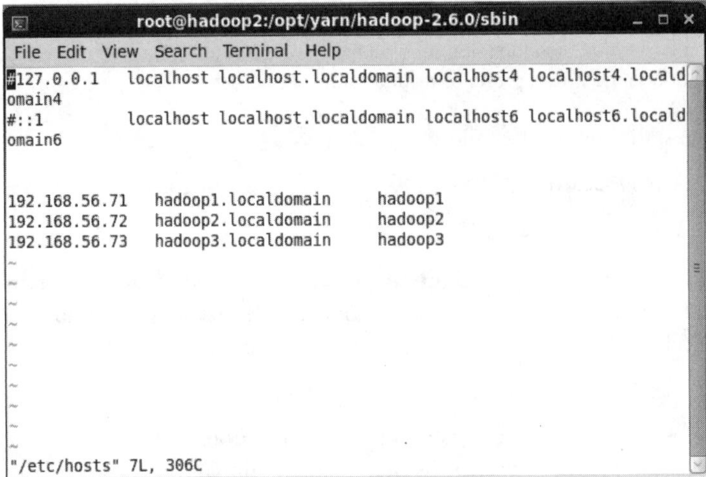

Figure 4.5 The /etc/hosts file, showing the hostnames and IP addresses for all three nodes in the cluster

Modifying the Hadoop Configuration

In our pseudo-distributed node, I was forced to use a replication factor of 1 since I had only a single node on which to store HDFS blocks. Now that I have three nodes, I can raise the replication factor in this fully distributed cluster by modifying the `dfs.replication` parameter in the hdfs-site.xml file. In addition to this `dfs.replication` parameter, let's add some more parameters that you'd normally specify in a real-life production cluster to raise your cluster to production grade.

A word of caution here regarding the configuration parameters: In this section, I introduce many key configuration parameters that determine how HDFS, MapReduce and YARN work. However, the configuration list isn't by any means exhaustive. There are hundreds of these parameters, such as the parameters for scheduling jobs through the Fair Scheduler and for setting up Kerberos security, as well as a whole host of configuration properties that affect Hadoop performance, and you'll run into them in the appropriate chapters.

The following sections show you how to

- Change the HDFS configuration
- Change the YARN configuration
- Change the MapReduce configuration

Changing the HDFS Configuration (hdfs-site.xml file)

In order to move to a fully distributed cluster from our pseudo-distributed cluster, you need to make a few changes to the HDFS configuration.

dfs.block.size

In the pseudo-distributed cluster, as I explained in Chapter 3, I haven't set the HDFS block size that Hadoop must use when creating a file, so it takes the default block size of 128MB (the default value is for the Hadoop 2.6 version—it may vary across the Hadoop releases). You can set the block size to a higher value, such as 256MB or 512MB, depending on the size of the input files your system is processing. You set the HDFS block size with the `dfs.block.size` parameter:

```
<property>
  <name>dfs.block.size</name>
  <value>134217728</value>
</property>
```

The default block size for new files is in bytes (134,217,728, which is 128MB). You can also specify the size with a case-insensitive suffix such as k (kilo-), m (mega-), g (giga-), t (tera-) or e (exa-) to set the block size (128k, 512m, 1g, etc.).

> **Note**
>
> When you change the block size, it applies only to new files—if you want to change the block size for existing data, you'll need to reload the data after setting the new block size.

In this example, the `dfs.block.size` parameter specifies a block size of 128MB. Note that an application can override this by specifying a different value, as shown here:

```
$ hdfs dfs -fs  -D dfs.block.size=2684354568 -put local_name hdfs_location
```

dfs.datanode.du.reserved

The `dfs.datenode.du.reserved` parameter specifies the amount of space on each storage volume that can't be used for HDFS file storage. By default, this parameter is set to 0, meaning all the space on a DataNode can be used for HDFS storage. It's best to leave about 20 percent of the space on each volume to non-HDFS uses, with a minimum of 10GB of space reserved for non-HDFS uses. Here's how you set this parameter:

```
<property>
<name>dfs.datanode.du.reserved</name>
<value>20</value>
</property>
```

Updating the HDFS Parameters

In addition to the new parameters, you'll also want to update the following parameters in the hadoop-site.xml file, since you're now working with a fully distributed "production" cluster.

- `dfs.replication`: As mentioned earlier, let's go ahead and change the value of the `dfs.replication` parameter from 1 to 3.

  ```
  <property>
     <name>dfs.replication</name>
     <value>3</value>
  </property>
  ```

When you were working with a single-node cluster, you really had no choice but to set the replication factor to 1. Now that you have a three-node cluster, it's time to set the HDFS block replication to the default value, which is 3.

- `dfs.name.node.dir`: This parameter specifies where in the local file system the NameNode stores the fsimage file. If you provide a comma-delimited list of directories, the fsimage file is replicated to all the directories you specify, providing redundancy for this important file. You must specify at least two disks or a RAID volume on the NameNode as the value for this parameter. You'll expose the cluster to a catastrophic data loss by not setting the recommended multiple disks for this crucial parameter.

```
<property>
  <name>dfs.namenode.name.dir</name>
  <value>file:///u01/dfs/nn,file:///u02/dfs/nn</value>
</property>
```

Note that if one of the directories is filled up, the NameNode doesn't crash—it continues to function normally and keeps writing to the other directory. If you specify only one directory, no such luck—the NameNode will stop. When you set the `dfs.namenode.name.dir` parameter, the NameNode writes synchronously to the edit log in all directories you specify for this parameter. You can choose to specify a separate path for the edit log directory with the `dfs.namenode.edits.dir` parameter, as shown here.

```
<property>
   <name>dfs.namenode.edits.dir</name>
   <value>file:///u01/dfs/nn/edits,file:///u02/dfs/nn/edits</value>
</property>
```

If you're using a single NameNode and a Secondary NameNode, there's no high availability for the NameNode, and that's how I've set up my cluster at this initial point. In Chapter 8, "The Role of the NameNode and How HDFS Works," I show you how to set up a high-availability HDFS NameNode, with an active and a Standby NameNode.

- `dfs.datanode.data.dir`: In our pseudo-distributed one-node cluster, you could avail yourself of storage on only a single node. Since you're now using three nodes for HDFS storage, you must add the data directories for all three nodes for the `dfs.datanode.data.dir` parameter.

```
<property>
    <name>dfs.datanode.data.dir</name>
<value>file:///u12/hadoop/dfs,file:///u11/hadoop/dfs,file:///u10/hadoop/
dfs,file:///u09/hadoop/dfs,file:///u08/hadoop/dfs,file:///u07/hadoop/
dfs,file:///u06/hadoop/dfs,file:///u05/hadoop/dfs,file:///u04/hadoop/
dfs,file:///u03/hadoop/dfs,file:///u02/hadoop/dfs,file:///u01/hadoop/dfs
</value>
</property>
```

- `dfs.permissions.superusergroup`: This parameter specifies the group that contains HDFS super users. In Hadoop, whichever user you start the NameNode as is deemed the super user for HDFS. In addition to this default super user of HDFS, you can specify a special super user group using this parameter (dfs.permissions.superusergroup). If you set this parameter, any user that's a member of this group will also be considered an HDFS super user. The default value of this parameter is supergroup. In our case, I name the group admingroup instead:

```
<property>
    <name>dfs.permissions.superusergroup</name>
    <value>admingroup</value>
</property>
```

Changing the YARN Configuration

In our simple YARN configuration for our pseudo cluster, we specified just two parameters in the yarn-site.xml file:

- yarn.nodemanager.aux-services: Our value for this parameter is "mapreduce_shuffle".
- yarn.nodemanager.aux-services.mapreduce.shuffle.class: Our value for this parameter is yarn.nodemanger.aux-services.mapreduce.shuffle.class. The default value is org.apache.hadoop.mapred.ShuffleHandler.

You really don't need to specify the value for the second parameter if you're using just the MapReduce framework, since the Java class for the MapReduce auxiliary service is the default value for this parameter anyway. You do need to add the appropriate value(s) for this parameter if other application frameworks are running under YARN, though.

Configuring the Memory-Related Parameters

If you don't set any memory-related configuration properties, the cluster will start up fine, but it may not perform efficiently, since it'll be using Hadoop's default values for all the memory related parameters. Thus, it's important to tweak these parameters.

Specify the following additional (and optional, but highly recommended in production settings) YARN parameters in the yarn.xml file.

- yarn.nodemanager.resource.memory-mb: This parameter specifies the total amount of RAM in MB available on this node for the tasks that YARN manages. You must include other Hadoop memory usage such as the memory used by the DataNode daemon in the category "non-YARN-managed work." So, if the node has a total RAM of 96GB, you can assign about 70 percent of it to YARN by assigning the value 68 (GB) for the yarn.nodemanager.resource.memory-mb parameter, as shown here.

```
<property>
   <name>yarn.nodemanager.resource.memory-mb</name>
   <value>68608</value>
</property>
```

The default value for the yarn.nodemanager.resource.memory-mb parameter is 8,192MB (8GB), which means that if your nodes have a large RAM capacity such as 64GB or 96GB you'll be wasting most of the memory as the default value for this parameter limits memory allocation for YARN jobs to just 8GB.

- yarn.nodemanager.resource.cpu-vcores: The number of CPU cores that can be allocated to YARN containers. The default value for this parameter is 8, and you must set it to one less than the number of physical cores on the node. The example below shows how to set the number of CPU cores to 24.

```
<property>
    <name>yarn.nodemanager.resource.cpu-vcores</name>
    <value>24</value>
</property>
```

- mapreduce.map.memory.mb and mapreduce.reduce.memory.mb: These two parameters specify the amount of memory to allocate for each map or reduce task (container size). The default for both parameters is 1GB and most clusters will need a higher value (between 2-4GB in most cases). The following examples show how to set the memory size for map and reduce tasks to 2GB each.

```
<property>
    <name>mapreduce.map.memory.mb</name>
    <value>2048</value>
</property>

<property>
    <name>mapreduce.reduce.memory.mb</name>
    <value>2048</value>
</property>
```

- mapreduce.map.java.opts and mapreduce.reduce.java.opts: Mapper and reducer processes run within a JVM. Besides memory for the JVM, the memory (2GB) you allocated for each map and reduce must also accommodate other requests for memory—this memory usage is called the overhead for the process. Use up all of this memory and the task won't have any memory for its overhead.

  In order to avoid the JVM taking up all of a task's memory allocation, you limit the size of the Java heap for mappers and reducers with the mapreduce.map.java.opts and the mapreduce.reduce.java.opts parameters:

```
<property>
   <name>mapreduce.map.java.opts</name>
   <value>1536</value>
</property>
<property>
   <name>mapreduce.reduce.java.opts</name>
   <value>-Xmx1536</value>
</property>
```

  A good rule of thumb here is to allocate 70-75 percent of the value you set for the mapreduce.map.memory.mb and mapreduce.reduce.memory.mb parameters as the values for the mapreduce.map.java.opts and mapreduce.reduce.java.opts parameters.

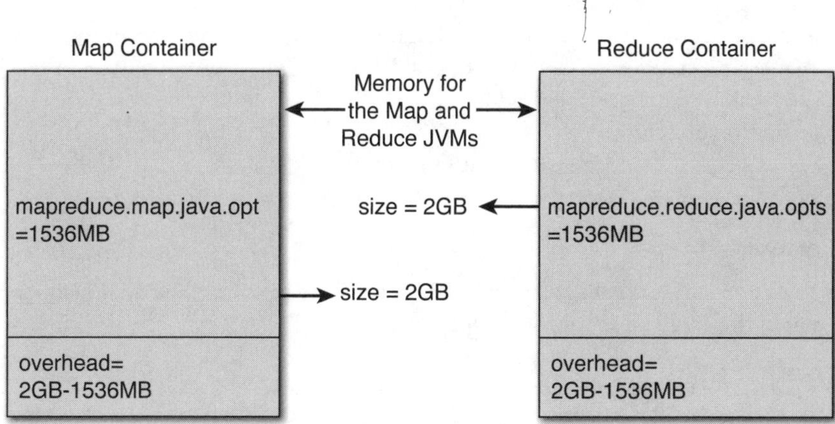

Figure 4.6 How you allocate memory to map and reduce containers, making sure that there's some memory set apart for overhead, after accounting for JVM memory

The memory settings I describe here configure the upper limit of the physical RAM that map and reduce tasks will use. The upper limit for the virtual memory for each Map and Reduce task is determined by the virtual memory ratio that you configure for a YARN container with the `yarn.nodemanager.vmem-pmem-ratio` property. The default value is 2.1, and you can set a different value:

```
<name>yarn.nodemanager.vmem-pmem-ratio</name>
<value>3.0</value>
```

Users are often unsure of how the memory allocated for map and reduce processes is related to the requirements for the JVM memory. Figure 4.6 explains this relationship and shows how you leave aside a certain portion of the memory for the map/reduce processes for overhead as well. The size of the map container is determined by the parameter `mapreduce.map.memory.mb`. In our example this parameter is sized at 2GB. The size of the reduce container is determined by the parameter `mapreduce.reduce.memory.mb`. In our example this parameter is sized the same as the map container, which is 2GB.

Configuring the Logging-Related Parameters

Hadoop produces voluminous logs, and they're quite critical when you're troubleshooting various types of issues. Following are the key parameters you must configure to get going with logging.

- `yarn.log.aggregation-enable`: This property is used by the NodeManagers on each DataNode to aggregate the application logs. When you enable log aggregation, Hadoop collects the logs for each container that is part of an application and moves these files to HDFS once the application is completed.

You can configure the `yarn.nodemanager.remote-app-log-dir` and `yarn.nodemanager.remote-app-log-dir-suffix` configuration properties to specify the location for the aggregated logs in HDFS. Here's how you enable log aggregation in your cluster:

```
<property>
   <name>yarn.log-aggregation-enable</name>
   <value>true</value>
</property>
```

- `log-aggregation.retain.seconds`: This property specifies how long Hadoop will retain the application logs in HDFS.

```
<property>
   <name>yarn.log-aggregation.retain-seconds</name>
   <value>604800</value>
</property>
```

- `yarn-nodemanager.remote-apps-log-dir`: This property specifies the directory in HDFS where the application log files are aggregated. The JobHistoryServer uses this directory to serve the application logs stored in HDFS. Here, I set this parameter to point to the /tmp/logs directory in HDFS:

```
<property>
   <name>yarn.nodemanager.remote-app-log-dir</name>
   <value>/tmp/logs</value>
</property>
```

- `yarn.nodemanager.log-dirs`: This property specifies the directories on the Linux file system where YARN sends the application log files. Since I've enabled log aggregation, once the application completes, YARN removes the local files and you can access them through the JobHistoryServer (from HDFS where the logs are aggregated). An example setting is /var/log/hadoop-yarn/container. Only the NodeManager uses these directories.

```
<property>
   <name>yarn.nodemanager.log-dirs</name>
   <value>/var/log/hadoop-yarn/container</value>
</property>
```

- `yarn.nodemanager.local-dirs`: YARN needs to store its local files such as intermediate output from MapReduce jobs somewhere on the local file system. This parameter specifies those local directories, as shown here:

```
<property>
    <name>yarn.nodemanager.local-dirs</name>
    <value>/u12/hadoop/yarn/nm,/u11/hadoop/yarn/nm,/u10/hadoop/yarn/nm,/u09/
hadoop/yarn/nm,/u08/hadoop/yarn/nm,/u07/hadoop/yarn/nm,/u06/hadoop/yarn/nm,/
u05/hadoop/yarn/nm,/u04/hadoop/yarn/nm,/u03/hadoop/yarn/nm,/u02/hadoop/yarn/
nm,/u01/hadoop/yarn/nm
</value>
</property>
```

YARN's distributed cache uses these local resource files as well.

- `yarn.application.classpath`: This property specifies the locations on the local file system for storing the Hadoop, YARN and HDFS common JAR files necessary for executing applications in the cluster.

```
<property>
    <name>yarn.application.classpath</name>
    <value>$HADOOP_CLIENT_CONF_DIR,$HADOOP_CONF_DIR,$HADOOP_COMMON_
HOME/*,$HADOOP_COMMON_HOME/lib/*,$HADOOP_HDFS_HOME/*,$HADOOP_HDFS_HOME/
lib/*,$HADOOP_YARN_HOME/*,$HADOOP_YARN_HOME/lib/*,/usr/lib/avro/avro.jar,/
usr/lib/avro/avro-mapred.jar,/usr/lib/mahout/lib/commons-lang3-3.1.jar
</value>
</property>
```

Both the ApplicationMaster for an application and the clients running that application need to know where on the local file system the various HDFS, YARN and Hadoop common JAR files are located. The `yarn.application.classpath` parameter specifies the values for all the locations needed by them to run the application.

Changing the MapReduce Configuration

Earlier, in our simple pseudo-distributed cluster, I specified only a single MapReduce-related configuration parameter in the mapred-site.xml file. This parameter was named `mapred.framework.name`, and the default value for this parameter is local. The parameter specifies the runtime framework for executing MapReduce jobs, and the possible values are local, classic or yarn. I had specified the value yarn for this parameter, to indicate that clients want to use the MapReduce execution framework.

In a production-grade cluster, you need to add three additional parameters to the mapreduce-site.xml file, at a minimum. The first parameter specifies a staging directory in HDFS for application-related information. The other two parameters specify the server/port information for the JobHistoryServer, which plays a huge role in troubleshooting and understanding how your applications performed.

- `yarn.app.mapreduce.am.staging-dir`: This is the staging directory used for submitting jobs. This points to an HDFS directory under which YARN stores all the application-related information, such as the temporary files created by running jobs, the job counters and the job configuration. Typically, you set this parameter to the value of the directory under root where you create the user's "home" directories. The common name used for this directory is /user (in HDFS), as shown here:

```
<property>
   <name>yarn.app.mapreduce.am.staging-dir</name>
   <value>/user</value>
 </property>
```

- `mapreduce.jobhistory.address`: The JobHistoryServer uses the pair of address/port you specify with this parameter for its internal communications. The default value for this parameter is `0.0.0.0:10020`, and you can configure it as shown here:

```
<property>
   <name>mapreduce.jobhistory.address</name>
   <value>hadoop03.localhost:10020</value>
</property>
```

- mapreduce.jobhistory.webapp.address: The JobHistoryServer uses the server/port combination you specify here for the JobHistoryServer web UI. Here's how you set this parameter. The server name in this example (hadoop03.localhost) points to the server where I'm running the JobHistoryServer daemon.

  ```
  <property>
    <name>mapreduce.jobhistory.webapp.address</name>
    <value>hadoop3.localhost:19888</value>
  </property>
  ```

  The default value for this parameter is 0.0.0.0:19888. The server name is the server where you're running the JobHistoryServer.

Note that when you set the first parameter (yarn.am.app.mapreduce.am.staging-dir), you also automatically set the location for two other directories in HDFS, which have to do with storing job-history files. Here are the two parameters, which by default (in the mapred-default.xml file) take their values from the yarn.am.app.mapreduce.am.staging-dir parameter's value:

- mapreduce.jobhistory.intermediate-done-dir: This is the directory where MapReduce jobs write their history files. The default value is ${yarn.app.mapreduce.am.staging-dir}/history/done.
- mapreduce.jobhistory.done-dir: This is the directory where the JobHistoryServer manages the history files. The default value for this parameter is ${yarn.app.mapreduce.am.staging-dir}/history/done_intermediate.

For all three of these HDFS storage locations that you specify (one staging and two history file storage locations), you must ensure that you create the necessary HDFS directories, which are the following:

- /user
- /user/history
- /user/history/done
- /user/history/done_intermediate

That's it—these few changes to our initial single-node (pseudo-distributed cluster) configuration let you move your cluster into production mode.

Starting Up the Cluster

You start up the YARN and Hadoop services using the same commands as you did for a pseudo-distributed cluster. The key difference is that the NodeManager (YARN service) and the DataNode (HDFS service) services will be running on multiple nodes.

As in the case of the single-node pseudo-distributed cluster, you must format the NameNode before using it for the first time in a new cluster. This step is identical to the one you performed on the single-node cluster, using the namenode -format command:

```
$ su - hdfs
$ /opt/yarn/hadoop2-6-0/bin/namenode -format
```

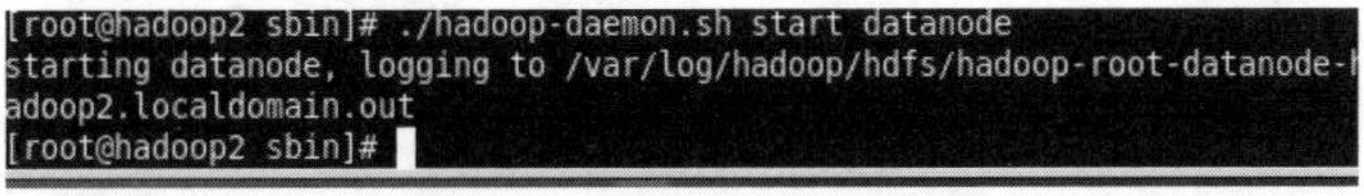

```
[root@hadoop2 sbin]# ./hadoop-daemon.sh start datanode
starting datanode, logging to /var/log/hadoop/hdfs/hadoop-root-datanode-h
adoop2.localdomain.out
[root@hadoop2 sbin]#
```

Figure 4.7 Starting the DataNode on a worker node

Once you format the NameNode, you're ready to start the Hadoop services. On server hadoop1, start the services as shown here:

```
$./hadoop-daemon.sh start namenode                    #1
$./yarn-daemon.sh start resourcemanager               #2
```

Figure 4.7 shows the DataNode startup command on one of the three worker nodes in our cluster.

On server hadoop2, start these services:

```
$./hadoop-daemon.sh start secondarynamenode           #3
$./mr-jobhistory-daemon.sh start historyserver        #4
```

Notes

#1 NameNode for managing HDFS

#2 ResourceManager for managing YARN resource allocation

#3 Secondary NameNode

#4 YARN JobHistoryServer service

On the servers hadoop1, hadoop2 and hadoop3, start the following services:

```
$./hadoop-daemon.sh start datanode                    #1
$./yarn-daemon.sh start nodemanager                   #2
```

Notes

#1 DataNode service

#2 NodeManager service—runs on all servers where you run a DataNode

When you're all done starting up the HDFS and YARN services, issue the `jps` command to make sure the services started correctly and have stayed up. One of the problems with the startup commands is that when you issue them, the prompt may return, indicating that everything went well, but the process may die unbeknownst to you!

Figure 4.8 shows the results of issuing the `jps` command on the worker node hadoop2.

```
[root@hadoop2 sbin]# jps
4073 Jps
4042 JobHistoryServer
3414 DataNode
3879 NodeManager
3530 ResourceManager
3771 SecondaryNameNode
[root@hadoop2 sbin]#
```

Figure 4.8 Making sure the Hadoop services are running with the help of the Linux `jps` command

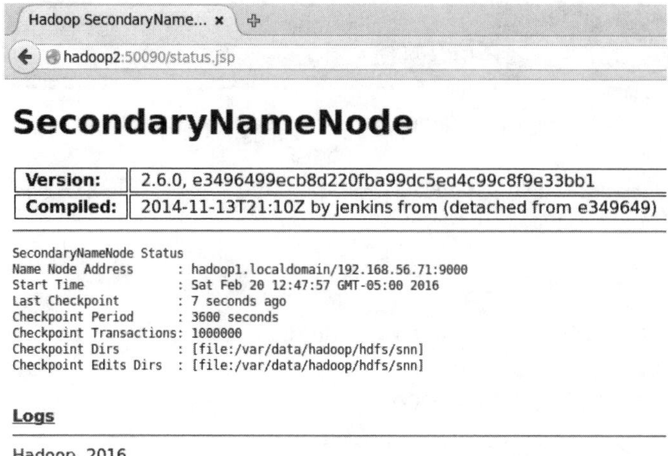

Figure 4.9 Viewing details about the Secondary NameNode, including checkpointing information, which is exclusive to the Secondary NameNode

You've already seen how you can view the NameNode information by accessing the NameNode web UI. Similarly, you can access the Secondary NameNode information by going to the Secondary NameNode web UI, as shown in Figure 4.9. Note that the Secondary NameNode web UI shows the checkpoint information, but the NameNode web UI doesn't.

Note that the commands for starting up a multinode cluster are identical to those you've used earlier to start up the single-node pseudo-distributed cluster. The shutdown commands are identical as well.

> **Note**
>
> There are two types of Hadoop log files you'll be spending a lot of your time and energy dealing with. First, there are the daemon log files pertaining to the various Hadoop daemons you just started up. In addition, MapReduce produces voluminous log files for the applications and tasks it runs.

Starting Up and Shutting Down the Cluster with Scripts

As you've learned in the previous section, Hadoop requires you to start several processes for the cluster to become operational. In my cluster here, there are only three nodes, so it's not really a big deal to start them manually one by one. But in a full-fledged cluster, you're going to have a large number of nodes and therefore a large number of processes to start up. Same goes for shutting down a cluster, where you'll need to stop all those processes manually. The smart thing to do would be to create a pair of scripts to start up and shut down your cluster.

First, create a simple script to start all cluster services, as shown here.

```
# vi startcluster.sh
#!/bin/bash

ssh hdfs@hadoop1 'hadoop-daemon.sh start namenode'                    #1
ssh hdfs@hadoop2 'hadoop-daemon.sh start standbynamenode'             #1
ssh hdfs@hadoop1 'hadoop-daemon.sh start datanode'                    #2
ssh hdfs@hadoop2 'hadoop-daemon.sh start datanode'                    #2
ssh hdfs@hadoop3 'hadoop-daemon.sh start datanode'                    #2
ssh yarn@hadoop2 'yarn-daemon.sh start resourcemanager'               #3
ssh yarn@hadoop1 'yarn-daemon.sh start nodemanager'                   #4
ssh yarn@hadoop2 'yarn-daemon.sh start nodemanager'                   #4
ssh yarn@hadoop2 'yarn-daemon.sh start nodemanager'                   #4
ssh mapred@hadoop2 'mr-jobhistory-daemon.sh start historyserver'      #5
```

Notes

#1 Starts the NameNode and the Standby NameNode services

#2 Starts the three DataNodes on the three cluster nodes

#3 Starts the ResourceManager

#4 Starts the NodeManager service on all three cluster nodes

#5 Starts the JobHistoryServer on hadoop2

Next, create a script named something such as stopcluster.sh script, shown next, to stop all the cluster services:

```
$ vi stopcluster.sh
ssh hdfs@hadoop1 'hadoop-daemon.sh stop namenode'                     #1
ssh hdfs@hadoop2 'hadoop-daemon.sh stop standbynamenode'              #1
ssh hdfs@hadoop1 'hadoop-daemon.sh stop datanode'                     #2
ssh hdfs@hadoop2 'hadoop-daemon.sh stop datanode'                     #2
ssh hdfs@hadoop3 'hadoop-daemon.sh stop datanode'                     #2
ssh yarn@hadoop2 'yarn-daemon.sh stop resourcemanager'                #3
ssh yarn@hadoop1 'yarn-daemon.sh stop nodemanager'                    #4
ssh yarn@hadoop2 'yarn-daemon.sh stop nodemanager'                    #4
ssh yarn@hadoop2 'yarn-daemon.sh stop nodemanager'                    #4
ssh mapred@hadoop2 'mr-jobhistory-daemon.sh stop historyserver'       #5
```

Notes

#1 Stops the NameNode and the Standby NameNode services

#2 Stops the three DataNodes on the three cluster nodes

#3 Stops the ResourceManager

#4 Stops the NodeManager service on all three cluster nodes

#5 Stops the JobHistoryServer on hadoop2

Performing a Quick Check of the New Cluster's File System

Once you've started up the new cluster, it's a good idea to check its status with a pair of everyday Hadoop commands. One is the `fsck` command, which works similar to the `fsck` Linux command and verifies the health of the HDFS file system. Issue the `hdfs fsck` command on the HDFS root directory, as shown here:

```
[root@hadoop2 sbin]# hdfs fsck /
```

> **Tip**
>
> Don't forget to specify `hdfs` while performing an HDFS file system sanity check. If you just execute `fsck /` and continue, you may corrupt the file system!

For now, this is good enough for us because HDFS is in a healthy state, essentially indicating that none of the HDFS blocks or files are corrupt. Chapter 10, "Data Protection, File Formats and Accessing HDFS," explains how the `fsck` utility can tell you if there are any corrupt blocks or missing replicas and how to handle those situations. Similarly, you can quickly run the highly versatile `hdfs dfsadmin` command with the `report` option, to ensure that you see the configured capacity in your HDFS file system.

```
$ hdfs dfsadmin -report
```

The `hdfs dfsadmin` utility can do much more than show the capacity of the HDFS file system. You'll learn all the capabilities of this useful utility in later chapters of this book.

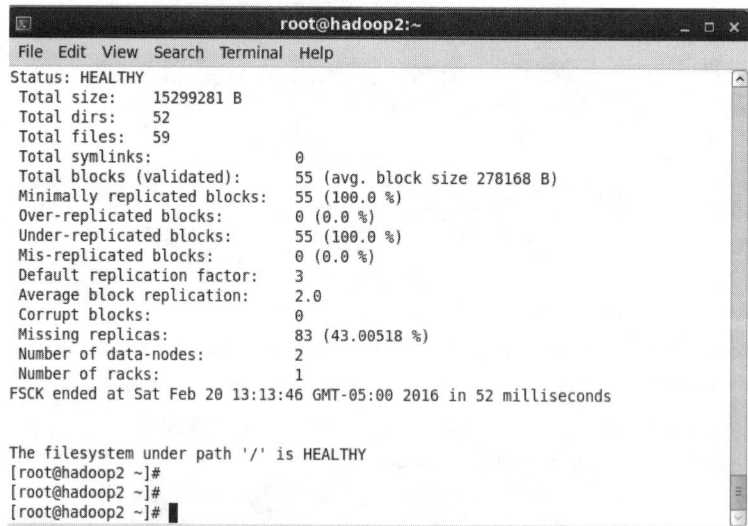

Figure 4.10 The output of the `fsck` command, showing that HDFS is healthy, with no corrupted data blocks

Configuring Hadoop Services, Web Interfaces and Ports

Hadoop provides great web UIs for accessing both HDFS and YARN services. For example, the ResourceManager web UI helps tremendously in tracking applications and jobs and accessing job logs from the web interface.

In the following sections, I cover

- Service configuration and web interfaces
- Setting port numbers for Hadoop services
- Configuring Hadoop clients

Service Configuration and Web Interfaces

In the three-node Hadoop cluster, I designated the first two nodes, hadoop1 and hadoop2, as master nodes. Normally, you don't run DataNode services on the master nodes, but since I have but three nodes, I use all three nodes for running the DataNodes. This way, I can use the default Hadoop replication factor of 3! The other two servers are the worker nodes (usually referred to as slave nodes).

Here's how I've set up the various services in the cluster:

- hadoop1: NameNode, ResourceManager, DataNode
- hadoop2: Standby NameNode, HistoryJobServer, DataNode
- hadoop3: DataNode

So, in our case, the server hadoop1 runs the NameNode and ResourceManager services as well as a DataNode. In a real-life multinode production cluster, you may or may not run DataNodes on the master nodes, which are typically dedicated to the hosting of critical cluster services such as the NameNode and the ResourceManager. Most clusters have anywhere from two to four master servers. Since most production clusters run high-availability NameNode and ResourceManager services, you can host the active and standby instances on separate master nodes.

Gateway Machines

It's common practice to set apart one or more machines in a Hadoop environment as gateway machines. You use these servers to access the Hadoop cluster but don't actually run DataNodes or other Hadoop services on them. You can install Pig and any other tools you need on the gateway server. Using a gateway server in this manner helps guard access to the Hadoop cluster. In a Hadoop cluster, you usually use gateway servers for Hadoop clients, Sqoop clients and Flume agents for staging data and for NFS gateway servers. An alternative name for a gateway server is *edge server.*

Hadoop Web Interfaces

Hadoop comes with great web interfaces that let you monitor the cluster by allowing you to review things such as the HDFS storage and YARN jobs running in your cluster. Let's review the key Hadoop web interfaces that you'll be using every day as an administrator. Some of these interfaces are helpful to users as well, helping them track their jobs and review the logs of their jobs.

The DataNode Web Interface

You can monitor the status of the HDFS service, as well as browse through its file system, through the web server exposed by HDFS. By default, this is on the NameNode server, accessible via port 50070. Since our NameNode is running on server hadoop1, you can get to the DataNode web UI by going to the following URL:

```
http://hadoop1:50070
```

Figure 4.11 shows the HDFS overview page, including the health, configured capacity and current usage of HDFS storage by the cluster. You can change the default port and address by modifying the `dfs.namenode.http-address` parameter in the hadoop-site.xml configuration file. If you want the NameNode to accept requests on all ports, you can do so by setting 0.0.0.0 as the value for the port number. The default value for this parameter is `0.0.0.0:50070`.

The Secondary NameNode's web UI shows you when it last performed a checkpoint operation of the HDFS metadata. You can't get this information from the NameNode's web UI.

The DataNode Web Interface

While the NameNode interface shows you the overall HDFS file system usage and other details, each of the DataNodes in a cluster has its own web interface. These interfaces

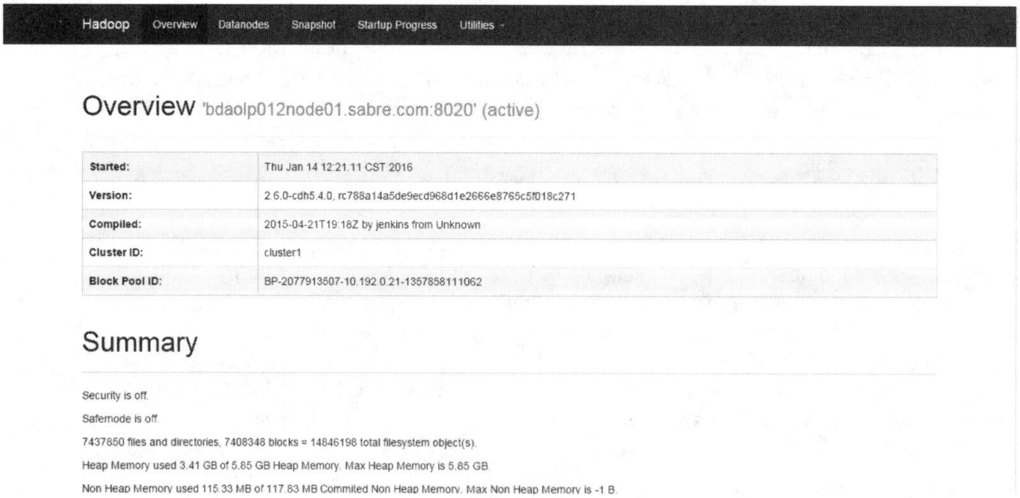

Hadoop   Overview   Datanodes   Snapshot   Startup Progress   Utilities

Overview 'bdaolp012node01.sabre.com:8020' (active)

Started:	Thu Jan 14 12:21:11 CST 2016
Version:	2.6.0-cdh5.4.0, rc788a14a5de9ecd968d1e2666e8765c5f018c271
Compiled:	2015-04-21T19:18Z by jenkins from Unknown
Cluster ID:	cluster1
Block Pool ID:	BP-2077913507-10.192.0.21-1357858111062

Summary

Security is off.

Safemode is off.

7437850 files and directories, 7408348 blocks = 14846198 total filesystem object(s).

Heap Memory used 3.41 GB of 5.85 GB Heap Memory. Max Heap Memory is 5.85 GB.

Non Heap Memory used 115.33 MB of 117.83 MB Commited Non Heap Memory. Max Non Heap Memory is -1 B.

Figure 4.11 The NameNode web UI

show you details of the HDFS file system on each server. You can access the DataNode web interface by going to

```
http://<datanode_server>:50075
```

You can change the port settings for this web interface by modifying the `dfs.datanode.http.address` configuration parameter in the hdfs-site.xml file.

DataNode web interfaces help you quite a bit by providing easy access to log files generated by various Hadoop daemons, which, as you'll learn, are highly useful when debugging and troubleshooting problems.

The YARN Web Interface

Like the NameNode and the DataNodes, the ResourceManager has its own web UI. You can access it by going to:

```
http://<host_name>:8088
```

The port number 8088 is the default for the ResourceManager web UI. You can change the default port by setting a new value for the parameter `yarn.resourcemanager.webapp.address` in the yarn-site.xml file. If by mistake you use one of the other port numbers shown in the yarn-site.xml file, you'll get the following error.

```
It looks like you are making an HTTP request to a Hadoop IPC port. This is not the
correct port for the web interface on this daemon.
```

Figure 4.12 shows the ResourceManager web UI's home page. This is a highly useful page, and it shows not only the number of applications running in the cluster but also the number of containers, current usage of memory and virtual cores. In Chapter 17, "Monitoring, Metrics and Hadoop Logging," which deals with monitoring and managing YARN jobs, you'll learn a lot more about how to effectively use the ResourceManager web UI for managing your jobs.

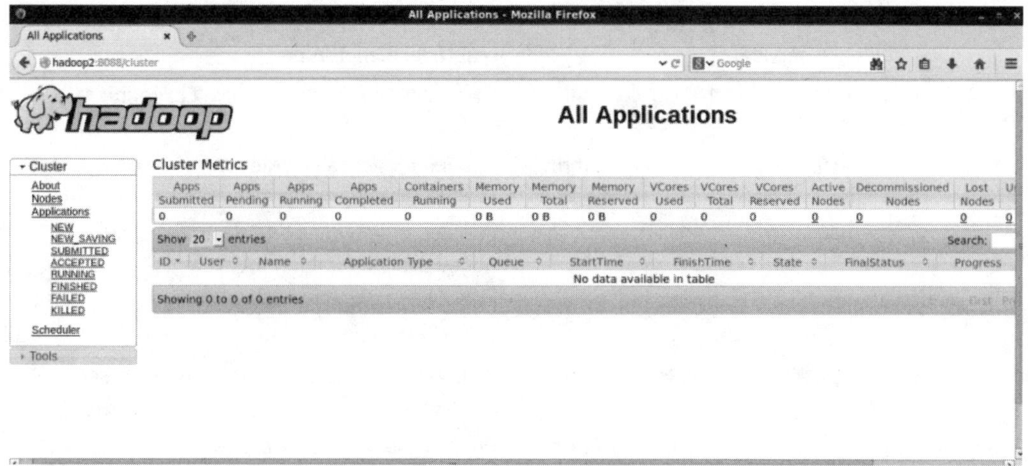

Figure 4.12 The ResourceManager YARN web UI

Setting Port Numbers for Hadoop Services

As you might have realized by now, Hadoop uses various ports for its services, and determining the correct port for the various services might be confusing. Table 4.1 shows the default port numbers for various Hadoop services.

Table 4.1 **Port Numbers for Common Hadoop Services**

Service	Default Port	Protocol	Description and Configuration Parameter
ResourceManager web UI	8088	http	Web UI for the ResourceManager yarn.resourcemanager.webapp.address
NodeManager web UI	8042	http	Web UI for the NodeManager yarn.nodemanager.webapp.address
NodeManager	8040	http	TPC port for resource localization yarn.nodemanager.localizer.address
History Job Server UI	19888	http	Web UI for Job History mapreduce.jobhistory.webapp.address
JobHistoryServer	10020	http	RPC port for clients to query job history mapreduce.jobhistory.address
ResourceManager UI	8031	http	YARN ResourceManager yarn.resourcemanager.resource-tracker.address
ResourceManager Admin	8033	http	ResourceManager admin interface yarn.resourcemanager.admin.address
ResourceManager	8032	http	Used by clients for app submission yarn.resourcemanager.address
ResourceManager	8030	http	Scheduler RPC port for ApplicationMaster yarn.resourcemanager.scheduler.address
ShuffleHandler (MapReduce service)	13562		Port used to serve Shuffled map outputs mapreduce.shuffle.port
HiveServer2	10000	thrift	Service for connecting to Hive Environment variable HIVE_PORT
Hive metastore	9083	thrift	Service for accessing Metadata hive.metastore.uris
ZooKeeper Server	2888		Port for ZooKeeper service communication hbase.zookeeper.peerport
ZooKeeper Server	3888		Port for ZooKeeper service communication hbase.zookeeper.leaderport
WebHcat Server	50111	http	Web API for Hcatalog and other Hadoop services templeton.port
MySQL	3306	http	Port for the MySQL database

You can change the port number for the services through the appropriate configuration parameter listed in Table 4.1.

I've listed the ports for important Hadoop services in Table 4.1. However, there are numerous other ports pertaining to services such as Hue, Kafka and Kerberos. A good resource for Hadoop ports is the following link from Hortonworks: https://docs.hortonworks.com/HDPDocuments/HDP2/HDP-2.4.0/bk_HDP_Reference_Guide/content/reference_chap2.html.

The HDFS service uses several ports for the various services such as the NameNode and the DataNodes. Table 4.2 summarizes the default port information for the HDFS services.

When connecting to certain ports, you might receive a bind exception error such as the following.

```
java.net.BindException: Address already in use
```

This usually occurs when the NameNode, DataNode or some other Hadoop service tries to use an already in-use port to listen for connections. Once you make sure that the hostname/IP address are correct, change the appropriate parameter for the service to point to a different, unused port. You can use the command `netstat -a -t --numeric-ports -p` to identify the ports in use on a server.

Table 4.2 **Port Numbers for HDFS Services**

Service	Default Port	Protocol	Description and Configuration Parameter
NameNode web UI	50070	http	HDFS web UI dfs.namenode.http.address
NameNode web UI (secure)	50470	https	HDFS web UI (secure) dfs.namenode.https.address
NameNode	8020/9000	ipc	File system embedded in URI fs.defaultFS
DataNode	50075	http	DataNode web UI dfs.datanode.http.address
DataNode (Secure)	50475	https	Secure HTTP service dfs.datanode.https.address
DataNode	50010	http	Data transfer dfs.datanode.address
DataNode	50020	Ipc	Block metadata operations dfs.datanode.ipc.address
DataNode	0.0.0.0:8010	ipc	Metadata operations dfs.datanode.ipc.address
Secondary NameNode	50090	http	Secondary NameNode UI dfs.datanode.secondary.http-address

Deploying HDFS and YARN in a Multihomed Network

By default, you specify HDFS endpoints as a specific IP address or hostname, meaning HDFS daemons will bind to a single IP address. You can set up things so that the cluster nodes are connected to multiple network interfaces, for security or performance reasons. Setting up support for more than one network interface is called a multihomed network. You can also do this to provide redundancy by letting a node use multiple network adapters to protect against a network adapter failure.

You must not confuse a multihomed network with the use of NIC bonding, which presents only a single logical network to the clients. With a multihomed network, you can connect to the HDFS daemons from more than one network. In order to allow a multihomed network, you need to configure the following parameters in the hdfs-site.xml file, so they all have a value of 0.0.0.0:

- `dfs.namenode.rpc.bind-host`
- `dfs.namenode.servicerpc-bind.host`
- `dfs.namenode.http-bind-host`
- `dfs.namenode.https-bind.host`

You can configure YARN for a multihomed environment. You can force YARN services to listen on all ports of a multihomed host by setting the bind-host parameter to the all-wildcard value 0.0.0.0. For example, if you set the value of the `yarn.resourcemanager.bind.host` parameter to 0.0.0.0, and the `yarn.resourcemanager.address` is configured as `rm.prodcluster.internal:9999`, the ResourceManager will listen on all host addresses on the port 9999.

By configuring the bind-host parameter (in the yarn-site.xml file) in the following way, you ensure that all ResourceManager services and web applications listen on all the interfaces in a multihomed network.

```
<property>
   <name>yarn.resourcemanager.bind-host</name>
   <value>0.0.0.0</value>
</property>.
```

Similarly, you can configure the `yarn.nodemanager.bind-host` property, also in the yarn-site.xml file, and the `mapreduce.jobhistory.bind-host` parameter (mapred-site .xml file) to the value 0.0.0.0 to ensure that the YARN and MapReduce daemons listen on all addresses and interfaces of a multihomed cluster.

Hadoop Clients

While the components of Hadoop such as HDFS and YARN run within the Hadoop cluster, users and applications need to access them from somewhere. A Hadoop client uses Hadoop APIs to access the storage and processing capabilities of the cluster. In order for a Hadoop client to work with the cluster components (HDFS and YARN), the client requires the Hadoop API, and you must also configure it so it can connect with the Hadoop components running in the cluster.

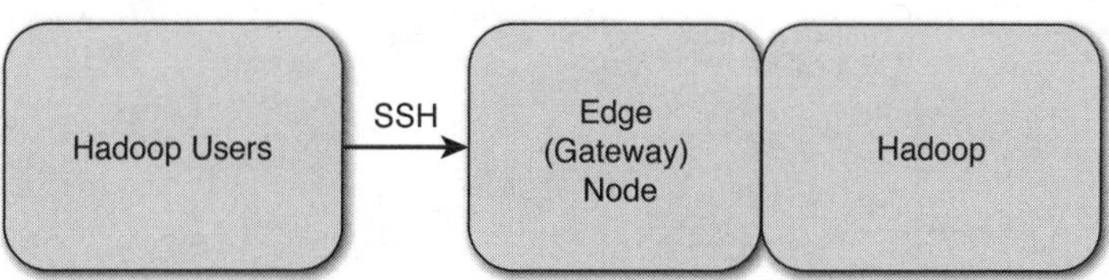

Figure 4.13 How Hadoop clients can access the Hadoop cluster

Figure 4.13 shows the current Hadoop client model, wherein clients can access HDFS and MapReduce (or other frameworks, now that we're in Hadoop 2) Java APIs to work with HDFS and YARN. Users log into edge servers through SSH and run their commands from the Linux shell prompt. APIs are mostly used through gateway or edge nodes. These nodes are technically outside the Hadoop cluster. However, they are considered to be inside the cluster in practice.

Some Hadoop Clients

You can consider MapReduce map and reduce tasks as Hadoop clients, since they use the Hadoop API (hadoop-client) to access the cluster storage and processing components. There are also both command-line Hadoop clients and server daemons that act as clients.

Command-line clients include the following:

- The Hadoop shell, also called `hdfs dfs`
- Pig shell
- Sqoop CLI

Server daemons include the following:

- Oozie
- Sqoop2
- Hiveserver2
- Flume agents

Configuring the Hadoop Clients

In order to connect to the HDFS storage component, a client needs to contact the NameNode service running in the cluster. Similarly, to process anything in the cluster, the client needs to contact the ResourceManager service. In order for the client to find the NodeManager and the ResourceManager services as well as any additional cluster services, you must provide the client with the Hadoop configuration files such as the hdfs-site.xml, mapred-site.xml and yarn-site.xml files.

In some cases, you may only need some of the Hadoop configuration files to be stored on a client, but you might as well simply copy over all your Hadoop configuration files to the client machines. Note that some clients may need additional configuration files that specify special configuration properties that apply only to them, such as the hive-site.xml and the pig.properties configuration files.

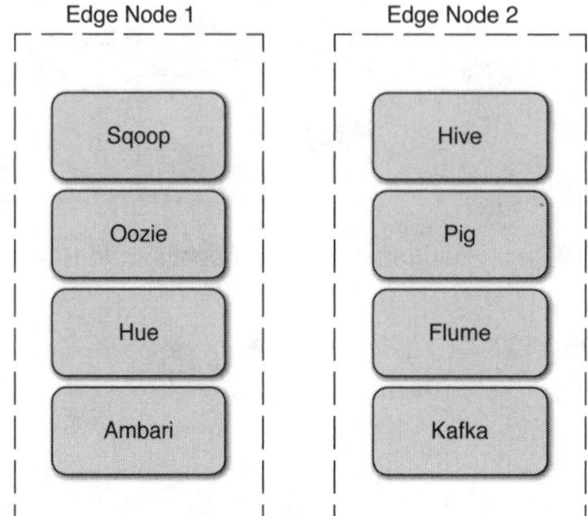

Figure 4.14 How you can deploy client applications and management tools on edge nodes in a Hadoop cluster

Where the Clients Are Deployed

End users can directly access a Hadoop cluster's storage and processing components by executing commands from their own machines through a command line interface such as the Pig shell or the Sqoop CLI. It's also common to denote one or more servers as gateway servers, also called edge nodes.

Figure 4.14 shows how you can have multiple edge nodes, each running a set of client applications such as Oozie, Sqoop and Pig, as well as management interfaces such as Hue. Users connect to the gateway servers and execute commands from there to access the Hadoop cluster. Users can access the gateway servers directly or through a browser. It is good to have dedicated edge servers since they ensure that your client apps and management tools aren't competing for resources with HDFS and YARN.

Summary

Here's what you learned in this chapter:

- Planning and configuring a Hadoop cluster depends on your specific requirements.
- Hadoop is highly flexible and you can choose the storage, processing and memory to fit your needs.
- Installing a fully distributed Hadoop cluster is only slightly more complex than installing the pseudo-distributed cluster.

II

Hadoop Application Frameworks

5

Running Applications in a Cluster—The MapReduce Framework (and Hive and Pig)

This chapter covers the following:

- The MapReduce application framework
- A brief introduction to Apache Hive
- A brief introduction to Apache Pig

As a Hadoop administrator, you'll be responsible for managing several types of data processing work in your Hadoop cluster. While MapReduce is on its way out and is fast being replaced by Apache Spark, I believe it's still important to learn the essentials of this processing framework, as it happens to be the most common processing framework in many Hadoop clusters even now. Over the next few years, however, MapReduce may be completely replaced by alternative frameworks such as Spark.

Hive and Pig are abstractions that use MapReduce as their underlying processing model. Understanding how these processing frameworks function is critical to your success as a Hadoop administrator, so I explain the basics of both Hive and Pig in this chapter.

The MapReduce Framework

Although MapReduce is eventually going to be supplanted by other processing frameworks such as Apache Spark, it's instructive to learn a bit about how the MapReduce processing model works. Most Hadoop clusters have a lot of MapReduce and Pig/Hive code running and administrators still need to understand the basics of MapReduce.

The MapReduce Model

A MapReduce job consists of two steps: map and reduce. Here's what the two processes do:

- Map: This step processes the original input file in a parallel fashion and transforms it into an intermediate output.
- Reduce: This summarization step processes all relevant records together.

The application developer provides the following four classes (they don't need to be coded in Java, but most MapReduce programming is Java-based) for enabling the MapReduce programming model:

- A class to read the input file and transform the input records into a key/pair value per record
- A mapper class
- A reducer class
- A class to transform the key/value pair generated by the reducer class into the final output records

Here's how the map and reduce processes perform computations:

1. The map process breaks large input files into multiple chunks, processing each chunk simultaneously with multiple mapper processes. The resulting output from the different chunks is partitioned into sets, which are sorted.
2. The reducer tasks take each of the sorted chunks and process them, creating the final output file.

When you initiate a MapReduce job, multiple mapper processes are simultaneously started on various nodes, with the number of mappers being dependent of the size of the input file. Each of the map tasks transforms a set of input records into key/value pairs, and the output of all map tasks is portioned and then sorted, with one partition per reduce task. The reducer tasks will then process each partition's sorted keys and values. As with the mappers, you can have multiple reducer classes. Note that not all MapReduce jobs will have a reducer component. It's possible to run jobs that use just the mapper processes and no reducers.

I admit that the preceding explanation may seem a bit confusing to readers who are new to the MapReduce programming model. In order to understand the model clearly, it also helps to break down a simple MapReduce program, such as the WordCount program, which is widely used to explain the MapReduce model.

The WordCount program is pretty simple: It analyzes a text document and counts how many times each word occurs in the document. The elements of the MapReduce program in a Hadoop environment follow.

1. Multiple map processes are needed to compute the distinct words in the document. The number of map processes is based on the input size. Let's assume that each mapper will process a single file and that there are 100,000 files altogether. If you have 10 DataNodes in your cluster, each node will process approximately 10,000 map tasks each. How many map processes run simultaneously will depend on the memory available on each node for MapReduce processing and the number of processors. If we assume each DataNode can process 20 map processes simultaneously, then each of these nodes will start with that number. As the first 20 mapper tasks finish, each DataNode will start the next batch of 20 mappers and so on.
2. Each map task processes a single file and extracts the key/value pairs: <{word}. 1>, as shown here:

```
<the, 1>
<the, 1>
<crux, 1>
<of, 1>
<the, 1>
<matter, 1>
<is, >
...
```

3. The reducer tasks will receive the <key,value> pairs in the following format:

```
<the, [1,1,1,1,1,...]
<crux, 1>
...
```

   As you can see, the mappers and reducers don't have a one-to-one relationship. It's usually a many-to-one relationship between the two. Thus, in our example, the key/value pairs received from a reducer can come from multiple mappers.
4. The next step is the "shuffle and sort" process, which collects the 1s for each word in the local file system where a reducer task will run. The shuffle and sort process sends data from the mappers to the reducer processes.
5. The reducer adds all the occurrences of a word (the "1" in the key/value pair) to get the total count of each word and sends the results to the output file as the following key/value pairs:

```
<the, 21000>
<crux, 1>
<of, 10900>
...
```

How MapReduce Works

Following are the key concepts regarding how MapReduce works in the Hadoop environment.

- Each mapper processes a single input split from the HDFS file system. Usually the input split is sized the same as a single HDFS block.
- Hadoop sends one record at a time to the mapper, with each record containing a key and a value.

- Mappers work on one record at a time and write the intermediate data to disk.
- The reducer aggregates the results, using the intermediate keys produced by the mapper.
- All values associated with the same intermediate key are sent to the same reducer.
- Reducers write the final output to the HDFS file system.

Although MapReduce may seem complex to beginners, it's at its heart very simple. The process is similar to the following Linux pipeline that finds unique words in a file.

```
cat /test/log  | grep '\hadoop'  \ sort  |  uniq -c > /tmp/outfile.txt
```

In this example, here's what the different commands in the Linux pipe do:

- `grep`: This performs the map task.
- `sort`: This performs the shuffle and sort.
- `uniq`: This is the reducer.

> **Note**
>
> Hadoop refers to each unit of work it performs as a job (same as an application). A job may consist of multiple tasks, and tasks may sometimes be attempted multiple times if a task fails for some reason.

Inputs and Outputs

MapReduce works exclusively with `<key, value>` pairs. It views the job inputs as a set of `<key, value>` pairs and outputs a set of `<key, value>` pairs as well. The map and reduce functions in a MapReduce program have the following general form:

- Map: `(k1, v1) => list(k2, v2)`
- Reduce: `(k2, list(v2) => list(k3, v3)`

Normally, the map input key value types (k1 and v1) differ from the map output types (v2, k2). Reduce input types must have the same types as the output of the map process. Reduce output types may be different (k3, v3).

Hadoop (MapReduce) Input and Output Processing

In order to understand how MapReduce processes vast amounts of data efficiently, you need to learn how MapReduce handles the I/O process. CPU-bound Hadoop systems aren't common, and I/O remains the main bottleneck. Following is a simple outline of the I/O processes used by a MapReduce job.

1. HDFS files are read as input to the mapper processes.
2. During the map phase, the input is split into chunks (called input splits or just splits), and Hadoop creates a separate map task to process each of these chunks of data.

3. Each of the map tasks processes the key/value pairs from the data chunk (input split) assigned to it and generates a set of intermediate key/value pairs.
4. The intermediate data is sorted by key, and the sorted data is partitioned into a number of chunks that match the number of reducer tasks.
5. The nodes on which the reducer processes run will merge the data on local disk, after sorting the data received from the mappers.
6. The reducers write their output to HDFS.

> **Note**
>
> A MapReduce job stores its intermediate data output from the map processes in the underlying file system of the local disk on the node on which the mapper runs.

Data Compression

Since I/O is the predominant operation in MapReduce, you need to focus on reducing both disk and network I/O to increase the cluster's throughput. A basic strategy you can use here is to compress data at various levels by compressing the input files, the intermediate mapper output and, finally, the MapReduce job output.

Hadoop environments use specialized file formats when dealing with data. SequenceFiles are a binary format to store binary key/value pairs. Apache Avro is a popular data format in many Hadoop environments. It offers a compact, fast binary data format and uses a container file to store persistent data. You don't need to generate code to read or write the data files or for using or implementing RPC protocols, since Avro is self-documenting. Note that sequence files support just the Java language, whereas you can use the Avro format with any language (so long as the Avro bindings exist).

A great advantage offered by MapReduce is that developers don't need to set up the housekeeping chores, as the MapReduce framework handles all the work behind the scenes. Developers can just focus on developing their Map and Reduce functions. While MapReduce programs are usually written in Java, you can write them in other languages by using Hadoop Streaming.

MapReduce Job Processing

When you run a MapReduce job, this is what happens:

1. Multiple map processes are started simultaneously, each of which reads an input split (part of the full import data) from an HDFS directory and processes the data, generating intermediate key/value pairs.
2. The reducer process swings into action next, by processing all key/value pairs with identical intermediate keys.
3. The reducer process writes the final output as key/value pairs to an output directory.

Each MapReduce map task will process a single input split, which is calculated by the client before submitting a job to the cluster. You can specify how to calculate the input split in the program, with the HDFS block size being the most common split size.

MapReduce is designed to take advantage of the data distributed across a Hadoop cluster. A massive data set is thus split into bite-size pieces spread throughout the cluster's DataNodes, and MapReduce processes this data in a parallel fashion. Here's a summary of the MapReduce application phases:

1. Determine the input splits.
2. Process each record in an input split with the help of a map task.
3. Combine the output of each map task.
4. Group the sorted data from each mapper's result set.
5. Use the reducer tasks (these are optional, and serve to aggregate the result sets of the mapper processes into a single output to be stored in HDFS.

Figure 5.1 shows how map and reduce tasks process data. In YARN, each mapper process runs in a container, which is a logical entity containing a specific amount of CPU and memory. The ApplicationMaster for an application requests the ResourceManager

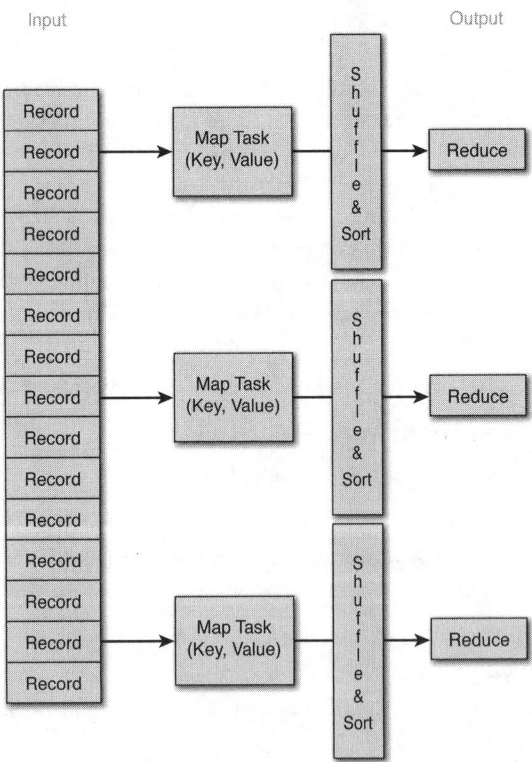

Figure 5.1 How the map and reduce tasks process data

for the allocation of a container for each Mapper process. The ResourceManager will then schedule the necessary resources and inform the ApplicationMaster as to which nodes it can ask the NodeManagers to launch the containers.

A Simple MapReduce Program

Let's use the well-known WordCount MapReduce program to understand how MapReduce does its work. The following program consists of a map class and a reduce class, which together process the data in the input file that's provided to the MapReduce job.

```
public class WordCount {
 public static class Map extends Mapper<LongWritable, Text, Text, IntWritable> {
    private final static IntWritable one = new IntWritable(1);
    private Text word = new Text();

    public void map(LongWritable key, Text value, Context context)
      throws IOException, InterruptedException {
        String line = value.toString();
        StringTokenizer tokenizer = new StringTokenizer(line);
        while (tokenizer.hasMoreTokens()) {
            word.set(tokenizer.nextToken());
            context.write(word, one);
        }
    }
 }

 public static class Reduce extends Reducer<Text, IntWritable, Text, IntWritable> {

    public void reduce(Text key, Iterable<IntWritable> values, Context context)
      throws IOException, InterruptedException {
        int sum = 0;
        for (IntWritable val : values) {
            sum += val.get();
        }
        context.write(key, new IntWritable(sum));
    }
 }

 public static void main(String[] args) throws Exception {
    Configuration conf = new Configuration();

    Job job = new Job(conf, "wordcount");

    job.setOutputKeyClass(Text.class);
    job.setOutputValueClass(IntWritable.class);

    job.setMapperClass(Map.class);
    job.setReducerClass(Reduce.class);

    job.setInputFormatClass(TextInputFormat.class);
    job.setOutputFormatClass(TextOutputFormat.class);

    FileInputFormat.addInputPath(job, new Path(args[0]));
    FileOutputFormat.setOutputPath(job, new Path(args[1]));

    job.waitForCompletion(true);
 }
}
```

In the following section, I explain exactly what the map and reduce classes do to process an input file and get you the output you're after.

Hadoop doesn't require you to specify the input and output directories on the command line. When you submit a job to the cluster, Hadoop places the job files in a temporary directory in the HDFS file system and the ResourceManager is made aware of this location. Hadoop also serializes the configuration of the job to an XML file and places that in an HDFS directory as well.

Understanding Hadoop's Job Processing—Running a WordCount Program

Let's understand how Hadoop processes a MapReduce job by running one of the example MapReduce programs that come with the Hadoop distribution. You can list the available examples by doing this:

```
$ hadoop jar $HADOOP_HOME/hadoop*examples.jar
```

It's standard practice in a Hadoop environment to run the well-known WordCount program to put Hadoop through its paces. The WordCount program accepts a text file as input and counts the number of occurrences of each word in that file. Figure 5.2 shows

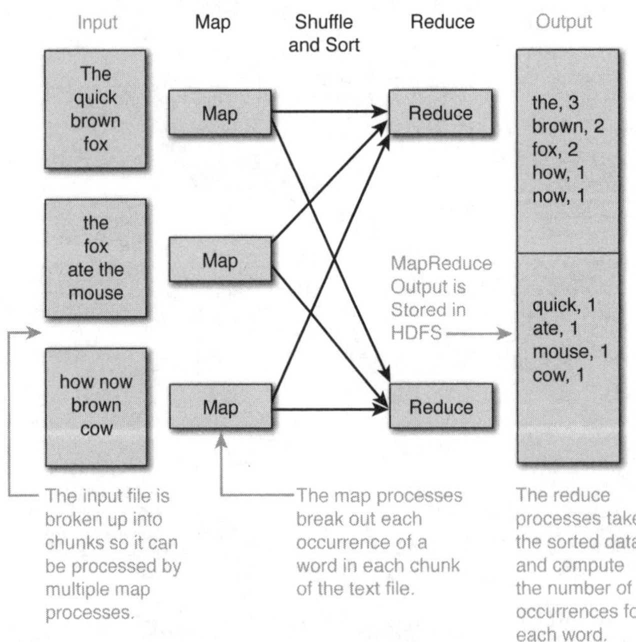

Figure 5.2 How the WordCount program processes a text file with multiple map and reduce processes

how the WordCount program uses map and reduce tasks to process data, sort it and store the results in HDFS.

For the following example, I chose to count the occurrences of each word in Shakespeare's collected works, which I downloaded from here:

```
http://www.gutenberg.org/cache/epub/100/pg100.txt
```

I renamed the downloaded text file to shakespeare.txt and placed it in the /tmp directory.

Once you download the text file, you must upload it to HDFS so MapReduce can work on it. You can copy the file to an HDFS directory by following these steps:

1. Make a directory in HDFS in which to store the text file.

   ```
   [root@hadoop2 sbin]# hdfs dfs -mkdir -p /input/shakes
   ```

2. Copy the text file shakespeare.txt from the /tmp directory to the new HDFS directory, /input/shakes, using the Hadoop file system command –`copyFromLocal`, which copies a file from the Linux file system to HDFS.

   ```
   [root@hadoop2 sbin]# hdfs dfs -copyFromLocal /tmp/shakespeare.txt /input/
   shakes/
   ```

3. Test that the file has been copied from the local directory to HDFS.

   ```
   [root@hadoop2 sbin]# hdfs dfs -ls /input/shakes/

   Found 1 items
   -rw-r--r--   3 root supergroup    5589889 2016-05-24 10:02 /input/shakes/
   shakespeare.txt
   [root@hadoop2 sbin]#
   ```

MapReduce Input and Output Directories

When you run a MapReduce job, the input directory must exist and it must contain the file you want MapReduce to process. There's also an output directory that you must name when you run the MapReduce job, but that directory must not exist, or your job will fail immediately!

Now that I've gotten my input directory set up in HDFS, I can run the example WordCount program on our text file, which consists of Shakespeare's collected works. Note that /input/shakes is the input directory and that's all you need to specify. Hadoop will find the shakespeare.txt file you placed there and analyze it. The job will create the output directory that you specify (shake_output in our example) and place the job's output in that directory.

How Hadoop Shows You the Job Details

Hadoop's job logging is quite voluminous, for both its daemons and for the jobs you run on Hadoop. When you run a job, Hadoop emits a bunch of output, as shown in the following example. The output includes valuable information for a developer or administrator who wants to understand the job execution flow and troubleshoot it.

To execute our MapReduce job, I run the following on the command line:

```
[root@hadoop2 sbin]# hadoop jar /opt/yarn/hadoop-2.6.0/share/hadoop/mapreduce/
    hadoop-mapreduce-examples-2.6.0.jar wordcount /shakes shake_output                              #A
16/05/22 10:44:00 INFO input.FileInputFormat: Total input paths to process : 1                      #B
16/05/22 10:44:01 INFO mapreduce.JobSubmitter: number of splits:1                                   #B
16/05/22 10:44:01 INFO mapreduce.JobSubmitter: Submitting tokens for job: job_1440603749764_0001    #C
16/05/22 10:44:03 INFO impl.YarnClientImpl: Submitted application  application_1440603749764_0001   #C
16/05/22 10:44:03 INFO mapreduce.Job: The url to track the job: http://hadoop1.localdomain:8081/
    proxy/application_1440603749764_0001/                                                           #D
16/05/22 10:44:44 INFO mapreduce.Job: Job job_1440603749764_0001 running in uber mode : false
16/05/22 10:44:44 INFO mapreduce.Job:  map 0% reduce 0%                                             #E
16/05/22 10:45:07 INFO mapreduce.Job:  map 67% reduce 0%
16/05/22 10:45:17 INFO mapreduce.Job:  map 100% reduce 0%
16/05/22 10:45:33 INFO mapreduce.Job:  map 100% reduce 100%                                         #E
16/05/22 10:45:34 INFO mapreduce.Job: Job job_1440603749764_0001 completed successfully             #F
16/05/22 10:45:36 INFO mapreduce.Job: Counters: 49                                                  #G
        File System Counters
                FILE: Number of bytes read=983187
                FILE: Number of bytes written=2178871
                HDFS: Number of bytes read=5590008
                HDFS: Number of bytes written=720972
                HDFS: Number of read operations=6

                HDFS: Number of write operations=2                                                  #G
        Job Counters
                Launched map tasks=1                                                                #H
                Launched reduce tasks=1
                Data-local map tasks=1
                Total time spent by all maps in occupied slots (ms)=30479
                Total time spent by all reduces in occupied slots (ms)=13064
                Total time spent by all map tasks (ms)=30479
                Total time spent by all reduce tasks (ms)=13064
                Total vcore-seconds taken by all map tasks=30479
                Total vcore-seconds taken by all reduce tasks=13064
                Total megabyte-seconds taken by all map tasks=31210496
                Total megabyte-seconds taken by all reduce tasks=13377536                           #H
        Map-Reduce Framework
                Map input records=124787                                                            #I
                Map output records=904061
                Map output bytes=8574733
                Map output materialized bytes=983187
                Input split bytes=119
                Combine input records=904061
                Combine output records=67779
                Reduce input groups=67779
                Reduce shuffle bytes=983187
                Reduce input records=67779                                                          #I
                Reduce output records=67779
                Spilled Records=135558                                                              #J
                Shuffled Maps =1
                                Merged Map outputs=1                                                #J
                GC time elapsed (ms)=454                                                            #K
                CPU time spent (ms)=10520
                Physical memory (bytes) snapshot=302411776
                Virtual memory (bytes) snapshot=1870229504
                Total committed heap usage (bytes)=168497152                                        #K

        File Input Format Counters                                                                  #L
                Bytes Read=5589889                                                                  #L
        File Output Format Counters                                                                 #M
                Bytes Written=720972                                                                #M
[root@hadoop2 sbin]#
```

Notes

#A Shows how to invoke the MapReduce job through Hadoop JAR files.

#B Shows the input paths and the number of splits—in this simple example, there's only one split, but in real life, there could be tens of thousands of splits.

#C Shows the job and application name, which you'll need to troubleshoot your job.

#D The URL for tracking the progress of this job.

#E Shows the progress of the job—when both maps and any reduces reach 100 percent execution, you're done!

#F Shows that the job finished successfully.

#G File system Hadoop counters, showing the bytes read and written and so on.

#H Hadoop job counters, showing the number of maps and reduces and the time taken for completing the map and reduce tasks.

#I Shows the number of input and output records.

#J Shows details about any spills (sorts) to disk and about the shuffles.

#K Shows CPU time spent by the job and the memory used by it.

#L Shows the number of total bytes read.

#M Shows the number of total bytes written.

Wow! That's quite a bit of output to find out the number of times a word occurs in the text file you provided. However, the job's output illustrates many key aspects of MapReduce programming, which you'll encounter over and over, even when running Pig and Hive jobs, which, as you know by now, use the MapReduce framework underneath.

You can check the job output by checking the output directory first, as shown here:

```
# hdfs dfs -ls /out/shake_output
```

You can copy the output files from HDFS to the Linux local file system, as shown here:

```
# hdfs dfs -get /out/shake_output
```

Use the Linux command `cat`, to view the output:

```
# cat shake_output
```

Alternatively, you can view the output files directly in HDFS, using the HDFS file system command, also called cat:

```
# hdfs dfs -cat /out/shake_output
```

You can view the results of your job in the ResourceManager (RM) web UI, by going to:

```
http://rm_host:8088/
```

Hadoop Streaming

Whether you use a MapReduce program or a Hive or Pig script, you're essentially using Java-based MapReduce underneath. However, Java isn't the only way to create map and reduce jobs in your cluster. You can also use **Hadoop Streaming**, which is a utility that allows you to use any executable or script as a mapper or reducer. Following is a simple example that shows how to use common Linux utilities such as cat (lists the contents of a file) and wc (counts the words in a file) to perform a MapReduce task.

```
$HADOOP_HOME/bin/hadoop jar $HADOOP_HOME/hadoop-streaming.jar \
    -input myInputDirs \
    -output myOutputDir \
    -mapper /bin/cat \
    -reducer /bin/wc
```

As you can see, both the mapper and the reducer are represented by operating system executables and not any custom code. The two executables, cat and wc, read an input file and display the output on the terminal (stdout).

How Hadoop Streaming Works

In our simple Hadoop streaming example, the job runs exactly as any Java-based MapReduce, with similar job progress output—in fact, there are no operational differences at all. Here's what the mapper and reducer tasks do:

- The mapper converts the input into lines and collects the output from standard output (stdout) and converts each of the lines into a key/value pair. This key/value pair is the output of the mapper process, just as in the case of the WordCount programs you've seen earlier in this chapter.
- The reducer task converts the key/value pair inputs into lines and sends them to standard input (stdin) of the reduce process. They then collect the output from the process's stdout and convert them into key/value pairs and these become the reducer's output.

Hadoop Streaming and Java Classes

When your mapper uses Hadoop streaming, it isn't imperative that you use non-Java executables or code for both the mapper and the reducer—you can mix and match! The following example shows how you can supply a Java class just for the mapper and use the operating system executable (wc) for the reducer.

```
$HADOOP_HOME/bin/hadoop  jar $HADOOP_HOME/hadoop-streaming.jar \
    -input myInputDirs \
    -output myOutputDir \
    -mapper org.apache.hadoop.mapred.lib.IdentityMapper \
    -reducer /bin/wc
```

You could easily replace the Java mapper with a mapper written in Python, by specifying `-mapper myPythonScript.py`. You can also use mappers and reducers written in other programming languages such as Ruby and PHP just as easily as we did with the OS executables. For example, the following two lines use PHP-based mappers and reducers.

```
-mapper /usr/local/hadoop/scripts/wc_mapper.php
-reducer /user/local/hadoop/scripts/wc_reducer.php
```

Now that you know how MapReduce works, let's take a quick look at two popular processing tools—Apache Hive and Apache Pig, both of which are abstractions that use MapReduce to perform their computations.

Apache Hive

Apache Hive provides a SQL interface that enables you to use HDFS data without having to write programs using MapReduce. It's important to understand that unlike Apache HBase, Hive is not a database. It simply provides a mechanism to project a database structure on data you store in HDFS and lets you query that data using HiveQL, a SQL-like language. Hive uses a type of SQL that lets you query HDFS data in ways that are similar to how you query data stored in a relational database.

While HiveQL doesn't have the full range of features available in SQL, it offers more than enough SQL capabilities for you to efficiently work with HDFS data. When you use a Hive query, Hive parses the SQL query and generates a MapReduce job to process the data to get you the query results. The main rationale for Hive is to reduce effort by doing away with developing MapReduce programs. It also provides a data warehouse capability when handling large amounts of data, is analyst friendly and is ideal for making use of HDFS data for business intelligence (BI) analysis.

It's important to understand that Hive, while it lets you use SQL-type queries to process HDFS data, isn't a database itself, although it does use the concept of database tables. Hive simply maps HDFS directories to tables.

If you've been using SQL to process data stored in relational databases, you can make a quick transition to Hive and start working with HDFS without having to learn any MapReduce programming.

Do note that you can't update data with HiveQL, as Hive doesn't support updates and deletes. Also, unlike the lightning quick results from SQL queries you may be used to, Hive seems to be plodding in comparison, often taking several minutes or hours to get the output you're looking for. Even for small queries, a Hive job needs to set the MapReduce engine in motion and that startup overhead does takes some time.

Hive saves you quite a bit of time as you can write Hive queries much faster than you can write MapReduce code. A word count program that takes about 50 lines of code in MapReduce needs only 5 lines when you do the same thing in Hive. Also, since Hive supports SQL syntax, you can integrate Hive with your BI tools. Hive allows to perform classic SQL operations such as joins.

Hive is a data warehousing infrastructure built on top of Hadoop to take advantage of the scalability and fault tolerance offered by Hadoop. Hive is designed for quick summarization of data and ad-hoc querying and analysis of large data sets using HiveQL. MapReduce programmers can also plug in custom map and reduce processes for enhancing Hive's capabilities.

It's important to remember that since MapReduce is essentially a batch processing framework, Hive queries generally run a long time when you're processing small amounts of data, due to the inherent overhead in submitting and scheduling MapReduce jobs.

As mentioned earlier in this book, Hive isn't a great tool when working with small data sets, as well as for OLTP queries.

Hive Data Organization

Hive uses a type of data organization that's very similar to that of traditional relational databases. Following is how Hive organizes its data.

- Databases: These are namespaces that demarcate different data units.
- Tables: These are units of data that have an identical schema, meaning the same number and type of columns.
- Partitions: Although not a requirement, you can subdivide a table into chunks using partition keys, to efficiently identify data that satisfies specific criteria.
- Buckets: As with partitions, buckets are also optional and let you subdivide a partition into smaller data units that share the same value of a hash function of a column in a table.

Working with Hive Tables

Hive lets you create two types of tables: external tables and managed tables. Managed tables are maintained by Hive itself. As mentioned earlier, when you use Hive, you store data in tables and, optionally, partitions and buckets. The following example shows how to create a simple Hive managed table:

```
CREATE TABLE page_view(viewTime INT, userid BIGINT,
                page_url STRING, referrer_url STRING,
                ip STRING COMMENT 'IP Address of the User')
COMMENT 'This is the page view table'
PARTITIONED BY(dt STRING, country STRING)
STORED AS SEQUENCEFILE;
```

You can view existing Hive tables by issuing the following command:

```
SHOW TABLES;
```

To view a table's partitions, issue the following command:

```
DESCRIBE page_view;
```

You can list the columns and column types in a table with the `DESCRIBE EXTENDED` command:

```
DESCRIBE EXTENDED page_view;
```

Loading Data into Hive

A common way to load data into Hive is to create an external table. You can create an external table that points to an HDFS directory. You can copy an external file into the HDFS location using either of the HDFS commands `put` or `copy`. Here, once I create the table named PAGE_VIEW_STG, I use the HDFS put command to load the data into the table.

```
CREATE EXTERNAL TABLE page_view_stg(viewTime INT, userid BIGINT,
                page_url STRING, referrer_url STRING,
                ip STRING COMMENT 'IP Address of the User',
                country STRING COMMENT 'country of origination')
COMMENT 'This is the staging page view table'
ROW FORMAT DELIMITED FIELDS TERMINATED BY '44' LINES TERMINATED BY '12'
STORED AS TEXTFILE
LOCATION '/user/data/staging/page_view';

hadoop dfs -put /tmp/pv_2016-03-09.txt /user/data/staging/page_view
```

Note that you can transform the initial data and load it into another Hive table, as shown in this example. The file /tmp/pv_2016-03-09.txt contains the page views served on 9 March 2016. These page views are loaded into the PAGE_VIEW table from the initial staging table named PAGE_VIEW_STG, using the following statement.

```
FROM page_view_stg pvs
INSERT OVERWRITE TABLE page_view PARTITION (dt='2016-03-09', country='US')
SELECT pvs.viewTime, pvs.userid, pvs.page_url, pvs.referrer_url, null, null, pvs.ip
WHERE pvs.country = 'US';
```

Querying with Hive

Let's illustrate how you query the data you've just loaded, with a couple of examples. The first example shows how to insert data into a table by using a query on the PAGE_VIEWS table.

```
INSERT OVERWRITE TABLE xyz_com_page_views
SELECT page_views.*
FROM page_views
WHERE page_views.date >= '2016-03-01' AND page_views.date <= '2016-03-09' AND
      page_views.referrer_url like '%xyz.com';
```

This query gets you all the page views for a specific time period that were referred from the domain xyz.com. You're able to successfully run this query using the DATE column because you had partitioned the table PAGE_VIEWS on that column.

The next query shows how to join two tables in Hive, which is a very common usage pattern. Often, the Hadoop administrator's assistance is called for to assist with the optimizing of Hive queries that involve complex joining of multiple tables.

```
INSERT OVERWRITE TABLE pv_users
SELECT pv.*, u.gender, u.age
FROM user u JOIN page_view pv ON (pv.userid = u.id)
WHERE pv.date = '2016-03-09';
```

The preceding query joins two tables, PAGE_VIEW and USER, to get you the breakdown of the page views by gender and age.

Apache Pig

Pig is a high-level framework for data processing that enables you to use a scripting language called Pig Latin to process data using MapReduce. Pig thus works as a wrapper for MapReduce code. It's important to remember that, just as in the case of Hive, Pig doesn't provide functionality beyond that offered by MapReduce. It certainly makes it a lot easier to use various types of data operations though.

Pig, being a procedural language, is easy to use and quite expressive when performing the data transformation steps. Its conciseness resembles that of a language such as Python.

Since Pig is procedural, you control the execution flow and it's quite easy to incorporate custom functions into the pipeline. Pig's lazy evaluation model, wherein the code doesn't get evaluated until you generate the output, means that the query optimizer can come up with more efficient plans, since it can optimize the entire program from the beginning to the end. You can let Pig ingest data from various sources such as files or streams and then use it to transform that data and store the results in HDFS. Pig jobs are transformed transparently into MapReduce jobs and Pig performs optimizations to efficiently process the data in a Hadoop cluster.

Pig Execution Modes

You can run Pig in two modes: local and MapReduce. In the local mode, Pig doesn't use the HDFS file system. It uses the local file system instead. Local mode is purely for development and prototyping purposes. It provides a shell called Grunt. Here's how you invoke Pig in the local mode:

```
$ pig -x local
...
grunt>
```

To run a pig script named test.pig instead of using the Grunt shell interactively, you execute the following:

```
$ pig local -x test.pig
```

Grunt helps you execute both interactive commands and Pig scripts.

In order to access a hadoop cluster, you invoke Pig in the MapReduce mode as shown here:

```
$ pig -x mapreduce
grunt>
```

If you want to execute a Pig script on the Hadoop cluster, do the following:

```
$ pig -x mapreduce test.pig
```

A Simple Pig Example

Let's see how Pig uses Pig Latin to work with data, by using our familiar WordCount problem. Let's say your input file is named input.txt, consisting of the following lines:

```
A =LOAD ' /input.txt';
B = FOREACH A generate FLATTEN (TOKENIZE(chararray)$0)) as word;
C = FOREACH C generate COUNT(b), GROUP;
STORE D into ' /wordcount';
```

You execute the script *wordcount.pig* across the cluster in the following way:

```
$ hdfs dfs copyFromLocal input.txt input/input.txt /
              bin/pig -x mapreduce wordcount.pig
```

Here's what happens when you execute this Pig script:

- The `LOAD` parameter in the wordcount.pig script loads the data from the file system.
- The `FLATTEN` operator eliminates nesting and the `FOREACH` operator transforms the data based on the columns.
- The `COUNT` function counts the number of elements in a bag and the `GROUP` operator groups rows that have identical key values.
- The `STORE` operator stores the output of the Pig job in HDFS. You can display the output in your terminal instead of storing it, by specifying the DUMP operator instead.

Pig will automatically generate parallel MapReduce tasks across the Hadoop cluster to count the number of words in the input file. Note how simple our Pig WordCount program is compared to the earlier program you've seen, which used MapReduce.

Summary

- Although MapReduce is increasingly being considered a legacy processing framework, it's important to understand how it works.
- Hive (and Pig) are often used for data processing of various types, but since it's MapReduce that runs underneath in both cases, it's useful to gain a thorough understanding of MapReduce processing.
- It's clear that Apache Spark is the future as of now, and the next two chapters introduce the Spark framework.

6

Running Applications in a Cluster—The Spark Framework

This chapter covers

- An introduction to the Spark framework
- The Spark stack
- Installing Spark
- Understanding cluster managers
- Spark and data access (loading data into Spark)

Spark is the most active open-source project relating to big data and is widely considered the successor to the MapReduce framework for processing big data. MapReduce is on its way out in many places, with Spark increasingly becoming the go-to processing framework in Hadoop environments. Four things set Spark apart from its predecessor MapReduce: speed, ease of use, a general purpose framework and built-in sophisticated analytical capabilities.

Although Spark can be run independent of Hadoop, using the Mesos framework for example, Hadoop environments can continue to use YARN and HDFS to support new Spark applications to process data fast.

In this, the first of four chapters in this book that are dedicated to Apache Spark, I explain the main benefits offered by Spark and why it's superior to MapReduce as a processing framework for big data environments. This chapter also shows how to install Spark and configure it.

I explain what a Spark stack is and discuss the key components, such as Spark Core, Spark Steaming and Spark SQL, that constitute the stack.

Spark works with more than one cluster manager, YARN being one of them. You'll learn how to use Spark with Spark's own Standalone Cluster, as well as with Apache Mesos.

Loading data into Spark is a key part of working with Spark, and this chapter explains how to load data from text files, HDFS and relational databases so you can process it with Spark.

What Is Spark?

Spark is an-open source computational framework that, like MapReduce, processes and analyzes huge amounts of data using commodity servers. Spark's API lets developers create distributed applications that make use of a cluster's resources without having to know all the low-level details about how to allocate the cluster's resources among the various applications.

Spark started as a research project in 2009, and its creators started the company named Databricks to promote and commercialize Spark. Spark is an open-source project (the fastest growing Apache project, in fact), and the project's committers include folks from Databricks, UC Berkeley, Hortonworks and Cloudera.

Spark was explicitly designed to overcome the inefficiency of the MapReduce model in performing interactive and iterative computations.

Spark supports a wide variety of workloads, including batch processing, streaming, business intelligence, graphs and, last but not least, machine learning.

You can run Spark on clusters of thousands of nodes (the largest known Spark cluster has 8,000 nodes). In large clusters, Spark has successfully worked with multiple petabytes of data.

In a Hadoop cluster, Spark and MapReduce can be used side-by-side to provide distributed data processing, as shown in Figure 6.1. You can run Spark on the same nodes as you run MapReduce, with YARN managing both processing frameworks, or you can dedicate some of the nodes in a Hadoop cluster exclusively to Spark. Hadoop's HDFS

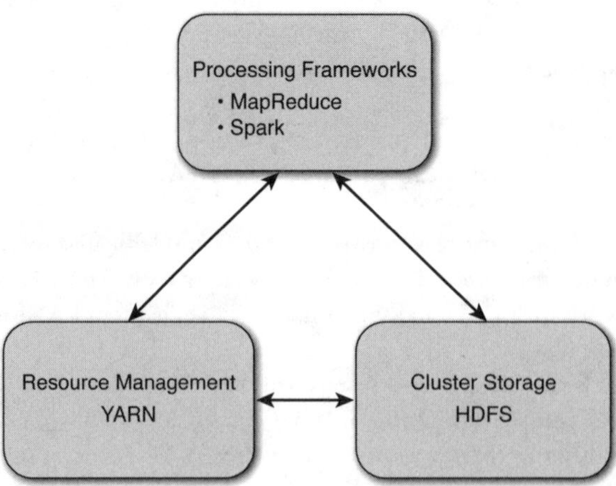

Figure 6.1 The distributed data processing frameworks (MapReduce and Spark)

storage and the YARN processing framework support both MapReduce and Spark in an identical fashion.

Languages such as Java and C++ aren't very useful for exploratory analysis, because they lack a REPL (read-evaluate-print loop) environment for working interactively with data. Data scientists find that Spark enables them to perform easy interactive data analysis, using Python or Scala, through the Spark shell. You can also use Spark SQL, which is a separate SQL shell with which to run SQL-based queries, either interactively or within the Spark shell as part of a Spark program.

Why Spark?

MapReduce has been justly famous for the past several years as the key processing framework in Hadoop clusters. Spark offers several benefits when compared to MapReduce, leading organizations to migrate to Spark applications. Following are the drawbacks of MapReduce programming that gave impetus to the development of Spark as an alternative:

1. Programmability: MapReduce requires several chaining steps to perform certain workloads. You also need specialized systems for different applications.
2. MapReduce writes intermediate data to disk between each computational step. This makes it quite inefficient for applications such as interactive analytics and iterative algorithms to reuse the data. Most machine learning algorithms tends to be iterative by design, making multiple passes over the same data.

Following is a summary of the many benefits of Spark over the MapReduce framework.

Speed

Spark is fast—no two ways about it. Spark set the official record in large-scale sorting in November 2014, breaking the previous petabyte sort record. Spark won the Daytona GraySort contest in 2014. The contest is named after the revered database guru Jim Gray, and its benchmark workload is extremely resource intensive (very high disk and network I/O) and measures how fast a system can sort 100TB of data (1 trillion records).

> **Note**
>
> Spark offers a 100X improvement in performance over MapReduce, offering near real-time processing capabilities.

The previous world record for computation speed was set by MapReduce, which used 2,100 nodes (50,400 physical cores) to sort 100TB of data in 72 minutes. An Amazon EC2–based Spark system sorted the same 100TB of data in a mere 23 minutes, meaning it used 10X fewer nodes but processed the data 3 times faster! It's noteworthy that Spark sorted all the data on disk (HDFS storage) and didn't use Spark's in-memory cache.

Hadoop is based on the idea that processing should move to where the data is, and Spark adds more power to this basic idea by processing data in memory and using execution plans to organize its work.

Some of the reasons for Spark's speed superiority over Hadoop MapReduce include the following:

- Use of memory for data storage. (Unlike MapReduce, which uses memory purely for computation, Spark uses it for both computing and for data storage during application processing.)
- Less expensive shuffle.
- Fewer I/O synchronization barriers.

Like MapReduce, Spark transforms a job into a directed acyclic graph (DAG) of multiple stages. The more complex the directed acyclic graph (DAG), the more the performance improvement of Spark as compared to MapReduce.

Spark also enables you to parallelize massive production data processing applications across a Hadoop cluster, while keeping you from having to deal with the networks, distributed programming and fault tolerance.

Spark can use memory-based computation. Regardless of whether data fits in memory, Spark is much faster than MapReduce. If data fits in memory it can be hundreds of times faster than MapReduce. Spark offers several features that MapReduce does, such as fault tolerance and scalability. However, two key factors account for the superiority of Spark: Spark's advanced execution engine and its in-memory cluster computing.

Spark can connect at run time to different storage sources such as HDFS, Cassandra, Amazon S3 and Apache HBase.

You can write Spark applications in Scala, Python or Java. I focus on Scala in this chapter and the rest of the book wherever I discuss Spark, since it's not only easier and more compact than Java but also offers superior performance.

Spark's Advanced Execution Engine

Spark uses a much more sophisticated job execution engine than MapReduce. MapReduce has limited optimization capabilities, as it always creates a DAG with the same two stages—map and reduce—for all jobs. If you want to perform advanced computation using complex algorithms, you need to split the job into multiple jobs and sequentially execute each of the jobs.

With Spark, unlike in MapReduce, you aren't limited to two stages per job—you can have any number of stages you want. Instead of splitting complex algorithms into multiple jobs, you can run jobs with multiple stages. This is a huge difference, leading to several optimizations not possible with MapReduce. Since Spark is aware that a job has multiple stages it uses this information to optimize the job execution—for example, by minimizing the shuffling of data and disk I/O.

Spark represents the future (as far ahead as we can see it right now, anyway!). YARN libraries such as Mahout and Hive will be ported to Spark. Far from being a replacement for Hadoop, Spark is poised to be a key part of the Hadoop ecosystem. MapReduce will continue to exist for quite a while—there's too much MapReduce code running in the world's Hadoop clusters for it to disappear anytime soon.

Spark's In-Memory Computation

I/O latency, which is the delay in transferring data from disk to memory, is always a significant component of the total job execution time. A MapReduce job often reads and writes data from and to disk multiple times in the course of its execution. You can implement the same job in Spark where it reads just once from disk. Once it reads the data, Spark caches the data in memory for further processing steps, thus minimizing disk I/O. Since reading from memory is at least 100 times faster than reading from disk, performance is increased dramatically.

> **Note**
>
> Persistence of data in memory means more efficient iteration for jobs such as machine learning.

Because Spark caches the data in memory, it doesn't have to write to disk or read data from disk during various intermediate operations. That's a key reason for the speed of Spark applications.

What happens when the data doesn't fit in memory? After all, you're processing terabytes of data while your server memory is limited to 128GB, 256GB, or 512GB in most cases. It's important to understand that Spark doesn't always decide to cache the data in memory. It determines when during the data processing pipeline it should cache and which data it should cache—sometimes it may not cache any data if it's making just a single pass over the data.

Spark is built to run on a cluster of servers and works well with distributed storage (such as HDFS) by supporting data locality, which is the moving of code to where the data is.

Ease of Use and Accessibility

Spark programs are much simpler than corresponding MapReduce applications. Spark's API is also much more wide ranging. You must break down every MapReduce job into map and reduce jobs, since MapReduce offers just the map and reduce operators.

> **Note**
>
> Compared to MapReduce job, a Spark job means a 10:1 reduction in the lines of code.

Spark is highly accessible: You can use Python-, Java-, Scala- and SQL-based API's to perform your processing. The efficacy and low cost of Spark has made it possible to perform computations that were previously deemed impractical or impossible.

Developers can be much more productive with Spark than with MapReduce.

Simplicity and Compactness

In earlier chapters, you've seen what the MapReduce code looks like—typically you'd need more than 50 lines of Java MR code to get the word count of a text. WordCount in Spark takes just three lines:

```
val f = sc.textFile(inputPath)
val w = f.flatMap(l => l.split(" ").map(word => (word, 1))).cache()
w.reduceByKey(_ + _).saveAsText(outputPath)
```

That's it!

The Hadoop MapReduce model is quite restrictive, which makes most algorithms harder to implement. Spark on the other hand uses fine-grained "combinators" for composing algorithms.

Spark is a much higher-level programming framework than MapReduce, allowing developers to focus on the application logic rather than the plumbing.

General-Purpose Framework

MapReduce was designed for batch processing—nothing else. Spark is a true general-purpose processing framework. You can use it for all the following types of processing:

- Batch processing
- Interactive analysis
- Stream processing
- Machine learning
- Graph computing

When you use MapReduce, you'd need to use additional frameworks for performing tasks other than batch processing. This hinders developer productivity, whereas with Spark you can use the same framework for all the work. This also means that you don't have to duplicate data by having to store it in multiple frameworks. For example, you can use MapReduce (batch processing) together with Storm (stream processing). However, this means that you need to set up and maintain a different cluster for each of the frameworks and maintain the code in both frameworks as well.

Spark involves far less complexity since by learning this one framework, you can build complex data processing pipelines that perform various types of tasks.

Spark can process data in any file format supported by Hadoop. It can process data in HDFS, HBase, Cassandra, Hive and any Hadoop InputFormat.

Spark is especially useful for running iterative data processing jobs and for interactive analysis. An iterative algorithm iterates over the same data multiple times, sometimes performing hundreds of iterations over the same data sets. Machine learning and graph processing are two well-known iterative algorithm-based applications.

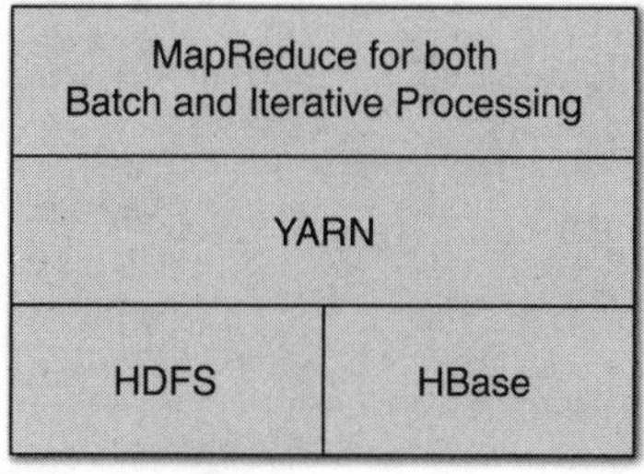

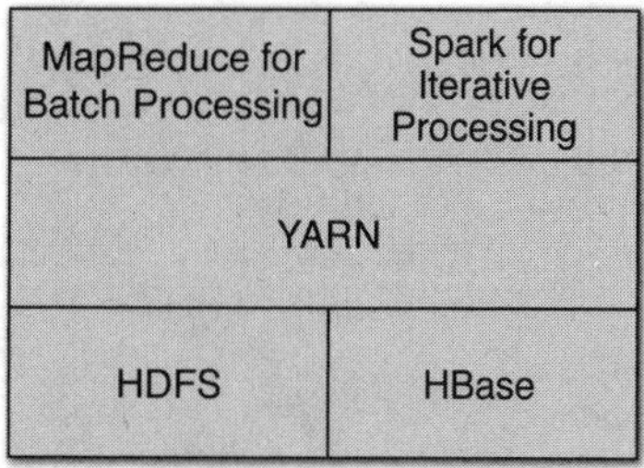

Figure 6.2 MapReduce and Spark together in a Hadoop Cluster, with MapReduce handling batch processing and Spark handling iterative processing

Spark and Hadoop

Most places that use MapReduce have found that it works great for several types of batch processing, but they run into issues when handling iterative processing. In most clusters, you have both MapReduce and Spark running together, with MapReduce handling batch processing and Spark handling interactive processing (such as machine learning jobs). Figure 6.2 shows this type of architecture.

> **Note**
>
> Spark is not a replacement for or rival to Hadoop—it complements existing clusters and works side by side with MapReduce and other traditional processing frameworks.

Spark doesn't require Hadoop. It happens to support several storage systems, including HDFS. It supports text files, SequenceFiles, Avro, Parquet and other Hadoop InputFormat-based files.

The Spark Stack

Spark is unique among the processing engines supported by YARN, in the sense that it contains several closely integrated components, each of which specializes in handling a different type of workload, such as machine learning or SQL processing. This benefits an organization that has to perform different types of data processing, as it doesn't need to run multiple software systems, one for each type of work.

A big benefit of the tightly integrated architecture employed by Spark is that your applications can combine different types of processing without difficulty. For example, an application can ingest data from a streaming source and employ machine learning algorithms to analyze the data in real time. You can then analyze the data using SQL in real time as well.

Figure 6.3 shows the basic architecture of the Spark stack when you run Spark on a Hadoop cluster.

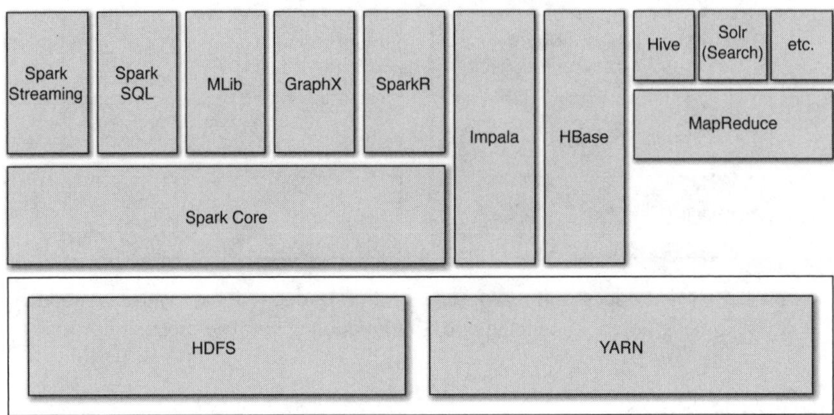

Figure 6.3 The Spark stack when running Spark on a Hadoop cluster, and how Spark and Hadoop are complementary tools in a Hadoop cluster

Following is what each of the components in the Spark stack does:

- Spark Core is Spark's main execution engine, and all of Spark's functionality rests on this engine. It provides the main Spark functionality, such as scheduling, memory management, fault recovery and handling storage. Spark Core has the following features:
  - In-memory computing for speedy processing.
  - General execution model that supports a huge variety of use cases.
  - Ease of development. Unlike MapReduce (Java only), you can use Scala, Python or Java to write the code.
- Spark SQL works with structured data and lets you query data via SQL and Hive query language (HQL). You can intersperse Spark SQL with Spark's resilient distributed datasets (RDDs), which are Spark's programming abstractions and represent collections of items distributed across a cluster that you can process in parallel. You can create the RDDs using Java, Scala or Python. This capability to combine SQL with Spark's native programmatic devices lets you combine SQL with analytics. This is what gives Spark a leg up on competing processing engines in a data warehouse setting. Note that you can create Spark RDDs not only from files in the HDFS file system but also from any storage system supported by Hadoop APIs, such as Amazon S3, Cassandra and Hive.

> **Note**
>
> Since Spark supports storage systems implementing the Hadoop API, it doesn't require Hadoop—it works with any storage system supported by the Hadoop APIs.

- Spark streaming lets you process streaming data such as the log files generated by web servers while providing you a high degree of fault tolerance throughput, just as Spark Core does.
- MLlib provides machine learning algorithms such as classification, clustering and collaborative filtering.
- GraphX lets you manipulate graphs such as those contained in a social network.
- Standalone scheduler, YARN and Mesos: Spark comes with a simple cluster manager called the standalone scheduler, which is a way to get acclimatized to using Spark. However, in order to run on massive clusters, you need a full-fledged cluster manager, such as Hadoop YARN or Apache Mesos. Spark will run on both YARN and Mesos.

As Figure 6.3 shows, the Spark ecosystem rests on a cluster at the bottom of the structure. In a development environment you don't need the cluster, but in a production system you do. The cluster takes care of the storage part, which is HDFS in a Hadoop cluster. Spark Core comes next, and on top of it you have Spark SQL, Spark Streaming, GraphX and MLlib.

Installing Spark

Installing Spark and getting it running is quite easy. In the following example, I use an Ubuntu server to install and configure Spark. Although you can build it from source code, I download the precompiled binaries from the Spark download site at `http://spark.apache.org`.

While I used `wget` (I could also have used `curl`) to get the Apache Hadoop tarballs from an Apache software mirror location, I do things a bit differently for Spark, as you'll see here.

1. First, make sure you have Java and Python in the path, and also set the `$JAVA_HOME` environment variable.
2. Go to the Spark downloads page at `http://spark.apache.org/downloads.html`.
3. Select the latest Spark release and make sure to it's a prebuilt package for Hadoop 2.4 or later. Download the package with the following command and then unpack the binaries. Finally, rename the folder containing the binaries to just `spark` for the sake of simplicity.

```
$ wget http://d3kbcqa49mib13.cloudfront.net/spark-1.4.0-bin-hadoop2.4.tgz
$ tar -zxf spark-1.4.0-bin-hadoop2.4.tgz
$ sudo mv spark-1.4.0-bin.-hadoop2.4 spark
```

Note that the latest Spark binaries are developed with a recent and stable Hadoop release.

1. Make a directory specific to your organization as the installation directory under the /opt directory (the/opt directory in Linux contains the add-on software

binaries). Once you do this, move the spark directory with the binaries under this new directory.

```
$ sudo mkdir -p /opt/mycompany
$ sudo mv spark /opt/mycompany
```

2. Make root the owner of the spark home directory. Also change the file permissions to 0755 (rwe, re, re).

```
$ sudo chown -R root:root /opt/mycompany/spark
$ sudo chmod -R 755 /opt/mycompany/spark
```

3. Do the following to set up a symbolic link to the Spark configuration directory:

```
$ cd /opt/mycompany/spark
$ sudo mv spark/conf/* /etc/spark
$ sudo ln -s /etc/spark conf
```

4. Add the spark path to the PATH variable in the .bashrc file.

```
$ echo "export PATH=$PATH:/opt/mycompany/spark/bin">> home/hduser/.bashrc
```

5. Create the log and tmp directories for Spark.

```
$ sudo mkdir -p /var/log/spark
$ sudo chown -R hduser:hduser /var/log/spark
$ sudo mkdir /tmp/spark
```

6. Finally, configure Spark to work with Hadoop and also to use its new log and tmp directories that I've created in the previous step.

```
$ cd /etc/spark
$ echo "export HADOOP_CONF_DIR=/opt/mycompany/hadoop/etc/hadoop" >> spark-
env.sh
$ echo "export YARN_CONF_DIR=/opt/mycompany/hadoop/etc/hadoop" >> spark-
env.sh
$ echo "export SPARK_LOG_DIR=/var/log/spark" >> spark-env.sh
$ echo 'export SPARK_WORKER_DIR=/tmp/spark" >> spark-env.sh
```

Now that the installation is complete, test it by running a local pyspark interpreter:

```
$ pyspark
Python 2.7.10 (default, Jun 23 2015, 21:58:51)
[GCC 4.2.1 Compatible Apple LLVM 6.1.0 (clang-602.0.53)] on darwin
Type "help", "copyright", "credits" or "license" for more information.
Using Spark's default log4j profile: org/apache/spark/log4j-defaults.properties
[... snip ...]
Welcome to
      ____              __
     / __/__  ___ _____/ /__
    _\ \/ _ \/ _ `/ __/  '_/
   /__ / .__/\_,_/_/ /_/\_\   version 1.5.2
      /_/

Using Python version 2.7.10 (default, Jun 23 2015 21:58:51)
SparkContext available as sc, HiveContext available as sqlContext.
>>>
```

Spark Examples

Spark comes with a bunch of examples, and you can use some of them to take your new Spark installation for a spin.

Spark's sample programs based on Scala, Java, Python and R are located in the examples/src/main directory. To run one of the sample programs (Scala) use `bin/run-example <class> [params]` in the top-level directory. Here's an example:

```
./bin/run-example SparkPi 10
```

Spark uses its spark-submit script (more about this in the next chapter) to run this program for you. If you want to try a Spark Python program that does the same things (calculate the value of Pi), do the following:

```
./bin/spark-submit  examples/src/main/python/pi.py 10
```

Key Spark Files and Directories

Spark's installation directories include the following:

- bin contains the executable files such as the program that starts the Spark shell.
- core, streaming and others contain the source code for the major Spark components.
- examples contains useful Spark standalone jobs you can use to learn Spark.

Compiling the Spark Binaries

Earlier, I used the Spark binaries that I've downloaded to install and configure Spark. In some situations—for example, where you need to compile Spark for a specific Hadoop version or want to add YARN and Hive integration—compiling the Spark source code is the way to go.

To install Spark using compiled binaries from source code, follow the same steps as in the example for the binary installaion, but add the following step in between steps 2 and 3.

```
$ mvn -Pyarn -Phadoop-2.4 -Dhadoop.version=2.4.0 -Phive -DskipTests clean package
```

The flags I added here will enable YARN and Hive and skip the tests. Of course, you'll need Maven on your server to do this. Everything else proceeds in the same fashion as before.

You've now installed and set up Spark to work on your test server (or laptop) in a "standalone mode." You can run sample code in this mode. You can also execute the `spark-submit` command to submit jobs to the YARN ResourceManager running in a pseudo-distributed mode.

Spark offers several example applications such as WordCount and Pi. You'll find the Scala- Java- Python- and R-based examples in the examples/src/main directory. You can run the Scala or Java example program to compute the value of Pi as follows:

```
./bin/run-example SparkPi 10
```

You can run the same job in Python like this:

```
./bin/spark-submit examples/src/main/python/pi.py 10
```

Reducing Spark's Verbosity

Since Spark and PySpark are quite verbose in their log messages, you can reduce the heavy output by editing the log4j settings as shown here:

```
$ cp $SPARK_HOME/conf/log4j.properties.template \
      $SPARK_HOME/conf/log4j.properties
```

In the log4j.properties file, replace all instances of INFO with WARN, in order to reduce the log output. The next time you run a PySpark command, the log messages will be much smaller.

Spark Run Modes

You can run Spark locally or on a cluster. When you want to run a distributed Spark application across a cluster, Spark needs a cluster manager. Spark comes with its own standalone cluster manager (also referred to as standalone scheduler and standalone mode), and using it is the easier way to set up your Spark cluster. In addition to the standalone cluster manager, Spark supports Hadoop's YARN and Apache Mesos as a cluster manager.

Just as you can learn Hadoop and YARN without ever installing a cluster (through a single-node pseudo-distributed cluster), you can use the standalone scheduler to get started with Spark without any cluster at all. You can upgrade to a distributed deployment such as Hadoop (or Mesos) later on. However, as with all the other stuff, our focus will be on using Spark in a Hadoop 2/YARN environment.

Local Mode

The local mode uses just a single server and so is a non-distributed mode. When running Spark locally you can run it with a single worker thread or with multiple worker threads. The local mode is really just for development and testing.

Cluster Mode

In a production setting, you always use a cluster manager to run Spark applications. A cluster manager is an external service that helps acquire resources on a cluster. As alluded to previously, there are three types of clusters on which Spark can be run:

- Spark standalone cluster: This comes with Spark. While it is quite easy to run, it has limited configuration options and isn't very scalable. You use this primarily for testing and development.
- Apache Mesos: This is the original platform that was supported by Spark and is not as commonly used as the next alternative, YARN.
- Hadoop YARN: Spark can be run side by side with other application frameworks such as MapReduce and Impala.

Regardless of which cluster manager you use, a Spark application works the same, since the applications don't care about how you manage the cluster—the Spark API is quite independent of the cluster manger you choose to use.

Understanding the Cluster Managers

This book is about administering Hadoop clusters, so I'm naturally interested in running Spark on YARN. However, it's a good idea to understand both the standalone cluster manager and Mesos as well, so that's what I do next—explain all three cluster managers.

The Standalone Cluster Manager

Spark can run on its own dedicated cluster, called a standalone Spark cluster. The standalone cluster manager is easy to set up out of the box after installing Spark.

In the following sections, I explain the architecture of the standalone cluster manager and how you set it up.

Architecture of the Standalone Cluster Manager

The standalone cluster manager uses worker and master processes to perform computations. The worker process manages the computing resources such as CPU/RAM on each of a cluster's nodes. The master node pools the resources and allocates them to competing applications.

A Spark application that you deploy on a standalone cluster manger uses the following entities:

- Driver program: This is the main Spark application that consists of the data processing logic.
- Executor: This is a JVM process that runs on each worker node and processes the jobs that the driver program submits.
- Task: A task is a subcomponent of a data processing job.

> **Note**
>
> A Spark application and the driver program are used as synonyms for each other.

Figure 6.4 shows the architecture of a standalone Spark cluster. The driver program uses a SparkContext object, which serves as the entry point into the Spark library, to connect to a cluster. The SparkContext object launches executors on the worker nodes and sends them the application code. The job is split into tasks and executed by the executor process in the worker nodes.

In a Spark standalone cluster, the Spark Master and Worker processes manage the Spark application processes.

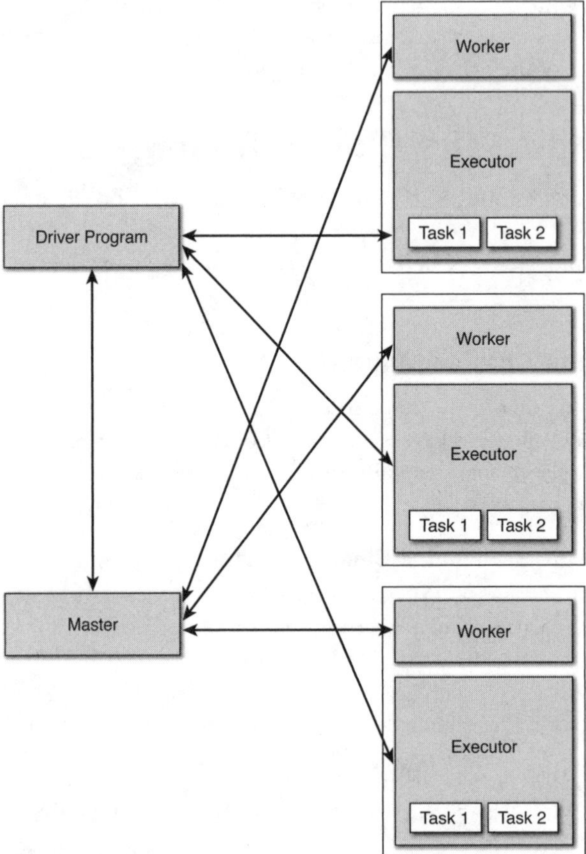

Figure 6.4 A standalone Spark cluster

How to Set Up a Standalone Spark Cluster

There really isn't a whole lot to setting up a standalone Spark cluster—the standalone mode is the default—so you must simply install the Spark binaries on all the cluster nodes and then start the master and worker processes in the cluster. The following steps show you how to do this in a setting with 1 master node and 5 worker nodes.

1. Install the Spark binaries on all six nodes (1 master and 5 worker nodes).
2. Make sure to place `/path/to/spark/sbin` in the path variable on all the nodes in the cluster.

```
$ echo "export PATH=$PATH:/path/to/spark/sbin/" >> /home/hduser/.bashrc
```

If you have no legacy MapReduce jobs and also no Hadoop cluster, and you just want to run jobs using the Spark framework, you can do so with the standalone Spark cluster.

Starting and Stopping the Master and Worker Processes

Once you install the binaries, go to one of the servers and start the master process.

```
$ /path/to/spark/sbin/start-master.sh
```

> **Note**
>
> By default, the master starts on port 7077. The workers use this port to connect to the master. The master has a web UI running on port 8088.

The next step is to start the worker processes on all the cluster nodes.

```
$ /path/to/spark/sbin/start-slave.sh <master-URL>
```

You can stop the master and worker processes (separately on each worker node) by executing the following two shell scripts provided by Spark:

```
$ /path/to/spark/sbin/stop-master.sh
$ /path/to/spark/sbin/stop-slave.sh
```

You can start all the worker processes as well as the master process with a single Spark-provided script. In order to do this, first setup a private-key-based SSH access from the master node to all the worker nodes (as I showed in Chapter 3, "Creating and Configuring a Simple Hadoop Cluster"). In addition, you need to create a file called slaves (/path/to/spark/conf/slaves) that lists all the hostnames on IP addresses of the cluster's worker nodes, with one server per line.

Using the Spark-provided scripts, you can start and stop the Spark standalone cluster in the following way:

```
$ /path/to/spark/sbin/start-all.sh
$ /path/to/spark/sbin/stop-all.sh
```

Configuring the Worker and Master Nodes

When you use the start-all.sh script, it starts the master and worker processes with default configurations. You must configure the Spark cluster configuration by editing the environment variable settings in the spark-env.sh file. You must do this on the master servers as well as on all the worker nodes. Spark provides a template file named /path/to/spark/conf/spark-env.sh that contains all the configuration variables you can set.

The easiest way to go about configuring the Spark cluster is to copy the spark-env.sh template, and edit the settings you want.

Spark on Apache Mesos

This book is about Hadoop, which has its own cluster manager (YARN) and hence doesn't need to use Apache Mesos to run Spark applications. However, I think as an administrator of a Hadoop cluster it's probably a good idea to acquire a rudimentary knowledge of how Spark runs in a Mesos cluster.

Apache Mesos is an open-source cluster manager that allows different distributed computing frameworks to share a cluster's resources. You can actually run Hadoop on Mesos if you want. Mesos supports Spark and other applications such as Kafka and Elasticsearch.

Mesos is becoming increasingly popular as a kind of an operating system to manage all types of computing resources in a data center. Mesos runs on Linux distributions and was built according to the same principles as the Linux kernel itself.

Setting Up Spark to Work with Mesos

Installing Mesos and configuring it to work with Spark is easy, as I show you in this section. You can set up multiple master services in Mesos for high availability using ZooKeeper to support high availability, just as you do for NameNode high availability in Hadoop. In our example, I use a single master to keep things simple.

Here are the steps you must follow:

1. Install Mesos.

   ```
   $ sudo apt-get -y update
   $ sudo apt-get -y install mesos
   ```

2. In order for Spark to connect and work with Mesos, you must make the Spark binaries avaialable to Mesos. You can do this by uploading the Spark binaries to HDFS:

   ```
   $ hdfs dfs -put spark-1.4.0-bin-hadoop2.4.tgz spark-1.4.0-bin-hadoop2.4.tgz
   ```

3. Configure Spark for Mesos by editing the spark-env.sh file to add the following:

   ```
   $ export MESOS_NATIVE_LIBRARY=/usr/local/lib/libmesos.so
   $ export SPARK_EXECUTOR_URI=hdfs://localhost:9000/user/hduser/
   spark-1.4.0-bin-hadoop2.4.tgz
   ```

Mesos is a good framework, but our focus in this book is on Hadoop and YARN. Let's look at how you run Spark on YARN.

Spark on YARN

Finally, I get to Spark on YARN, which is my main concern in this book. In Chapter 2, "An Introduction to the Architecture of Hadoop," you learned the architecture of Hadoop, including how YARN operates as a kind of an operating system for the cluster by managing the cluster's computing resources.

If you have legacy MapReduce jobs running in your Hadoop cluster and you foresee them running for a good while, YARN will be great as the cluster manager for Spark.

When you run Spark on YARN, the ResourceManager and the NodeManagers running on the worker nodes manage the Spark application processes. YARN's ResourceManager is the counterpart to the Mesos master, and the NodeManager does the same work as Mesos's slave processes.

Most Hadoop clusters have started off running MapReduce applications and have been moving over to Spark applications. MapReduce is viewed as a legacy application framework now. YARN lets you run both MapReduce and Spark applications in the same cluster.

Why YARN Is Better than the Spark Standalone Cluster Manager

Using YARN as Spark's cluster manager rather than the Spark standalone cluster manager offers several benefits to you, as I summarize here.

- It's quite common to run MapReduce, Spark and other frameworks such as Tez together on the same cluster. YARN lets all these applications dynamically share the same pool of cluster resources.
- You can use the YARN schedulers such as the Capacity Scheduler and the Fair Scheduler to categorize and prioritize your cluster workloads.
- When you run the Spark applications through a Spark standalone cluster, the application will run an executor process on every node—in a YARN cluster, you get to choose the number of executors.
- It's easy to secure the authentication between the processes by Kerberizing (enabling Kerberos on) your Hadoop cluster.

How YARN and Spark Work Together

A Spark application acts as the client and submits a job to YARN's ResourceManager. As you learned in Chapter 2, YARN contains an application-specific ApplicationMaster that owns and executes the job in the cluster. It's the ApplicationMaster that negotiates resources required to run the job from the ResourceManager. Once it gets the resources, the ApplicationMaster launches containers on the cluster's nodes, in coordination with the NodeManagers running on each of the nodes.

Everything regarding the creation of the ApplicationMaster and the allocation of resources works the same way for MapReduce and Spark applications. In this context, it's important to realize that the ApplicationMaster is provided by the processing framework's libraries. Spark provides its own ApplicationMaster through its libraries.

Chapter 7, "Running Spark Applications," shows how to deploy Spark applications in a Hadoop cluster managed by YARN.

Setting Up Spark on a Hadoop Cluster

When you run Spark on Hadoop with YARN as the cluster manager, the ResourceManager acts as the Spark master and the NodeManagers on all the nodes act as the executors. Each of the Spark executors will run inside a YARN container.

In order to set up Spark in your Hadoop cluster, you need to ensure that the binary distribution of Spark that you installed has YARN support, as I showed earlier in this chapter. Once you install Spark, all you need to do is configure it to work with HDFS and YARN by setting these environment variables:

- `HADOOP_CONF_DIR`: You configure this variable to allow Spark to write to HDFS.

  ```
  export HADOOP_CONF_DIR=/opt/mycompany/hadoop/etc/hadoop
  ```

- `YARN_CONF_DIR`: You configure this variable so Spark can connect to the YARN ResourceManager.

  ```
  export YARN_CONF_DIR=/opt/mycompany/hadoop/etc/hadoop
  ```

Spark and Data Access

Spark can use data from various sources by connecting with the data sources. Spark works with Hadoop's HDFS storage as well as other data sources such as relational databases and Amazon's S3 storage. Spark will work with any Hadoop-supported storage, meaning that the storage format must be able to work with the following Hadoop interfaces.

- `InputFormat`: This interface creates the InputSplits from the input data and divides it into records.
- `OutputFormat`: This interface writes data to storage.

In the following sections, I describe how to load data for Spark from various sources.

Loading Data from the Linux File System

You've already seen how to load data from the local directory on a Linux server. You usually do this for small jobs where you want to test out some new applications or something like that. Theoretically, you can load any size data into a cluster from the local file system, but then you must ensure that each of the cluster's nodes can access the directory where you stored the data.

Here's a simple example that shows how you can load data from a text file on the local file system into a Spark RDD.

```
scala> val words = sc.textFile(file://home/bduser/words)
```

Loading Data from HDFS

HDFS is the most popular storage platform for Spark, owing to Spark being increasingly used to replace MapReduce programs that were running on a Hadoop cluster.

Spark supports Hadoop's InputFormat, and the default `InputFormat` is `TextInputFormat`. Spark uses the `sc.textFile` method to read the data with `TextInputFormat` and creates an RDD of strings.

Accessing Data from a Text File

In our Spark WordCount example shown earlier, I used a text file stored on the local file system as the source for the data. When you want to use HDFS, you use the same WordCount program but load the words directory from HDFS:

```
scala> val words = sc.textFile("hdfs://localhost:9000/user/hduser/words")
```

Your complete WordCount program when using Scala will then look like the following:

```
scala> sc.textFile("hdfs://localhost:9000/user/hduser/words"). flatMap(
_.split("\\W+")).map( w => (w,1)). reduceByKey( (a,b) => (a+b)).foreach(println)
```

Accessing Entire Text Files at One Time

Often you may need to access an entire file by processing multiple lines as a record. You can use the `SparkContext.wholeTextFiles` format in cases such as this. Each text file is stored as an element of the RDD.

Let me use a weather data set that you can get from the following location to illustrate how to load entire files at a time:

```
ftp://ftp.nc.dc.noaa.gov/pub/data/noaa
```

The following steps show how to download the zipped files in the gzip format (.gz) and load them into HDFS.

1. Download the files:

   ```
   $ wget -r ftp://ftp.ncdc.noaa.gov/pub/data/noaa/
   ```

2. Load the downloaded data into HDFS:

   ```
   $ hdfs dfs -put ftp.ncdc.noaa.gov/pub/data/noaa weather/
   ```

3. Start the Spark shell and load the data for the year 1950 into an RDD:

   ```
   scala> val weatherFileRDD = sc.wholeTextfiles
   ("hdfs://localhost:9000/user/hduser//weather/1950")
   ```

4. To avoid recomputation each time you access it, you can cache the data in the RDD:

   ```
   scala> val weatherRDD = weatherFileRDD.cache
   ```

5. Load the first element of the data set:

   ```
   scala> val firstElement = weatherRDD.first
   ```

6. Read the value for the first element of the RDD:

   ```
   scala> val firstValue = firstElement._2
   ```

7. Split `firstValue` by lines:

   ```
   scala> Val firstVals = firstValue.split(\\n)
   ```

8. Wind speed occupies positions 66-69 in the text of the weather data files. You can find the wind speed by doing this:

   ```
   scala> val windSpeed = firstVals.map(line => line.substring(65,69)
   ```

Often you need to load data in a specific format, and the TextInputFormat may not allow that. You can use Spark's `SparkContext.newAPIHadoopFile` method for these cases.

Note

You can also load data from Amazon Simple Storage Service (S3) into a Spark RDD and process it.

Loading Data from a Relational Database

Spark's JdbcRDD feature lets you load relational database tables as RDDs. If you want to load a lot of data into HDFS from a relational database, a tool such as Apache Sqoop is best, as I explain in Chapter 12, "Moving Data Into and Out of Hadoop."

However, if you want to load a bit of data from a relational database directly for some ad-hoc analysis, JdbcRDD will work very well. JdbcRDD is an RDD that will execute a SQL query on a JDBC connection to a relational database such as a MySQL database and fetch the results as well.

> **Note**
>
> It's better to use Spark SQL's JDBC data source rather than load data directly from a relational database, as you can take advantage of DataFrames (see Chapter 7).

In the following example, I show how to load data from a table in a MySQL database.

1. Download the MySQL connector mysql-connector-java-x.x.xx-bin.jar from the location `http://dev.mysql.com/downloads/connector/j/`.
2. Launch the Spark shell and make the MySQL driver available to it:

   ```
   $ spark-shell -jars /path-to-mysql-jdar/mysql-connector-java-5.1.29-bin.jar
   ```

3. Create Spark variables to hold the database credentials and the JDBC URL:

   ```
   scala> val url="jdbc:mysql://localhost:3306/hadoopdb"
   scala> val username = "hduser"
   scala> val password = "******"
   ```

4. Import the JdbcRDD and the JDBC classes, and then create an instance of the JDBC driver:

   ```
   scala> import org.apache.spark.rdd.JdbcRDD
   scala> import java.sql.{Connection, DriverManager, ResultSet}
   scala> Class.forName("com.mysql.jdbc.Driver").newInstance
   ```

5. Load the JdbcRDD:

   ```
   scala> val myRDD = new JdbcRDD( sc, () =>
   DriverManager.getConnection(url,username,password) ,
   "select first_name,last_name,gender from person limit ?, ?",
   1, 5, 2, r => r.getString("last_name") + ", " + r.getString("first_name"))
   ```

6. Run the following queries to check the data load:

   ```
   scala> myRDD.count
   scala> myRDD.foreach(println)
   ```

7. You can save the RDD to HDFS for permanent storage:

   ```
   scala> myRDD.saveAsTextFile("hdfs://localhost:9000/user/hduser/person")
   ```

Summary

Here's what you learned in this chapter:

- Spark is replacing MapReduce as the go-to processing framework in Hadoop environments.
- Spark can coexist with MapReduce in a Hadoop cluster.
- Spark can be run in its own standalone cluster or in a cluster such as Hadoop or Mesos.
- You gain several benefits, such as security, when you run Spark in a YARN-managed Hadoop cluster.
- You can load data into Spark from various sources, such as text files, HDFS, Amazon Simple Storage Service (S3) and relational databases.

7

Running Spark Applications

This chapter covers the following:

- The Spark programming model
- Working with resilient distributed datasets (RDDs)
- Programming Spark
- Structure of a Spark application
- Using the Spark shell
- Running Spark applications

The previous chapter explained the architecture of Spark, showed how to install Spark and explained the various ways in which you can run Spark, including on a YARN-based Hadoop cluster.

This chapter is all about Spark programming. You learn about the Spark programming model and how RDDs are at the heart of everything you do with Spark.

You learn about running Spark code interactively using the Spark shell, as well as how to run applications through the spark-submit script.

Spark SQL and Spark Streaming are two important components of the Spark stack, and this chapter provides an introduction to both.

The Spark Programming Model

Before you start programming with Spark, let's review some important features of Spark programming, such as functional programming and the unique Spark programming model.

Spark Programming and RDDs

At the heart of Spark processing is the RDD, which is a distributed collection of elements or objects. You perform all your work in Spark by creating, transforming and manipulating RDDs. Spark Core will take care of distributing the data contained in the RDDs and parallelizing your operations across the cluster. You can include Python, Java or Scala objects in an RDD or even user-defined classes.

An RDD, as mentioned earlier, is simply a collection of objects that's split into partitions, to be computed on different nodes in the cluster. The most common way to create an RDD is by loading an external dataset, for example, by loading data contained in a text file, as an RDD of strings. Here's an example that shows how to create an RDD of strings using `SparkContext.textFile()`:

```
>>>lines = sc.textFile("/path/to/README.md")
```

Once you create an RDD, you can perform operations called **transformations** and **actions** on the RDD. A transformation lets you create an RDD from an existing RDD. Using our first RDD, you can create a new RDD that'll contain just the strings that contain the word "Python" as shown here (I'm using Python here, but you can do equivalent things with either Java or Scala):

```
>>>pythonLines = lines.filter(lambda lines: "Python" in line)
```

Actions compute results based on an RDD. The computed result is either stored in HDFS (or any external storage system) or returned to the driver program. Here's an example that shows how to return the first element of an RDD:

```
>>>pythonlines.first ()
U'## Interactive Python Shell
```

Each time you execute an action on an RDD, Spark recomputes the RDDs. If you plan on reusing the RDD, you can request that Spark store the RDD contents in memory. You can also store the data on disk instead of memory. If you're going to query some data repeatedly, it makes sense to load that subset of data into memory.

Spark and Scala

You can write Spark applications in three different languages: Scala, Python and Java. I use Scala in this book, since it has several performance benefits over the other two languages, besides being much simpler to code than Java applications.

My advice to Spark users (and administrators) is to invest some time in learning the essence of Scala—although you can work with Spark without knowing Scala, you can read Spark source code if you know Scala, as Spark is written in Scala. The methods in Spark RDDs are patterned after Scala collections APIs. RDD functions such as map, filter and reduce have specifications similar to equivalent Scala functions.

Another big advantage offered by Scala is the fact that the Spark shell is quite helpful for debugging and development efforts. Spark is an interpreted language; hence the shell. As Java is a compiled language, there's no shell for it.

While Python is easy to learn and includes several data-science-related tool kits, such as SciPy, numPy and pandas, Spark code written in Python is slower than the same code written in a JVM (Java Virtual Machine), which Scala uses. Also, many of Spark's features are first written in Scala, so if you use Python, you're always going to be behind! However, I must note that with Spark 2.0, the performance difference among the supported languages is smaller than before.

Spark provides all the scalability and fault tolerance of MapReduce but also goes way beyond MapReduce in many ways. It can support a more general execution format of a general directed acyclic graph (DAG) of operators, rather than the monolithic map and reduce format. Instead of writing intermediate results to disk like MapReduce, it can pass the results to the next step in the pipeline. Spark also offers in-memory processing, by enabling users to store data at any point in the processing pipeline to memory, avoiding the need to repeatedly recompute the same result or load it back from disk. Spark can read and write in all the data formats supported by MapReduce, such as Avro and Parquet. It also can work with HBase and Cassandra and is able to ingest continuously streaming data from Flume and Kafka.

Functional Programming

Spark depends on functional programming, which uses functions as the basic programming input. Functions have no state or side effects and consist of just input and output.

Passing Functions as Parameters

Spark uses functions as parameters, and most RDD operations accept the functions as parameters. It applies functions to each of the RDD's records. Here's an example in Scala:

```
scala> def toUpper(s):
         return s.upper()
scala> mydata = sc.textFile("purplecow.txt")
scala> mydata.map(toUpper).take(2)
```

Anonymous Functions

You can also use anonymous functions, which are functions defined inline without an identifier. You do this mostly for short one-off functions. Here's an example in Scala:

```
Scala> mydata.map(line => line.toUpperCase()).take(2)
```

You can use an underscore(_) to represent anonymous parameters:

```
Scala> mydata.map(_.toUpperCase()).take(2)
```

> **Note**
>
> In order to create production-grade applications and deploy them in a production setting, you must use integrated development environments (IDEs) and build tools.

Programming Spark

You define RDDs in code on a driver machine and Spark will then lazily evaluate and execute the RDDs across the cluster.

Spark is an optimized engine that supports general execution graphs over RDDs. In a nutshell, here are the steps for how you program something with Spark:

1. Define one or more RDDs through any of the methods available to do so, including creating them from data stored on disk (HDFS or local disk), parallelizing a collection in memory or transforming an existing RDD.
2. Invoke various operations on the RDDs by passing functions (**closures**) to each of an RDD's elements. Spark makes available to you over 80 high-level operators.
3. Perform actions such as `count`, `collect` and so on on the RDDs you derive from Step 3. Due to Spark's lazy evaluation model, computing in the cluster begins only after the actions start their work.

When Spark runs its functions on the worker nodes, it copies the variables used in that function to the worker nodes. Two types of shared variables are restricted, however:

- Broadcast variables: These variables send large sets of read-only data, such as lookup tables, to the workers once.
- Accumulators: These are variables that worker nodes may add to associative operations. The Spark driver uses them as counters, as these are read-only to the driver.

Spark's Lazy Execution Model

Spark uses a lazy execution model, which means that it will wait to process the data in an RDD until it performs an action—that is, a transformation isn't executed until the action requires it.The following example illustrates how lazy execution works.

```
scala> val mydata =sc.textFile("purplecow.txt")
scala> val mydata_uc = mydata.map(line => line.toUpperCase())
Scala> val mydata_filt = mydata_uc.filter(line => line.startWith("I")
Scala> mydata_filt.count()
3
scala>
```

In this example, there are three RDDs: `mydata`, `mydata_uc` and `mydata_filt`. All three code lines that start with `val` are assignment operations. Spark's lazy execution model means that Spark will actually process something only when you perform an **action** on an RDD—in this case, the `count()` operation on the RDD `mydata_filt`.

Chaining Transformations

Spark lets you chain transformations. You can chain all the different statements in the previous section into one simple statement in Scala:

```
scala> sc.textFile("purplecow.txt").map(line => line.toUpperCase ()).filter(line
=> line.startsWith("I").count()
```

RDD Lineage

Spark maintains the lineage of each RDD that you create (lineage in this context refers to the ancestor RDDs for an RDD). You can view the lineage of any RDD by using `toDebugString` as shown here:

```
scala>  val mydata_filt =
     | sc.textFile("purplecow.txt").
     | map(line => line.toUpperCase()).
     | filter(line => line.startsWith("I"))
16/04/27 10:52:39 INFO SparkContext: Created broadcast 0 from textFile at
<console>:22
mydata_filt: org.apache.spark.rdd.RDD[String] = MapPartitionsRDD[3] at filter at
<console>:24
scala>
Scala> mydata_filt.todeBugString
```

> **Note**
>
> Spark uses a process called pipelining while it transforms RDDs. Pipelining means that, whenever possible, Spark performs sequences of RDD transformations by row, without storing any data.

Spark Applications

A Spark application consists of a driver program, which acts as your main function and performs parallel operations on a cluster. Spark applications rely on two abstractions:

- RDDs
- Shared variables

In the following sections, you'll learn the essentials of Spark RDDs. Chapter 20, "Optimizing Spark Applicators," explains shared variables.

As alluded to previously, the heart of Spark is the RDD. An RDD is a "fault-tolerant collection of elements" that Spark works on in parallel. An RDD is an abstraction that represents a read-only collection of elements that are partitioned across a cluster's nodes and which can be operated on in parallel. The term RDD stands for the following:

- Resilient: Spark recreates the data in memory if it's lost, thus providing fault tolerance.
- Distributed: Data is distributed across a cluster and accessed via parallel operations similar to those of MapReduce.
- Dataset: You can create the dataset programmatically or get them from a data file.

Spark can also save an RDD in memory for reuse across parallel operations. RDDs are written to distributed storage such as HDFS. An RDD can also automatically recover from a node failure.

> **Note**
>
> Most of your work with Spark involves performing various operations on RDDs.

Basics of RDDs

An RDD can hold various types of elements such as the following:

- Primitive types: Integers, characters, etc.
- Sequence types: Strings, lists, arrays, dicts, etc.
- Scala and Java objects if serializable.

Creating an RDD

You can create RDDs in two ways:

- You can parallelize an existing collection in the Spark driver program (that is, from data in memory).
- You can reference an external data set stored in a relational database, HDFS or a shared file system. Any data storage system that supports the Hadoop InputFormat will do the job.

Creating an RDD with Parallelization

The Spark driver program can create a parallelized collection with the help of SparkContext's `parallelize` method. Use this method when testing your Spark programs or when you want to generate data programmatically.

The following example shows how to create a parallelized collection that holds the numbers 1 through 5.

```
val data = Array(1,2,3,4,5)
val distData = sc.parallelize(data)
```

This code creates the distributed dataset named `distData`. You can now perform operations on this dataset in parallel. For example, you add the elements of the array by calling `distData.reduce((a,b) => a + b)`.

Here's another example:

```
scala> myData = ["Alice","Nick","Sam","Nina"]
Scala> myRdd = sc.parallelize(myData)
scala> myRdd.take(2)
['Alice', 'Nick']
```

Spark automatically sets the number of partitions into which the dataset should be split (so it can work on the pieces in parallel), based on your cluster. However, you can pass a second parameter to the `parallelize` method to set the number of partitions, as shown here:

```
val distData = sc.parallelize(data, 20)
```

This example shows how to create 20 partitions to process the dataset.

Creating an RDD from a Text File

You can provide a single file, a wild carded list of files or a list of comma-separated files. Let's take a simple example to show how you can create an RDD from data inside a text file.

```
scala> val mydata = sc.textFile("purplecow.txt")
```

Figure 7.1 shows how Spark has converted the text file purplecow.txt to the RDD mydata.

All of the following are valid ways to specify the text file or files:

```
-sc.textFile("myfile.txt")
-sc.textFile("mydata/*.log")
-sc.textFile("myfile1.txt,myfile2.txt")
```

Using a relative URI, you reference a file as just myfile.txt, for example. In order to reference this file through its absolute URI, do this:

```
File://home/test/myfile.txt
```

The text file myfile.txt is for line-delimited text files only. It maps *each line* in the source text file to a separate element in the RDD you create—so, if the text file has 10,000 lines, the RDD based on this text file will have 10,000 elements.

If you have a multiline input format such as JSON, use the `sc.wholeTextfiles` method. This method maps the entire contents of a text file in a specified directory to an RDD

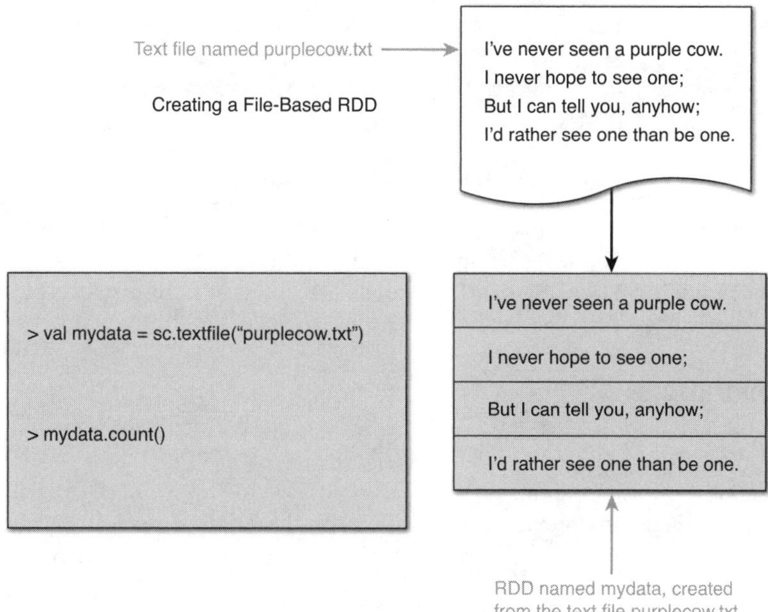

Figure 7.1 A file-based RDD

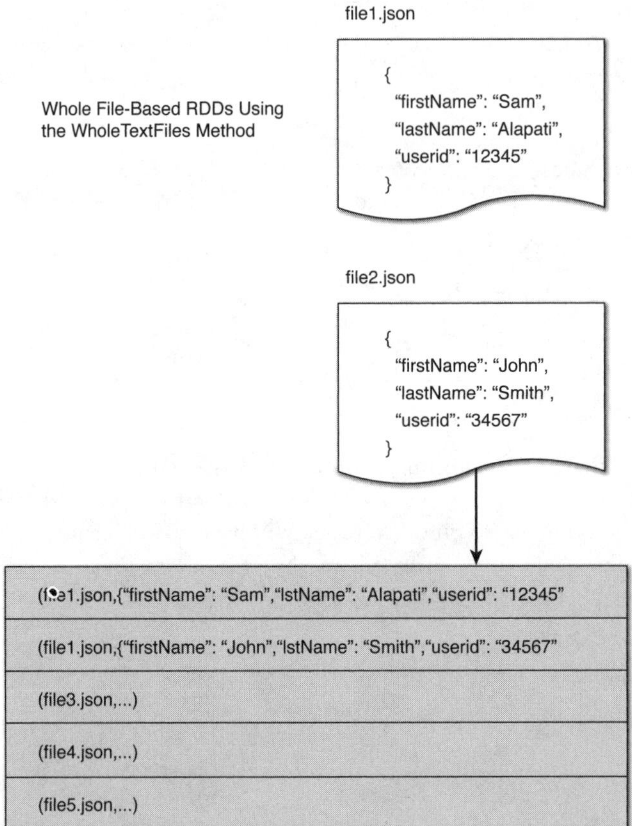

Figure 7.2 The `sc.wholeTextfiles` method.

element. That is, each file will correspond to a single RDD element. Obviously, you use this method only if the files are small, since each element must fit in memory. Figure 7.2 shows the `sc.wholeTextfiles` method in action.

RDD Operations

There are two types of operations you can perform with RDDs:

- Actions: Operations in this category just return a value from an RDD, such as the `count()` operation, for example, which returns the count of some data element.
- Transformations: These operations define a new RDD based on the RDD you're operating on.

Figure 7.3 shows the two types of RDD operations.

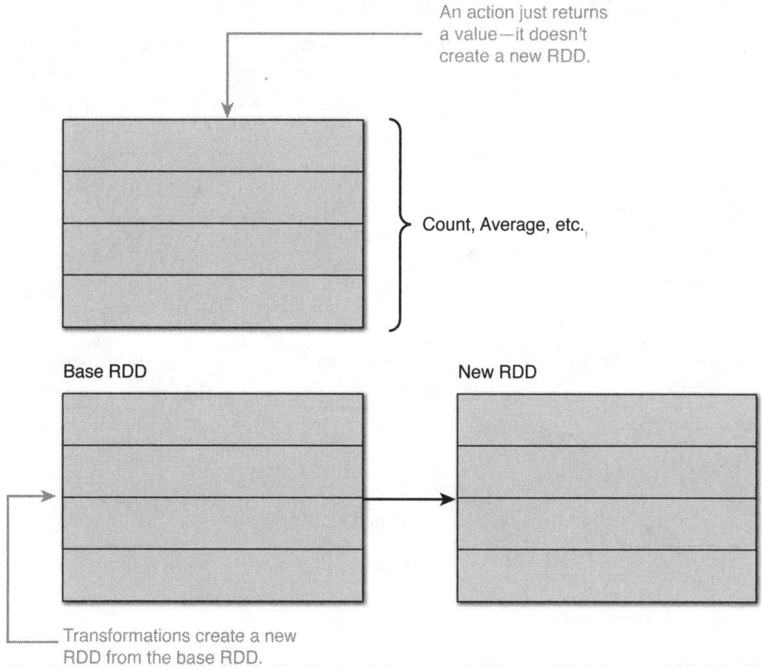
An action just returns a value—it doesn't create a new RDD.
Count, Average, etc.
Base RDD
New RDD
Transformations create a new RDD from the base RDD.

Figure 7.3 The two types of RDD operations: actions and transformations

Common RDD Operations That Involve Actions

Spark offers several RDD transformations or operations, making it easy to manipulate data. Here are a few of the RDD operations.

- `count()`: Returns the number of elements
- `saveAsTextFile(file)`: Saves to a text file
- `take(n)`: Returns the array of the first n elements
- `first`: Returns the RDD's first element
- `top(n)`: Returns the RDD's largest n elements

Here are some examples of RDD operations in action (in Scala):

```
scala> val mydata = sc.textFile ("purplecow.txt")
scala> mydata.count()
4
scala> for (line <- mydata.take(2))
          Println(line)
I've never seen a purple cow.
I never hope to see one.
```

Common RDD Operations That Involve Transformations

A transformation is a Spark action that creates a new RDD based on the RDD you're working on. Since an RDD is immutable, Spark won't change the data in the original RDD; rather, it creates a new RDD that contains the modified or transformed data.

Following are some common RDD transformations:

- `map(function)`: Returns a new RDD by running a function on each record in the original RDD.
- `sample`: Creates a new RDD as a subset (sample) of elements from the original RDD.
- `filter(function)`: Creates a new RDD by either including or ignoring records in the original RDD.
- `flatMap`: Is similar to map, but each input item can be mapped to 0 or more output items. Therefore, the function should return a sequence rather than a single item.
- `distinct`: Filters out duplicates.
- `sortBy`: Uses the function you provide to perform a sort.

Here's an example that uses two common transformation operations—`flatMap` and `distinct`:

```
sc.textFile(file) .
flatMap(line=> line.split(' ')).
distinct()
```

Figure 7.4 shows the effect of the `flatMap` and `distinct` transformations. Together they yield the unique words in a text file.

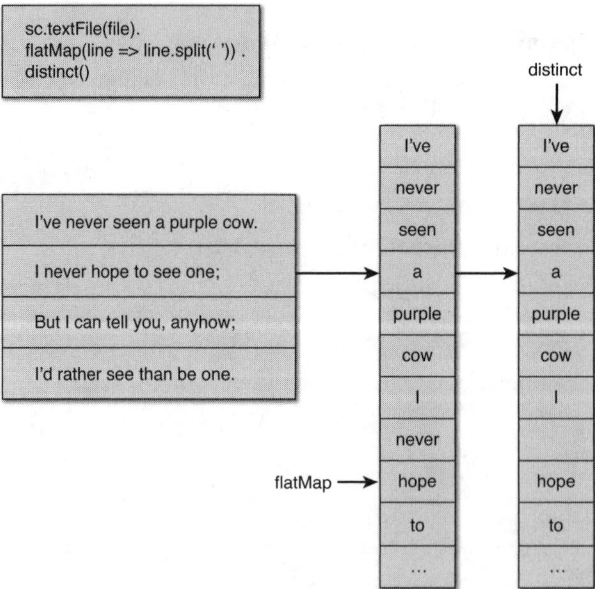

Figure 7.4 Using the `flatMap` and `distinct` transformations with a text file

RDDs with Additional Functionality

You can create two types of RDS with additional functionality compared to that of a normal RDD:

- Pair RDD: This is an RDD consisting of key/value pairs. Spark offers several operations when working with pair RDDs—it implements MapReduce with pair RDDs. However, unlike MapReduce, which lets you use only a single map and a reduce phase per job, Spark lets you chain multiple map and reduce operations, to perform algorithms such as join and sorting. There are several additional functions such as sorting, joining, grouping and counting that you can use with pair RDDs.
- Double RDD: This is an RDD that consists of numerical data. There are several double RDD functions, which are convenience functions such as the mean, sum and variance functions, that work with RDDs that are comprised of doubles.

RDD Persistence

An important capability of Spark is its capability to persist or cache a dataset in memory. Each node stores partitions of the dataset in memory and reuses them in subsequent actions on the dataset. Cached data sets, of course, speed up processing, and thus caching is a key element in the efficient computation of iterative algorithms, as well as interactive usage.

You mark an RDD for persistent storage with the `persist()` or `cache()` methods. Spark uses a fault-tolerant strategy wherein if a partition of an RDD is lost, Spark will automatically recompute it.

When you use the `cache()` method on a dataset, the default behavior is to store the data in memory. Spark also lets you persist an RDD using other storage levels. You can, for example, persist the dataset on disk or store it off-heap in Tachyon. For example, the `DISK_ONLY` storage level lets you store the RDD partitions only on disk, and the `MEMORY_AND_DISK` storage level stores RDDs as deserialized Java objects in the JVM. However, if the RDD doesn't fit in memory, it stores the partitions that don't fit on disk.

You can also choose to persist data in memory and on disk so the same dataset can be used multiple times, by specifying `.persist(StorageLevel.MEMORY_AND_DISK_SER)`. Spark will gracefully spill data to disk when datasets are too large for memory across all the worker nodes. Subsequent queries can read data directly from the persisted data rather than read the entire dataset again.

Architecture of a Spark Application

A Spark application consists of several individual components that together perform the work required by the application. In the following sections, let's learn the basic Spark terminology pertaining to application execution and understand the key components of a Spark application.

Spark Terminology

Here are the common terms used in Spark application execution, starting from the broader to the narrower units of an application:

- Application: Contains one or more jobs that are managed by a single driver
- Job: A set of tasks to be executed following an action
- Stage: A set of tasks in a job that Spark can execute in parallel
- Task: An individual unit of work that's assigned to a single executor

Components of a Spark Application

A distributed Spark application that runs in a cluster consists of five key components:

- A driver program
- A cluster manager
- Worker processes running on worker nodes
- Executors running on worker nodes
- Tasks running on worker nodes

You'll learn a bit about each of the key components of a Spark application in the following sections.

The Driver Program

A driver program is the application that contains the processing code that Spark will execute on each of the worker nodes in a cluster. The driver program can launch more than one job on the cluster.

Cluster Managers

When you run Spark in a distributed fashion over a cluster of nodes, you need a cluster manager to manage the cluster resources. As you know by now, Spark supports three types of cluster managers:

- Standalone Spark cluster
- Mesos
- YARN (Hadoop)

While both Mesos and Hadoop YARN let you run Spark and other application frameworks such as MapReduce together, our focus will be on using Spark with YARN as the cluster manager. I described all three cluster managers earlier in this chapter.

Workers

Worker processes run on each of the worker nodes in a cluster and provide the CPU, memory and storage resources necessary to execute Spark applications.

Executors

For each application, Spark creates an executor, which is a Java Virtual Machine (JVM) process, on each of the worker nodes in the cluster. The executor process executes the application code and also caches data in memory or disk storage when necessary. Each application has its own executors—when the application completes, the executor processes go away.

Tasks

A Spark task is the smallest unit of work Spark can perform within an executor. A task represents a unit of work that's sent to one executor. Executors contain multiple threads, and each task is executed by one of these threads on a worker node. Tasks perform computations and either return results or perform operations on the output such as the shuffle operation.

Jobs and Stages

A job is a parallel computation that consists of a set of tasks. The number of tasks per job depends on the number of data partitions. The number of data partitions thus determines the degree of parallelism in a Spark job.

A stage is how a job divides its tasks into smaller sets of tasks that are dependent on each other.

Running Spark Applications Interactively

You can either run a Spark application in the interactive mode through the Spark shell or submit the job. You use Spark's interactive shell to run Spark applications locally or across a distributed cluster.

Usually you use the interactive mode of running Spark applications when you are in the data exploration phase. Another common reason for doing this is when you perform ad-hoc analysis of data.

The recommended way in production most of the time is to submit the Spark application to the cluster. You use the spark-submit script to submit applications.

In this section we concentrate on running Spark applications interactively through the Spark shell.

Spark Shell and Spark Applications

Let's look at the difference between running a job through Spark shell or through Spark applications in a little more detail:

- The Spark shell is for interactive exploration and manipulation of data—you can use a Python or Scala shell.
- A Spark application is an independent program that runs on its own. You use such applications to perform heavy-duty data processing such as ETL processing and streaming. You can write a Spark application in Scala, Python or Java.

Each Spark application you run needs to be initialized. Before a Spark application can be run, it must create a `SparkContext` object. The `SparkContext` obtains the necessary information to help Spark access a cluster.

Spark's interactive shell lets you combine operators and actions in a REPL (read-evaluate-print loop) that you can evaluate on the cluster, with control returning to you. `SparkContext` gets added to your environment, which lets you start interacting with Spark and the RDDs you create and modify.

Here's how a Spark application creates a SparkContext:

```
val conf = new SparkConf().setAppName(appName).setMaster(master)
new SparkContext(conf)
```

The `master` attribute is a Spark, Mesos, or YARN cluster URL. It can also be a local "string" to run in local mode.

A Bit about the Spark Shell

The Spark shell is generally for development and testing and not for application deployment, but it's quite powerful. The Spark shell is actually a wrapper around the Scala shell. You can certainly develop applications with the Spark shell. I show you how to use the Spark shell to run a simple Spark WordCount program.

In order to run the WordCount program, I need a text file as data, which Spark will analyze to count the number of times each word occurs in that text file. Note that you can use a very large file in a compressed format if you want by loading it in HDFS first. Spark makes use of its compression codecs to unzip the file based on the file extension, such as .gz, for example.

As I mentioned earlier, you can use the interactive shell to run applications locally or across a cluster. In the following sections, I show you how to run applications locally and in a distributed fashion.

Using the Spark Shell

You use the Spark shell to work interactively with Spark. Sometimes a developer may not want to run an entire program at once—they'd like to enter each line of code to see the results. The Spark shell is ideal for those types of testing and development efforts. Internally, spark-shell invokes the spark-submit script to do its work.

> **Note**
>
> Every Spark application you run requires a SparkContext—it's the main entry point to the Spark API.

The Spark shell lets you perform interactive exploratory analysis through its REPL. The REPL interface here is a modified version of the interactive Scala REPL.

The SparkContext is the entry point to the Spark API. A special SparkContext is pre-created for you inside the Spark shell, within a variable named "sc." The following output from spark-shell shows the SparkContext named "sc" in a Scala Spark shell.

```
$ spark-shell
...
16/04/27 10:46:26 INFO SparkILoop: Created sql context (with Hive support)..
SQL context available as sqlContext.

scala>
```

> **Note**
>
> In some environments, after you enter the `spark-shell` command, the scala prompt (`scala>`) doesn't appear until you hit ENTER.

Running a Program Locally from the Spark Shell

Let's run a simple program from spark-shell so as to get our feet wet. You don't need to create a SparkContext when using the Spark shell—Spark provides a preconfigured SparkContext called "sc." When you submit applications later on with the spark-submit script, however, you must create your own SparkContext.

Follow these steps to run the WordCount program locally on a single node from spark-shell.

1. Start the Spark shell.

```
$ spark-shell
16/04/27 12:52:19 INFO HttpServer: Starting HTTP Server
Welcome to
      ____              __
     / __/__  ___ _____/ /__
    _\ \/ _ \/ _ `/ __/  '_/
   /___/ .__/\_,_/_/ /_/\_\   version 1.3.0
      /_/

Using Scala version 2.10.4 (Java HotSpot(TM) 64-Bit Server VM, Java 1.8.0_45)
Type in expressions to have them evaluated.
Type :help for more information.
16/04/27 12:52:24 INFO SparkContext: Running Spark version 1.3.0
16/04/27 12:52:25 INFO Utils: Successfully started service 'sparkDriver' on
port 29755.
16/04/27 12:52:26 INFO SparkUI: Started SparkUI at http://hadoop09.example
.com4040
16/04/27 12:52:27 INFO Client: Will allocate AM container, with 896 MB memory
including 384 MB overhead
16/04/27 12:52:27 INFO Client: Submitting application 2992 to ResourceManager
16/04/27 12:52:41 INFO SparkILoop: Created sql context (with Hive support)..
SQL context available as sqlContext.

scala>
```

2. Load the text file you want to analyze in a directory such as /tmp/words. Store the text file in this directory as test.txt.

3. Now, load the words directory as a Spark RDD.

```
scala> val words = sc.textFile("hdfs://localhost:9000/user/hduser/words")
```

4. Break up the lines in the text file into words.

```
scala> val wordsFlatMap = words.flatMap(_.split(\\w+))
```

5. For each occurrence of a word as the key, convert word to (word, 1).

```
scala> val wordsMap = wordsFlatMap.map(w => (w, 1))
```

6. Using the `reduceByKey` method, add the number of occurrences of each word as a key.

```
scala> val wordCount = wordsMap.ReduceByKey ( (a,b) => a+b))
```

7. Sort the output.

```
scala> val wordCountSorted = wordcount.sortByKey (true)
```

8. Finally, print the resulting RDD.

```
scala> wordCountSorted.collect.foreach (println)
```

9. Check the output.

You can actually run the whole thing in one fell swoop:

```
Scala> sc.textFile("hdfs://localhost:9000/user/hduser/words"),
flatMap(_.split(\\w+)).map (w => (w, 1)).reduceByKey((a,b) => a+b)).
sortByKey(true).collect.foreach(println)
```

> **Note**
>
> The applications you write and test in the local mode during development will run as is on a cluster—there's no need to change a thing. This means you can use small datasets to quickly prototype something and later run the application on a large cluster.

Running `spark-shell` on a Cluster

In the previous section I showed how to start spark-shell on a single node. You can start the Spark shell on a cluster as well. Both PySpark and spark-shell (remember there's no shell for Java) have a `--master` option that lets you specify the values `yarn`, `spark`, `mesos` or `local`. The value `local` for the master option is the default. Here are the values you can specify for the `--master` option:

- `yarn` (only in the *client* mode when using the Spark shell)
- `spark` or `mesos`: The cluster manager URL
- `local`: Run locally without distributed processing
- `local[n]`: Run locally with n worker threads
- `local[*]`: Run locally with the same number of threads as processing cores on that node (default value)

The following example shows how to start the Spark shell, in a Hadoop cluster managed by YARN, in the client mode:

```
$ spark-shell --master yarn -deploy-mode client
```

Once you get the Spark shell prompt, everything works the same way as it did in the previous example, where I showed you how to use the shell in the local mode (single node).

Overview of Spark Cluster Execution

When you submit a Spark application to a cluster (for example, YARN), Spark manages everything through the driver program of the application. The `SparkContext` object in the main program (called the driver program) manages the application, which runs as an independent set of processes on a cluster.

> **Note**
>
> In the cluster mode, the driver runs on a different server than the client.

When it runs on a cluster, the SparkContext can connect to various types of cluster managers, such as YARN. When the driver program runs, the Spark framework initializes the executor processes on the cluster's nodes where Spark will process your data.

Here's what happens when you submit an application to a cluster.

1. The driver launches and invokes the Spark application's main method (there's one in each Spark application).
2. The driver requests resources by asking the cluster manager (YARN) to launch executor processes.
3. On behalf of the driver program, the cluster manager launches the executors.
4. The driver executes the application logic and sends tasks to the executors.
5. The executors perform the actual computations by running the tasks and saving the results.
6. Once the main method exits or calls `SparkContext.stop`, the driver terminates all outstanding executors and this releases all the resources granted by the cluster manager. If you've enabled dynamic allocation, executors are released after they remain idle for a specified time after the application completes its run.

A key point to understand here is that the driver must run close to the worker nodes to take advantage of data locality.

Creating and Submitting Spark Applications

Just as you used a SparkContext when using Spark through its interactive shell, you use one when you run a Spark application. The only difference is that you create your own

SparkContext when running an application. By tradition you name the SparkContext sc, and you call sc.stop when the program ends.

Here's how our old warhorse the venerated WordCount program looks when run as a Spark application:

```
import org.apache.spark.SparkContext
import org.apache.spark.SparkContext._
object WordCount {
def main(args: Array[String]) {
if (args.length < 1) {
System.err.println("Usage: WordCount <file>")
System.exit(1)
}
val sc = new SparkContext()
val counts = sc.textFile(args(0)).
flatMap(line => line.split("\\W")).
map(word => (word,1)).reduceByKey(_ + _)
counts.take(5).foreach(println)
sc.stop()
}
}
```

Building the Spark Application

If you're building a Scala or a Java Spark application, you must compile the application and assemble it into a JAR file that you send to the worker nodes. You can use Maven (or SBT—Scala Build Tool), or an IDE such as IntelliJ or Eclipse for the builds. Here's an example:

```
$ spark-submit -master 'local[5]' -class WordCount MyJarFile.jar fileURL
```

Running an Application in the Standalone Spark Cluster

You deploy a Spark application on the standalone Spark cluster with the spark-submit script. You can run (deploy) a Spark application in one of two modes: client mode or cluster mode. The default mode is client. Following is the difference between the client and the cluster modes of operation:

- Client mode: The client here is the spark-submit script. In the client mode, the Spark application (aka the "driver program") runs in the client process that is running the spark-submit script.
- Cluster mode: In the cluster mode, the Spark application (the driver program) runs on one of the worker nodes in the cluster.

> **Note**
>
> Since the default mode is the client mode, you can skip the deploy_md parameter when running in the client mode.

You can find all the command-line options for the spark-submit script by executing the script with the -help flag:

```
# spark-submit --help
Usage: spark-submit [options] <app jar | python file> [app arguments]
Usage: spark-submit --kill [submission ID] --master [spark://...]
Usage: spark-submit --status [submission ID] --master [spark://...]
Options:
  --master MASTER_URL         spark://host:port, mesos://host:port, yarn, or
local.
  --deploy-mode DEPLOY_MODE   Whether to launch the driver program locally
("client") or
                              on one of the worker machines inside the cluster
("cluster")
 ...
```

You can launch an application in the cluster mode with the following command:

```
$ /path/to/spark/bin/spark-submit --deploy-mode cluster \
                                  --master <master-URL> \
                                  </path/to/app-jar> [app-arguments]
```

Once you launch a Spark application as shown here, the spark-submit script quits. Before it quits, though, the spark-submit script prints a submission ID.

You can use the submission-id to track the status of the driver program running on one of the worker nodes (cluster mode), as shown here;

```
$ /path/to/spark/bin/spark-submit --status <submission-id>
```

Using spark-submit to Execute Applications

Use the spark-submit script to submit jobs to a cluster. The spark-submit command is the common tool you use to submit a Spark job against *any* cluster manager, including Spark's own cluster managers, YARN or Mesos.

Here's an example that shows how to run an application through the spark-submit script for Scala and Java:

```
$ spark-submit -class WordCount MyJarFile.jar fileURL
```

Here's an example that shows how to submit a Python program with spark-submit:

```
$ spark-submit test_script.py
```

> **Note**
>
> A Spark application consists of a driver program and executors on the cluster you're using.

Using Help to Find Out the Options

Use the spark-submit -help command to view all the available options for running spark-submit. Here, I show partial output for this command to show just those settings that are relevant to a YARN cluster:

```
$ spark-submit --help
Usage: spark-submit [options] <app jar | python file> [app arguments]
Usage: spark-submit --kill [submission ID] --master [spark://...]
Usage: spark-submit --status [submission ID] --master [spark://...]
```

```
YARN-only:
  --driver-cores NUM        Number of cores used by the driver, only in cluster mode
                            (Default: 1).
  --executor-cores NUM      Number of cores per executor (Default: 1).
  --queue QUEUE_NAME        The YARN queue to submit to (Default: "default").
  --num-executors NUM       Number of executors to launch (Default: 2).
  --archives ARCHIVES       Comma separated list of archives to be extracted into the
                            working directory of each executor.
$
```

Of the flags shown here for the spark-submit script, the --master flag and the execution-related flags are crucial.

The --master flag

The --master flag is for specifying the cluster URL, and it points to the cluster manager. This flag could point to a single node (local) or to a distributed cluster. You specify the cluster URL through the --master flag. For example, you can submit a job to the Spark standalone cluster in the following way:

```
$ spark-submit --master spark: //host:7077
```

Following are the possible values you can specify for the --master flag.

- spark:host:port: Connects to a Spark standalone cluster (default port is 7077).
- mesos://host:port: Connects to a Mesos cluster (default port is 5050).
- yarn: Connects to a Hadoop cluster. The cluster location is specified by the HADOOP_CONF_DIR or the YARN_CONF_DIR environment variables. yarn-client URL is the same as yarn with -deploy-mode client. yarn-cluster URL is the same as yarn with -deploy-mode cluster.
- local: Runs in the local mode (single node). This is the default value for the --master flag.
- local(n): Runs in local mode with n cores.
- local(*): Runs in the local mode with as many nodes as the server has.

Running a Spark Application in the Local Mode

Just as you did with spark-shell, you use the spark-submit command with the --master option. By choosing the value local for the --master option, you run Spark applications locally.

You can use the following options for the local option:

- local [*]: Runs locally with the same number of threads as the processing cores (default value)
- local[n]: Runs locally with n number of threads
- local: Runs locally with just one thread

Following is an example that shows how to run a Spark application locally with five threads:

```
$ spark-submit -master 'local [5]' \  --class \
  WordCount MyJarFile.jar fileURL
```

Running Spark Applications on Mesos

The URL for the Mesos master is `mesos://host:5050`. You can run Spark applications by doing the following from a Scala program:

```
val conf = new SparkConf().setMaster("mesos://host:5050")
val SparkContext = new SparkContext(conf)
```

You can run the applications from the Spark shell by doing this:

```
$ spark-shell -master mesos://host:5050
```

Mesos can run in two modes—fine-grained and coarse grained:

- Fine-grained mode is the default, wherein each Spark task will run as a separate Mesos task.
- Coarse-grained is a mode in which there's only a single Spark task running on each Mesos server.

In order to run in the coarse-grained mode, set the following property:

```
conf.set("spark.mesos.coarse", "true")
```

Running Spark Applications in a YARN-Managed Hadoop Cluster

As in the case of a standalone cluster, YARN supports both a client and a cluster mode deployment of Spark applications. Here's how the two modes work:

- In the client mode the Spark driver program runs inside the client process that deploys the Spark application and not in the YARN cluster. The client mode operation uses the ApplicationMaster just for requesting resources from YARN (from the ResourceManager).
- In the cluster mode operation, the Spark driver program runs within the Spark-specific ApplicationMaster process, which is managed by YARN on the cluster. The client will go away after launching the application.

In order to run Spark applications in your Hadoop cluster, you must set either the `HADOOP_CONF_DIR` or the `YARN_CONF_DIR` environment variable in the spark-env.sh file, so it points to the directories where you've stored the client-side Hadoop configuration files. The configuration in this directory is used by Spark to write to HDFS storage and to connect to YARN's ResourceManager. The configuration is distributed to the entire cluster so all containers used by Spark use an identical configuration.

The following sections explain how to launch Spark applications on YARN in the client and the cluster modes.

Launching a Spark Application on YARN in the Client Mode

You launch a Spark application in the client mode with the following command:

```
$/path /to/spark/bin/spark-submit -class path.to.main.C$ spark-submt -lass  \
  --master yarn -deploy-mode client </path/to/app-jar>  [app-args]
```

Here's an example:

```
$ spark-submit --class org.apache.spark.examples.SparkPi \
             --master client \
             --deploy-mode cluster \
             --driver-memory 4g -\
             --executor-memory 2g \
             --executor-cores 1 \
             --queue myqueue \
             lib/spark-examples*.jar \
             10
```

Launching a Spark Application on YARN in the Cluster Mode

The syntax for the command to launch Spark in the YARN cluster mode is:

```
$/path /to/spark/bin/spark-submit -class path.to.main.Class  \
  --master yarn -deploy-mode cluster </path/to/app-jar>  [app-args]
```

Here's an example:

```
$ spark-submit --class org.apache.spark.examples.SparkPi \
             --master yarn \
             --deploy-mode cluster \
             --driver-memory 4g -\
             --executor-memory 2g \
             --executor-cores 1 \
             --queue myqueue \
             lib/spark-examples*.jar \
             10
```

Figure 7.5 shows how Spark runs in a Hadoop cluster managed by YARN in the cluster mode. There is one ApplicationMaster per job and a NodeManager runs on each DataNode.

Just note the following key YARN-related Spark configuration parameters for now. I'll have a lot more to say about these in Chapter 19, "Configuring and Tuning Apache Spark on YARN," which is dedicated to the tuning of Spark on YARN.

- `--num-executors`: Configures how many executors are allocated
- `--executor-memory`: Memory (RAM) allocated per executor
- `--executor-cores`: CPU cores allocated per executor

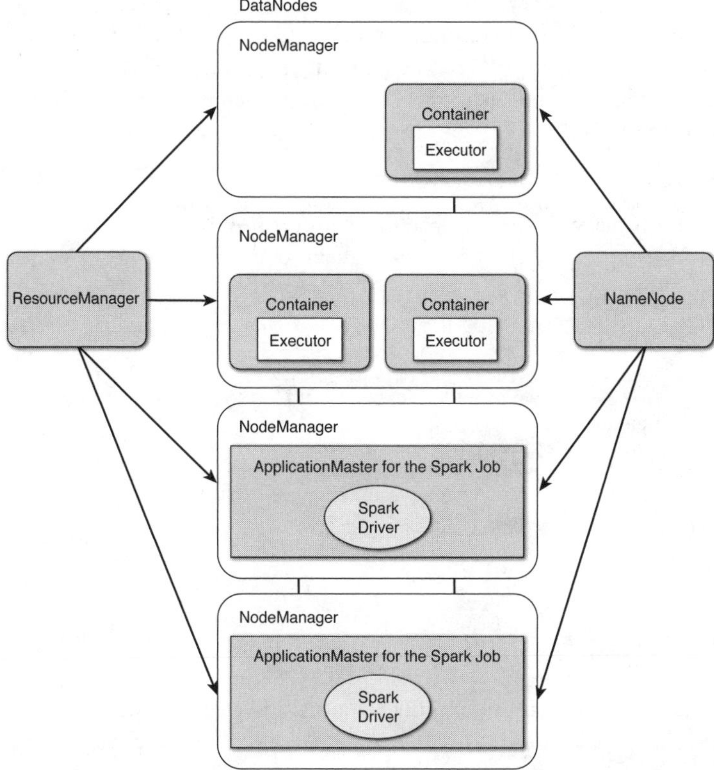

Figure 7.5 Spark on YARN in the cluster mode

HDFS and Spark

If you are using HDFS as the data source for Spark, you must include the following two files in the Spark class path:

- hdfs-site.xml: Contains default behavior for the HDFS client
- core-site.xml: Sets the default file system name

In order for Spark to see these files, you must set the `HADOOP_CONF_DIR` environment variable in the $SPARK_HOME/spark-env.sh file such that it points to the location of these two files.

Using the JDBC/ODBC Server

Spark offers a JDBC server that acts as a standalone Spark driver program that clients can share. Business intelligence (BI) tools can also connect to the Spark cluster through the JDBC server.

Spark's JDBC server works very similarly to the HiveServer2 server in Hive. As with HiveServer2, it uses the Thrift communication protocol and is called the Thrift Server.

You can start the Spark JDBC server with the start-thriftserver.sh script in the sbin directory under Spark home. As with HiveServer2, the default port is 10000. Here's how you start the JDBC server:

```
./sbin/start-thriftserver.sh --master sparkMaster
```

Once the JDBC server starts up, you can connect to it using the Beeline client program. This opens up a SQL shell that lets you run commands on the JDBC server:

```
$ ./bin/beeline -u jdbc:hive2://localhost:10000
Spark assembly has been built with Hive, including Datanucleus jars on classpath
scan complete in 1ms
Connecting to jdbc:hive2://localhost:10000
Connected to: Spark SQL (version 1.2.0-SNAPSHOT)
Driver: spark-assembly (version 1.2.0-SNAPSHOT)
Transaction isolation: TRANSACTION_REPEATABLE_READ
Beeline version 1.2.0-SNAPSHOT by Apache Hive
0: jdbc:hive2://localhost:10000> show tables;
+---------+
| result  |
+---------+
| test    |
+---------+
1 row selected (1.188 seconds)
0: jdbc:hive2://localhost:10000>
```

In the Beeline client, you can execute the usual HiveQL commands to create and query tables, such as the `CREATE TABLE` and `SHOW TABLES` commands.

> **Note**
>
> In addition to the JDBC server, Spark SQL also offers a `spark-shell` script that launches a simple shell that connects to the Hive metastore. This is okay for developing on a local basis, but in a cluster with multiple users, you must use the JDBC server with the Beeline client.

Configuring Spark Applications

So far, you've learned about launching Spark applications in various ways. As an administrator, one of your main responsibilities is to configure Spark applications so they run well—that is, they run in the most efficient manner possible, using as few resources as possible, and get done fast. Configuring Spark applications so they run optimally in a production environment requires you to learn how to set a bunch of Spark configuration properties.

Spark Configuration Properties

Chapter 19 contains a detailed explanation of all Spark configuration parameters that affect Spark application performance when running in a YARN-managed Hadoop cluster. For now, I show a couple of parameters that you can set to configure the location for storing intermediate files and to allocate memory for the executor processes.

- `spark.local.dir`: Specifies the location for storing local files such as shuffle output
- `spark.executor.memory`: Specifies how much memory is to be allocated to each executor

Specifying Configuration when Running `spark-submit`

You can declare the configuration parameters when submitting an application. You can do this in four different ways:

- By submitting them on the command line
- By explicitly setting the configuration values in a SparkConf
- Using a custom properties file
- Using the site defaults properties file

I show examples for these four options in the following sections.

Using the `spark-submit` Script

You can specify the configuration properties when you execute the `spark-submit` script as shown here, by passing the properties as flags to the `spark-submit` script:

```
$ spark-submit -driver-memory 1000M
```

Setting Properties in SparkConf

You can set some configuration properties directly in a SparkConf which you pass to your SparkContext. You can, for example, set some common properties such as the master URL and the application name in this way. Here's an example:

```
val conf = new SparkConf()
                    .setMaster("local[2]")
                    .setAppName("CountingSheep")
val sc = new SparkContext(conf)
```

Using a Properties File

When you run the `spark-submit` script, instead of specifying properties on the command line, you can specify a properties file as shown here:

```
$ spark-submit -properties-file filename
```

You must first add the configuration properties you want in the properties file you specify, as shown here:

```
spark.master       spark://masternode:7077
spark.local.dir    /tmp
spark.ui.port      4444
```

> **Note**
>
> You can view the configuration options by running `spark-submit` with the `-verbose` option—this tells you where Spark is getting the configuration properties from.

Using the Site Defaults Properties File

Spark provides a template file for specifying Spark application configuration properties. You can use this file as shown here:

```
$SPARK_HOME/conf/spark-defaults.conf
```

The precedence for evaluating the configuration properties is as follows:

1. Properties set by SparkConf
2. Properties you specify at the command line
3. Properties you set with a custom properties file
4. Properties in the site defaults properties file

Monitoring Spark Applications

You can track a Spark application through a web UI, which runs on port 4040 by default. The web UI will show

- Information relating to the running executors
- List of the scheduler stages and tasks
- Summary of the RDD sizes and the memory usage

You can get to the web UI of a running application by using the URL `http://spark_driver_HOST:4040` in your web browser.

What's interesting is that each Spark application that's running (same as a SparkContext) launches a web UI of its own, each of them using a different port starting with 4040. You can view the status of all running Spark applications in a Spark standalone cluster by going to the Spark Master UI:

```
http://spark_master:18080
```

In a YARN managed Hadoop cluster, go to the YARN applications page instead. The URLs I provided are only for tracking running applications. To view information on completed Spark applications, you need to access the Spark History Server at

```
http://spark_history_server:18088
```

Handling Streaming Data with Spark Streaming

Steaming data is the process of chopping up a continuous flow of input data into discrete units. We all use streaming data on a regular basis in our day-to-day lives. When you watch a streaming video, you don't download the entire movie at once. The movie data is streamed in small chunks that keep showing you the movie while in the background the rest of the movie is continually being downloaded.

Streams can come from various sources, such Twitter, Kafka or Flume. Streaming enables you to process data in real time (real time analytics), which is a key objective for many types of analysis, such as weather data and electronic stock trading data.

Spark Streaming is a Spark component that lets you perform real-time analytics with Apache Spark. Using its streaming capability, Spark can ingest live data streams to provide you real-time analytics with minimal latency of just a few seconds.

How Spark Streaming Works

Streaming is the continuous inflow of some data, which Spark divides into discrete time-based slices, called batch intervals, to process the data. You specify the length of the time slices when you create the `StreamingContext`. `StreamingContext` is a wrapper around SparkContext and acts as the entry point to Spark Streaming.

Each of the batches the streaming data is cut up into will end up as a separate Spark RDD. So, Spark Streaming takes streaming data, chunks it up into small batches and feeds it to the Spark engine for analysis. Figure 7.6 shows the idea behind Spark Streaming.

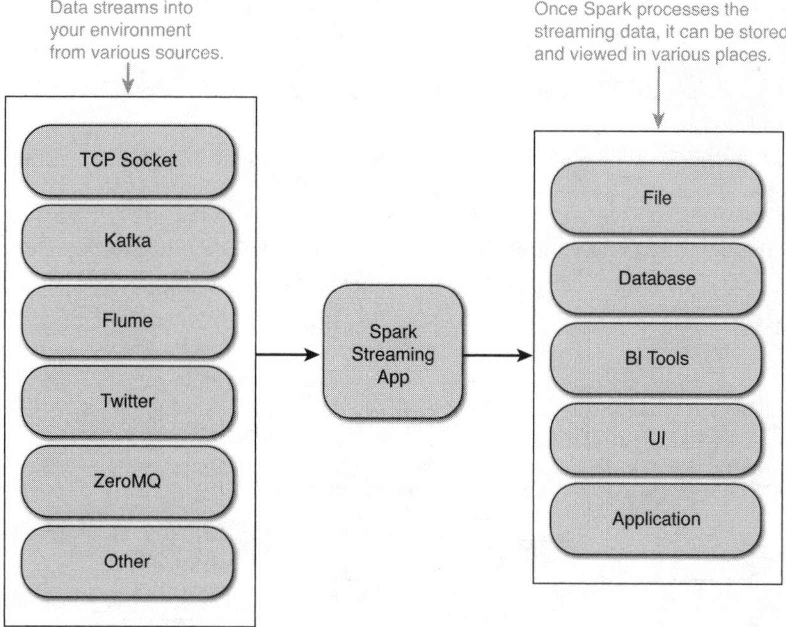

Figure 7.6 Spark Streaming—how it works

Micro-batching

When you determine a batch interval (called a micro-batch) for analyzing the streaming data, Spark Streaming gathers the incoming streaming data for the duration of the batch interval (say three seconds) and sends the data to Spark for processing. The length of the batch interval depends on how fast Spark can process the micro-batches—of course, if Spark is having a problem keeping up with data chunks for three-second intervals, you may need to raise the interval to something like five seconds.

How Spark Processes the Micro-batches

The micro-batches sent to Spark Core by Spark Steaming are of course a stream of RDDs (see Figure 7.7). Spark Streaming represents the RDDs in the form of an abstraction called a Discretized Stream (DStream). By operating on this logical entity, you'll be actually operating on the underlying RDDs.

There are two basic types of Spark Streaming sources:

- Basic sources: These include file and socket connections.
- Advanced sources: These include streaming solutions such as Apache Kafka and Apache Flume.

Windowed Computations

Using Spark Streaming's **windowed computations**, you can apply transformations over a sliding window of data. You use the following two parameters to configure the sliding window:

- Window length: This parameter specifies the duration of the window, such as 1 minute, for example.
- Sliding interval: This parameter determines the frequency of the operations, such as 10 seconds, for example.

Both the window length and sliding interval parameters must be a multiple of the batch interval. In addition, the window length needs to be a multiple of the sliding interval.

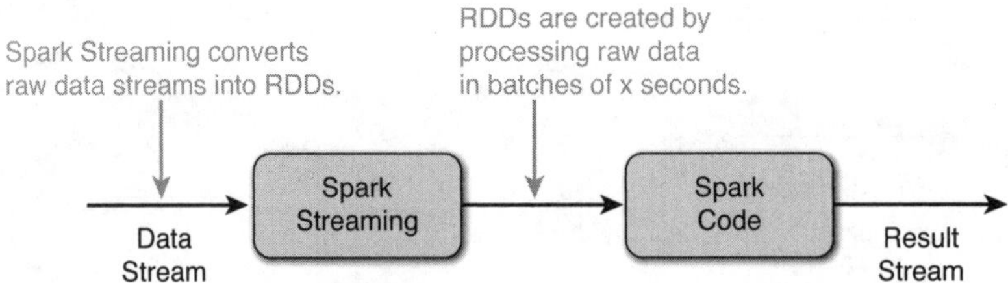

Figure 7.7 Micro-batching and Spark Streaming

A Spark Streaming Example—WordCount Again!

I use a simple streaming example where I input some text in a terminal and watch the Spark Streaming application capture the stream and process it in a different terminal. Just make sure the Spark shell has enough memory.

In one window of your server, start the Netcat server:

```
$ nc -1k 8585
```

In a different window, start up the Spark shell with sufficient memory to handle our streaming data.

```
$ spark-shell -driver-memory 1G
```

1. Perform some Spark imports for an implicit conversion:

   ```
   scala> import org.apache.spark._
   scala> import org.apache.spark.streaming._
   scala> import org.apache.spark.streaming.StreamingContext._
   ```

2. Use a three-second batch interval and create the `StreamingContext` with that value:

   ```
   scala> val ssc = new StreamingContext(sc, Seconds(3))
   ```

3. Create a `SocketTextStream` DStream on my server specifying 8585 as the port and with `MEMORY_ONLY` caching:

   ```
   scala> val lines = ssc.socketTextStream("localhost",8585)
   ```

4. Using `WordsFlatMap`, chunk the input lines into separate words:

   ```
   scala> val wordsFlatMap = lines.flatMap(_.split(" "))
   ```

5. Convert the words to (word, 1) by outputting 1 each time a word occurs as the key:

   ```
   scala> val wordsMap = wordsFlatMap.map( w => (w,1))
   ```

6. Use the `reduceByKey` method to count the number of occurrences of each word as the key:

   ```
   scala> val wordCount = wordsMap.reduceByKey( (a,b) => (a+b))
   ```

7. Start the `StreamingContext`:

   ```
   scala> ssc.start
   ```

8. On the first server where you have Netcat running, enter the following line:

   ```
   # nc -lk 8585
   to be or not to be
   ```

9. In the Spark shell, the WordCount program prints the word count for the text you entered:

   ```
   -------------------------------------------
   Time: 1461605982000 ms
   -------------------------------------------
   (not,1)
   (or,1)
   (be,2)
   (to,2)
   ```

```
16/04/25 12:39:42 INFO JobScheduler: Finished job streaming job
1461605982000 ms.0 from job set of time 1461605982000 ms
16/04/25 12:39:42 INFO ShuffledRDD: Removing RDD 51 from persistence
list
```

Twitter is a great platform for testing your Spark big data streaming applications. Over a half a billion tweets are sent each day, so you have lots of data to work with. You can bring Twitter data to Spark and make use of the live data feeds to find tweets trending in the past few minutes. It's common to use Apache Kafka, a distributed, partitioned, replicated commit log service, together with Spark Streaming.

Using Spark SQL for Handling Structured Data

You use Spark SQL for handling structured and semi-structured data. Any data that has a schema (known set of columns for each record or row) is considered structured data. Spark SQL helps you both load and query structured data.

Spark uses an abstraction called DataFrames, which are akin to relational database tables, to make it easy to work with structured data. Spark can handle many types of structured data formats such as JSON, Hive tables, Parquet files and so on.

Spark SQL lets you query the data, using SQL, in two different ways:

- You can query using SQL statements from within a Spark application.
- You can query using external BI tools such as Tableau, which can connect to Spark SQL through JDBC (or ODBC).

DataFrames

Spark SQL relies on the logical concept just alluded to, called a DataFrame, which is nothing but an extension of our old friend the RDD. DataFrames are aware of the schema of their rows. DataFrames are RDDs of row objects, with each row pointing to a record. Since a DataFrame is schema aware, it stores data much more efficiently than a simple RDD. The schema awareness of the DataFrame is what makes it possible to run SQL queries on the data.

You can create DataFrames from all of the following:

- External data sources
- Regular RDDs
- Query results

You can register the DataFrame as a table and run SQL queries off it.

HiveContext and SQLContext

Earlier, you learned how SparkContext serves as an entry point to the Spark API. Similarly, when programming with Spark SQL, you can use one of two entry points: `SQLContext` or `HiveContext`. Here are the differences between the two entry points:

- `SQLContext`: Basic and provides a subset of the Spark SQL functionality
- `HiveContext`: Provides access to HiveQL and related Hive functionality

The recommended approach is to use `HiveContext`, as HiveQL is the best way to work with Spark SQL.

Connecting Spark SQL to Hive

Spark SQL will work just fine even if you aren't currently using Hive. However, if you want to connect Spark SQL to your Hive installation, copy the Hive configuration file (hive-site.xml) to the SparkConf directory ($SPARK_HOME/conf).

Working with Spark SQL

The best way to use Spark SQL is to invoke it from within Spark applications to load and query your data.

In order to use Spark SQL from a Spark application, you must construct a `HiveContext` (assuming you want Hive-related functionality—otherwise use `SQLContext` instead) based on the SparkContext. This will enable you to use the Spark SQL functionality.

With the help of `HiveContext`, you can build DataFrames and operate on them with SQL. You can also use regular RDD operations to work with the DataFrames, since RDDs form the basis for a DataFrame.

Initializing Spark SQL

Before you can start using Spark SQL, you must initialize it by adding the following to the Spark application:

```
// Import Spark SQL
import org.apache.spark.sql.hive.HiveContext
```

You issue these commands in order to import the implicits used to convert regular RDDs into DataFrames, so you can query them. You must first construct an instance of the HiveContext:

```
// Create a Spark SQL HiveContext
val hiveCtx = ...
// Import the implicit conversions
import hiveCtx.implicits._
```

Now that you've added the imports, you're ready to create the HiveContext:

```
val sc = new SparkContext(...)
val hiveCtx = new HiveContext(sc)
```

You're now ready to load data and query it, using the HiveContext (or SQLContext).

Loading the Data

Let's load some Twitter data (JSON format) and name it by registering it as a temporary table. This will enable you to query the table named tweets in this example.

```
val input = hiveCtx.jsonFile(inputFile)
// Register the input schema RDD
input.registerTempTable("tweets")
```

> **Note**
>
> Temporary tables are what they say they are—they disappear once the Spark application exits.

Loading the data as shown here returns a DataFrame. Registering a DataFrame (using the `registerTempTable()` method) as a temporary table lets you query it through `HiveContext.sql` (or its counterpart, `SQLContext.sql`). You can reference the table with its name, if you pass a value for it thus:

```
registerTempTable("mytable").
```

Querying the Data

You can now query the data using a SQL statement as shown here:

```
// Select tweets based on the retweetCount
val topTweets = hiveCtx.sql("SELECT text, retweetCount
    FROM tweets
    ORDER BY retweetCount
    LIMIT 10")
```

Operations on DataFrames

DataFrames offer several transformations that work on themselves. Here are some basic DataFrame operations:

- `select()`: Selects specific fields or functions, as in `df.select("name. df("age")+2`
- `show()`: Shows the DataFrame's contents, as in `df.show()`
- `filter()`: Selects rows meeting a criterion, as in `df.filter(df("age") >19)`
- `groupBy`: Groups together on a column (you must add an aggregation such as `min()` or `max()` to this), as in `df.groupBy(df("name")).max()`

Creating DataFrames

Earlier, I showed an example that helped me load data into a table and query it. Loading and saving data is one way to create a DataFrame. The other is to create one from an RDD. Let me explain both methods in more detail in the following sections.

Loading and Saving Data for DataFrames

It's easy to load structured data using Spark SQL, since it lets you get data from various sources such as Hive tables, JSON and Parquet files. Spark SQL also includes a DataSource API, which lets data sources such as Avro, Cassandra, Elasticsearch and others integrate with Spark SQL. When loading data from a Hive table, Spark SQL can use all storage formats that Hive supports, such as RCFiles, ORC, Avro, Parquet and ProtoBuf (Protocol Buffers).

Using an RDD to Create a DataFrame

As with Hive, Spark SQL leverages user-defined functions (UDFs) to reduce coding burden. You can use both Spark SQL's UDFs and your current Hive UDFs.

You can register UDFs easily by passing a function:

```
hiveCtx.udf.register("strLenScala", (_: String).length)
val tweetLength = hiveCtx.sql("SELECT strLenScala('tweet') FROM tweets LIMIT 10")
```

Summary

Here's what you learned in this chapter:

- Functional programming and a lazy execution model are two important components of Spark programming.
- You perform all your work with Spark by creating, transforming and manipulating Spark RDDs.
- The Spark shell is useful for testing and interactive usage.
- Use the `spark-submit` script to run Spark applications.
- You can run Spark applications in the local or cluster mode.
- You can perform real-time analytics with Spark Streaming.
- Use Spark SQL to handle structured data.
- DataFrames are similar to relational database tables and make it easy to work with structured data.

III

Managing and Protecting Hadoop Data and High Availability

8

The Role of the NameNode and How HDFS Works

As you learned in earlier chapters, HDFS is one of the two main architectural pillars of Hadoop 2, the other being YARN. In this chapter, I start off with an explanation of the interaction between the NameNode and the DataNodes and go on to discuss the theory behind how clients read from and write to HDFS. I then discuss HDFS features such as archival storage and HDFS cache management.

This chapter discusses the following topics pertaining to HDFS:

- The interaction between the NameNode and the DataNodes
- HDFS data organization
- How clients read and write HDFS data
- HDFS recovery processes
- Hadoop archival storage

You also learn how to use advanced features such as HDFS's centralized cache management, which enables you to cache frequently used data to enhance application efficiency, and the short-circuit local reads feature, which lets clients bypass the DataNodes and read data directly from the file system.

Finally, you'll learn how to use the new Hadoop heterogeneous storage feature to optimize HDFS storage, by storing your data in multiple tiers of data storage.

HDFS—The Interaction between the NameNode and the DataNodes

HDFS is a distributed, fault-tolerant file system, explicitly designed to work with large data sets. An HDFS instance usually contains several nodes, each of which stores a small portion of its data. By its design, HDFS is suitable for batch processing rather than interactive use because the focus is on providing high throughput rather than low latency. HDFS relaxes some of the POSIX semantics to gain the increased throughput it requires. HDFS employs a write-once-read-many access mode for the files it stores. Once a file is created, written to and stored, its contents can't be modified, except for appends, thus furthering its goal of providing high throughput.

HDFS supports common file system operations such as operations that read and write files and create and delete directories. You don't need to be aware of the fact that HDFS stores multiple replicas of its data blocks. You simply refer to files and directories in HDFS by paths in the HDFS namespace. User applications access files stored in HDFS by using the HDFS *client*, which is a library that exports the HDFS file system interface.

In a Hadoop cluster, there's a single NameNode that acts as the master server, manages the file system namespace and controls client access to the files stored in HDFS. DataNodes run on almost all nodes of the cluster (they can run on every node, but it's common to designate 2-4 nodes as the master servers, to run critical services such as the NameNode and the ResourceManager) and manage the storage on each node where they run. The NameNode manages the metadata concerning HDFS files and stores it in an image file. The DataNodes manage the actual data inside an HDFS file and store the files in the servers where the DataNodes run.

HDFS stores data in HDFS files, each of which consists of a number of blocks (default size is 128MB). As you know by now, blocks are replicated on multiple DataNodes. The NameNode performs the following functions with regard to HDFS:

- Executes all HDFS operations, such as opening and closing files and directories
- Maps the blocks to the DataNodes
- Maintains the metadata, such as the files that belong to each block location of the block replicas, a file's current state and access control information

The DataNodes serve all read and write requests from clients. Upon being instructed by the NameNode, they also perform operations such as block creation and deletion, as well as replication. Clients communicate with DataNodes directly to create, read, write and transfer block replicas. The DataNode daemon maintains an open socket for communication with clients and other DataNodes. It lets the NameNode know the server and port information, so it can be sent to clients and other DataNodes. Keeping the server sockets open helps clients read and write efficiently.

Interaction between the Clients and HDFS

Applications incorporate the HDFS client library into their address space, and it's the client library that manages communications between the application on one hand and the NameNode and the DataNode on the other. HDFS exposes file block locations through its API, which enables MapReduce and other application frameworks to schedule tasks near where the data is located, making for more efficient reads. The API also enables applications to set the replication factor for its files.

NameNode and DataNode Communications

DataNodes aren't connected directly to the NameNode but communicate with them as the need occurs. Here are the ways in which DataNodes communicate with the NameNode:

- Initial registration: When the DataNode is started (or restarted), it registers with the NameNode to let it know that it's available to handle HDFS read and write operations.
- Periodic heartbeats: All DataNodes periodically (every three seconds, by default) send a heartbeat containing statistical usage information for that DataNode to the NameNode. This heartbeat lets the NameNode know that it can send commands such as block replication or deletion to the DataNodes.

  > **Note**
  >
  > The `-getDatanodeInfo` *<datanode_host:ipc_port>* command shows whether a DataNode is alive.

  If the NameNode doesn't receive a heartbeat for a long time, it requests an immediate block report from the DataNode. If the NameNode doesn't recognize the DataNode, either because the NameNode has restarted, or because the network connection with the DataNode has timed out, it asks the DataNode to register again. If a DataNode fails to send its periodic heartbeat even after a long time (such as ten minutes), the NameNode will mark that DataNode as dead and issues commands to other DataNodes to replicate the data stored on the dead DataNode, to bring the replication factor of the blocks to the configured number of replicas.
- Periodic block report: By default, each DataNode sends a block report to the NameNode every hour. The block report lets the NameNode synchronize the replica information that exists on the NameNode with that on the DataNodes. Block reports piggyback on the periodic heartbeats sent by the DataNodes to the NameNode.
- Completion of a replica write: After successfully writing a block replica, the DataNode sends a message to the NameNode.

Figure 8.1 shows how the DataNodes communicate regularly with the NameNode, sending it both a frequent heartbeat that indicates that the DataNodes are alive, as well as a periodic block report. It's this block report that the NameNode uses to build its metadata and keep it up to date.

In a high availability setup, where you have both an active and a Standby NameNode running, the DataNodes will send their block reports to both of the NameNodes. This way, the Standby NameNode is ready at all times to take over from the active NameNode. Figure 8.2 shows how the DataNodes send block reports to both NameNodes.

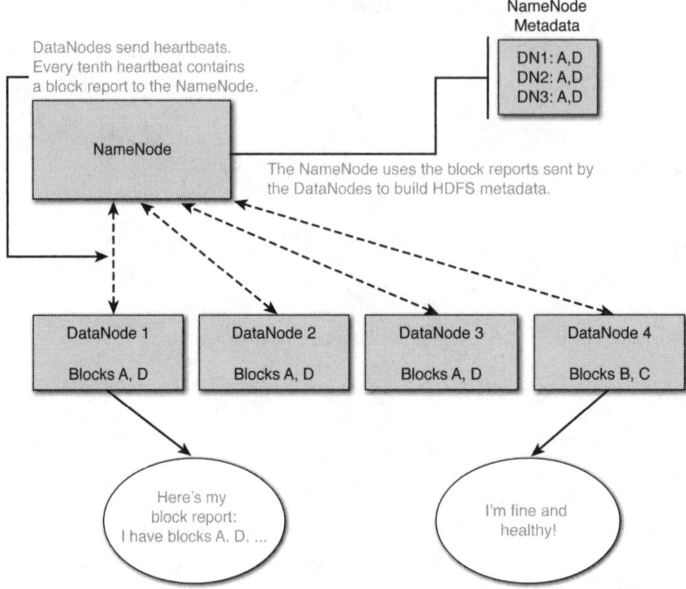

Figure 8.1 How the DataNodes send heartbeats and block reports to the NameNode

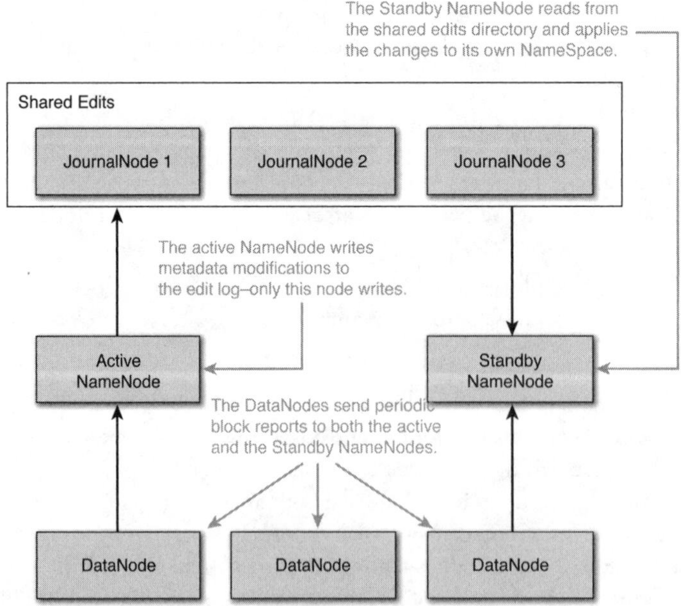

Figure 8.2 In a high availability architecture, the DataNodes send block reports to both the active and the Standby NameNodes.

Rack Awareness and Topology

Both HDFS and YARN are *rack-aware* (actually switch-aware), meaning that they have an idea as to where the cluster nodes are located relative to each other. HDFS uses rack awareness for fault-tolerance purposes, by ensuring that it places one block replica on a different rack. Thus, if a network switch fails and an entire rack goes down, you are still guaranteed access to the data.

The ResourceManager capitalizes on its rack awareness to optimally allocate resources to clients by steering them to the nodes that are closest to the data. The NameNode and the ResourceManager daemons obtain the rack information by invoking an API, which also resolves DNS names to a rack ID.

> **Note**
>
> Since Hadoop places data blocks in only two unique racks rather than three different racks (using the default replication factor of 3), total network bandwidth usage is reduced when reading data.

It's common to arrange the nodes in a Hadoop cluster into multiple racks. By default, even if you have nodes that belong to multiple racks in your cluster, Hadoop assumes that all nodes belong to the same rack.

Figure 8.3 shows how Hadoop's rack awareness helps build redundancy in a cluster by configuring multiple racks. Configuring multiple racks is beneficial, since network

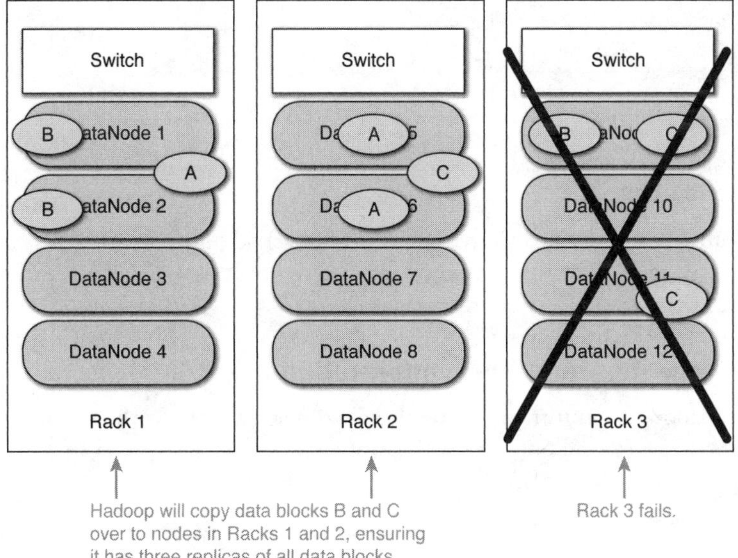
Switch
Switch
Switch
DataNode 3
DataNode 4
DataNode 7
DataNode 8
Rack 1
Rack 2
Rack 3
Hadoop will copy data blocks B and C over to nodes in Racks 1 and 2, ensuring it has three replicas of all data blocks.
Rack 3 fails.

Figure 8.3 How configuring multiple racks enhances redundancy in a cluster through rack awareness

traffic among nodes in the same rack is less intense than the traffic among nodes that belong to different racks. If you configure multiple racks, the NameNode will attempt to place data replicas on multiple racks, thus providing you with higher fault tolerance as well.

How to Configure Rack Awareness in Your Cluster

Hadoop provides a script named *topology.py* to help you configure rack awareness in your cluster. Hadoop uses the script to determine the location of nodes in a rack. The script uses a text-based control file that you edit by adding the node information (IP addresses) of all nodes in your cluster.

Once you execute the topology.py script, it uses the IP addresses you provide in the rack information file and returns a list of the rack names for each rack. In order to configure the use of the topology.py script, you must first specify the script file name in the core-site.xml file, as shown here:

```
<property>
<name>net.topology.script.file.name</name>
<value>/etc/hadoop/conf/topology.py</value>
</property>
```

And here's a sample topology.py script:

```
#!/usr/bin/env python
import sys
DEFAULT_RACK = "/prod/default-rack"
HOST_RACK_FILE = "/etc/hadoop/conf/host-rack.map"
host_rack = {}
for line in open(HOST_RACK_FILE):
   (host, rack) = line.split()
   host_rack[host] = rack
for host in sys.argv[1:]:
   if host in host_rack:
      print host_rack[host]
   else:
      print DEFAULT_RACK
```

By default, every rack in a cluster has the same rack id—*default-rack*. This means that if you don't set the `net.topology.script.file.name` parameter, Hadoop will return a value of `/default-rack` for all of the cluster nodes.

Finding Your Cluster's Rack Information

When the Hadoop administrator configures the topology script, each node in the cluster will run the script to find out its rack ID, as shown here:

```
10.1.1.160,/rack01
10.1.1.161,/rack01
10.1.1.162,/rack02
10.1.1.163,/rack02
10.1.1.164,/rack03
10.1.1.165,/rack03
```

You can execute the command dfsadmin -printTopology to access your cluster's rack information:

```
$ hdfs dfsadmin -printTopology

Rack: /prod011
   10.192.0.21:50010 (prod011node01)
   10.192.0.22:50010 (prod011node02)
   10.192.0.23:50010 (prod011node03)
   10.192.0.24:50010 (prod011node04)
...
Rack: /prod012
   10.192.0.51:50010 (prod012node01)
   10.192.0.52:50010 (prod012node02)
   10.192.0.53:50010 (prod012node03)
   10.192.0.54:50010 (prod012node04)
...
$
```

How Hadoop Distributes the Data Replicas

In small cluster architectures, all of the cluster's nodes reside in a single rack. In this case, locality is simple to determine—a node is either "on-machine" or "off-machine." Hadoop doesn't distribute the replicas of a file evenly across the racks in a cluster. When you load new data into HDFS, it places one copy in a DataNode on the local rack, the second replica in a different node on a remote rack, and the third replica on a different node on the same remote rack (assuming the default replication of three). Thus, you end up with the following distribution for the replicas:

- One third of the replicas are written to one node
- Two thirds of the replicas are written to one rack
- One third of the replicas are distributed evenly across the other racks

The goal here is to improve write performance by minimizing inter-rack writes. You're far less likely to lose an entire rack than a single node. By placing the data on two unique racks instead of three you ensure that you'll need less network bandwidth when reading data.

Regardless of where the replicas are placed, if the switch doesn't work, then the data becomes unavailable.

In a larger Hadoop setup, you'll have a larger number of nodes, distributed among multiple racks. In that situation, you should exploit the multiple-rack architecture by ensuring that the replicas of data blocks are saved on different racks to enhance data availability, even when an entire rack goes down.

Getting the Rack Information for a Cluster

You can use the commands fsck and dfsadmin to test that you have configured the rack information correctly. The fsck command should show the number of racks in your cluster at the very end of its output, as shown here:

```
$ hdfs fsck /
...
Number of data-nodes:        24
Number of racks:              3
```

```
FSCK ended at Mon Mar 02 22:11:50 CST 2015 in 42261 milliseconds

The filesystem under path '/' is HEALTHY
$
```

The `dfsadmin -report` command will also show the rack information for each node in a cluster, as shown here (partial output for a large cluster):

```
$ hdfs dfsadmin -report
Name: 10.192.0.61:50010
Hostname: hadoop012node011
Rack: /prod02
...
Last contact: Mon Mar 02 22:13:49 CST 2015

Name: 10.192.0.59:50010
Hostname: hadoop012node09
Rack: /prod01
...
Last contact: Mon Mar 02 22:13:48 CST 2015
$
```

HDFS reliability, as well as performance, depends critically on how it places the replicas. Rack-aware replica placement improves the reliability and availability of data. If you configure a rack topology by defining a rack topology script, you're protected even if an entire rack fails. Hadoop places the first copy of a data block on the same node where the client is running and the other two replicas in two different nodes from a different rack. (If the client is external to the cluster, then the first block is placed on a randomly chosen node in the cluster.) Thus, losing an entire rack all of a sudden isn't going to cause data loss. Losing multiple nodes in multiple racks could still theoretically cause data loss, but this is a highly unlikely event.

Let's say your cluster nodes are spread out among three racks. If you haven't configured the cluster with a rack topology script, Hadoop's decision without any block placement policy is to randomly write the block replicas to any three cluster nodes. This is so because in the absence of a rack topology script, Hadoop can't know in which rack a node is, so it assumes that all cluster nodes belong to the same rack.

HDFS Data Replication

HDFS organizes its data into files and directories, similar to how the Linux file system organizes its files and directories. You access HDFS files from the command line using an interface called the FS shell. Using the FS shell is somewhat similar to using other Linux shells such as the bash shell. Scripting languages can use FS shell commands to access data stored in HDFS. HDFS provides a Java API for applications, and you can also use an HTTP browser to view HDFS files.

The following sections cover

- How HDFS data is organized into data blocks
- HDFS data replication and data protection
- Block and replica states

HDFS Data Organization and Data Blocks

The primary organizational unit of storage in Hadoop is a *data block*, which is the size of the minimum chunk of data that you can write to or read from a disk. Users deal with data at the file level, but maintenance tools such as `fsck` work at the block level. The default Hadoop block size is 128MB and it's quite common to use a much larger block size such as 256MB.

The reason Hadoop uses large block sizes is because it deals with huge amounts of data, a large block size minimizes the cost of disk seeks and data transfers depend mostly on the rate at which you can transfer data (disk transfer rate). Hadoop will try to spread the chunks around among the cluster's DataNodes. If a file is smaller than the block size, it occupies only the space it needs and not the entire block.

Clients writing data to an HDFS file first write the data to a temporary local file. Once the size of that local file crosses the size of a single HDFS block, the client contacts the NameNode and requests that it create a file in HDFS. The NameNode adds the filename to the namespace and allocates a data block in HDFS for it. The NameNode informs the client of the block number and a list of DataNodes on which the block can be stored and replicated by the client.

Data Replication

Unlike many other distributed file systems, Hadoop doesn't rely on a data protection mechanism such as RAID. Instead, it replicates data on multiple nodes for reliability. In addition to providing reliability, this key strategy also multiplies the data transfer bandwidth and increases the chances of moving computation to where the data is stored, which happens to be a key principle of Hadoop.

Once the client gets the DataNode and block information from the NameNode, it flushes data from the local file to HDFS. It sends the contents of the data block from the local file to the first DataNode in the list of DataNodes it receives from the NameNode. Data replication happens simultaneously with the writing of the first copy (replica) of the data block to the first DataNode.

Each DataNode that'll store a replica (except the last one) will receive data from the previous DataNode in the list and simultaneously transmit that data to the next DataNode. As the first DataNode starts receiving the data, it writes a chunk of it to its own disks and sends it along to the second DataNode. The second DataNode, in turn, will write that portion and flush it to the third DataNode.

The NameNode sends its block replication and invalidation commands by piggybacking those commands when it replies to a DataNode heartbeat message. When a DataNode doesn't send any heartbeats for a set length of time (ten minutes by default), the NameNode assumes that the DataNode is dead, as shown in Figure 8.4. When a block is unavailable for any reason, Hadoop simply reads the block's replica from a different node. If block corruption makes one of the blocks unusable, Hadoop automatically replicates that block from one of the other good replicas.

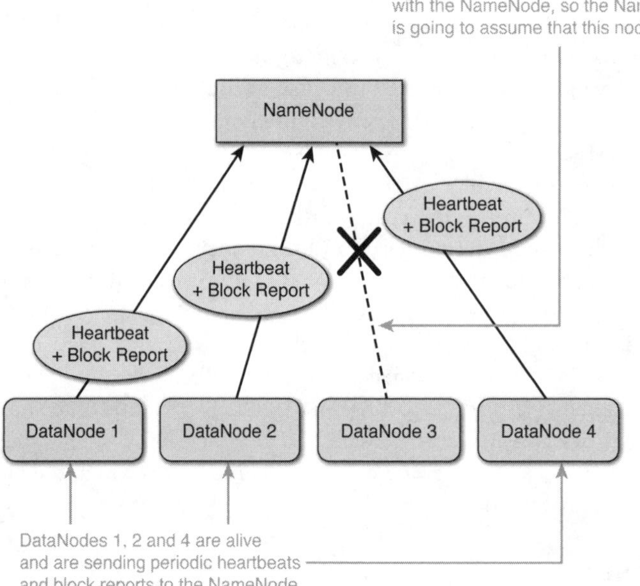

Figure 8.4 How the NameNode finds out that a DataNode isn't alive any longer, through missing heartbeats from the DataNode

A key question here is whether you should always set your replication factor to the default level of three. Three replicas are most commonly configured by users, but if the data isn't critical, you can drop the replication factor to two to save storage. On the other hand, if you're making heavy use of some files (hot files), you can configure more than three replicas, so that multiple nodes can share the load of reading the data from those hot files.

HDFS Replication Factor and Data Protection

Let's say you go with the default HDFS replication factor of three in your cluster. If one of your cluster's racks isn't reachable due to a network issue, such as a faulty switch, you can't access the replicas of the data stored on that rack.

However, processing won't really be affected as Hadoop will distribute a block on multiple racks to guard against data unavailability for any reason. Hadoop will simply go read one of the other two replicas of the data an application might need. Remember that Hadoop's policy for placing the replicas across the DataNodes in a cluster uses the following strategy:

1. Place the first replica on the same node where the client is running. If the client is running from outside the cluster, the first block is placed on a random node in the cluster.

2. Place the second replica on a DataNode in a randomly chosen rack that's different from the rack where the first node was placed.
3. Place the third replica on a random DataNode on the remote rack chosen in Step 2.

Figure 8.5 shows the Hadoop block placement policy in action. Once the faulty switch is replaced, the affected rack gradually (and automatically) rejoins the cluster. Note that no more than one replica of a block is placed on any node, and no more than two replicas are placed on any rack. Placing data on multiple racks provides security against major hardware failures. Rack awareness helps the NameNode find the blocks nearest to the client during read operations. This strategy of data locality is a key Hadoop principle.

> **Note**
>
> Remember that when you use the `hdfs dfs` commands to remove files, *all* replicas of a file are deleted, regardless of the file's replication factor.

While availability is safeguarded by the use of multiple replicas, if you lose all three replicas due to the (unlikely) failure of all DataNodes with a replica of a block, or if you accidentally delete all replicas, the data is deemed corrupted and can't be recovered.

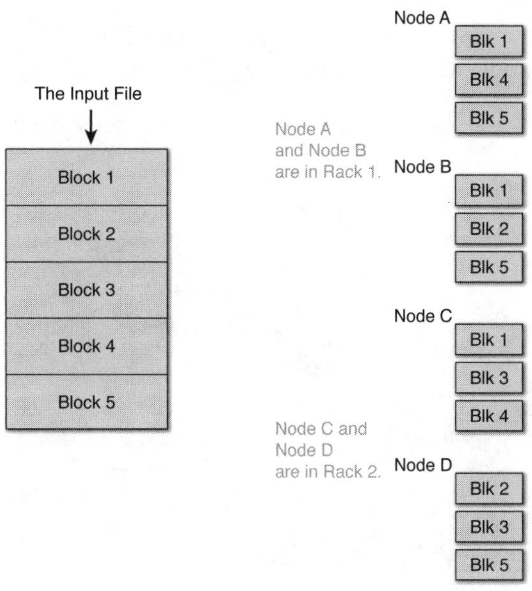

Figure 8.5 How Hadoop places multiple replicas across the DataNodes in a cluster

Block and Replica States

So, far, I've been talking about blocks and replicas as if they're synonymous—actually there's a difference. To distinguish between the two, you can refer to data being stored in blocks when referring to them with reference to the NameNode and use the term replicas to refer to the blocks that are being actually stored in the DataNodes.

Replica States

DataNodes store the replica's state to disk. A replica being stored on a DataNode can be in various states. Following are the possible replica states in a DataNode.

- Finalized: A finalized replica of a block is one where the writes to a replica are completed and the replica's length is finalized. All replicas with an identical generation stamp (GS) will have identical data.
- RBW (Replica Being Written): An RBW replica is one where data is currently being written and is always the last block of an open file. Thus the block isn't in a finalized state. It doesn't matter if the file was newly created or is being appended to.
- RWR (Replicas Waiting to be Recovered): When you restart a DataNode after a failure, all replicas on that DataNode are changed to the RWR state. These replicas eventually will be removed or participate in the lease recovery process.
- RUR (Replica Under Recovery): A replica is in this state when it's participating in block recovery.
- Temporary: A temporary replica is similar to an RBW, with the difference that clients can't see the data. If the replication of the block fails, the replica is deleted.

Figure 8.6 shows the replicas transitioning among the multiple states.

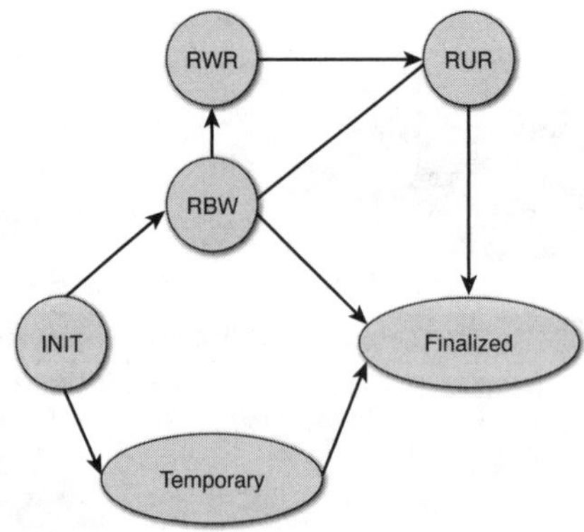

The order in which the blocks are ranked is
Finalized > RBW > RWR > RUR> Temporary.

Figure 8.6 Replica state transitioning

Where the HDFS Data Blocks Are Stored in the Linux File System

DataNodes have no awareness of HDFS files and store all HDFS data in the local file system on the servers where they run. The parameter `dfs.data.dir` in the hdfs-site.xml file specifies the local file system directories where the DataNodes store the HDFS data. The DataNodes store each block replica of HDFS data in a separate file in the local file system. Each DataNode periodically generates a lot of HDFS block replicas corresponding to each of the files on the local file system and sends a block report to the NameNode.

On each of your DataNodes, you should see the following directory layout:

```
/[mountpoint}/dfs/dn/current/{blockpool}/current
/[mountpoint}/dfs/dn/current/{blockpool}/previous
```

The following displays of the Linux file system storing HDFS data exhibit how HDFS stores its data blocks:

```
# cd current
# pwd
/u04/hadoop/dfs/current/BP-2077913507-10.192.0.21-1357858111062/current
# ls
dfsUsed  finalized  rbw  VERSION
# ls -altr
total 32
drwxr-xr-x 258 hdfs hadoop 12288 Apr 25 21:09 finalized
-rw-r--r--   1 hdfs hadoop    27 May 19 10:57 dfsUsed
drwxr-xr-x   4 hdfs hadoop  4096 May 19 10:57 .
-rw-r--r--   1 hdfs hadoop   143 May 19 10:58 VERSION
drwxr-xr-x   4 hdfs hadoop  4096 May 19 10:58 ..
drwxr-xr-x   2 hdfs hadoop  4096 May 26 03:20 rbw

# cd /u04/hadoop/dfs/current/BP-2077913507-10.192.0.21-1357858111062/current/
finalized/subdir210/subdir13
# ls -altr
total 24
-rw-r--r--   1 hdfs hadoop   2053323 May 11 13:05 blk_1096785957_1099623703765.meta
-rw-r--r--   1 hdfs hadoop 262824271 May 11 13:05
drwxr-xr-x   2 hdfs hadoop      4096 May 11 13:05 .
[root@hadoop011node16 subdir13]#
```

As you can see, each block replica in the HDFS data directory on the local file system has two files—a data file (blk_1096785957) that contains the actual data, and a small metadata file that describes the data in the data file. The block's metadata includes checksums for the data in the data file and its generation stamp. Note that the size of the data file (blk_1096785957, sized 262824271 bytes) is the same as the block size for the file (256MB in my case). If a block replica were to be half full, however, it takes up only half of the block size on the local file system.

If you need to, you can freely move the block pair of files between disks. Make sure you bring down the DataNode first, though! You may also move an entire subdirectory such as subdir999 between disks. You normally don't ever need to do this, but if there's severe space crunch in a directory, you can move the directories around without a problem.

Finalizing an Upgrade

Although you aren't supposed to see any data blocks stored in the /[mountpoint}/dfs/dn/current/{blockpool}/previous directory, you may find data in there following a failed Hadoop version upgrade or an upgrade that was not finalized as it was supposed to. You can run the following command in such a case to finalize the NameNode upgrade.

```
$ hdfs dfsadmin -finalizeUpgrade
```

Restart the NameNode after the command finishes. You'll see the following output in the DataNode logs after you run the command:

```
INFO org.apache.hadoop.hdfs.server.common.Storage: Finalizing upgrade for storage
directory
```

You'll notice that the data blocks in the "previous" directory are gone.

Block States

NameNodes don't store the state of a block to disk. Figure 8.7 shows how the blocks transition through various states. From the point of view of a NameNode, a block can be in the following states:

- Under Construction: A block is in this state while data is being written to it. A block in this state keeps track of the locations of all valid RBW replicas in the current write pipeline, as well as the locations of its RWR replicas. Readers can view the data in this block, and both the block's length and its generation stamp could change.
- Under Recovery: When a client's lease on a file expires, and the last block in that file is in the Under Construction state, when block recovery starts, the state of the file is changed to Under Recovery.
- Committed: When a client asks the NameNode to add a new block to the file it's writing to, or to close the file, blocks in the Under Construction state transition to the Committed state. In this state, the block's data and generation stamp are frozen. This state also means that the DataNodes have reported that fewer Finalized replicas exist than what's required by the replication factor.
- Complete: When enough DataNodes report that they have Finalized replicas of the same generation state and length, a block transitions from the Committed state to the Complete state. If a client requests a new block and the previous block isn't in the Complete state, the block may be forced to the Complete state even if the minimum number of replicated blocks don't exist for the block.

How Clients Read and Write HDFS Data

When working with HDFS, it's important to understand the mechanism behind a client's read and write operations. The following sections provide a high-level view of how clients actually read and write data.

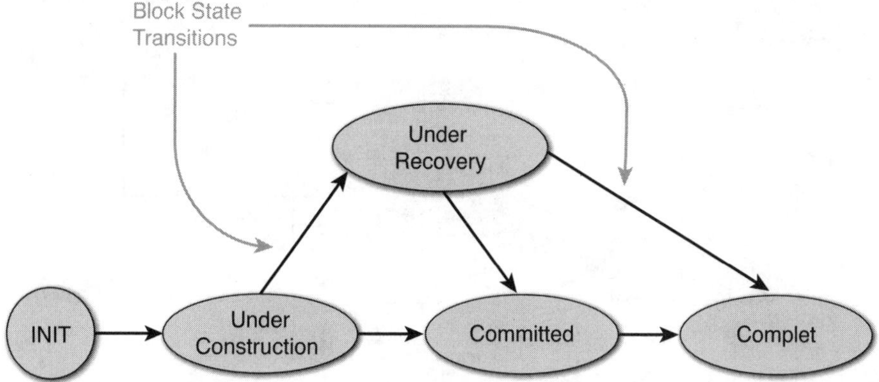

Figure 8.7 How data blocks transition through multiple states

How Clients Read HDFS Data

The following is a high-level description of the process through which clients read HDFS data.

1. When a client makes a request for reading some HDFS data, it first contacts the NameNode to find out the locations of the first few blocks of the file it wants to read.
2. The NameNode returns the addresses of all DataNodes that store a copy of those first few blocks, ranking the DataNodes in order of their closeness to the client.
3. The client then reads the data from the DataNodes in the preferential order presented to it. Should the first DataNode fail during the read (say, because the DataNode is dead), the client automatically connects to the next DataNode in the list and reads the block.
4. When the client reads the block, it also verifies that the block's current checksum is the same as the original checksum calculated when the block was first stored on disk. If the checksums differ, again the client will move to a different DataNode in the list to read the data. The client also informs the NameNode that it found a potentially corrupt block and the NameNode will replicate the corrupt block to another node. Note that by default, a DataNode will verify checksums for all blocks it stores every three weeks.
5. If the read request emanated from one of the cluster's DataNodes, the first choice of the client would be to see if that DataNode itself can satisfy the read request, without having to go to a non-local DataNode.
6. As the client starts reading through the first few blocks, it requests that the NameNode send it the locations for the next set of data blocks. The NameNode will send the best (based on proximity) list of DataNodes for each data block.

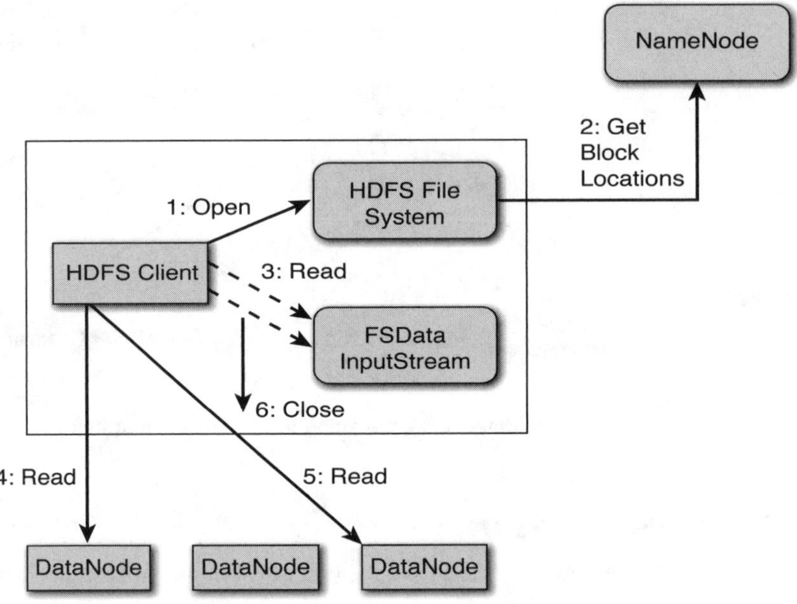

Figure 8.8 How clients read HDFS data

Figure 8.8 shows how the clients, DataNodes and NameNode interact to facilitate the reading of HDFS data.

The key things to remember here are that data blocks don't travel through the NameNode, which merely services requests from the client for the location of the data blocks. Clients contact the DataNodes to retrieve the data they are looking for. The clients request the DataNode to read the blocks and the DataNode will read the file's data blocks on disk and transmit the data to the client via TCP socket. Since the NameNode doesn't actually have to serve any data, scalability is enhanced because you can serve larger requests for data simply by adding more DataNodes to the cluster.

> **Tip**
>
> Data never travels through the NameNode during either a write or a read operation.

How Clients Write Data to HDFS

Let's first understand, in a nutshell, what happens when a client wants to write data to HDFS. When you issue a command to write to HDFS from the command line, through the web or programmatically, a number of steps are involved in writing the data, as summarized in the following list.

1. The first thing the client does is create the file and connect to the NameNode for that namespace.
2. The NameNode, after verifying that the file doesn't already exist and the client has sufficient permissions to create the file, records the new file in its metadata and sends the block name and list of DataNodes to the client. This list of DataNodes is called a pipeline, and for the default replication factor of three, there are three DataNodes in the pipeline. The pipeline specifies the DataNodes on which the clients can place the block replicas.
3. The file the client wants to write out to HDFS is split into blocks and these blocks are stored on HDFS on various DataNodes. The client connects to the first DataNode in the pipeline and starts writing the data blocks on that node.
4. The first DataNode will connect to the second DataNode in the list and forward it the data blocks as it receives them.
5. The second DataNode in turn connects to and forwards the data to the next DataNode in the pipeline.
6. When all three (by default) replicas are completely written to the client, an acknowledgment packet is relayed through the pipeline of DataNodes to the client, to indicate that the block was successfully written to all nodes. The client will start writing the next block at this point.
7. When all block replicas are written, the block is committed in the edit log by the NameNode and marked as "written."
8. When the client completes writing data to the file, it closes the file. This requires that all the file's blocks have been replicated the minimum number of times. The client may have to wait to close the file if there are any DataNode failures in the process.
9. The client informs the NameNode that the file writing was successfully completed.

Note the following:

- The writing of the block replicas is done asynchronously.
- The client doesn't have to send the data blocks it's writing to all the DataNodes. It just sends them to one of the DataNodes in the list provided by the NameNode, and it's the responsibility of that DataNode to send the data blocks along to the other DataNodes in the pipeline.
- Each DataNode will also save a checksum of each data block it stores. When this block is read, its checksum is verified to ensure that the block is complete and isn't corrupt.
- The NameNode creates metadata from the block reports it receives from the DataNodes.

Figure 8.9 shows how clients write data to HDFS files.

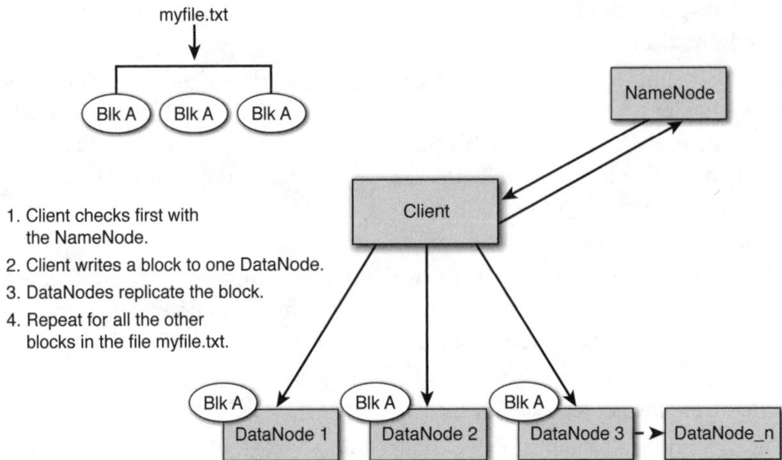

Figure 8.9 How Hadoop clients write data to HDFS files.

HDFS stores the data blocks such that the availability of one or more nodes won't cause a data loss. Hadoop automatically replicates any lost blocks. Data replication ensures both availability and data locality, which helps enforce a guiding principle of Hadoop, which is to bring processing to the data and not the other way round, as it is in traditional database systems.

How the Block Size and the Replication Factor Are Determined

The number of replicas the client stores in HDFS is based on the configuration setting `dfs.replication`, whose default value is 3. The `fs.block.size parameter` determines the block size. Any changes you make to these two parameters will affect only newly added data blocks. The settings for existing blocks already in HDFS aren't affected by these changes.

The NameNode lets the client know the configured values for both the `dfs.replication` and the `fs.block.size` parameters. Both of these parameters settings are made at the file level, and the client can override them at the file level. Based on the configured values for these parameters, the client will break up the file into the appropriate number of blocks and store the configured number of block replicas in HDFS.

Where the Client Writes the Data

Once the client receives the list of DataNodes to which they can write data from the NameNode, it writes the blocks in a sequential fashion to the nodes in that list. The way the client writes a block to multiple nodes is called *replication pipelining*. The pipelining ensures that the block writes satisfy the configured replication setting.

Whenever a client creates a new file block or opens a file for append, the write operation creates a pipeline of DataNodes to store the replicas. The replication factor for the cluster determines the number of DataNodes in this pipeline. All following writes to

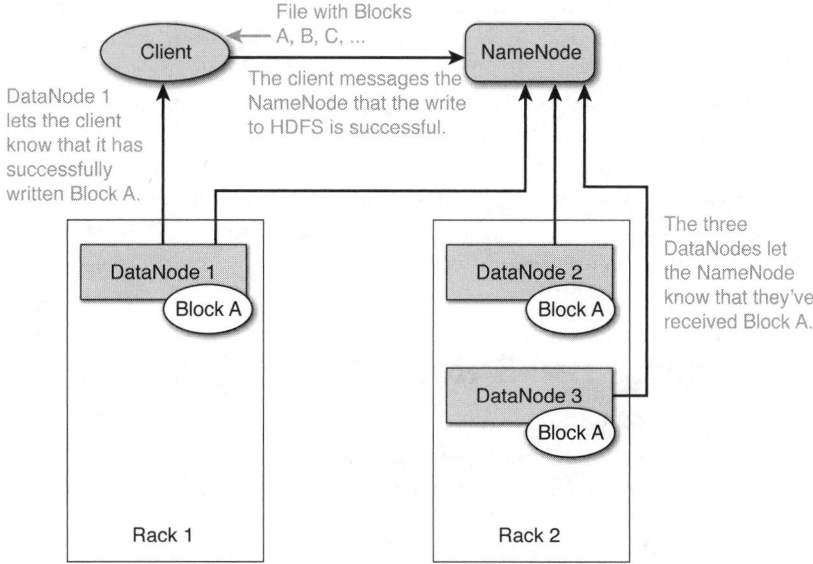

Figure 8.10 Hadoop uses data pipelining to nodes while writing data by first writing to one DataNode and having that DataNode pass the data blocks to the next DataNode in the pipeline.

that block go through the replication pipeline. Each of the DataNodes in the replication pipeline buffers each data packet as it's received and starts transferring the packets as soon as they receive a complete data packet. Regardless of the status of the transmission, the client starts to transmit the next packet, without waiting for an acknowledgment from the DataNodes. To ensure data integrity, clients also send a checksum along with the data to the DataNodes for each block they're writing to HDFS.

Once a data block is completely sent to a DataNode, it's the turn of the DataNode to report to the NameNode that it has stored the new data block. This process repeats for all subsequent blocks in a file. When all the blocks are written to HDFS, the NameNode finalizes its metadata and updates the edits file (serves as the transaction log for the main metadata file called *fsimage*).

Figure 8.10 shows how Hadoop uses data pipelining.

Considerations During a Write

The write algorithm that HDFS uses ensures that data is stored on multiple racks, and it attempts to minimize the cost of writing. The HDFS write algorithm dictates that the client should attempt to write to a specific DataNode, provided the node has enough free space and is in a healthy state.

If a DataNode in the current replication pipeline fails during the data transfer, the client moves down the list of DataNodes handed to it and picks another DataNode to write the block. The current replication pipeline is closed and another pipeline is opened with a different set of two good DataNodes, and the data is written to those two nodes. The NameNode understands that the data has been replicated only to two nodes instead of the default number of three nodes. It will replicate the data to a third node automatically to maintain the correct replication factor for the data.

Note that the write algorithm doesn't ensure that the data transfer keeps the HDFS data evenly balanced across a cluster's nodes. That's the reason you need to run the balancer yourself (explained in Chapter 9, "HDFS Commands, HDFS Permissions and HDFS Storage," in the section "Running the Balancer Tool to Balance HDFS Data") to keep HDFS data evenly distributed.

Understanding HDFS Recovery Processes

A key requirement of HDFS operations is fault tolerance. Clients such as Flume clients need to write continuously; hence, their streaming writes to HDFS must be successful, even when one or more DataNodes in a pipeline fail. HDFS must ensure that the writes don't fail.

HDFS uses the concepts of *lease recovery, block recovery* and *pipeline recovery* to provide fault tolerance by ensuring that writes are durable and consistent even when the network or the DataNodes fail in the cluster. I review these key terms in detail in the following sections. Before we do that, it's a good idea to familiarize ourselves with the concept of a *generation stamp* for a block.

The following sections cover

- Generation stamps
- Lease recovery
- Block recovery
- Pipeline recovery

Generation Stamp

The NameNode maintains a monotonically increasing 8-byte number called the generation stamp (GS) for each block. Both data blocks and replicas have a GS. If a replica's GS is older than the block's GS, it means the replica is stale. The GS is also helpful in detecting outdated replicas on long-dead DataNodes when the DataNodes rejoin the cluster.

Lease Recovery

A client is required to obtain a lease on an HDFS file before it can write to it. This lease acts as a lock on that file, preventing multiple simultaneous writes to it. As long as an HDFS client holds the lease on a file, no other client is allowed to write to the file. If the client doesn't renew the lease in a predefined length of time, the lease expires and HDFS will close the file and release the lease, so other clients obtain a lease on it for their writes. This process is called a *lease recovery*.

A lease manager in the NameNode process is in charge of management of leases, such as renewing leases and removing leases. Clients with multiple open files periodically request the NameNode to renew all the leases they currently hold.

The lease manager uses both soft and hard limits to set the expiration of leases. The soft limit is 1 minute and the hard limit is 1 hour. HDFS guarantees exclusive access to a file until the soft limit expires. If the soft limit expires and a client hasn't either renewed the lease or closed the file, another client can take over the lease. If the client hasn't renewed the lease within the hard limit of an hour, the lease manager working on behalf of the NameNode will close the lease and recover the lease. Figure 8.11 shows how lease expiries and renewals are handled.

A lease recovery can be set in motion either when the hard limit for the lease expires or when the soft limits expire. As with relational databases, writers don't block readers—when clients are writing to a file on which they hold a lease, concurrent readers can read the same file.

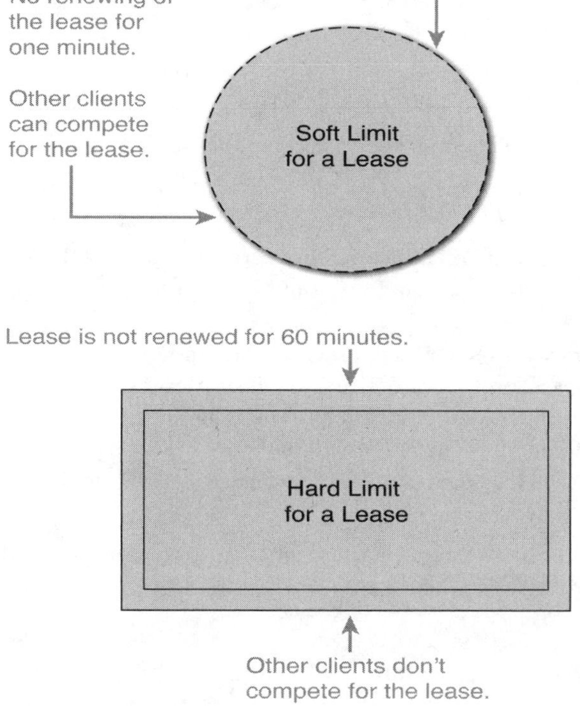

Figure 8.11 How Hadoop resolves client lease renewals

Block Recovery

Block recovery is only set in motion following a lease recovery. When a lease recovery occurs, it's possible that the last block that was being written to may not have been sent to all the DataNodes that are part of the pipeline. Block recovery is the process that ensures that when a file is closed during lease recovery, all replicas of the last block are of the same length. If the file's last block is not in the Complete state defined earlier, block recovery is triggered on that last block of the file.

For block recovery, the NameNode finds which DataNodes contain the last block of the file for which lease recovery was performed and selects one of the DataNodes as the primary DataNode. This primary DataNode coordinates the block-recovery work with the rest of the DataNodes in the pipeline, and the following steps occur:

1. The primary node gets a new generation stamp from the NameNode.
2. The primary node gets block information from each of the DataNodes.
3. The primary node computes the minimum length of the block.
4. The primary node updates the DataNodes with the new generation stamp and the minimum block length.
5. The primary node reports to the NameNode when it completes this process.
6. The NameNode updates its internal block information for the state of this block and removes the lease on the file so other writers can write to the file.
7. The NameNode commits the changes to the edit log.

Pipeline Recovery

If a DataNode fails while it's in the midst of writing to a file, HDFS attempts to recover from the error to enable the client to continue their writes to that file, in a process called *pipeline recovery*.

When a client writes to an HDFS file, it writes in sequential blocks. The data is broken up into packets of about 64K in size. That packet is made up of chunks that are usually 512 bytes in size and propagated to the DataNodes in the write pipeline, which comprises three nodes by default. How the pipeline recovery works depends on the stage in which the block finds itself in the write pipeline, the three stages being

- Setting up of the pipeline
- The data streaming stage
- The close stage

It's during the close stage that the replica is finalized and the pipeline is shut down.

If a DataNode goes bad during the flow through the pipeline, it's removed from the pipeline and the client may build a new pipeline with the surviving DataNodes. Similar to how the lease manager manages leases, a replication monitor replicates blocks to ensure that the replication factor is satisfied. During pipeline recovery, a client may or may not replace bad DataNodes when rebuilding a new pipeline.

You can configure the `dfs.client.block.write.replace-datanode-on-failure.policy` configuration parameter to influence how the DataNode replacement policy works during a pipeline failure.

In the following sections, you'll learn a bit about the three stages of the pipeline recovery process.

The Pipeline Setup Stage

The pipeline setup stage is when the clients send a write request through the pipeline and receive acknowledgments from all nodes in the pipeline, indicating that the pipeline is ready for the client to commence writing. If a pipeline encounters an error during this stage, and the client is writing a new block, the client asks the NameNode for a new block and a list of DataNodes on which it can find the blocks. Thus, a new pipeline is started instead of the failed pipeline. If, on the other hand, the pipeline was created for appending to a block, the client rebuilds the pipeline with the surviving DataNodes.

The Data Streaming Stage

Clients buffer data in packets (chunks of data) and send the data through the pipeline once the packets are filled up. How failures during the data streaming stage are handled depends on whether the client or the DataNode detects the failure. If the client detects the failure, it constructs a new pipeline with the surviving good DataNodes and starts sending data packets with a new GS. If it's the DataNode that detects the failure, it removes itself from the pipeline by closing its connections.

Close Stage

The close stage is where the replica is finalized and the pipeline is shut down. When a client sends a close request, all the DataNodes in the pipeline transition the replica into the Finalized state. Once they report this to the NameNode, if the right number of DataNodes (based on the configured replication factor) has reported a Finalized state for their replicas, it transitions the block's state to Complete.

If a client encounters a failure in the close stage, it rebuilds the pipeline with the surviving DataNodes. Each of the DataNodes will ensure that it finalizes its replica of the block.

Centralized Cache Management in HDFS

Often, several files, such as small Hive fact tables, are accessed frequently by applications. You can use Hadoop's centralized cache management to explicitly cache specific paths. You can cache data at the file or directory level. When you cache a path, the NameNode instructs the DataNodes that have the blocks in that file on their disks to cache the blocks, essentially pinning those blocks in memory.

> **Note**
>
> Tests by Cloudera's engineers show that applications such as Impala have increased their speed up to 59X when reading from cache as compared to reading from disk.

When the amount of the working set is greater than RAM, servers evict data from memory to make room for fresh data. Caching large datasets used for querying isn't as efficient, since you most likely won't be repeatedly reading those same data sets. You can consider caching data for critical workloads with stringent SLAs to keep those data sets from contending for disk I/O. Caching is especially helpful in clusters with disk contention.

Hadoop and OS Page Caching

Hadoop DataNodes already use the operating system page cache, which caches all recently accessed data on the local file system. However, in a distributed system such as Hadoop, OS page caching isn't quite adequate. Since there's no global information about the in-memory state of each DataNode, when provided a choice of multiple HDFS replicas, a client is unable to schedule its tasks for cache locality. Performance suffers, because the client schedules tasks without awareness of the cache locality.

When a client runs a query, the application scheduler chooses a block replica location and runs the task on that DataNode, pulling the replica into the OS page cache. However, the scheduler is unaware of the replicas stored in the page cache and can't place tasks to exploit the cache locality. Another problem is that since most OS page caches use a modified version of the LRU (least recently used) algorithm to determine data they should retain in memory, they are likely to evict users' working sets of data from the cache. Another reason the OS page cache isn't great is that it's less efficient than reading directly from memory, which offers "zero-read copy" performance.

The Key Principles Behind Centralized Cache Management

The NameNode's centralized cache management feature is based on the following key principles:

- Knowledge of the state of the centralized cache, which helps in scheduling jobs based on cache locality
- Predictable performance for mixed loads, due to the awareness of the cluster cache state
- Zero-copy reads made possible by pinning the current data set in the local cache instead of flushing it out to disk

The *cache pool* sets a limit on the amount of memory you can use. Users manage caching through *cache directives*. A cache directive specifies the following:

- The HDFS file or directory to cache, indicated by a path
- The cache replication factor (from 1 to the file's replication factor)
- The cache pool for the directive

How Centralized Cache Management Works

Now that you've learned the principles behind centralized cache management, it's time to learn how it actually works:

1. When an HDFS client caches a file it sends a cache directive to the NameNode, requesting it to cache that file.
2. The NameNode sends cache commands to a DataNode.
3. The DataNode sends back a cache report once it caches the data.
4. Application schedulers can find the cache information from the NameNode and schedule tasks for cache locality.

The DataNodes store the data off-heap, which means that caching large amounts of data won't adversely affect garbage collection. HDFS maps the cached blocks from the page cache into a client's address space directly, avoiding the overhead of context switching involved in repeated read system calls. Zero-copy reads are the result, and they are named thus because they spend very little time copying data, leaving most CPU cycles free for "real work." One of the other benefits of centralized cache management is that that since DataNodes checksum the data when they cache it, clients can skip the checksum verification when they read that data.

You can potentially improve the read performance of applications by co-locating tasks with a cached block replica. Applications can then query the set of cached block locations when deciding where to place the tasks. Cluster memory application is also more efficient, since you can pin only one of the three (default) replicas of a block, thus avoiding the possibility of pulling all the replicas of a block into the buffer cache, following repeated reads of a block.

The following sections cover

- Configuring caching
- Cache directives
- Cache pools
- Using the cache

Configuring Caching

You use the `hdfs cacheadmin` command-line interface to configure caching. The `cacheadmin` command lets you configure both *cache directives* and *cache pools*, which are the two key components you must configure in order to cache HDFS data.

When you implement HDFS caching, you must increase the OS limits for locked memory. Set the `dfs.datanode.max.locked.memory` parameter to the maximum amount of memory a DataNode can use for caching data. You must specify this attribute in bytes, although the memory lock limit shown with a `ulimit -l` command displays the limit in kilobytes. In a Linux system, when you set this parameter, you may also need to increase the *max locked memory* attribute in the /etc/security/limits.conf file.

Cache Directives

In order to cache a file or a directory, you must cache the appropriate path to the file or directory with a cache directive. Remember that if you cache a specific path, only the files at that level are cached and not the files underneath that directory. You can additionally specify a replication factor and expiration time when you cache a file or directory.

You add a cache directive with the `addDirective` attribute of the `cacheadmin` command. Here's the syntax:

```
$ hdfs cacheadmin -addDirective -path <path> -pool <pool-name> {force}
[-replication <replication>] [-ttl <time-to-live>]
```

As mentioned earlier, `path` refers to either a file or a directory. The `poolname` attribute points to the pool to which you want to add this directive (the following section shows how to create a cache pool). By default, the replication factor for a cached file or directory is one, but you can specify a higher replication factor if you wish. You can specify the number of replicated data blocks on specific nodes in the cluster. Also, by default, a directive never expires, but you can specify how long a directive will remain valid, with the `ttl` (time-to-live) attribute.

You can remove one or more cache directives with the `–removeDirective` or the `–removeDirectives` attribute. You can list all cache directives with the `-listDirectives` option. You can optionally specify the following:

- The `stats` flag to view the cache directive statistics
- The `path` attribute to see only the directives under a specific path
- The `pool` attribute to list just the directives in a specific cache pool

Cache Pools

You configure cache pools, which are simply administrative entities, to manage a set of cache directives. By setting appropriate permissions, you can restrict access to the pool to specific users and groups or allow users to add or remove cache directives you've configured. The total amount of memory in all cache pools in a cluster will be equal to the amount of aggregate memory you've reserved for HDFS caching.

You create a cache pool with the `addPool` attribute of the `hdfs cacheadmin` command, and I show the syntax of the command here:

```
$ hdfs cacheadmin -addPool <name> [-owner <owner>] [-group <group>] [-mode <mode>]
[-limit <limit>] [-maxTtl <maxTtl>
```

All the attributes are self-explanatory except the `limit` attribute, which is optional, and this attribute lets you specify the maximum number of bytes that can be cached by all cache directives together in this cache pool.

Once you configure HDFS block caching, MapReduce and other job frameworks can utilize the cache by scheduling jobs on the nodes where blocks are cached, reducing the need for I/O for reading data.

Using the Cache

The following example shows how create a cache pool and add a cache directive for an HDFS file.

1. Add a cache pool named testPool.

```
$ hdfs cacheadmin -addPool testPool
Successfully added cache pool testPool.
$
```

2. Add a cache directive.

```
$ hdfs cacheadmin -addDirective -path /user/test.txt -pool testPool
Added cache directive 1
$
```

3. List the pools with the -listPools command.

```
$ hdfs cacheadmin -listPools -stats testPool
Found 1 result.
NAME      OWNER  GROUP  MODE            LIMIT  MAXTTL  BYTES_NEEDED  BYTES_
CACHED  BYTES_OVERLIMIT  FILES_NEEDED  FILES_CACHED
testPool  hdfs    hdfs   rwxr-xr-x   unlimited   never          37565
37565              0             1             1
$
```

4. Issue the dfsadmin -report command to check if the report shows the cache.

```
$ hdfs dfsadmin -report
...
Non DFS Used: 0 (0 B)
DFS Remaining: 94222279700 (87.75 GB)
DFS Used%: 0.94%
DFS Remaining%: 99.06%
Configured Cache Capacity: 1908408320 (1.78 GB)
Cache Used: 40960 (40 KB)
Cache Remaining: 1908367360 (1.78 GB)
Cache Used%: 0.00%
Cache Remaining%: 100.00%
Last contact: Tue May 26 15:37:14 EDT 2015
...
$
```

The dfsadmin -report command shows that HDFS is indeed aware of the cache pool and the cache directive you created. The file *test.txt* that I cached with a directive is in the cache, since Cache Used is now 40960 bytes, whereas it was zero before I created the cache pool and the cache directive.

Short-Circuit Local Reads

If the client reading HDFS data is located on the same server as the DataNode, clients can directly read the file, which is quicker than the DataNode transmitting the data to the client. Short-circuit reads are those reads made by the clients directly from the local file system while bypassing the DataNode using UNIX domain sockets, which offer a pathway for communication between clients and DataNodes. Short-circuit reads aren't enabled by default. In order to use short-circuit reads, you need to configure the following on the client as well as on the DataNodes.

```
<property>
  <name>dfs.client.read.shortcircuit</name>
  <value>true</value>
</property>
<property>
  <name>dfs.domain.socket.path</name>
  <value>/var/lib/hadoop-hdfs/dn_socket</value>
</property>
```

Short-circuit local reads offer both improved performance and enhanced security. A key principle of Hadoop is data locality, whereby HDFS attempts to handle most reads as local reads by reading data from the same node where the client (reader) is located.

Hadoop Archival Storage, SSD and Memory (Heterogeneous Storage)

Frequently, organizations find that they have quite a bit of historical data occupying expensive storage. The typical data usage pattern in an organization is for new incoming data to be heavily used by applications, leading this data to be branded "hot." Over time, stored data is accessed a few times a week instead of several times a day, and is considered "warm" data. Over the next few weeks and months, the data usage falls even more, becoming "cold" data. If you rarely use the data, such as querying it but once or twice a year, you can even create a fourth data classification based on its age, and call this set of rarely queried older data "frozen."

Hadoop lets you assign historical data to less expensive storage, to be used as archival or cold storage, as opposed to hot or active current data. You can set up *storage policies* and transition older data from expensive and high-performing hot storage to less expensive storage with lower performance capabilities.

Hadoop 2.5, 2.6 and 2.7 all offer support for heterogeneous storage polices, where you can store HDFS data not only on the default traditional disk storage type, but also on SSD (solid state disks).

The following sections cover

- Performance characteristics of different storage types
- The architecture of heterogeneous storage
- Storage types
- Storage policies
- Implementing archival storage

Performance Characteristics of Storage Types

In order to understand heterogeneous storage policies and Hadoop archival storage, it's helpful to compare the performance characteristics of different storage types. You can compare alternative storage media on the basis of cost, the durability of the media and their performance. Cost is usually measured in cost per megabyte of storage. Durability is related to the failure rate of the storage media. Performance is measured on the basis of throughput (maximum read/write rate in megabytes/second) and I/O operations per second, which are limited by how fast the media can serve a request to read and write data.

Hard disk drives (HDD), the standard disk storage devices for Hadoop, offer a fairly high throughput and are inexpensive. The high throughput they offer is ideal for batch processing. However, disks can fail at any time.

SSDs offer great throughput and I/O per second but are several times more expensive than disk storage devices. As with disks, SSD devices have a moderate failure rate, and can fail at any time.

RAM-based storage offers extremely high performance for all types of work, but is extremely expensive. RAM doesn't provide durable storage as everything is stored in memory.

The driving factor behind using heterogeneous storage is cost—the cost per gigabyte of storage of the archive tier that has little processing power is 3-4 times cheaper than the cost of normal disk storage. Classifying your storage into multiple tiers based on the processing power of the nodes leads to an optimal use of storage. Hadoop provides a special mover tool to move some or all replicas of data blocks to a lower-cost storage as the frequency of usage of that data diminishes over time.

The Need for Heterogeneous HDFS Storage

Traditionally Hadoop was used for batch processing, where disk storage offered the high sequential throughput required by batch work. Hive and other applications that use Hadoop for interactive processing are more dependent for their performance on high random I/O performance, offered by storage such as SSD. While you can't build an entire cluster with SSD devices due to their high cost, it's ideal to have multiple storage types available in the same cluster so different types of applications can choose the storage device that's best for them.

It's common to store different types of data sets in a Hadoop cluster, with different teams running various types of workloads to process the data. Here's the typical progression of data usage over time:

- Initially, after new data is loaded, it tends to be used heavily, and the data sets are considered *hot*.
- Over a period of a few weeks or so, the frequency of usage of this data goes down and it transitions into *warm* data.
- Over a period of a few months, the data usage drops down even further, and this data is deemed *cold* data.
- Over a very long time period, this data is rarely used and can be deemed *frozen*, because it's accessed only on rare occasions.

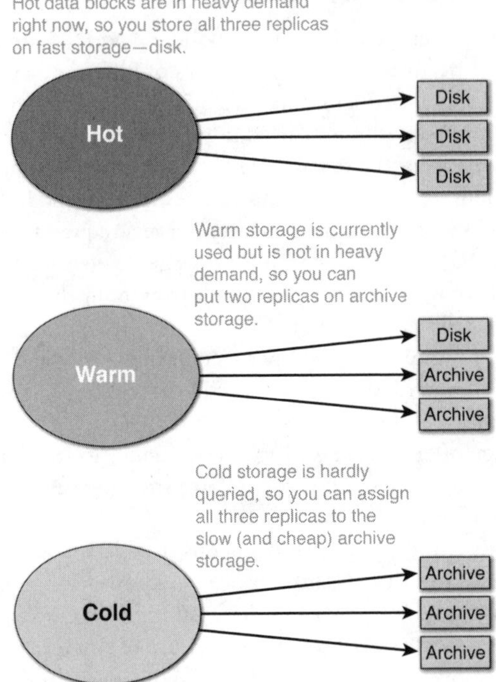

Figure 8.12 Hot, warm and cold data and how the various types of data are stored on disk and archive storage based on how recent the data is

Figure 8.12 shows the various types of data in a Hadoop cluster and how it's assigned to different types of storage. Hadoop's heterogeneous storage capability lets you create and maintain multiple tiers of storage to reflect the changing usage patterns of HDFS data over time.

Changes in the Storage Architecture

In earlier Hadoop releases, the NameNode and the HDFS clients looked upon the DataNode as a monolithic storage unit, without any awareness of the storage types used by the DataNodes. Hadoop 2.5 and later versions have made fundamental changes to the HDFS storage architecture so the DataNode lets the NameNode know the different storage types and their usage statistics. This enables the NameNode to choose a DataNode with a specific storage type when placing block replicas.

DataNodes send heartbeats (health reports) every three seconds by default using a TCP handshake to the NameNode, to announce that they're alive and in a healthy state, and this heartbeat also contains a summary storage report including the capacity and usage information. In addition, the DataNodes also send periodic block reports (listing all blocks on that DataNode) to the NameNode (every tenth heartbeat includes a block report, so block reports are made at 30-second intervals), and these reports could be full block reports or incremental block reports.

In earlier Hadoop releases, both storage reports and block reports used to contain only aggregated information about the storage types. In Hadoop 2.5 and later releases, the DataNodes show the usage statistics and block reports differentiated by the *storage types* they use.

Space quota schemes have also been extended to add per-storage-type space quotas for each HDFS directory. If a parent directory doesn't specify a per-storage-type quota, then the per-storage-type space quota you create on that directory will be enforced. If the parent directory already has a per-storage-type space quota specified for it, then the minimum space quota on the parent or subdirectory will be the space quota that HDFS will enforce. Therefore, an administrator can specify a per-storage-type space quota of zero on a parent directory to prevent the subdirectories from using any space in that specific storage type.

Storage Preferences for Files

Applications can specify a *Storage Preference* when creating a file, to send a hint to HDFS about the application's preference for where it wants the block replicas to be stored. Applications can also modify the Storage Preference for existing files. The Storage Preference can include the replication factor as well as the target storage type of the file's block replicas.

When an application specifies a Storage Preference, HDFS will try to satisfy the preference, subject to the availability of storage space as well as the availability of the space quota. If a target storage type doesn't have enough free space to satisfy a preferred storage type, a different storage type will be chosen. For example, if an application prefers the SSD storage type, and there's not enough SSD storage to go around, HDFS will store the replicas on a *fallback storage* medium such as HDD.

Setting Up Archival Storage

To enable the maintenance of different storage types, Hadoop lets you use not only disk for storage, but also alternative storage media such as SSD and memory. You can combine different storage policies with the alternative storage types to set up Hadoop archival storage in your environment.

Configuring Multiple Storage Tiers for HDFS

The HDFS administrator must configure a couple of things for implementing heterogeneous HDFS storage. Here are the configuration parameters you need to configure in the *hdfs-site.xml* file:

- `dfs.storage.policy.enabled`: This parameter lets you enable and disable heterogeneous storage policies. The default value for this parameter is true.
- `dfs.datanode.data.dir`: This parameter is set on each of the DataNodes, and you should assign the storage locations with a tag indicating the storage type. This lets the storage policies place the data blocks on different storage types according to the storage policy.

The dfs.datanaode.data.dir parameter must be familiar to you by this point—it's the parameter that specifies the local storage directories used for HDFS. Under heterogeneous storage, you can add an enum called StorageType to specify the storage tier—for example, ARCHIVE. You simply prefix the local directory location with [ARCHIVE] to denote that this directory belongs to the ARCHIVE storage tier. Here are some examples:

- Specify [DISK]file:///grid/dn/disk0 for a storage location /grid/dn/disk0 on DISK storage type.
- Specify [SSD]file:///grid/dn/ssd0 for a DataNode storage location /grid/dn/ssd0 on DISK storage type.
- Specify [ARCHIVE]file:///grid/dn/archive0 for a DataNode storage location /grid/dn/archive0 on ARCHIVE storage type.
- Specify [RAM_DISK]file:///grid/dn/ram0 for a DataNode storage location /grid/dn/ram0 on RAM_DISK storage type.

Note

If you don't tag a storage type, the default storage type of a DataNode's storage location will be the traditional DISK storage type.

Let's say your cluster has 50 nodes, each with 100TB of storage, thus giving you a total of 5PB of storage. If you now add another 20 nodes each with 100TB of storage, you can form an ARCHIVE tier by tagging this new storage as ARCHIVE. You tag the new storage by prefixing all the new local storage directories with [ARCHIVE]. You'll now have two tiers of storage in your cluster, with 5PB in the DISK tier and 2PB in the ARCHIVE tier.

Different Storage Types

Originally you could use only a single physical storage type—DISK for HDFS data. DISK is the default storage type, but now you can also use a new storage type called ARCHIVE, which has very high storage density (petabytes of storage) but low processing capabilities.

In addition to the DISK and ARCHIVE storage types, you can also use SSD and RAM_DISK as alternative storage types. Both SSD and RAM_DISK offer better performance than traditional disk storage. The ARCHIVE storage type is also disk-based storage, and supports archival storage by providing high storage density with low computing power. You can summarize the available HDFS storage types in the following way:

- DISK: The default storage type, corresponding to the standard disk-based storage used by HDFS
- ARCHIVE: Archival disk-based storage that uses densely packed storage nodes to store historical or less frequently used data

- SSD: Flash storage that uses SSD storage to store data for read/write workloads that require a low latency
- RAM_DISK: In-memory storage that provides single replica writes to RAM, with asynchronous writes to disks for persisting data

Earlier in this book, you learned how you can assign disk volumes on the host system as storage mount points for HDFS storage, by configuring the dfs.data.dir parameter in the hdfs-site.xml file. Starting with Hadoop 2.5, you can tag these storage volumes with a StorageType enum, to signify the specific type of storage the mount points represent, such as archival storage and flash storage.

The key idea here is to store heavily used (hot) data on the nodes with superior computing power in the DISK storage tier. So, if you're using the default HDFS replication factor of three, you can keep all three replicas of hot data on the DISK tier. As far as warm data is concerned, you can keep two out of the three replicas on the DISK tier and move one of the replicas to the ARCHIVE tier. For data classified as cold data, you can move two replicas to the ARCHIVE tier and keep just one replica in the DISK tier. If you have data that is almost purely historical, you can classify it as FROZEN data and move all three replicas to the ARCHIVE tier.

Multiple Storage Policies

HDFS storage polices let you store different files in different storage types, according to a predetermined policy. You can set the following types of storage policies.

- Hot: These are for data you're currently using for processing. All replicas are stored on storage type DISK.
- Cold: This is the storage with limited computing power, for data that needs to be archived, with all replicas being stored in ARCHIVE storage type–based media.
- Warm: One replica is stored on disk (DISK storage type) and the others in archive storage (ARCHIVE storage type).
- ALL_SSD: All replicas are stored in SSD (policy enforced during the creation of the file).
- ONE_SSD: One replica is stored in SSD and the other replicas in DISK (policy enforced during the creation of the file).
- Lazy_Persist: Used for writing blocks with a single replica in memory. This is meant for applications that write temporary or easily reproducible data. The replica is first sent to the RAM_DISK storage type, and later moved to DISK.

Figure 8.13 shows how a storage policy will determine how many block replicas will go on the various types of available HDFS storage.

A storage policy contains a list of storage types for placing the blocks, and there are two separate lists of storage types called fallback storage types, one for file creation and

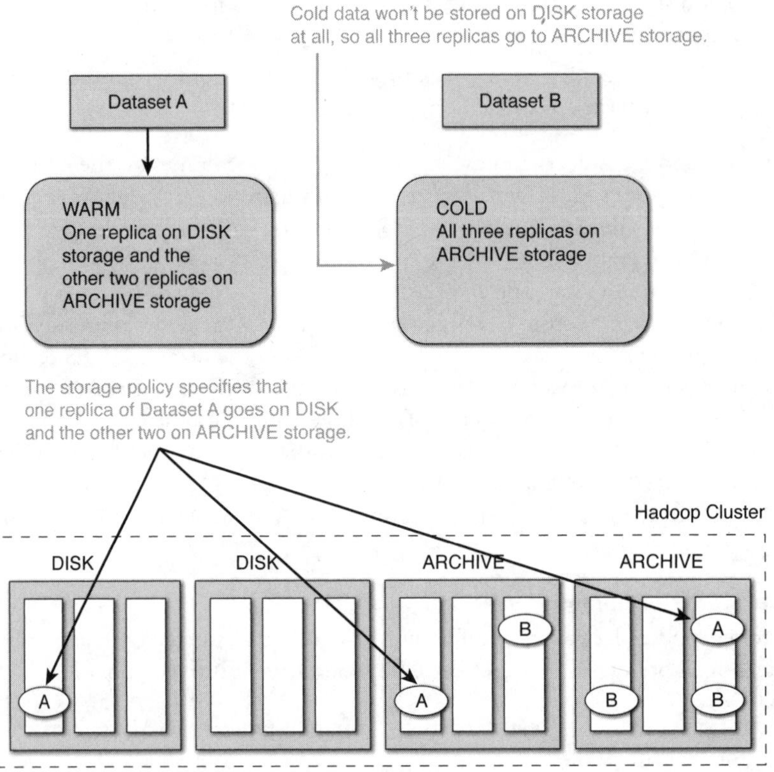

Figure 8.13 Storage policies that assign data blocks to different types of storage

the other for replication. When the storage types of block placement run out of space, blocks are placed in the fallback storage types for file creation and replication. Here's what a storage policy looks like (shows only three types of storage policies):

Policy ID	Policy Name	Block Placement (n replicas)	Fallback storage for creation	Fallback storage for replication
2	Hot (default)	DISK: n	none	ARCHIVE
5	Warm	DISK: 1, ARCHIVE: n-1	ARCHIVE, DISK	ARCHIVE, DISK
7	Cold	ARCHIVE:n	none	none

You can list all the storage policies by issuing the following command:

```
$ hdfs storagepolicies -listPolicies
```

The default storage policy is to store all replicas on DISK. The scope of a storage policy encompasses a directory and all files within that directory.

The `hdfs storagepolicies` command has other uses besides letting you find the current storage policies in place. Here's the syntax of the command:

```
$ hdfs storagepolicies
Usage: bin/hdfs storagepolicies [COMMAND]
          [-listPolicies]
          [-setStoragePolicy -path <path> -policy <policy>]
          [-getStoragePolicy -path <path>]
          [-help <command-name>]
$
```

Managing Storage Policies

As mentioned earlier, the `dfs.storage.policy.enabled` parameter is by default set to true, meaning that the storage policy feature is enabled. You can disable the feature by setting the parameter to false. When you create an HDFS directory or file, it doesn't have a storage policy attached to it. You can specify the storage policy by using the `dfsadmin -setStoragePolicy` command, as shown here:

```
$ dfsadmin -setStoragePolicy <path> <policyName>
```

In this command, the `path` attribute can refer to either a file or a directory and the `policyName` attribute must specify one of the storage polices I listed earlier.

You can determine the current storage policy for a file or a directory with the following command:

```
$ hdfs dfsadmin -getStoragePolicy <path>
```

Moving Data Around

You can migrate data from a hot to a warm and then to a cold storage policy. Note that you can move one, two or all replicas of a data set to a different storage tier to optimize your use of HDFS storage capacity. You can keep some replicas of a specific set of data on one type of storage tier and the rest on other storage types. Applications that access the data are completely oblivious to the fact that you're using multiple storage tiers. Since the `ARCHIVE` tier isn't designed to have much (or any) processing power, mapper tasks running on the nodes providing the `DISK` storage will need to read the data from the nodes providing the `ARCHIVE` storage. This of course means that your cluster will incur additional network traffic to move the data around.

Here's a summary of how storage policies work:

- When you update storage policies for a file or a directory, HDFS doesn't automatically enforce the new storage policy.
- You can not only enforce a storage policy when you create a file but also at a later time.
- When you store data for the first time in your cluster, it's stored in the default `DISK` tier.
- Based on the classification of the data (specified by the storage policies you configured), one or more replicas are moved over time to the `ARCHIVE` tier.

The new *mover* tool moves data from one storage tier to another. It works very similarly to the HDFS balancer tool, except that it moves block replicas across different storage types.

You can scan the HDFS files with the *mover* tool to determine whether the block placement matches the storage policies you've configured. If a block is not currently placed according to the storage policy you've configured, the mover will—what else—move the replicas to the appropriate storage type. Here's how you invoke the mover tool to migrate data in the cluster.

```
$ hdfs mover [-p <files/dirs> | -f <local file name>] mover
```

This command will use the root directory (/) as the default path. Here's an explanation of the key options you can specify with the mover command:

- You can specify a list of HDFS files or directories for migration by specifying the `-p` option, which accepts a space-separated list of files and directories.
- You can also use a local file with the list of HDFS files and directories to migrate the data to and specify the file with the `-f` option.
- In addition to the HDFS path and destination parameters, the mover also accepts the `replica count` as a parameter.

You can periodically run the mover to migrate all files to the storage type you configured with your storage policies.

If you've denoted some data as belonging to the `ARCHIVE` storage type and subsequently find applications using this data much more than what you had anticipated, you can reclassify that data as Warm or Cold. You can move one or more replicas to the faster `DISK` storage without incurring the additional network overhead involved in reading data from the `ARCHIVE` nodes.

Suppose the administrator applies the cold storage policy to a data set that she wants to store on the archival storage tier nodes. Since the dataset already exists, it falls to the mover to enforce the cold storage policy by moving the archived data from warm storage to cold storage. It's a good practice to move all your cold data into a Hadoop archive.

Implementing Archival Storage

You set up archival storage separately on each DataNode. Here are the steps to do so.

1. Stop the DataNode:

   ```
   $ $HADOOP_PREFIX/sbin/hadoop-daemon.sh stop datanode
   ```

2. Assign the archive storage type to the DataNode by specifying the `dfs.name.dir` parameter in the hdfs-site.xml file. Since `DISK` is the default storage type, you don't have to set `DISK` as the storage type. However, if you choose to specify a DataNode with the `ARCHIVE` storage, you must insert `[ARCHIVE]` at the beginning of the local file system path, as shown here:

```
<property>
<name>dfs.data.dir</name>
<value>[ARCHIVE]file:///u01/data/dfs/</value>
</property>
```

3. Set the storage policy with the `-setStoragePolicy` command as shown here:

```
$ hdfs dfsadmin -setStoragePolicy /cold1  COLD
```

4. Start the DataNode:

```
$ $HADOOP_PREFIX/sbin/hadoop-daemon.sh start datanode
```

5. Since you updated the storage policy on a file or directory, you must use the HDFS mover tool to migrate blocks according to the new storage policy you've configured:

```
$ hdfs move  /cold1/testfile
```

---

iNotify in HDFS

Applications that run on HDFS often use some type of indexing or cache part of the data. This means that those applications must constantly update their caches and indices as new files are added or deleted. Consequently, applications had to perform inherently inefficient periodical scans to keep themselves abreast of all HDFS changes. In Hadoop 2.6 there's a brand new feature called HDFS iNotify that sends notifications to the applications when any HDFS-related file system changes occur.

The HDFS iNotify feature is used in cases such as when an application needs to monitor file and directory changes in a Hive database. Applications such as Solr also need notifications of file and directory changes. There's a Hadoop Event Notification System offered by a third party, but with Hadoop 2.6, HDFS notifications become an integral part of Hadoop.

Summary

Here's what you learned in this chapter:

- As a Hadoop administrator, you'll be spending a lot of time working with HDFS.
- Clients, DataNodes and the NameNode interact to perform read and write operations.
- Heterogeneous storage policies help you optimize your storage profile by using appropriate storage types based on various data classifications.

There's a whole lot more to HDFS than what I discussed in this chapter! This chapter is one of four chapters in this book that deal with HDFS in depth. Chapter 9, "HDFS Commands, HDFS Permissions and HDFS Storage," Chapter 10, "Data Protection, File Formats and Accessing HDFS," and Chapter 11, "NameNode Operations, High Availability and Federation," cover several other important aspects of working with HDFS.

9

HDFS Commands, HDFS Permissions and HDFS Storage

This chapter covers the following:

- Working with HDFS
- Using HDFS shell commands
- Managing HDFS permissions and users
- Managing HDFS storage (including rebalancing of data)
- Granting users permissions and quotas

Working with HDFS is one of the most common tasks for someone administering a Hadoop cluster. Although you can access HDFS in multiple ways, the command line is the most common way to administer HDFS storage.

Managing HDFS users by granting them appropriate permissions and allocating HDFS space quotas to users are some of the common user-related administrative tasks you'll perform on a regular basis. The chapter shows how HDFS permissions work and how to grant and revoke space quotas on HDFS directories.

Besides the management of users and their HDFS space quotas, there are other aspects of HDFS that you need to manage. This chapter also shows how to perform maintenance tasks such as periodically balancing the HDFS data to distribute it evenly across the cluster, as well as how to gain additional space in HDFS when necessary.

Managing HDFS through the HDFS Shell Commands

You can access HDFS in various ways:

- From the command line using simple Linux-like file system commands, as well as through a web interface, called WebHDFS
- Using the HttpFS gateway to access HDFS from behind a firewall

- Through Hue's File Browser (and Cloudera Manager and Ambari, if you're using Cloudera, or Hortonwork's Hadoop distributions)

Figure 9.1 summarizes the various ways in which you can access HDFS. Although you have multiple ways to access HDFS, it's a good bet that you'll often be working from the command line to manage your HDFS files and directories. You can access the HDFS file system from the command line with the `hdfs dfs` file system commands.

File Systems other than HDFS

It's important to keep in mind that HDFS file systems are only one way that Hadoop implements a file system. There are several other Java implementations of file systems that work with Hadoop. These include local file systems (file), WebHDFS (WebHDFS), HAR (Hadoop archive files), View (viewfs), S3 (s3a) and others. For each file system, Hadoop uses a different URI scheme for the file system instance in order to connect with it. For example, you list the files in the local system by using the file URI scheme, as shown here:

```
$ hdfs dfs -ls file:///
```

This will get you a listing of files stored on the local Linux file system.

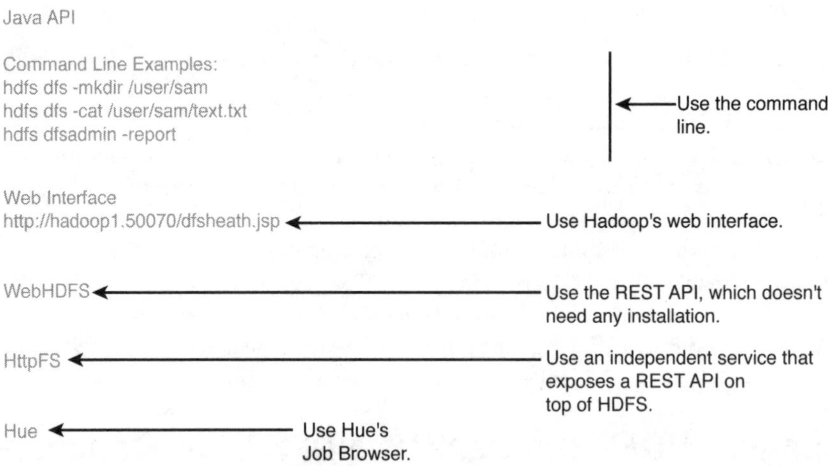

Figure 9.1 The many ways in which you can access HDFS

Using the `hdfs dfs` Utility to Manage HDFS

You use the `hdfs dfs` utility to issue HDFS commands in Hadoop. Here's the usage of this command:

```
hdfs dfs [GENERIC_OPTIONS] [COMMAND_OPTIONS]
```

Using the `hdfs dfs` utility, you can run file system commands on the file system supported in Hadoop, which happens to be HDFS.

You can use two types of HDFS shell commands:

- The first set of shell commands are very similar to common Linux file system commands such as `ls`, `mkdir` and so on.
- The second set of HDFS shell commands are specific to HDFS, such as the command that lets you set the file replication factor.

You can access the HDFS file system from the command line, over the web, or through application code. HDFS file system commands are in many cases quite similar to familiar Linux file system commands. For example, the command `hdfs dfs -cat /path/to/hdfs/file` works the same as a Linux `cat` command, by printing the output of a file onto the screen.

Internally HDFS uses a pretty sophisticated algorithm for its file system reads and writes, in order to support both reliability and high throughput. For example, when you issue a simple `put` command that writes a file to an HDFS directory, Hadoop will need to write that data fast to three nodes (by default).

You can access the HDFS shell by typing `hdfs dfs <command>` at the command line. You specify actions with subcommands that are prefixed with a minus (-) sign, as in `dfs -cat` for displaying a file's contents.

You may view all available HDFS commands by simply invoking the `hdfs dfs` command with no options, as shown here:

```
$ hdfs dfs
Usage: hadoop fs [generic options]
        [-appendToFile <localsrc> ... <dst>]
        [-cat [-ignoreCrc] <src> ...]
```

Figure 9.2 shows all the available HDFS `dfs` commands.

However, it's the `hdfs dfs -help` command that's truly useful to a beginner and even quite a few "experts"—this command clearly explains all the `hdfs dfs` commands. Figure 9.3 shows how the help utility clearly explains the various file copy options that you can use with the `hdfs dfs` command.

> **Note**
>
> Several Linux file and directory commands have analogs in HDFS. These include the familiar `ls`, `cp` and `mv` commands. However, a big difference between Linux file and HDFS file system commands is that there are no directory-location-related commands in HDFS. For example, there's no HDFS `pwd` command or `cd` command.

```
bash-3.2$ hdfs dfs
Usage: hadoop fs [generic options]
        [-appendToFile <localsrc> ... <dst>]
        [-cat [-ignoreCrc] <src> ...]
        [-checksum <src> ...]
        [-chgrp [-R] GROUP PATH...]
        [-chmod [-R] <MODE[,MODE]... | OCTALMODE> PATH...]
        [-chown [-R] [OWNER][:[GROUP]] PATH...]
        [-copyFromLocal [-f] [-p] [-l] <localsrc> ... <dst>]
        [-copyToLocal [-p] [-ignoreCrc] [-crc] <src> ... <localdst>]
        [-count [-q] [-h] <path> ...]
        [-cp [-f] [-p | -p[topax]] <src> ... <dst>]
        [-createSnapshot <snapshotDir> [<snapshotName>]]
        [-deleteSnapshot <snapshotDir> <snapshotName>]
        [-df [-h] [<path> ...]]
        [-du [-s] [-h] <path> ...]
        [-expunge]
        [-get [-p] [-ignoreCrc] [-crc] <src> ... <localdst>]
        [-getfacl [-R] <path>]
        [-getfattr [-R] {-n name | -d} [-e en] <path>]
        [-getmerge [-nl] <src> <localdst>]
        [-help [cmd ...]]
        [-ls [-d] [-h] [-R] [<path> ...]]
        [-mkdir [-p] <path> ...]
        [-moveFromLocal <localsrc> ... <dst>]
        [-moveToLocal <src> <localdst>]
        [-mv <src> ... <dst>]
        [-put [-f] [-p] [-l] <localsrc> ... <dst>]
        [-renameSnapshot <snapshotDir> <oldName> <newName>]
        [-rm [-f] [-r|-R] [-skipTrash] <src> ...]
        [-rmdir [--ignore-fail-on-non-empty] <dir> ...]
        [-setfacl [-R] [{-b|-k} {-m|-x <acl_spec>} <path>]|[--set <acl_spec> <pa
th>]]
        [-setfattr {-n name [-v value] | -x name} <path>]
        [-setrep [-R] [-w] <rep> <path> ...]
        [-stat [format] <path> ...]
        [-tail [-f] <file>]
        [-test -[defsz] <path>]
        [-text [-ignoreCrc] <src> ...]
        [-touchz <path> ...]
```

Figure 9.2 The hdfs dfs commands.

```
-copyFromLocal [-f] [-p] [-l] <localsrc> ... <dst> :
  Identical to the -put command.

-copyToLocal [-p] [-ignoreCrc] [-crc] <src> ... <localdst> :
  Identical to the -get command.

-count [-q] [-h] <path> ... :
  Count the number of directories, files and bytes under the paths
  that match the specified file pattern.  The output columns are:
  DIR_COUNT FILE_COUNT CONTENT_SIZE FILE_NAME or
  QUOTA REMAINING_QUOTA SPACE_QUOTA REMAINING_SPACE_QUOTA
        DIR_COUNT FILE_COUNT CONTENT_SIZE FILE_NAME
  The -h option shows file sizes in human readable format.

-cp [-f] [-p | -p[topax]] <src> ... <dst> :
  Copy files that match the file pattern <src> to a destination.  When copying
  multiple files, the destination must be a directory. Passing -p preserves status
  [topax] (timestamps, ownership, permission, ACLs, XAttr). If -p is specified
  with no <arg>, then preserves timestamps, ownership, permission. If -pa is
  specified, then preserves permission also because ACL is a super-set of
  permission. Passing -f overwrites the destination if it already exists. raw
  namespace extended attributes are preserved if (1) they are supported (HDFS
  only) and, (2) all of the source and target pathnames are in the /.reserved/raw
  hierarchy. raw namespace xattr preservation is determined solely by the presence
  (or absence) of the /.reserved/raw prefix and not by the -p option.
```

Figure 9.3 How the hdfs dfs -help command helps you understand the syntax of the various options of the hdfs dfs command

In the following sections, I show you how to

- List HDFS files and directories
- Use the HDFS STAT command
- Create an HDFS directory
- Remove HDFS files and directories
- Change file and directory ownership
- Change HDFS file permissions

Listing HDFS Files and Directories

As with regular Linux file systems, use the `ls` command to list HDFS files. You can specify various options with the `ls` command, as shown here:

```
$ hdfs dfs -usage ls
Usage: hadoop fs [generic options] -ls [-d] [-h] [-R] [<path> ...]
bash-4.2$
Here's what the options stand for:
-d: Directories are listed as plain files.
-h: Format file sizes in a human-readable fashion (eg 64.0m instead of 67108864).
-R: Recursively list subdirectories encountered.
-t: Sort output by modification time (most recent first).
-S: Sort output by file size.
-r: Reverse the sort order.
-u: Use access time rather than modification time for display and sorting.
```

Listing Both Files and Directories

If the target of the `ls` command is a file, it shows the statistics for the file, and if it's a directory, it lists the contents of that directory. You can use the following command to get a directory listing of the HDFS root directory:

```
$ hdfs dfs -ls /
Found 8 items
drwxr-xr-x   - hdfs   hdfs                0 2013-12-11 09:09 /data
drwxr-xr-x   - hdfs   supergroup          0 2015-05-04 13:22 /lost+found
drwxrwxrwt   - hdfs   hdfs                0 2015-05-20 07:49 /tmp
drwxr-xr-x   - hdfs   supergroup          0 2015-05-07 14:38 /user
...
#
```

For example, the following command shows all files within a directory ordered by filenames:

```
$ hdfs dfs -ls /user/hadoop/testdir1
```

Alternately, you can specify the HDFS URI when listing files:

```
$ hdfs dfs -ls hdfs://<hostname>:9000/user/hdfs/dir1/
```

You can also specify multiple files or directories with the `ls` command:

```
$ hdfs dfs -ls /user/hadoop/testdir1 /user/hadoop/testdir2
```

Listing Just Directories

You can view information that pertains just to directories by passing the -d option:

```
$ hdfs dfs -ls -d /user/alapati
drwxr-xr-x   - hdfs supergroup          0 2015-05-20 12:27 /user/alapati
$
```

The following two ls command examples show file information:

```
$ hdfs dfs -ls /user/hadoop/testdir1/test1.txt
$ hdfs dfs -ls /hdfs://<hostname>:9000/user/hadoop/dir1/
```

Note that when you list HDFS files, each file will show its replication factor. In this case, the file test1.txt has a replication factor of 3 (the default replication factor).

```
$ hdfs dfs -ls /user/alapati/
-rw-r--r--   3 hdfs supergroup         12 2016-05-24 15:44 /user/alapati/test.txt
```

Using the hdfs stat Command to Get Details about a File

Although the hdfs dfs -ls command lets you get the file information you need, there are times when you need specific bits of information from HDFS. When you run the hdfs dfs -ls command, it returns the complete path of the file. When you want to see only the base name, you can use the hdfs -stat command to view only specific details of a file.

You can format the hdfs -stat command with the following options:

```
%b  Size of file in bytes
%F  Will return "file", "directory", or "symlink" depending on the type of inode
%g  Group name
%n  Filename
%o  HDFS Block size in bytes ( 128MB by default )
%r  Replication factor
%u  Username of owner
%y  Formatted mtime of inode
%Y  UNIX Epoch mtime of inode
```

In the following example, I show how to confirm if a file or directory exists.

```
# hdfs dfs -stat "%n" /user/alapati/messages
messages
```

If you run the hdfs -stat command against a directory, it tells you that the name you specify is indeed a directory.

```
$ hdfs dfs -stat "%b %F %g %n %o %r %u %y %Y" /user/alapati/test2222
0 directory supergroup test2222 0 0 hdfs 2015-08-24 20:44:11 1432500251198
$
```

The following examples show how you can view different types of information with the hdfs dfs -stat command when compared to the hdfs dfs -ls command. Note that I specify all the -stat command options here.

```
$ hdfs dfs -ls /user/alapati/test2222/true.txt
-rw-r--r--   2 hdfs supergroup         12 2015-08-24 15:44 /user/alapati/test2222/
true.txt
$

$ hdfs dfs -stat "%b %F %g %n %o %r %u %y %Y" /user/alapati/test2222/true.txt
12 regular file supergroup true.txt 268435456 2 hdfs 2015-05-24 20:44:11 1432500251189
$
```

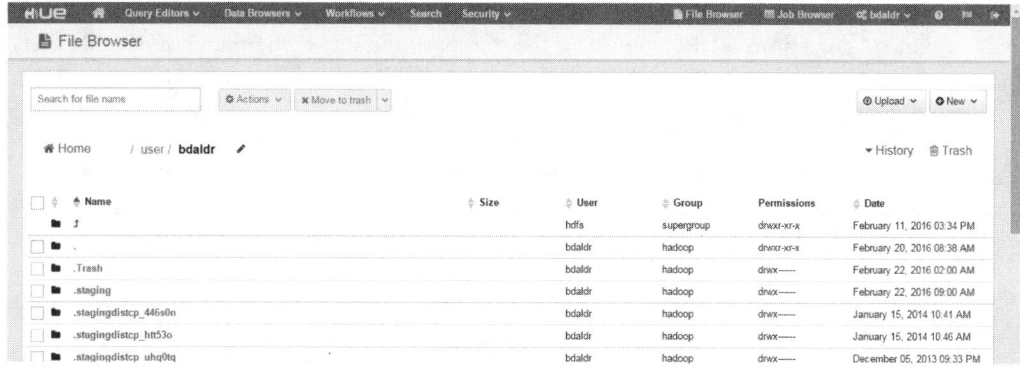

Figure 9.4 Hue's File Browser, showing how you can access HDFS from Hue

I'd be remiss if I didn't add that you can also access HDFS through Hue's Job Browser, as shown in Figure 9.4.

Creating an HDFS Directory

Creating an HDFS directory is similar to how you create a directory in the Linux file system. Issue the `mkdir` command to create an HDFS directory. This command takes path URIs as arguments to create one or more directories, as shown here:

```
$ hdfs dfs -mkdir /user/hadoop/dir1 /user/hadoop/dir2
```

The directory /user/hadoop must already exist for this command to succeed.

Here's another example that shows how to create a directory by specifying a directory with a URI.

```
$ hdfs dfs -mkdir hdfs://nn1.example.com/user/hadoop/dir
```

If you want to create parent directories along the path, specify the `-p` option, with the `hdfs dfs -mkdir` command, just as you would do with its cousin, the Linux `mkdir` command.

```
$ hdfs dfs -mkdir -p /user/hadoop/dir1
```

In this command, by specifying the `-p` option, I create both the parent directory hadoop and its subdirectory dir1 with a single `mkdir` command.

Removing HDFS Files and Directories

HDFS file and directory removal commands work similar to the analogous commands in the Linux file system. The `rm` command with the `-R` option removes a directory and everything under that directory in a recursive fashion. Here's an example.

```
$ hdfs dfs -rm -R /user/alapati
15/05/05 12:59:54 INFO fs.TrashPolicyDefault: Namenode trash configuration:
Deletion interval = 1440 minutes, Emptier interval = 0 minutes.
Moved: 'hdfs://hadoop01-ns/user/alapati' to trash at: hdfs://hadoop01-ns/user/
hdfs/.Trash/Current
$
```

I issued an `rm -R` command, and I can verify that the directory I want to remove is indeed gone from HDFS. However, the output of the `rm -R` command shows that the directory is still saved for me in case I need it—in HDFS's trash directory. The trash directory serves as a built-in safety mechanism that protects you against accidental file and directory removals. If you haven't already enabled trash, please do so ASAP!

Even when you enable trash, sometimes the trash interval is set too low, so make sure that you configure the `fs.trash.interval` parameter in the hdfs-site.xml file appropriately. For example, setting this parameter to 14,400 means Hadoop will retain the deleted items in trash for a period of ten days.

You can view the deleted HDFS files currently in the trash directory by issuing the following command:

```
$ hdfs dfs -ls /user/sam/.Trash
```

You can use the `-rmdir` option to remove an empty directory:

```
$ hdfs dfs -rmdir /user/alapati/testdir
```

If the directory you wish to remove isn't empty, use the `-rm -R` option as shown earlier.

If you've configured HDFS trash, any files or directories that you delete are moved to the trash directory and retained in there for the length of time you've configured for the trash directory. On some occasions, such as when a directory fills up beyond the space quota you assigned for it, you may want to permanently delete files immediately. You can do so by issuing the `dfs -rm` command with the `-skipTrash` option:

```
$ hdfs dfs -rm /user/alapati/test -skipTrash
```

The `-skipTrash` option will bypass the HDFS trash facility and immediately delete the specified files or directories.

You can empty the trash directory with the `expunge` command:

```
$ hdfs dfs -expunge
```

All files in trash that are older than the configured time interval are deleted when you issue the `expunge` command.

Changing File and Directory Ownership and Groups

You can change the owner and group names with the `-chown` command, as shown here:

```
$ hdfs dfs -chown sam:produsers  /data/customers/names.txt
```

You must be a super user to modify the ownership of files and directories.

HDFS file permissions work very similar to the way you modify file and directory permissions in Linux. Figure 9.5 shows how to issue the familiar `chmod`, `chown` and `chgrp` commands in HDFS.

```
bash-3.2$ hdfs dfs -chmod 600 /user/sg221771/test2222/test1.txt
bash-3.2$  hdfs dfs -chown sg221771:sg221771 /user/sg221771/test2222/test1.txt
bash-3.2$  hdfs dfs -chgrp hadoop  /user/sg221771/test2222/test1.txt
bash-3.2$
```

Figure 9.5 Changing file mode, ownership and group with HDFS commands

Changing Groups

You can change just the group of a user with the chgrp command, as shown here:

```
$ sudo -u hdfs hdfs dfs -chgrp marketing /users/sales/markets.txt
```

Changing HDFS File Permissions

You can use the chmod command to change the permissions of a file or directory. You can use standard Linux file permissions. Here's the general syntax for using the chmod command:

```
hdfs dfs -chmod [-R] <mode> <file/dir>
```

You must be a super user or the owner of a file or directory to change its permissions.

With the chgrp, chmod and chown commands you can specify the -R option to make recursive changes through the directory structure you specify.

In this section, I'm using HDFS commands from the command line to view and manipulate HDFS files and directories. However, there's an even easier way to access HDFS, and that's through Hue, the web-based interface, which is extremely easy to use and which lets you perform HDFS operations through a GUI. Hue comes with a File Browser application that lets you list and create files and directories, download and upload files from HDFS and copy/move files. You can also use Hue's File Browser to view the output of your MapReduce jobs, Hive queries and Pig scripts.

While the hdfs dfs utility lets you manage the HDFS files and directories, the hdfs dfsadmin utility lets you perform key HDFS administrative tasks. In the next section, you'll learn how to work with the dfsadmin utility to manage your cluster.

Using the dfsadmin Utility to Perform HDFS Operations

The hdfs dfsadmin command lets you administer HDFS from the command line. While the hdfs dfs commands you learned about in the previous section help you manage HDFS files and directories, the dfsadmin command is useful for performing general HDFS-specific administrative tasks. It's a good idea to become familiar with all the options that are available for the dfsadmin utility by issuing the following command:

```
$ hdfs dfsadmin -help
hdfs dfsadmin performs DFS administrative commands.
Note: Administrative commands can only be run with superuser permission.
The full syntax is:
hdfs dfsadmin
        [-report [-live] [-dead] [-decommissioning]]
        [-safemode <enter | leave | get | wait>]
        [-saveNamespace]
...
$
```

```
        [-triggerBlockReport [-incremental] <datanode_host:ipc_port>]
        [-help [cmd]]

-report [-live] [-dead] [-decommissioning]:
        Reports basic filesystem information and statistics.
        Optional flags may be used to filter the list of displayed DNs.

-safemode <enter|leave|get|wait>:  Safe mode maintenance command.
                Safe mode is a Namenode state in which it
                        1.  does not accept changes to the name space (read-only)
                        2.  does not replicate or delete blocks.
                Safe mode is entered automatically at Namenode startup, and
                leaves safe mode automatically when the configured minimum
                percentage of blocks satisfies the minimum replication
                condition.  Safe mode can also be entered manually, but then
                it can only be turned off manually as well.

-saveNamespace: Save current namespace into storage directories and reset edits log.
                Requires safe mode.

-rollEdits:     Rolls the edit log.

-restoreFailedStorage:  Set/Unset/Check flag to attempt restore of failed storage replica
s if they become available.

-refreshNodes:  Updates the namenode with the set of datanodes allowed to connect to the
namenode.
```

Figure 9.6 The `dfsadmin -help` command reveals useful information for each `dfsadmin` command.

> **Note**
>
> You've already seen a couple of the `dfsadmin` administrative commands in action (such as `dfsadmin -report` and `dfsadmin -printTopology`) in earlier chapters. This book explains the rest of the `dfsadmin` commands in the appropriate context in various chapters.

If you issue the `dfsadmin` command with no options, it will list all the options that you can specify with the command. The `dfsadmin -help` command is highly useful, since it not only lists the command options, but also shows you what they are for and their syntax as well. Figure 9.6 shows a portion of the `dfsadmin -help` command.

There are several useful `dfsadmin` command options. In the next few sections, let's look at the following command options (other sections of this chapter and other chapters will discuss several other command options).

- `dfsadmin -report`
- `dfsadmin -refreshNodes`
- `dfsadmin -metasave`

The `dfsadmin -report` Command

The `dfsadmin` tool helps you examine the HDFS cluster status. The `dfsadmin -report` command produces useful output that shows basic statistics of the cluster, including the status of the DataNodes and NameNode, the configured disk capacity and the health of the data blocks. Here's a sample `dfsadmin -report` command:

```
$ hdfs dfsadmin -report

Configured Capacity: 2068027170816000 (1.84 PB)                          #A
Present Capacity: 2068027170816000 (1.84 PB)
DFS Remaining: 562576619120381 (511.66 TB)                               #A
DFS Used: 1505450551695619 (1.34 PB)                                     #B
DFS Used%: 72.80%                                                        #B
Under replicated blocks: 1                                               #C
Blocks with corrupt replicas: 0
Missing blocks: 1
Missing blocks (with replication factor 1): 9                            #C

-------------------------------------------------
Live datanodes (54):                                                     #D

Name: 10.192.0.78:50010 (hadoop02.localhost)                             #E
Hostname: hadoop02.localhost.com
Rack: /rack3                                                             #E
Decommission Status : Normal                                             #F
Configured Capacity: 46015524438016 (41.85 TB)                           #G
DFS Used: 33107988033048 (30.11 TB)
Non DFS Used: 0 (0 B)
DFS Remaining: 12907536404968 (11.74 TB)
DFS Used%: 71.95%
DFS Remaining%: 28.05%                                                   #G
Configured Cache Capacity: 4294967296 (4 GB)                             #H
Cache Used: 0 (0 B)
Cache Remaining: 4294967296 (4 GB)
Cache Used%: 0.00%
Cache Remaining%: 100.00%                                                #H
Xceivers: 71
Last contact: Fri May 01 15:15:59 CDT 2015

...
```

Notes

#A Configured capacity for HDFS in this cluster

#B HDFS used storage statistics

#C Shows if there are any under-replicated, corrupt or missing blocks

#D Shows how many DataNodes in the cluster are alive and available

#E The hostname and rack name

#F Status of the DataNode (decommissioned or not)

#G Configured and used capacity for this DataNode

#H Cache usage statistics (if configured)

Note

You can view the same information as that shown by the `dfsadmin -report` command on the NameNode web status page, which is at `http://<namenode IP>:50070/dfshealth.jsp`.

The dfsadmin -report command shows HDFS details for the entire cluster, as well as separately for each node in the cluster. The output of the DFS command shows the following at the cluster and the individual DataNode levels:

- A summary of the HDFS storage allocation, including information about the configured, used and remaining space
- If you've configured centralized HDFS caching, the used and remaining percentages of cache
- Missing, corrupted and under-replicated blocks

As you'll learn later in this book, the dfsadmin -report command's output helps greatly in examining how balanced the HDFS data is, as well as helps you find out the extent of HDFS corruption (if it exists).

The dfsadmin -refreshNodes Command

The dfsadmin -refreshNodes command updates the NameNode with the list of DataNodes that are allowed to connect to the NameNode.

The NameNode reads the hostnames of the DataNode from the files pointed to by the dfs.hosts and the dfs.hosts.exclude configuration parameters in the hdfs-site.xml file. The dfs.hosts file lists all the hosts that are allowed to register with the NameNode. Any entries in the dfs.hosts.exclude file point to DataNodes that need to be decommissioned (you finalize the decommissioning after all the replicas from the node that is being decommissioned are replicated to other DataNodes).

The dfsadmin -metasave Command

The dfsadmin -metasave command provides more information than that provided by the dfsadmin -report command. This command gets you various block-related pieces of information such as:

- Total number of blocks
- Blocks waiting for replication
- Blocks that are currently being replicated

Here's how you run the dfsadmin -metasave command:

```
$ sudo -u hdfs hdfs dfsadmin -metasave test.txt
Created metasave file test.txt in the log directory of namenode hadoop1
.localhost.com/10.192.2.21:8020
Created metasave file test.txt in the log directory of namenode hadoop02
.localhost.com/10.192.2.22:8020
$
```

When you run the dfsadmin -metasave command, it creates a file in the /var/log/hadoop-hdfs directory on the server where you executed the command. The output file will contain the following information regarding the blocks:

```
58 files and directories, 17 blocks = 75 total
Live Datanodes: 1
Dead Datanodes: 0
```

```
Metasave: Blocks waiting for replication: 0
Mis-replicated blocks that have been postponed:
Metasave: Blocks being replicated: 0
Metasave: Blocks 0 waiting deletion from 0 datanodes.
Metasave: Number of datanodes: 1
127.0.0.1:50010 IN 247241674752(230.26 GB) 323584(316 KB) 0% 220983930880(205.81 GB)
Sat May 30 18:52:49 PDT 2015
```

Managing HDFS Permissions and Users

HDFS as a file system is somewhat similar to the POSIX file system in terms of the file permissions it requires. However, HDFS doesn't have the concept of users and groups as in the other file systems. It's important to understand the nature of the HDFS super user and how to manage the granting of permissions to users. You also need to learn how to set up users so they're ready to read data and write to the HDFS file system.

In the following sections, I explain these topics:

- HDFS file permissions
- Creating HDFS users

HDFS File Permissions

In a Linux system, you create OS users and make them members of an existing operating system group. In Hadoop, you associate a directory with an owner and a group. You need not actually "create" either the users or the groups. Rather, you use the concept of users and groups to set file and directory permissions. The following sections show how file and directory permissions work in HDFS.

HDFS Permission Checking

The HDFS configuration parameter `dfs.permissions.enabled` in the hdfs-site.xml file determines whether permission checking is enabled in HDFS:

```
<property>
<name>dfs.permissions.enabled</name>
<value>true</value>
</property>
```

The default value of the parameter is `true`, meaning permission checking is enabled. If you set this parameter to `false`, you turn HDFS permission checking off. Obviously, you can do this in a development environment to overcome frequent permission-related error messages, but in a production cluster, you need to keep it at its default setting.

HDFS File and Directory Permissions

HDFS uses a symbolic notation (`r, w`) to denote the read and write permissions, just as a Linux operating system does.

- When a client accesses a directory, if the client is the same as the directory's owner, Hadoop tests the owner's permissions.
- If the group matches the directory's group, then Hadoop tests the user's group permissions.

- If neither the owner nor the group names match, Hadoop tests the "other" permission of the directory.
- If none of the permissions checks succeed, the client's request is denied.

Although there's an **execute** (x) permission for a file, it's ignored for files, and as far as directories go, the execute permission implies that you can access the subdirectories of that directory. Unlike in the underlying Linux operating system, Hadoop has nothing like the UIDs (User IDs) or GIDs (Group IDs) to identify users and groups. HDFS simply stores users and groups of a directory or file as strings.

A user can write to an HDFS directory only if that user has the correct permissions. In this example, the Linux root user tries to copy a file to a user's HDFS directory and fails due to lack of permissions.

```
[root@hadoop01]# hdfs dfs -put test.txt /user/alapati/test2222/
put: Permission denied: user=root, access=WRITE, inode="/user/alapati/
test2222":hdfs:supergroup:drwxr-xr-x
[root@hadoop01]#
```

Permission Denied Errors in HDFS

You may receive the permission denied error when you're issuing an HDFS command from the command line, as in the previous example, or even when you're trying to browse the HDFS file system through the NameNode web page. For example, you may receive the following error when you try to browse files through the web UI.

```
Permissiondenied:user=alapati,access=READ_EXECUTE,inode="/user":hadoop:hdfs:drwx.------
```

In this case, you need to change the access privileges on the HDFS directory /user, after logging in as the user `hdfs`, from the command line:

```
$ hdfs dfs -chmod -R 755 /user
```

Running administrative commands as the root user or any other non-privileged (from the perspective of Hadoop) user will result in errors. If you run the Hadoop file system checking command `fsck` as the root user, you'll get the following error:

```
$ su root
$ hdfs fsck /
...
FSCK ended at Sun May 29 14:46:27 CDT 2016 in 39473 milliseconds
Permissiondenied:user=root,access=READ_EXECUTE,inode="/lost+found/user":hdfs:supergroup:drwxr--r--

Fsck on path '/' FAILED
#
```

The `FAILED` result you get from running the `fsck` command here doesn't mean the file system is corrupt! It simply means that you failed to execute the `fsck` command. A similar thing happens when you run the `dfsadmin -report` command as any user other than the HDFS super user, hdfs:

```
$ hdfs dfsadmin -report
------------------------------------------------
report: Access denied for user root. Superuser privilege is required
#
```

In both the cases described here, the right thing to do is to either log in as the user hdfs and execute the commands, or if you have the sudo privileges to the hdfs user account, run the commands as follows:

```
$ sudo -u hdfs hdfs fsck /
$ sudo -u hdfs hdfs dfsadmin -report
```

Using Access Control Lists (ACLs) to control permissions

Unlike the regular Linux or UNIX permissions mode, Access Control Lists (ACLs) let you define permissions for some of a group's members. For example, you can grant or deny write permissions on a file only to specific users or groups. ACLs are disabled by default, but you can enable them by configuring the NameNode appropriately with the `dfs.namenode.acls.enabled` configuration parameter.

Chapter 15, "Securing Hadoop," which deals with Hadoop security, discusses ACLs in more detail.

HDFS Users and Super Users

Typically, database administrators create users in their databases, with each user having specific privileges and/or roles that enable them to perform various actions in the database. In the context of Hadoop, *creating* a user is kind of a misnomer, as HDFS really doesn't have anything that lets you create user identities as you would on Linux systems. It also doesn't enable you to create any groups.

In the default mode of authentication, called simple authentication, Hadoop relies on the underlying operating system to determine client identities. If you set up a **Kerberized** system (a system that has been set up to authenticate connections through Kerberos), then Kerberos will determine the client identities. Chapter 15 shows how to set up Kerberos for user authentication.

Note that you don't need to create an operating system account on the underlying Linux system for your HDFS users to be able to access and use HDFS. It's a good practice to create OS accounts for all Hadoop users who'll be using the local file system on the gateway servers for their Hadoop-related work.

Creating HDFS (and Hadoop) Users

In order to enable new users to use your Hadoop cluster, follow these general steps.

1. Create an OS account on the Linux system from which you want to let a user execute Hadoop jobs. Before creating the user, you may have to create the group as well:

   ```
   $ group add analysts
   $ useradd -g analysts alapati
   $ passwd alapati
   ```

   Here, **analysts** is an OS group I've created for a set of users. The `passwd` command lets me set a password for the user.

2. Make sure that you've set the permissions on the Hadoop temp directory you've specified in the **core-site.xml** file, so all Hadoop users can access it:

```
<property>
  <name>hadoop.tmp.dir</name>
  <value>/tmp/hadoop-$(user.name)</value>
</property>
```

3. If the file permissions on the HDFS temp directory aren't 777, make them so:

```
$ hdfs -dfs -chmod -R 777  //tmp/hadoop-alapati
```

4. In order to "create" a new HDFS user, you need to create a directory under the /user directory. This directory will serve as the HDFS "home" directory for the user.

```
$ hdfs dfs -mkdir /user/alapati
```

5. By default, when you create a directory or a file, the owner is the user that creates the directory (or file) and the group is the group of that user, as shown here.

```
# sudo -u hdfs
# hdfs dfs -ls /user
Found 135 items
drwxr-xr-x   - hdfs       supergroup          0 2016-05-28 08:18 /user/alapati
....
```

   In this case, I used the hdfs account to create the directory, so the owner is hdfs and the group is supergroup. Change the ownership of the directory, since you don't want to use the default owner/group (hdfs/supergroup) for this directory.

```
$ su hdfs
$ hdfs dfs -chown -R alapati:analysts
$ hdfs dfs -ls /user/
$ drwxr-xr-x   - alapati   analysts          0 2016-04-27 12:40 /user/alapati
```

6. You can check the new directory structure for the user with the following command:

```
$ hdfs dfs -ls /user/alapati
```

   User alapati can now store the output of his MapReduce and other jobs under that user's home directory in HDFS.

7. Refresh the user and group mappings to let the NameNode know about the new user:

```
$ hdfs dfsadmin -refreshUserToGroupMappings
```

8. Set a space quota for the new directory you've created:

```
$ hdfs dfsadmin -setSpaceQuota 30g /user/alapati
```

The new user can now log into the gateway servers and execute his or her Hadoop jobs and store data in HDFS.

User Identities

Hadoop supports two modes of operation—**simple** and **Kerberos**—to determine user identities. The simple mode of operation is the default. You specify the mode of operation with the `hadoop.security.authentication` property in the hdfs-site.xml file.

When operating in a non-Kerberos (or non-Kerberized) cluster, the host operating system determines the client identities. In a Kerberized cluster, user identities are based on the user's Kerberos credentials, as explained in Chapter 15. Users determine their current Kerberos principal through the `kinit` utility, and the Kerberos principal is then mapped to an HDFS username.

The HDFS Super User

Since Hadoop doesn't have the concept of a user identity, there's no fixed super user for Hadoop. The system super user for Hadoop is simply the operating system user that starts the NameNode. The HDFS super user doesn't have to be the root user of the NameNode host. If you wish, you can allocate a set of users to a separate super user group.

You can make a set of users members of a super user group by setting the `dfs.permissions.supergroup` configuration parameter in the hdfs-site.xml file, as shown here.

```
<property>
  <name>dfs.permissions.superusergroup</name>
  <value>supergroup</value>
</property>
```

In this example, supergroup is the name of the group of super users in the cluster. The following example shows that the user hdfs belongs to the group supergroup:

```
# hdfs dfs -ls /
Found 7 items
drwxr-xr-x   - hdfs   hdfs                 0 2014-06-25 16:39 /data
drwxr-xr-x   - hdfs   supergroup           0 2015-05-05 15:46 /system
drwxrwxrwt   - hdfs   hdfs                 0 2015-05-09 09:33 /tmp
drwxr-xr-x   - hdfs   supergroup           0 2015-05-05 13:20 /user
...
#
```

A lot of the administrative HDFS commands need to be run as the "hdfs" OS user, which is the default HDFS super user. If you run these commands as any other user, including the root user in a Linux system, you'll get the following error:

```
Access denied for user root. Superuser privilege is required.
```

The root user in Linux is indeed a super user but only for the local file system. It's user hdfs who's king when it comes to the HDFS file system. You can perform administration-related HDFS commands only as the hdfs user or by sudoing to that user. You can use the Linux sudo command to use the privileged administrative commands, as shown in the following example.

```
$ sudo -u hdfs hdfs dfs -rm /user/test/test.txt
```

In this example, the OS user was granted sudo privileges to the HDFS account and thus is able to run HDFS file commands as the HDFS super user hdfs.

Managing HDFS Storage

You deal with very large amounts of data in a Hadoop cluster, often ranging over multiple petabytes. However, your cluster is also going to use a lot of that space, sometimes with several terabytes of data arriving daily. This section shows you how to check for used and free space in your cluster, and manage HDFS space quotas. The following section shows how to balance HDFS data across the cluster.

The following subsections show how to

- Check HDFS disk usage (used and free space)
- Allocate HDFS space quotas

Checking HDFS Disk Usage

Throughout this book, I show how to use various HDFS commands in their appropriate contexts. Here, let's review some HDFS space and file related commands. You can view the `help` facility for any individual HDFS file command by issuing the following command first:

```
$ hdfs dfs -usage
```

Let's review some of the most useful file system commands that let you check the HDFS usage in your cluster. The following sections explain how to

- Use the `df` command to check free space in HDFS
- Use the `du` command to check space usage
- Use the `dfsadmin` command to check free and used space

Finding Free Space with the `df` Command

You can check the free space in an HDFS directory with a couple of commands. The `-df` command shows the configured capacity, available free space and used space of a file system in HDFS.

```
# hdfs dfs -df
Filesystem                      Size              Used         Available  Use%
hdfs://hadoop01-ns  2068027170816000  1591361508626924  476665662189076   77%
#
```

You can specify the `-h` option with the `df` command for more readable and concise output:

```
# hdfs dfs -df -h
Filesystem          Size   Used  Available Use%
hdfs://hadoop01-ns  1.8 P  1.4 P    433.5 T   77%
#
```

The `df -h` command shows that this cluster's currently configured HDFS storage is 1.8PB, of which 1.4PB have been used so far.

Finding the Used Space with the `du` Command

You can view the size of the files and directories in a specific directory with the `du` command. The command will show you the space (in bytes) used by the files that match the file pattern you specify. If it's a file, you'll get the length of the file. The usage of the du command is as follows:

```
$ hdfs dfs -du URI
```

Here's an example:

```
$ hdfs dfs -du /user/alapati
67545099068  67545099068  /user/alapati/.Trash
212190509    328843053    /user/alapati/.staging
26159        78477        /user/alapati/catalyst
3291761247   6275115145   /user/alapati/hive
$
```

You can view the used storage in the entire HDFS file system with the following command:

```
$ hdfs dfs -du /
414032717599186  883032417554123  /data
0                0                /home
0                0                /lost+found
111738           335214           /schema
1829104769791    5401313868645    /tmp
325747953341360  690430023788615  /user
$
```

The following command uses the -h option to get more readable output:

```
$ hdfs dfs -du -h /
353.4 T  733.6 T  /data
0        0        /home
0        0        /lost+found
109.1 K  327.4 K  /schema
2.1 T    6.1 T    /tmp
277.3 T  570.9 T  /user
$
```

Note the following about the output of the du -h command shown here:

- The first column shows the actual size (raw size) of the files that users have placed in the various HDFS directories.
- The second column shows the actual space consumed by those files in HDFS.

The values shown in the second column are much higher than the values shown in the first column. Why? The reason is that the second column's value is derived by multiplying the size of each file in a directory by its replication factor, to arrive at the actual space occupied by that file.

As you can see, directories such as /schema and /tmp reveal that the replication factor for all files in these two directories is three. However, not all files in the /data and the /user directories are being replicated three times. If they were, the second column's value for these two file systems would also be three times the value of its first column.

If you sum up the sizes in the second column of the `dfs -du` command, you'll find that it's identical to that shown by the `Used` column of the `dfs -df` command, as shown here:

```
$ hdfs dfs -df -h /
Filesystem              Size     Used  Available  Use%
hdfs://hadoop01-ns   553.8 T  409.3 T    143.1 T   74%
$
```

Getting a Summary of Used Space with the du -s Command

The `du -s` command lets you summarize the used space in all files instead of giving individual file sizes as the `du` command does.

```
$ hdfs dfs -du -s -h /
131.0 T  391.1 T  /
$
```

How to Check Whether Hadoop Can Use More Storage Space

If you're under severe space pressure and you can't add additional DataNodes right away, you can see if there's additional space left on the local file system that you can commandeer for HDFS use immediately. In Chapter 3, I showed how to configure the HDFS storage directories by specifying multiple disks or volumes with the `dfs.data.dir` configuration parameter in the hdfs-site.xml file. Here's an example:

```
<property>
<name>df.data.dir</name>
<value>/u01/hadoop/data,/u02/hadoop/data,/u03/hadoop/data</value>
</property>
```

There's another configuration parameter you can specify in the same file, named `dfs.datanode.du.reserved`, which determines how much space Hadoop can use from each disk you list as a value for the `dfs.data.dir` parameter. The `dfs.datanode.du.reserved` parameter specifies the space reserved for non-HDFS use per DataNode. Hadoop can use all data in a disk above this limit, leaving the rest for non-HDFS uses. Here's how you set the `dfs.datanode.du.reserved` configuration property:

```
<property>
<name>dfs.datanode.du.reserved</name>
<value>10737418240</value>
<description>Reserved space in bytes per volume. Always leave this much space
free for non-dfs use.
</description>
</property>
```

In this example, the `dfs.datanode.du.reserved` parameter is set to 10GB (the value is specified in bytes). HDFS will keep storing data in the data directories you assigned to it with the `dfs.data.dir` parameter, until the Linux file system reaches a free space of 10GB on a node. By default, this parameter is set to 10GB. You may consider lowering the value for the `dfs.datanode.du.reserved` parameter if you think there's plenty of unused space lying around on the local file system on the disks configured for Hadoop's use.

Storage Statistics from the `dfsadmin` Command

You've seen how you can get storage statistics for the entire cluster, as well as for each individual node, by running the `dfsadmin -report` command. The `Used`, `Available` and `Use%` statistics from the `dfs -du` command match the disk storage statistics from the `dfsadmin -report` command, as shown here:

```
bash-3.2$ hdfs dfs -df -h /
Filesystem            Size   Used  Available  Use%
hdfs://hadoop01-ns  1.8 P  1.5 P    269.6 T   85%
```

In the following example, the top portion of the output generated by the `dfsadmin -report` command shows the cluster's storage capacity:

```
bash-3.2$ hdfs dfsadmin -report
Configured Capacity: 2068027170816000 (1.84 PB)
Present Capacity: 2067978866301041 (1.84 PB)
DFS Remaining: 296412818768806 (269.59 TB)
DFS Used: 1771566047532235 (1.57 PB)
DFS Used%: 85.67%
...
```

You can see that both the `dfs -du` command and the `dfsadmin -report` command show identical information regarding the used and available HDFS space.

Testing for Files

You can check whether a certain HDFS file path exists and whether that path is a directory or a file with the `test` command:

```
$ hdfs dfs -test -e /users/alapati/test
```

This command uses the `-e` option to check whether the specified path exists.

You can create a file of zero length with the `touchz` command, which is identical to the Linux `touch` command:

```
$ hdfs dfs -touchz /user/alapati/test3.txt
```

Allocating HDFS Space Quotas

You can configure quotas on HDFS directories, thus allowing you to limit how much HDFS space users or applications can consume. HDFS space allocations don't have a direct connection to the space allocations on the underlying Linux file system. Hadoop lets you actually set two types of quotas:

- Space quotas: Allow you to set a ceiling on the amount of space used for an individual directory
- Name quotas: Let you specify the maximum number of file and directory names in the tree rooted at a directory

The following sections cover

- Setting name quotas
- Setting space quotas

- Checking name and space quotas
- Clearing name and space quotas

Setting Name Quotas

You can set a limit on the number of files and directory names in any directory by specifying a **name quota**. If the user tries to create files or directories that go beyond the specified numerical quota, the file/directory creation will fail. Use the `dfsadmin` command `-setQuota` to set the HDFS name quota for a directory. Here's the syntax for this command:

```
$ hdfs dfsadmin -setQuota <max_number> <directory>
```

For example, you can set the maximum number of files that can be used by a user under a specific directory by doing this:

```
$ hdfs dfsadmin -setQuota 100000 /user/alapati
```

This command sets a limit on the number of files user alapati can create under that user's home directory, which is /user/alapati. If you grant user alapati privileges on other directories, of course, the user can create files in those directories, and those files won't count against the name quota you set on the user's home directory. In other words, name quotas (and space quotas) aren't **user specific**—rather, they are **directory specific**.

> **Warning**
>
> If you create a user's home directory but fail to grant the user a space quota, the user has unlimited storage in HDFS. Not good!

Setting Space Quotas on HDFS Directories

A **space quota** lets you set a limit on the storage assigned to a specific directory under HDFS. This quota is the number of bytes that can be used by all files in a directory. Once the directory uses up its assigned space quota, users and applications can't create files in the directory.

> **Note**
>
> HDFS space quotas are based on limits on HDFS storage that can be used by a directory—and not by a user.

A space quota sets a hard limit on the amount of disk space that can be consumed by all files within an HDFS directory tree. You can restrict a user's space consumption by setting limits on the user's home directory or other directories that the user shares with other users. If you don't set a space quota on a directory it means that the disk space quota is unlimited for that directory—it can potentially use the entire HDFS.

Hadoop checks disk space quotas recursively, starting at a given directory and traversing up to the root. The quota on any directory is the minimum of the following:

- Directory space quota
- Parent space quota

- Grandparent space quota
- Root space quota

Managing HDFS Space Quotas

It's important to understand that in HDFS, there must be enough quota space to accommodate an entire block. If the user has, let's say, 200MB free in their allocated quota, they can't create a new file, regardless of the file size, if the HDFS block size happens to be 256MB. You can set the HDFS space quota for a user by executing the `setSpaceQuota` command. Here's the syntax:

```
$ hdfs dfsadmin -setSpaceQuota <N> <dirname>...<dirname>
```

The space quota you set acts as the ceiling on the total size of all files in a directory. You can set the space quota in bytes (b), megabytes (m), gigabytes (g), terabytes (t) and even petabytes (by specifying p—yes, this is big data!). And here's an example that shows how to set a user's space quota to 60GB:

```
$ hdfs dfsadmin -setSpaceQuota 60G  /user/alapati
```

You can set quotas on multiple directories at a time, as shown here:

```
$ hdfs dfsadmin  -setSpaceQuota 10g /user/alapati /test/alapati
```

This command sets a quota of 10GB on two directories—/user/alapati and /test/alapati. Both the directories must already exist. If they do not, you can create them with the `dfs -mkdir` command.

> **Caution**
>
> The space quota includes all replicated data. If you set the quota at 30GB for a user, that user can exhaust her quota by storing 10GB of actual data in her HDFS directory (using the default replication factor of three, HDFS stores 10 X 3= 30GB of data).

You use the same command, `-setSpaceQuota`, both for setting the initial limits and modifying them later on. When you create an HDFS directory, by default, it has no space quota until you formally set one.

You can remove the space quota for any directory by issuing the `-clrSpaceQuota` command, as shown here:

```
$ dfsadmin -clrSpaceQuota /user/alapati
```

If you remove the space quota for a user's directory, that user can, theoretically speaking, use up all the space you have in HDFS. As with the `-setSpaceQuota` command, you can specify multiple directories in the `-clrSpaceQuota` command.

Things to Remember about Hadoop Space Quotas

Both the Hadoop block size you choose and the replication factor in force are key determinants of how a user's space quota works. Let's suppose that you grant a new user a space quota of 30GB and the user has more than 500MB still free. If the user tries to load a 500MB file into one of his directories, the attempt will fail with an error similar to the following, even though the directory had a bit over 500MB of free space.

```
org.apache.hadoop.hdfs.protocol.DSQuotaExceededException: The DiskSpace quota
       of /user/alapati is exceeded: quota = 32212254720 B = 30 GB but
       diskspace consumed = 32697410316 B = 30.45 GB
```

In this case, the user had enough free space to load a 500MB file but still received the error indicating that the file system quota for the user was exceeded. This is so because the HDFS block size was 128MB, and so the file needed 4 blocks in this case. Hadoop tried to replicate the file three times since the default replication factor was three and so was looking for 128*12=1556MB of space, which clearly was over the space quota left for this user.

> **Note**
>
> The disk space quota is deducted based not only on the size of the file you want to store in HDFS but also the number of replicas. If you've configured a replication factor of three and the file is 500MB in size, three block replicas are needed, and therefore, the total quota consumed by the file will be 1,500MB, not 500MB.

The administrator can reduce the space quota for a directory to a level below the combined disk space usage under a directory tree. In this case, the directory is left in an indefinite **quota violation state** until the administrator or the user removes some files from the directory. The user can continue to use the files in the overfull directory but, of course, can't store any new files there since their quota is violated.

Checking Current Space Quotas

You can check the size of a user's HDFS space quota by using the `dfs -count -q` command as shown in Figure 9.7.

When you issue a `dfs -count -q` command, you'll see eight different columns in the output. This is what each of the columns stands for:

- `QUOTA`: Limit on the files and directories
- `REMAINING_QUOTA`: Remaining number of files and directories in the quota that can be created by this user
- `SPACE_QUOTA`: Space quota granted to this user
- `REMAINING_SPACE_QUOTA`: Space quota remaining for this user
- `DIR_COUNT`: The number of directories
- `FILE_COUNT`: The number of files
- `CONTENT_SIZE`: The file sizes
- `PATH_NAME`: The path for the directories

The `-count -q` command shows that the space quota for user bdaldr is about 100TB. Of this, the user has about 67TB left as free space.

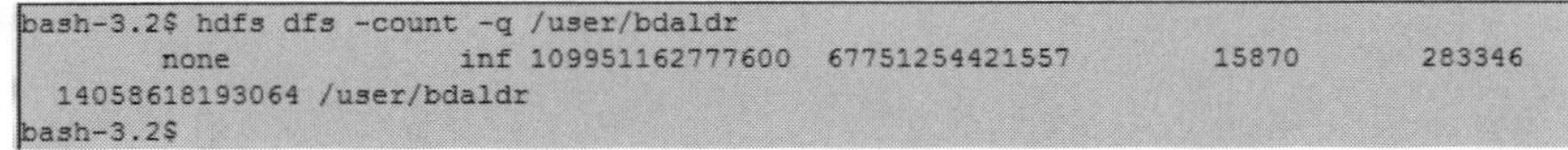

bash-3.2$ hdfs dfs -count -q /user/bdaldr
none inf 109951162777600 67751254421557 15870 283346
14058618193064 /user/bdaldr
bash-3.2$

Figure 9.7 How to check a user's current space usage in HDFS against their assigned storage limits

Clearing Current Space Quotas

You can clear the current space quota for a user by issuing the `clrSpaceQuota` command as shown here:

```
$ hdfs dfsadmin -clrSpaceQuota
```

Here's an example showing how to clear the space quota for a user:

```
$ hdfs dfsadmin -clrSpaceQuota /user/alapati
$ hdfs dfs -count -q /user/alapati
        none             inf            none             inf            2
0                 0 /user/alapati
$
```

The user still can use HDFS to read files but won't be able to create any files in that user's HDFS "home" directory. If the user has sufficient privileges, however, she can create files in other HDFS directories. It's a good practice to set HDFS quotas on a per-user basis. You must also set quotas for data directories on a per-project basis.

Rebalancing HDFS Data

Over time, the data in the HDFS storage can become skewed, in the sense that some of the DataNodes may have more data blocks compared to the rest of the cluster's nodes. In cases of extreme skew, the read and write activity is overly busy on the nodes with more data, and the sparsely populated nodes remain underutilized.

HDFS data also gets unbalanced when you add new nodes to your cluster. Hadoop doesn't automatically move existing data around to even out the data distribution among a cluster's DataNodes. It simply starts using the new DataNode for storing fresh data.

> **Note**
>
> It's a good practice to run the HDFS balancer regularly in a cluster.

Hadoop doesn't seek to achieve a fully balanced cluster. This state of affairs is quite hard to achieve in a cluster with continuous data flows. Instead, Hadoop is satisfied when the space usage on each DataNode is with within a certain percentage of space used by the other DataNodes. In addition, it also makes use of a threshold size to give you flexibility with the balancing of data.

Hadoop makes available a useful tool, called the **balancer**, to let you rebalance a cluster's block distribution so all DataNodes store roughly equal amounts of data.

The following sections cover

- Reasons for an unbalanced HDFS
- Using Hadoop's balancer tool
- Setting the proper threshold value
- When to run the balancer
- Making the balancer run faster

Reasons for HDFS Data Imbalance

There's no guarantee that HDFS will automatically distribute data evenly among the DataNodes in a cluster. For example, when you add a new node to the cluster, all new blocks could be allocated to that node, thus making the data distribution lopsided. When the NameNode allocates data blocks to the nodes, it considers the following criteria to determine which DataNodes get the new blocks.

- Uniformly distributing data across the cluster's DataNodes
- Keeping one of the replicas of a data block on the node that's writing the block
- Placing one of the replicas on the same rack as the node writing the block, to minimize cross-rack network I/O
- Spreading the block replicas across racks to support redundancy and survive the loss of an entire rack

Hadoop considers a cluster balanced when the percentage of space in a given DataNode is a little bit above or below the average percentage of space used by the DataNodes in that cluster. What this "little bit" is, is defined by the parameter `threshold size`.

Running the Balancer Tool to Balance HDFS Data

The aforementioned HDFS **balancer** is a tool provided by Hadoop to balance the data spread across the DataNodes in a cluster by moving data blocks from the over-utilized to the under-utilized DataNodes. Figure 9.8 shows the idea behind the balancer tool. Initially Rack 1 and Rack 2 have data blocks. The new rack, Rack 3, has no data initially—only newly added data will be placed there. This means adding nodes leads to an unbalanced cluster. Data is moved from the nodes with data to the new nodes, which have no data until you move data over to them from the current DataNodes or wait for new data to come in. When you run the balancer, Hadoop moves data blocks from their existing locations to the nodes that have more free space, all nodes will have roughly the same amount of used space.

You can run the balancer manually from the command line by invoking the balancer command. The `start-balancer.sh` command invokes the balancer. You can also

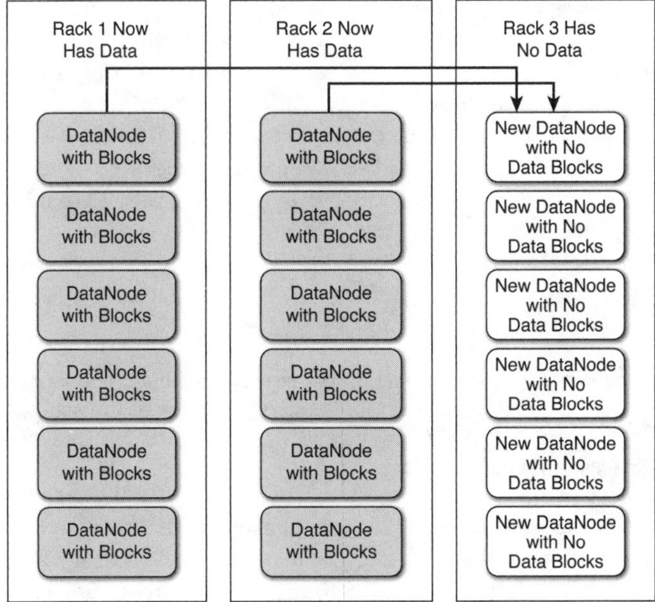

Figure 9.8 How the balancer moves data blocks to the under-utilized nodes from the over-utilized nodes

run it by issuing the command `hdfs -balancer`. Here's the usage of the `balancer` command:

```
$ hdfs balancer --help
Usage: java Balancer
        [-policy <policy>]       the balancing policy: datanode or blockpool
        [-threshold <threshold>]        Percentage of disk capacity
        [-exclude [-f <hosts-file> | comma-separated list of hosts]]      Excludes
the specified datanodes.
        [-include [-f <hosts-file> | comma-separated list of hosts]]      Includes
only the specified datanodes.
```

The `threshold` parameter denotes the percentage deviation of HDFS usage of each DataNode from the cluster's average DFS utilization ratio. Exceeding this threshold in either way (higher or lower) would mean that the node will be rebalanced.

The default DataNode policy is to balance storage at the DataNode level. The balancer doesn't balance data among individual volumes of the DataNode, however. The alternative **blockpool policy** applies only to a federated HDFS service.

Setting the Proper Threshold Value for the Balancer

You can run the `balancer` command without any parameters, as shown here:

```
$ sudo -u hdfs hdfs balancer
```

This balancer command uses the default threshold of 10 percent. This means that the balancer will balance data by moving blocks from over-utilized to under-utilized nodes, until each DataNode's disk usage differs by no more than plus or minus 10 percent of the average disk usage in the cluster.

Sometimes, you may wish to set the threshold to a different level—for example, when free space in the cluster is getting low and you want to keep the used storage levels on the individual DataNodes within a smaller range than the default of plus or minus 10 percent. You can do so by specifying the threshold parameter, as shown here:

```
$ hdfs balancer -threshold 5
```

> **Tip**
>
> How long the balancer will run depends on the size of the cluster and how unbalanced the data is. When you run the balancer for the very first time, or you schedule it infrequently, as well as when you run it after adding a set of DataNodes, it will run for a very long time—often several days.

The amount of data moved around during rebalancing depends on the value of the threshold parameter. If you use the default value of 10 and the average DFS usage across the cluster is, for example, 70 percent, the balancer will ensure that that each DataNode's DFS usage lies somewhere between 60 and 80 percent of that DataNode's storage capacity, once the balancing of the HDFS data is completed.

When you run the balancer, it looks at two key HDFS usage values in your cluster:

- Average DFS used percentage: The average DFS used percentage in the cluster can be derived by performing the following computation:

  ```
  Average DFS Used = DFS Used * 100/Present Capacity
  ```

- A Node's used DFS percentage: This measure shows the percentage of DFS used per node.

The balancer will balance a DataNode only if the difference between a DataNode's used DFS percentage and the average DFS used (by the cluster) is greater than the threshold value. Otherwise, it won't rebalance the cluster.

As noted previously, if you run the balancer without specifying a threshold value, it'll use the default value of 10 as the threshold. In our case, it won't perform any balancing, ending up as shown here (assuming all the DataNodes have a similar DFS usage as that of Node10):

```
$ hdfs balancer
15/05/04 12:56:36 INFO balancer.Balancer: namenodes  = [hdfs://hadoop01-ns]
15/05/04 12:56:36 INFO balancer.Balancer: parameters = Balancer
.Parameters[BalancingPolicy.Node, threshold=10.0, number of nodes to be excluded = 0,
number of nodes to be included = 0]
Time Stamp               Iteration#  Bytes Already Moved  Bytes Left To Move
Bytes Being Moved
'''
```

```
The cluster is balanced. Exiting...
May 4, 2015 12:56:37 PM  Balancing took 1.47 seconds
$
```

The balancer ran, but it wound things up pretty quickly, because it found that all nodes in the cluster have a usage that's within the threshold value—the cluster is already balanced!

In our case, for balancing to occur, you must specify a threshold value that's <=2. Here's one way to run it:

```
$ nohup su hdfs -c "hdfs balancer -threshold 2" > /tmp/balancer.log/stdout.log
2>/tmp/balancer.log/stderr.log &
```

Specifying `nohup` and `&` will run the job in the background and get back control of the shell. Since a balancer job can run for quite a long time in a cluster, it's a good idea to run it in this way.

Using `hdfs dfsadmin` to Make Things Easier

In our example, we used a single node, Node10, to check that node's DFS used percentage. We then figured out that we must set the threshold to a value that is <= 2 based on this node's DFS used percentage. But you can't run the balancer on a specific node. So, how do you determine the threshold value when you have a larger number of nodes? It's easy. Just pick the lowest DFS used percentage of a node in the entire cluster. You don't have to spend a lot of time figuring out the DFS used percentages for each node. Use the `hdfs dfsadmin -report` command to find out everything you need in order to figure out the right threshold value.

In this example, there are 50 nodes in the cluster. I can run the `dfsadmin` command as follows, capturing the output in a file, since the command will print out the DFS usage reports for each node separately.

```
[root@hadoop01]# sudo -u hdfs hdfs dfsadmin -report > /tmp/dfsadmin.out
```

Look at the very top of the command's output (in the file dfsadmin.out), where you'll find the DFS used statistics for the entire cluster:

```
Configured Capacity: 608922615386112 (553.81 TB)
Present Capacity: 607364914327552 (552.40 TB)
DFS Remaining: 166697481228288 (151.61 TB)
DFS Used: 440667433099264 (400.78 TB)

DFS Used%: 72.55%
```

The smaller the value of the threshold parameter, the more work the balancer will need to perform and the more balanced the cluster will be. However, there's a catch here: If you have a heavily used cluster with numerous writes and deletes of data, the cluster may never reach a fully balanced state, and the balancer will be merely moving around data from one node to another.

When you start the balancer, you'll see the following type of output. Note how the balancer determines how many nodes are overutilized or underutilized. It'll move data from the overutilized nodes to the rest of the cluster nodes. It also determines the actual amount of data that needs to be moved around to balance the cluster's data distribution.

```
30/05/2016 10:02:26 INFO balancer.Balancer: 4 over-utilized:              #A
[10.192.0.55:50010:DISK, 10.192.0.24:50010:DISK, 10.192.0.54:50010:DISK,
10.192.0.25:50010:DISK]
30/05/2016 10:02:26 INFO balancer.Balancer: Need to move 8.05 TB to make the
cluster balanced.                                                           #A
30/05/2016 09:07:21 INFO Balancer: Decided to move 10 GB bytes from         #B
10.192.0.55:50010:DISK to 10.192.0.116:50010:DISK
30/05/2016 09:07:21 INFO balancer.Balancer: Decided to move 10 GB bytes from
10.192.0.25:50010:DISK to 10.192.0.115:50010:DISK
30/05/2016 09:07:21 INFO balancer.Balancer: Decided to move 10 GB bytes from
10.192.0.24:50010:DISK to 10.192.0.118:50010:DISK
30/05/2016 09:07:21 INFO balancer.Balancer: Decided to move 10 GB bytes from
10.192.0.54:50010:DISK to 10.192.0.110:50010:DISK
30/05/2016 09:07:21 INFO balancer.Balancer: Will move 40 GB in this iteration
30/05/2016 09:07:22 INFO balancer.Dispatcher: Successfully moved
blk_1155910122_1099683676641 with size=17370340 from 10.192.0.54:50010:DISK to
10.192.0.110:50010:DISK through 10.192.0.54:50010                          #B

May 30, 2016 10:34:10 PM  Balancing took 14.56153333333334 minutes         #C
$
```

Notes

#A Points out the four DataNodes that are currently overutilized. Their HDFS usage percentage is higher than the average HDFS usage for the cluster.

#B Shows how the balancer moves the data from overutilized to underutilized DataNodes.

#C Shows the completion of the balancing once the data is evenly spread across all DataNodes.

Tip

To keep the balancer from running for a very long time, specify a higher threshold first and then drop the threshold to a lower value the next time you run the balancer.

Iterative Movement of Blocks

The goal of the balancer is to move data from the overutilized nodes to the underutilized nodes, thus balancing the DFS usage across the cluster. When you start the balancer, it starts by moving some data from nodes whose DFS usage is higher than the threshold and moves that data to nodes whose DFS usage is below the threshold. The balancer is rack aware and thus will generate minimal inter-rack traffic. The balancer works in an iterative fashion, moving a certain amount of data per iteration as the output of the balancer run shows (e.g., "Will move 40GB in this iteration").

When to Run the Balancer

A couple of guidelines as to when to run the balancer are appropriate. In a large cluster, run the balancer regularly. You can schedule a cron job to perform the balancing, instead of manually running it yourself. If a scheduled balancer job is still running when the next job needs to start, no harm's done, as the second balancer job won't start.

It's a good idea to run the balancer right after adding new nodes to the cluster. When you add a large number of nodes at once and run the balancer afterwards, it'll take quite a while to complete its work.

Making the Balancer Run Faster

Ideally you must run the balancer during periods when the cluster is being lightly utilized, but the overhead is usually not high. You can adjust the bandwidth of the balancer to determine the number of bytes per second that each DataNode in the cluster can use to rebalance its data.

The default value for the bandwidth is 10MB per second and you can raise it to make the balancer complete its work faster. You can raise the bandwidth up to about 10 percent of your network speed without any noticeable impact on the cluster's workload. You can set the network bandwidth used by the balancer with the help of the `hdfs dfsadmin` command, as shown here:

```
$ hdfs dfsadmin -setBalancerBandwidth <bandwidth in bytes per second>
```

The `-setBalancerBandwidth` option enables you to change the network bandwidth consumed by each DataNode in your cluster during an HDFS block balancing operation. The bandwidth you specify here is the maximum number of bytes per second that will be used by each DataNode in the cluster. If you're using a shell script to invoke the balancer periodically, you can specify the bandwidth option in the script before invoking the balancer. Here's an example showing how to change the bandwidth to 20MB.

```
$ hdfs dfsadmin -setBalancerBandwidth 20971520
Balancer bandwidth is set to 20971520 for hadoop01.localhost/10.192.0.22:8020
Balancer bandwidth is set to 20971520 for hadoop01.localhost/10.192.0.51:8020
$
```

Make sure that you have adequate bandwidth before increasing the bandwidth. You can find out the speed of your NIC card by issuing the following command:

```
$ ethtool eth0
...
Speed: 1000Mb/s
Duplex: Full
...
$
```

In this example, the network has a speed of 1,000MB per second, so it's safe to set the balancer bandwidth to about 10 percent of it, which is 100MB per second.

When the balancer runs for a long time, you can schedule it to run with different bandwidths during peak and off peak times. You can run it with a low bandwidth during peak times and run it with a higher bandwidth during periods when the cluster is less busy. For example, during peak times, you can schedule a cron job such as the following for the balancer (bandwidth of 10MB):

```
$ su hdfs -c 'hdfs dfsadmin -setBalancerBandwidth 10485760'
$ nohup su hdfs -c 'hdfs balancer' > /tmp/balancerstderr.log 2>
/tmp/balancerstdout.log &
```

You can at the same time schedule a different cronjob to run at off-peak times, with a higher (20MB) setting for the bandwidth parameter:

```
$ su hdfs -c 'hdfs dfsadmin setBalancerBandwidth 20971520>'
$ nohup su hdfs -c 'hdfs balancer' > /tmp/balancerstderr.log 2>
/tmp/balancerstdout.log &
```

Only one balancer job can run at a time. When the second (off-peak) job starts, it stops the first balancer job and starts a new balancer job with the higher bandwidth setting.

Reclaiming HDFS Space

Oftentimes you can conserve HDFS storage space by reclaiming used space where you can. There are two ways in which you can reclaim space allocated to HDFS files:

- You can remove the files or directories once you're done processing them.
- You can reduce the replication factor for a file.

Removing files works well with the raw data files you load into HDFS for processing, and the reduction of the replication factor is a good strategy for handling older and less-critical HDFS files.

Removing Files and Directories

Periodic removal of unnecessary data is an operational best practice. Often, data needs to be retained only for a specific period of time. You can stretch your storage resources by removing any files that are just sitting in HDFS and eating up valuable space.

Decreasing the Replication Factor

You can configure the replication factor at the cluster level by setting the `dfs.replication` parameter in the hdfs-site.xml file, as explained in Chapter 4, "Planning for and Creating a Fully Distributed Cluster." The setting you configure with the `dfs.replication` parameter sets a global replication factor for the entire cluster.

It's important to understand that while you can set the replication factor at the cluster level, you can modify the replication factor for any existing file, with the `-setRep` command. This offers great flexibility, as you can set the replication factor based on the importance and usage of data. For example, you can lower the replication factor for historical data and raise the replication factor for "hot" data, so more nodes can process the data.

You can change the global replication factor anytime by configuring the `dfs.replication` parameter. Hadoop will either add or remove replicas across the cluster based on whether you increase or decrease the global replication factor.

Note how this behavior is different from how the `fs.block.size` parameter works. The `fs.block.size` parameter sets the block size for the cluster. When you change the value of this parameter, it won't change the block size of files already in HDFS. It'll use the new block size only for new files that are stored in HDFS.

Applications can also specify the replication factor on a per-file basis. You can change the replication factor for a file anytime with the `hdfs dfs -setRep` option. You can change the replication factor for a single file with this command:

```
$ hdfs dfs -setRep -w 2 /data/test/test.txt
```

You can change the replication factor for all files in a directory by adding the `-R` option as shown here:

```
$ hdfs dfs -setRep -w 2 -R /data/test
```

You can reduce the amount of HDFS space occupied by a file by simply reducing the file's replication factor. When you reduce the replication factor using the `hdfs dfs -setrep` option, the NameNode sends the information about the excess replicas to the DataNodes, which will remove the corresponding blocks from HDFS.

Here's an example showing how to reduce the replication factor from the default level of 3 to 2:

1. Issue the following command to check the current replication factor for the file.

   ```
   $ hdfs dfs -ls /user/hive/warehouse/customer/year=2016/month=12/day=31
   -rw-r--r--   3 alapati   analysts   60226324 2016-02-01 01:07
   /user/hive/warehouse/customer/year=2015/month=01/day=31/
   CustRecord-20150131_040_28049_20150131235718-000001-0.avro
   ```

   The number 3 next to the file permission list indicates the replication factor for this file.

2. Change the replication factor from 3 to 2 with the following command:

   ```
   $ hdfs dfs -setrep -R -w 2
   /user/hive/warehouse/customer/year=2015/month=12
   ```

   You can check to make sure that the replication factor has been changed to 2 from 3.

   ```
   $ hdfs dfs -ls /user/hive/warehouse/shoprecord/year=2016/month=01/day=31
   -rw-r--r--   2 alapati analysts   60226324 2016-02-01 01:07
   /user/hive/warehouse/customer/year=2015/month=01/day=31/CustRecord-
   20160131_040_28049_20160131235718-000001-0.avro
   ```

3. Optionally, you can also add the -w flag with this command, to wait for the replication to complete, but this takes a long time for some files. You can see that the replication factor has changed to 2 for the file.

```
$ hdfs dfs -ls
/user/hive/warehouse/customer/year=2016/month=01/day=31
-rw-r--r--   2 alapati analysts   60226324 2015-02-01 01:07
/user/hive/warehouse/customer/year=2015/month=01/day=31/
ShoppingRecord-20160131_040_28049_20160131235718-000001-0.avro
```

In the example here, I changed the replication factor for a file. If you specify a directory instead of a file, the `setrep` command will recursively change the replication factor for all files that are under the directory name you specify.

Although I discussed reducing the replication factor as a way to conserve storage, for important data, you can also try increasing the replication factor. You can also set a higher replication factor for data that's in demand (hot data).

Summary

Here's what you learned in this chapter:

- The `hdfs dfs` command is your ally in performing day-to-day work with HDFS files and directories
- The `hdfs dfsadmin` command is highly useful for checking the status of the DataNodes and the way HDFS data is spread across the DataNodes
- By granting space and file quotas, you can control HDFS usage.
- RThe `hdfs du` and `hdfs df` commands are handy for finding out how your cluster is using its storage
- Balancing your cluster's data on a regular basis provides computational benefits by evenly spreading HDFS data across all the nodes of your Hadoop cluster.

10

Data Protection, File Formats and Accessing HDFS

This chapter covers the following:

- Safeguarding HDFS data using trash and HDFS snapshots
- Ensuring data integrity with file system checks (`fsck` command)
- File-based formats supported by Hadoop
- Choosing the optimal file format
- The Hadoop small files problem and merging files
- Using Hadoop archives to manage small files
- Using Hadoop WebHDFS and HttpFS

As a Hadoop administrator, one of your key tasks is to safeguard Hadoop data. In this chapter, I build on the HDFS introduction I provided in the last chapter and show you how to protect the data stored in HDFS from corruption and accidental deletion of files. You'll learn how to use an important HDFS utility, `fsck`, to check the integrity of HDFS data. I also show how to effectively configure the HDFS trash feature that saves accidentally (or otherwise) deleted files from oblivion. You'll learn how protect HDFS data through the use of HDFS snapshots.

Hadoop can use various types of file formats, with different compression capabilities. The choice of the right file format and the right compression format play a huge role in performance. This chapter details the most common Hadoop file formats. You can compress HDFS data at various levels, and the chapter shows you how to configure compression. You can access HDFS data from outside the Hadoop cluster, through web-based utilities such as WebHDFS and HttpFS, and this chapter shows how to use these tools effectively.

Safeguarding Data

HDFS offers two highly useful features that help guard against deletions of files and directories by users:

- The trash feature stores deleted files and directories for a specified period in a special trash directory before permanently removing them.
- The HDFS snapshot feature lets you make a read-only point-in-time copy of HDFS files or directories that you can revert to if necessary.

Using HDFS Trash to Prevent Accidental Data Deletion

When you delete a file from HDFS, you'll free up blocks associated with that file. However, this freeing up of space won't occur immediately, since HDFS doesn't immediately remove the files you delete. Rather, it renames them and places them in the trash directory. If you configure the retention period to say, six hours, the deleted files stay in the trash directory for six hours, after which the NameNode deletes the file from its namespace. You can restore a deleted file back to its original or a different directory as long as it's still in the trash directory. Thus, the trash feature is a safety device that protects you from the accidental removal of a file. As I just alluded to, you can configure the time interval for which deleted files stay in the trash directory.

Things to Remember about Trash

HDFS trash is a user-level feature, meaning that only files you remove with the HDFS `dfs` file system commands are stored in trash. If you programmatically remove an HDFS file, it's deleted permanently right away! If you want to protect against accidental or wrong file removals through a program, you can do so. You need to create a trash instance and call `moveToTrash()` with the path of the file you want to delete. If trash isn't enabled, the `moveToTrash()` method returns `false`.

Configuring Trash

The HDFS trash feature protects you against accidental deletion of both files and directories. You can enable the trash feature by setting the parameter `fs.trash.interval` (in minutes)in the core-site.xml file, as shown here.

```
<property>
  <name>fs.trash.interval</name>
  <value>1440</value>
</property>
```

By default the trash interval is zero (`fs.trash.interval=0`), so files are deleted permanently immediately, without storing them in the trash directory. By setting 1,440 minutes as the value for the `fs.trash.interval` parameter, I ensured that deleted files are retained in HDFS for one day.

In addition to the `fs.trash.interval` parameter, you can also configure the `fs.trash.checkpoint.interval` parameter when configuring trash in your cluster. This second parameter specifies how often the NameNode checks the trash directory. Trash checkpointing is the process where the current subdirectory is periodically renamed with a timestamp. If you set this parameter to one hour, then the NameNode checks the trash directory every hour and removes files that have been there longer than 1,440 minutes, which is my configured trash interval in this example.

Note that it isn't enough to set the `fs.trash.interval` parameter on the NameNode. You must also set it on all the client nodes from which your clients may access HDFS. Otherwise, you may see files being deleted immediately when clients delete files! The trash interval starts ticking from the time the file was moved to trash, which is whenever you delete a file.

If you've enabled trash, and a file or directory is deleted from HDFS, it doesn't disappear—it's automatically moved to the trash directory under the user's home directory. Here's an example:

```
$ hdfs dfs -rm /user/test/test.txt
15/05/28 08:52:10 INFO fs.TrashPolicyDefault: Namenode trash configuration:
Deletion interval = 1440 minutes, Emptier interval = 0 minutes.
Moved: 'hdfs://hadoop01-ns/user/test/test.txt' to trash at: hdfs://hadoop01-ns/
user/hdfs/.Trash/Current
$
```

The deleted files will actually be located in the /.Trash/.Current/user/test subdirectory of the user's home directory, as shown here:

```
$ hdfs dfs -ls /user/hdfs/.Trash/Current/user
Found 1 items
drwxr-xr-x   - hdfs supergroup 0 2015-05-28 08:52 /user/hdfs/.Trash/Current/user/
test/test.txt
$
```

The file you just deleted, test.txt, which is now in the `.Current` subdirectory, will be permanently deleted and the NameNode will remove the file from the HDFS namespace once the configured time interval for trash elapses. To restore a deleted file from the trash directory, simply copy it to any location in HDFS, as shown here:

```
$ hdfs dfs -cp /user/hdfs/.Trash/Current/user/test/test.txt /user/test/
```

You can empty the trash directory with the following command:

```
$ hdfs dfs -expunge
```

This command deletes all files that are older than the trash interval you've configured. The expunge command will let you reclaim HDFS space occupied by files in the trash directory.

> **Note**
>
> The trash feature allows you to selectively delete some files from HDFS. You can first delete a directory and then restore the files you want from the trash directory.

Bypassing Trash

Sometimes, you may want to bypass the trash facility, because you're deleting some data for good and you want it be gone once and for all. If trash is enabled, the deleted files will continue to occupy the blocks associated with the file and you can't free up the space. If you're performing a regular deletion of files for conserving HDFS space, specify the `-skipTrash` option when deleting files, as shown here:

```
$ hdfs dfs -rm -r -skipTrash /user/test
```

Since I specified the `-skipTrash` option, trash is bypassed, and the deleted file is immediately removed, space occupied by the file is freed up and the NameNode namespace is updated. You can use the `-skipTrash` option when deleting files from a user's directory that exceeds its granted space quota.

If you issue the following command, it removes not only every file stored in the trash directory but the trash directory itself!

```
$ hdfs dfs -rm -r -skipTrash /user/alapati/.Trash
```

Not to worry though, since as soon as you remove any new file, Hadoop will recreate the .Trash/Current directories under your home directory.

Using HDFS Snapshots to Protect Important Data

You can use HDFS snapshots to protect a cluster against errors, as well as to recover from disaster. You can create snapshots of an entire file system or a subtree.

Neither the DataNodes nor the block management layer has any knowledge of the snapshots, with the NameNode storing all the snapshot metadata.

By default, HDFS directories aren't enabled for snapshots, but you can create snapshots on an HDFS directory once you formally set the directory as snapshottable. You can choose to make specific directories or the entire file system snapshottable.

You won't be copying any blocks when you make a director snapshottable. The snapshot files will only contain the block list and the size of the files. You can specify any HDFS directory as snapshottable. In order to delete a snapshottable HDFS directory, it mustn't contain any snapshots.

Snapshots allow you to query previous versions of data. You can access current data without a slowdown, but accessing snapshot data involves some slowdown.

In order to access the snapshot of a directory that you've made snapshottable, you use the path component .snapshot, as shown here.

```
/test1/file1 .snapshot/s0/file1
```

In this example

- /test1 is a snapshottable directory
- /test1/file1 is a file under /test1
- s0 is a snapshot of /test1
- The path /test1/.snapshot/s0/file1 points to the snapshot copy of /test1/file1

In the following sections, I cover

- Working with HDFS snapshots
- Creating and removing snapshots
- Listing snapshots
- Getting a snapshot difference report
- Recovering a deleted file from a snapshot

Working with HDFS Snapshots

You can manage HDFS snapshots with simple commands, such as the examples shown in this section. But before you can play with HDFS snapshots, you must enable the creation of snapshots in a directory. Use the `dfsadmin` utility to make an HDFS directory snapshottable. Use the `-allowSnapshot` command to allow the creation of snapshots under a directory. The syntax of the command is as follows:

```
[-allowSnapshot <snapshotDir>]
```

And here's an example:

```
$ hdfs dfsadmin -allowSnapshot /user/test
Allowing snapshot on /user/test succeeded
$
```

In this command, the snapshot name is optional, and if you omit it, Hadoop will generate a default name for it using a timestamp from when the command was executed. This command makes the /user/test directory snapshottable, meaning you can now create snapshots on this directory. You can reverse the ability to create snapshots on a directory with the `–disallowSnapshot` command. The syntax of this command is as follows:

```
[-disallowSnapshot <snapshotDir>]
```

Creating and Removing Snapshots

Once you've made an HDFS directory snapshottable, use the `dfs` utility to execute the `-createSnapshot` command to create a snapshot of the now snapshottable directory, as shown in this example.

```
$ hdfs dfs -createSnapshot <path> [,snapshotName>]
```

Here's an example showing how to create a snapshot on the /user/test directory.

```
$ hdfs dfs -createSnapshot /user/test Snap1
Created snapshot /user/test/.snapshot/Snap1
$
```

The snapshot is named Snap1 in this example. If you don't specify a snapshot name, which is an optional attribute for the command, you'll still create a snapshot, but it will now have a Hadoop-generated name, as shown here.

```
$ hdfs dfs -createSnapshot /user/test
Created snapshot /user/test/.snapshot/s20150509-140236.074
$
```

It's easier to refer to a snapshot with a name provided by you than with a system-generated one, so use a snapshot name when creating a snapshot.

As mentioned earlier, all snapshots are created under the target directory, within a directory named .snapshot.

You can remove a snapshot with the deleteSnapshot command:

```
$ hdfs dfs -deleteSnapshot /user/test Snap1
```

Listing Your Snapshots

You can use the normal HDFS file commands when dealing with .snapshot paths. To list all snapshots under a directory, issue the ls command.

```
$ hdfs dfs -ls /user/test/.snapshot
Found 1 items
drwxr-xr-x   - hdfs supergroup          0 2015-05-28 08:44 /user/test/.snapshot/
Snap1
$
```

In order to find all the snapshottable directories where a current user is allowed to create snapshots, issue the lsSnapshottbleDir command:

```
$ hdfs lsSnapshottableDir
drwxr-xr-x 0 hdfs     supergroup 0 2015-05-09 14:11 0 65536 /user/test
```

In this case, I have just one snapshottable directory. If you have multiple snapshottable directories, you can optionally specify the path of the snapshottable directory and the snapshot name as well, as shown in the following syntax statement.

```
hdfs lsSnapshottableDir $path $snapshotName
```

Getting a Snapshot Difference Report

You can get a snapshot difference report to view the differences between two snapshots, a starting and ending snapshot, by issuing the following command.

```
hdfs snapshotDiff $path $fromSnapshot $toSnapshot
```

The fromSnapshot parameter species the name of the starting snapshot and the parameter toSnapshot specifies the name of the ending snapshot. Here's an example:

```
$ hdfs snapshotDiff snap1 snap2
```

When you issue this command, you'll see output like the following:

```
Difference between snapshot snap1 and snapshot snap2 under
directory /test:
M           .
        ./file1
        ./subdir1
+       ./file2
+       /subdir2
```

The symbol M in the output for this command indicates that the file or directory was modified. The + (plus) and – (minus) signs indicate which files and directories were removed or added in the second snapshot. If you see the symbol `R`, it means that the file or directory was renamed.

You can list all files in a snapshot in the following manner:

```
$ hdfs dfs -ls /foo/.snapshot/s0
```

You can copy a file from a snapshot, in this case snapshot `s0`, in the following way.

```
$ hdfs dfs -cp -ptopax /foo/.snapshot/s0/bar /tmp
```

The options -ptopax mean that the timestamps, ownership, permissions, ACLs and XAttrs are all preserved in the copied snapshot.

Removing a Snapshottable Directory

You can test whether the snapshottable directory works as promised by trying to delete a snapshottable directory that has a file inside it. Earlier, I showed how you could remove an empty snapshottable directory with the `deleteSnapshot` command. Let's see what happens when issuing a `rm -r` command to delete a snapshottable directory that contains files.

```
$ hdfs dfs -rm -r /user/test

15/05/28 08:50:32 INFO fs.TrashPolicyDefault: Namenode trash configuration:
Deletion interval = 1440 minutes, Emptier interval = 0 minutes.

rm: Failed to move to trash: hdfs://hadoop01-ns/user/test: The directory
/user/test cannot be deleted since /user/test is snapshottable and already has
 Snapshots

$
```

As you can see, Hadoop has refused to delete the directory because it's snapshottable and it contains a directory. You can't remove the directory, either as the HDFS super user or as the owner of the directory. A snapshottable directory can't be deleted or renamed until you delete all snapshots.

Recovering a Deleted File from a Snapshot

Let's see what happens when you remove a file from a snapshottable directory.

```
$ hdfs dfs -rm /user/test/test1.txt
```

Hadoop does as you wish and removes the file. Since this file was in a snapshottable directory, you can recover the deleted file without any problem! To do this, follow these steps.

1. Find the file you wish to recover by looking for it in the snapshot subdirectory:

   ```
   $ hdfs dfs -  test/.snapshot
   ```

   As you can see, the subdirectory you need to check is named `.snapshot`, and under it is the file that you removed from HDFS. You can even view the contents of the file to ensure everything is intact.

2. Recover the deleted file from the snapshot by copying the file to its original location:

```
$ hdfs dfs -cp /user/test/.snapshot/Snap1/test.txt /user/test/test.txt
```

Your deleted file is back without a problem!

When you create an HDFS snapshot, the blocks in the DataNodes aren't copied, and there is no data copying whatsoever. The snapshot files merely record the block list and the file size. Normal HDFS operations go on as usual. Any modifications to a snapshotted file are stored in reverse chronological order, so you can access current data directly. The snapshot data is figured by subtracting any modifications from the current data.

Users can be enabled to take their own snapshots, with administrators managing the snapshots by specifying where the users can take the snapshots. Files and directories in a snapshottable directory are immutable, and you can't add or remove anything from the directories.

Snapshots and HDFS Backups

In the previous section, I showed you how to recover a deleted file, say due to a user error, with the help of an HDFS snapshot. You can also use HDFS snapshots to back up critical data. Using the trash facility guards against accidental deletion of files and directories works only for CLI-based deletions. Snapshots enable point-in-time recovery and periodic snapshots from which to restore data. There's no recovery involved in accessing data in the snapshots.

Ensuring Data Integrity with File System Checks

Linux system administrators run the `fsck` command to repair file system corruption on an ext3 or ext4 file system. The `fsck` utility examines the on-disk structures and can fix them if they're corrupted. HDFS offers a similar `fsck` command, which helps determine files missing blocks or containing corrupt blocks.

Unlike the Linux `fsck` command, the `hdfs fsck` command doesn't try to repair the errors but provides options to fix the corruption. Here's an example that shows how to check the entire HDFS file system—that is, the entire file system namespace—by specifying / as the path under which Hadoop must check the file system.

> **Note**
>
> When you run the `fsck` command right after adding a DataNode back to the cluster, the `fsck` report normally reports over-replicated blocks—this is corrected over time.

Instead of issuing the command `hdfs fsck`, you can issue it in the following format:

```
hdfs fsck / | egrep -v '^\.+$' | grep -v eplica
```

This gets rid of the lines of dots that preceded the actual output of the `fsck` command. Following are the results of our example.

```
$ hdfs fsck / | egrep -v '^\.+$' | grep -v eplica
Connecting to namenode via http://hadoop01.localhost:50070
```

```
FSCK started by hdfs (auth:SIMPLE) from /10.192.0.23 for path /
 at Mon May 30 13:54:08 CDT 2016
$ hdfs fsck /
........
.........Status: HEALTHY
 Total size:    146228151045063 B
 Total dirs:    28152
 Total files:   1077255
 Total symlinks:                0
 Total blocks (validated):      1170946 (avg. block size 124880354 B)
 Minimally replicated blocks:   1170946 (100.0 %)
 Over-replicated blocks:        0 (0.0 %)
 Under-replicated blocks:       0 (0.0 %)
 Mis-replicated blocks:         0 (0.0 %)
 Default replication factor:    3
 Average block replication:     2.9950006
 Corrupt blocks:                0
 Missing replicas:              0 (0.0 %)
 Number of data-nodes:          18
 Number of racks:               1
FSCK ended at Fri May 01 09:45:41 CDT 2015 in 18069 milliseconds
The filesystem under path '/' is HEALTHY
$
```

Note that the total size of the cluster (in bytes) shown by the following line at the top shows actual size of all HDFS files and not their replicated size. If your replication factor is three for HDFS, then the total actual size used by HDFS is three times this number.

```
Total size:    146228151045063 B
```

The actual size occupied by HDFS will be about 438TB in this example.

If you've configured HDFS snapshots, you can add the option `-includeSnapshots` when running the `fsck` command. This option ensures that `fsck` includes the snapshot data if a directory path has snapshottable directories under it. The `-list-corruptfileblocks` option in the `fsck` command will print all missing blocks and the files of which they are a part.

HDFS Data Corruption

HDFS file corruption could have a serious impact on the availability of data. In the following sections, I explain how to detect HDFS data corruption and what to do about it.

The easiest way to check if there's corruption in HDFS is to run the `fsck` command. The `fsck` command will run through all the HDFS blocks and report whether the file system is healthy. If the `fsck` command reports an unhealthy HDFS system, you most likely will see the following types of messages in the `fsck` command output:

```
There are 1 missing blocks. The following files may be corrupted:

blk_1088616699 /user/alapati/.staging/job_1424873694018_0438/libjars/hbase-
common.jar
Please check the logs or run fsck in order to identify the missing blocks. See the
Hadoop FAQ for common causes and potential solutions.
```

And the fsck command reports that the HDFS file system that HDFS is corrupt, as shown in the following example.

```
$ sudo -u hdfs hdfs fsck /
Status: CORRUPT
 Total size:    360430 B
 Total dirs:    0
 Total files:   1
 Total symlinks:                0
 Total blocks (validated):      1 (avg. block size 360430 B)
  ********************************
  CORRUPT FILES:        1
  MISSING BLOCKS:       1
  MISSING SIZE:         360430 B
  CORRUPT BLOCKS:       1
  ********************************
 Minimally replicated blocks:   0 (0.0 %)
 Over-replicated blocks:        0 (0.0 %)
 Under-replicated blocks:       0 (0.0 %)
 Mis-replicated blocks:         1 (100.0 %)
 Default replication factor:    3
 Average block replication:     0.0
 Corrupt blocks:                1
 Missing replicas:              0
 Number of data-nodes:          54
 Number of racks:               3
FSCK ended at Fri May 01 12:13:54 CDT 2015 in 1 milliseconds
The filesystem under path '/user/alapati/.staging/job_1424873694018_0438/libjars/
hbase-common.jar' is CORRUPT
$
```

Handling HDFS Corruption

If you're concerned about some blocks being corrupt, you can run the fsck command with the -list-corruptfileblocks option as shown here:

```
$ hdfs fsck -list-corruptfileblocks
Connecting to namenode via http://hadoop1.localhost:50070
The list of corrupt files under path '/' are:
blk_1088616699  /user/alapati/.staging/job_1424873694018_0438/libjars/hbase-
common.jar
The filesystem under path '/' has 1 CORRUPT files
$
```

There are two ways to handle corrupt files. One way is for you to run the fsck command with the -move option to move the corrupted files to the /lost+found directory. This is better than deleting the corrupted file from the HDFS file system with the hdfs -dfs -rm command. Also, remember that when you remove a corrupted file from HDFS with the rm command, the corrupted file is shown as corrupt, because it goes into the trash directory, if you've configured one.

A better way to remove the corrupted files is by specifying the -delete option with the fsck command, as shown here:

```
$ fsck -delete
```

While the `fsck` command issued without any options (besides the file system to check) lets you know the health status of that file system, specifying the `-blocks` option gets you a block report and the `-locations` option prints out locations for every block. Here's an example:

```
$ hdfs fsck /user/alapati/.staging/job_1424873694018_0438/libjars/hbase-common.jar
-blocks -locations
Connecting to namenode via http://hadoop01.localhost:50070
FSCK started by hdfs (auth:SIMPLE) from /10.192.0.22 for path /user/alapati/
.staging/job_1424873694018_0438/libjars/hbase-common.jar at Mon May 30 12:13:54
CDT 2016
.
/user/alapati/.staging/job_1424873694018_0438/libjars/hbase-common.jar:
CORRUPT blockpool BP-2077913507-10.192.0.21-1357858111062 block blk_1088616699

/user/alapati/.staging/job_1424873694018_0438/libjars/hbase-common.jar:
Replica placement policy is violated for BP-2077913507-10.192.0.21-
1357858111062:blk_1088616699_1099615351525. Block should be additionally
replicated on 1 more rack(s).

/user/alapati/.staging/job_1424873694018_0438/libjars/hbase-common.jar: MISSING 1
blocks of total size 360430 B.
0. BP-2077913507-10.192.0.21-1357858111062:blk_1088616699_1099615351525
len=360430 MISSING!
```

The output of the previous command helps you find out where the corrupted blocks are (on which node in the cluster). You can then use the block numbers to go to the NameNode and check its logs to see where the blocks are (or were) located. If you find that the problem was due to a DataNode being down or a missing mount point, the corruption will go away once you fix the problem.

When you see a message stating that a block is missing as shown here, unfortunately, it means just what it says!

```
MISSING 1 blocks of total size 360430 B
BP-2077913507-10.192.0.21-1357858111062:blk_1088616699_1099615351525 len=360430
MISSING!
```

Regardless of the replication factor of the missing block, all replicas of that block are gone and the NameNode is not aware of any DataNode that has a replica of this block. It's possible that the DataNode that stores a replica of this block is down or unreachable, and when you are able to access that DataNode again, the block is replicated as many times as specified by its replication factor. You consequently also won't find the block listed as corrupt when you rerun the `fsck` command.

It's possible that a block is not missing but is replicated fewer times than it's supposed to be. In this case, you'll see output similar to the following:

```
BP-2077913507-10.192.0.21-1357858111062:blk_1088616699_1099615351525 len=360430
repl=3 [10.192.0.21:50010, 10.192.0.25:50010, 10.192.0.30:50010]
BP-2077913507-10.192.0.21-1357858111062:blk_1088616699_1099615351525 len=360430
repl=3 [10.192.0.21:50010]
```

The entries in the square brackets are the DataNodes that hold the block. The first entry lists three such DataNodes. The second entry lists only one DataNode, which indicates that while the replication factor is three, only a single replica of the block exists (on node 10.192.0.21). The remaining two blocks are missing. Unless you have hard drive issues on the target servers, over time the cluster will automatically replicate this block two more times. If you run the `fsck` command at this point, you won't find the block listed as corrupt.

If all replicas of a data block are either missing or corrupt, it means that there's no readable replica—in effect the data on the data block can't be read. A missing data block has no live replicas. This may be due to corruption or because the DataNode on which the block lives is offline. If you see the file system corrupt message for many blocks at once, it means several DataNodes are unavailable simultaneously. If you have stored any data with a replication factor of just one, you may see the missing blocks messages even when a single node is lost or is functioning incorrectly.

The `fsck` Command Options

Here's a brief summary of the important options you can specify with the `hdfs fsck` command.

- `fsck /`: Performs an HDFS file system check
- `fsck / -files`: Displays files being checked
- `fsck / -files -blocks`: Displays files and blocks
- `fsck / files -blocks -locations`: Displays files, blocks and their locations
- `fsck / -files -blocks -locations -racks`: Displays files, blocks, locations and racks
- `fsck -locations`: Shows locations for every block
- `fsck - move`: Moves corrupted files to the /lost+found directory
- `fsck -delete`: Deletes corrupt files
- `fsck -list-corruptfileblocks`: Lists missing blocks and the files they belong to

Handling Files That Are Unrecoverable

A corrupted file is an HDFS file where all replicas of a block are missing. You can use the `fsck -move` command to move all corrupted files to the /lost+found directory. You can execute the `fsck -delete` command to delete the corrupted files from HDFS.

If you can't find at least one DataNode that contains any of the missing or corrupt blocks of a file pointed out by the `fsck` utility, that file doesn't exist in HDFS any longer and is lost for good. In this case, use the `fsck -move` command to move the parts of the file with missing blocks to the /lost+found directory, as shown here.

```
$ hdfs fsck -move <file_name>
```

Here's an example:

```
$ hdfs fsck -move /user/alapati/.staging/job_1424873694018_0438/libjars/hbase-
common.jar
Connecting to namenode via http://hadoop01.localhost:50070
FSCK started by hdfs (auth:SIMPLE) from /10.192.0.23 for path /user/alapati/
.staging/job_1424873694018_0438/libjars/hbase-common.jar at Mon May 04 13:22:09
CDT 2015
drwxr--r--   - hdfs supergroup          0 2015-05-04 13:22 /lost+found/user/
alapati/.staging/job_1424873694018_0438/libjars

$ hdfs dfs -ls /lost+found/user/alapati/.staging/job_1424873694018_0438/libjars
Found 1 items
drw-r--r--   - hdfs supergroup          0 2015-05-04 13:22 /lost+found/user/
alapati/.staging/job_1424873694018_0438/libjars/hbase-common.jar
```

If you store an HDFS file with a replication factor of two and two of the DataNodes go down, potentially you could end up with corrupted HDFS files. Similarly, if you have stored any HDFS files with a replication factor of 1, even the loss of a single DataNode can result in missing blocks showing up when you check your file system with the `hdfs fsck` command.

By running the `fsck -delete` command, you ensure that the missing files are removed from the HDFS metadata. If you don't remove them, it's possible that a process may get stuck trying to read the missing files. Make sure that the unimportant files are the only ones showing up in the `fsck` command output before you issue the `fsck -delete` command. You may still find that `fsck` reports the deleted files. When you run `fsck` subsequently, it should report a healthy HDFS.

To proactively catch potential HDFS corruption, run the `hdfs fsck` command on a regular basis, just as you'd run the HDFS `balancer` command (to ensure that the HDFS data is balanced across all nodes), using a `cron` job. The overhead of the `fsck` file checks isn't really significant, but on a busy cluster, you may want to schedule the job during off-peak times, just as you schedule the balancer jobs.

Handling Under-Replicated Files

Hadoop is good about replicating blocks to meet the configured replication factor for files. When a DataNode crashes, files on that node are usually replicated in a short time. Hadoop is aware of the missing DataNode since it ceases getting the heartbeats from the DataNode. The replication starts in a little over ten minutes after the DataNode crash.

Data Compression

Compression is used for efficiently storing data blocks. Compression is highly recommended as it reduces the size of the files on disk and also speeds up both disk and network I/O.

You must weigh the following when deciding on a compression format:

- CPU required for compressing and decompressing the data
- The network bandwidth consumed by the transmission of data across the cluster

- Disk I/O required for reading and writing the data
- Whether the file is splittable

Note

If the blocks in a file are independently compressible, then those file formats support block-level compression. If a file format doesn't permit block compression, and you compress that file, that file isn't splittable. If you are dealing with a large file, this will affect performance because when reading the compressed file, Hadoop must start at the beginning of the file, even if it wants to simply read a block at the very end of the file.

As you'll learn, the choice of a compression format involves tradeoffs between speed and the size of the compressed output. Faster compression and decompression speeds usually are associated with larger compressed files.

Regardless of the compression format, however, since the files are significantly smaller than uncompressed files, I/O bound jobs tend to finish faster when you compress the input files.

Common Compression Formats

The most common compression formats are gzip, bzip2, LZO and Snappy. Let's quickly review these compression formats.

- gzip: This compression format is based on the deflate algorithm and uses the file extension .gz. It's a non-splittable format.
- bzip2: It's highly efficient in terms of storage savings and is also fast in both compressing data and decompressing data. This is a splittable format.
- LZO: It's composed of multiple small blocks of compressed data, which allows jobs to be split across the block boundaries. Its decompression speed is about twice as fast as that of bzip2. However, the compressed files are about 50 percent larger than files compressed with the bizip2 format. LZO files are splittable only if they're indexed.
- Snappy: Snappy offers reasonable compression of data, since its compression ratio is less efficient than that of several other compression formats. However, the compression is done at higher speed. Although Snappy compressed files are usually 10 to 50 percent larger than a gzip compressed file, for example, it's much faster, with a compression rate of about 250MB per second and a decompression rate of about 500MB per second.

Note

The Text file type is an unstructured file format. Avro, Parquet, RCFile and SequenceFile are all structured formats.

Evaluating the Various Compression Schemes

As you've learned, you can employ various compression algorithms for data. Here are some observations regarding the various compression strategies:

- LZO is good for general formats.
- Snappy and LZO both are optimized for speed but aren't very effective at compressing data. Snappy is faster than LZO in decompressing data.
- Snappy is recommended for container formats like Avro, and gzip is generally not recommended as an output format because it's not splittable. Snappy is a better performer than LZO in most cases.
- gzip offers a better compression ratio, but it uses more CPU resources than Snappy and LZO. You can consider gzip for compressing data that's accessed infrequently. For data you access frequently. Snappy or LZO are better options.
- bzip2 offers a better compression ratio than gzip2, but for some types of files, it's slower when compressing and decompressing the data.
- If you want the MapReduce compressed data to be in a splittable format, you should consider bzip2, LZO and Snappy, since they're all splittable. gzip isn't splittable.
- Your choice of a file format has serious performance implications. Query performance is directly related to the amount of resources in the form of CPU and I/O that you need to expend to deserialize compressed data.

The appropriate file format and compression codec you choose will depend on your data sets. Hive can import files stored in the gzip and bzip2 compression format into tables directly. When you execute queries the compressed files are decompressed and provided to the mapper tasks. However, gzip and bzip2 compression schemes don't allow the file to be split and processed within a single mapper. Therefore, files stored in the gzip/bzip2 format are loaded into Hive tables using a SequenceFile or Avro or Parquet format, all of which are splittable and assignable to different mappers.

You can move data from one file format or compression codec to another by creating a new Hive (or Impala) table with the new file format or compression codec and then copying the data from the current table to a new table with an `INSERT` statement.

Compression at Various Stages for MapReduce

You can compress data at the input, intermediate or output stages. It's a good practice to consider compressing data at each of the three stages, to reduce both disk and network I/O. You'll almost always have enough available CPU cycles to handle the overhead involved in compressing and decompressing data.

MapReduce Input and Output

MapReduce jobs involve a heavy amount of I/O processing, so any reduction in the I/O will improve job performance. Compressing data is a great way of reducing MapReduce I/O. MapReduce involves I/O at several steps during its processing:

- Reading input data files from HDFS
- Writing mapper output to the local file system
- Merging sorted data received from the mappers on the local file system for use by the reducers
- Reducers reading data from their local file system
- Reducers writing output back to HDFS

These steps are all operations that involve the usage of disk. Besides disk usage, there's also network I/O involved during the retrieval of files by the reducers from the nodes where the mappers are running. Compressing data is a great way to reduce the I/O involved in processing.

Compressing Input Data

You can compress input files when storing data in HDFS. Mappers need to perform less I/O when reading the compressed input blocks. Since compression reduces the bytes you need to read from HDFS, reads are faster, but decompressing the files involves CPU overhead.

MapReduce automatically decompresses data as it reads the input files. It uses the filename extension to determine which compression codec to use. For example, it identifies a file ending with the .gz extension as a gzip-compressed file, and reads the file with the gzip codec.

Compressing Intermediate Mapper Output

Input files aren't the only ones that benefit from compression. You can also compress the intermediate files generated by MapReduce jobs. During MapReduce processing, mappers produce intermediate files on the local file system of the nodes where the mappers run. The destination reducers will then partition the intermediate output files and sort them according to the reducer keys, following which the reducers download the files over HTTP. Compressing intermediate output will reduce both disk I/O due to mappers writing to disk as well as network I/O when reducers transfer the partitioned files from the mapper nodes to the nodes where the reducers are running.

You should consider compressing intermediate data for all MapReduce jobs that generate more than a tiny amount of map output. Using LZO compression will hasten job completion by reducing the amount of disk I/O incurred during the shuffle phase. You can enable compression by setting the configuration parameter `mapred.compress.map.output` to true in the mapred-site.xml file.

If your job outputs are large, LZO compression will reduce the number of writes, especially if you're using the default replication factor of three.

Note that even if MapReduce reads and writes uncompressed data, it can benefit from compressing the mapper's intermediate output. For example, if you use LZO compression or Snappy, you gain performance improvements through reducing the amount of data transferred.

Compressing MapReduce Job Output

You can compress map output before it's written to disk. This is not only faster but involves less data transferred to the reducer, as well as consumes less storage space. By default, output is not compressed, and you can enable compression by setting the `mapred.compress.map.output` parameter to true. You specify the actual compression codec with the parameter `mapred.map.output.compression.codec`.

Some MapReduce jobs use a reduce phase and some don't. Regardless, there's output that can be compressed. If it's a map-only job, you can compress the mapper output, and if the job uses a reducer, you compress the reducer output.

You can compress either the MapReduce intermediate data or the output data, or even both intermediate and output data. The following example shows how to compress both intermediate as well as output data when running a MapReduce job:

```
hadoop jar hadoop-examples-.jar sort "-Dmapreduce.compress.map.output=true"
      "-Dmapreduce.map.output.compression.codec=org.apache.hadoop.io.compress
.GzipCodec"
      "-Dmapreduce.output.compress=true"
      "-Dmapreduce.output.compression.codec=org.apache.hadoop.io.compress
.GzipCodec" -outKey
      org.apache.hadoop.io.Text -outValue org.apache.hadoop.io.Text input output
```

How to Enable Compression

Hadoop comes with several codecs to enable you to compress (and decompress) data. A codec is an implementation of the `CompressionCodec` class, and you can specify the appropriate compression codecs in the core-site.xml file by specifying the property `io.compression.codecs`. For example, you can specify Snappy compression by specifying the Snappy CompressionCodec implementation class in the core-site.xml file, by specifying the class `org.apache.hadoop.io.compress.SnappyCodec`.

Since compression isn't enabled by default, you must enable it by setting both of these parameters to true in the `mapred-site.xml` file.

- `mapreduce.map.output.compress`: Compresses the intermediate mapper output
- `mapreduce.output.fileoutputformat.compress`: Compresses the MapReduce job output

The `mapreduce.map.output.compress` parameter determines whether the map output should be compressed before it's sent across the network. The default value for this parameter is `false`. The `mapreduce.output.fileoutputformat.compress` parameter determines whether the job output should be compressed and is set to `false` by default.

It's important to understand that if you enable compression but don't specify the compression codecs with the `io.compression.codecs` parameter, Hadoop will still compress the output, using a default codec. The default Hadoop compression codec is org.apache.hadoop.io.compress.Defaultcodec, which uses the deflate compression format. The deflate compression format is the same as gzip without the additional headers.

You can configure the type of compression you want by choosing the appropriate compression codec. The following compression codecs are available:

```
org.apache.hadoop.io.compress.DefaultCodec
org.apache.hadoop.io.compress.GzipCodec
org.apache.hadoop.io.compress.BZip2Codec
org.apache.hadoop.io.compress.DeflateCodec
org.apache.hadoop.io.compress.SnappyCodec
org.apache.hadoop.io.compress.Lz4Codec
```

As mentioned earlier, the configuration property io.compression.codecs (in the mapred-site.xml file) lets you configure the types of compression codecs you want to use. For this parameter, you provide a list of comma-separated compression codec classes that Hadoop is allowed to use for compression and decompression of data.

You can configure the use of multiple compression codecs in your cluster, as shown here:

```
<property>
  <name>io.compression.codecs</name>
  <value>
org.apache.hadoop.io.compress.DefaultCodec,org.apache.hadoop.io.compress
.GzipCodec,org.apache.hadoop.io.compress.BZip2Codec,org.apache.hadoop.io.compress
.DeflateCodec,org.apache.hadoop.io.compress.SnappyCodec,org.apache.hadoop
.io.compress.Lz4Codec
  </value>
</property>
```

In this example, I enabled the use of multiple compression codecs in my cluster. MapReduce jobs in my cluster can use any of these compression codecs. As explained earlier, if you enable compression but don't specify a particular codec to use, Hadoop uses the default codec (org.apache.hadoop.io.compress.DefaultCodec). You can change the default codec to an alternative codec by configuring one or both of the following two parameters in the mapred-site.xml file:

- mapreduce.output.fileoutputformat.compress.codec: Sets the default codec for the job output
- mapreduce.map.output.compress.codec: Sets the default codec for the intermediate output produced by the mappers

If you don't frequently process the stored data, and the compression factor is high, or the data arrives in a compressed format, then that data is a good candidate for compressing. This is particularly true if you're using a compression format such as Snappy, whose decompression speed is quite high. You end up gaining a lot while paying a small price for compression. On the other hand, if you can only gain meager benefits because the data isn't very redundant and compressed data isn't in a splittable format, it may not be such a good idea to use compression.

Compression for Spark

Spark comes with its own compression-related configuration parameters. For example, you can compress broadcast variables before sending them, by setting the `spark.broadcast.compress` property (the default value is `true`, anyway).

Spark lets you compress internal data such as RDD partitions, broadcast variables and shuffle outputs through the `spark.io.compression.codec` property. Spark provides three codecs: lz4, lzf and Snappy (default). You may optionally use fully qualified class names when specifying the codecs, such as the following:

```
org.apache.spark.io.LZ4CompressionCodec
org.apache.spark.io.LZFCompressionCodec
org.apache.spark.io.SnappyCompressionCodec
```

Data Serialization

In its raw form, data is a sequence or stream of bits. When data is sent to HDFS from an external source, it's in this raw form that data moves through the network and is stored on disk. Serialization is the process of converting structured data to its underlying raw form and deserialization is the opposite process of reconstructing a structured form of data from its raw form. Once you choose the right type of file format, you may also choose the type of serialization you want.

Hadoop uses the writable interface for serializing and deserializing data. Hadoop's serialization is more compact than Java serialization and thus more efficient. You can integrate any type of alternative serialization framework with MapReduce jobs. Many of these frameworks are more compact and faster in serializing and deserializing data.

Typically, serialization and deserialization (SerDe) is used to read and write data to a Hive table. The SerDe module is located between the file format of the data and the object representation of the rows in the Hive table. Here's how we can summarize how serialization/deserialization works:

- Serializer: Row Object => Serializer => <key,value> => OutputFormat => HDFS File
- Deserializer: HDFS File => InputFileFormat => <key,value> => Deserializer => Row Object

Parquet data, for example, is serialized using a Parquet file format. Parquet, therefore, can't read files serialized with the Avro SerDe, and the same thing does for Avro, which can't read Parquet files.

Hadoop File Formats

Although administrators often focus their time and energies on cluster management, it's important that they devote adequate attention to the selection of the optimal Hadoop file formats. The file formats you choose for your data have a significant impact on both performance and storage.

The problem here is that there's no file format out there that is best in both performance and storage requirements. Some file formats lend themselves better to compression, and thus are appropriate if reducing storage for that data is your key concern. Similarly, a file format may lead to lower throughput because changes in the schema (such as adding new columns) may lead to the reprocessing of vast amounts of data.

Hadoop supports the following data formats:

- Text files
- SequenceFiles
- Record columnar (RC) and optimized row columnar (ORC) files
- Avro
- Parquet

One of the key points you must remember with regard to data formats is that most of us deal with structured data as well as semi-structured data that is quite likely to undergo structural changes over time, with the addition, modification and removal of fields. It's also possible that the formats may vary across records.

Hadoop lets you work with several data formats, including regular text files, SequenceFiles, Avro, ORC and Parquet. The various formats determine how Hadoop reads, splits and writes files.

It's common in many environments to transform the input data from their original format such as XML files to a more useful format such as the Avro file format. You can also compress the files, using various compression formats, such as Snappy, bzip and bzip2. Thus, you end up with various choices, such as Avro or Avro with Snappy Compression, for example.

I discussed compression in detail in the preceding sections. In addition to the file format you select, you can also specify a SerDe to determine how a table's records ought to be serialized and deserialized. For example, Hive comes with an AvroSerDe, where the Avro format stores data in a binary format.

Criteria for Determining the Right File Format

Following are some of the common criteria used to determine the right file format for data for Hadoop applications.

Flexibility of the File Format

Some file formats are more amenable than others to enabling schema evolution over time. If you anticipate that your data will add or delete fields, it'll be nice if your file format can read the historical data without your having to modify the code. Ideally, you should be able to read all your historical data, even though the current schema has changed over time, without having to rewrite code.

Compression Capabilities

When using large files, you need to be wary about the disk storage that you're going to need. If a file is 10GB, since each file will be replicated three times, you'll actually need 30GB of disk storage to store that file. Obviously, anything that can conserve your disk storage is going to be a great thing. It's common in many environments to transform the input data from their original formats, such as converting input files in the XML format to Avro files for MapReduce processing.

There are several types of compression that are available. The most commonly used compression types are Snappy, bizp, bzip2 and deflate.

Splittability

A file is considered splittable if Hadoop can read the data from any specific point in the file. If Hadoop can't process a file by starting at any arbitrary point in the file, that file isn't splittable. In a splittable format, a file can be split reliably into pieces called splits at the record boundaries. A splittable file format can easily seek to the beginning of a record from any point in the file. Since MapReduce splits files in order to read the data in parallel with multiple mappers, splittable files are a vital requirement for it.

SequenceFiles, Avro, RC and ORC are container file formats that support both compression and splitting. They all help solve Hadoop's "small files problem," which I explain later in this chapter.

The compression format you use has a significant bearing on how MapReduce processes the input files, depending on whether the compression format supports splitting.

Performance

Compressing data has a bearing on performance, and you need to differentiate between write and read performance in this context. Some file formats perform great for reading the compressed data but offer less efficient write performance. Typically, uncompressed data such as writing to a CSV file is much faster than writing to a compressed file, as there's no overhead of compression. The same compressed CSV file also proves to be less efficient for reading data, since reading from a compressed file is usually slower as compared to reading from an uncompressed original file.

File Size

As mentioned earlier, it's advantageous to use large splittable files as small files aren't conducive to efficient processing. Hadoop works best with large files—processing large numbers of tiny files will adversely affect performance. Ideally, you should have large files that are splittable, so you can take advantage of Hadoop's parallel processing architecture.

Compatibility with the Processing Tools

A key criterion when choosing a file format is the format's compatibility with various tools used in the Hadoop environment, such as Hive and Pig. Hadoop components support multiple data formats such as text files, SequenceFiles and RC files. Hive, for example, can load data into the Text, Parquet, Avro, RC file and SequenceFile formats. I discuss the file formats supported by Hadoop in the next section.

File Formats Supported by Hadoop

It might seem to you that since Hadoop is a big data tool, you can store all the data you need without worrying about space. Unfortunately, that isn't true, and it's very easy to exhaust space by loading and storing data. You can save space by compressing the data, and for doing that, you need to store the data in container formats such as a SequenceFile or the Avro file format.

Hadoop is quite flexible regarding the storage formats of data. You can use various file formats by explicitly specifying the format in a SQL statement, such as `STORED AS PARQUETFILE`, or by using an installed interface such as Avro.

In the following sections, I briefly review the data formats supported by Hadoop.

Text Files and Binary Formats

The text file format is the default storage format and represents data stored in a delimited form, with a separate line for each record and with new lines separating the records. Here's an example:

```
...
ROW FORMAT DELIMITED
  FIELDS TERMINATED BY ',' ESCAPED BY '\\'
  LINES TERMINATED BY '\n'
  NULL DEFINED AS '\N'
```

You can specify the termination character as a tab or a carriage return character or an octal or hexadecimal value, and the data mustn't contain any delimiter characters.

In a text file, every record is a line of text. Text files are most commonly CSV, TSV or JSON records. Text and CSV files are common and are used often when transferring data from relational databases or loading data into other databases. Text format is convenient when exchanging data with applications or scripts that generate or read delimited files, and it is readable by humans and parsable as well.

The text file format, while it can be processed by almost all tools, isn't as efficient as a binary storage format, because unlike the latter, it requires type conversions for all non-character columns. The text file format also doesn't support block compression. Not being able to use block compression means that reading large uncompressed CSVs is much slower when compared to read performance of other compressed data formats.

CSV files don't store metadata, and therefore you must have that information with you when working with these types of files. CSV files don't offer full support for schema evolution, because while you can add new fields, you can do so only by adding them at the end of a record. You can't delete existing fields.

JSON data fully supports evolving schemas, as it stores metadata with the data. As with text files, JSON records don't support block compression and thus aren't splittable.

Your data might come in a format readable by humans. However, for efficient processing by applications, it's smarter to convert them into a binary format since they store data much more efficiently on disk (fewer bytes to store the same data) and, therefore, are faster to write out the data to disk. In addition, many binary formats can compress data before writing it out to disk.

Binary formats are also better at error detection during writes. The fact that binary records detect and ignore error-ridden files makes them a better candidate for writing to HDFS when compared to regular text files if, during a write, a file ends up with incomplete or corrupt records, say due to a block allocation.

Avro and Protobuf are popular binary formats used in several Hadoop environments. There are also binary columnar formats such as RC file, ORC file and Parquet.

SequenceFiles

SequenceFiles provide persistent data structures for storing binary key/value pairs. These files are row-based and are frequently employed by MapReduce jobs to transfer data among themselves. SequenceFiles support splitting, even when you compress the data. SequenceFiles are used as containers to store small files. A SequenceFile is a flat file that contains key/value pairs. It's common during data ingestion to use a SequenceFile as a container and store the file-related metadata such as the filename and creation time as the key and consider the file's contents as the value.

SequenceFiles are more compact than text files and work well with the output of MapReduce programs. In order to lower its I/O footprint, you can compress SequenceFiles on file or block level. SequenceFiles are a common data format used to write files to HDFS.

SequenceFiles are commonly used to combine multiple small files into a single large file, to get around the well-known *small file problem* in Hadoop.

SequenceFiles let you store any arbitrary data in a binary format and have a structure that's similar to a text file (CSV file). This type of file maintains the necessary metadata to recognize the record boundaries and thus lets you store data that can be split on record boundaries. Contrast this with a text file, where newlines determine record boundaries, and therefore an arbitrary DFS block is processed by looking for new lines to find the beginning and end of a record. If the data is in binary format, however, it's impossible to read an arbitrary block.

Since SequenceFiles don't store metadata, their support for schema evolution is limited—you can only append new fields to the existing schema.

SequenceFiles can store either text or binary data:

- Text SequenceFile: The main rationale for this format that stores delimited text data in a SequenceFile format is to enable the compression of the textual data, which in a regular text file will remain unsplittable.
- Binary SequenceFile: Stores data in a binary format that needs minimal conversion processing during reads. From the performance point of view, this is better than using the text file storage format. A Parquet file, which I explain shortly, offers even better performance.

SequenceFiles can be split into configurable blocks. SequenceFiles support binary compression, and you can use Snappy, gzip, deflate or bzip2 compression. Reading SequenceFiles is somewhat complex, so they're most commonly used just for handling intermediate data storage during MapReduce processing.

A MapFile is a sorted and indexed SequenceFile. MapFiles are special forms of SequenceFiles and allow random access to data stored in a sorted SequenceFile. A MapFile is a set of two SequenceFiles stored together in a directory with the same name as that of the MapFile. The name of the MapFile is denoted by the variable `${map.file.name}`, and it consists of a file named *data* which is a SequenceFile with the data sorted by keys. The second file, named *index*, is also a SequenceFile that contains a fraction of the keys.

RC Files and ORC Files

The record columnar (RC) file and optimized row columnar (ORC) file formats are efficient binary formats that store data in a columnar format and offer several benefits.

The RC file is a high-performance flat file-storage format that stores data in the form of binary key/value pairs. It partitions rows into row splits and then partitions the row splits in the columnar format. It stores the row split metadata as the record key and the data of the row split as the value.

RC files split the data horizontally into row groups and store sets of rows in each group. For example, rows 1 to 100 may be stored in one group and rows 101 to 200 in another group. Each HDFS file consists of one or more row groups. RC files save this row group data in a columnar format. That is, instead of storing rows 1 through *n* serially, they store the first column values across all rows, then the following columns across all rows as well.

Since the row groups of various files are distributed redundantly across the cluster, Hadoop can process the data in parallel. Each node in the cluster skips the unnecessary columns in a query and just reads the pertinent columns only. Since compression takes advantage of the similarity of data in the columns, compression is more efficient.

RC files support Snappy, bzip, deflate and bzip 2 compression and, in addition to significant benefits on the compression side, offer significant performance benefits for querying data. However, the write performance when writing to and RC file involves significant overhead in terms of both memory and CPU when compared to non-columnar data formats, thus leading to slower writes.

The key problem with the RC file format is that currently the existing SerDes in Hive and other Hadoop tools don't support full schema evolution. This means that if you add fields to the file you may have to rewrite all the existing RC files you store now.

The ORC file format is an improvement over RC files. It stores collections of rows and, within those collections, stores the actual data in a columnar format. As with RC files, the columnar format enables the parallel processing of data across the cluster.

An ORC file stores records in a columnar format, with each column contiguously stored for all the rows, thus increasing the efficiency of aggregate queries that are I/O-intensive in nature. ORC files are very similar to RC files and provide better compression than the latter. However, ORC files don't support full schema evolution, while RC files do.

ORC files are quite similar to SequenceFiles but offer more optimizations and are especially useful in Hive, where their capabilities of compression, predicate push-down and so on lead to tremendous improvements in query performance.

ORC files include lightweight indexing that enables them to skip all blocks containing rows that aren't relevant for a query. The format also comes with a set of elementary statistics on columns, such as the minimum, maximum, count and sum. The format allows the parallel processing of row collections, since it's splittable.

Parquet File Format

Parquet offers a columnar storage format that supports encoding schemas as well as efficient compression, thus providing faster query performance. Parquet supports the Snappy and gzip compression formats. The columnar format adopted by Parquet, however, leads to slower write performance when compared with non-columnar storage formats. Parquet files offer limited schema evolution support—you can add new columns at the end of the current column.

Since Parquet is a columnar storage format, it works well with structured data that include some repetition of data. It's quite efficient in how it uses disk I/O when you query specific columns. If you want to retrieve an entire record at a time, however, Parquet doesn't perform too well, owing to its somewhat complex format. Parquet format is suitable for storing nested information in records.

Hive and Pig both support the Parquet file format, and it's quite easy to add the format to your Hive and Pig scripts or commands.

Avro Files

Avro is one of the more popular Hadoop storage formats. Avro makes it easy to represent complex data stores by using Avro SerDes. In many ways, Avro is similar to SequenceFiles. While the SequenceFile format is also a binary format, it supports only the Java language. You can use an Avro file with any language for which Avro bindings exist.

Avro files are row-based and offer a compact and fast binary format for storing data. Avro files are splittable, support block compression and support the Snappy, bzip, deflate and bzip2 compression types. Avro lets you serialize data to a very compact binary format based on the schema you specify.

Avro's model is JSON-like, but you represent it in a compact binary form as well. Avro offers the following benefits:

- Offers direct mapping between itself and JSON
- Very compact format that is ideal for high volume data transfers
- Very fast performance
- Contains bindings for a large number of programming languages so you don't need to write separate code for different data streams
- Contains a rich, extensible schema language
- Offers the best compatibility over time for evolving data

Unlike the other storage formats discussed here, Avro fully supports schema evolution by letting you add, delete, modify and rename the fields in a schema. Avro makes this possible by storing the metadata along with the data, as well as enabling you to specify a separate independent schema for reading the Avro file.

Avro uses schemas during reading and writing of data, which makes possible a compact representation of the serialized objects. The schemas are self-describing and are described in a JSON format.

Note

The Avro format is splittable and can detect incomplete or corrupt data in a file.

Avro's serialization format is quite similar to that of Protocol Buffer (protobuf). Avro is very compatible with Hadoop because the Avro container is based on Hadoop's SequenceFile and is integrated fairly well with MapReduce. Since Avro has a self-describing schema using JSON, it's ideal for long-term data storage, as storage formats usually change over time. Avro is beneficial if your data has a lot of structure and you expect that structure to change.

Popular tools such as Pig and Hive support reading and writing data in the Avro format. You don't need to write fancy Java (or Python) code to see what's in a binary file. Avro comes with its own command line tools that let you read, write and convert data to and from binary Avro files.

Handling Format Changes

Since you're going to be handling data that comes in from external sources over which you have no real control, you must be concerned with future changes in the structure of the data. Hive, for example, applies the table schema only when you're reading data, and queries may fail when new data does not match the queries that you're trying to run.

Avro can easily handle changes to the data structure. Suppose you create a Hive table using an Avro schema stored in a file named `twitter.avsc`, where `avsc` is the standard file extension for AVRO schemas. You store this file in HDFS and then create a Hive table that uses this schema. You can then create a Hive table that uses the Avro schema you stored. Let's say you add a new field, thus updating your Avro schema. You'll find that the Hive table definition has also been automatically updated to reflect the schema change.

The Ideal File Format

Well, the heading of this section is somewhat misleading, as there's no one ideal file format for Hadoop processing! Your choice will depend on the type of data you handle and also whether the data format is compatible with your processing and querying tools. The size of the data files and whether schemas evolve over time are also important factors in the choice of a data format.

The selection of the file format depends on your use case. If all you want to do is move data from Hadoop to a relational database, good old-fashioned CSV files will be fine. Text files are good for the quick movement of large amounts of data to HDFS. The text format is somewhat inefficient, but it's easily readable as well as parsable. SequenceFiles work well when data sets are shared between MapReduce jobs.

If the structure of the input data is constantly evolving, you should consider using a format such as Avro, which fully supports schema evolution.

If query performance is your main concern, ORC and Parquet may be better than Avro. However, the write performance when using ORC or Parquet will be slower. Both of these formats require additional parsing to format data, which leads to longer time to read the data.

Finally, specific Hadoop distribution such as Cloudera or Hortonworks, for example, may support specific file formats.

When it comes to reading data, remember the following:

- Parquet and ORC provide optimal read performance but make you pay the cost of poorer write performance.
- Columnar formats such as Parquet or ORC files are good for queries that are specific to a few columns or a few groups of columns.
- Regardless of the file format, compressing data means longer query times.
- Text files are usually slower to read.

Most likely, you're going to have to deal with various types of data such as XML files, web server logs in plain text and so on. It may be useful to use a mix of plain text files and one or more container file formats. In general, you are better off converting all XML documents into a container format such as Avro to overcome Hadoop's small file problem. JSON documents in general aren't affected so much by the small files problem. You can store small log files from web servers as plain text files.

In many ways, more important than the specific file format you end up choosing is the fact that you must endeavor to keep the file format consistent.

The Hadoop Small Files Problem and Merging Files

Ideally, as you know by now, you should use large files in HDFS, with each file around the size of the block size (default is 128MB, with 256MB commonly used as the block size). Small files are files that are much smaller than the HDFS block size. You may be using small files due to several reasons, such as the source system generating small files and their being loaded directly into HDFS. Also when Hadoop ingests real-time data, the ingestion processes are running continuously, grabbing small chunks of new data each time.

Small files in Hadoop mainly pose two problems. The first problem is performance related—too many small files means that you'll spend a lot of time in disk seeks. Many small files increase random disk seeks, which are much less efficient than performing a sequential read to read one very large file that contains the same data.

The second problem is that a large number of small files will stress the NameNode's memory. Remember that for fast access, the NameNode holds all metadata in its RAM. Even a small file will take up a block to store its information in the namespace, just as a large file will. Each file, directory and block in HDFS is an object in the NameNode's memory and takes up about 150-200 bytes of RAM on average.

Let's say you have a set of 20,000 small files, each about 1MB. The NameNode will need to store the metadata for 20,000 files as well as 20,000 blocks—that is, a total of 40,000 pieces of metadata information. If you store the same data in a 10GB file, you end up with just one file name and 40 blocks (assuming the block size of 256MB), for a total of just 41 pieces of metadata information. Clearly, small files impose a huge burden on the NameNode's memory!

If you end up with 60 million small files in your system, you'll need about 18-20GB of memory for the NameNode to handle the huge number of objects in its namespace.

DataNodes continuously report the block information to the NameNode. With numerous small files, there's a lot more reporting of data from the DataNodes to the NameNode, stressing your network bandwidth.

There are two well understood approaches to reducing the impact of a large number of files on the NameNode's memory footprint. The first involves using a federated NameNode architecture, as explained in Chapter 11, "NameNode Operations, High Availability and Federation." The second is the use of Hadoop archive (HAR) files, a way to archive or consolidate several files into a single archive file. Let's quickly review the two approaches to reducing the adverse impact of a large number of small files on the NameNode's performance.

Using a Federated NameNode to Overcome the Small Files Problem

A federated NameNode architecture helps you overcome the small files problem by portioning the metadata over multiple NameNodes. However, the problem is that if the same data is shared across multiple applications, this partitioning may not be ideal. The number of small files remains the same; you are merely apportioning the large number of files to multiple NameNodes.

Using Hadoop Archives to Manage Many Small Files

Hadoop archive (HAR) files get around the limitation imposed by too many small files by packing small files (files sized much smaller than the HDFS block size) more efficiently into larger files in HDFS, thus diminishing the usage of the NameNode namespace. Instead of a larger number of small files, the NameNode just needs to be aware of a few HAR files. These HAR files can be accessed by specifying `har:///` instead of `hdfs:///` as a prefix. By decreasing the load on the NameNode, the scalability of your system will be higher. Your MapReduce jobs will process just as usual, since HAR files are transparent to them, and the jobs access the original small files in a parallel fashion.

A HAR file imposes a kind of file system on top of HDFS and lets you archive a large number of files into a small number of HDFS files. Clients see and can access all the original files with a `har:/// URL`, and the number of files in HDFS is drastically diminished.

Although HAR files don't offer any performance gains in reading HDFS files, they are ideal for archiving purposes. If you rarely access the small files, the HAR files will serve the purpose of limiting the namespace for a large number of files.

The following sections cover each of the following:

- The HAR format
- How Hadoop archives work
- Creating a HAR file
- Using a HAR file
- Querying HAR files using Hive external tables
- Accessing HAR files from Pig

The HAR Format

A HAR file has a file extension of .har and consists of two types of files—index files and part files. The index files contain the original directory tree structure and the status of the files contained in the HAR file, while the part files contain the file data. The HAR file format is laid out in the following manner:

```
foo.har/_master_index      //stores the hashes and effects
foo.har_index              //stores the status of the files
foo.har/part-[1,,n]        //stores the file data
```

How Hadoop Archives Work

Since the HAR file is integrated with HDFS, the archived files and directory structures are exposed transparently to the users. Let's say you copy an HDFS file to a local directory as follows:

```
$ hdfs dfs -get hdfs://namenode/foo/file-1 localdir
```

Let's now create a HAR file named bar.har from the foo directory. You can now copy the original file as follows using the HAR file instead:

```
$ hdfs dfs -get har://namenode/bar.har/foo/file-1 localdir
```

Due to their transparency, HAR files are compatible with Hadoop APIs and MapReduce, as well as applications such as Pig and DistCp.

Creating a HAR File

HAR archive files are created in the HDFS file system from preexisting HDFS directories. You create a HAR file with the Hadoop archiving tool, which involves MapReduce to create the archive file. Here's the syntax for using the archiving tool.

```
$ hadoop archive -archiveName name -p <parent> <src> <dest>
```

In this command, `archiveName` is the name of the HAR file, and you specify the extension .har to denote that it's a HAR file. The `<parent>` argument specifies the path to the location where the HAR files are archived. The file list is split into map task inputs, with each map task creating a part file (default size is 2GB) from a subset of the source files. A reduce task will collect the metadata output by the mappers and create the index file for the HAR file. All source files are retained after the creation of the HAR archive file.

Let's say you want to archive two directories named /user/hadoop/dir1 and /user/hadoop/dir2 in the /user/test/foo.bar archive. You issue the following command to generate the archive.

```
$ hadoop archive -archiveName foo.har -p /user/hadoop dir1 dir2 /user/test
```

Since Hadoop archives are immutable, you can't rename an archive.

Using HAR Files

Hadoop archives are exposed as a file system, and MapReduce can use all input files in the archives as input. In order for MapReduce to use the files stored in the archive foo.har, you must specify the input directory as `har://user/test/foo.har`.

When you archive files into a .har file, the original files remain in place and aren't deleted. If you need to conserve HDFS space, you can manually delete the source files. HAR is designed to act as a file system, and you can't extract the original files from the HAR archive by issuing a command such as `tar -xvf`, for example. However, you can use regular HDFS file commands to look up the HAR files. Simply add `har:` before the HAR file name. The URI for a HAR file is

```
har://scheme=hostname:port/archivepath/fileinarchive
```

If you don't specify a scheme, Hadoop assumes the underlying file system, in which case the URI looks like this:

```
har:///archivepath/fileinarchive
```

For example, to view an archive you created, issue the following command.

```
$ hdfs dfs -ls har:///user/text/foo.bar/
Output:
har:///user/test/foo.har/dir1
har:///user/test/foo.har/dir2
```

You can copy an archived file inside a HAR file by using the `cp` command, which essentially unarchives the file.

```
$ hdfs dfs -cp har:///user/test/foo.har/dir1 hdfs:/user/test/newdir
```

You can use the DistCp (distributed copy) command to perform the unarchiving in parallel:

```
$ hadoop distcp har:///user/text/foo.har/dir1 hdfs:/user/test/newdir
```

Some Caveats

HAR files are meant to efficiently store data and don't offer performance benefits for reading the files in the archive. Reading files in a HAR archive may be slower than reading other files because you need two index file reads plus the data file read for each HAR file access. As an alternative to HAR files, you may use Avro to combine files or write a MapReduce job to combine multiple files into a SequenceFile. You may also look into an open-source utility such as `filecrusher` to combine small files.

Handling the Performance Impact of Small Files

While a federated NameNode architecture or the HAR archives may help you with the namespace issue involved in handling small files, you must also consider alternative methods to reduce the performance impact of many small files. Following are some of the ways you can improve performance when dealing with small files.

Using SequenceFiles

A SequenceFile uses key/value pairs, with the keys denoting file names and the values the content of the files. SequenceFiles are very useful when you need to merge small files but still keep them logically separate. For instance, you can store HTML files as key/value pairs in a SequenceFile and process them with MapReduce.

SequenceFiles are ideal when ingesting a large number of small files at once, because MapReduce jobs need to launch just a single job to process a file instead of assigning a separate mapper for each of the numerous small files. This advantage disappears if you're ingesting the small files a few at a time, because you can't append to an HDFS file. Also, if you're using Hive, note that Hive sees the entire contents of the file as a single row. In addition, Hive tables have access only to the value and not the key of the SequenceFile, which is the filename of the SequenceFile. You'll need to write custom Hive SerDes to overcome these limitations.

Extensible binary formats such as Avro, Parquet, Thrift or protobuf are all good candidates for storing data on disk. Note that regardless of which of these you choose to use, each record is an Avro, Thrift, or protobuf struct stored in a SequenceFile. Parquet provides features such as predicate push-down, which Avro and other formats lack.

Consolidating the Batch Files

You can also consolidate a large number of small files by rewriting those files into a few large files. You can write simple Pig programs to consolidate multiple text files. You can also use the open-source Filecrush project to consolidate the small files. You can merge a large number of small files into fewer files either before or after getting them into HDFS.

In addition to the use of SequenceFiles and the consolidation of batch files, there are several alternative ways to reduce the adverse performance impact of small files. You can, for example, stream the small files into HBase and use the HBase tables for processing, instead of the original files. If you're using Amazon EMR, you may also use S3DistCp, which lets you process numerous small files by concatenating the files and processing them using Amazon EMR. This approach is quite similar to the consolidation of the batch files before processing them.

Alternatively, your development team can use `CombineFileInputFormat`, which reads multiple files and merges them for use by a single map task, without ever writing the merged file to disk. You'll therefore still have to deal with the large number of small files and their impact on the NameNode's memory.

Finally, you can append the content of the small files to an existing file, but tools such as Flume, Sqoop, Hive, Spark, Pig and MapReduce don't support the append option. You may have to custom develop a complex system to successfully append data to an existing file.

Using Hadoop WebHDFS and HttpFS

WebHDFS and HttpFS are both HTTP/HTTPS REST interfaces to Hadoop. Both interfaces enable you to read HDFS data and to write to it, as well as perform several administrative commands relating to HDFS. You can use both interfaces by embedding them in programs or scripts or through command-line tools such as `curl` or `wget`.

WebHDFS doesn't support the high-availability NameNode architecture. You can use HttpFS for those environments.

WebHDFS—The Hadoop REST API

When applications that are running within a Hadoop cluster want to access HDFS data, they use Hadoop's native client libraries to work with HDFS. However, you may need to access HDFS from outside the cluster in order to process data as well as store and retrieve HDFS data.

If the applications want to use the native HDFS protocol, you must install Hadoop on the servers where the applications run and also provide a Java binding with the applications.

Hadoop's WebHDFS offers a powerful set of HTTP REST APIs. Representational State Transfer (REST) is an architectural style for building large-scale web services that enable applications to access and work with HDFS remotely. In addition to facilitating external access to HDFS, WebHDFS is also helpful when you're trying to work with two Hadoop clusters, each running a different version of Hadoop. Since WebHDFS is independent of MapReduce and the HDFS versions, as it employs REST APIs, it can be used to work with the two clusters. It can be used, for example, when you need to perform a data copy between the two clusters using the DistCp utility.

When using WebHDFS to remotely access HFDS data, you don't need to install Hadoop on the client. You use well-known tools such as `curl` and `wget` to access the HDFS data. WebHDFS supports all HDFS operations you can perform by connecting directly to a Hadoop cluster.

WebHDFS uses the basic HTTP operations `GET`, `PUT`, `POST` and `DELETE` in order to remotely manipulate the HDFS file system. For example

- `HTTP GET` supports the `OPEN`, `GETFILESTATUS` and `LISTSTATUS` commands
- `HTTP PUT` supports the `CREATE`, `MKDIRS` and `SETPERMISSIONS` commands
- `HTTP POST` supports the `APPEND` operation
- `HTTP DELETE` supports the `DELETE` operation

Using WebHDFS

Using WebHDFS is simple. All you need to do is replace the HDFS file system URIs with the HTTP URLs. Suppose your HDFS URI looks like the following.

```
hdfs://<HOST>:<RPC_PORT>/<PATH>
```

A WebHDFS file system URI has the following format instead:

```
webhdfs://<HOST>:<HTTP_PORT>/<PATH>
```

In your REST API, you must insert the prefix `/webhdfs/v1` in the path and append a query at the very end (after `?op=`), as shown here.

```
http://<HOST>:<HTTP_PORT>/webhdfs/v1/<PATH>?op=<hdfs query here>
```

The HTTP URL shown here is the standard format for accessing HDFS using the WebHDFS REST API.

Setting Up WebHDFS

In order to use WebHDFS, you must add the following configuration parameter to the hdfs-site.xml file:

```
<property>
  <name>dfs.webhdfs.enabled</name>
  <value>true</value>
</property>
```

You must restart HDFS (all NameNodes and DataNodes) after adding the new configuration parameter. If your Hadoop cluster is Kerberized, you need to configure the following two parameters as well, in order to use WebHDFS.

```
dfs.web.authentication.kerberos.principal     // HTTP Kerberos principal
dfs.web.authentication.kerberos.keytab        // Kerberos keytab file
```

In a non-Kerberized cluster, authentication is based on the "user name" query parameter. In a Kerberized cluster, it depends on Kerberos credentials instead.

Using the WebHDFS API

You can access and transfer data using regular HDFS CLI commands or use standard Linux/UNIX tools such as `curl` or `wget`. The following sections show how to perform common file system operations using both methods.

Using WebHDFS through HDFS Commands

If you have Hadoop command line tools installed on your local client, you can use regular HDFS file commands to list HDFS files or to copy the files. The following URL will let you access HDFS:

```
webhdfs://localhost:14000/<path>
```

The following command lists all the files and directories in the HDFS directory named /user:

```
$ hdfs dfs -ls webhdfs://hadoop02.localhost:14000/user
```

Note that you specify the NameNode but don't use the usual port number, which is 8020. Instead, you specify the port number 14000.

You can copy a file from the local system to HDFS in the following way:

```
$ hdfs dfs -put webhdfs://hadoop02.localhost:14000/user/<username>/test.txt
```

You can execute the same -put command as a different Hadoop user by specifying the `HADOOP_USER` option as shown here:

```
$ HADOOP_USERNAME=hdfs dfs -ls webhdfs://hadoop02.localhost:14000/user
```

You can copy a file from HDFS to your local file system as follows:

```
$ hdfs dfs -get webhdfs://hadoop02.localhost:14000/user/<username>/test.txt  test.txt
```

You can remove a file from HDFS by issuing the following command:

```
$ hdfs dfs -rm webhdfs://hadoop02.localhost:14000/user/<username>/test.txt
```

Understanding the WebHDFS Commands

WebHDFS is really quite comprehensive and includes numerous commands that help you access and work with HDFS data. Let's review the most common ways to access HDFS with the WebHDFS REST API, using the `curl` tool. You need to make sure that `curl` is already installed on your server first. `curl` commands are simple to use and you can use them to get data into or out of HDFS. Here are the `curl` options you need to be familiar with:

- `-L`: Asks `curl` to follow redirects
- `-X`: Indicates the HTTP method to use
- `-H`: Adds a header to the request
- `-T`: Points to an upload file

The standard format for a URL is the following:

```
http://host.port/webhdfs/v1/?op=operation&user.name=username
```

You can read a file in HDFS by specifying `OPEN`. Suppose you want to read the contents of a file named test1.txt from the HDFS /tmp directory. You can issue the following `curl` command to read the file.

```
$ curl -i -L \
http://hadoopNameNode:50070/webhdfs/v1/tmp/test1.txt?op=OPEN&user.name=
hadoopUserName
```

Here, replace *`hadoopNameNode`* with your NameNode's server name and *`hadoopUserName`* with any Hadoop user that has read permissions on the test1.txt file.

If the NameNode (default port is 50070) redirects the request with a location URL that points to a DataNode, you must then use that URL to execute the WebHDFS file system operations on a DataNode. In this case, you'll specify the port 50075, which is the default port number for a DataNode.

The following `curl` command lets you view the contents of a file named test1.txt.

```
# curl -i -L \

http://hadoop01.localhost:50070/webhdfs/v1/tmp/test1.txt?op=OPEN&user.name=alapati

HTTP/1.1 307 TEMPORARY_REDIRECT
...
Content-Type: application/octet-stream
Access-Control-Allow-Methods: GET
...
A|1|2|3
B|4|5|6
#
```

Make sure you use the active NameNode's address, not the Standby NameNode's address, if you have an HA NameNode setup. Your read request is redirected to a DataNode where the file can be read.

Checking the Status of a Directory

You can check the status of an HDFS directory with the `LISTSTATUS` command:

```
$ curl -i -L "http://$<<Host_Name>:$<Port>/webhdfs/v1/foo?op=LISTSTATUS"
```

You can list the status of an HDFS file with the `GETFILESTATUS` command:

```
$ curl -i -L "http://$<<Host_Name>:$<Port>/webhdfs/v1/foo?op=GETFILESTATUS"
```

Here's an example.

```
[root@hadoop01 ~]# curl -i "http://hadoop01.localhost:50070/webhdfs/v1/tmp?user
.name=alapati&op=GETFILESTATUS"
HTTP/1.1 200 OK
Cache-Control: no-cache
)
...
{"FileStatus":{"accessTime":0,"blockSize":0,"childrenNum":62,
"fileId":16393,"group":"hdfs","length":0,"modificationTime":
1431361777691,"owner":"hdfs","pathSuffix":"","permission":
"1777","replication":0,"type":"DIRECTORY"}}
[root@hadoop01 ~]#
```

The `LISTSTATUS` command gets you the same results as the HDFS command `dfs -ls`:

```
# curl -i "http://hadoop01.localhost:50070/webhdfs/v1/tmp?user
.name=alapati&op=LISTSTATUS"
HTTP/1.1 200 OK
Expires: Mon, 30 May 2016 13:50:10 GMT
Date: Mon, 30 May 2016 13:50:10 GMT
...
{"FileStatuses":{"FileStatus":[
{"accessTime":0,"blockSize":0,"childrenNum":1064,"fileId":1970264,"group":"hdfs",
"length":0,"modificationTime":1432993768677,"owner":"hdfs","pathSuffix":
".cloudera_health_monitoring_canary_files","permission":"1777","replication":0,
"type":"DIRECTORY"},
...
```

```
{"accessTime":1417766804894,"blockSize":268435456,"childrenNum":0,"fileId":
7463010,"group":"hdfs","length":0,"modificationTime":1417766804915,
"owner":"hdfs","pathSuffix":"test_hdfs","permission":"644","replication":3,
"type":"FILE"}
]}}
#
```


Creating a Directory

You must specify the PUT option to perform any operations that involve writing and renaming a file or creating a new HDFS directory. Create a directory with the MKDIRS command, as shown here:

```
$ curl -i -X  PUT
http://$<<Host_Name>:$<Port>/webhdfs/v1/foo2?op=MKDIRS&permissions=711
```

This command creates a directory and also sets permissions on it.

Reading a File

Specify the -L option with the curl command so as to follow the HTTP temporary redirect URL. Here's an example:

```
$ curl -i -L "http://localhost:50070/webhdfs/v1/tmp/webhdfs/webhdfs-
test.txt?op=OPEN&user.name=alapati"

HTTP/1.1 307 TEMPORARY_REDIRECT
...
```

Using the OPEN command is identical to issuing the dfs -cat command.

Creating a File

Creating a file requires two steps. First you run the command against your NameNode, and then you follow the redirection to execute the WebHDFS API against the DataNode referred to by the NameNode, as follows.

First:

```
curl -i -X PUT
"http://hadoop01.localhost:50070/webhdfs/v1/tmp/webhdfs/webhdfs-test.txt?user
.name=alapati&op=CREATE"
HTTP/1.1 307 TEMPORARY_REDIRECT
...
```

Next:

```
$ curl -i -T webhdfs-test.txt "http://hadoop01.localhost:50075/webhdfs/v1/tmp/
webhdfs/webhdfs-test.txt?op=CREATE&user.name=alapati&overwrite=false"
HTTP/1.1 100 Continue
...
```

You can check the results of the CREATE command with the dfs -ls command.

Removing a Directory

You can delete an HDFS directory by issuing the DELETE command and specifying the directory name. However, the target directory must be empty. If you have files inside the directory you want to remove, first remove the files and then remove the directory itself. Here's an example that shows how to do this.

```
First:
$ curl -i -X DELETE "http://hadoop01.localhost:50070/webhdfs/v1/tmp/webhdfs-new/
webhdfs-test.txt?op=DELETE&user.name=alapati"
Next:
$ curl -i -X DELETE "http://hadoop01.localhost:50070/webhdfs/v1/tmp/webhdfs-
new?op=DELETE&user.name=alapati&destination=/tmp/webhdfs-new"
HTTP/1.1 200 OK
```

Check Directory Quotas

You can check the quota on an HDFS directory with the following command:

```
$ curl -i -L
"http://hadoop01:14000/webhdfs/v1/user/<username>/?op=GETCONTENTSUMMARY&user
.name=alapati&overwrite=false"
```

Most of the WebHDFS commands help users perform various tasks with HDFS, but as an administrator, you can use WebHDFS to perform several administrative operations. Here's a command that shows how to get a content summary of an HDFS directory, including information such as number of files, space quotas and space consumed:

```
$ curl -i "http://<HOST>:<PORT>/webhdfs/v1/<PATH>?op=GETCONTENTSUMMARY"
```

Using HttpFS Gateway to Access HDFS from Behind a Firewall

HttpFS is a Java application that runs on Apache Tomcat. HttpFS lets you remotely access the HDFS file system through the WebHDFS REST API. HttpFS uses HTTP REST calls that map to HDFS file system operations.

You can set up an HttpFS server to provide a REST HTTP gateway that supports HDFS file system operations. Since HttpFS is a proxy, it doesn't require clients to access every machine in the cluster, unlike WebHDFS.

HttpFS is useful in environments where firewall restrictions make it difficult to access HDFS data. You can set up an HttpFS server as the only system allowed to access the cluster through the firewall in such cases.

HttpFS involves a little bit more work to get going, because you must first install and configure an HttpFS server. You must then enable proxy access to HDFS for an HttpFS user, so the user running the HttpFS server can access HDFS on behalf of other users. The client only needs access to the HttpFS server since it's the HttpFS server that accesses HDFS.

Hue contains an HDFS browser that uses HttpFS in an HA NameNode setup to access the HDFS file system. In an HDFS HA setup, you can't use WebHDFS to access HDFS through Hue's file browser. In a non-HA setup, however, you may use either WebHDFS or HttpFS to access HDFS.

Configuring HttpFS

As mentioned earlier, HttpFS uses a server to provide the gateway to HDFS. You must download the HttpFS zip file from Apache and unzip the file in the HttpFS configuration directory. Make sure that you configure the httpfs.hadoop.config.dir property in the hdfs-site.xml file to point to the location of the Hadoop configuration directory in your cluster.

1. You must first install HttpFS by downloading and unzipping the HttpFS binaries:

   ```
   $ tar xvzf httpfs-2.5.1.tar.gz
   ```

   You can download the binaries from http://hadoop.apache.org.

2. Once you download and unzip the HttpFS binaries, start the HttpFS server as shown here.

   ```
   $ bin/httpfs.sh start
   ```

3. Edit the Hadoop core-site.xml file as follows to define the Linux user that will run the HttpFS server:

   ```
   <property>
       <name>hadoop.proxyuser.#HTTPFSUSER#.hosts</name>
       <value>httpfs-host.foo.com</value>
     </property>
     <property>
       <name>hadoop.proxyuser.#HTTPFSUSER#.groups</name>
       <value>*</value>
     </property>
   ```

   Here, #HTTPUSER# is a placeholder for your Linux user that will run the HttpFS server as a proxy user.

4. Restart the NameNodes to activate the proxy user you've configured. Now you can start the HttpFS server as shown here:

   ```
   $ sbin/httpfs.sh start
   ```

Using HttpFS to Access HDFS

Use the Linux curl command to access HDFS through HttpFS. The following example show how to get the contents of the /user/foo/README.txt file.

```
$ curl http://httpfs-host:14000/webhdfs/v1/user/foo/README.txt
```

And the following command shows the contents of the /user/foo directory in JSON format:

```
$ curl http://httpfs-host:14000/webhdfs/v1/user/foo?op=list
```

You can create a directory by specifying the MKDIRS operation, as shown here:

```
$ curl -X POST http://httpfs-host:14000/webhdfs/v1/user/foo/bar?op=mkdirs
```

Since the HttpFS REST API returns JSON objects, you may want to pipe those objects to the python -m json.tool to get the output into an easily readable format, as shown in the following example.

```
$ curl -s "http://httpfs-host:14000/webhdfs/v1/\
     User/sam?op=LISTSTATUS&user.name=sam"\
| python -m json.tool
```

The `curl` command shown here will return a JSON object showing the status of the directories under the /user/sam path in HDFS.

Differences between WebHDFS and HttpFS

A key difference between WebHDFS and HttpFS is that using HttpFS, a single node will act as a gateway and the main transfer conduit for the data to the client node from where you issue the HttpFS command. On the other hand, WebHDFS needs access to all of a cluster's nodes, and data read from a node is directly sent from that node.

If you're transferring very large files, HttpFS can prove to be a chokepoint. The best thing to do is test both in your environment and pick whichever works best for you.

Summary

Here's what you learned in this chapter:

- Using the HDFS trash feature prevents accidental data deletion.
- HDFS snapshots help you safeguard important data.
- You can use the `fsck` command to detect HDFS corruption and fix it.
- Hadoop supports many file formats, and the choice depends on your use cases.
- Hadoop has difficulty dealing with small files, and you can overcome that problem using Hadoop archives.
- You can communicate remotely with HDFS through WebHDFS and HttpFS.

11

NameNode Operations, High Availability and Federation

This chapter covers the following topics:

- Understanding NameNode operations
- Different types of NameNodes
- The checkpointing process
- Configuring HDFS High Availability
- Setting up federated HDFS

As you know by now, HDFS stores metadata on the NameNode, and the application data is stored on the DataNodes. The NameNode detects failed DataNodes, unavailable replicas and other causes of data corruption. In case the data isn't replicated the configured number of times, it's the NameNode that ensures that enough copies of the good replicas are copied over to the DataNodes.

The main job of the NameNode is to store the HDFS metadata, which includes the directory tree, file permissions and mapping of HDFS files to the block IDs on the DataNodes. Two entities are involved in maintaining the HDFS namespace:

- The fsimage file: This file contains the most recent checkpointed namespace.
- The edit log: This is a set of log files that contain a record of the changes made to the namespace after the latest checkpoint.

While the fsimage file is the master file for the namespace metadata, due to its usually large size (it could run into hundreds of megabytes and even several gigabytes in most decent sized clusters), it's not practical to write all modifications to the namespace directly to the fsimage file. When the namespace is modified in any way, say, by the creation of an HDFS directory, the NameNode records the change in the edit log so the change is permanently stored on disk.

When you restart a NameNode after a crash or after scheduled maintenance, the NameNode loads the fsimage file into memory and then replays the transactions from the edit log that record the most recent metadata operations in the cluster. The NameNode thus starts up with the most up-to-date version of its metadata.

In this chapter, you'll learn all about NameNode metadata and how Hadoop ensures that it's continuously updated and available.

You'll also learn how to put HDFS into **safe mode**, which is a read-only mode, when performing maintenance tasks.

Probably the most important topic this chapter deals with is the NameNode high availability feature available in Hadoop 2, which involves running two NameNodes—one an active NameNode and the other a Standby NameNode. If the active NameNode needs to be stopped or crashes, it's automatically (or manually) failed over to the Standby NameNode, which becomes the active NameNode.

In a large environment with a lot of HDFS data and a large number of processes accessing that data, you may want to consider federating the NameNode. A federated NameNode uses multiple NameNodes to provide scalability, performance and isolation.

Understanding NameNode Operations

In Hadoop, the DataNodes are the workhorses, since they store the data blocks and also retrieve them when clients or the NameNode ask them do so. The NameNode keeps track of all the data blocks by maintaining information about which blocks make up the individual files. If you happen to lose the server where the NameNode is running and don't have a backup of the metadata, your HDFS files are deemed lost, since there's no way for Hadoop to reconstruct the HDFS files from the blocks stored on the DataNodes.

The HDFS file system metadata is stored in two different files: the fsimage and the edit log. The fsimage is a point-in-time snapshot of the HDFS metadata. However, the format of the fsimage file is more suited to reading than writing small updates, which involves creating a new fsimage file every time the namespace is modified by even a tiny change, such as the renaming of an HDFS file.

To keep things simple and efficient, all HDFS file changes are logged in an edit journal conveniently named the edit log. The edit log consists of a set of files called the edit log segments, which together contain all the namespace changes made since the creation of the fsimage file. The edit log stores all changes since the last checkpoint, which is defined as the last time when the contents of the edit log file were merged with the latest fsimage file.

Both the fsimage and the edit log are stored on the server running the NameNode daemon. If the NameNode crashes, it restores its state by loading the fsimage file and then replaying all the operations in the edit log. These operations are called edits or transactions. The replaying of the edits from the edit log lets the NameNode update the state of the namespace and ensure that it matches the actual current status of the HDFS file system.

HDFS Metadata

The NameNode's primary job is to store the HDFS namespace. HDFS metadata, or what is the same thing, the HDFS namespace, is a hierarchy of files and directories represented by inodes. Inodes store attributes such as permissions, modifications, access times and disk space quotas. The namespace also includes information showing the mapping of files to block IDs.

The NameNode stores the HDFS metadata while the DataNodes store the actual HDFS data. When clients connect to Hadoop to read and write data, they connect first to the NameNode, which lets the clients know where the actual data blocks are stored or on which DataNodes they should write their data.

HDFS Metadata includes the following information:

- HDFS file locations
- Names of the HDFS data blocks
- Locations of the HDFS data blocks
- File ownership and permissions

The metadata file fsimage includes all the metadata listed above, *except* the location of the HDFS data blocks.

The NameNode maintains the namespace tree, as well as the mapping of data blocks to the DataNodes in a cluster.

The inodes and the list of blocks together define the metadata of the namespace and are called the image (fsimage). The NameNode stores the entire image in its memory and stores a record of the image on the NameNode's file system. This persistent record of the namespace is called a **checkpoint**.

The NameNode writes changes to the HDFS file system to a journal, named the edit log. The checkpoint combined with the journal gives the current in-memory image of the NameNode. It's important to understand that the NameNode doesn't ever change its checkpoint while it's running. A new checkpoint is only created when the NameNode starts, or when requested by you, or by the Secondary or Standby NameNode. When the NameNode starts up, it initializes the namespace image from the checkpoint on disk and replays all changes from the journal. Before it starts serving clients, it creates a new checkpoint (fsimage file) and an empty journal (edits file).

> **Tip**
>
> The fsimage file contains the mapping between the data blocks stored on the DataNodes and the HDFS files. If this file is lost or corrupted, your HDFS data stored on the DataNodes can't be accessed—it's just as if all that data has disappeared!

When clients write data to HDFS, the write operations change the HDFS metadata, of course, and those changes are recorded to the edit log by the NameNode. Simultaneously the NameNode will also update its in-memory representation of the metadata.

Every client transaction is recorded in the write-ahead journal by the NameNode, which flushes and syncs the journal (edit log) before sending an acknowledgement to the client. The NameNode processes requests from multiple clients in the cluster, so in order to optimize the process of saving those transactions to disk, it batches multiple client transactions together.

More about the fsimage and the Edit Log

The fsimage and the edit log are the two key constructs associated with HDFS metadata. The NameNode stores both of these in the directory specified by the configuration parameter `dfs.namenode.name.dir` in the hdfs-site.xml file. Following are the contents of the directory specified by this parameter in my cluster:

```
# pwd
/opt/hadoop/dfs/nn/current
# ls -altr
total 1105192
-rw-r--r-- 1 hdfs hadoop      1432 Aug 15 00:22
edits_0000000000594347899-0000000000594347912
-rw-r--r-- 1 hdfs hadoop        10 Aug 15 00:24 seen_txid
-rw-r--r-- 1 hdfs hadoop      1531 Aug 15 00:24
edits_0000000000594347913-0000000000594347927
-rw-r--r-- 1 hdfs hadoop   1048576 Aug 15 00:24
edits_inprogress_0000000000594347928
drwxr-xr-x 3 hdfs hadoop      4096 Aug 15 00:34 ..
-rw-r--r-- 1 hdfs hadoop        62 Oct 15 10:57 fsimage_0000000000686020016.md5
-rw-r--r-- 1 hdfs hadoop 564821977 Oct 15 10:57 fsimage_0000000000686020016
-rw-r--r-- 1 hdfs hadoop       184 Oct 15 11:57 VERSION
-rw-r--r-- 1 hdfs hadoop        62 Oct 15 11:57 fsimage_0000000000686033110.md5
-rw-r--r-- 1 hdfs hadoop 564691172 Oct 15 11:57 fsimage_0000000000686033110
drwxr-xr-x 2 hdfs hadoop      4096 Oct 15 11:57 .
#
```

The Secondary NameNode (or the Standby NameNode) has an identical file structure. Note that the edit log consists of multiple edit segments, each of which is a file starting with "edits_". The fsimage file, of course, starts with "fsimage_".

Downloading the Latest fsimage File

You can use the `dfsadmin` command option `–fetchImage` to download the latest fsimage file to a local directory.

```
# hdfs dfsadmin -fetchImage /tmp
```

This command downloaded the fsimage file named fsimage_0000000000074283613 to the /tmp directory.

The NameNode stores only the file system layout data such as the files, blocks, directories and permissions in the fsimage file on disk. It keeps the actual block locations only in its memory. When a client seeks to read a file, the NameNode informs the client where the file's blocks are located. At this point, the client doesn't need to communicate further with the NameNode regarding the transferring of the data itself.

Because of the critical nature of NameNode metadata, you should configure more than one directory as the value for the `dfs.namenode.name.dir` configuration parameter. Ideally, you must configure one of the locations on NFS.

You can view the contents of an fsimage file to examine the cluster's namespace using the **Offline Image Viewer** (OIV). This tool dumps the contents of the fsimage file to a human-readable format and lets you examine the HDFS namespace through the read-only WebHDFS API. The fsimage file tends to be quite large, and the OIV helps you quickly process the file's contents. As the name of the tool indicates, you can view the image file offline with it.

The NameNode Startup Process

Understanding how the NameNode starts up goes a long way toward understanding the nature of NameNode operations. A key function of the NameNode is to let applications know the data blocks they need to process. It maintains ready access to the exact location of all data blocks by keeping the block locations and the block-to-file mappings in memory.

When you start up the NameNode, the following things happen:

1. The NameNode reads into memory the contents of the image file it has, thus obtaining the HDFS file system state.
2. The NameNode loads the edit log and replays the edit log (the transactions in the edit log segments) to update the metadata it loaded into memory in step 1.
3. The NameNode also updates the fsimage file with the updated HDFS state information.
4. The NameNode starts running with a fresh, empty edits file.
5. The DataNode daemons connect to the NameNode and send it block reports that list all data blocks stored by a DataNode.

Once the startup process completes, the NameNode will have full knowledge of the HDFS data, and it can now start serving HDFS data to clients. When HDFS data is modified, the edit log is updated with the information and the changes are also made in the block locations and metadata that the NameNode stores in RAM for quick access.

The key point to understand here is that the NameNode writes all namespace modifications to the edit log, but it doesn't merge those changes with the fsimage file during runtime.

> **Note**
>
> DataNode daemons send the NameNode a heartbeat every three seconds by default, to let it know that they're alive. You can configure a different frequency for the heartbeats. By default, the DataNodes also send a block report to the NameNode every hour, to let the NameNode know which file blocks the DataNodes are storing. This ensures that the NameNode always has the latest picture of the HDFS storage.

How the NameNode and the DataNodes Work Together

When you start up a DataNode, it connects to the NameNode and performs a handshake to verify the namespace ID and the DataNode's software version. If one of these doesn't match the ID and version stored in the NameNode, the DataNode shuts down.

When you format the NameNode, a namespace ID is generated and assigned to the file system instance and stored on all the cluster nodes. This is done to ensure that DataNodes with other namespace IDs don't join the cluster by mistake.

After the initial handshake to register themselves with the NameNode, the DataNode stores a unique ID internally, called the storage ID. This storage ID is assigned only once to each DataNode when it first registers with the NameNode and never changes. Even if you change the IP address or the DataNode's port number following this, the DataNode will always be able to join the cluster without a problem.

Following the initial registration with the NameNode, all DataNodes send two pieces of information to the NameNode: periodic **heartbeats** that show they're alive and a **block report** that shows block information. The block reports sent by the DataNodes enable the NameNode to know which block replicas are stored on each DataNode. The block report contains the block ID, a generation stamp (GS) and the length of each block replica a DataNode stores. DataNodes send out a block report to the NameNode every hour and also when they register with the NameNode.

The heartbeats sent to the NameNode by the DataNodes serve to confirm that a DataNode and its block replicas are available. In addition to the DataNode's health status, a heartbeat also contains information about total storage capacity and the storage currently in use and the number of currently ongoing data transfers.

The NameNode uses this storage-related information from the DataNodes during its block-allocation and load-balancing work.

The NameNode uses the heartbeat sent by the DataNodes for other purposes as well. It never directly sends requests to the DataNodes, instead using its replies to the DataNode heartbeats to send requests to the DataNodes. This is called "piggybacking the heartbeats." The requests sent by the NameNode this way may include instructions to replicate a DataNode's block replicas to other DataNodes, or to remove its block replicas or even to shut down the DataNode. It may also request an immediate block report from the DataNodes, should it need it.

DataNodes send a heartbeat to the NameNode every three seconds by default. You can set the heartbeat interval in the hdfs-site.xml file by configuring the parameter `dfs.heartbeat.interval`.

If the NameNode doesn't receive any heartbeats for a specified time, which is ten minutes by default, it assumes the DataNode is lost and that the block replicas hosted by that DataNode are unavailable. The NameNode then sets in motion the process of replicating the data blocks stored on the lost node to other DataNodes in the cluster. The NameNode will then do the following:

1. It determines the blocks that were stored on the DataNode.
2. It checks to see which DataNodes have copies of those blocks.

3. It tells those other DataNodes to start copying the data blocks to other nodes in the cluster to maintain the replication factor for those blocks.

Now that the NameNode has ensured the data blocks are correctly replicated, what happens when the lost DataNode joins the cluster again? The NameNode realizes that certain data blocks are over replicated and tells the DataNodes to remove the over-replicated copies. All this is automatic, and you don't need to do a thing to ensure that the data is correctly replicated following the removal or addition of a DataNode. This is one of the many things that make the administration of Hadoop a delight!

The Checkpointing Process

Checkpointing is the process that creates a new fsimage by merging the current fsimage and the edit log. Once the edit log reaches a specified threshold or when a certain period of time elapses, the new entries in the edit log are committed to the fsimage file.

While the edit log segments (files that together comprise the edit log) are quite small (tens or hundreds of bytes) in comparison with the fsimage file, if you don't regularly update the fsimage file with the edit log transactions, the edit log could get pretty large itself! Of course, this will delay the restart of the NameNode. Checkpointing periodically merges the latest fsimage file with the edit log, creating a brand new up-to-date fsimage. This helps the NameNode load its final in-memory state directly from the fsimage file instead of having to replay a vast number of files from the edit log.

You might be thinking at this point that the NameNode might be tasked with the periodic updating of the fsimage file. Actually, this isn't the case. Checkpointing is a resource intensive operation and may also lead to the restricting of user concurrent access. During checkpointing, the NameNode won't be able to allow client operations such as reading and writing HDFS files. That's the reason the NameNode relies on either the Secondary NameNode or the Standby NameNode (in a high-availability setup) to take care of checkpointing.

In Hadoop 2, the checkpointing functions can be handled by any one of the following four daemons:

- Secondary NameNode
- Checkpoint node
- Backup node
- Standby NameNode

The last one, the Standby NameNode, is present only in an HDFS high-availability environment, of course. I briefly review these daemons in the next section.

The Need to Keep the fsimage File Updated

Earlier in this chapter, you learned about the sequence of steps the NameNode goes through when you restart it. The drawback of this sequence of steps is that if you don't start up the NameNode for a long time, you've got a big problem on your hands! The startup is going to take a long time, and the NameNode isn't available (it'll be in the safe mode) until it completes reading and merging all changes since its last start. Hadoop lets the Standby NameNode (or the Secondary NameNode) regularly update the fsimage file, so an updated fsimage is always ready for the NameNode following a restart.

Secondary, Checkpoint, Backup and Standby Nodes

As mentioned in the previous section, you can configure checkpointing through the Secondary NameNode, checkpoint node, backup node or Standby NameNode. The Secondary NameNode checkpoint node and backup nodes all perform somewhat similar functions, and thus you don't need to run all three of these services on a cluster. Most commonly, you run the Secondary NameNode in a non-HA-enabled cluster. In a high-availability NameNode configuration, you won't need a Secondary NameNode, since the Standby NameNode will take over its functions.

Secondary NameNode

The Secondary NameNode, contrary to what its name suggests, doesn't really function as a NameNode. The Secondary NameNode's job is to perform periodic checkpoints of the namespace.

The Secondary NameNode doesn't upload the checkpointed fsimage file to the active NameNode as a matter of course. In order to use the checkpointed file, you must physically move the file over to the NameNode server.

You run the Secondary NameNode on a server configured identically to the server on which the NameNode runs. The Secondary NameNode maintains a directory identical to the one the NameNode maintains, thus facilitating the reading of the checkpointed image file by the NameNode when necessary.

Checkpoint Node

The checkpoint node performs the same function as the Secondary NameNode—that is, it checkpoints the namespace on a regular basis, helping keep the size of the edits file down. As with the Secondary NameNode, the checkpoint node downloads the edits file from the NameNode, merges it with the image file and sends back the updated image file to the NameNode. You can have multiple checkpoint nodes for safety, if you wish, as long as you have no backup nodes registered.

The key difference between the Secondary NameNode and the checkpoint node is that, unlike the Secondary NameNode, the checkpoint node actually uploads the new updated image file to the active NameNode.

Backup Node

The backup node is an extension of the checkpoint node. The backup node, while ultimately providing essentially the same functionality as the Secondary NameNode or checkpoint node, employs a different mechanism. This node maintains an in-memory copy of the latest namespace and ensures that it's synchronized with the NameNode's namespace. It achieves this by getting a stream of the namespace changes from the NameNode.

The backup node then stores these changes to disk and applies them to its in-memory copy of the namespace. Since the backup node doesn't have to transfer and then merge the fsimage and edits filed from the NameNode, it's much more efficient than the checkpoint node for performing the checkpointing duties.

Since the backup node always has a backup of the namespace in its memory, it's called a "backup" node! When the backup node performs a checkpoint, it doesn't need to download the fsimage and the edit log from the NameNode—it simply saves its own namespace to the local fsimage file and zeroes out the edit log file. If you start up a backup node, there's no need to start a checkpoint node or a Standby NameNode in your cluster.

If you startup a backup node, you can run the NameNode without any requirements to store the namespace on its own disk system. The NameNode only maintains the latest namespace in-memory in this case. The backup node will take care of the actual storage of the fsimage and the edit log files on disk. In order to do this, you start the NameNode as follows, after starting the backup node.

```
$ hdfs namenode -backup
$ hdfs namenode -importCheckpoint
```

Since you're choosing not to store the namespace on the active NameNode, you must also remove the `dfs.name.dir` parameter in the hdfs-site.xml file.

> **Note**
>
> If you run the backup node, you can't run the checkpoint node.

Standby NameNode

The Standby NameNode is the hot standby for the NameNode service. In its capacity as a Standby NameNode, it also performs the checkpointing duties normally performed by one of the other types of NameNodes. Therefore, in a high-availability environment, you shouldn't run the backup node, checkpoint node or Secondary NameNode. Later in this chapter, you'll learn how to configure and manage a Standby NameNode.

Configuring the Checkpointing Frequency

The checkpointing process is highly configurable. By default, the Secondary NameNode will checkpoint every hour or after every 1 million transactions, whichever occurs first. You can configure the frequency of checkpointing by basing it on either of the following two criteria:

- Time elapsed since the last checkpoint. You configure this with the `dfs.namenode.checkpoint.period` configuration parameter.
- Number of edit log transactions since the last checkpoint. You set this with the `dfs.namenode.checkpoint.txns` parameter.

If either the elapsed time or the number of edit transactions since the last checkpoint exceeds their respective configured values, the checkpointing node (could be the Standby NameNode, the Secondary NameNode, the checkpoint node or the backup node) will set the checkpointing process in motion. As mentioned earlier, the Secondary NameNode performs the checkpointing by default, and in a high-availability setup, it's the Standby NameNode that checkpoints.

If for any reason the checkpointing process isn't working right, you may have a lot of catching up to do, especially in a large, busy cluster. Make sure that the periodic checkpoints are occurring. You can check the checkpoint time by viewing the NameNode web UI.

If you monitor the NameNode logs during a startup, you may notice the statement "replaying edit logs." This means the NameNode is replaying the necessary edit logs based on its "last checkpoint" information. Once it replays all the necessary edit logs, it updates its namespace information.

How long will this process take? It depends on when the most recent checkpointing was performed and the number of changes in your cluster since that time, as indicated by the number of edit logs generated since the last checkpoint.

Go to the directory configured in the `dfs.namenode.name.dir` parameter to view the fsimage and the edit log files. The last successful checkpoint time is shown by the creation time of the latest fsimage file. You can figure out how long it takes for the NameNode to create its fresh namespace information by checking to see how many edit log segments (edits files) are present in this directory. If the cluster stopped checkpointing a few months ago and you never caught it, the NameNode will need to process through thousands of edit log segments, making the cluster unavailable for days!

> **Note**
>
> If the checkpoint process fails for any reason, the NameNode server can end up with a very large edit log with numerous edits segments, which you may not be aware of until the disk space is exhausted and the NameNode crashes. It's no fun to restart the NameNode in this situation, as it may take hours for it to replay the accumulated edit log files, which may run into hundreds of gigabytes!

In some clusters, mostly non-production-related, it's possible that a Secondary NameNode hasn't been configured, hasn't been running or, although it was running, failed to perform its main duty of performing checkpointing operations. As you know by now, if the NameNode has been running for a long time and needs to be restarted, it'll then be looking at a massive amount of edit log segments that need to be replayed. Hadoop provides a couple of useful parameters that help you configure how many extra edit logs (and how many extra edits) are retained:

- `dfs.namenode.num.extra.edits.retained` (default value of 1,000,000): This parameter specifies the number of extra transactions to be retained beyond the minimum necessary for restarting the NameNode. This is useful for cases where the remote Standby NameNode has been offline for a while and needs to access a larger backlog of edits in order to restart. The default value for this parameter is 1 million edits. Since the average edit is a few hundred bytes in size, the default value of 1 million edits means the total size of the retained edits will be a few hundred megabytes or a few gigabytes at the most.

- `dfs.namenode.max.extra.edits.segments.retained` (default value of 10,000): This parameter specifies the maximum number of extra edit log segments that should be retained over and above what is required for restarting the NameNode.

The two parameters listed here work in tandem to keep the total extra edits and the extra edits files at a reasonable level.

Managing Checkpoint Performance

On large clusters a checkpointing operation can consume critical I/O and network resources when copying very large fsimage files (several GB in size) to the NameNode. You can control the transfer speed of the fsimage file by configuring the following parameters.

- `dfs.image.transfer.bandwidthPerSec`: This configuration attribute allows you to specify the maximum amount of bandwidth (in bytes per second) for transferring the fsimage and edits files. This parameter is designed to help you keep NameNode operations responsive during the checkpointing process. The default value is 0, meaning that there's no throttling.
- `dfs.image.transfer.timeout`: This parameter sets the socket timeout (in milliseconds) for transferring the image. The timeout prevents the clients from hanging when the sender fails during the transfer of the image. The default value is 60,000 milliseconds.

> **Note**
>
> NameNode logs are always quite exhaustive, even in the literal sense, since they consume lots of disk space. Configure plenty of space for handling the NameNode logs. Because the NameNode rolls over its logs very quickly (a few minutes), you won't have the necessary diagnostic data that you'll need for troubleshooting in current logs if you don't size the NameNode logs big enough. Big is a relative term of course, but in general, a size of 250MB or higher should be ideal.

The Mechanics of Checkpointing

Checkpointing is a resource-intensive operation and may also lead to restricting user concurrent access. During checkpointing, the NameNode won't be able to allow client operations such as reading and writing HDFS files. That's the reason the NameNode relies on either the Secondary NameNode or the Standby NameNode (in a high-availability setup) to take care of the checkpointing work.

In the following two sections, you'll learn the checkpointing mechanics, first with a Standby NameNode and then with a Secondary NameNode.

Checkpointing with a Standby NameNode

When you configure high availability for the NameNode service, edits are stored in shared storage that is accessible to both the active and Standby NameNodes. The Standby NameNode doesn't concern itself with handling client requests. Its main job is to keep its version of the namespace updated by regularly performing checkpoints—that is, by updating the fsimage by replaying the edits being written to the shared edits directory by the active NameNode.

> **Note**
>
> Creating a new fsimage file with the latest namespace through checkpointing is essentially the same as running the command `hdfs dfsadmin -saveNameSpace`.

Here are the steps involved in checkpointing with a Standby NameNode:

1. The Standby NameNode checks whether the time elapsed since the last checkpoint or the number of accumulated edits matches the configured checkpoint thresholds for these two conditions.
2. The Standby NameNode saves its namespace data to a new intermediate file named `fsimage.ckpt_txid`. The `txid` part in the filename refers to the ID of the most recent edit log transaction. After writing an MD5 file for this fsimage file, it renames the file to fsimage_.xxxx.
3. The Standby NameNode sends an HTTP `GET` message to the active NameNode's `GetImageServlet (/getimage?putimage=1)`.
4. The Active NameNode will do its own `GET` operation to the Standby NameNode's `GetImageServlet`. It renames the newly retrieved fsimage file to an intermediate name (fsimage.ckpt), creates an MD5 file for it and then renames it fsimage_.xxxx

> **Note**
>
> When a checkpoint is in progress, you can't fail over to the Standby NameNode or access the Standby web UI. Fortunately, the checkpointing process lasts for a very short time.

Now that you've seen how checkpointing works with a Standby NameNode, let's see how it works with a Secondary NameNode.

Checkpointing with a Secondary NameNode

The checkpointing process run by the Secondary NameNode is different initially, as it and the active NameNode don't share an edits directory. Here's the checkpoint procedure when using a Secondary NameNode:

1. The Secondary NameNode checks whether the time elapsed since the last checkpoint or the number of accumulated edits meets the configured checkpoint threshold.
2. The Secondary NameNode retrieves the most recent edit log transaction ID through an RPC call to the NameNode.
3. The Secondary NameNode requests the NameNode to roll the current edits file by ending the current edit log segment and starting a new edit segment.

4. The NameNode continues writing edits to the new edit log segment and the Secondary NameNode compacts the old edit logs. The Secondary NameNode also obtains the transaction IDs of the current fsimage file and the rolled edit log segment.
5. Using the two transaction IDs retrieved in step 4, the Secondary NameNode performs a GET to the NameNode's `GetImageServlet` to get the fsimage and edit files.
6. The Secondary NameNode replays the edit log segments so it can catch up with the current transaction ID and refresh its namespace.
7. The Secondary NameNode writes its refreshed namespace to a new fsimage file.
8. The Secondary NameNode performs an HTTP `GET` operation (`/getimage?putimage=1`) to the NameNode. The NameNode will in turn perform its own `GET` operation to the Secondary NameNode and download the new fsimage file.
9. Finally, the NameNode replaces its previous fsimage file with the new fsimage file. It also replaces the previous edits file with the new edits file it created in step 3.

NameNode Safe Mode Operations

Safe mode is a NameNode state in which the node doesn't accept any changes to the HDFS namespace, meaning HDFS will be in a read-only state. Safe mode is entered automatically at NameNode startup, and the NameNode leaves safe mode automatically when the configured minimum percentage of blocks satisfies the minimum replication condition.

The NameNode can enter the safe mode automatically, or you can place it in the safe mode before performing certain maintenance operations, such as backing up the HDFS metadata. The following sections explain both of these cases.

Automatic Safe Mode Operations

When you start up the NameNode, it doesn't start replicating data to the DataNodes right away. The NameNode first automatically enters a special read-only state of operation called safe mode. In this mode, the NameNode doesn't honor any requests to make changes to its namespace. Thus, it refrains from replicating, or even deleting, any data blocks until it leaves the safe mode.

As you learned earlier in this chapter, the DataNodes continuously send two things to the NameNode—a heartbeat indicating they're alive and well and a block report listing all data blocks being stored on a DataNode. Hadoop considers a data block "safely" replicated once the NameNode receives enough block reports from the DataNodes indicating they have a minimum number of replicas of that block.

Hadoop makes the NameNode wait for the DataNodes to report blocks so it doesn't start replicating data prematurely by attempting to replicate data even when the correct number of replicas exists on DataNodes that haven't yet reported their block information. When a preconfigured percentage of blocks are reported as safely replicated, the

NameNode leaves the safe mode and starts serving block information to clients. It'll also start replicating all blocks that the DataNodes have reported as being under replicated.

You can't write HDFS data while the NameNode is in safe mode. If you attempt to perform a write operation, you'll get the following error:

```
$ hdfs dfs -copyFromLocal test.txt /tmp/
     copyFromLocal: org.apache.hadoop.hdfs.server.namenode.SafeModeException:
Cannot create
     file/tmp/.bash_history. Name node is in safe mode.
```

While the NameNode automatically enters and transitions out of safe mode upon restarting, sometimes you may need to put the NameNode into safe mode. You need to put the NameNode into safe mode whenever you want to freeze the namespace. Thus, safe mode can be seen as a tool to put your cluster in maintenance mode.

Placing the NameNode in Safe Mode

Sometimes, you may want to perform administrative actions that require HDFS to be in the read-only mode. You can explicitly put the NameNode in safe mode during those operations. Once you're done performing the administrative actions, you can take the NameNode out of safe mode.

Use the `dfsadmin -safemode` command to manage safe mode operations for the NameNode. You can check the current safe mode status with the `-safemode get` command:

```
$ hdfs dfsadmin -safemode get
  Safe mode is OFF in hadoop01.localhost/10.192.2.21:8020
  Safe mode is OFF in hadoop02.localhost/10.192.2.22:8020
$
```

You can place the NameNode in safe mode with the `-safemode enter` command:

```
$  hdfs dfsadmin -safemode enter
Safe mode is ON in hadoop01.localhost/10.192.2.21:8020
Safe mode is ON in hadoop02.localhost/10.192.2.22:8020
$
```

Finally, you can take the NameNode out of safemode with the `-safemode leave` command:

```
$ hdfs dfsadmin -safemode leave
Safe mode is OFF in hadoop01.localhost/10.192.2.21:8020
Safe mode is OFF in hadoop02.localhost/10.192.2.22:8020
$
```

The `-safemode wait` command makes the NameNode wait to resume its operations until HDFS finishes all of its data replication.

```
$ hdfs dfsadmin -safemode wait
```

This command blocks all access to the NameNode until it exits safe mode.

You already know that the NameNode will automatically enter the safe mode every time you start it up. In addition, the NameNode will also enter the safemode when the server on which the NameNode is running runs out of disk space.

The NameNode stores its metadata in the directory you specify with the `dfs.namenode.name.dir` parameter. The amount of space the NameNode can use for its metadata storage depends on a key parameter named `dfs.namenode.du.reserved`. This parameter specifies the threshold for free space to be reserved by Hadoop for the NameNode to write its namespace information. By default, this parameter is about 100MB (104,857,600 bytes).

If the free space on the server where the NameNode stores its metadata information falls below the threshold specified by the `dfs.namenode.du.reserved` parameter, the NameNode will immediately enter the safe mode, as you'll see in the following messages.

```
Space available on volume /u05 is 103645184, which is below the configured
reserved amount 104857600
NameNode low on available free space. Entering safe mode.
STATE* Safe mode is ON
Resources are low on NN. Please add or free up more resources then turn off
safe mode manually. NOTE:  If you turn off safe mode before adding resources,
the NN will immediately return to safe mode.
```

As the messages clearly inform you, there's no way you can manually take the NameNode out of safe mode until you add more disk space to the partition or volume on which you ran out of space. Once you've taken care of the space issue, you can take the NameNode out of safe mode with the `dfsadmin -safemode leave` command.

> **Note**
>
> The dfs.datanode.du.reserved parameter specifies the threshold of free space on the entire system, not on any specific volume.

You can put the NameNode into the safe mode for purposes other than backing up its metadata. If a large number of DataNodes in your cluster fail, Hadoop will immediately swing into action by replicating large amounts of data to the remaining DataNodes in the cluster. A good strategy to avoid the large-scale data replication is to start up the NameNode in safe mode and then go about bringing up the failed DataNodes.

> **Note**
>
> The NameNode logs, the `dfsadmin safemode` command and the NameNode UI all show the current state of the NameNode.

How the NameNode Transitions Through Safe Mode

Following is a quick rundown of how the NameNode transitions through safe mode to a fully "open" mode.

1. When you enter the safe mode of operations, both the NameNode and the DataNodes are in the running state. NameNode reads the latest checkpoint to initialize the NameNode's namespace information.
2. The NameNode may replay some edit logs to create fresh namespace information based on the checkpoint information.

3. NameNode creates a new checkpoint (that is, a new fsimage file that's a compaction of the previous fsimage file and all transactions applied from the edit logs) and saves it.
4. The ports to the DataNodes, NameNode web UI and Secondary NameNode are opened to start communications.
5. The NameNode enters safe mode—no HDFS read and write operations are permitted at this point.
6. The NameNode exits the safe mode—HDFS reads and writes are allowed.

If there are a large number of edit logs, say because the Secondary NameNode was out of commission for a while, the NameNode could stay in the safe mode status quite a while.

If you've configured multiple redundant storage locations for the fsimage file, the NameNode writes in a parallel fashion to all the fsimage files but remains in safe mode until it completes writing to all locations. Until then, there can't be any client connections to HDFS.

You can track the NameNode restart process immediately upon starting it by checking the NameNode web UI. The UI will display the percentages of completion in the process of loading the fsimage and loading the edits.

During the NameNode restart process, in the NameNode web UI, completed phases are displayed in bold text. Currently the running phase is shown in italics and the yet-to-begin phases are shown in gray text. The UI will also show other bits of information such as where the active NameNode is loading the fsimage and edits files from, and the size of those files. It also shows all the locations where the NameNode is writing the fsimage to, as well as the size of the fsimage file.

Backing Up and Recovering the NameNode Metadata

Since the NameNode metadata is absolutely critical to your cluster operations, you should periodically back it up. Here are the steps to back up the NameNode metadata.

1. Put the cluster in safe mode:

```
$ hdfs dfsadmin -safemode enter
Safe mode is ON in hadoop02.example.com/10.192.2.22:8020
Safe mode is ON in hadoop02.example.com/10.192.2.21:8020
$
```

2. Back up the metadata with the -saveNameSpace command:

```
$ hdfs dfsadmin -saveNamespace
Save namespace successful for hadoop02.example.com/10.192.2.22:8020
Save namespace successful for hadoop02.example.com/10.192.2.21:8020
$ hdfs dfsadmin -safemode leave
Safe mode is OFF in hadoop02.example.com/10.192.2.22:8020
Safe mode is OFF in hadoop02.example.com/10.192.2.21:8020
$
```

The -saveNameSpace command saves the current namespace (HDFS metadata) to disk, and also resets the edit log. Since this command requires HDFS to be in safe mode, you must make sure to exit safe mode after executing the -saveNameSpace command.

3. The dfsadmin -metasave command helps you save the NameNode's primary structures to a text file, as shown here:

   ```
   $ hdfs dfsadmin -metasave mymeta.txt
   Created metasave file mymeta.txt in the log directory of namenode
   hadoop02.example.com/10.192.2.22:8020
   Created metasave file mymeta.txt in the log directory of namenode
   hadoop02.example.com/10.192.2.21:8020
   $
   ```

   In this example, the dfsadmin -metasave command stores the following primary data structures to the file named *mymeta.txt* in the directory you specified for the hadoop.log.dir parameter (in our case this is /var/log/hadoop-hdfs). A primary data structure in this context is of the following types:

   - DataNode heartbeats sent to the NameNode
   - Blocks awaiting replication
   - Blocks that are currently being replicated
   - Blocks awaiting deletion

4. Here's the top portion of the mymeta.txt file created with the -metasave command:

   ```
   Note 2222102 files and directories, 2148293 blocks = 4370395 total
   Live Datanodes: 17
   Dead Datanodes: 1
   Metasave: Blocks waiting for replication: 79
   /user/sam/pos_poc/hive/hostsession_bbis_prod/date=2014-05-26/hostmessage_
   data_attempt_1408991795079_0265_r_000029_0.avro: blk_1074299104_1099524502475
   MISSING (replicas: l: 0 d: 0 c: 0 e: 0)
   /user/sam/pos_poc/hive/hostsession_bbis_prod/date=2014-05-27/hostmessage_
   data_attempt_1408991795079_0266_r_000013_0.avro: blk_1074299273_1099524502644
   MISSING (replicas: l: 0 d: 0 c: 0 e: 0):
   ```

It's not a good idea to edit the metadata files, as you could end up losing data. For example, the VERSION file protects DataNodes belonging to a different namespace from registering with a NameNode. This is a built-in safety device, and by editing the VERSION file to match the namespace IDs of the DataNodes and the NameNode, you can end up corrupting the data.

Using the getconf Command to Get the NameNode Configuration

The hdfs getconf utility gets you NameNode configuration information, as explained here.

```
$ hdfs getconf -namenodes
hdfs getconf is utility for getting configuration information from the config
file

hadoop getconf
        [-namenodes]            gets list of NameNodes in the cluster.
        [-secondaryNameNodes]   gets list of secondary NameNodes in the cluster.
        [-backupNodes]          gets list of backup nodes in the cluster.
        [-includeFile]          gets the include file path that defines the
                                DataNodes that can join the cluster.
```

```
        [-excludeFile]         gets the exclude file path that defines the
                               DataNodes that need to decommissioned.
        [-nnRpcAddresses]      gets the namenode rpc addresses
        [-confKey [key]]       gets a specific key from the configuration
```

Here's an example:

```
$ hdfs  getconf -namenodes
hadoop01.localhost hadoop02.localhost
$
```

This example assumes a high-availability NameNode setup, wherein there are two NameNodes: an active and a Secondary NameNode.

Earlier, I mentioned that you can configure a Standby NameNode to provide high availability for the NameNode. The next section shows how to configure and set up HDFS high availability.

Configuring HDFS High Availability

A NameNode outage, regardless of whether it's planned or not, means that users can't use HDFS. If the NameNode server (host on which the NameNode runs) is lost, all HDFS files are for all practical purposes lost as well, since there's no way to access the HDFS metadata.

If you have just a single NameNode, an outage means that you're going to spend significant time starting up a new NameNode service on a different server and wait for it to start accepting client requests.

NameNodes are usually architected to run on more robust servers than the DataNodes, so they may not fail often. However, you must also consider the fact that you'll be taking the NameNode down once in a while to perform various maintenance tasks—such as patching the OS of the server on which the NameNode service is running, for example—and each time you take it down, there's an outage, albeit planned. Obviously, availability of the Hadoop cluster is weakened due to its dependence on the NameNode service.

Due to the critical importance of the metadata managed by the NameNode, you must make the NameNode immune to failure by building resiliency for the NameNode service. In Hadoop 2, you can run two NameNodes simultaneously to provide high availability for HDFS, with one of the NameNodes serving as the active NameNode and the other as the Standby NameNode. While configuring a high-availability (HA) NameNode service is purely optional, this architecture is recommended for a production environment.

The Standby NameNode doesn't merely sit idle until it's called upon to take over from the active NameNode and become the active NameNode. Besides providing high availability, the Standby NameNode provides other services. In a HA architecture, the Standby NameNode takes over the task of performing checkpoints of the namespace from the Secondary NameNode.

In most cases, the standby will transition to active status within about a minute or so. It can transition this quickly because it has the up-to-date namespace state stored in its memory, with consists of the latest edit log data, as well as the most up-to-date block mapping.

You can also take advantage of the HDFS high-availability capability when you need to perform any maintenance work on the server hosting the active NameNode.

The NameNode uses the edit log to get the latest state of HDFS metadata. The key to supporting NameNode high availability is to make sure the edit log is shareable (highly available) between the active and Standby NameNodes. Hadoop lets you enable the sharing of the edit log in two different ways:

- You can set up a Quorum Journal Manager (QJM) to enable the sharing of the edit log.
- Alternatively, you can set up a shared NFS directory to enable the sharing of the edit log between the two NameNodes.

Setting up high availability through the QJM is the recommended approach. In the following sections, you'll learn how to configure HDFS HA using the QJM. Many of the configuration steps are quite similar in both approaches, so if you understand the following discussion, you can easily set up HA using the alternative shared NFS directory approach.

NameNode HA Architecture (QJM)

When you're running an HA NameNode service, there are two NameNodes, but only one of them is active at any time, in terms of handling HDFS client operations. As its name indicates, it's the job of the active NameNode to interact with the clients. The Standby NameNode doesn't handle client requests—it simply ensures that its state is synchronized with that of the active NameNode.

When you use the QJM to synchronize the two NameNodes in an HA environment, you'll have a set of JournalNode (JN) daemons running in the cluster, in addition to the two NameNode services. When the active NameNode modifies the HDFS metadata, it writes the changes to all, or at least a majority of, the JNs.

Following are the main components of the Hadoop NameNode HA architecture (with two NameNodes):

- The ZooKeeper Failover Controller (ZKFC) controls the NameNode failover process.
- JNs hold the shared edit logs.
- A pair of NameNodes run in an the active/standby mode.

Using Apache ZooKeeper as a Coordinator

Apache ZooKeeper is used for coordination purposes in an HA environment. ZooKeeper monitors the active NameNode and handles the failover mechanism when the active NameNode becomes unavailable. Both the active and the Standby NameNode run a ZKFC to monitor the NameNodes and to initiate the failover tasks. It's the ZKFC that informs the ZooKeeper instances when a NameNode fails, which leads to those instances electing a new active NameNode to take over from the failed active NameNode.

The Role of the JournalNodes

In a typical HA environment, one of the NameNodes is in the active state and the other is in a standby state. The active NameNode attends to client operations, while the Standby NameNode waits to take over from the active NameNode in case of a failover.

In order to be able to take over from the active NameNode, the Standby NameNode must maintain state. The way the Standby NameNode synchronizes its state with that of the active NameNode is by both nodes communicating through a set of daemons called JournalNodes (JNs).

All changes made by the active node are written to a majority of the JNs. In order to obtain a quorum of these nodes, you always run an odd number of JNs, such as 3 or 5. The Standby NameNode monitors the JNs and applies all edits made to the JNs to its own namespace.

Before a failover, the Standby NameNode ensures that it has read all edits from the JNs before it makes itself the active NameNode.

> **Note**
>
> In order to ensure that the Standby NameNode always has up-to-date information regarding all blocks and thus minimize the time failover, the DataNodes send the block locations as well as their health status (heartbeats) to both the active and the Standby NameNodes.

It's the job of the JNs to ensure that only one NameNode writes changes to the namespace at any time, in order to avoid ending up with an inconsistent namespace.

You need a minimum of three JNs to support NameNode HA. When there are changes to HDFS, the active NameNode writes journal entries to the majority of the JN services.

When a failure occurs, the Standby NameNode reads the completed journal entries (that is, where a majority of the JNs have a completed entry) to make sure that when it transforms into an active NameNode, its state is fully consistent with the cluster's state.

How High Availability Works

Clients connect to the active NameNode, but the DataNodes will send their heartbeats to both the NameNodes. The active NameNode writes its metadata to the JNs, and the Standby NameNode stays in sync with the active NameNode by continuously reading the metadata from the JN.

> **Note**
>
> There are two types of failover: automatic failover, which is detected and initiated by HDFS, and manual failover, which is initiated by the administrator and can be due to maintenance work.

The JNs provide the shared edits storage. The active NameNode writes to this storage and the Standby NameNode reads from it, to keep current with the HDFS changes being made by the active NameNode. Here's how high availability for HDFS works:

1. The active NameNode writes all metadata changes to (a majority of) the JN's Journal Manager, which is part of the NameNode. It waits for a majority of the JNs to acknowledge success. The majority acknowledgment is to ensure that a single failed JN won't adversely affect the NameNode latency.
2. The Standby NameNode monitors the JNs for changes to the edit log.
3. When the Standby NameNode notices changes to the edit log, it updates its namespace with the changes it notices.
4. When a failover is imminent, the Standby NameNode first ascertains that it has up-to-date metadata based on the changes to the edit log in the JNs.
5. Once the Standby NameNode verifies it has the most recent changes in the edit log, it's ready to be converted into the active NameNode.
6. The new active NameNode (former Standby NameNode) will commence writing namespace changes to the JNs.

As far as provisioning the servers for the Standby NameNode is concerned, ensure that the machine on which it runs is identical to the server on which you're running the active NameNode, since the Standby NameNode could be called upon to replace the active NameNode anytime.

As mentioned earlier, the active NameNode needs to write to a majority of the JNs, so you'd need an odd number of JN daemons running. You must therefore configure a minimum of three JN daemons.

When the active NameNode writes edit logs to the JNs, it uses the `QuorumGeneralManager` to write data to a majority of the JNs to achieve high availability. The greater the number of JNs, the higher the number of failures your cluster can survive and still maintain a high-availability HDFS service.

Luckily, you don't need to run the JN daemons on dedicated servers—simply run them on any of the master cluster nodes.

> **Note**
>
> The DataNodes will send block reports to both the active and Standby NameNodes.

Setting Up an HDFS HA Quorum Cluster

Now that you've learned about the basic architecture of QJM-based HDFS high availability, let's learn how to set up a high-availability NameNode service. In an HA NameNode setup, you create a **logical nameservice**, formally called a nameservice ID, to point to the HDFS instance, which consists of both the active and the Standby NameNodes.

In a HA configuration, you must also add a **logical NameNode ID** to tell the two NameNodes apart from each other. To configure the HA NameNode service, you must make a few configuration changes in the hdfs-site.xml configuration file. Since you're distinguishing between the two NameNodes with their own IDs, you can use the same hdfs-site.xml file to configure settings for both NameNodes.

Configuring an HA NameNode service involves the configuration of several name- and address-related attributes, as well as some failover attributes. To keep things clear, let's approach these two sets of configuration parameters separately.

Configuring the HA Name and Address Attributes

Following are the name- and address-related HA configuration parameters you add to the hdfs-site.xml file to set up NameNode high availability.

1. Create a logical name for the nameservice. Using the `dfs.nameservices` configuration parameter, you can specify an arbitrary name for the nameservice. In this example `prodcluster` is the logical name for the nameservice. Here's how to set the logical name with the `dfs.nameservices` attribute:

   ```
   <property>
      <name>dfs.nameservices</name>
      <value>prodcluster</value>
   </property>
   ```

   This parameter sets a unique nameservice ID (`prodcluster`), which is used by the two NameNodes as well as Hadoop clients.

2. Configure the `fs.defaultFS` attribute to setup a default path prefix for HDFS. By using the logical name you specified earlier (`prodcluster`), you ensure that Hadoop clients will access the HA-enabled nameservice.

   ```
   <property>
     <name>fs.defaultFS</name>
     <value>hdfs://prodcluster</value>
   </property>
   ```

   The logical URI specified here will define a virtual NameNode and resolves to the active NameNode, for example, `hdfs: //prodcluster`, as in our example.

3. Uniquely identify each NameNode. You've already configured the logical name with which to identify the HA nameservice (`prodcluster`). You must also create unique identifiers for each of the NameNodes in the HA configuration by configuring the `dfs.ha.namenodes.<xxxx>` property as shown here.

   ```
   <property>
     <name>dfs.ha.namenodes.prodcluster</name>
     <value>nn1,nn2</value>
   </property>
   ```

   I chose to name the two NameNodes `nn1` and `nn2`. When I set the other HA configuration attributes next, I can specifically refer to each of the NameNodes by their unique NameNode IDs. The DataNodes (and clients) will identify a NameNode through its ID.

4. Provide the URI to identify the set of JournalNodes. In our case, there are going to be three JournalNodes, so we need to configure the addresses in the following way.

```
<property>
  <name>dfs.namenode.shared.edits.dir</name>
  <value>qjournal://node1.example.com:8485;node2.example.com:8485;
  node3.example.com:8485/prodcluster</value>
</property>
```

The list of JNs you specify here is used by the NameNodes. The attribute `dfs.namenode.shared.edits.dir` points to our three JNs, running on three different servers. Configuring this parameter is a bit tricky! The correct format to use here is `qjournal://{semicolon-separated list of journal-server:port entries}/journalId)`. The Journal ID is a unique identifier for this nameservice, and although it isn't mandatory, it probably is a good idea to just use the nameservice ID as the Journal ID as well.

Although you need to specify the three addresses for our three JournalNodes, make sure to configure just one of the addresses as a URI. In this case, the third JN's URI (`node3.example.com:8485/prodcluster`) points to the group of JNs. I used our cluster's nameservice ID (`prodcluster`) as the Journal ID in this example, but you may specify any other logical name you wish.

5. You must also provide the specific location on the JNs where the cluster will store the edits file as well other local state information needed by the JNs.

```
<property>
  <name>dfs.journalnode.edits.dir</name>
  <value>/path/to/journal/node/local/data</value>
</property>
```

   This property is used by the JNs. You can't specify multiple locations for the storage directories, as redundancy is provided by using multiple JNs. If you wish additional redundancy, you can configure this directory on a local RAID array.

6. Configure RPC addresses for the two NameNodes. You must supply the full address and the IPC port for both NameNodes, as shown here.

```
<property>
  <name>dfs.namenode.rpc-address.prodcluster.nn1</name>
  <value>machine1.example.com:8020</value>
</property>

<property>
  <name>dfs.namenode.rpc-address.prodcluster.nn2</name>
  <value>machine2.example.com:8020</value>
</property>
```

   The RPC addresses are used by both NameNodes and clients.

7. As with the RPC addresses, you must also specify the HTTP addresses where the NameNodes will listen.

```
<property>
      <name>dfs.namenode.http-address.prodcluster.nn1</name>
  <value>hadoop01.localhost:50070</value>
```

```
</property>
<property>
  <name>dfs.namenode.http-address.prodcluster.nn2</name>
  <value>hadoop02.localhost:50070</value>
</property>
```

The HTTP addresses are used by the NameNodes.

8. Configure the Java class for HDFS clients to use when contacting the active NameNode.

```
<property>
  <name> dfs.client.failover.proxy.provider.prodcluster </name>
  <value>org.apache.hadoop.hdfs.server.namenode
.ha.ConfiguredFailoverProxyProvider</value>
</property>
```

The `dfs.client.failover.proxy.provider.prodcluster` property specifies the Java class that HDFS clients use to determine which of the two NameNodes is currently acting as the active NameNode.

Configuring the HA Failover Attributes

The NameNode handles the heartbeats from the DataNodes and passes back its current HA state. When the active NameNode goes down for any reason, it may potentially serve out-of-date read requests (stale data) to clients. In order to avoid this, it's advisable to have a **fencing** mechanism for use during a failover.

Fencing ensures that only a single NameNode runs in the active mode at any point in time. You do this by configuring a fencing process for the storage directory shared by the NameNodes. During a failover, if the failed NameNode still is in the active state, the fencing process will prevent that node from accessing the storage directory. Instead, it allows the former Standby NameNode, which is the current active NameNode, to complete the failover process.

> **Note**
>
> Fencing prevents the well-known **split-brain scenario**, wherein more than one node can write to the JournalNodes, causing potential file system metadata corruption.

The attribute `dfs.ha.fencing.methods` lets you specify a set of scripts or Java classes that will be used to fence the active NameNode during the failover. Hadoop attempts each of the fencing methods you configure in the order you list until one of them indicates that fencing has succeeded. Configure a fencing method that's guaranteed to return success as the last fencing method in the set of scripts or Java classes you provide. This ensures that the system is available even if all the fencing mechanisms fail.

You can use one of two methods for configuring the fencing of the NameNode:

- `sshfence` kills the process after connecting to the active NameNode.
- `shell` executes a shell command to fence the active NameNode.

The sshfence method will kill the process listening on the NameNode port after using SSH to connect to the Active NameNode. You configure the sshfence option by setting sshfence as the value for the dfs.ha.fencing.methods attribute, as shown here.

```
<property>
  <name>dfs.ha.fencing.methods</name>
  <value>sshfence</value>
</property>
```

The dfs.ha.fencing.methods parameter value is used for both of the NameNodes as well as by the ZKFCs.

When using the sshfence fencing method, you must also configure the hdfs.ha.fencing .ssh.private-key-files attribute, which lets you provide a list of SSH private key files that enable the use of SSH:

```
<property>
  <name>dfs.ha.fencing.ssh.private-key-files</name>
  <value>/home/exampleuser/.ssh/id_rsa</value>
</property>
```

This property specifies the location of the SSH key used for SSH-based fencing and is used by both NameNodes and the ZKFCs. This file must be readable by the HDFS user, and it allows automation of SSH with no passphrase.

The alternative fencing method, simply called **shell**, uses an arbitrary shell command to fence the active NameNode, and you can configure it as shown here:

```
<property>
  <name>dfs.ha.fencing.methods</name>
  <value>shell(/path/to/my/script.sh arg1 arg2 ...)</value>
</property>
```

If you're testing the HA NameNode setup, you can specify shell(/bin/true) as your fencing method, but note that it won't perform any fencing during a failover. It's a good idea to use sshfence as your fencing method. This requires generating an SSH key and configuring its location.

In order for a NameNode to successfully failover, one of the fencing methods you configure must be successful. Fencing is deemed successful if the shell command returns an exit code of 0.

After making the configuration changes in the hdfs-site.xml file on one of your servers, you can copy it over to the rest of the nodes.

> **Note**
>
> It'll only take you a few minutes to configure high availability with Cloudera Manager or Ambari. The documentation is very good for both of these products, and the steps are quite simple to follow. My goal, however, isn't merely to help you set up high availability; it's to help you understand exactly how it all works.

Deploying the High-Availability NameNodes

Once you've configured the JournalNodes, it's time to get the HA NameNode service going. Follow these steps to deploy the two HA NameNodes.

1. On each of your JournalNodes, create the shared edits directories where the JournalNodes will share the metadata. Once you create the shared edits directory on all Journal Nodes, change the ownership of the shared edits directory to the user hdfs and the group hadoop.

   ```
   $ mkdir -p /var/data/dfs/jn
   $ chown -R hdfs:hadoop /var/data/dfs/jn
   ```

2. Start up the JournalNode daemons using the following command on each of the three servers where you've configured a JournalNode.

   ```
   $ hdfs hadoop-daemon.sh start journalnode
   ```

   You can confirm that the JournalNodes are running as supposed with the `"jps | grep JournalNode"` command.
3. Once all JournalNodes have successfully started up, the final step is to synchronize the state of the active and Standby NameNodes. In case you're setting up a fresh cluster, you must format one of the NameNodes, as shown in Chapter 3, "Creating and Configuring a Simple Hadoop Cluster." If you're adding high availability to an existing cluster, you mustn't format the NameNodes!
4. Run the following command on the current single NameNode:

   ```
   $ hdfs namenode -initializeSharedEdits -force
   ```

   Running this command will initialize all JournalNodes with the edits data recorded after the most recent checkpoint from NameNode `nn1` to the edits directory of all the JournalNodes.
5. Run the following command on the new unformatted NameNode in order to bootstrap it before starting it:

   ```
   $ hdfs namenode -bootstrapStandby -force
   INFO util.ExitUtil: Exiting with status 0
   ```

   This command synchronizes the namespace metadata stored on disk on both the NameNodes by copying the latest fsimage file from `nn1` (active) to `nn2` (Standby). It formats the storage on the Standby NameNode first and afterwards copies the latest namespace snapshot from the active NameNode.
6. Make sure the ZooKeeper services are running on all the nodes on which services are configured to run. If they are not, start the ZooKeeper service on all the ZooKeeper hosts. The following command formats the znode in the ZooKeeper server that tracks the status (active/Standby) of your NameNodes. The ZKFCs use the znode to track the active and the Standby NameNodes.

   ```
   $ hdfs zkfc -formatZK -force
   ```

7. Finally, start up the first NameNode, which is nn1 in our example, as shown here:

```
$ /usr/lib/hadoop/sbin/hadoop-daemon.sh start namenode
```

8. Check to make sure that NameNode nn1 is running successfully.
9. You must now initialize the second NameNode, which is named nn2 in our example. Format this NameNode and copy the latest checkpoint from nn1 to nn2, as shown here, with the -bootstrapStandby command:

```
$ hdfs namenode -bootstrapStandby [-force]  [-nonInteractive]
```

   The -bootstrapStandby command gets the checkpointed fsimage file from the first NameNode, nn1. It also makes sure that nn2 has received all the corresponding edit logs from the JournalNodes. This command will succeed only if the JNs are currently initialized and provide the edit logs requested by nn2.
10. At this point, you're ready to start the second NameNode, nn2, with the usual start command:

```
$ /usr/lib/hadoop/sbin/hadoop-daemon.sh start namenode
```

11. Start all the DataNodes by issuing the following command:

```
 $ su - hdfs -c "/usr/lib/hadoop/sbin/hadoop-daemon.sh -config
/etc/hadoop/conf start datanode"
```

12. Restart all the NodeManagers, the JobHistoryServer and the ResourceManager, as well.

   Initially, both of the NameNodes are in the standby state! If you attempt to list any files in HDFS, you'll get an error because neither of your NameNodes are in active status. You can check the status of the NameNodes, nn1 and nn2, with the following commands:

```
 $ hdfs haadmin -getServiceState nn1
   Standby
 $ hdfs haadmin -getServiceState nn2
   Standby
```

13. Now you need to transition one of our two NameNodes to the active state by failing over the NameNode:

```
$ hdfs haadmin -failover -forcefence- -forceactive nn2 nn1
```

   Your cluster is now running with an HA NameNode service. You can verify the HA NameNode configuration by issuing the hdfs getconf command as follows:

```
$ hdfs getconf -namenodes
hadoop02.localhost hadoop01.localhost
$
```

14. Verify that the two NameNodes are now running as they're expected to, with nn1 in the active state and nn2 in the standby state, using the following commands:

```
 $ hdfs haadmin -getServiceState nn1
   Active
 $ hdfs haadmin -getServiceState nn2
   Standby
$
```

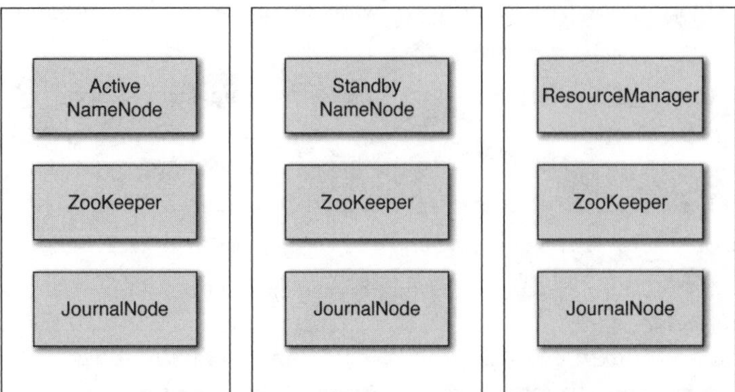

Figure 11.1 A typical Hadoop HA NameNode architecture with multiple ZooKeeper instances to support HA

Namenode `nn1` is now running in the active state. You can also check the status of each NameNode by accessing their web pages. One of the NameNodes must show that it's in the active and the other node, in the standby state. Figure 11.1 shows a typical high-availability architecture, with two NameNodes and three ZooKeeper instances.

What Our High-Availability Configuration Looks Like

At the end of the HA NameNode configuration exercise, our cluster with the three nodes named hadoop1, hadoop2 and hadoop3 has the services shown in Figure 11.2 running on each of the nodes.

Here's a summary of the HA NameNode configuration on my cluster now:

- There are two NameNodes, on hadoop1 and hadoop2, in an active/passive configuration.
- There are three JournalNodes, one on each of the three nodes of my cluster.
- The ZKFC daemons run on the same nodes as the two NameNodes, to support automatic failover.
- There are three ZooKeeper servers, to provide a quorum to support the ZKFC daemons.

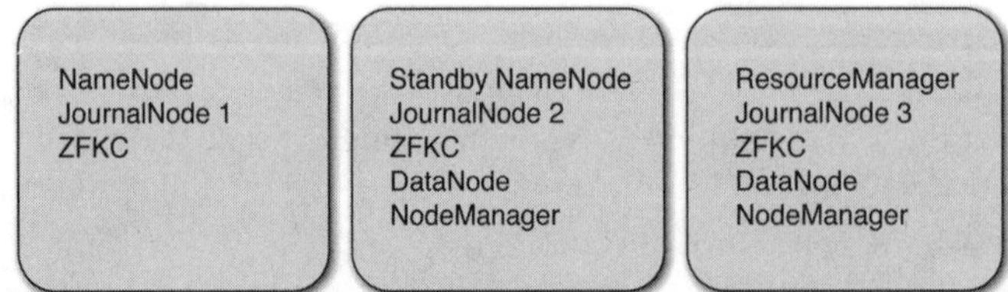

Figure 11.2 The Hadoop services on any three-node cluster after setting up quorum-based NameNode high availability

Testing the HA NameNode Setup

You can run some tests to make sure all the processes that are expected to be running are indeed running. Use the jps command to check the processes.

When I issue the jps command, I see the following services on the three nodes of my cluster:

- hadoop1: NameNode, JournalNode, ZKFC, QuorumPeerMain, DataNode, NodeManager
- hadoop2: NameNode, JournalNode, ZKFC, QuorumPeerMain, DataNode, NodeManager
- hadoop3: JournalNode, QuorumPeerMain, DataNode, ResourceManager, JobHistoryServer, NodeManager

Notice the new processes named QuorumPeerMain on hadoop1, hadoop2 and hadoop3—this process runs the ZooKeeper server on those three nodes.

In an HA NameNode setup, you'll have two NameNode UIs, one for the active and the other for the Standby NameNode. If you access the web UIs, you'll see that the very first line in the web UI shows the following for the two NameNodes:

```
NameNode 'hadoop1:8020'
(active)
NameNode 'hadoop2:8020'
(standby)
```

You can test the HA configuration by bringing down each of the NameNodes one by one and restarting them, with the following commands.

```
$ $HADOOP-PREFIX/sbin/hadoop-daemon.sh stop namenode
$ $HADOOP-PREFIX/sbin/hadoop-daemon.sh start namenode
```

You'll notice that the NameNodes switch between the active and standby states. You can stop and start a NameNode anytime you wish—it won't have any impact on the cluster operations. That's the whole point in setting up an HA NameNode service!

Managing an HA NameNode Setup

In an HA NameNode configuration, the active NameNode must at all times be able to write to a majority of the JNs. You must ensure that the JNs are running before you start up the NameNodes. In an HA NameNode setup, you must start up the NameNodes, JNs and DataNodes in the following order.

1. Start all JNs.
2. Start the active NameNode.
3. Start the Standby NameNode.
4. Start all DataNodes.

Errors When Querying the Standby NameNode

The Standby NameNode is, as its name indicates, merely a node that's waiting to take over as the active NameNode on short notice. The active NameNode serves all client requests. When users mistakenly connect to the Standby NameNode for metadata operations, they get an error message:

```
{"RemoteException":{"exception":"StandbyException","javaClassName":"org.apa
che.hadoop.ipc.StandbyException","message":"Operation category READ is not
supported in state standby"}}
```

In the standby mode, the NameNode can only perform HA-related functions such as a failover. It's not designed to share client-related and namespace-related work with the active NameNode. If you need to execute a command that must access the currently active NameNode in a cluster, such as a `curl` command, you can write a script to poll both the NameNodes in an HA cluster to find the NameNode that's currently in the active state.

Using the `dfsadmin` Command in an HA NameNode Environment

You must specify the `-fs` option when issuing any `dfsadmin` commands, so as to specify the RPC address or service RPC address of the NameNode. If you don't set the `-fs` option, the following commands will fail over to the active NameNode and perform the operation there.

- `-setQuota`
- `-clrQuota`
- `-setSpaceQuota`
- `-clrSpaceQuota`

You must run refresh options such as `-refreshNodes` or `-refreshServiceAcl` on both the active and Standby NameNodes.

When the Standby NameNode takes a checkpoint, it saves the data to its local storage and also uploads it to the other NameNode. That is, it applies the edit logs to its fsimage file, and then it uploads the image file to the active NameNode to speed up failovers and avoid long delays for updating the fsimage file on the active NameNode.

The NameNode checks its HA state and doesn't serve any requests when it's in the standby state. All operations are permitted in the active NameNode, but read and write operations aren't allowed in the standby state.

HA Manual and Automatic Failover

Now that you've configured high availability for your NameNodes, it's time to learn how to set up automatic failover, as well as how to manually failover a NameNode from an active to a standby status. In a QJM-based HA setup, the NameNode transitioning to the active state will take over the responsibility of writing to the JournalNodes, since the

JournalNodes don't allow multiple NameNodes to write namespace changes. This means that the original NameNode (active) can't continue in the active state simultaneously.

Configuring Automatic Failover

The NameNode HA setup you've configured is only capable of a manual failover by the administrator. The next step is to learn how to configure automatic failover from the active to the Standby NameNode.

The ZooKeeper service is at the heart of automatic NameNode failover. While you don't need ZooKeeper to set up NameNode high availability, you do need it to set up automatic failover. ZooKeeper sets off the failover by notifying the Standby NameNode when the active NameNode's ZooKeeper session expires for a reason such as the crash of the server on which the active NameNode runs. The Standby NameNode will then take an exclusive lock in ZooKeeper to convert itself into the active NameNode.

> **Note**
>
> Since ZooKeeper instances aren't resource hungry, you can simply install them on the same nodes as the master daemons.

ZooKeeper uses the aforementioned special component named the Zookeeper Failover Controller (ZKFC) that runs on both NameNodes to monitor NameNode state. The ZKFC verifies that the active NameNode is healthy through periodic pings, and as long as the active NameNode is healthy, ZFKC holds a session open for it in ZooKeeper. When the currently active NameNode is unhealthy, ZooKeeper fails over from the active to the Standby NameNode.

The time it takes to automatically failover from the Standby to the active NameNode is determined by the value of the `ha.zookeeper.session-timeout.ms` parameter, whose default value is five seconds. Before configuring and deploying automatic failover through ZooKeeper, you need to stop all Hadoop services in the right order. Once you stop the services, follow these steps to configure automatic failover:

1. Configure your cluster for automatic failover by adding the following parameter to the hdfs.site.xml file on both of the servers hosting the NameNodes:

   ```
   <property>
      <name>dfs.ha.automatic-failover.enabled</name>
      <value>true</value>
   <property>
   ```

2. Configure the `ha.zookeeper.quorum` parameter in the core-site.xml file to indicate where the ZooKeeper services are running:

   ```
   <property>
     <name>ha.zookeeper.quorum</name>    <value>zk1.localhost.com:2181,zk2
   .localhost.com:2181,zk2.lcoalhost.com:2181</value>
   <property>
   ```

   ZKFC uses this information, and this is required only when configuring automatic failover.

3. Start the ZooKeeper service with the following command:

```
$ /usr/local/zookeeper/bin/zkServer.sh start /usr/local/zookeeper/conf/
zoo.cfg

JMX enabled by default
Using config:
Starting zookeeper ... STARTED
$
```

   You can check that ZooKeeper has successfully started up with the following command:

```
$ ps -ef | grep zoo | grep -v grep
```

4. Initialize the ZooKeeper state on both of the NameNodes:

```
$ hdfs zkfc -formatZK
```

5. Start the ZKFC service on both NameNode hosts:

```
$ /usr/lib/ahdoop/sbin/hadoop-daemon.sh start zkfc
```

   You must start the ZKFC service on both NameNode servers. The server where you start the ZFKC service first will be the active NameNode.

6. Test that automatic failover works by killing the active NameNode's PID at the OS level. You should see the Standby NameNode transition to the active state shortly.

```
$ hdfs haadmin -getServiceState nn1
active
$ ps -ef | grep namenode | grep -v grep
$ kill -9 $PID_of_Active_Namenode
$ hdfs haadmin -getServiceState nn2
active
$ $HADOOP_PREFIX/sbin/hadoop-daemon.sh start namenode
```

   The previous command starts the nn1 namenode service that I killed earlier.

7. Get the state of nn1:

```
$ hdfs haadmin -getServiceState nn1
standby
```

The haadmin -getServiceState command verifies that that the NameNodes failed over successfully.

High Availability and Manual Failover Commands

Once you configure NameNode HA, you have access to a set of HA-related haadmin commands, which are summarized as follows.

- haadmin -failover: Use this command to initiate a failover between the two HA NameNodes. If nn1 is in standby state, the command will transition nn2 to the active state. If nn1 is in the active state, the command will attempt to transition `nn1` gracefully to the standby state. If the attempt fails, Hadoop will try one of the fencing methods you configured with the `dfs.ha.fencing.methods` parameter in order, until one of them succeeds. The NameNode `nn2` will *not* be transitioned to the active state if no fencing method succeeds.

- `haadmin -checkHealth`: Lets you check the health of a NameNode and returns 0 if that NameNode is healthy. Note that currently this command will always return success, unless the NameNode is completely down.
- `haadmin -transitionToActive`: Transitions the Standby NameNode to the active status.
- `haadmin -transitionToStandby`: Set monospace Transitions the active NameNode to the standby status.
- `haadmin -getServiceState`: Shows the current status of either of the two NameNodes. Often some jobs need to verify whether they're connected to the current active or standby NameNode. This command is very useful for confirming that you are connected to an active NameNode.

HA NameNode architecture doesn't help you scale—it provides you high availability of the NameNode. For scalability, you can set up a federated NameNode, to which we turn next.

HDFS Federation

The NameNode stores a reference to all files and data blocks in its memory. If you have a large number of HDFS files, lack of sufficient memory could limit the size to which you can scale. Once you reach a set number of data blocks, the NameNode simply can't scale up.

Hadoop 2 lets you configure multiple NameNodes, called federated NameNodes. You can **federate** the NameNode in order to expand your Hadoop cluster to a very large size. Along with multiple NameNodes, you also will have multiple namespaces, with parts of the total HDFS storage apportioned to each nameservice.

Federation is a very simple concept—you create multiple NameNode instances running on separate nodes, with each of the NameNodes responsible for a portion of the HDFS file blocks, as part of its own namespace. For example, one of the NameNodes will manage all files under the /user namespace and the other all files under /share.

The DataNodes of course will store the data blocks from all namespaces, while each NameNode maintains its own namespace and its own image and edits files.

In order to access a federated HDFS, clients make use of client-side mount tables to map file paths to the different NameNodes. You can configure this using the ViewFileSystem and the `viewfs:// URIs`.

In a very large cluster, the namespace may be so large that it becomes difficult for a single NameNode to efficiently manage it. As a result, large Hadoop clusters won't easily scale beyond three to four thousand nodes.

In an HDFS federation (also called NameNode federation) setup, the multiple NameNodes work independent of each other, all of them accessing the same storage, without any communication among themselves. In this architecture, the DataNodes will send their heartbeats and block reports to all NameNodes that are part of the federated NameNode architecture.

Federated namespaces provide scalability, isolation and performance benefits. A federated NameNode service is ideal for large clusters that need to deal with a very large number of large files. You get better throughput since multiple NameNodes can work with the DataNodes. You can also set up things such that you allocate different namespaces to different sets of applications.

Architecture of a Federated NameNode

HDFS, the storage component of Hadoop, can be best viewed as a combination of a namespace and a storage service. The storage service is called the Block Storage Service. The namespace contains information about the files, directories and data blocks that are part of your HDFS storage system.

The Block Storage Service consists of two main components—physical storage and block management. Physical storage is simply how the DataNodes store the HDFS blocks on the underlying Linux (or other OS) file system. Block management refers to block-related operations such as the creation, deletion and modification of data blocks and the replication and the placement of the replicas among the cluster's nodes.

In very large Hadoop environments there are thousands of DataNodes with millions of files and data blocks ranging over petabytes of storage. In such environments, while you can scale HDFS by adding new nodes, the namespace can't keep up with the increase in storage. The single namespace's throughput is designed to support only about 60,000 tasks, thus affecting performance as you scale higher.

Each namespace in a federated architecture will be assigned a block pool, which is a specific set of HDFS blocks that belong to a single namespace. A namespace (metadata) and its block pool are together referred to as a **namespace volume**.

Each namespace volume is a self-contained management unit, with each of the namespaces managing its own block pool independent of the other block pools, enabling it to generate its own block IDs for the new blocks without coordinating with the rest of the namespaces.

If one of the federated NameNodes goes down and you don't have a standby configured for it, you can't access the data blocks that belong to that NameNode's namespace. Thus, a federated architecture for your NameNode service doesn't buy you high availability; instead, it provides scaling capabilities, besides enhancing performance as well as providing isolation between different sets of users.

Summary

Here's what you learned in this chapter:

- HDFS metadata is absolutely critical to the functioning of your cluster. No metadata, no cluster! You must set up a high-availability system with the Standby NameNode taking care of the regular updating of the HDFS namespace.
- You've spent a lot of time reviewing the details of the checkpointing process, but you really can't know too much about this process, in light of how critical a process it is.
- While the federated NameNode architecture isn't really very popular in real life, it's helpful to know that it's there for you if your use case requires it.

IV

Moving Data, Allocating Resources, Scheduling Jobs and Security

12

Moving Data Into and Out of Hadoop

This chapter covers the following topics:

- Using HDFS commands to move data to and from Hadoop clusters
- Using Sqoop to move data between Hadoop and relational databases
- Ingesting external data with Apache Flume and Apache Kafka

In this chapter, I explain some of the most common ways to move data into and out of HDFS, such as using HDFS file and directory commands and the DistCp (Distributed Copy) tool, which helps you move data between Hadoop clusters. In addition, the chapter shows how to use Apache Sqoop to move data between HDFS and a relational database, and how to use Apache Flume to capture log data in near real time and store it in HDFS. I also briefly describe how to set up and use Apache Kafka, which is a popular data ingestion tool in Hadoop environments.

One of the things that'll be quickly apparent to you when working with Hadoop is that you can use a dizzying array of tools to load data into HDFS. Apache Hadoop itself contains tools like DistCp to let you transfer data between clusters. You can also use tools such as Flume for data movement. Storm and Kafka are both good tools for processing streaming data.

Introduction to Hadoop Data Transfer Tools

You often need to move large data sets into your cluster when you initially populate your cluster. Later on, there will be times when you need to move large amounts of data into and out of the cluster. There are several good tools available that make your life easier, but you need to know when and how to use each of these data migration tools. Typically, you use bulk data transfers to populate your cluster after setting it up. Later on, you'll be updating the cluster (HDFS) with periodic batch updates. You may also stream in new data in real time, as the data arrives. So, you need tools that can help with all three of the data transfer modes: bulk, batch and streaming.

Following is a summary of the various data transfer tools I discuss in this chapter:

- Hadoop's built-in tools to move data: HDFS has several built-in commands to copy and move data from the local file system to HDFS as well as between two HDFS directories, or even between two Hadoop clusters.
- Tools for bulk data loading: DistCp is a bulk data loading tool that ships with Hadoop, and it offers effective data transfer capabilities to move data between Hadoop clusters.
- Tools for moving data to and from a relational database: Apache Sqoop lets you easily import and export data from and to various popular relational databases.

> **Note**
>
> One of the concerns with DistCp is its potential to saturate your cluster's network when moving large data. Make sure you don't use too many parallel copy processes to avoid network saturation. In addition, DistCp has also been known to timeout sometimes, causing the entire job to fail. It's therefore a good idea to check out the DistCp options to increase the timeout duration as well as to turn off checksumming.

- Tools for handling streaming data: Apache Flume is a commonly employed event transport system that uses the push mode to write streaming data such as web server logs to your HDFS system. Apache Kafka is an alternative streaming data movement candidate and uses a publish-subscribe messaging mechanism. Apache Storm is another great tool for event stream processing, which involves responding to individual events within a reasonable timeframe. We discuss Apache Flume in detail in this chapter.

If your goal is to load data from flat files or semi-structured/unstructured files, you can simply use HDFS shell commands or Hadoop's DistCp utility.

Let's start our exploration of the data movement tools available to us with a quick overview of the HDFS commands you can use to move around data.

Loading Data into HDFS from the Command Line

Loading data into HDFS using HDFS commands is the easiest way to move data from the local file system into HDFS.

You'll often use HDFS file system commands to copy data into and out of HDFS. Let's review all the ways in which you can move data from the command line.

Using the `-cat` Command to Dump a File's Contents

The `-cat` command copies source paths to stdout. The command concatenates the source files and displays the contents. This command is handy when you want to view the contents of a script or an output file and works similarly to Linux's cat command. Here are a couple of examples:

```
hadoop fs -cat hdfs://nn1.example.com/file1
hadoop fs -cat file:///file1 /user/sam/file2
```

Testing HDFS Files

You can test whether a file exists in HDFS by issuing the following command:

```
$ hdfs df -test -e /user/alapati/file.txt
```

You can test whether a file is empty with the -test -z option:

```
$ hdfs dfs -test -z /user/alapati/file.txt
```

You can check whether a file is a directory by issuing the -test command with the -d option:

```
$ hdfs dfs -test -d /user/alapati/testfile
```

Issue the dfs -stat command to find various file-related statistics, such as whether it's a file or a directory:

```
$ hdfs dfs -stat /user/alapati/file.txt
```

You can create an empty file with the -touchz command:

```
$ hdfs dfs -touchz /user/alapati/file.txt
```

The -touchz command is, of course, the counterpart of Linux's familiar touch command.

Defining Files as URIs

Specifying filenames isn't the only way to refer to the target files. You can also specify the file as a URI (Uniform Resource Identifier). URIs indicate a file's source and destination in HDFS and include the server name, file path, file name and a source identifier.

You may specify the URI for both local and HDFS files. When you want to point to a file in HDFS, use hdfs: in front of the URI, and when you want to point to a file from the local file system, specify file: instead. In the following example, the server is localhost and the file I'm interested is in the HDFS directory /users/sam.

```
hdfs://<server-name>:<port-name>/<TargetDirPath>
hdfs://localhost:9000/users/sam
```

Here's an example that shows the contents of a file by specifying a URI:

```
$ hdfs dfs -cat file://localhost:9000/home/sam/scripts/test.pig
$ hdfs dfs -cat hdfs://localhost:9000/users/sam/scripts/test.output
```

The first example shows the contents of the file test.pig, which is in the local directory /home/sam/scripts. The second example does the same for a file stored in the HDFS directory /users/sam/scripts.

Copying and Moving Files from and to HDFS

Hadoop provides several built-in file system commands that make your life easy when copying and moving files between the local file system and HDFS, as well as within the HDFS file system itself.

You can use either the HDFS –put or the -copyFromLocal command to move a file or even a directory from the local file system into HDFS and vice versa. The -put command copies a single source file or even multiple files from the local file system to HDFS.

Here's the syntax of the hdfs dfs -put command:

```
Usage:
dfs fs -put <localsrc> ... <HDFS_dest_Path>
```

Since the -put command lets you also read from the standard input and write to an HDFS file, in order to test the -put command, you can do the following:

```
# echo -e "A|1|2|3\nB|4|5|6" | hadoop fs -put - /tmp/test1.txt
```

The following example shows how to copy a file from the local file system into HDFS with the –put command:

```
$ hadoop dfs -put /var/hadoop/logs /users/sam/
```

If the file you're copying already exists, you'll receive an error:

```
$ hdfs  dfs -put /tmp/test.txt /user/
put: '/user/test.txt': File exists
$
```

If the file you're copying from the local file system to HDFS exists, add the -f option to overwrite the file, as shown here:

```
$ hadoop dfs -put -f /var/hadoop/logs  /users/sam
```

You can copy multiple files with a single -put command, as shown here:

```
$ hdfs dfs -put /tmp/file1.txt /tmp/file2.txt /users/sam/
```

You can use a wildcard (*) to copy multiple files to a target directory:

```
$ hdfs dfs -put /tmp/file* /users/sam/
```

This command copies all files in the /tmp directory whose filenames start with "file" to the HDFS directory /users/sam.

You can copy an entire local directory over to HDFS with the -put command, as shown here:

```
$ hdfs dfs -put /home/data/customer /user/alapati/customer
```

The following shows the syntax for the copyFromLocal command and a simple example of the command's usage.

```
$ hdfs dfs -copyFromLocal <local_FS_filename> <target_on_HDFS>
$ hdfs dfs -copyFromLocal /var/log/test.txt
/user/sam/test.txt
```

The -copyFromLocal command works the same as the -put command, the only difference being that it's restricted to copying from a local file system to HDFS, whereas the -put command can copy files from HDFS to the local file system as well.

You can use the pipe symbol (|) with the less command to review a file, as shown here:

```
$ hdfs dfs -cat /user/sam/testfile | less
```

You can extract a zip file and load it into HDFS with the -put command in a single step, as shown in the following example:

```
$ gunzip -c testfile.gz | hdfs dfs -put - /user/sam/testfile
```

The following example shows how to load an Avro file into HDFS, to make the data available for processing by MapReduce jobs:

```
$ hdfs dfs -copyfromLocal /src/text/avro/twitter/.avro  /test/input
```

When copying files, make sure you already have the target HDFS directory in place, or create one if you don't have it, before attempting the copy of a file or directory:

```
$ hdfs dfs -mkdir /user/sam
```

If you want to move a large file into HDFS but you really don't want to consume three times the size of the file in HDFS storage (assuming you're using the default replication factor of three), you can overwrite the default replication factor when copying a file by specifying the replication factor with the -D option, as shown here.

```
$ hdfs dfs -D dfs.replication=1 -copyFromLocal bigfile.txt /user/alapati
```

The -copyToLocal command is analogous to the -copyFromLocal command. It copies a file from HDFS to the local file system. You can move data between two Hadoop clusters with the help of the -copyFromLocal and the -copyToLocal commands, as shown here:

- Use the -copyToLocal command to move data from the first cluster's HDFS to a local file system.
- Use the -copyFromLocal command to move the data from the local file system to the second cluster's HDFS.

Using the -get Command to Move Files

You can use the -get command to copy HDFS files to the local file system. Here are some examples showing how to use the -get command to download files from HDFS to a local file system.

```
$ hdfs dfs -get /user/sam/output.txt /home/
$ hdfs dfs -get  /user/alapati/.staging/job_1430256400174_0444/
job_1430256400174_0444_1.jhist
/tmp/
```

The first command will copy the HDFS file output.txt to your current local file system location, under the /home directory. If you specify a directory as the target in your `-get` command, Hadoop will put the entire directory on your local file system.

Moving Files from and to HDFS

The HDFS `-mv` command lets you move a file from one HDFS directory to another, and works similarly to the Linux `mv` command.

```
$ hdfs dfs -mv /users/sam/scripts/test1.txt /users/sam/tmp/test1.txt
```

You can use the `-getmerge` command to concatenate multiple HDFS files into a single file in the local system. The syntax for the `-getmerge` command is as follows:

```
hdfs dfs -getmerge <src> <localdst> [adnl]
```

The optional attribute `adnl` lets you add a new line at the end of each file you are concatenating. The following example shows how to merge files from the HDFS directory /user/hadoop/dir1 into the local directory named samplefile2.txt.

```
$ hdfs dfs -getmerge /user/hadoop/dir1/  ./Samplefile2.txt
```

Hadoop's DistCp command is a much faster way to move large amounts of data within a cluster or between two clusters. I will discuss DistCp later in this chapter.

Using the `-tail` and head Commands

You can use the `-tail` command to view a (HDFS) file's last portion, as shown here:

```
$ hdfs dfs -tail /users/sam/text1.txt
```

If you'd like to watch the contents of a file as data is being added to it, specify the `-f` option as shown here:

```
$ $ hdfs dfs -tail -f /users/sam/output.txt
```

Although there's an HDFS `-tail` command that works similarly to the Linux `tail` command, there's no equivalent to the Linux `head` command in HDFS. You can view the topmost portion of an HDFS file by piping the contents of the file and then using the Linux `head` command to view the file's contents, as shown here.

```
$ hdfs dfs -cat /users/sam/text1.txt | head
```

You can also use Linux's pipe mechanism to pipe a command's output into an HDFS file, as shown here:

```
$ hdfs dfs -cat /local/text1.txt | hadfs dfs -put - /user/sam/myfile.txt
```

This command will output the contents of the local file test1.txt into the HDFS file channel named myfile.txt.

Copying HDFS Data between Clusters with DistCp

Hadoop offers a great tool called DistCp to help you move data between two Hadoop clusters or from one location in HDFS to another location within the same Hadoop cluster. Most commonly, you use DistCp for moving data between two different clusters. DistCp is quite powerful because it uses MapReduce underneath to perform parallel loading of data.

DistCp works great for moving large amounts of data in both bulk and batch modes. Bulk mode is when you want to load a cluster with a lot of initial data from a source, and batch mode is when you want to perform regular exports and imports of data to and from HDFS.

How to Use the DistCp Command to Move Data

DistCp will turn out to be your best friend when it comes to moving data, especially between different Hadoop clusters. Let's learn the most common DistCp commands you'll be using often in your cluster to move data.

The syntax for the DistCp command is simple:

```
$ distcp srcdir destdir
```

In the syntax

- `srcdir` is a fully qualified path to the source directory. When moving data between clusters, the path will include the NameNode host and port information for the source cluster.
- `destdir` is a fully qualified path to the destination directory. When moving data between clusters, the path will include the NameNode host and port information for the destination cluster.

Note that you can also specify an Amazon S3 path such as `s3://bucket-name/key`. Here's an example that shows how to use DistCp to copy data:

```
$ hadoop distcp hdfs://nn1:8020/source hdfs://nn2:8020/destination
```

The following example shows how to use DistCp to move data from one cluster to another.

```
hadoop distcp hdfs://nn1:8020/user/hadoop/dir1/\
dfs://nn2:8020/user/hadoop/dir2/
```

Note that you must specify absolute paths to the HDFS data. In the syntax for the command, here's how you specify the source and destination:

```
hdfs://nn1:8020/source /* this is the data source
hdfs://nn2:8020/destination /* this is the destination
```

In the command, `nn1` and `nn2` refer to the NameNodes from two different Hadoop clusters.

Note

It's important to understand that DistCp uses MapReduce underneath to move the data between the two HDFS file systems, one on the source cluster and the other in the destination cluster. When you issue the command, DistCp will make the namespace under the source directory (/source) into a temporary file and partition the file's contents among a set of map processes. The mappers will then copy chunks of data from the source to the target.

You can specify multiple source directories, as shown here:

```
hadoop distcp hdfs://nn1:8020/source/a hdfs://nn1:8020/source/b hdfs://
 nn2:8020/destination
```

You can alternatively specify multiple source directories within a text file, and pass the file name as a parameter to the DistCp command, as shown here:

```
hadoop distcp -f hdfs://nn1:8020/srclist hdfs://nn2:8020/destination
```

Here, I specify a file named `srclist` with the `-f` option. The `srclist` file will contain the source directory information as follows:

```
hdfs://nn1:8020/source/a
hdfs://nn2:8020/source/b
```

If you're using DistCp to move data between two clusters enabled with NameNode high availability, one way to specify the NameNode correctly is to first verify which of the two NameNodes is currently active Namenode, and specify the host for that NameNode in your DistCp command. The other way is to use the nameservice instead of the hostname in the DistCp command. Recall that you can specify the logical name for the nameservice with the `dfs.nameservices` property (in the hdfs-site.xml file).

A DistCp Example

DistCp is typically used to move data between two clusters, as shown in the following example. Here, I'm using DistCp to "refresh" a Hive table partition in my test cluster with data from the production cluster.

```
$ hadoop distcp -overwrite
hdfs://hadoop01.localhost:8020/user/hive/warehouse/custrecord/year=2015/month=
05/day=08*
hdfs://hadoop01.localhost:8020/user/hive/warehouse/custrecord_prod/year=2015/m
onth=05/day=08

15/05/18 15:06:35 INFO tools.DistCp: Input Options:
DistCpOptions{atomicCommit=false, syncFolder=false, deleteMissing=false,
 ignoreFailures=false, maxMaps=20, sslConfigurationFile='null',
copyStrategy='uniformsize', sourceFileListing=null, sourcePaths=[hdfs://ahdoop01
.localhost:8020/user/hive/warehouse/custrecord/yea
year=2015/month=05/day=08*], targetPath=hdfs://hadoop01.localhost:8020/user/hive/
warehouse/custrecord_prod/
year=2015/month=05/day=08, targetPathExists=false,

...

BYTESCOPIED=1095967454036
```

```
BYTESEXPECTED=1095967454036

COPY=2530

$
```

How to Use DistCp to Move Data within a Cluster

Here's an example that shows how you can use DistCp to perform a data move within the same Hadoop cluster. Let's say that you want to increase the block size of your input datasets to 256MB from 128MB to reduce the number of mapper tasks. When you change the block size, it affects only new data you load into HDFS. Current data will continue to use the smaller block size. You can use DistCp to change the block size of the old files in HDFS. Here's the command for doing this:

```
$ hdfs distcp -D dfs.block.size=$[128*1024*1024] /pth/to/source_data
/path/to/data-with-larger-block-size
```

Once DistCp finishes running, you can verify that you've copied all the files you need and remove the original data that was stored with the smaller block size. This example, although not very common, is provided to illustrate the potential uses to which you can put DistCp in your cluster.

> **Note**
>
> DistCp uses Mapreduce for its work. Therefore, you may need to increase the memory allocation for mappers when copying very large files.

DistCp Options

When you move data with the help of the DistCp utility, you can customize the data transfers with the help of several DistCp command options. Following is a list of the most useful of these options.

- `-p`: Modification times are preserved when you specify this option.
- `-i`: This option tells DistCp to ignore any failures. It also saves the logs from a failed copy.
- `-log`: This option lets you specify a directory for a log file.
- `-m`: This option specifies the maximum number of mappers for a copy.
- `-overwrite`: This option overwrites the destination.
- `-update`: This option overwrites the destination if the source file size is different from the target file size.
- `-f <urilist uri>`: This option lets you specify a fully qualified URI to list all the source files instead of specifying them on the command line.
- `-delete`: This option deletes files from the destination (but not from the source). Trash will be used if you've enabled it.
- `-sizelimit <n>`: This option specifies the maximum size of the copy in bytes.
- `-filelimit`: This option lets you limit the total number of files.

Of these options I've listed here, the –update and the -overwrite options require some elaboration, as explained in the following sections.

Default Behavior of DistCp When Copying Files and Directories

If you specify neither the -overwrite nor the -update options in the following example, by default DistCp will create the directories first and second on the target cluster, under the directory named /target. So, if you issue the following DistCp command, you'll see the ensuing list of contents under the /target directory on the target cluster.

```
$ hadoop distcp hdfs://nn1:8020/source/first  hdfs://nn1:8020/source/second  \
hdfs://nn2:8020/target

hdfs://nn2:8020/target/first/1
hdfs://nn2:8020/target/first/2
hdfs://nn2:8020/target/second/10
hdfs://nn2:8020/target/second/20
```

The Update and Overwrite Options

You must specify the -update option in the following cases:

- When you're copying files that don't already exist on the target cluster
- When the files exist but the file contents are different

The -overwrite option will overwrite target files if they exist.

Since the -update and -overwrite options tend to be quite tricky in practice, let's use some examples to understand these two options further.

Let's say you're copying files from two directories named /source/first and /source/second on the source cluster, to a directory named /target on the target cluster. The source directory paths are as follows:

```
hdfs://nn1:8020/source/first/1
hdfs://nn1:8020/source/first/2
hdfs://nn1:8020/source/second/10
hdfs://nn1:8020/source/second/20
```

If you add either -update or -overwrite, only the contents of the source directories are copied over. The source directories themselves aren't copied to the target cluster. So, if you issue the following DistCp command, you'll see the ensuing contents under the /target directory.

```
$ hadoop distcp -update hdfs://nn1:8020/source/first  hdfs://nn1:8020/source/
second  hdfs://nn2:8020/target
hdfs://nn2:8020/target/1
hdfs://nn2:8020/target/2
hdfs://nn2:8020/target/10
hdfs://nn2:8020/target/20
```

Because of the way the –update command works, if there's a file with the same name under the /first and the /second directories on the source cluster, DistCp will abort the copy process.

Let's use another example to understand how DistCp decides whether it should skip a file copy or not, and whether it should overwrite a file. In this example, I issue the DistCp command without the -update or -overwrite option:

```
$ hadoop distcp hdfs://nn1:8020/source/first  hdfs://nn1:8020/source/second
\
hdfs://nn2:8020/target
```

Here are the files and their sizes in the two directories on the source cluster:

```
hdfs://nn1:8020/source/first/1   32
hdfs://nn1:8020/source/first/2   32
hdfs://nn1:8020/source/second/10 64
hdfs://nn1:8020/source/second/20 32
```

And here's the same information under the /target directory in the target cluster:

```
hdfs://nn2:8020/target/1    32
hdfs://nn2:8020/target/10   32
hdfs://nn2:8020/target/20   64
```

The target cluster will end up with the following set of files after DistCp finishes the copy:

```
hdfs://nn2:8020/target/1    32
hdfs://nn2:8020/target/2    32
hdfs://nn2:8020/target\10   64
hdfs://nn2:8020/target/20   32
```

DistCp does the following in this situation:

- It copies the file to /target/2 because it didn't exist prior to the copy.
- It overwrites the files /target/10 and /target/20 since their contents are different.
- It skips the file /target/1 because its file length and contents are identical to the source file.

Ingesting Data from Relational Databases with Sqoop

Sqoop, short for "SQL to Hadoop," is a commonly used and powerful tool for moving bulk data to and from relational databases. Often you'll find that the value of big data is significantly enhanced when it's combined with enterprise analytical databases and warehouses. Sqoop is an important ally in combining big data with traditional enterprise data stores.

There are many cases where you'd like to import data directly into HDFS from a relational database management system (RDBMS)or to send the output of your Hadoop processing directly to an external database or data warehouse. Sqoop takes care of the headaches involved in moving data between Hadoop and the databases.

Sqoop provides an easy way to import the external data residing in databases over to HDFS, where you can process it with Pig (a high-level data pipeline system used to query and manipulate data) and Hive (which helps you write SQL-like queries that are converted into MapReduce) jobs, and then export the output of these jobs to the same or a different database.

Sqoop can import and export data from relational databases, data warehouses and NoSQL systems. Sqoop offers two-way replication of data and incremental updates. Sqoop supports multiple, commonly used data formats such as Avro and SequenceFiles and is well integrated with tools such as Hive and Oozie, Hadoop's popular job scheduler.

In the following sections, I discuss:

- Sqoop's architecture
- Deploying Sqoop
- Using Sqoop to move data
- Importing data with Sqoop
- Importing Data into Hive
- Exporting Data with Sqoop

Sqoop Architecture

Sqoop takes advantage of Hadoop's MapReduce framework for all its heavy lifting. This means that you reap all the benefits of the MapReduce framework—such as MapReduce's parallel processing capabilities, as well as its excellent fault tolerance capabilities—when you employ Sqoop to move data around.

Figure 12.1 shows the basic architecture of Sqoop. Sqoop clients perform all exports and imports of data through Hadoop map tasks.

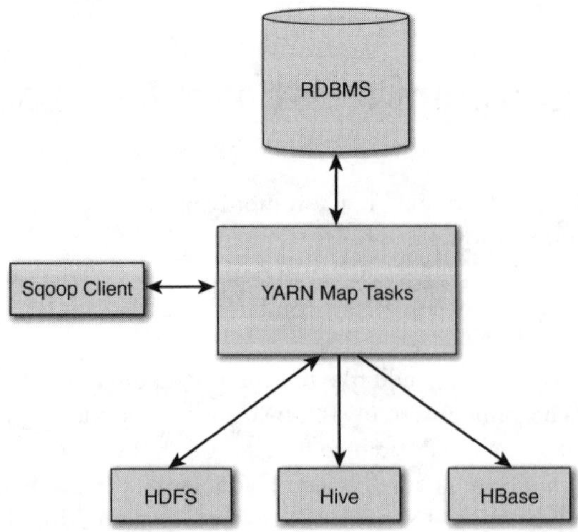

Figure 12.1 The basic architecture of Sqoop and how it works with an RDBMS to move data

It's important to remember that while Sqoop can directly import data from an RDBMS into HDFS, Hive and HBase, you can't export data from Hive and HBase directly to an RDBMS. (That's why the arrows to Hive and HBase in Figure 12.1 aren't bidirectional, as is the arrow to HDFS.) Instead, you perform all exports from HDFS. When you export Hive tables from your Hadoop cluster to an RDBMS, you do so by pointing to the HDFS directories that store the Hive tables (by default: /user/hive/warehouse).

Deploying Sqoop

As Sqoop is not a cluster service, you need to install it on just one node within your cluster. Sqoop just needs the Hadoop binaries and configuration files on the server where you install it. To work with Sqoop, you must first download and install the Sqoop binaries and also the Java Database Connectivity (JDBC) drivers for the specific RDBMS you're going to use, since Sqoop doesn't come with the JDBC drivers.

Sqoop Connectors and Drivers

You can use any RDBMS that supports JDBC to import and export data with Sqoop. JDBC lets applications access and inspect data stored in a relational database. Sqoop also comes bundled with special connectors for Oracle, Microsoft SQL Server, MySQL, PostgreSQL and Netezza. The special connectors are used to provide additional functionality beyond that provided by the standard JDBC standard drivers and help improve the performance of Sqoop's imports and exports.

It's a bit tricky to figure out which connectors and drivers you need for Sqoop to work with a specific database or warehouse product (such as Teradata), due to the various options and choices. It's good to remember that although Sqoop is bundled with special connectors for many databases, it doesn't come with the JDBC drivers that are required for the Sqoop connectors to function. This is so because the JDBC drivers are subject to licensing requirements by the RDBMS vendors.

Following are your three options, then, regarding the Sqoop connectors and JDBC drivers:

- If Sqoop is bundled with a special connector that works with your database, you need to get the JDBC driver from your database provider. You must get the JAR file for the driver and install it in the $SQOOP_HOME/lib directory. `SQOOP_HOME` is the directory where you installed Sqoop. This is the approach I use in the following section to install the JDBC driver for the MySQL database.
- For databases such as Couchbase and Teradata, which don't have a bundled Sqoop special connector, you need to get both the JDBC driver and the special connector for Sqoop from the vendor.
- If a database has no special Sqoop connector, whether bundled with Sqoop or not, do both of the following:
    - Download and install the vendor's JDBC driver.
    - Use Sqoop's generic JDBC connector.

Using Sqoop to Move Data

Sqoop is really a collection of tools such as import and export, and therefore, you can alias scripts using the `sqoop-(toolname)` syntax, as in `sqoop-import` and `sqoop-export`, for example. The command line program for invoking Sqoop is named `sqoop`. This is a wrapper that runs the bin/hadoop script that comes with Hadoop.

> **Note**
>
> Two simple commands go a long way when working with Sqoop. You can issue the command `sqoop help` to see all the Sqoop options. In order to view the specific options for just the import or export capability, type `sqoop help import` or `sqoop help export`. Use the `sqoop version` command to check the Sqoop version.

By default, Sqoop will use the value you set for the `$HADOOP_HOME` environment variable. If you want to point to an alternative Hadoop installation, you must configure the `HADOOP_COMMON_HOME` and the `HADOOP_MAPRED_HOME` environment variables, as shown here:

```
$ export HADOOP_COMMON_HOME=/path/to/different/hadoop
$ export HADOOP_MAPRED_HOME=/path/to/different/hadoop-mapreduce
```

Let's start with a simple command that shows all databases in an RDBMS, which is MySQL in our case. You use the `list-databases` command for this, as shown here:

```
sqoop  list-databases /
    --connect jdbc.mysql://hadoop01   /
    --username root /
    --password password
```

This command gets you a list of all databases on the host you specify.

You can list all the tables in a database by issuing the `list-tables` command:

```
sqoop  list-tables /
    --connect jdbc.mysql://hadoop01/db1
    --username root /
    --password password
```

This command shows all tables in the database named db1.

Now that you've learned how the sqoop command works, let's see how you can use it perform the two most important things Sqoop can do for you—import and export data.

Importing Data with Sqoop

As mentioned earlier, Sqoop leverages Hadoop MapReduce (actually just the map part of the framework) to perform its data imports (as well as exports). Figure 12.2 shows how Sqoop uses Hadoop map tasks to import data into HDFS and Hive tables. Here's the high-level sequence of steps in a Sqoop import operation:

1. Sqoop uses the special connector for the RDBMS to get the table metadata for the tables involved in the import. In this example, it's the metadata for a single table named `CUSTOMERS`. This metadata helps map the data types from the RDBMS table (`CUSTOMERS`) to Java data types.

2. Using the metadata it retrieved in step 1, Sqoop generates and compiles the Java class that it will use in the MapReduce job that is submitted to import the data.
3. Hadoop map tasks use the Sqoop-generated Java class to import data from the `CUSTOMERS` table.
4. Sqoop uses multiple map tasks to import the data from the `CUSTOMERS` table in the MySQL database (or another RDBMS) to HDFS (or Hive or HBase).

Let's learn how Sqoop imports data with a simple example that shows how to import data from a MySQL database into HDFS. You use Sqoop's `import` command to perform the data import from a MySQL database. The import example is shown right after Figure 12.2.

> **Note**
>
> You can get the entire list of Sqoop import and export parameters by typing `sqoop help import` or `sqoop help export`.

Every Sqoop `import` command has two basic parts: a set of generic arguments and a set of arguments pertaining to the import. Here's the general syntax of the `import` command:

```
sqoop import  {generic arguments}    {import arguments}
```

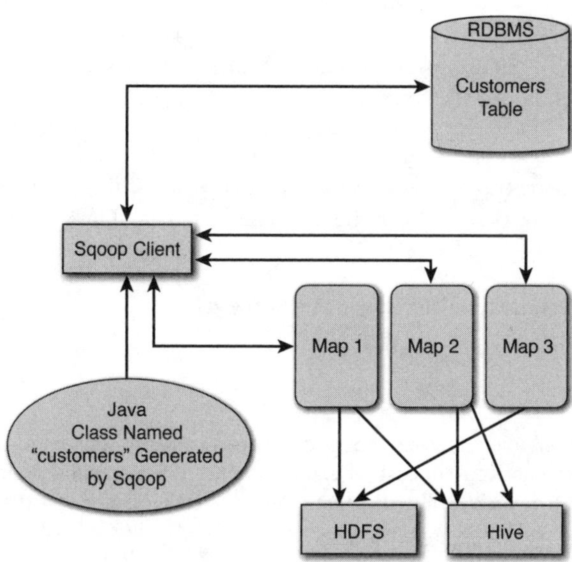

Figure 12.2 How Sqoop uses Hadoop map tasks to import data from an RDBMS into HDFS

Here's the Sqoop import command in action.

```
sqoop import \
   --connect jdbc:mysql://mysql.example.com/sqoop \
   --username sqoop \
   --password sqoop \
   --table tableName \
   --target-dir  /user/data/test
```

In this example, I chose not to specify either a class name or a location for the Java code that Sqoop will generate and for importing data through Hadoop Map tasks.

You can specify the name of a custom class by adding the –`class-name` command line argument. By default Sqoop places the generated Java code in the current working directory. You can specify a different location by adding the –`bindir` argument to the import command. When I add these two parameters to our previous import example, this is what the `import` command will look like:

```
sqoop import \
   --connect jdbc:mysql://mysql.example.com/sqoop \
   --username sqoop \
   --password sqoop \
   --table tableName
   --target-dir  /user/data/test
   --class-name  myClassName
   --bindir .
```

- The `-class-name` attribute points to the name of the Java class that Sqoop generates as part of this import.
- The `-bindir` attribute specifies the location for the class and JAR files pertaining to the Java code.

When you issue a Sqoop `import` command, Sqoop chops up the dataset into multiple partitions and launches map-only jobs to transfer the data chunks into HDFS, with Sqoop inferring the data types from the database metadata. Thus, a Sqoop import is a two-step process:

1. Sqoop gathers the required metadata for the data it's importing.
2. Sqoop submits the mapper jobs to the Hadoop cluster.

> **Note**
>
> It's important to understand that Sqoop doesn't directly connect to the relational database or warehouse to import (or export) the data. Sqoop simply runs a MapReduce job that will connect to the database, read the table and import the data into HDFS.

You can check your HDFS home directory after the import completes to make sure that you can see the `SUCCESS` and the `part*` files.

The `success` and `part*` files are similar to those that you received following the WordCount example in Chapter 5. This is no surprise, as Sqoop uses MapReduce to perform the actual imports.

Using an Options File

Instead of specifying all the import connection options each time you run an import job, you can simplify things by using an **options file**, inside which you place the connection-related parameters. Here's how to specify an options file.

```
$ bin/sqoop import
     --options-file /opt/option-file.txt
     --table testTable
     --target-dir   /user/sam/testTable
```

This is much simpler than the previous import example, since the options file (in this example named option-file.txt) contains the following connection information:

```
connect jdbc:mysql://localhost/db1
   username root
   password password
```

Note that the imported data is loaded into the HDFS directory specified by the `-target-dir` parameter, which in our case points to the `/user/sam/testTable` directory. As your import job starts importing data into this directory, other clients will be able to see the blocks in that file and may begin to process it before the import has completed.

In order to avoid complications, import data into a temporary directory. Once the import completes, you can simply move data from the temporary directory to where you really want it to end up. This move is very quick (it requires only file metadata updates and no data moves). You can include the HDFS data move operation at the very end of the job that sets off the import.

How Sqoop Imports Data

When you issue an `import` command, this is how the data import process proceeds:

1. Sqoop connects to the relational database (such as MySQL or Oracle).
2. Sqoop fetches the table's metadata, such as the columns and their data types.
3. Sqoop generates a Java class and compiles it.
4. Sqoop connects to the Hadoop cluster.
5. Sqoop generates a MapReduce job.
6. Sqoop executes a MapReduce job in the Hadoop cluster.
7. MapReduce performs the import process with the help of map processes (no reducers) using the metadata generated in step 1.
8. MapReduce generates the output as a set of files in HDFS.

Sqoop leaves the actual transferring of the data to the Hadoop mappers and merely oversees the entire process. By default, an import will get all of a table's records, but you can limit the data, as explained later. The output file will have the records in the original order of the columns in the database. Because Sqoop imports data in a parallel fashion, the HDFS output is also in multiple files, such as delimited text files, binary Avro files and SequenceFiles.

Specifying the Password

In our example, I specified the password at the command line itself, but you have other options. You can specify --P instead of --password, so Sqoop can prompt you for the password. Alternatively, you can store the password in a file somewhere in HDFS and specify the --password-file option so Sqoop can read the password from there.

You can also store the password in the Sqoop metastore, although it is less secure. You do this by setting the sqoop.metastore.client.record.password property in the sqoop-site.xml file.

The password stored in the metastore isn't encrypted. Therefore, use this method only if you can restrict access to the metastore server.

How to Share the Sqoop Metastore between Clients

As explained in the previous section, you can store passwords in the Sqoop metastore without having to provide them each time you run a Sqoop import or export job. You can share the Sqoop metastore among clients. In order to do this, you must know how to start the Sqoop metastore. You can start the Sqoop metastore with the following command:

```
$ sqoop metastore
```

Once you start the Sqoop metastore service, the embedded HSQLDB becomes accessible to users. The default port for the metastore is 16000. You can modify it with the sqoop.metastore.server.port property in the sqoop-site.xml file. Users can connect to the metastore by specifying the -meta-connect parameter as shown here:

```
meta-connect jdfs.hsqldb:hsql://metastore.exmple.com:16000/sqoop
```

You don't need to specify the --meta-connect parameter if you store the value in the sqoop-site.xml file, as shown here:

```
<property>
<name>sqoop.metastore.client.autoconnect.url</name>
<value>jdbc:hsqldb:hsql://your-metastore:16000/sqoop</value>
</property>
```

Setting Delimiters for Output and Input

By default, the output files generated by MapReduce (these files contain the imported data) use comma-separated (,) fields separating the records with new lines (\n). You can explicitly specify delimiters, as well as field-enclosing characters and escape characters, to handle delimiters (such as commas) in the fields. You can change the default file and line delimiters by setting any of the following formatting options at the command line:

- --fields-terminated-by <char>: Custom field delimiting character, such as a comma.
- --lines-terminated-by <char>: Custom line or record terminator character, such as the new-line character.

- `--enclosed-by <char>`: Custom field-enclosing character, such as double quotes.
- `--optionally-enclosed-by <char>`: If the data includes the enclosed-by `<char>` such as double qutoes, for example, then write the characters. Otherwise, ignore the characters.
- `--escaped-by <char>`: Custom escaped character (\:), used to avoid ambiguity when parsing or writing data to HDFS. For example, you can specify this option when importing a string with double quotes inside it, and Sqoop will write the field to HDFS by adding a backslash before the double quotes in the string.

You can specify `fields-terminated-by '\t'`, for example, when working with Hive and Pig, to separate the HDFS file's fields with the tab character. The list of formatting options I showed here is for formatting Sqoop output. There are also similar **input parsing** options, which are counterparts to the output formatting options, and work in the same fashion. Here's the list of input parsing options you can specify:

- `--input-fields-terminated-by <char>`
- `--input-lines-terminated-by <char>`
- `--input-enclosed-by <char>`
- `--input-optionally-enclosed-by <char>`
- `--input-escaped-by <char>`

By default, an output file is in the delimited text format, but you can import data into a binary format such as a SequenceFile or an Avro binary format, as shown here.

- `as-avrodatafile`: Stores output file in an Avro file format
- `as-sequencefile`: Stores output in a SequenceFile format
- `as-textfile`: Stores output in a delimited text format

The Avro file format uses a schema to describe the data structures in an Avro file and encodes it in a JSON string. Sqoop automatically generates the Avro schema from the metadata it retrieves from the relational database server.

Compressing the Table Data

Sqoop takes advantage of the built-in support MapReduce has for compression and provides various options to compress the data it imports from a database. If you specify just `-compress` while importing data, Sqoop compresses the output files with the gzip code, resulting in HDFS output files with a gz extension. You can specify an alternative compression codec such as bzip2 instead, as shown here.

```
sqoop import ...
compress -compression-codec org.apache.hadoop.io.compress.Bzip2Codec
```

> **Tip**
>
> Regardless of which file format you use, such as Avro, SequenceFile or text file, you can specify the --`compress` command line argument to compress the data you import from a database. By default, the compression will use the gzip format. You can specify an alternative format by adding the `-compression-codec` argument at the command line when performing the Sqoop import.

Make sure that the parameter `mapred.output.compress` is set to `true` (default value) in the mapred-site.xml file.

Selecting the Target Directory in Which to Store the Imported Data

In our simple import example, I didn't specify a target directory where Sqoop should store the imported data. So, where does Sqoop place the imported data? By default, it stores the data in the user's home directory with the same name as the imported table. So, if user `sam` is the one performing the Sqoop import, the table data will be placed in the HDFS directory /user/sam/TableName. You can specify an alternative directory with the `--target-dir` parameter.

> **Tip**
>
> Make sure the directory you specify with the `-target-dir` parameter doesn't already exist in HDFS. Otherwise Sqoop will throw an error, just as Hadoop does when a MapReduce output directory is already present!

If you don't want to use your HDFS home directory, you can specify that all Sqoop imports go into a special directory with the parameter `--warehouse-dir`. Sqoop will then load the imported data under the directory you specify for the `--warehouse-dir` parameter, in a subdirectory named the same as the imported table. Make sure you don't use the Hive warehouse directory, which is /user/hive/warehouse by default, for your temporary location.

Specifying the Access Mode

Sqoop uses the JDBC access mechanism by default, but for those databases such as MySQL that permit a non-JDBC access, you can specify the parameter `direct` to select the non-JDBC access mechanism.

You can use the high-performance capabilities of a database such as MySQL by specifying the `direct` parameter during an import. Note that the `direct` option is meant to be used along with the `direct-split-size` command line argument (`--direct-split-size <n>`).

Selective Imports of a Table's Data

The first Sqoop import example you saw earlier in this chapter will import all of the target table's rows. You can import only some of the rows of a table by specifying a `WHERE` clause. Simply add a `WHERE` clause such as the following to the `import` command, to selectively import the table's rows:

```
sqoop import \
  --connect jdbc:mysql://mysql.example.com/sqoop \
  --username sqoop \
  --password sqoop \
  --table customers \
  --where "state = 'Texas'"
```

You can alternatively import only selected *columns* of a table, by specifying the `-columns` attribute as shown here:

```
sqoop import \
  --connect jdbc:mysql://mysql.example.com/sqoop \
  --username sqoop \
  --password sqoop \
  --table customers \
  --columns customer_id, address, state
```

Sqoop assumes that the HDFS data that you're importing and the target table to which you're exporting that data have an identical number of columns in the table, and that they're ordered the same way as well. Your target database must allow the inserting of rows with specific columns. It must also allow a NULL value for the columns you aren't exporting or define a default value for those columns.

Sqoop lets you express any condition in the `WHERE` clause that the source relational database supports, in addition to special functions and user-defined functions. Due to the nature of Sqoop's parallel data transferring mechanism, ideally you should filter the data on the source table first and save the data in a temporary table before importing it.

Sqoop allows you to specify the `query` parameter with the `import` command, which lets you import the data that results from executing the SQL query that you specify. Here's an example:

```
sqoop import
--connect jdbc:mysql://mysql.example.com/sqoop \
--username sqoop \
--password sqoop \
--query 'select students.student_id, \
         counties.county, \
         students.city \
         FROM students \
JOIN counties USING(county_id) \
         WHERE $CONDITIONS' \
--split-by-id \
--target-dir cities
```

Specifying the `query` argument is also called a **free form import** and is one of Sqoop's most powerful features. Free form import lets you specify an arbitrary query for importing data instead of using a regular table import. It replaces the arguments such as `table`, `columns` and `where`, which are the parameters that you need to specify when restricting the data you're importing. Often, a free form import is slower than an alternative table import that imports the same data.

When you perform a free form import, you are required to specify two parameters, and optionally, a third parameter (in addition to the query parameter, of course), as shown in our example:

- --split-by-id: Use this parameter to specify the column that Sqoop will use to split the data into several parallel tasks. Note that we specified the parameter but didn't specify any column. In this case, the parameter will default to the primary key of the main table in the join.
- --target-dir: This parameter specifies the HDFS directory where the imported data is stored. You can't use the parameter -warehouse-dir to store the data with a free-form import.
- $CONDITIONS (optional parameter): You can make Sqoop split the query into several chunks, each of which can be imported in parallel, by specifying this parameter. The $CONDITIONS parameter acts as a placeholder in the WHERE clause that you specify, and Sqoop generates conditions to substitute for the placeholder, with each condition specifying the data chunk to be moved by an import task. If you omit the $CONDITIONS parameter, Sqoop will not parallelize the import job and will simply use a single mapper to perform the import. If your join is fairly complex, you ought to parallelize it.

Getting Data from All the Tables

You can use Sqoop to import all tables from the target database into HDFS with the import-all-tables command:

```
sqoop import-all-tables \
--connect jdbc:mysql://mysql.example.com/sqoop \
--username sqoop \
--password sqoop
```

This example shows how to import all tables from a database into HDFS. Sqoop stores data for each table in a separate HDFS directory.

In essence this command will sequentially import an entire database in one fell swoop.

If you want to import most, but not all the tables from a database, add the --exclude-tables option to the previous import command, as shown here:

```
sqoop import-all-tables \
   --connect jdbc:mysql://mysql.example.com/sqoop \
   --username sqoop \
   --password sqoop \
   --exclude-tables customers,sales
```

This command will get you the data from all tables from the database, with the exception of the customers and sales tables.

Creating Sqoop Jobs

For one-off imports, you can simply run a Sqoop `import` (or `export`) command from the command line. However, if you need to run the same Sqoop job frequently, it's a good idea to create a Sqoop **job**, by storing the `import` (or `export`) command in the built-in Sqoop metastore. All you need to do to create a Sqoop job is specify the attributes `job` and `-create <jobname>` when running a Sqoop command, in this case a Sqoop `import`. In the following example, I named the Sqoop job `testjob`.

```
sqoop job  \
--create testjob \
--username sqoop \
--password sqoop
--import  \
--table testTable
```

You can view the stored Sqoop jobs by issuing the following command:

```
$ bin/sqoop job -list
```

You can view the parameters of a job you saved by specifying the `-show` attribute:

```
$ bin/sqoop job -show testjob
```

Finally, you can execute a saved job by specifying the `-exec` attribute:

```
$ bin/sqoop job -exec testjob
```

You can delete a Sqoop job by specifying the `-delete` option at the command line. Saving jobs to the metastore is especially useful when performing incremental imports and exports, which I explain in the following sections. This is due to the fact that a saved Sqoop import job will store not only the commands to rerun the import job but also the last value of the column that you want to incrementally import.

Controlling Job Parallelism

Sqoop uses MapReduce processes to perform its imports, and by default, for each import (and export), it runs four map tasks, with each of the four tasks importing roughly a quarter of the data.

You can tell Sqoop to utilize more mappers by specifying the `-num-mappers` attribute. Sqoop uses the primary key column of the source table by default, to consider how to split work among the mappers. If the source table doesn't have a primary key column, you can specify the parameter `--split-by <column-name>` to specify the column on which to split the work among the mappers.

In the following example, I specify 12 as the value for the `-num-mappers` parameter, meaning I want Sqoop to use 12 parallel map tasks.

```
sqoop import \
--connect jdbc:mysql://mysql.example.com/sqoop \
--username sqoop \
--password sqoop \
--table tableName \
--num-mappers 12
```

Remember that if the table is missing a primary key column and you're thinking of specifying the `--split-by` parameter, check to ensure that the column's values are somewhat equally distributed. Otherwise, you'll end up with some map tasks that take much longer to complete when compared to the rest of the mappers.

> **Tip**
>
> Remember that the parallelism option doesn't really mandate that the job use the degree of parallelism you specify—it's only a *directive* that Sqoop is at liberty to ignore by spawning fewer mappers than what you assume.

When specifying parallelism, it's a good idea to also keep in mind the potential extra load on the target database. It's a good strategy to start with a small value and move up to a larger number for the `--num-mappers` parameter.

Performing Incremental Imports

Sometimes you'd like to import just the newly added or modified rows from a table. You don't want to have to import the entire table just to capture the newly updated or added rows. Sqoop provides options to perform incremental imports, allowing you to import just the new inserts and updates into HDFS.

You make use of the following three parameters when performing incremental imports.

- `--incremental`: This parameter tells Sqoop that it should perform an incremental import. An incremental import can be performed in two different modes. You can specify append as the value for the `--incremental` parameter when Sqoop is getting all new rows and no currently existing rows are modified. Alternately, you can specify an incremental import with the `lastmodified` option, which means that Sqoop should import only those rows which were updated after the most recent import.
- `--check-column`: This column's value determines the rows Sqoop will import.
- `--last-value`: You use this parameter to let Sqoop know the value of the column (`check-column`) from the most recent import you've performed. If a record has a check column value greater than the value for the `--last-value` parameter, Sqoop will import it.

By specifying the `last-modified` attribute for the `--incremental` parameter, you can import both newly added as well as any updated records. In order for you to do this, the source table must have a timestamp column.

As in the `append incremental` mode, Sqoop prints out the value of the `--last-value` parameter at the end of an incremental import. Sqoop performs two separate MapReduce jobs here to get you the data you need. It imports the changed data first and saves it in a temporary HDFS directory. A second job will merge the old and the new data while saving only the last updated values for each row.

Let's say you run the same incremental job again or whenever the import is scheduled to run again. This will generate a new file under the HDFS directory customer, with the new customer table data. You can merge the multiple files with the help of Sqoop's merge command as explained next.

Using the Sqoop Merge Command

When you use the incremental import in the lastmodified mode, each import creates a separate file. You can use Sqoop's merge command to combine new data sets with the old data sets. The way this works is that whenever the primary keys in the two datasets match, the data from the older data set is overwritten by the data from the newer dataset. Here's an example showing how to use the merge command when using incremental imports.

```
$ sqoop merge
  --new-data /user/alapati/customer/part-m-00001
  --onto /user/alapati/part-m-00000
  --target-dir /user/alapati/customer/MERGED-CUSTOMERS
  --jar-file customer.jar
  --class-name   customer
  --merge-key customer-id
```

Note that the --merge-key attribute states that the primary key customer-id should be used to match the rows from the older dataset with those from the new dataset.

Importing Data into Hive

Sqoop can automatically create Hive tables to store the data it imports from a relational database. Before we learn how to import data into Hive tables with Sqoop, let's quickly review how to create a Hive table and how you load data from HDFS into a Hive table. Doing this will get you ready for using Sqoop to do the same.

You load data from either the local file system or from HDFS into a Hive table with Hive's load data statement, as shown here:

```
hive> load data local inpath  './examples.files.test1.txt' overwrite into table test;
hive> load data inpath '/users/sam/test1.txt overwrite into table test;
```

The first load statement loads data into the Hive table named test, from a file in the local file system. The second load statement loads the same Hive table using data from a file stored in HDFS.

Now, on to how you can do the same things with Sqoop, this time by getting data from a relational database such as MySQL. Importing data into Hive is really the same as importing data into HDFS and then manually asking Hive to create and load the Hive table (or Hive partition).

However, manual loading into Hive requires you to know the type mapping between data and the serialization format and delimiters. Sqoop takes care of all this for you when you use it to load data directly into Hive. It populates the Hive metastore with the necessary table metadata and invokes the commands to load the table. All you need to do is specify the hive-import option when running a Sqoop import.

Sqoop first imports the data to a temporary location in HDFS. It then generates a query for creating a table and also another query for loading the data from the temporary HDFS location, using the Hive load data inpath statement to move the data into the Hive warehouse directory in HDFS. You can specify the temporary location with either the --target-dir parameter or the --warehouse-dir parameter. I explained both of these Sqoop parameters earlier in this chapter.

By default, Sqoop appends new data it imports to the existing data in the Hive table. By specifying --hive-overwrite, you can tell Sqoop to truncate the data and load it with fresh data. This essentially replaces the existing table. The --overwrite parameter is handy when you need to refresh a Hive table's data on a regular basis.

There are two different ways in which you can get data from a relational database into Hive. Both of these are quite simple and are essentially the same as importing data into HDFS, which you already know. Following is an explanation of the two methods.

The First Method

The first method is to import the MySQL (or other database) table data into a file such as /user/sam/customers. Once you import the data into HDFS, you can create an external Hive table as shown here:

```
hive> CREATE EXTERNAL TABLE student(id int, name string)
      ROW FORMAT DELIMITED FIELDS TERMINATED BY ','
      LINES TERMINATED BY '\n    STORED AS TEXTFILE
      LOCATION '/user/sam/customers';
```

The LOCATION parameter tells Hive where to look in HDFS to access the data you've imported from MySQL.

The Second Method

The alternative way to load data into Hive from an external relational database is to specify the --hive-table argument in the Sqoop import command and let Sqoop both create the table and load it from the HDFS directory into which it imports the table data from the RDBMS. In this case the HDFS data is loaded into the Hive warehouse directory. If the Hive table doesn't already exist, you can create it at the same time as you're loading data by specifying the --create-hive-table argument at the command line.

The following example shows how to create a Hive table and load data into it from a MySQL table:

```
sqoop import
  --connect jdbc:mysql://mysql.example.com/sqoop
  --username sqoop
  --password sqoop
  --table testtable
  --hive-table testTable
  --create-hive-table
  --hive-import
  --hive-home /path/to/hive_home
```

Once this import is complete, you can access the Hive table just as if you performed a direct load into a Hive table. As with a regular import into HDFS, if the target table doesn't have a primary key column, you must specify a split-by option to specify a column whose value Sqoop will take into account when dividing the job into multiple map tasks.

Sqoop converts the data from the native data types into corresponding Hive data types, using the native Hive delimiter set. If the data consists of new lines or other Hive delimiter characters, you can remove the characters in order to correctly populate the Hive table.

If the target table already exists in Hive, Sqoop imports data into that table. If that table doesn't exist, Sqoop creates it, using the metadata it fetches for that table. For a new Hive table, Sqoop converts the source table's data types into Hive-compatible data types. If the default mapping doesn't work for you, you can overwrite it as follows, by specifying the parameter `--map-column-hive` in your Sqoop `import` command:

```
sqoop import \
  ...
  --hive-import \
  --map-column-hive id=STRING,price=DECIMAL
```

In this example, I changed the Hive data type for the column `id` to `STRING` and the column `price` to `DECIMAL`.

Using Partitioned Hive Tables

Sqoop can automatically import data into a Hive table partition. If you want Sqoop to load data directly into a Hive partition, specify the following parameters:

- `--hive-partition-key`: This parameter names the partition column.
- `--hive-partition-value`: This parameter specifies the desired value.

For example, to load data into a partition named 2016-04-23 for a partition column named day, you can run the import command as follows:

```
sqoop import \
  --connect jdbc:mysql://mysql.example.com/sqoop \
  --username sqoop \
  --password sqoop \
  --table cities \
  --hive-import \
  --hive-partition-key day \
  --hive-partition-value "2016-04-23"
```

As Sqoop has no way of knowing into which partition it should import data, you must specify the name and value of the partition with the two parameters shown here. You can't simply specify the column name for a partitioned table import.

Exporting Data with Sqoop

Exporting with Sqoop means you get data from HDFS into a relational database (RDBMS) table. When you export an HDFS file to an RDBMS, a MapReduce (map-only) job processes a set of text-delimited files in HDFS and converts them into table rows in the target RDBMS, using `INSERT` statements. Exporting data has many parallels to importing data.

How to Export Data with Sqoop

Let's use a simple example to learn how to use Sqoop to export data into a MySQL database table:

```
sqoop export  \
   --connect jdbc:mysql://mysql.example.com/sqoop \
   --username sqoop \
   --password sqoop  \
   --table testTable \
   --export-dir /user/alapati/testTable
```

This `export` command exports the data in the HDFS directory /user/alapati/testTable into the MySQL database's table named testTable. You must have the table ready in MySQL before you run the Sqoop export. If the table isn't present in the database already, make sure you create it, with the same target columns and in the same order. Also ensure that the table is created with the correct SQL data types. For your export job to succeed, no input row can violate a primary key or other database constraint.

The parameter `--export-dir` points to the location of the input files in HDFS from which Sqoop will export the data, and the `--table` parameter points to the database table into which you are exporting the data. Both of these parameters are mandatory, and you can also specify one or more of the parameters listed here:

- `--direct`: Specifies the direct mode so you can complete the export faster. A direct-mode export to most databases is more efficient than a comparable JDBC-based export.
- `-m, --num-mappers <n>`: Lets you specify the number of mappers for the export process.
- `--update-mode <mode>`: Specifies how an update will be performed when new rows are found with non-matching keys in the database. The two values for `<mode>` are the default value of `updateonly` and `allowinsert`.
- `--update-key <col-name>`: A column used to identify the records you want to update during the `update-mode`. You can supply a comma-separated list to update multiple columns at once.
- `--staging-table <staging-table-name>`: The name of the staging table used to stage data before inserting it into the target table. This ensures that the export is an "all-or-nothing" affair. The export data is moved from the staging table to the target table after the entire data export completes successfully. This avoids partial exports and potential data corruption in the target table.

> **Tip**
>
> If you specify the `--staging-table` option, the target database will need storage for two copies of the data, one the staging table and the other, the actual target table. Also, the `--staging-table` option is only available with the `INSERT` mode and not in the update, update insert or direct mode, or when you call a stored procedure during an export.

- `--clear-staging-table`: If you specify a staging table, that table must exist before starting the Sqoop export. The staging table needs to be empty and you can specify the `--clear-staging-table` option to let Sqoop clean up the staging table by truncating the table.

How Sqoop Export Works

Here's what happens when you run a Sqoop export job. Sqoop will do the following:

- Validate the metadata of the MySQL table.
- Execute the MapReduce job, which will transfer the data in each record from the HDFS file and translate it into an `INSERT` command before appending it to the target table.

Note that Sqoop appends data to the target table. By specifying the `--update-key` argument with your export command, you can instead have Sqoop update the target rows in the database table.

> **Tip**
>
> By default, Sqoop uses four map jobs for both an import and an export. You can specify the number of map jobs to perform a Sqoop export (as well as an import). Of course, the more the mappers, the faster your export. However, as is true so often with the map tasks, there's a tradeoff—the more mappers, the more load on the cluster, and if there's a resource crunch, the whole cluster might be affected. In addition, too many map jobs may make it harder for the target database to handle the extra work!

When you start a Sqoop export job, multiple mapper tasks are started to perform the export, and if one or more of them fails, you'll end up with a partial export of rows to the target table. If you rerun your export, it may fail because rows already exist. In order to avoid this situation, you can specify the `--staging-table` argument with your exports. Sqoop will then store the data into a staging table first, before moving it to the target table. To ensure that the staging table is empty, specify the `--clean-staging-table` argument when you issue the export command.

Figure 12.3 shows the basic steps involved in a Sqoop export from HDFS to a database.

Performing Batch Exports

By default, Sqoop exports will insert each row as a separate `INSERT` statement. If you want to export millions of rows to a database, the SQL `INSERT` command will be painfully slow, as it needs to insert data one row at a time! You can change this default behavior in three different ways, so Sqoop can insert multiple rows at a time during an export:

- Enable JDBC batching.
- Specify the number of records to be inserted with an `INSERT` statement.
- Specify the number of rows to be inserted per transaction.

I briefly explain the three techniques in this section, starting with JDBC batching.

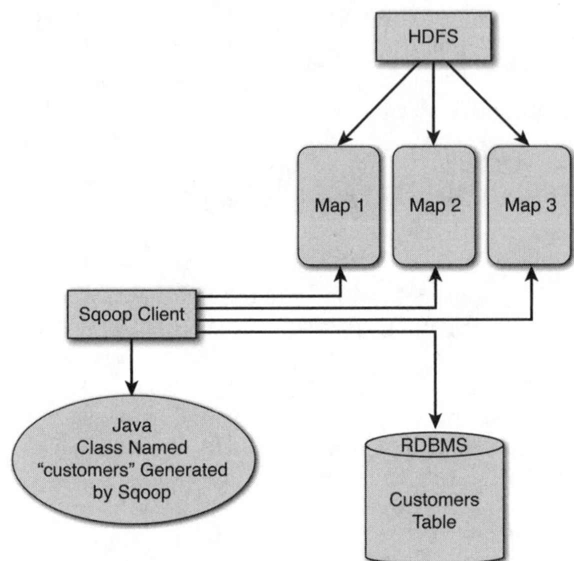

Figure 12.3 How Sqoop exports data from HDFS to a relational database (or data warehouse)

You can enable JDBC batching during an export by specifying the --batch parameter, as shown here:

```
sqoop export \
  --connect jdbc:mysql://mysql.example.com/sqoop \
  --username sqoop \
  --password sqoop \
  --table customers \
  --export-dir customers \
  --batch
  ....
```

When you specify the --batch parameter, your mileage may vary, because some JDBC drivers serialize rows in an internal cache before sending it to the database server, slowing down the export. Specifying the --batch parameter means that the map tasks will batch multiple INSERT statements together before sending them to the database, instead of using the default mode of single row inserts.

Alternatively, you can specify the property sqoop.export.records.per.statement to dictate the number of records per INSERT statement, as shown here, where I specify ten records per INSERT statement:

```
sqoop export \
Dsqoop.export.records.per.statement=10 \
  ...
```

Tip

Sqoop lets you specify certain properties at the command line by using the `-D <property=value>` argument. This will let you avoid having to set these parameters in the sqoop-site.xml file (in the $SQOOP_HOME/conf directory by default). You can check out the command line arguments that start with the `-D` option by issuing the `sqoop help export` command.

Adding the `--batch` parameter makes Sqoop generate a query with multiple rows in a single `INSERT` statement before sending it to the database server. Most databases support the use of multiple rows in a single `INSERT` statement, but not all do. The insert may fail on some databases because it exceeds the database's maximum query size.

Finally, you may also specify the number of rows to be inserted per transaction by adding the `sqoop.export.statements.per.transaction` property, as shown here:

```
sqoop export \
   Dsqoop.export.statements.per.transaction=10 \
   ...
```

The `sqoop.export.statements.per.transaction` parameter lets you group a set of insert statements to be run together, before committing the transaction. Thus, this strategy reduces the overhead of starting and completing each `INSERT` transaction separately. While you can generally increase insert performance by setting this parameter, you should also remember that each RDBMS may behave differently in how it handles this parameter. Test before you try this in production!

While I've presented several options here for enhancing Sqoop export performance, you'll be able to find the best option for you by testing these options in your own environment.

Simultaneously Updating or Inserting Data

When you use Sqoop to export data to a relational database such as MySQL, Sqoop leverages the SQL `INSERT` statement to append the data to the target table.

What if you want to update data instead of appending it? Sqoop takes care of this with its `--update-key <column(s)>` command line argument, which lets Sqoop generate a SQL `UPDATE` statement during an export, instead of the usual `INSERT` statement. So, in order to let a Sqoop export command generate a SQL `UPDATE` statement, you run the export as follows:

```
sqoop export
  ...
  --update-key customer_id \
...
```

If the target table (`CUSTOMER`) in the RDBMS has a record with the matching value in the column `CUSTOMER_ID` for the export data stored in HDFS (in the directory specified by the `export-dir` parameter), the table `CUSTOMERS` in the RDBMS is updated.

However, what happens if there's no matching record? You want to make sure that you don't let any data fall through the cracks. Obviously, if the data in HDFS is new, there won't be a matching record for the CUSTOMER_ID column in the RDBMS table CUSTOMERS and you ought to insert this new data into that table. Fortunately, you don't need to worry as Sqoop takes care of this eventuality as well.

> **Note**
>
> You can move data into and out of HDFS effortlessly using the Sqoop UI (through the Hue interface), which lets you move data with the mere click of a few buttons.

Sqoop offers an UPSERT (update or insert, depending on the situation) capability that lets it insert a row if it's new or update it if the row already exists. You can use this in cases when the data includes rows that you need to update with newer data from Hadoop as well as brand new rows. Obviously you can't simply specify the update mode in this scenario.

There really isn't actually a Sqoop export command named UPSERT. You must specify allowinsert as the value for the --update-mode parameter to perform simultaneous inserts (depending on the value of the matching columns) of new rows and updates of existing rows.

```
sqoop export
  ...
  --table customers
  --update-key id
  --update-mode allowinsert
...
```

The --update-mode <mode> attribute can have one of two possible values:

- The default value is updateonly and allows only updates, as the attribute value indicates.
- The allowinsert value specifies the UPSERT mode.

Some databases may not support the UPSERT option, so be sure to check your database documentation first before specifying it during an export operation.

Using Stored Procedures during Exports

You can use stored procedures during exports, by replacing the --table parameter with the --call parameter, followed by the name of the stored procedure you want Sqoop to invoke (--call <stored procedure>), as shown in the following example:

```
sqoop export \
  --connect jdbc:mysql://mysql.example.com/sqoop \
  --username sqoop \
  --password sqoop \
  --call populate_cities...
```

When you specify a stored procedure, Sqoop will call the stored procedure with column values as a separate parameter, instead of issuing insert statements for each row of data. For each record in the directory you specify with the --export-dir parameter, Sqoop will call the stored procedure populate_cities.

Exporting Data from Hive to a Database

You can't really directly export data from a Hive table into a database table using Sqoop (or Sqoop 2). You can, however, effectively do so by exporting data from the HDFS directory where Hive stores its table data. You can extract the data as text or as an Avro file. The following example shows how to export data from a Hive table named `testTable` into a MySQL table.

```
$ bin/sqoop export
--connect jdfs:mysql://localhost/test_db
--table invoice
--export-dir/user/hive/warehouse/invoice
--username root --password password
--m 12
--input-fields terminated by '001'
```

In this `export` command, I specify the path to the Hive warehouse where I stored the table named `invoice`. I also specified `'001'` as the field delimiter—Hive allows several other types of delimiters as well. This `export` command will load the Hive table invoice into the MySQL table, also named invoice.

Sqoop will read the records one by one from the /user/hive/warehouse/invoice table and insert them into the MySQL table. If you need to export an HBase table to an RDBMS, you can extract the data in a fashion similar to HDFS and then use Sqoop to export the data to the RDBMS.

Using Sqoop as a Service with Sqoop 2

Sqoop 2 is a new version of Sqoop that utilizes a client-server design and lets you run Sqoop as a service on its own dedicated server. Just as HiveServer2 is the centralized Hive server, Sqoop 2 is the centralized Sqoop server. Since the Sqoop 2 server does most of the work, it has a thin client. Other clients can also communicate with the Sqoop 2 server, using its JSON-REST protocol. Sqoop requires a client-site installation and configuration, whereas Sqoop 2 is installed and configured only on the server. One of the big drawbacks of Sqoop is that there really is no way to manage resources when working with relational databases. Sqoop 2 administrators can manage resources by limiting connections to the databases.

Using Sqoop means that you must install all connectors and JDBC drivers on each client. Each of the clients also needs its own connections to the database. If you use Sqoop 2, you don't need to install the connectors and drivers on the clients, as they are installed on the Sqoop server already. You also need database connectivity for just the Sqoop 2 server and not for each of the clients. Whereas traditional Sqoop clients were limited to the command-line interface CLI, in Sqoop 2, clients can use a CLI, browser, REST interface browser or another client to connect to the Sqoop server when working with databases.

While Sqoop 2 is definitely the future of the Apache Sqoop project, as of now, Sqoop 2 lacks some key capabilities offered by Sqoop (Sqoop 1 if you will). You may use Sqoop 2 if it contains the functionality you need. Otherwise, you must use Sqoop 1 for all your Sqoop-related work.

Sqoop 2 supports interaction through the command line but adds a web UI with a simple user interface to easily set up import and export jobs. Since the UI is built on a REST API, a command line client with similar functionality can use the UI. Sqoop 2's UI will walk you through the settings of import and export jobs, letting you eliminate incorrect options.

Sqoop 2 is architected differently than Sqoop 1. Since Sqoop 1 and Sqoop 2 use different code paths, there are different features available with each of them. While Sqoop 2 comes with a UI, there's none for Sqoop 1. The only way to run Sqoop 1 jobs from Hue is either by scheduling an Oozie job or by going through the Job Designer application. Sqoop 2 jobs can't yet be run from Oozie.

While you can use both Sqoop 1 and Sqoop 2 from the command line, there's a major difference. Sqoop 1 doesn't offer an interactive command line interface, while Sqoop 2 does.

Sqoop 2 currently has the following limitations:

- Unlike Sqoop, Sqoop 2 doesn't allow you to transfer data from a relational database to Hive or HBase. You can, however, get around this limitation by importing data from the RDBMS to HDFS, and then manually loading the data into Hive or HBase using the appropriate commands (`LOAD DATA` in Hive, for example).
- Again, unlike Sqoop, Sqoop 2 doesn't support connectors for all major relational databases. As a workaround, you can use the generic JDBC Connector, which works with several popular relational databases, but its performance lags behind that of Sqoop's specialized connectors.

Ingesting Data from External Sources with Flume

A prime use case for big data is the capture and analysis of data coming in through high-throughput data streams such as application log data. Apache Flume is a popular tool often used for collecting log data from multiple sources, aggregating it and storing it in HDFS. While Flume is often used to transport log data, you can transport any type of data you like. Flume offers the following benefits:

- It's architected for handling streaming data flows.
- It's simple to use.
- It's highly reliable (Flume stores a central list of ongoing data flows in ZooKeeper for redundancy).
- It contains extensions that enable online analytic applications that process data streams.

Unlike Sqoop and other data-migration tools, Flume is ideal for handling live transactions and can write log entries in near-real time—as the entries are being written to an access log, for example.

Flume is ideal for the ingestion of large volumes of log files in real time, from sources such as web servers and mail servers, which generate millions of log events on a daily basis. It's ideal for aggregating and moving streaming data from multiple sources into HDFS or HBase.

If you're moving only a small amount of data to HDFS, you can use WebHDFS (see Chapter 10, "Data Protection, File Formats, and Accessing HDFS") instead of Flume. Flume is designed for continuously ingesting data into HDFS and is perfect for handling massive amounts of log data. If the amount of data you need to move is small, Flume isn't worth the effort to configure and deploy it.

Flume Architecture in a Nutshell

A flume **agent** (running in a JVM), which is a daemon, is the basic unit of Flume. An agent consists of three components: **sources**, **channels** and **sinks**:

- Sources write events to one or more channels, which are holding areas for events.
- Events are passed from the sources to the sinks through channels.
- Sinks are the ultimate repository for the data Flume transmits.

The Flume agent is a JVM process that hosts the three components (sources, channels and sinks) through which the Flume data events flow. Note that a sink can also be a follow-on source of data for other Flume agents, or write data to HDFS and S3.

Figure 12.4 shows the Flume data flow model. The Flume agent is a JVM that runs Flume. The Flume sinks for each **agent node** send data to **collector nodes**. The collector nodes aggregate data from multiple agents and write it to HDFS so it can be analyzed with Pig, Hive and other tools.

Key Components of Flume

Apache Flume has three main components—sources, channels and sinks:

- Sources receive or retrieve data and send it along to channels.
- Channels act as a transient store for events within the agent and queue the transitory data. Channels serve as intermediary conduits between sources and sinks and are useful for holding data in queue when the ingest rate of data exceeds the outflow rate. Although there's an experimental hybrid memory and file channel, the two main channels are a non-durable memory-based channel and a durable file-system-based channel. The choice of channel type will depend upon your specific needs, risk tolerance and how you handle failures.

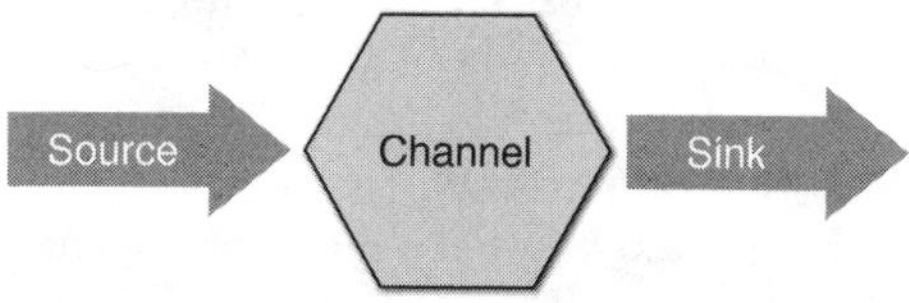

Figure 12.4 The Flume data-flow model showing how sources, channels and sinks interact

- Sinks take the data held temporarily by the channels and process it. A sink can remove an event from a channel and send it to another Flume agent or to the event's final destination, such as HDFS. A sink is sometimes an intermediate store, and at other times, the final destination of the events being captured. You can specify various types of sinks: The HDFS (type-hdfs) sink writes events to HDFS and supports creating text and SequenceFiles, and you can specify compression for both file types.

Simply put, a Flume source is the *source* of the streaming input, the channel acts as the temporary *buffer* for the data and the sink defines the final *destination* of the incoming streaming data. The clients send data events to the source, which sends those events to the channel buffer, and from there the data flows to the sink, which is the final destination for the data.

In addition to knowing how sources, channels and sinks work, you must understand several key Flume concepts including events, interceptors, channel selectors and sink processors.

- An **event** is the payload delivered by Flume, and it consists of a body (the actual payload) and possibly some headers. An event is the basic data unit handled by Flume processes—for example, a log record. The event body is a byte array and the headers are a map with string keys and values. Headers are for routing purposes (for example, `hostname=mywebserver.myhostname.com`) and for tracking the priority of the events being sent. Events are transmitted from their point of origination, also referred to as a client, to the source. A number of events together constitute a transaction, which has a unique ID.

> **Note**
>
> Flume events are designed for small events and usually are about 1–2KB in size. Thus, large events such as video and audio events won't work well with Flume.

- An **intercept** is a point in the data flow where you can inspect and alter events.
- A **channel selector** takes care of the moving data from a source to one or more channels.
- A **sink processor** is the mechanism that lets you create failover paths for sinks or load balance multiple Flume events across multiple sinks.

Sources write events to a channel and the events stay in the channel until a sink removes the events through a transaction. If there's a network failure, the events are queued in the channels until the sink can write them to HDFS.

Important Things about the Flume Agent

Here are the key things you need to know about a Flume agent:

- At a minimum, a Flume agent consists of a single source, a channel and a sink.
- Each source, channel and sink must be uniquely named.

- A Flume agent can have multiple sources, channels and sinks.
- You can configure multiple Flume agents to run multiple sets of channels and sinks to either replicate or selectively route events.
- You can chain agents to form a tiered collection topology with multiple hops until the events are stored in their ultimate data store—for example, HDFS.
- While a source can send data to multiple channels, a sink can receive data only from one channel.
- You can send data to multiple sinks such as HDFS sinks and Cassandra sinks.

Flume **topologies** can be extremely flexible, and there's no standard architecture. Flume architecture supports tiered data collection, with multiple Flume agents in a tiered fashion. You can chain multiple Flume agents to build complex data workflows. In a chained-agent architecture, the sink for one agent can send data to the source from a different agent. Avro is commonly used to send data across networks, since it's known as an efficient serialization mechanism for transforming data into a compact binary format.

Configuring the Flume Agent

Once you download and extract the Flume binaries, in order to run a Flume job, you need to configure the Flume agent.

The file flume.conf is the key file for you—it's where you configure the Flume agent by specifying the properties of the sources, channels and sinks, as well as how they are connected together to form a Flume data flow. You can either edit the file directly or, to make things a bit easier, copy the flume-conf.properties.template file to the flume.conf file, as shown here:

```
$ cp flume-conf.properties.template  flume.conf
```

The Flume architecture I described earlier as consisting of the three components—sources, channels and sinks—is converted into a functioning model by the Flume agent configuration, with is stored in a local text file that's similar to a Java properties file.

The Flume configuration file flume.conf uses key/value pairs that you pass to the agent when it starts up. Flume monitors this configuration property file for changes every 30 seconds. You can configure multiple Fume agents in a single Flume agent configuration file. You configure each Flume agent with the following three parameters:

```
agent.sources=<list of sources>
agent.channels=<list of channels>
agent.sinks=<list of sinks>
```

Each configuration item in a Flume configuration file lets Flume know the kind of source, channel and sink it's using. You configure properties for the sources, channels and sinks in the configuration file.

In a Flume agent, sources, channels and sinks all have unique names within that agent's context. You can specify a name for the agent as well, but I chose to simply use "agent" as the agent's name. For example, if you are moving Apache web server HTTP access logs, you can name your channel "access" and configure the channel as

```
agent.channels.access
```

In this example, `agent.channels.access` is a configuration item. More specifically, when you configure a channel, you need to specify the type of channel. I chose to specify an in-memory channel (there are other types of channels, as I explain later), so the complete configuration for our channel named "access" is going to be

```
agent.channels.access.type=memory
```

Similarly, you configure a `capacity` parameter for the memory channel you've configured with the following:

```
agent.channels.access.capacity=200
```

The capacity of a channel specifies the maximum number of events the channel can hold at any time.

A Simple Flume Example

Let's use a very simple example to understand how to configure a Flume agent. In this example, we have the following:

- A single agent named "agent1"
- A source named "netcatSource", a channel named "memChannel" and a sink named ..."logsink"
- The channel type is `memory`
- The sink type is `logger`, a sink that's commonly used for debugging event flows and for testing

Sources need a type, and in our example, it is Netcat, which opens a socket and listens for events through the open socket. The Flume agent will connect to the Netcat utility to send Flume events. There can only be a single sink since we have a single channel. In this example, the Flume agent receives service requests from a specified port and turns each line of text it receives into an event. The events are stored in a memory channel named "memChannel." These events are then retrieved by the memory-based sink and shown to you.

Open the configuration file flume.conf, and add the following configuration to the file:

```
# You must define the sources, channels and sinks on a per-agent basis, in this
case for the Flume agent named agent1
agent1.sources=netcatSource
agent1.channels=memChannel
agent1.sinks=logsink

# configure the source
agent1.sources.netcatSource.type=netcat
```

```
agent1.sources.netcatSource.channels=memchannel
agent1.sources.netcatSource.bind=0.0.0.0
agent1.sources.netcatSource.port=44444

#configure the channel
agent1.channels.memChannel.type=memory

# Configure the sink
agent1.sinks.logsink.type=logger
agent1.sinks.logsink.channel=memChannel
```

In this example, the agent configuration you specify in the flume.conf file does the following:

- It configures an agent named "agent1."
- It contains properties for each source, channel and sink in agent1.
- It specifies the connection properties—for example, the source listens for data (messages to `netcat`) on port 44444.
- It contains a channel that buffers event data in memory (and not disk).
- It configures a sink that logs event data to the console.

Once you configure the Flume agent, follow these steps to test your configuration:

1. Start the Flume agent, to test your configuration. To start the agent, use the shell-script `flume-ng`, located in Flume's bin directory. Issue the `agent` command from the command line, as shown in the following example.

   ```
   $ ./bin/flume-ng agent -n agent1 -c conf -f /home/flume/flume.conf -
   Dflume.root.logger=INFO, console
   ```

   The `agent` command has two required parameters: an agent name and a configuration file to use. If you've configured only a single agent, you can omit the agent's name.
2. Check the Flume agent's log to make sure that the source, channel and sink have all successfully started up. If you didn't specify the `-Dflume.root.logger` property, the output will go to the log/flume.log file.
3. Telnet to port 44444 from a different terminal and type the following Netcat (nc) command, to send a simple string message and hit `Return`.

   ```
   $ nc localhost 12345
   It's time for big data!
   OK
   ```

The agent confirms the acceptance of the text you typed by printing it on the screen, along with an `OK` message to indicate that all went well. In the agent log, you can see your message:

```
2016-21-05 11:52:45:11,215 (SinkRunner-PollingRunner
DefaultSinkProcessor) [INFO -
org.apache.flume.sink.LoggerSink.process(LoggerSink.java:70)] Event: {
headers:{} body: 48 65 6C 6C 6F 20 57 6F 72 6C 64          It's time for
big data!}
```

You can find all the event-processing messages from the source and the sink in the /opt/apache-flume/bin/logs.flumelog file.

In our example, the source of the Flume agent's data was Netcat. You can alternatively specify Exec, Avro, Thrift, Syslog, HTTP, JMS, a spooling directory source or twitter-source as your source type. You can even write a custom source type.

If you specify Exec, you must provide an executable command that will be executed to get the data to the Flume agent. For example, you can specify a command such as `tail -F /tmp/access_log`, which grabs the web server access logs. Each time the command executes, the Flume agent receives an event.

> **Tip**
>
> Watch your Java Heap size (`-Xms` and `-Xms`) closely when using a memory channel; if you raise the size of the memory channel significantly, you may need to raise the Java heap size.

Using Flume to Move Data to HDFS

This book is primarily for Hadoop administrators, so let's discuss a very common use for Flume in Hadoop environments, where Flume is commonly used to write dynamically generated data into HDFS, such as the access logs from a company's web servers. Flume is capable of writing various HDFS file formats such as text, SequenceFile, JSON, Avro and so on.

In order to configure a Flume data capture and storage flow, you must modify the Flume agent configuration file. You can configure one or more Flume agents in a single Flume agent property file (`flume.conf`).

Each of the Flume agents must have its own named sources, channels and sinks. When you configure multiple Flume agents in a single configuration file, before you start a Flume agent you must pass an argument at the command line to tell Flume which Flume agent it should start.

Let's create a Flume agent configuration file for moving the dynamic data to HDFS. I named the Flume agent "hdfs1" in this example, but you can name it anything. The following code shows the Flume configuration file.

```
# Configure the Flume agent, sources, channels and sinks
hdfs1.sources = execSource
hdfs1.channels = fileChannel
hdfs1.sinks = hdfsSink

# Configure the source
hdfs1.sources.execSource.type = exec
hdfs1.sources.execSource.command = tail -F /var/log/messages
hdfs1.sources.execSource.channels = fileChannel

#Configure the channels
hdfs1.channels.fileChannel.type = FILE
hdfs1.channels.fileChannel.capacity = 1000000
hdfs1.channels.fileChannel.maxFileSize= 10737418240
```

```
#Configure the Sinks
hdfs1.sinks.hdfsSink.type = hdfs
hdfs1.sinks.hdfsSink.hdfs.path = hdfs://<Name Node IP>/user/flume/messages
hdfs1.sinks.hdfsSink.hdffs.filePrefix = flume-
hdfs1.sinks.hdfsSink.hostname = localhost
hdfs1.sinks.hdfsSink.port = 6000
hdfs1.sinks.hdfsSink.batch-size = 100
hdfs1.sinks.hdfsSink.channel = fileChannel
```

Here's what the Flume agent configuration parameters mean:

- Channel: The channel type is a file and not memory. The file is configured to store 1 million events.
- Sources: I've specified `exec` as the source type—in our first small example I used `Netcat`. When you specify `exec` as the source type, you must specify the actual command to be executed in the `hdfs1.sources.execSource` command attribute. The `exec` source executes a command you specify and consumes the output. In this example, the executable command is `tail -F /var/log/messages`. The user running this must be able to read from the /var/log/messages file.
- Sinks: Our sink type is HDFS, so the data is going to be stored in the /user/flume/messages directory in HDFS, as specified by the `hdfs1.sinks.hdfsSink.hdfs.path` attribute in the flume.conf file.

Now that our Flume agent is configured, run the Flume agent as shown here:

```
$ flume-ng agent  \
    --conf  /etc/flume-ng/conf  \
    --conf-file  hdfs1.cfg  \
    --Dfile.root.logger=DEBUG, INFO, CONSOLE \
    --name hdfs1
```

Tip

Ensure that the Flume sinks can keep up with the sources, thus keeping the channels from becoming a chokepoint. If you suspect that the channel is the issue, specify a memory sink to verify that the channel isn't the cause of the problem.

When you start the Flume agent (hdfs1), Flume validates its configuration file and shows you the sources, channels and sinks you've configured in the flume.conf file.

Our example here is quite elementary and uses a single agent with one source and one sink, but you could build complex processing topologies with Flume, as mentioned earlier.

A More Complex Flume Example

In our two examples, I used only a single Flume agent. However, you can chain multiple Flume agents together, where the sink of one agent sends data to the source of another sink. You need to do this often when you want to first collect data such as log data and store it in a central location such as HDFS. You can then use HDFS as the source for sending out that data to other targets, which will serve as the sinks.

The Avro file format is the standard method used to send data across the network with Flume. In the example I discuss in this section, a source tails a log file. New log lines are queued up in a channel, from where a sink extracts them and writes them to HDFS.

There are two Flume agents in this setup:

- The first Flume agent, called simply "agent," runs on the web server whose access logs we're interested in. It retrieves the log lines from the `/var/logs/httpd/access_log` file and sends them to the second Flume agent.
- The second Flume agent, which is typically referred to as a "collector," stores the log lines in HDFS.

Configuring the Web Server Flume Agent

Since I'm using two Flume agents, I need two configurations, one for each agent. I can put both configurations in a single file, or I can use a separate config file for each of the agents. In this case, I'm using separate configuration files, but it doesn't really matter. For the first agent running on the web server, the /opt/flume/conf/flume-webagent.conf file has the following configuration:

```
webagent.sources = apache
webagent.sources.apache.type = exec
webagent.sources.apache.command = tail -F var/log/httpd/access_log
webagent.sources.apache.batchSize = 1
webagent.sources.apache.channels = memoryChannel
webagent.sources.apache.interceptors = itime ihost itype
#
webagent.sources.apache.interceptors.itime.type = timestamp
#
webagent.sources.apache.interceptors.ihost.type = host
webagent.sources.apache.interceptors.ihost.useIP = false
webagent.sources.apache.interceptors.ihost.hostHeader = host
#
webagent.sources.apache.interceptors.itype.type = static
webagent.sources.apache.interceptors.itype.key = log_type
webagent.sources.apache.interceptors.itype.value = apache_access_combined

#
webagent.channels = memoryChannel
webagent.channels.memoryChannel.type = memory
webagent.channels.memoryChannel.capacity = 100

## Send to Flume Collector on 1.2.3.4 (Hadoop Slave Node)
# agent.sinks = AvroSink
webagent.sinks.AvroSink.type = avro
webagent.sinks.AvroSink.channel = memoryChannel
webagent.sinks.AvroSink.hostname = 1.2.3.4
webagent.sinks.AvroSink.port = 4545
```

This configuration file is quite simple:

- It specifies exec as the source type, with a single source, Apache, which refers to the Apache HTTP Server.
- It has a single memory channel (no files) to hold the log entries.
- It has a single Avro sink.

Once the first Flume agent is running, it starts sending log entries to a different Flume agent running on the Hadoop cluster.

Start up the first agent as shown here:

```
$ cd /opt/flume
$ bin/flume-ng agent  -f  conf/flume-webagent.conf   -n webagent
```

I specify webagent as the Flume agent's name, since that's the name we configured in the flume-webagent.conf file. Once you have the first Flume agent running, configure the second Flume agent, which stores the access log data in HDFS. The following section explains how to do this.

Configuring the Collector Agent

Following is the configuration for the "collector" agent.

```
# collector.sources = AvroIn
collector.sources.AvroIn.type = avro
collector.sources.AvroIn.bind = 0.0.0.0
collector.sources.AvroIn.port = 4545
collector.sources.AvroIn.channels = memChannel1 memChannel2

## Source writes to 2 channels, one for each sink (Fan Out)
collector.channels = memChannel1 memChannel2

# collector.channels.memChannel1.type = memory
collector.channels.memChannel1.capacity = 100

collector.channels.memChannel2.type = memory
collector.channels.memChannel2.capacity = 100

## Sinks
collector.sinks = LocalOut HadoopOut

## Optionallly write to the Local Filesystem (For Debugging purposes)
#
collector.sinks.LocalOut.type = file_roll
collector.sinks.LocalOut.sink.directory = /var/log/flume
collector.sinks.LocalOut.sink.rollInterval = 0
collector.sinks.LocalOut.channel = memChannel1

## Write to HDFS
collector.sinks.HadoopOut.type = hdfs
collector.sinks.HadoopOut.channel = memChannel2
collector.sinks.HadoopOut.hdfs.path = /flume/events/%{log_type}/%{host}/%y-%m-%d
collector.sinks.HadoopOut.hdfs.fileType = DataStream
collector.sinks.HadoopOut.hdfs.writeFormat = Text
collector.sinks.HadoopOut.hdfs.rollSize = 0
collector.sinks.HadoopOut.hdfs.rollCount = 10000
collector.sinks.HadoopOut.hdfs.rollInterval = 600
```

Here's what the flume-connector.conf file shows:

- The Flume agent runs on port 4545.
- We have two sink collector channels, `memChannel1` and `memChannel2`.
- Flume will store a maximum of 100 entries in the two channels.

In this example, the source accesses two Avro network events, sending the events along to two different memory channels, `memChannel1` and `memChannel2`. Each of the two memory channels stores data in a different sink, with `memChannel1` writing to a directory (optional, for debugging purposes) and `memChannel2` writing to HDFS.

Start the second Flume agent as shown here:

```
$ bin/flume-ng agent  -c conf -f  /etc/flume-ng/conf/flume-connector.conf  -n
collector
```

Now that both Flume agents are running, you can view the logs stored in HDFS by issuing the command `hdfs dfs -ls /flume`. If you've configured the **file roll** sink as well, you can find the logs in the /var/log/flume directory in case you need to debug or test things.

Ingesting Data with Kafka

Apache Kafka is a publish-subscribe messaging system used instead of traditional message brokers such as JMS due to the higher throughput and reliability it offers. Kafka is highly fault tolerant and can handle huge amounts of messages for low-latency analysis in your Hadoop system, by allowing parallel data loads into Hadoop. In a Hadoop 2 environment, you can use Kafka along with Apache Storm and Apache Spark for real-time analysis of streaming data.

While Kafka is similar to Flume in some ways because it can process streaming data, in its architecture it really resembles well-known messaging systems such as ActiveMQ and Rabbit MQ.

Apache Kafka is especially designed for handling streaming data. While it's often called a messaging system, and does provide many capabilities of a typical messaging system, it's fundamentally different in the sense that it provides a different abstraction of a structured commit log of updates.

Benefits Offered by Kafka

Kafka offers the following features that make it highly desirable in situations where you need a high throughput with reliable message delivery. You can summarize Kafka's benefits thus:

- Performance: High throughput for publishing and subscribing messages even when handling very large amounts of stored messages.
- Data consistency: You don't need to implement functionality for checking data consistency since Kafka takes care of it for you.

- Scalability: Kafka is a distributed system, without any downtime
- Reliability: Kafka provides fault-tolerant data replication and balances the message consumers when failure occurs, in addition to offering delivery guarantees.
- Durability: Kafka stores messages on disk.
- Real-time: Due to the speed with which Kafka handles messages, it supports real-time use cases.

Due to the benefits Kafka offers, it is widely used for work involving the tracking of website activity, the collection and monitoring of metrics and aggregating logs, and stream processing. Following are some key use cases for Kafka:

- Analyzing meter and sensor data from grid points
- Capturing solar and wind energy production data (transient sources)
- Forecasting data for weather, energy production and energy markets
- Working with activity data such as log data
- Capturing event messages
- Application performance tracing

How Kafka Works

The key to understanding how Kafka works is realizing that it is Kafka's **commit log abstraction** that makes possible a reliable and highly efficient way of distributing changes to consumers. Figure 12.5 shows the Kafka commit log abstraction. Data producers send streaming records which are appended to the commit log and consumers

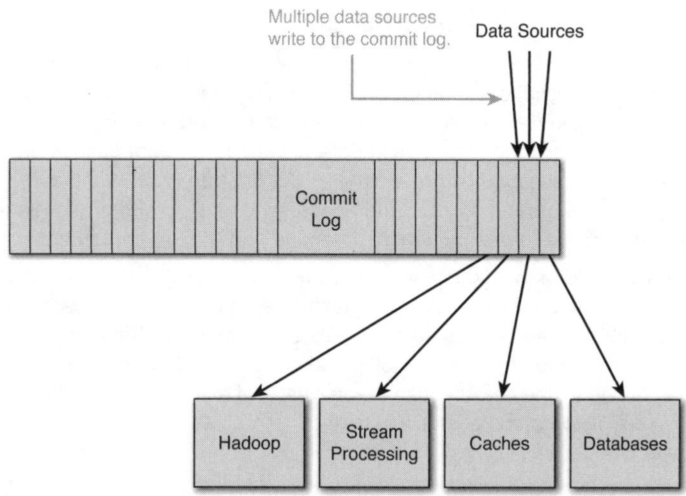

Figure 12.5 Kafka's commit log abstraction

can stream the updates to the log with very low latency. Since consumers advance through the commit log independent of each other, a reliable and ordered stream of updates is sent to each consumer.

Database updates need to be delivered in the order they occur. Kafka's commit log can be spread over a cluster, with each part of the log replicated for fault-tolerance. The cluster helps parallel and ordered transmitting of data to multiple customers. The Kafka cluster can grow in size or shrink, without applications being aware of the changes. Even when a Hadoop cluster working with data from Kafka goes down for a while, there's nothing to worry about, as the Kafka cluster safely persists all changes. All these capabilities set Kafka apart from typical enterprise messaging systems.

As with typical messaging systems, Kafka's design involves four key components—**topics**, **producers**, **consumers** and **brokers**. Here's how the four key components interact:

- A topic is a user-defined category to which messages are published.
- Producers publish messages to the topics.
- Consumers subscribe to those topics to access the published messages.
- Brokers are servers that manage all the work related to the messaging, which involves the persistence and replication of messages in various topics.

Consumers are responsible for keeping track of the messages they consume. Consumers keep track of the messages they consume by tracking what's called an **offset**, which is a sequential number identifying a message. Consumers can easily get to any message stored on disk by supplying the message's offset value. Unlike in traditional messaging systems such as JMS, the broker is relieved of the duty of tracking message consumption. This design feature is at the heart of Kafka's ability to scale with the number of consumers.

Kafka—A Real-Time Messaging Solution

In addition to its high reliability and throughput, Kafka stands out for its ability to provide a real-time publish-subscribe solution for very large data volumes. You can use multiple producers, such as the web applications generating logs, producers generating web analytics logs and so on. Producers send data to various types of consumers, including offline consumers who may store them in HDFS or in an RDBMS. Near real-time consumers may store data in a NoSQL database such as Cassandra and real-time consumers filter messages in the in-memory database and trigger alert events.

Offline analysis provided by Hadoop and other systems isn't adequate for handling large amounts of data generated by a users' web activity such as logins and page visits, as well as social networking activities such as likes and comments. Kafka offers a way to combine both online and offline processing and not only load data parallely into HDFS, but also partition real-time consumption over a cluster of machines. LinkedIn uses Kafka for streaming activity data and operational metrics, as well as streaming data to Hadoop for offline analysis.

Setting Up an Apache Kafka Cluster

Although this isn't really a full-fledged introduction to Kafka, let me briefly describe how you go about setting up an Apache Kafka cluster.

You can create the following types of Kafka clusters:

- Single node–single broker
- Single node–multiple broker
- Multiple node–multiple broker

To keep things simple, let's learn how to create a single node–single broker cluster. Before we do that, however, we need to first install Apache Kafka, so let's start with that.

Installing Apache Kafka

In order to create our simple Kafka cluster, let's start by installing Kafka. Here are the steps.

1. Download the current stable version of Kafka from `http://apache.kafka.org` and extract it into a directory such as /opt, as shown here.

   ```
   # tar xvzf kafka-0.8.0-incubating-src.tgz
   ```

2. Once you untar the zipped file, you must build the source binaries using the tool, since Kafka is implemented in Scala. Change the current directory to go to the one where you downloaded Kafka. Run the following command from there to build Kafka.

   ```
   # ./sbt update
   ```

3. The `update` downloads all dependencies necessary to build Kafka. Run the following command to compile the source code.

   ```
   $ ./sbt package
   ```

4. Run the following command to produce the dependency artifacts.

   ```
   $ ./sbt assembly-package-dependency
   ```

Apache Kafka is now installed on your server, and you can move on to the building of the Kafka cluster.

Creating the Single Node–Single Broker Cluster

Kafka comes with the files necessary for defining the minimal properties you need to get a single node–single broker cluster going. These files include basic configuration for ZooKeeper, Kafka brokers and so on. You'll need to do the following to set up and test a working Kafka cluster.

- Set up ZooKeeper.
- Start a Kafka broker.
- Create a Kafka topic.

- Start a producer to send messages.
- Start a consumer to consume the messages.

Since this is going to be a single-node cluster, it's good to open up four different terminals on your server, one each for running the ZooKeeper server, the broker, the producer and the consumer. This way, when you're done setting up the Kafka cluster by creating all these entities, you can enter messages from the terminal where the producer is running, and see them show up on the terminal running the consumer!

Setting up the ZooKeeper Services

Creating a functioning Apache Kafka cluster requires you to set up the ZooKeeper server for storing the cluster coordination information such as status, configuration, location information and so on.

You learned how to setup the ZooKeeper service and you also learned how to use it to support NameNode high availability in Chapter 11. You can use the same ZooKeeper servers for supporting an Apache Kafka cluster as well. However, Kafka also comes with a small default ZooKeeper configuration file that launches a single local ZooKeeper instance. This ZooKeeper instance coordinates the flow of activity between the Kafka brokers and the Kafka consumers.

In this example, I use the default ZooKeeper configuration file provided by Kafka. This file contains the following configuration properties:

```
dataDir=/tmp/zookeeper
clientPort=2181
```

Start the ZooKeeper server as shown here.

```
[root@localhost]# bin/zookeeper-server-start.sh
config/zookeeper.properties
```

Now that ZooKeeper is running, time to start up the Kafka broker.

Starting the Kafka Broker

You can start the Kafka broker with its default configuration file, which contains the following configuration items:

- `broker.id=0`
- `log.dir=/tmp/kafka8-logs`
- `zookeeper.connect=localhost:2181`

There's a single broker in this cluster and its ID is 0. It connects to the ZooKeeper service using the port 2181.

Start the Kafka broker with the following command:

```
# bin/kafka-server-start.sh config/server.properties
```

Now that both ZooKeeper and the Kafka broker are running, you can create Kafka topics.

Creating a Kafka Topic

You create Kafka topics using a command line utility provided by Apache Kafka. The following example creates a simple topic with a single partition and replica.

```
# bin/kafka-create-topic.sh -zookeeper localhost:2181 -replica 1 -
partition 1 -topic testtopic
```

I named our topic *testtopic* in this example.

I'm almost done! Once the topic is successfully created, you start a producer to send messages to the Kafka cluster.

Starting the Producer

In a real Kafka cluster, you'll usually have multiple brokers, producers and consumers. In our case, it's enough to start a single producer, as shown here.

```
[root@localhost]# bin/kafka-console-producer.sh -broker-list
localhost:9092 -topic testtopic
```

You need the following two parameters to start the command line producer client:

- `broker-list`: The server and port information for the brokers (`localhost` and `9092` in our example)
- `topic`: The name of the topic (`testtopic` in our example)

What I created here is a command line producer client that accepts your input from the command line and publishes it to the cluster as messages. The consumer will then consume the messages. But first we need to create and start the consumer, which is our next and last step in the cluster configuration.

The producer client is now running, so you can start sending messages. Type something like the following message on the terminal where the producer is running:

```
Hola Kafka, Como Esta?
```

Starting a Consumer

In order to consume the messages sent by the producer, you need a consumer. Start the consumer as shown here.

```
# bin/kafka-console-consumer.sh -zookeeper localhost:2181 -topic testtopic -from-
beginning
```

The consumer runs with the default configuration properties from the `consumer.properties` file, as shown here:

```
groupid=test-consumer-group
zookeeper.connect=localhost:2181
```

As soon as the consumer starts running, you'll see the message you typed in the producer server appear on the screen. An Apache Kafka cluster sure is easy to set up, isn't it?

This example showed how to set up and use a single node–single broker Kafka cluster. Setting up a single node–multiple broker cluster isn't really much different. You just need to create multiple brokers on the same node, using unique values for all the configuration properties (such as unique broker IDs, for example) listed in the server.properties file, which specifies the broker configuration. Since you have multiple brokers, you need to name the different server properties files server1.properties, server2.properties and so on, depending on how many brokers you want to start. When you start the brokers, you need to start each of them in the following way, with a unique port for each of the brokers.

```
# bin/kafka-server-start.sh config/server1.properties
# bin/kafka-server-start.sh config/server2.properties
```

Since you have multiple brokers (two in this example) you can create a new topic with multiple partitions and replicas as well, as shown here.

```
# bin/kafka-create-topic.sh -zookeeper localhost:2181 -replica 2 -
partition 2 -topic testtopic2
```

Assuming you're running a single producer, it needs to connect to all the brokers you start. You do this by specifying the different brokers with the --broker-list parameter when you start the producer, as shown here.

```
# bin/kafka-console-producer.sh -broker-list localhost:9092,
localhsot:9093 -topic testtopic
```

The single consumer you created earlier will be able to consume messages as before, after it subscribes to the topic created earlier. The procedure to start the consumer is no different from how you start it in a single-broker setup.

To set up a multiple node–multiple broker Kafka cluster, you need to install Kafka on each of the cluster nodes. All the brokers will also need to connect to the same ZooKeeper service. Kafka lets you create complex architectures, such as multiple producers connecting to different sets of brokers and so on. It also lets you configure all its components such as the brokers, consumers, producers and topics in a much more complex way by offering a richer set of configuration properties than what you saw here. This was, after all, just a mere introduction to setting up an Apache Kafka cluster!

Integrating Kafka with Hadoop and Storm

Kafka is ideally suited for integrating with Hadoop and Storm, as well as other tools such as Apache Flume, another important log-processing tool. There are several use cases that merit integrating Kafka with Hadoop and Storm. For example, you may be storing heaps of raw cluster clickstream data from web sites in a Hadoop cluster and processing the data with MapReduce and Hive jobs. However, there's no real-time use of this humongous amount of clickstream data flowing into your system. By integrating Storm and Hadoop with Kafka, you can perform both batch processing and real-time data processing. Kafka, for example, can provide critical real-time business intelligence to a real-time data processing framework such as Apache Storm, which can capitalize on this intelligence and take appropriate actions.

Integrating Kafka with Hadoop and Storm (and Flume) requires significant awareness of the enterprise architecture as well as expertise in working with the various data ingestion tools that are involved. You can architect the integrations in a highly complex fashion. For example you can have Flume stream data to Kafka and then let Kafka stream the data to Storm for processing. Storm can then be architected to stream the processed data into HDFS for analytical use and into Spark or a NoSQL database for real-time processing. Our goal here is to get a rudimentary idea of how and why one may want to integrate Kafka with Hadoop and other data processing frameworks.

Integrating with Hadoop

You can use Kafka to build data pipelines that enable real-time processing and load the data into Hadoop for offline processing. A Hadoop producer publishes HDFS data to the Kafka cluster, and a Hadoop consumer pulls data into HDFS from a Kafka cluster. Kafka provides the source code for creating Hadoop producers and consumers, and you can also use third-party solutions for integrating Kafka and Hadoop.

Let's understand a bit about how the Kafka-provided Hadoop producers and consumers work:

- A Hadoop producer serves as a conduit for publishing data from the Hadoop cluster to the Kafka cluster. One way to send data from Hadoop to Kafka is to write Pig scripts for the Kafka producers in an Avro binary format, where rows indicate a single message, and push the data to the Kafka cluster. In this approach, you use an `AvroKafkaStorage` producer to write to various topics and brokers in the same Pig script. An alternative approach is to use the Kafka `OutputFormat` class to publish HDFS data to the Kafka cluster. Kafka's `OutputFormat` class extends Hadoop's `OutputFormat` class when writing messages to a Hadoop cluster.
- A Hadoop consumer moves data from Kafka to Hadoop. The consumer is a Hadoop job that pulls the data from the Kafka brokers and loads it parallely to HDFS.

Integrating with Storm

Apache Storm uses entities called spouts and bolts to do its work. Spouts are sources of continuous streams of log data and bolts consume the data sent to them by the spouts, with a Storm topology defining how data flows from the spouts to the bolts. As with the Kafka integration with a Hadoop cluster, you need two clusters to be running simultaneously: a Kafka cluster and a Storm cluster.

You can use the Kafka Spout code available from Apache Kafka to integrate Storm with a Kafka cluster. The Kafka Spout continuously reads data from a Kafka cluster. The Kafka Spout stores the message offset and other message consumption tracking information in Zookeeper's root path. By default, this message offset is stored in the Storm cluster's ZooKeeper znodes. You can also store the data in other ZooKeeper clusters, by configuring the Kafka Spout.

You need to provide the configuration information for the Kafka Spout to connect to the Kafka cluster. Here are the essential configuration parameters:

- A list of the Kafka brokers
- The number of partitions per host
- The topic name to use to pull messages
- The root path to ZooKeeper for the Kafka Spout to store its consumer offset
- The ID for the consumer that will store the consumer offset in ZooKeeper

Once you have all the configuration parameters, you can initialize the KafkaSpout class instance as follows.

```
spoutConfig spoutconfig = new SpoutConfig(
    ImmutableList.of("localhost:9092", "localhost:9093"),
2,
:"testtopic",
"/kafka-storm",
"consumerID");
KafkaSpout kafkaSpout = new KafkaSpout (spoutConfig);
```

I provided a rudimentary introduction here to both Kafka and its integration with Storm and Hadoop, and there's quite a bit more to it. LinkedIn engineers have created Camus, which also provides a data pipeline from Kafka to HDFS. There's an Apache Camel-Kafka integration as well. You can also integrate Kafka with Apache Spark streaming.

Summary

Here's what you learned in this chapter:

- As a Hadoop administrator, you'll be using Hadoop's built-in HDFS file system commands often to move data into and out of your cluster.
- DistCp is your friend when it comes to moving vast amounts of data fast between two clusters or within the same cluster.
- Sqoop is a versatile tool for efficiently moving large data sets between your Hadoop cluster and just about any relational database.
- Flume is a very popular log ingesting tool and is a mainstay of many companies when it comes to the processing of vast amounts of log data.
- Kafka is a messaging system often used to ingest data into Hadoop environments due to its high throughput and reliability.

13

Resource Allocation in a Hadoop Cluster

This chapter covers the following:

- Understanding how Hadoop manages resources among its users
- Using the Fair Scheduler to allocate resources
- Using the Capacity Scheduler to allocate resources
- Comparing the Fair Scheduler and the Capacity Scheduler

This chapter and the next together deal with two very important areas of day-to-day Hadoop administration—resource allocation among competing users, and scheduling jobs in your Hadoop cluster. This chapter is dedicated to resource allocation among the multiple tenants of a Hadoop cluster.

Resource allocation is a crucial part of Hadoop administration. There are strict limits to the amount of memory and CPU cores that can be used by running jobs in your cluster. Since you have finite resource limits, you're often required to prioritize jobs that various users submit to your cluster. In an organization, there are usually several departments or groups who want to use your cluster to perform various tasks. It's your job to ensure that the competing groups get appropriate resources to complete their jobs within their service level agreements (SLAs). Hadoop's built-in resource schedulers, such as the Fair Scheduler and the Capacity Scheduler, make life easy for you when it comes to allocating the finite resources at your command. They enable you to allocate those resources in an orderly, optimal, fair and balanced manner that fully uses all the available cluster resources while granting specific resource guarantees to user groups in the cluster.

Resource Allocation in Hadoop

Resource allocation refers to the allocation of scarce, finite computing resources, such as CPU time, memory, storage space and network bandwidth, among the users that utilize a Hadoop cluster.

The two most important resources that you have control over are processing power (CPU) and memory (RAM).

In a theoretical world, with an infinite set of resources, you can imagine all these groups of users, each with their own deadlines, priorities and SLAs, working happily together with no potential conflicts regarding individual (or group-level) resource usage. In real-life, alas, every resource is finite—and it's your job to apportion the limited resources available to you among the multiple competing user groups, so they can all "live" together happily, making sure that the critical jobs of each group are allocated sufficient resources to finish within their deadlines.

Managing Cluster Workloads

As just alluded to, as a Hadoop administrator, one of your key tasks is to balance workloads so you can meet both your SLAs and your users' expectations. Hadoop makes it easy for you to manage cluster workloads by providing a couple of very powerful resource schedulers, the Fair Scheduler and the Capacity Scheduler, both of which I explain later in this chapter.

Hadoop resource schedulers are components that are responsible for assigning tasks to available YARN containers on various DataNodes. The scheduler is a plug-in within the ResourceManager.

You can look at Hadoop schedulers as tools that let multiple tenants of a cluster share a cluster and use the cluster resources in an efficacious and timely manner, while being mindful of the total allocated capacity of a cluster. Resources in this context usually refer to memory (RAM) and processing power (CPU cores), although future releases will also explicitly include disk storage as a resource.

I'll take a typical scenario in our own cluster at work, where we deal with various user groups with different SLAs that they need to meet. In addition to these user groups, we also have several data scientists that execute long-running jobs in the cluster that can take 24 hours or more to finish at times. The users who need to meet strict SLAs can't afford jobs to run past the job windows, whereas the data scientists and analysts basically want us to allocate resources fairly so their jobs don't take forever.

Our biggest practical concern is that if we give a lot of resources to the data scientists, their jobs will take up so much of the resources (their data sets are usually very large) that the critical jobs that have strict SLAs will run past their assigned job windows. We use resource allocation strategies based on one of the Hadoop resource schedulers (specifically, the Fair Scheduler, the topic of the next section) and use weights and other priority allocation attributes to make sure that jobs with SLAs get done on time, and during the times when these jobs aren't running, the data scientists' resource allocation is ramped up, so their jobs can finish in a reasonable time.

> **Note**
>
> The Capacity Scheduler is the default scheduler for Apache Hadoop, although for some Hadoop distributions such as Cloudera's, the Fair Scheduler is the default scheduler.

Resource scheduling lets you prioritize the various tasks running in your cluster.

Hadoop's Resource Schedulers

Hadoop comes with three different types of resource schedulers that help you assign resources to applications and users. The three available resource schedulers are:

- First-in, first-out (FIFO) scheduler: This is a simple early Hadoop scheduler, and it uses a single queue for all jobs. There's no concept of priority in choosing a job for execution, with the oldest jobs getting chosen first from the head of the queue.
- Capacity Scheduler: This scheduler submits your jobs to queues, each of which is guaranteed a minimum amount of resources such as RAM and CPU. The queues with a greater gap between their used capacity and their granted resources are offered priority in the allocation of new resources as those resources are released by completing jobs. If it has excess capacity, the scheduler shares it among the cluster users, just as the Fair Scheduler does. It uses the concepts of reservation and preemption (which means that containers from other applications may need to be killed if necessary to make room for the new applications) to return the guaranteed capacity to the queues.
- Fair Scheduler: This scheduler assigns jobs to queues (the term *queues* is used interchangeably with *pools* for this scheduler), with guaranteed minimum resources. The scheduler picks up the jobs with the greatest time deficit for allocating resources that are freed by other applications. This scheduler can also allocate excess capacity from a pool to other pools. The Fair Scheduler uses the concept of **priority** to support the importance of an application within a pool. It uses the concept of **preemption** to support fairness among different resource pools.

As you'll learn in the following sections, except in the case of the FIFO scheduler, which isn't appropriate for most production environments, all schedulers revolve around the crucial concept of a job queue.

Queues are the very heart of a resource scheduler, and both the Capacity Scheduler and the Fair Scheduler use the concept of a queue. Why is the queue such an important concept in scheduling cluster jobs? The simple answer is that queues enable you to optimize a cluster's resources.

Let's say your organization has a set of groups such as marketing, sales and human resources, all with different SLAs and, thus, differing expectations of how fast they expect their jobs to complete. Using a job queue lets you share your cluster among these groups in an organized manner. Queues enable you to guarantee minimum levels of capacity for them and also divert unused cluster resources for overloaded queues, thus optimizing the cluster's resource utilization.

The big difference between the two schedulers is that the Capacity Scheduler provides stringent guarantees for queues by actually reserving queue capacity. Small jobs you submit to a dedicated queue can start right away as their resources aren't given to other queues but kept idle, so the queue can have them any time its runs an application. This comes at a cost, though, since the reserved capacity isn't allocated to other queues when the queue isn't in use.

The Fair Scheduler doesn't reserve any resources for queues—it's dynamic in nature, meaning that if you submit a job to a queue, the scheduler ensures that the job starts receiving resources in a fair fashion, conforming to the configurations you set in place.

By assigning jobs to predefined queues and not directly to the users, you ensure fairness and stability in your cluster, by preventing a single application (or a mere handful of them) from grabbing a disproportionate share of the cluster's resources. Queues thus promote an orderly sharing of cluster resources and prevent resource usage beyond the guaranteed resource limits that you set for the queues.

Often, Hadoop administrators seek to find out which of the two schedulers we explained in this chapter is better. There's no hard and fast answer to such a question. To be honest, there are more similarities than serious differences between the two schedulers, as the two implement the same things—priority and resource guarantees—in different ways. At work, we use the Fair Scheduler in our production clusters and are quite happy with how it helps us allocate resources to our users.

The following sections explain these three Hadoop schedulers:

- The FIFO scheduler
- The Capacity Scheduler
- The Fair Scheduler

The FIFO scheduler is primitive and is really not used much in production settings. I therefore discuss the Capacity Scheduler and the Fair Scheduler in more detail.

The FIFO Scheduler

The first-in, first-out (FIFO) scheduler uses a simple first come, first served strategy to schedule the jobs. This scheduler just places all applications into a single queue and executes them in the order the applications are submitted to YARN. Requests that come in after a previous request are satisfied only after the first request is fully satisfied. Since this is the default scheduler, it works out of the box and you don't need to make any specific configuration changes in the mapred-site.xml file.

In the FIFO scheduler, if two users submit separate jobs, and the first job needs all the cluster resources to complete its work, all tasks from the first job have to complete before the second job's tasks are executed. The FIFO scheduler, although it's the default scheduler, is really meant for use in a simple proof-of-concept or development Hadoop cluster, where you don't want to bother with the configuration steps involved in using one of the other two schedulers—the Capacity Scheduler and the Fair Scheduler.

Let's take a scenario where a data scientist runs a job that requires 200,000 maps to complete. You can get at the approximate number of map tasks for a job by dividing the total size of the data by the HDFS block size. In this case, let's say the data is about 60TB and the HDFS block size is 256MB. Dividing 60TB by 256MB will give you approximately 250,000 map tasks to process the entire data. If your cluster has a maximum capacity to run about 5,000 containers at any given time, this means that this data scientist's job will monopolize the entire cluster for a very long time (if the average completion time for a map task is 5 minutes, you can expect to take at least 4 hours to complete), and no other jobs can start in the meanwhile. Of course, if some of the waiting jobs need to meet SLAs, all hell breaks loose!

For all production servers, you should configure and use one of the other schedulers provided by Hadoop—the Capacity Scheduler and the Fair Scheduler. Both of these schedulers are quite sophisticated and allow you to control various aspects of resource allocation in a shared Hadoop cluster (which most clusters are). Both of these schedulers overcome the drawbacks of the default FIFO scheduler and enable multiple groups to share a cluster while maintaining some type of guarantees regarding the resource allocation for various users and groups. These two schedulers are the topics for our next two sections.

The Capacity Scheduler

The Capacity Scheduler is a Hadoop-provided resource scheduler that helps you allocate resources while maximizing the cluster's throughput and its utilization. Let's take a scenario where you have three different groups in your organization—sales, marketing and research. It's often the case that the three groups use the Hadoop resources in different ways. For example, the sales team might need way more resources around the holidays. Similarly, the marketing group might need vastly more processing power during the time periods when a new sales campaign runs.

A situation where you may want to consider the Capacity Scheduler is if you really know your cluster workloads and utilization patterns intimately and want to use this knowledge to allocate resources among your users. In some clusters this knowledge is easy to come by and in others not so much.

The essential concept behind the Capacity Scheduler is this: It uses dedicated queues to which you assign jobs. Each queue has a predetermined amount of resources allocated to it. However, you pay in terms of the cluster's resource utilization, since you're reserving and guaranteeing queue resource capacities.

The goal of the Capacity Scheduler is to enable multiple tenants (users) of an organization to share the resources of a Hadoop cluster in a predictable fashion. Hadoop achieves this goal by using job queues.

Clients schedule jobs by assigning them to a specific named queue, which is an ordered list of Hadoop jobs to be sequentially executed one after the other.

The scheduler provides guaranteed capacity for the job queues, while providing **elasticity** for the utilization of the cluster by the queues. Elasticity in this context means that the assignment of the resources isn't set in concrete. As the queues wend their way through the cluster, it's common for some queues to be overloaded and for some others to be relatively idle. The Capacity Scheduler realizes this and automatically transfers the unused capacity of the lightly used queues to the overloaded queues. What do you get as a result? Your cluster utilization will stay up all the time and at the same time providing a predictable completion time for critical Hadoop jobs.

Let's use a simple scenario to explain how the Capacity Scheduler functions. Let's say you have set up five job queues, with each queue being assigned 20 percent of the total capacity of the cluster for processing jobs. If Queue 1 is overloaded, the Capacity Scheduler reclaims free resources from Queues 2, 3 and 4 and assigns them to Queue 1, which needs extra resources due to the overload to meet the capacity guarantee.

The Capacity Scheduler is designed to accommodate the needs of multiple tenants in an organization that shares a Hadoop cluster, ensuring that each tenant's applications are allocated resources in a timely manner. The goal is to maximize the throughput and efficiently use the cluster's allocated resource capacities. The Capacity Scheduler enables multiple units in an organization to use a single cluster by offering each unit a **capacity guarantee**. The individual units are allowed to use any excess capacity that isn't being used by other units.

The Capacity Scheduler relies on job queues to facilitate the sharing of a cluster's resources. It guarantees minimum capacity levels for all of a cluster's job queues. If there's any unused capacity left over from a job queue, the scheduler makes the excess capacity available to queues that are overloaded, thus optimizing the usage of a cluster's resources. In addition to guaranteeing a minimum capacity for each queue, the scheduler also can specify a queue's **maximum capacity**, which is the absolute ceiling on the resources that can be allocated to a queue above and beyond its guaranteed capacity level.

The Capacity Scheduler sets stringent resource limits to ensure that no single application, user or queue (to be defined shortly) consumes a disproportionate amount of the cluster resources. It also sets limits on how many applications a single user or queue can run at a given time.

Queues and Subqueues

The Capacity Scheduler relies on the concept of a **queue** to control resource allocation in a cluster. A (job) queue is an ordered list of jobs. A queue is allocated a certain portion of your cluster's resources. When you create a queue, you allocate it a certain portion of your cluster's resources. User applications will then be submitted to this queue to access the queue's allotted resources. Here's what you need to understand regarding queues:

- You may configure soft limits as well as optional hard limits on a queue's capacity.
- Applications submitted to a queue will run in a FIFO order.
- Once the applications submitted to a queue start running, they can't be preempted, but as the tasks complete, any free resources will be assigned to queues running below the capacity allowed to them.
- If a queue isn't using all the resources allotted to it, it has excess resources that other queues in the cluster may use, thus optimizing the cluster's resource utilization.

The Capacity Scheduler supports using hierarchical queues to ensure that that an organization's (in a multitenant setup, there are multiple organizations that share the same cluster) resources are shared among its subqueues before other queues are allowed to use the free resources.

Creating the Queues

A job queue is where everything starts. You set up the queues in the capacity-scheduler .xml file, which is located by default in the /etc/hadoop/conf directory. The queue named `root` is pre-defined for you, and all queues you create will be considered child queues under this parent root queue.

Any child queue that you create will be named relative to a queue path that shows the full path of a queue's hierarchy, starting at the root queue. A top-level child queue is one that is directly underneath the root queue. Under each top-level child queue, you may create subqueues.

Use the YARN configuration property `yarn.scheduler.capacity.<queue-path>.queues` to configure the queues.

A Simple Example Showing How to Create a Queue

The following example shows you how to create a Capacity Scheduler configuration with three top-level child queues named `queue1`, `queue2` and `queue3`. Two of the child queues, `queue1` and `queue2`, also have subqueues defined under them.

```
<property>
  <name>yarn.scheduler.capacity.root.queues.root.queues</name>
  <value>queue1,queue2,queue3</value>
 </property>
<property>
  <name>yarn.scheduler.capacity.root.queues.queue1.queues</name>
   <value>queue1a,queue1b</value>
 </property>

<property>
  <name>yarn.scheduler.capacity.root.queues.queue2.queues</name>
  <value>queue2a,queue2b</value>
 </property>
```

Our configuration here creates the following queues:

- Three child queues named `queue1`, `queue2` and `queue3` under the `root` queue
- Two subqueues named `queue1a` and `queue1b` under the child queue named `queue1`
- Two subqueues named `queue2a` and `queue2b` under the child queue named `queue2`

Note how `root` is always the top queue under which all queues are created. Also, a child queue may or may not have any subqueues underneath it.

Now that you've learned how to create a queue, a natural question is "How do I map users to a queue?" You use the `yarn.scheduler.capacity.queue-mappings` property in the capacity-scheduler.xml file to map a user, a set of users or a group to a queue. The following example shows how to configure this property:

```
<property>
   <name>yarn.scheduler.capacity.queue-mappings</name>
   <value>u:user1:queue1,g:group1:queue2,u:%user:%user,u:user2:%primary_group</
value>
</property>
```

In this example, u denotes a user and g a group. The user named `user1` is mapped to `queue1` and `group1` to `queue2`. The user named `user2` is mapped to a queue with the same name as the primary group of the user in Linux. YARN evaluates the mappings in this property from left to right and uses the first valid mapping it finds.

Hierarchical Queues

In order to control resource allocation at a fine-grained level, you can also configure subqueues called **hierarchical queues** under each queue, thus allowing applications from a specific organizational unit to efficiently utilize all the resources allocated to that unit.

A queue's excess or free resources are allowed to be used by other queues only after its subqueues (called **leaf queues**) have satisfied their resource needs.

In addition to the assigned and maximum capacities for a queue, an administrator can also limit the following:

- The maximum amount of resources a specific user can use
- The number of pending tasks per queue (or per user)
- The number of active (or accepted) jobs per queue (or per user)
- Capacity guarantees and elasticity

Capacity Guarantees

The primary goal of the Capacity Scheduler is to ensure predictability in resource sharing. It seeks to achieve this predictability by providing **capacity guarantees** for the job queues you configure. Applications sent to a queue will be able to access the queue's capacity.

Each queue is allocated a portion of the cluster capacity, so a specific capacity is at the queue's disposal. You can configure both soft and hard (optional) limits on the capacity that you allocate for a queue.

Queue Elasticity

In order to fully utilize a cluster's resources, the scheduler also provides **elasticity** to the queues—a queue can always utilize resources beyond its configured capacity if there are idle resources in the cluster.

Elasticity in this context refers to the fact that the cluster can allocate resources that are more than (or less than) the original assignments, based on the availability (or non-availability) of resources in the cluster. This means that overloaded job queues can potentially use unused capacity of other queues in the cluster, thus leading to an optimal use of the cluster resources.

Of course, as the other queues ramp up and ask for their guaranteed capacity, Hadoop will reclaim the excess resources allocated to the first queue. In order to prevent a queue from using way more resources than its allocated capacity, you can set an upper bound on the elasticity of a queue, as I explain later in this section.

Elements of the Capacity Scheduler

Now that you've learned about the basic configuration elements of the Capacity Scheduler, let's explore how you actually go about setting up a scheduler in your cluster. In order to get going, you need to do two things:

- Set up the queues.
- Configure the capacity of the queues.

The queue element in the configuration file for the Capacity Scheduler (capacity-schduler.xml) is the crucial unit of scheduling in the Capacity Scheduler—everything revolves around it. So, to configure the Capacity Scheduler, you must first configure the queues. You can have multiple queues in a scheduler, and each queue has the following properties:

- A queue name and the full queue path name
- A list of the child queues and applications
- A list of users and their resource allocation limits
- The guaranteed and maximum capacities of the queue
- The state of the queue (running or stopped)
- Access controls to the queue in the form of Access Control Lists (ACLs)

You specify all of these properties in the configuration file for the scheduler named capacity-scheduler.xml, usually located in the /etc/hadoop/conf directory. The property `yarn-admin.acl` in the yarn-site.xml file governs who can update this file through the `rmadmin -refreshQueues` command.

Setting Up the Queues

Let's use a scenario to explain how to set up job queues. Let's say you have three major groups—Research, Support and Production—in your organization. Furthermore, the Research group also has two groups in it named Analytics and Data, and the Support group has two groups named Training and Services. You need to create Capacity Scheduler queues and subqueues for these groups and subgroups in order to allocate resources to them in your cluster.

The first step is to create queues for our three top-level groups, Research, Support and Production, as shown here:

```
<property>
  <name>yarn.scheduler.capacity.root.queues</name>
  <value>support,research,production</value>
  <description>The top-level queues below root.</description>
</property>
```

Each of the three top-level queues is a child of the parent queue in the cluster, which is the `root` queue—that's the reason you create the three queues as shown here with the `yarn.scheduler.capacity.root.queues` property.

The Capacity Scheduler supports **hierarchical queues**. Hierarchical queues help in making sure that resources are used by and among a group's subqueues before another group is permitted to use the first group's unused resources. Once you create the top-level queue, you must create the child-queues under each of them—in our case, for the Research and Support groups, both of which have subgroups. Here's how you configure the child queues:

```
<property>
  <name>yarn.scheduler.capacity.support.queues</name>
  <value>training,services</value>
  <description>child queues under support</description>
</property>

<property>
  <name>yarn.scheduler.capacity.research.queues</name>
  <value>analytics,data</value>
  <description>child queues under Research</description>
</property>
```

It's important to understand a bit more about how queues and child queues work with regards to the handling of applications submitted by the cluster's users. Following are the key things you need to remember regarding the queues in our example here:

- Queues can be either parent or leaf (child) queues.
- The root queue represents the cluster itself and you can't submit jobs directly to this queue.
- Two of the top-level queues—Research and Support—are also parent queues since they have leaf queues underneath them.
- You can't submit jobs directly to the parent queues.
- There are two leaf queues under both the Research and Support queues—you submit jobs only to the child queues.
- In our case, one of the queues, Production, has no leaf queue. It's considered a leaf queue of the root queue, so you can directly submit jobs to this queue.

You allocate resources to each top-level queue in terms of percentages of the total cluster capacity. Since top-level queues usually have leaf queues, you can also configure resource percentages for the leaf queues as well. The resources you guarantee to each top-level queue are shared among the leaf queues of that queue. At any given point in time, if a top-level queue is using resources below what you allocated to it, the cluster will allocate those "free" resources to other queues in the cluster.

Now that you've created the queues, it's time to configure the resource limits for those queues.

Configuring Queue Capacities

Let's say that, based on the needs of our organizational groups, you decide to allocate resources in a 6:1:3 ratio to the three groups. Percentages are kind of abstract. So, let's see what this means in real terms. If your cluster capacity is 1,000GB (represents the total memory available in the cluster), the Research group gets 600GB, the Support group gets 100GB and the Production group gets 300GB.

This means that you must configure the `yarn.scheduler.capacity.<queue-path>.capacity` parameter properties as follows:

```
yarn.scheduler.capacity.root.research.capacity = 60
yarn.scheduler.capacity.root.support.capacity = 10
yarn.scheduler.capacity.root.production.capacity = 30
```

The numbers 60, 10 and 30 represent percentages of the total capacity in your cluster. All capacities in any queue (or child queue) must always add up to 100. Note that when actually configuring these properties in the capacity.scheduler.xml file, you use the typical XML format to specify each of these properties, as in:

```
<property>
 <name> yarn.scheduler.capacity.root.research.capacity</name>
 <value>60</value>
</property>
```

You configure all the other scheduler properties I show in this section in the same format.

Recall that you can create subqueues or child queues within each queue. So, let's go ahead and assume that the Research group has two teams, Analytics and Data, and you want to allocate resources to them in a 1:4 ratio, as shown here:

```
yarn.scheduler.capacity.root.research.analytics.capacity = 20
yarn.scheduler.capacity.root.research.data.capacity = 80
```

Since the Research group has been allocated 600GB (60 percent of 1,000GB), the Analytics leaf queue will have 20 percent of the 600GB, which is 120GB, and the Data subgroups under Research will receive 80 percent of the 600GB, which is 480GB.

Similarly, the Support group has two subgroups, Training and Services. Assuming you want them to share the parent queue equally, you allocate resources to these two leaf queues in a 1:1 ratio. Here's how you create two leaf queues for the Support group:

```
yarn.scheduler.capacity.root.support.training.capacity = 50
yarn.scheduler.capacity.root.support.services.capacity = 50
```

You learned earlier that the Support group is allocated 10 percent of the total cluster capacity, which amounts to 100GB (10 percent of 1,000GB).

The Production group has no subgroups, and therefore you don't need to create any leaf queues for it. Figure 13.1 shows our simple Capacity Scheduler queues and subqueues, with their allocated resources.

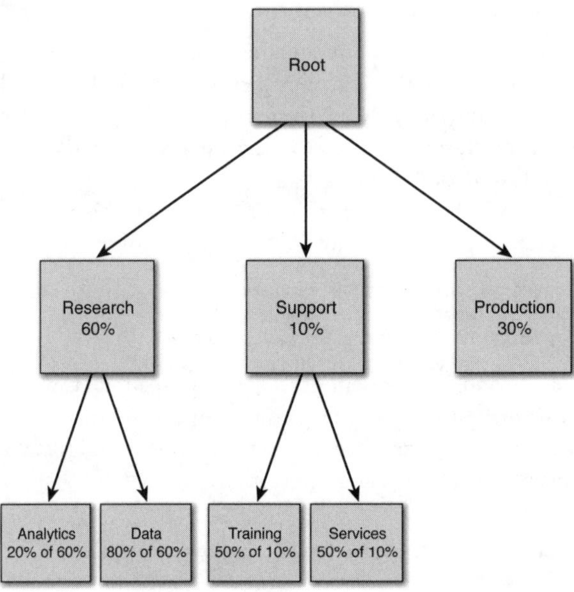

Figure 13.1 How the Capacity Scheduler queues and subqueues are set up

How the Cluster Allocates Resources

The first principle for resource allocation among the queues is that Hadoop never lets capacity sit idle—if a queue isn't using its configured capacity, other queues are handed those resources, even if means that those queues will be using resources beyond their configured capacity. This is the principle of elasticity, which I described earlier, in action.

Hadoop determines how to apportion resources among the cluster's queues based on how much of its configured capacity each queue is currently using. It allocates available resources among the queues by first allocating resources to the queues using the least amount of their configured capacity.

The lower the current used capacity of a queue, the higher the priority it gets for receiving additional resources from the cluster. Once a parent queue receives additional resources, it uses exactly the same principle by allocating those resources first to those leaf queues that are currently using the least amount of their allocated capacity.

Let's look at a scenario where there are no Research group jobs running, meaning that all of the allocated capacity of the Research group, 600GB, is free. Let's also assume that the other two top-level groups, Support and Production, are fully using their configured capacity. Two users, A and B, now submit an application each to the Analytics leaf queue, which is under the top-level queue, named Research.

Even though the Analytics group was configured for only a total of 120GB, since no jobs are running in the other leaf queue of the Analytics top-level queue (Research), the scheduler allocates 120GB to each of the two users.

This is how the principle of elasticity works—since there's excess capacity in the parent queue, the users are allowed to go beyond their configured capacity. If the Support and Production groups are idle, then the two users from the Research group can go beyond the capacity limit of their immediate parent—the Research queue—and theoretically use all of the cluster's resources.

> **Note**
>
> The most important operational element regarding the use of the Capacity Scheduler in my experience is the balancing of the concepts of capacity and elasticity. There's a built-in tradeoff between these two: If you set rigid capacity limits (through configuring maximum capacity), the queues become less elastic, thus negating one of the key goals of the Capacity Scheduler.

If more users submit jobs to the Analytics queue, they can take up all of the resources allocated to the leaf queue named Data, since no one has submitted jobs to that queue.

All of this is well and good when no one submits jobs to the Data leaf queue. What happens when someone does submit a job to this queue, since the queue's resources have been commandeered by the jobs running in the Analytics leaf queue? Well, the job must wait until containers start getting released from the running jobs in the Analytics queue. Over time, the two leaf queues will stabilize at the 1:4 resource ratio you had configured. If you don't want the user to wait to use the "guaranteed capacity" promised to the Data queue, you must enable preemption. I'll discuss the concept of preemption in more detail later in this chapter.

Limiting User Capacities

Okay, so you know how to create queues and leaf queues and how to configure capacities for them. Now it's time to talk about those all-important entities in a cluster—the users! It's users who submit jobs to the queues that you configure.

The Capacity Scheduler uses the FIFO principle (not the FIFO scheduler!), so jobs submitted earlier will be accorded a higher priority than jobs submitted later.

You can control the resources allocated to a user running jobs within a leaf queue. You can limit how much of a leaf queue capacity a user can consume with the following parameter:

```
yarn-scheduler.capacity.root.support.user-limit-factor
value: 2
```

In the example, I show how to set the maximum capacity for a specific user within the Support leaf queue. If you set the value for this parameter so it's greater than one, the user can consume resources beyond the leaf queue's capacity limit. The default value for this parameter is one, meaning a user can consume (if it's available) all of a leaf queue's configured capacity. You can set this parameter higher or lower than one. If you set it to four, the user can use up to four times the queue's configured capacity, and if you set it to 0.25, the user is limited to just a quarter of the configured capacity for the queue.

The hard limit on a user's capacity is set with the maximum-capacity (yarn-scheduler .capacity.<queue-path>.maximum-capacity) parameter. You set this parameter if you want to ensure that a user doesn't try and grab all of the parent queue's capacity. In our case, the Analytics leaf queue has 120GB out of its parent Research queue's configured capacity of 600GB. You can specify that any user submitting jobs to the Analytics leaf queue can't take up more than 50 percent of the Research queues capacity, as follows:

```
yarn-scheduler.capacity.root.research.analytics.maximum-capacity
value:50
```

Let's say you've configured a leaf queue that can take up 500GB of RAM altogether. What happens if 20 users submit jobs to this queue? Surely, you don't want to let all 20 users take up just 25GB of RAM for their containers—that would be too slow. You can configure the minimum percentage of resources allocated to a leaf queue user with the following property:

```
yarn-scheduler.capacity.root.support.services.minimum-user-limit-percent
```

If I set the value of this parameter (again, this applies to the Services leaf queue under the Support top-level group) to 20, it means that a user running applications through this queue is allocated a minimum of 20 percent of the capacity you've allocated to the Services leaf queue. The very first user that submits jobs to this leaf queue can use 100 percent of the leaf queue's resource allocation. Finally, as other users start submitting jobs to this queue, each user stabilizes at 20 percent usage of the queue—that is, five users can use the queue at any time. Other users must wait until resources are freed up by the first five users.

Limiting the Number of Applications

It's possible for a single user or queue to monopolize a cluster's resources and degrade its performance. To avoid potential excessive use of the cluster, you can limit the maximum number of applications that can be scheduled in the cluster at any given time. Use the yarn.scheduler.capacity.maximum-applications parameter to impose a ceiling on the number of applications that can be submitted through the Capacity Scheduler. The default value for this parameter is 10,000.

Once you set the maximum number of applications you can run in your cluster through the yarn.scheduler.capacity.maximum-applications parameter, you can set a limit on the apps you can run in the queues as well. Here's an example showing how to set the hard limit on the number of applications you can submit to the Research Queue:

```
<property>
  <name>yarn.scheduler.capacity.research.maximum-applications</name>
  <value>absolute-capacity * yarn.scheduler.capacity.maximum-applications</value>
</property>
```

Although you can specify a precise hard limit on the maximum number of applications that can be run at any given time with the yarn.scheduler.capacity.<queue-path> .maximum-applications parameter, you can also indirectly control the number of applications running in your cluster. You do this by setting the yarn.scheduler.capacity .maximum-am-resource-percent parameter.

As you learned in Chapter 3, "Creating and Configuring a Simple Hadoop 2 Cluster," each application in YARN needs an ApplicationMaster container. The parameter `yarn.scheduler.capacity.maximum-am-resource-percent` sets the limit on the amount of the cluster resources that can be used by all running ApplicationMasters. The default value for this parameter is 10 percent, meaning all the ApplicationMasters together can't take more than 10 percent of the cluster's resources (RAM memory allocation for the `AppMaster` container, which is the very first container created for an application).

Preempting Applications

Preempting an application means containers from other applications may need to be killed if necessary, to make room for the new applications.

If you don't want late-arriving applications to a specific leaf queue to wait because the running applications in other leaf queues are taking up all the allotted resources, you can use preemption. Under these situations, although you've "guaranteed" a set capacity for a queue, there are no free resources available to be allocated to this leaf queue. The ApplicationMaster container is killed only as a last resort, with preference being given to killing containers that haven't been executed yet.

YARN can preempt jobs in two ways:

- Minimum share preemption: When a pool is operating below its configured minimum share
- Fair share preemption: When a pool is operating below its fair share

Of these two, minimum share preemption is stricter and kicks in immediately when a pool starts operating below its minimum allocated share for a specific period, which is set by the minimum share preemption timeout parameter. Fair share preemption is far less aggressive—it kicks in only after a pool goes to below half of its fair share for a specific period (set by the fair share preemption timeout), before job preemption begins. Once preemption starts, a pool that's currently below its minimum allocated share can go up to its minimum share, whereas a pool that's now below 50 percent of its fair share will go all the way up until it hits its full fair share.

You can set several preemption-related configuration parameters in the yarn-site.xml file. By default, preemption is enabled, and you can disable it by setting the `yarn.resourcemanager.scheduler.monitor.enable` parameter to `false`. You can also set the speed of preemption—that is, the maximum percentage of resources preempted in a single round of periodic monitoring, by configuring the `yarn.resourcemanager.scheduler.monitor.capacity.preemption.total_preemption_per_round` parameter.

Now that you know how the Capacity Scheduler works, it's time to learn how to enable it and create queues for the scheduler. The following sections explain:

- Enabling the Capacity Scheduler
- Creating the job queues
- Configuring the job queues

- Modifying the queues
- Administering the queues

Enabling the Capacity Scheduler

You must configure the ResourceManager in order to enable and start using the Capacity Scheduler in your cluster. Add the following value for the `yarn.resourcemanager.scheduler.class` configuration property in the yarn-site.xml file, as shown here, to use the Capacity Scheduler:

```
<property>
<name> yarn.resourcemanager.scheduler.classs</name>    <value>org.apache.hadoop
.yarn.server.resourcemanager.scheduler.capacity.CapacityScheduler</value>
<property>
```

A Typical Capacity Scheduler

Now that you've learned how to set up queues and configure them, let's see what an actual capacity-scheduler.xml file looks like.

In the previous section, I created three resource queues for the Capacity Scheduler. However, these are very simple queues and use default values for their resource allocation, application limits and permissions. In order to use the Capacity Scheduler effectively in a production setting, you must configure a minimal set of configuration properties, as explained here.

I use the same groups and queues that I had used in our examples earlier in this chapter in the following sample capacity-scheduler.xml file.

I break up the typically long capacity-scheduler.xml file into more easily digestible chunks to explain how everything works.

1. The three configuration properties listed here specify the following, respectively:
   - Maximum ApplicationMaster (AM) resource percentage
   - The maximum number of applications
   - Who can administer the queue (the value * indicates that anyone belonging to the specified group can administer this queue)

   ```
   yarn.scheduler.capacity.maximum-am-resource-percent=0.2
   yarn.scheduler.capacity.maximum-applications=5000
   yarn.scheduler.capacity.root.acl_administer_queue=*
   ```

2. The following property configures our three parent queues of Research, Support and Production under the root queue.

   ```
   yarn.scheduler.capacity.root.queues=research,support,production
   ```

3. You allocate the Research group 60 percent of the total resources and also specify how the Research group splits its allocated resources between its component child queues, which are the Analytics and Data leaf queues.

   ```
   yarn.scheduler.capacity.root.research.capacity=60
   yarn.scheduler.capacity.root.research.maximum-capacity=100
   ```

```
yarn.scheduler.capacity.root.research.queues=Analytics,Data
yarn.scheduler.capacity.root.research.state=RUNNING
yarn.scheduler.capacity.root.research.user-limit-factor=1
yarn.scheduler.capacity.root.research.minimum-user-limit-percent=20
yarn.scheduler.capacity.root.research.Analytics.capacity=20
yarn.scheduler.capacity.root.research.analytics.maximum-capacity=100
yarn.scheduler.capacity.root.research.analytics.state=RUNNING
yarn.scheduler.capacity.root.research.analytics.user-limit-factor=1
yarn.scheduler.capacity.root.research.data.capacity=80
yarn.scheduler.capacity.root.research.data.maximum-capacity=100
yarn.scheduler.capacity.root.research.data.state=RUNNING
yarn.scheduler.capacity.root.research.data.user-limit-factor=1
```

There are several interesting things you should note regarding the configuration of the queues:

- Note how the root and the leaf queues all specify the capacity of that queue with the `yarn.scheduler.capacity.<queue-path>.capacity` property. This property sets the queue capacity in percentage terms, as in 20 (20 percent). The capacities of all queues at each level must sum to 100. Applications in a queue may consume more resources than what you configure here, providing there are free resources.
- Similarly, note how you set the maximum capacity for all queues with the `yarn.scheduler.capacity.<queue-path>.maximum.capacity` property. This property specifies the maximum capacity of the queue in percentage terms. By default, the value for this parameter is -1, meaning it's disabled (no maximum value). If there are free resources in the cluster, additional resources can be allocated to a queue until it reaches its maximum capacity.
- You use the `yarn.scheduler.capacity.<queue-path>.minimum-user-limit-percent` property to set the limit on the percentage of resources allocated to a user at any given time. The *minimum* value for the user limit is what you set with this property. The *maximum* value depends on the number of users running applications in the cluster. The default value is 100, meaning there are no user limits. For example, if you set a value of 25 for this parameter, when two users submit their applications to this queue, each of the users is limited to 50 percent of the queue's allotted resources. When a third user submits an application to the queue, all three users are limited to 33 percent of the queue's resources.

4. The following set of properties show how to allocate the Support group 10 percent of the total resources and also specify how this group splits its allocated resources between its component child queues, which are the Training and Services leaf queues.

```
yarn.scheduler.capacity.root.support.capacity=10
yarn.scheduler.capacity.root.support.maximum-capacity=100
yarn.scheduler.capacity.root.support.queues=training, services
yarn.scheduler.capacity.root.support.state=RUNNING
yarn.scheduler.capacity.root.support.user-limit-factor=1
yarn.scheduler.capacity.root.support.training.capacity=20
yarn.scheduler.capacity.root.support.training.maximum-capacity=100
yarn.scheduler.capacity.root.support.training.state=RUNNING
```

```
yarn.scheduler.capacity.root.support.training.user-limit-factor=1
yarn.scheduler.capacity.root.support.services.capacity=80
yarn.scheduler.capacity.root.support.services.maximum-capacity=100
yarn.scheduler.capacity.root.support.Data.state=RUNNING
yarn.scheduler.capacity.root.support.Data.user-limit-factor=1
```

5. The following set of properties shows how to allocate the Production group the remaining 30 percent of the cluster resources. Since the Production group has no leaf queues, it doesn't have to split its allotted resources among subgroups.

```
yarn.scheduler.capacity.root.production.capacity=30
yarn.scheduler.capacity.root.production.maximum-capacity=30
yarn.scheduler.capacity.root.production.state=RUNNING
yarn.scheduler.capacity.root.production.user-limit-factor=1
```

Note that the Production group can't go beyond 30 percent of the cluster resources ever, since it runs long-running data-science-related Production jobs.

Although I didn't show them in our example capacity-scheduler.xml file, you can set a limit on the number of applications with the `yarn.scheduler.capacity.maximum-applications` property. This property specifies a hard limit on the number of applications that can be active (in the running or pending state) in a cluster. Note that this parameter sets the limit on the total number of applications you can submit to the cluster. You can override this at the queue level by setting the `yarn.scheduler.capacity.<queue-path>.maximum-applications` parameter.

There's always a default queue when you use the Capacity Scheduler. Any application that doesn't specify a queue goes into the default queue. You can use the default queue for running ad-hoc jobs that anybody in your cluster can run, and these jobs can be preempted to make room for the more important queues that you've configured, which may be subject to strict SLAs. This is a good way to handle excess capacity in your cluster.

Modifying the Queue Configuration

Whenever you modify the capacity-scheduler.xml file, you must let the ResourceManager know about the changes you made, by running the `yarn` command `rmadmin -refreshQueues`, as shown here:

```
$ $HADOOP_YARN_HOME/bin/yarn rmadmin -refreshQueues
```

Administering the Queues

You can stop and start queues at any time at the root, parent and leaf queue levels. If you stop the root or the parent queue, the leaf queues becomes inactive, though technically they're in the running state.

There are two formal queue states: `RUNNING` and `STOPPPED`. By setting the `yarn.scheduler.capacity.root.support.queue` property in the capacity-scheduler.xml file to the value `STOPPED` or `RUNNING`, for example, you can stop and start the Support leaf queue that we discussed in our examples.

If you stop a queue while it's running, the currently running applications are allowed to complete and no new apps can be submitted to this queue. You can restart the queue by setting the `yarn.scheduler.capacity.root.support.queue` property to `RUNNING`.

As with any configuration change you make to the capacity-scheduler.xml file, you must enable the change by running the following command:

```
$ yarn rmadmin -refreshQueues
```

You can configure Capacity Scheduler queue administrators to perform queue management actions such as submitting apps to a queue, killing applications, stopping queues and viewing queue information. You can configure the administrators by setting the `yarn.scheduler.capacity.root<queue-path>.acl_administer_queue` configuration parameter.

For example, you can control queue administrators for the Support group as follows:

```
<property>
  <name> yarn.scheduler.capacity.root.support.acl_administer_queue</name>
  <value>support-group</value>
</property>
```

This means that members of the support-group can administer the Support queue.

You can also control who can submit jobs to a queue with similar ACLs. For example, the following property limits access to the Support queue to the users sam and nina and any members of the support-group only:

```
<property>
  <name> yarn.scheduler.capacity.root.support.acl_submit_applications</name>
  <value>sam,nina,support-group</value>
</property>
```

The `yarn.scheduler.capacity.<queue-path>.acl-submit-applications` property shown in this example specifies the ACL that controls which user can submit an application to a queue. If you don't specify a value, the ACL is derived from the parent queue in the hierarchy. The default value is * for the root queue, which means any user.

Regular users are prevented from viewing or modifying the applications submitted by other users. As an administrator, you can do the following with regards to queues and jobs:

- Change the definition and properties of queues at run time
- Stop a queue to prevent new applications from being submitted
- Start a stopped queue backup

> **Tip**
>
> Even when you stop a queue, already running applications in that queue will keep running until they finish.

You can monitor the status and settings of the Capacity Scheduler queues through the Scheduler page in the ResourceManager web UI's Applications page. The Scheduler button is on the left, at the very end of the menu.

Now that you've learned how to use the Capacity Scheduler, it's time to learn about the other major Hadoop resource scheduler—the Fair Scheduler.

The Fair Scheduler

You can use the Fair Scheduler instead of the Capacity Scheduler, described in the previous section, to control how Hadoop allocates your cluster's resources. The Fair Scheduler is a built-in Hadoop resource scheduler whose goal is to let smaller jobs finish fast (short response times) and provide a guaranteed service level for production jobs.

Let's take an example from a typical medium-to-large-size Hadoop cluster, say with 500-600 nodes and 4,000-5,000 jobs running daily and about 50-100 users. You typically run various types of data-science-related applications such as statistical reports, optimization, spam detection and so on.

The jobs aren't usually of the same type—some are production jobs that involve data imports and hourly reports. Some other jobs are run by the data analysts who are running ad-hoc Hive queries and Pig jobs. Usually there are some long-running data analyses or machine learning jobs running at the same time. The question before you as a Hadoop administrator is how to allocate the resources of the cluster in an efficient manner among these competing jobs.

The essential idea behind the Fair Scheduler is this: You don't need to reserve a predefined amount of capacity to groups or queues. The scheduler dynamically distributes the available resources among all the running jobs in a cluster. When a large job starts first, and it happens to be the only job running, it starts using all the cluster's resources by default (unless you specify maximum resource limits). Subsequently, when a second job starts up, it is allocated roughly half of the total cluster resources (by default)—now both jobs share the cluster resources on an equal basis. This is the concept of "fairness" that led to naming this scheduler the *Fair* Scheduler.

The Fair Scheduler ensures that resource allocation for applications is "fair," meaning that all applications get roughly equal amounts of resources over time. When we talk about resources in the context of the Fair Scheduler, I'm referring to memory only. However, you can also employ a variation of the Fair Scheduler called the **Dominant Resource Fairness** (**DRF**) scheduler, which uses both memory and CPU as resources. Dominant Resource Fairness is a concept wherein the YARN schedulers examine each user's dominant (defined as the higher proportion of resource usage in the cluster when compared to the resource usage of all other users) resource and use it as a measure of the resource usage by that user.

> **Note**
>
> By default, DRF isn't used by YARN, and only memory resources are considered, with CPU being totally ignored. You can enable DRF for the Fair Scheduler by setting the element `defaultQueueSchedulingPolicy` to `drf` in the fair-scheduler.xml file. To do the same with the Capacity Scheduler, you set the value of the element `yarn.scheduler.capacity.resource-calculator` to `org.apache.hadoop.yarn.util.resource.DominantResourceCalculator` in the capacity-scheduler.xml file.

The goal of the Fair Scheduler is to allow short interactive jobs to coexist with long-running jobs. It also attempts to allocate resources proportionally to users and ensure that the cluster is effectively used. Fairness in this context means that resources are allocated to queues that are most underserved—the scheduler always tries to allocate containers to queues with the fewest resources allocated. You can assign weights to the queues to determine which application gets what proportion of the cluster resources.

The Fair Scheduler allocates all the cluster resources to an application when that application is the only one running. As new applications are started up, resources are taken from the first application and allocated to the newer apps, so that eventually all applications are using about the same proportion of a cluster's resources. However, "fair" in this context doesn't mean that all queues are accorded equal importance—usually you configure weights for various queues, to denote priorities.

By default, the Fair Scheduler allows all applications to run. You can, however, limit the number of running applications on a per-user or per-queue basis. You do this to limit the stress on the system when a user submits a large number of applications at once.

When you restrict the number of applications a user can submit, the additional applications that users submitted will wait in the queue until some of the earlier apps submitted by the same user finish.

The Fair Scheduler can use different scheduling policies. The default scheduling policy is fair sharing, using just memory as a resource. There's also a FIFO policy that isn't used much. It's quite common to use the third type of scheduling policy, DRF, which allocates both memory and CPU resources to applications.

Under fair sharing, you can also prioritize applications by assigning weights that determine the fraction of the cluster resources that applications are assigned. A queue with a higher weight will receive greater attention compared to a queue with a lesser weight.

By default, all queues have a weight of 1. You can assign different weights to allow a queue to get more resources than others. For example, by setting a queue's weight to four, you specify that the queue receives roughly four times the resources of all queues that have a weight of one, the default value for all queues.

Queues

Queues enable the scheduler to allocate resources. All cluster users are assigned to a queue named "default." You can arrange queues in hierarchies and also configure them with weights in order to fine-tune resource allocation in a cluster.

In order to ensure that specific users or applications always get the resources they need, the Fair Scheduler lets you assign guaranteed minimum shares to queues.

An application or user is always guaranteed a minimum share, but the scheduler ensures that queues don't sit idle with unused resources. When any of the queues that are assigned guaranteed resources turn out to have surplus resources because the queues aren't running applications, the cluster assigns the surplus resources to other applications.

Applications are submitted to a specific queue, with each user getting their own queue by default. You can also create custom queues to guarantee minimum resources and set weights for each queue to set the priority.

The Fair Scheduler relies on resource queues or pools that are built in a hierarchical fashion. All queues descend from the same ancestor named the **root** queue. The descendent queues are called **leaf** queues, on which the actual applications are scheduled. Leaf queues can have more levels of child queues of their own.

You define queues in the fair.scheduler.xml file (also called the **allocation file**) and name them with the parent queue at the beginning of the queue name, as in `root.queue1`, `root.parent1.queue2`, for example. It's understood that you can leave off the `root` part of a queue name when referring to it. Hadoop distributes the cluster resources among the root queue's children in a fair manner.

Configuring the Fair Scheduler

You enable the Fair Scheduler in your cluster by specifying the configuration parameter `yarn.resourcemanager.scheduler.class` in the yarn-site.xml file as follows:

```
<property>
<name>yarn.resourcemanager.scheduler.class</name>
<value>org.apache.hadoop.yarn.server.resourcemanager.scheduler.fair
.FairScheduler</value>
</property>
```

Also in the yarn-site.xml file, specify the location of the allocation file (fair-scheduler.xml) for the Fair Scheduler, as shown here:

```
<property>
<name>yarn.scheduler.fair.allocation.file</name>
<value>/etc/hadoop/conf/fair-scheduler.xml</value>
</property>
```

You configure the Fair Scheduler itself by setting scheduler-related configuration properties in the yarn-site.xml file. In addition, you create an allocation file for the scheduler, usually named fair-scheduler.xml, for specifying how the scheduler allocates resources by configuring properties pertaining to users and their queues, weights and capacities.

Hadoop automatically reloads the fair-scheduler.xml file every ten seconds, so any changes you make to the Fair Scheduler configuration are made effective almost immediately. There's no need to run the `yarn rmadmin` command as is the case when you modify the configuration for the Capacity Scheduler.

Configuring the Scheduler in the yarn-site.xml file

As mentioned earlier, you use the yarn-site.xml file to configure the Fair Scheduler. Here's how to configure YARN to use the Fair Scheduler as its resource scheduler:

```
<property>
   <name>yarn.resourcemanager.scheduler.class</name>
   <value>org.apache.hadoop.yarn.server.resourcemanager.scheduler.fair
.FairScheduler</value>
</property>
```

By default, the property yarn.scheduler.fair.user-as-default-queue is set to the value true, which means that if a specific queue name isn't specified during job submission, the name of the user submitting the job is treated as the queue name. If you set this parameter to false, all jobs submitted to your cluster will share the default queue, which, not surprisingly, is named "default."

Also by default, the yarn.scheduler.fair.preemption property is set to the value false, meaning that by default, there's no preemption of applications.

An important property that you need to remember in this context is yarn.scheduler.fair.allow-undeclared-pools. If you set this property to true, new queues can be created at the time applications are submitted. This could be due to the submitter requesting a new queue, or because of the user-as-default-queue property. If you set the property to false (default value), applications can't create new queues on the fly at the time they're submitted.

Now that you've configured the yarn-site.xml file for the Fair Scheduler, let's learn how to configure the Fair Scheduler queues by specifying various configuration properties in the fair-scheduler.xml file.

Configuring the Queues in the fair.scheduler.xml File

The fair-scheduler.xml file consists of various types of elements, such as the queue, user and queuePlacementPolicy elements. You can specify values for various queue, user and scheduling policy related elements in the fairscheduler.xml file.

> **Note**
>
> The user element determines how the individual users can behave, and there's only a single property named maxRunningApps that you can configure under this element.

The userMaxAppsDefault element specifies the default maximum number of running applications for a user if you don't explicitly specify a limit yourself. You can control the maximum number of applications that a queue can run by setting the limit with the queueMaxAppsDefault element.

By default, the Fair Scheduler uses the "fair" scheduling policy to allocate resources in a fair manner across queues and applications. You can configure one of the two alternative scheduling policies, fifo or drf, at the cluster level by setting the defaultQueueSchedulingPolicy element. You can override this cluster-level setting by setting the schedulerPolicy element as shown here:

```
<property>
  <name>schedulerPolicy</name>
  <value>drf</value>
</property>
```

The schedulingPolicy element determines the scheduling policy of the queue. As discussed earlier, you can choose among the fifo, fair and drf (dominant resource fairness) scheduling policies.

In the preceding, I replaced the default fair scheduling policy with the drf scheduling policy.

> **Tip**
>
> It's quite important to remember that the minimum and maximum amounts of memory and virtual cores you can configure for a pool override any weight settings you specify. It doesn't really matter if a queue has a higher weight than other queues if you've limited its maximum resources. In order for an application to get disproportionally more resources than another queue, it must have both a higher weight *and* a higher `minResources` or `maxResources` setting.

How Jobs Are Placed into Queues

Under the Fair Scheduler, applications can run on the basis of any of the following:

- The user submitting the application
- The group of the submitting user
- A specific pool
- The default pool

> **Note**
>
> Remember that a pool and a queue are synonyms when we are dealing with the Fair Scheduler.

Rules help you place applications in pools based on the runtime configuration of the application or the name of the user running the application. For example, to submit a YARN application to a specific pool, a user can specify the `mapreduce.job.queuename` property.

As an administrator, you can configure policies to automatically place applications in specific queues. The `defaultQueueSchedulingPolicy` element lists rules that dictate how applications are placed into queues. All rules accept a "create" argument that defaults to true, meaning the rule can create a new queue. Here are the valid rules you may specify:

- `specified`: The application is placed in the queue it requests.
- `user`: The application is placed in the queue that has the same name as the user who submits the application. This queue is under the root queue.
- `nestedUserQueue`: The application is placed in a queue with the name of the user under a queue suggested by the nested rule. While under the `user` rule a user queue can be created only under the root queue, the `nestedUserQueue` rule allows the creation of the user queue under any parent queue.
- `primaryGroup`: The application is placed in the queue named after the primary group (Linux or UNIX) of the user submitting the application.
- `secondaryGroupExistingQueue`: The application is placed in a queue named after the secondary group of the user submitting the application.
- `default`: The application is placed in the queue specified by the default rule's `"queue"` attribute. If a `"queue"` attribute wasn't specified, the application is placed in the `root.default` queue.
- `reject`: The application is rejected when none of the rules apply.

The scheduler evaluates the rules you specify in the fair-scheduler.xml file in the order in which you specify them to determine which pool an application should run in. If a rule is satisfied, it doesn't evaluate any subsequent rules.

Note that there's always a `root.default` queue. By placing applications in the default queue, you can ensure that they're sharing resources on a fair basis. This means that resources are shared fairly among the applications and not the users. You can configure the applications to run the `root.default` queue in two different ways. You can set the following property in the fair-scheduler.xml file:

```
<queuePlacementPolicy>
   <rule name="default"/>
</queuePlacementPolicy>
```

Alternatively, you can just set the `yarn.scheduler.fair.user-as-default-queue` property to the value `false` in the yarn-site.xml file, to make the applications run in the `default.root` queue rather than in a queue named after the user, such as `root.sam.queue`.

Configuring the Scheduling Policy

You can configure policies that place an application you submit into an appropriate queue, based on your username and group, as well as the queue requested by the application. Scheduling policies use rules to sequentially evaluate and place a new application into a queue.

In the fair.scheduler.xml file, you can set the following values for the scheduling policies for a queue:

- `fifo`: First-in, first-out is a policy that gives preference to applications that start before others. Applications starting later are granted resources only if the applications that started before them have surplus resources.
- `fair`: The fair Share policy is the default.
- `drf`: Dominant resource fairness is another option.

Although I said that you can specify one of the three values listed here, in reality, you can use any class that extends `org.apache.hadoop.yarn.server.resourcemanager.scheduler.fair.SchedulingPolicy`.

Application Preemption in the Fair Scheduler

You can configure task preemption to ensure that key jobs are processed on time. However, preemption isn't arbitrary—it's used to kill containers for queues that are using more than their fair share of resources.

If you enable preemption in your cluster, the Fair Scheduler will preempt applications in other queues if a queue's minimum share isn't met for some period of time.

Preemption ensures that your key production jobs aren't delayed because other less important jobs are already running in the cluster. The Fair Scheduler kills the most recently launched applications to minimize the waste of resources in the cluster. To enable preemption, set the yarn.scheduler.fair.preemption property to true in the yarn-site.xml file.

Security and Resource Pools

You can set up authorization controls for resource pools so only specific users (and groups) can submit jobs to a specific pool. Use the <aclSubmitApps> element to specify who can submit jobs to a queue.

When users attempt to submit jobs to a resource pool for which they aren't authorized, you'll see the following message in the audit log:

```
2016-01-20 19:48:24 INFO USER=sam IP=192.168.56 OPERATION=Submit Application Request
  TARGET=ClientRMService RESULT=SUCCESS APPID=application_1437386054526_0004
2015-10-20 19:48:24 WARN USER=sam OPERATION=Application Finished - Failed
  TARGET=RMAppManager RESULT=FAILURE  DESCRIPTION=App failed with state: FAILED
  PERMISSIONS=User sam cannot submit applications to queue root.prod
  APPID=application_1437386054526_0004
```

The aclSubmtApps element lets you list the users and/or groups that can submit applications to a queue, thus enabling you to secure your resource pools.

A Sample fair-scheduler.xml File

I fully understand if you're a bit overwhelmed and confused at this point! In reality, though, the fair-scheduler.xml file isn't hard to configure at all, as the following example shows.

```
<?xml version="1.0"?>
<allocations>
  <queue name="top_user_queue">
    <minResources>204800 mb,120 vcores</minResources>
    <maxResources></maxResources>
    <maxRunningApps>50</maxRunningApps>
    <weight>4.0</weight>
    <minSharePreemptionTimeout>180</minSharePreemptionTimeout>
    <schedulingPolicy>drf</schedulingPolicy>
    <aclSubmitApps>*</aclSubmitApps>
    <aclAdministerApps>*</aclAdministerApps>
   </queue
<queue name="random_user_queue">
    <maxResources>327680 mb, 600 vcores</maxResources>
    <maxRunningApps>2</maxRunningApps>
    <weight>1.0</weight>
    <schedulingPolicy>fifo</schedulingPolicy>
    <aclSubmitApps>admin</aclSubmitApps>
    <aclAdministerApps>admin</aclAdministerApps>
 </queue>
  <queuePlacementPolicy>
        <rule name="specified" create="false"/>
        <rule name="user" create="false"/>
        <rule name="default" create="true"/>
    </queuePlacementPolicy>
</allocations>
```

Here's an analysis of our fair-scheduler.xml file:

- `top_user_queue`: This queue is named `root.top_user_queue` and is based on the username `top_user`, which I specified with the `queue_name` property. For this queue, I've set up the following:
  - `minResources`: This property specifies the minimum resources the queue can use, in terms of memory and virtual cores. However, the actual minimum share is determined by the specific scheduler policy you choose to use. Assuming you chose the single-resource fairness policy (memory-based), if the memory usage of the queue is below its memory share, it's considered unsatisfied. If more than one queue has yet to meet its minimum share, the ResourceManager allocates resources to the queue with the smallest ratio between its current resource usage and its minimum. The scheduler first allocates minimum resources to all queues before it offers additional resources to queues. If there isn't enough memory available in the cluster to satisfy the `minResources` setting for a queue, that queue can't launch an application—its attempt to do so will fail. When there are no applications running under this queue, the scheduler doesn't allocate or reserve any resources for the queue. However, the moment an application is started under this queue, the scheduler will provide the minimum resources (200GB and 100 virtual cores in our example) to this queue.
  - `maxResources`: This queue has no maximum—so, it can potentially use all of a cluster's resources if there are no other queues running in the cluster. Otherwise, you can set the `maxResources` attribute to limit the maximum resources a queue is allowed to use (virtual cores and memory for containers) in terms of containers allocated to the queue. This property sets the maximum limit on the number of containers allocated to a queue.
  - `maxRunningApps`: This property sets a ceiling on the number of applications that can run simultaneously under a queue.
  - `weight`: This attribute enables you to allocate more resources to a specific queue in comparison with the other queues. This makes it possible for you to specify non-proportional sharing of the cluster resources by the various queues that you configure. The default weight is 1, and therefore, a queue with a weight of four will receive four times as many resources as a queue for which you specify no weights. In this case, a value of four indicates higher priority than other queues that are at the default weight of one.
  - `minSharePremptionTimeout`: the amount of time (in seconds) a queue can remain below its minimum share before it takes resources from other queues by preempting application containers. In our example, we set the timeout to three minutes (180 seconds)

> **Note**
>
> The `minResources`, `maxResources` and `weight` elements let you allocate resources across the pools.

    - `schedulingPolicy`: This is set to `drf`.
    - `aclSubmitApps` and `aclAministerApps`: Anyone can submit apps or perform administrative tasks for this queue.
- `random_user_queue`: This queue is named `root.random_user_queue` and is configured as follows:
    - `minResources`: None.
    - `maxResources`: 320GB RAM and 600 virtual cores.
    - `weight`: One.
    - `schedulingPolicy`: `fifo`.
    - `aclSubmitApps` and `aclAministerApps`: Only the admin user can submit apps or perform administrative tasks for this queue.
- `queuePlacementPolicy`: There are three rules: `specified`, `user` and `default`. The first rule is evaluated, but since neither `top_user` nor `random_user` specify the pool when submitting their applications, the second rule (`user`) is evaluated. This rule says to use the `root.<username>` pool, but only if it exists (`create=false`). Both `top_user` and `random_user` have queues named after them (`root.top_user` and `root.random_user`), so this rule is satisfied for both. The third rule, which states that the application should run in the default pool, is ignored (not evaluated).

Submitting Jobs to the Scheduler

Once you configure the Fair Scheduler for the first time, restart the ResourceManager as shown here:

```
$ service hadoop-yarn-resourcemanager restart
```

You can now test drive your new resource scheduler by submitting a job to the `random_user_queue` that you just configured:

```
$ hadoop jar /usr/lib/hadoop-mapreduce/hadoop-mapreduce-examples.jar
wordcount -D mapreduce.job.queue_name=random_user_queue /input /output/
```

Moving Applications between Queues

An administrator can move an actively running application to a higher or lower priority queue by issuing the following `yarn` command:

```
$ yarn application -movetoqueue appID -queue targetQueueName
```

Monitoring the Fair Scheduler

As with the Capacity Scheduler, use the ResourceManager web UI at `http://<URL-for ResourceManager>/cluster/scheduler` to view queues and other information pertaining to the Fair Scheduler. You can see the following from this UI:

- Total resource allocation to containers within a queue
- Number of active applications in a queue

- Number of pending applications waiting to receive containers
- Minimum and maximum guaranteed resources configured for the queues
- Instantaneous and steady fair shares

Comparing the Capacity Scheduler and the Fair Scheduler

The Capacity Scheduler and the Fair Scheduler have some crucial differences, but also many similarities. I list the key similarities and differences in this section.

Similarities between the Two Schedulers

Both the Fair Scheduler and the Capacity Scheduler have an identical goal: Allow long-running jobs to complete in a decent time while simultaneously enabling users running queries to get their results back quickly. That is, we're talking about supporting the coexistence of batch and short-lived jobs.

The two schedulers have several things in common, and I list the major similarities here:

- Both schedulers support hierarchical queues.
- All queues descend from a root or default queue.
- You can submit applications only to the leaf queues.
- Both queues support minimum and maximum capacities.
- Both queues support maximum application limits on a per-queue basis.
- Both schedulers let you move applications across queues.

Differences between the Two Schedulers

Although there are many similarities between the Capacity Scheduler and the Fair Scheduler, there are important differences as well, as summarized here.

- The Fair Scheduler contains scheduling policies that determine which jobs get resources each time the scheduler allocates resources. You can use the three types of scheduling policies—`fifo`, `fair` (the default scheduling policy) and `drf`—by specifying the policy with the `defaultQueueSchedulingPolicy` top-level element. The Capacity Scheduler, on the other hand, always schedules jobs within each queue with the FIFO principle.
- The Fair Scheduler enables multiple queue placement policies, which dictate where the scheduler places new applications among the queues based on users, groups or the queue requests made by applications. You can submit applications to a non-existent queue by setting the `create` flag, which creates a new queue.
- The Capacity Scheduler chooses jobs with the highest gap between currently used and granted capacity—that is, the most underserved queues are offered resources

before other queues. The Fair Scheduler, on the other hand, selects jobs on the basis of the highest time deficit.

- The Fair Scheduler allocates excess capacity among jobs, whereas the Capacity Scheduler allocates the excess capacity among the cluster's tenants.
- The Fair Scheduler uses preemption to support fairness among the queues and assigns priorities to users through weights. The Capacity Scheduler, on the other hand, uses preemption to return guaranteed capacity back to the queues.

Summary

Here's what you learned in this chapter:

- Allocating cluster resources efficiently among the cluster's tenants is a key task for Hadoop administrators.
- Leave the FIFO scheduler alone, as it isn't designed for supporting real-life production environments.
- The Fair Scheduler and the Capacity Scheduler are the two main Hadoop resource schedulers. While there are some differences between the two schedulers, both of them strive to optimally allocate the cluster resources among multiple users.
- It's always a good idea to create queues and pools and assign users to these entities. You can then assign jobs to the queues and pools, rather than assigning jobs directly to users.
- At a practical level, there are more similarities than differences between the Capacity Scheduler and the Fair Scheduler. Either one will work fine for most environments, although you can use the Capacity Scheduler where you really are familiar with the resource requirements of your user groups.

14

Working with Oozie to Manage Job Workflows

This chapter covers the following:

- Setting up Apache Oozie
- Understanding Oozie job flows
- Creating and configuring Oozie workflows
- Creating time-based and data-based Oozie coordinators

Managing Hadoop job scheduling is probably one of the most important, if not *the* most important, tasks of a Hadoop administrator. Apache Oozie is a general-purpose job orchestration and workflow scheduling system for running multistage Hadoop jobs (MapReduce, Pig, Hive, etc.).

In order to efficiently analyze the vast quantities of data sets you store in HDFS, you will need to perform multiple actions sequentially, in the form of a workflow. You can write your own job scripts, of course, but it's far better to use Oozie, a workflow engine and job scheduler that's been designed expressly for use with Hadoop jobs.

Instead of you having to run the various stages of a multistage Hadoop job separately, Oozie lets you run the chained jobs as part of a single Oozie job, which makes the starting, stopping, pausing and resuming of job flows much easier.

Oozie lets you either run a workflow by itself or schedule it through an Oozie coordinator job. You can also set job SLAs as part of an Oozie workflow or coordinator application.

Using Apache Oozie to Schedule Jobs

Apache Oozie is a workflow engine and scheduler built explicitly for Hadoop environments. Oozie is especially designed to perform large-scale job orchestrations. It's much more sophisticated and has numerous capabilities for job execution and management when compared to a mere job scheduler.

Apache Oozie offers a command line utility named `oozie` to help you execute and manage jobs in your cluster. The `oozie` command line interface is very powerful and lets you create and administer complex job schedules.

Oozie lets you run one-off jobs manually, in the form a workflow, or schedule the execution of one or more arbitrarily complex workflows through Oozie **coordinator jobs**. Coordinator jobs can be triggered either by frequency (time-based) or by the availability of necessary input data (data-based).

Oozie is a great tool for job scheduling in a Hadoop environment since it supports just about any type of Hadoop job you want to run, out of the box. These jobs include Spark, MapReduce, Pig, Hive, Sqoop and DistCp. Not only that, Oozie lets you run system-based jobs such as Java programs and regular shell scripts. Oozie also helps you set SLAs for your jobs, monitor running jobs and receive alerts when a job flow exceeds the SLA limits.

In the Hadoop environment, it's often the case that you can't completely process a set of data with just a single MapReduce, Hive or Pig job. It's more likely that you'd need to run multiple MapReduce, Hive and Pig jobs together, with later jobs consuming the intermediate data produced by the initial jobs. You thus need to string together multiple MapReduce, Hive or Pig jobs and coordinate their execution.

You can write complex shell scripts or other server-based solutions to put together a job stream, but there are several problems with this approach. Tracking the job errors and recovering from failures are two major issues resulting from this approach, as well as efficiently monitoring the progress of all the jobs. These mechanisms also usually don't allow you to troubleshoot running jobs, and they can't support thousands of concurrent jobs either.

An **Oozie workflow** is an application that consists of a set of actions arranged in a directed acyclic graph (DAG). A DAG-based workflow won't permit loops within the workflow. An Oozie workflow has two types of nodes, **control nodes** and **action nodes**, as explained here:

- The control nodes determine the execution flow of actions, and are named **start**, **end**, **fork**, **join**, **decision**, and **kill**. The start and end control nodes define when the workflows starts and ends. The fork and join control nodes let Oozie execute the work in parallel. The decision nodes act like a switch or case statement, in that they select a specific execution path within a workflow, based on information from the job.
- The action nodes perform the actual work, such as copying HDFS files, and include MapReduce, Streaming, Java, Pig, Hive, Spark and Sqoop imports and exports; and Shell, SSH and DistCp actions.

Oozie workflows enable great flexibility in job creation. They let you define condition-based decisions and let you specify alternate paths (with forked actions) for parallel execution of commands.

Let's take a common scenario in a real-life Hadoop cluster that illustrates how condition-based decision making and forked paths of parallel execution give you the flexibility you need when creating complex data-analysis jobs.

You run a Pig job first to analyze some data in a pipeline. The Pig job execution is followed by a decision tree. The control flow for the job could go straight to an HDFS operation such as a file copy operation, or it may go to a fork action, depending on the output of the Pig job. If the control flow passes to the fork action instead of going straight to the HDFS operation, two jobs are run concurrently—a Hive query and a MapReduce job. Once these two jobs complete, the control flow goes to the HDFS operation, and once this operation completes, the workflow is deemed to be successfully completed.

In order to successfully string multiple jobs together, you need a **job coordinator**, and that's where Oozie shines big time. There are three types of Oozie jobs:

- Workflow job: This is an Oozie job (an application) you run on demand.
- Coordinator job: This an Oozie job that you schedule for periodic execution, similar to jobs run by a Linux `crontab`.
- Bundle job: This is a collection of coordinator jobs managed as a single Oozie job.

Oozie can help you schedule and launch tens of thousands of Hadoop jobs daily. Oozie job bundles help you efficiently chain together hundreds of coordinators and workflows. For example, Yahoo's Oozie team runs an Oozie bundle that consists of over 200 coordinators and a workflow with 85 fork/join pairs.

While Oozie isn't the only Hadoop-related job scheduler out there (there are others, such as Azkaban and Luigi), it's the most feature rich scheduling tool available by far. In addition, Hue and Oozie are integrated extremely well, which means you can configure, schedule and monitor all your Hadoop jobs from a web UI.

Oozie Architecture

An Oozie environment consists of the following components:

- The Oozie server
- The Oozie client
- The Oozie web service
- The relational database to store the Oozie metadata (can be Derby, MySQL, PostgreSQL, Oracle, etc.)

In the following sections, let's learn about these important components.

The Oozie Server

The Oozie server schedules Oozie jobs and executes them. While it acts as a server for Oozie clients, the Oozie server itself is a Hadoop client. You can configure the server with a web UI for monitoring Oozie jobs by adding a JavaScript library called extJS. You can install the Oozie server on any node in the cluster, but when dealing with a large and busy system, it's better to install it on a dedicated server.

> **Note**
>
> The Oozie server can be accessed at http://<OOZIE_HOSTNAME>:11000/oozie.

The Oozie server should use the same release Hadoop JAR files as those used by the Hadoop services in your cluster. In addition, you must configure the cluster's hdfs-site .xml file to allow the Oozie service user, which is typically an OS user named oozie, to serve as a proxy user for the Hadoop services.

The Oozie Client

Oozie clients, users and applications can connect to the Oozie server using one of the following methods, as long as the client application has network access to the Oozie web service:

- The `oozie` command line interface (CLI)
- The Oozie HTTP REST API that enables you to write client applications in multiple languages
- The Oozie Java client API that you can use in any Java-based application

Both the command line interface `oozie` and the Oozie Java API rely on the Oozie HTTP REST API to communicate with the Oozie server.

In addition to the previously listed options for interacting with the Oozie server, you can also use the Oozie web console to get a read-only view of the current status of the Oozie server. You can't do much else from this simple console, but you can monitor your Oozie jobs from there if you wish.

Finally, I would be remiss if I didn't mention the Hue interface, which is a popular way of working with Oozie. Hue's Oozie editor and dashboard are excellent, both for creating Oozie jobs and scheduling them, as well as for monitoring their status. A big benefit is that the Oozie editor lets you avoid having to manually configure the Oozie XML files.

The Oozie Database

As I mentioned earlier, as far as the Oozie database goes, you can select any relational database, such as Derby, PostgreSQL, MySQL or Oracle. Oozie comes with both the required JAR file and the configuration for the default Derby database, and you are expected to modify these in order for Oozie to work with other databases.

The Oozie server, which is a Java web application, runs on the Apache Tomcat web server by default. The Oozie server is stateless, and that means it doesn't store any user or job information between requests. It stores the state information relating to running and completed jobs in the Derby database by default. Using a relational database to store

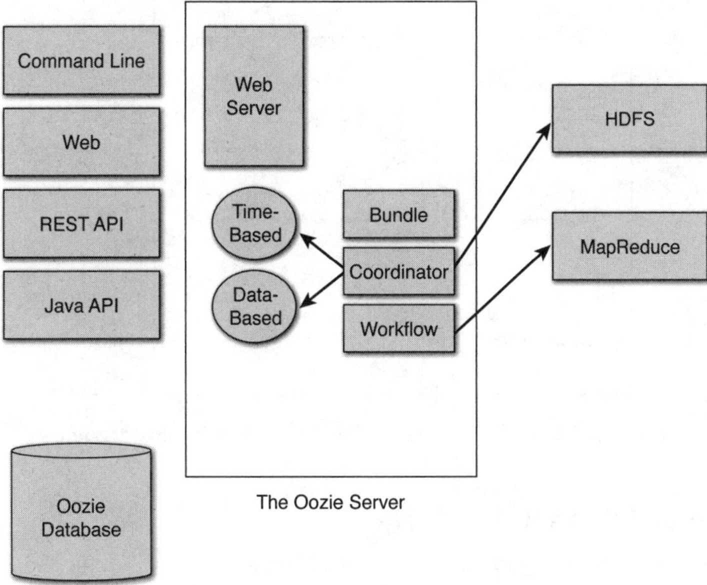

Figure 14.1 The Oozie server and how it works with the Oozie clients, database and HDFS

job information rather than storing the information in memory helps Oozie scale to very high levels of usage, even hundreds of thousands of jobs, with a very light footprint.

Figure 14.1 shows the Oozie server as well as other Oozie components (client, database) and how they interact with Oozie clients such as Java/REST APIs, web interface and the CLI on the one hand, all of which run applications through Oozie, and MapReduce and HDFS on the other.

> **Note**
>
> Oozie comes with an embedded Tomcat Server that manages all data flows to and from the Oozie server.

Deploying Oozie in Your Cluster

In order to use the Oozie server, you need to install it along with its database on some server, not necessarily a node in your Hadoop cluster. Oozie doesn't require the Hadoop binaries for it to do its job-creation and scheduling work; it just requires the Hadoop clients. It's customary to set up Oozie on one of the edge servers of a cluster.

Figure 14.2 shows how Oozie is typically deployed in a Hadoop cluster. Since Oozie doesn't absolutely require a dedicated server for itself (although in busy, large environments it's good to do so), you can run Oozie from the same edge servers you run applications such as Hive and Pig from which interact with the Hadoop cluster.

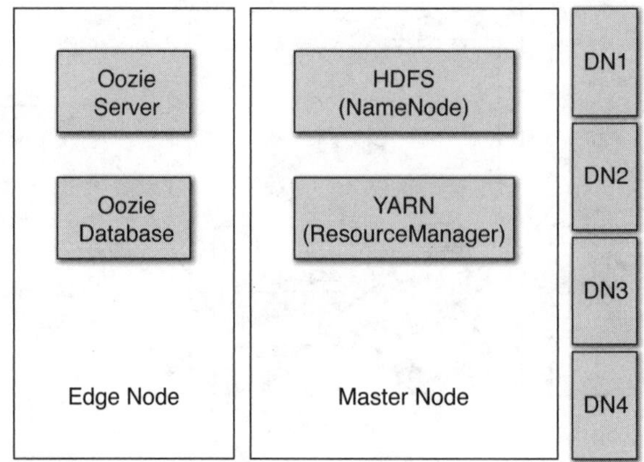

Figure 14.2 Typical Oozie server deployment on an edge node

Installing and Configuring Oozie

In order to effectively set up Oozie in your environment, it's important to understand how Oozie is installed and configured. As you learned earlier, Oozie actually consists of an Oozie server, an Oozie client and an Oozie database. Let's learn how to install and configure these components so you can start scheduling Hadoop jobs through Oozie.

Installing Oozie

In order to install the Oozie server, you must build it. Follow these steps to install and build Oozie in your cluster:

1. Download the latest Oozie source code:

```
$ curl -O http://www.us.apache.org/dist/oozie/4.2.0/oozie-4.2.0.tar.gz
```

2. Unzip the source code zip file:

```
$ tar xvf oozie-4.2.0.tar.gz
$ cd oozie-4.2.0
```

3. Invoke the `mkdistro` utility to build the Oozie binary package:

```
$ bin/mkdistro.sh -DskipTests
[INFO] Scanning for projects...
....
[INFO] BUILD SUCCESS
[INFO] --------------------------------
...
$
```

Installing the Oozie Server

The Oozie binary package that you installed in the previous section is missing three key sets of JAR and library files:

- The Hadoop JAR files
- The JDBC JAR files
- The extJS package you need for setting up the Oozie web UI

In the directory where you unpacked the TAR file, find the directory named libext/. You'll need to copy the three sets of required JAR and library files into this directory. Once you do this, the Oozie setup scripts inject the libraries into the WAR file it came with and create a brand new WAR file that you can then deploy in a web server.

As far as the required Hadoop JAR files go, you can copy them from the directory specified by <HADOOP_INSTALLATION_DIR>, or use the JAR files for Hadoop that are found in the Oozie build directory.

1. The JDBC JAR files you need to get depend on the type of database you want to use. In my case, I'll be using a MySQL database to store the job state information for Oozie. Therefore, I need to add the MySQL JDBC driver to the Oozie WAR file. First, I download the JDBC package as shown here:

   ```
   $ curl -O http://cdn.mysql.com/Downloads/Connector-J/\
   mysql-connector-java-5.1.25.tar.gz
   ```

2. Extract the mysql-connector-java-5.1.25.tar file and move it to the libext/ directory where you unpacked the Oozie TAR file.
3. Download extJS 2.2 from `http://extjs.com/deploy/ext-2.2.zip` and copy it to the same libext/ directory as in step 2. The ExtJS library isn't bundled with Oozie due to licensing reasons.

   ```
   $ cd <INSTALLATION_DIR>/oozie-4.2.0/libext
   $ cp <EXT_JS_DIR>/ext-2.2.zip .
   $ ls -1
   ...
   ```

   You're now ready to create a new Oozie WAR file that contains the necessary libraries and JAR files.

   > **Tip**
   >
   > Oozie ignores any values you set for the OOZIE_HOME environment variable—it automatically computes its home.

4. Create a new Oozie WAR files as shown here:

   ```
   $ cd ..
   $ bin/oozie-setup.sh prepare-war
     setting CATALINA_OPTS="$CATALINA_OPTS -Xmx1024m"

     INFO: Adding extension: <INSTALLATION_DIR>/libext/activation-1.1.jar
     INFO: Adding extension: <INSTALLATION_DIR>/libext/avro-1.7.4.jar

   New Oozie WAR file with added 'ExtJS library, JARs' at
     <INSTALLATION_DIR>/oozie-server/webapps/oozie.war

     INFO: Oozie is ready to be started
   $
   ```

By default, the Oozie server uses the port 11000. The default administration port is 11001. Note that you can configure Oozie to use Kerberos for authentication if you've Kerberized your Hadoop cluster (as Chapter 15, "Securing Hadoop" explains, a Kerberized Hadoop cluster is one that uses Kerberos to authenticate its users).

Configuring Hadoop for Oozie

The owner of the Oozie service, which is usually the OS user oozie, serves as a proxy user for accessing Hadoop and running jobs in the cluster. You therefore need to next configure the cluster so Oozie can serve as the proxy user for the end users. In order to do this, you must add the following two properties to the core-site.xml file.

```
<!-- OOZIE -->
<property>
  <name>hadoop.proxyuser.[OOZIE_SERVICE_OWNER].hosts</name>
  <value>[OOZIE_SERVICE_HOSTNAME]</value>
</property>

<property>
  <name>hadoop.proxyuser.[OOZIE_SERVICE_OWNER].groups</name>
  <value>[OOZIE_SERVICE_OWNER_GROUP] </value>
</property>
```

In my case, the core-site.xml file looks as follows after making the appropriate changes:

```
<property>
   <name>hadoop.proxyuser.oozie.hosts</name>
   <value>localhost</value>
</property>

<property>
   <name>hadoop.proxyuser.oozie.groups</name>
   <value>users </value>
</property>
```

Now that I've configured Oozie for working with Hadoop, I'll fire up Oozie so I can start scheduling jobs in the cluster.

Starting and Stopping Oozie

You can start and stop the Oozie server with the oozied.sh script. Start the server as shown here:

```
$ bin/oozied.sh start
Setting OOZIE_HOME:          <INSTALLATION_DIR>
Setting OOZIE_CONFIG:        <INSTALLATION_DIR>/conf
Sourcing:                    <INSTALLATION_DIR>/conf/oozie-env.sh
  setting CATALINA_OPTS="$CATALINA_OPTS -Xmx1024m"
..
Using CATALINA_PID: <INSTALLATION_DIR>/oozie-server/temp/oozie.pid
$
```

The previous command will run Oozie as a background process. You can run the following command to start Oozie as a foreground process:

```
$ bin/oozied.sh start
```

You can check the status of the Oozie server by issuing the `-status` command with the Oozie command line tool named `oozie`:

```
$ bin/oozie admin -oozie http://localhost:11000/oozie -status

 System mode: NORMAL
$
```

You can examine the Oozie log file (logs/oozie.log) to ensure that the startup was correct. You can also check Oozie's status through its web UI by using the following URL:

```
http://localhost:11000/oozie
```

If everything went right, you should see a `NORMAL` status.

Configuring a MySQL Database for Oozie

Oozie, by default, is configured to use the embedded Derby database. However, you can use MySQL, Oracle or PostgreSQL instead, especially if you're using Oozie in a production environment. If you're using any relational database other than the default Derby database, you need to configure the database for Oozie.

Installing the Oozie Client

If you're installing Oozie for testing purposes on a single server, you don't need to worry about installing the Oozie client, since the server install also installs the client as well. However, in a cluster, you install the Oozie server on a master node in your Hadoop cluster, and install the Oozie client on servers from which users will access Oozie. Oozie also provides a separate client install archive that you can use to install just the client part of Oozie on your cluster's nodes. Here's how you do it:

```
$ tar xvf oozie-client-4.0.1.tar.gz
```

It's a good idea to add the location of the Oozie client to the `PATH` environment variable:

```
$ export PATH=<CURRENT_WORKING_DIR>/oozie-client-4.0.1/bin:$PATH
```

You can verify that you installed the Oozie client correctly by running the following command:

```
oozie admin -status
     -oozie <OOZIEURL>
```

When you try to access the Oozie server through an Oozie client, it tries to find the Oozie web server URL either at the command line or in the Linux environment of the user issuing the command. Therefore, it is good to add the following to the environment:

```
$ export OOZIE_URL=<OOZIE_Server_URL>
```

Now that you have configured the Oozie server and the Oozie client and tested them, it's finally time to get to work with Oozie. This involves the creation and scheduling of Oozie workflows, coordinators, and optionally, bundles.

Understanding Oozie Workflows

An Oozie job is similar to the Linux executables you use such as `ls` or `echo`. Taking this analogy further, an Oozie job corresponds to a Linux process.

In order to schedule your Hadoop jobs, you create an Oozie application, and each execution of the application is an Oozie job. Similarly, each execution of an Oozie coordinator application is an Oozie job. As mentioned earlier, an Oozie job can be a workflow, a coordinator or a bundle. In this section, we show how to create and use an Oozie workflow.

An Oozie workflow is a Hadoop job with several steps or stages. In other words, it's a set of tasks that are to be executed in a specific order. An Oozie workflow is the heart of an Oozie scheduling application—individual action nodes constitute an Oozie workflow and it is these action nodes that perform the actual processing of the work. You can build coordinators to schedule the workflows once you create the Oozie workflows.

More formally, a workflow is a collection, or rather, a sequence of action and control nodes in a directed acyclic graph, with each action being a Hadoop job such as a MapReduce, Pig, Hive, Spark, DistCp or Sqoop job.

Workflows, Control Flow, and Nodes

An Oozie workflow consists of several nodes, which can be action nodes or control nodes, which can include start and end control nodes, fork and join control nodes, and **decision nodes** (where control flow can go in one or another direction). The lines in the graph that connect the nodes show the sequence of the actions as well as the direction of the control flow. Since an Oozie workflow is a directed acyclic graph, you can't have any loops within the workflow.

Figure 14.3 shows the basic Oozie DAG with a start, end and kill node (and an action node). The job flow goes from the action node to either the end node or the kill node. If the action completes successfully, the job flow goes to the end node, and if it errors, it goes to the kill node, which has instructions on what to do in the case of an error.

There are several types of control nodes in a workflow, with the workflow type determining the order in which actions are executed. Here are the types of workflow nodes:

- Start and end nodes: Define when a workflow begins and ends
- Fork and join nodes: Let you run actions in a parallel fashion
- Decision nodes: Select the execution paths within a workflow based on the job-processing activity

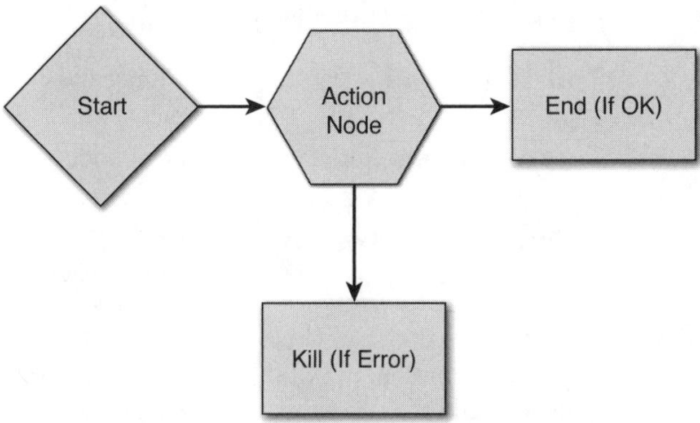

Figure 14.3 A simple Oozie DAG showing the start, end and kill control nodes and an action node

An Oozie workflow consists of multiple stages of a job presented to a Hadoop cluster. As mentioned earlier, the actions can be either Hadoop jobs such as a Hive or Sqoop action or a non-Hadoop job such as a shell script or email notification.

> **Note**
>
> All Oozie job definitions—for workflows, coordinators and bundles—are written in XML. These XML files use the Hadoop Process Definition Language (hPDL) schema.

Defining the Workflows with the workflow.xml File

In order to create an Oozie workflow, you place the workflow definition in an XML file usually named workflow.xml. A workflow.xml file has the following sections:

- Global configuration
- Control nodes
- Action nodes

When you have multiple action nodes, with each node representing an action such as a MapReduce or Hive job, the scheduler needs to know the order in which it should execute the actions. The actions are dependent on each other, and if a preceding action in the DAG doesn't complete, the action following it won't start. While the action nodes actually specify the actions which perform the work, the control nodes manage the flow of execution.

> **Tip**
>
> Remember that you can't define a workflow with looping constructs, meaning you can't run the same operation over and over until it meets a specific condition.

There are several types of control nodes in a workflow:

- Two control nodes named start and end define the beginning and end of an Oozie workflow.
- Two other control nodes, named the fork and join control nodes, enable the parallel execution of jobs.
- As alluded to previously, there are other control nodes called decision control nodes that select specific execution paths based on certain conditions within the job.

Figure 14.4 shows a typical Oozie workflow. This workflow starts by running a Pig script first. Once the Pig script completes running, the workflow faces a decision tree. Depending on the output, the control flow could transfer either to HDFS for file operations such as a `copyToLocal` operation, or it can go to a fork action. If the control flow goes to the fork action, two jobs—a Hive query and a MapReduce job—are started in parallel. Once these two jobs are completed, the control flow goes to HDFS (through an HDFS operation). The workflow as a whole is deemed complete after all the HDFS file operations are completed.

Tip

Action nodes are the key to an Oozie workflow because they perform the actual processing of work. I discuss action nodes in great detail, since that's where the real Oozie action is! Understanding how to configure and parameterize the various types of Oozie actions is the most significant aspect of Oozie job scheduling. Once you understand how to define actions correctly, creating the Oozie workflows and coordinators is but a simple step, since those are mostly wrappers for the Oozie actions.

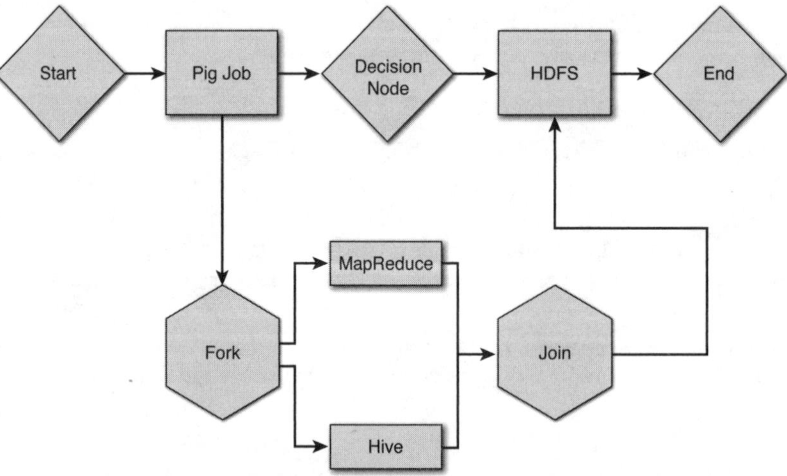

Figure 14.4 How an Oozie workflow is structured with decision (action) and control nodes. In this case the Pig job could either just write straight to HDFS or use a fork node to perform a MapReduce and Hive job before writing the results to HDFS.

Let's first review how some common types of action nodes work before you start creating and scheduling an Oozie workflow.

How Oozie Runs an Action

Oozie job execution works differently from normal user job execution. When a user executes a job, it runs from where the client starts the job execution. A user can actually log into one of the cluster nodes or run the job from a gateway node. As you can recall from Chapter 4, "Planning for and Creating a Fully Distributed Cluster," a gateway node is a server that doesn't need to have Hadoop services running on it. Also called an edge server, this server is meant for launching Hadoop jobs. In either case, the client's program runs the job in the cluster and retrieves the results.

When you run the same job through Oozie, it starts a map-only Hadoop job called a **launcher** to run the job actions. When you run an Oozie job through Hue or with the Oozie CLI, the Oozie client submits the job to the Oozie server, but the Oozie server doesn't actually launch the job on the machine where it runs. Instead, it starts the launcher job on the Hadoop cluster.

The launcher job runs in the cluster and invokes the necessary client libraries for MapReduce, Hive or Pig, depending on the type of job action you specify. The goal here is to keep the Oozie server out of the job-execution process—it merely executes the workflow, leaving the actual execution of the action code to the Hadoop cluster.

Since the Oozie server executes the launcher job on the Hadoop cluster, you must make available the code for all actions and the related configuration files on HDFS so the launcher can access the job information. The launcher job itself runs in its own YARN container, and the container is killed once the Oozie actions are completed.

Configuring the Action Nodes

Each Hadoop job you specify in an Oozie workflow, such as a Sqoop or Hive job, is specified as an action node in the Oozie workflow.xml file. A workflow is thus a package of action nodes, together with a set of control nodes, that specify the start and end of the job, as well as where the job can be forked into parallel branches that can execute simultaneously.

MapReduce and other Hadoop components such as Hive and Pig have their own specialized way of defining an Oozie action. In order to understand how to work well with action nodes, which are the most important part of an Oozie workflow, I'll explain how to create the action nodes for four types of Oozie actions:

- MapReduce
- Hive
- Pig
- Shell

Working with the other Oozie actions is very similar, with minor changes.

Each Oozie action, such as a MapReduce or a Hive action, requires an ordered sequence of XML elements. In order to define an Oozie action you must specify some or all of these XML elements for the action you want Oozie to perform. Some of the elements are common to all Oozie actions, but some are specific to a particular action.

The two required elements—`<job-tracker>` and `<name-node>`—aren't specific to just MapReduce action types, as you can guess. They are top-level XML elements common to all Oozie action types and specify the master services for Hadoop's processing (YARN) and storage (HDFS) systems. In Hadoop 2, of course, there's no job tracker, whose functions have been taken over by the ResourceManager. Hue lets you specify either job-tracker or resource-manager—there's no difference.

Action Nodes for MapReduce Jobs

Suppose you're running a MapReduce job from the command line as follows:

```
$ hadoop jar /user/sam/testApp.jar testAppClass \
   /user/sam/input  /user/sam/output test
```

You can convert this MapReduce job into an Oozie job with the following Oozie workflow action node definition (the actual complete workflow.xml file for the job will include additional elements such as job configuration and control nodes such as `<start>` and `<end>`.

```
<action name="testMapReduceAction">
 <map-reduce>
    <job-tracker>jt.mycompany.com:8032</job-tracker>
    <name-node>hdfs://nn.mycompany.com:8020</name-node>
    <prepare>
       <delete path="hdfs://nn.mycompany.com:8020/hdfs/user/sam/data/output"/>
    </prepare>
    <job-xml>/testjob.xml</job-xml>
       <configuration>
         <property>
           <name>mapred.mapper.class</name>
           <value>org.myorg.TestJob.Map</value>
           </property>
         <property>
           <name>mapred.reducer.class</name>
           <value>org.myorg.TestJob.Reduce</value>
         </property>
         <property>
            <name>mapred.input.dir</name>
            <value>/hdfs/user/sam/data/input</value>
        </property>
        <property>
           <name>mapred.output.dir</name>
           <value>/hdfs//user/sam/data/output</value>
         </property>
     </configuration>
     <file>testDir1/testFile.txt#file1</file>
   </map-reduce>
   <ok to="success"/>
<error to="fail"/>
</action>
```

This MapReduce job action uses several, but not all, of the action XML elements I listed earlier. To be precise, besides the two required elements (<job-tracker> and <name-node>), it uses the <action>, <action-type>, <prepare>, <job-xml>, <configuration> and <file> XML elements. Here are the key points about the MapReduce action described in the worklfow.xml file:

- The <action> element is common to all action types and starts with the <action> tag. The <action> element represents the application or command you want to execute. The name attribute lets you name the action. In this case, I named the action testMapReduceAction.
- Every type of action node has three common subelements:
  - <action-type>: You don't actually specify an element named <action-type>. You specify the actual type of action instead, which is MapReduce in our case. Therefore, everything within the <map-reduce> and </map-reduce> elements is part of the <action-type> element.
  - <ok>: This subelement indicates what to do following the exit of the job action after the action succeeds.
  - <error>: This subelement indicates what to do following an error.
- The <job-tracker> and <name-node> elements are required elements, and they point to the URLs for the ResourceManager and the NameNode on the cluster where Oozie is executing this job action.
- The <prepare> element is optional. In this case, I used it to delete the HDFS output directories before the MapReduce job is launched, since the job will fail if the output directory already exists in HDFS.
- The two elements <job-xml> and <configuration> provide the Hadoop-related job configuration properties.
- The <file> and <archive> attributes are optional: they let you specify the native Hadoop packaging for libraries, archives, scripts and data files for a MapReduce job. Most commonly, you package all the mapper and reducer classes for a MapReduce action into a JAR file and submit it to the Oozie action.

In the action node definition shown earlier, there's no reference to the testApp.jar that you had to specify at the command line. Where did it go? You must copy the JAR file to the /lib subdirectory under the root directory of the workflow application in HDFS. Oozie will automatically look for the JAR file in that directory.

Action Nodes for a Hive Job

Specifying a Hive action isn't a whole lot different from specifying a MapReduce action. As with MapReduce, you must package all the necessary configuration files, libraries and code for any UDFs (user-defined functions) and deploy the package to HDFS.

All the action elements you saw earlier for a MapReduce action are present for a Hive action as well, such as `<job-tracker>` and `<name-node>`. You must specify the Hive configuration file, named hive-config.xml, as the value for the `<job-xml>` element. There are three elements that are specific to Hive—`script`, `param` and `argument`—and here's what they stand for:

- `script`: This is a required element and specifies the Hive script (HQL) that you want Oozie to execute.
- `param`: There can be multiple `param` elements, which let you specify Hive script parameters.
- `arguments`: This element lets you parameterize the Hive script using variable substitution.

Let's say you're running the following Hive job from the command line:

```
$ hive -hivevar country=us -f hive.hql
```

I'm using `-hivevar` since I'm parameterizing this job with the variable `country`. My Oozie Hive workflow action will look as follows:

```
<action name="testHiveAction">
  <hive>
    <job-tracker>jt.mycompany.com:8032</job-tracker>
    <name-node>hdfs://nn.mycompany.com:8020</name-node>
    <job-xml>hive-config.xml</job-xml>
    <script>hive.hql</script>
    <argument>-hivevar</argument>
    <argument>country=us</argument>
  </hive>
 <ok to="success"/>
 <error to="fail"/>
</action>
```

Note how I use the `<argument>` elements to parameterize the Hive job. In this case, I specified hive-confg.xml as the value for the `<job-xml>` element and only specified some of the Hive configuration parameters for Hive. Instead I can simply point to the location of the complete Hive configuration file, which is the hive-site.xml file—there's no difference.

As I did earlier for MapReduce, I need to place the hive-conf.xml file, the hive.hql file and any related files in HDFS under the root directory of the Hive workflow.

Pig Action

A Pig action is very similar to that for Hive. Suppose you're executing a Pig script from the command line as follows:

```
$ pig -f pig.script -param country=us \
  -param output=hdfs://nn.mycompany.com:8020/hdfs/user/sam/pig/output
```

Here's the Oozie Pig action configuration that corresponds to the Pig script execution from the command line:

```
check<action name="testPigAction">
    <pig>
      <job-tracker>jt.mycompany.com:8032</job-tracker>
      <name-node>hdfs://nn.mycompany.com:8020</name-node>
      <prepare>
        <delete path="hdfs://nn.mycompany.com:8020/hdfs
      <script>/testpigscript.pig</script>
        <argument>param</argument>
        <argument>country=us</argument>
        <argument>param</argument>
        <argument>output=hdfs://nn.mycompany.com:8020/hdfs/user/sam/pig/output</
argument>
     </pig>
     <ok to=end"/>
     <error to="fail"/>
</action>
```

Note how I specify separate <param> elements for configuring the country argument and the output directory.

The Shell Action

You can run Linux commands as well as Perl and Python scripts through Oozie's shell action. The elements for a shell action remain the same as those for a MapReduce action, with the following additional elements.

- exec: This is a required element and specifies the shell command or Perl or Python executable.
- argument: This lets you specify the arguments for the shell command you are executing.
- env-var: This specifies the Linux environment variables such as PATH, for example.
- capture-output: This element captures the shell command output (stdout) and provides it to the workflow application.

Let's say you want to run the following Python script through Oozie:

```
$ export TZ=PST
$ python test.py 05/26/2016
```

Here's what the shell action for the Python script execution looks like:

```
<action name="testShellAction">
   <shell xmins=url:oozie:shell-action:0.2>
         ...
        <exec>/usr/bin/python</exec>
        <argument>test.py</argument>
        <argument>05/26/2016/argument>
        <env-var>TZ=PST</env-var>
       <file>test.py#test.py</file>
       <capture-output/>
   </shell>
  <ok to="success"/>
  <error to="fail/>
</action>
```

The File System Action

Let's say you want to perform some HDFS file operations as part of a workflow. You can run HDFS commands using the fs action. In addition to a required <name-node> element and the usual <job-xml> and <configuration> elements, an fs action uses HDFS file system commands you're likely already familiar with: mkdir, delete, move, chgrp, chmod and touchz. Here's a typical fs action inside a workflow .xml file.

```
<action name="myFSAction">
  <fs>
    <name-node>hdfs://nn.mycompany.com:8020</name-node>
    <delete path='/hdfs/user/sam/logs'/>
    <mkdir path='hdfs/user/sam/' permissions='777' dir-files='true'>
<recursive/></chmod>
  </fs>
    <ok to="success"/>
    <error to="fail/>
</action>
```

> **Tip**
>
> Unlike the other Oozie actions you've seen, Oozie launches the fs action commands on the machine where the Oozie server runs and not the launcher. If you're performing a huge HDFS delete or move operation, it's possible that the Oozie server's performance may be negatively impacted!

I've spent considerable time explaining how to configure Oozie actions, since they are really everything in an Oozie job. There are several other Oozie action types such as email and ssh actions, and they all basically work the same way as the actions I described here.

Now that you know how action nodes work in an Oozie workflow, it's time to move on to creating actual Oozie workflows by configuring the workflow.xml file for a Hadoop job.

> **Note**
>
> You define any of the three types of Oozie jobs—workflows, coordinators and bundles—through individual XML files (such as workflow1.xml, coordinator1.xml and bundle1.xml). Once you define the workflow/coordinator/bundle job, you configure the job using a combination of command line options and property files.

Creating an Oozie Workflow

An Oozie workflow consists of a set of actions encoded by XML nodes. There are multiple types of nodes in a workflow definition, with each type of node representing a specific type of action or control directive.

The workflow.xml file contains the configuration for an Oozie workflow, and it is in this file that you configure each Hadoop job you want to run through Oozie. The name workflow.xml is based on convention—you can name it anything you want. Here's the structure of a simple Oozie workflow.xml file:

```
<workflow-app xmlns=url:oozie:workflow:0.5 name=testWF">
<global>
      ...
</global>
<start to= />
<action name="TestPigAction">
      <pig>
      ...
     </pig>
 </action>
<ok to=done"/>
<error to="done"/
<action name ="TestFSAction">
   <FS>
            ..
  </FS>
<ok to=done"/>
<error to="done"/
</action>
   <end name="done"/>
</workflow-app>
```

As mentioned earlier, an Oozie workflow can contain multiple actions. Each action and control node requires a unique identifier. Oozie uses these identifiers to determine which node is processed next. Oozie goes down the workflow.xml file, processing each action based on the action's location in the workflow.xml file. Our simple workflow shown here consists of the following nodes:

- Two action nodes: There's a Pig action that runs a Pig script and an `fs` action that performs some HDFS operations. You must always name an action node. In our case, the two action nodes are identified by their names: TestPigAction and TestFSAction.
- Two control nodes: There's a `<start>` and an `<end>` control node in the workflow, indicating where the workflow will begin and end. No `name` identifier is required for the `<start>` node, since it's the starting point for any workflow; however, the `<end>` control node does require a `name` identifier.

Each workflow.xml file for a workflow you want to create must start with the root element `<workflow-app>`. Note that you provide a name for your workflow in this element. In our case, the workflow is named `testWF`. In the `<workflow-app>` element, the `xmlns` attribute specifies the schema URL that Oozie uses to perform XML schema validation of the workflow.xml file.

The workflow.xml sample shown here consists of three key sections:

- Action nodes
- Control nodes
- Job configuration

You've already learned how to configure the action nodes for various types of Oozie actions such as MapReduce, Hive, Pig, file system and shell actions. Let's learn how to configure the control nodes and the job configuration sections in a workflow.xml file.

Configuring the Control Nodes

Control nodes specify how a workflow begins and ends, as well as how the execution flow proceeds, with optional control structures. The following sections describe the various control nodes you can specify.

<start> and <end>

The <start> and <end> control nodes specify the beginning and end of a workflow and are mandatory. There should be a matching pair of <start> and <end> nodes in each workflow.

The <start> node is defined as follows:

```
<start to="mapReduce"/>
```

This <start> element uses the to attribute to make Oozie go to the action node named mapReduce and start executing the workflow.

> **Note**
>
> You don't need to identify the <start> node with an identifier, since Oozie knows that this is the starting point for the workflow.

The <end> node is defined as follows:

```
<end name="done"/>
```

When the Oozie job reaches the <end> control node, it completes execution and shows the status as SUCCEEDED.

<fork> and <join>

The <fork> control node enables Oozie to run jobs in parallel. Multiple independent execution paths can be specified. The <join> control node is somewhat of an end point to the <fork> control node. If you specify the <fork> control node, you must also specify a <join> node—this control node is where all paths of a <fork> node converge.

Figure 14.5 shows conceptually how the join, fork and decision nodes work together to support multiple workflows based on what actually happens when the workflow commences execution.

A simple example of a <fork> and <join> control node setup is where a workflow begins with the <start> node and uses a set of <fork> nodes, one to run a MapReduce job and the other to run a Hive job.

The <join> node is where the two jobs converge, before the <end> node completes the job. You can have nested <fork> and <join> nodes, but remember that each set of <fork> and <join> nodes is a different pair, and you must specify them together.

Here's a workflow with a set of <fork> and <join> control nodes.

```
<workflow-app ...
<global>
....
<global/>
```

```
<start to="testForkActions"/>
<fork name="testForkActions">
       <path name="testPath1"/>
       <path name="testPath2"/>
</fork>
<action name="testAction1">
     ...
     <ok to=testJoinActions"/>
     <error to="testJoinActions
</action>
<action name="testAction2">
     ...
     <ok to=testJoinActions"/>
     <error to="testJoinActions
</action>
<join name="testJoinActions" to="done"/>
<end name="done"/>
</workflow-app>
```

Here's what you need to understand regarding the <fork> and <join> nodes in this example:

- There's one <fork> action named `testForkActions`.
- The <fork> action contains two <path> elements.
- Each of the two <path> elements stands for a parallel executing path of the parent <fork> node.
- Each of the two <path> elements contains a single <action> node, but you can include multiple actions if you wish.
- The final <action> node under each <path> element (here we have only a single <action> node under the <path> element) must point to the <join> node.
- There's a single <join> node named `testJoinActions` where all execution paths under the <fork> node `testForkActions` end. You can specify multiple <join> nodes within a workflow.

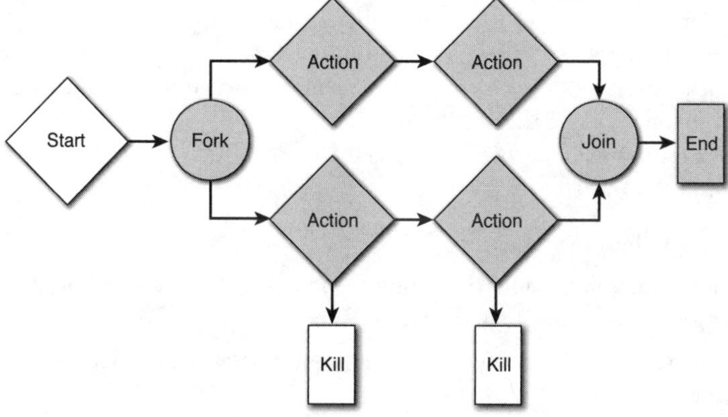

Figure 14.5 How Oozie supports multiple workflows through the use of the join, fork and decision nodes

<ok>, <error> and <kill>

When you run a workflow in your cluster, you want to know if the job succeeded or failed. Think of a scenario when you want to perform a subsequent processing step after the job succeeds. You can add the logic for the subsequent steps in the workflow configuration.

Similarly, when a job fails, you want to take specific actions, such as re-running it, for example. In both cases, you assign the next processing step to a different node. Here's how the <ok>, <error> and <kill> nodes work:

- If the Oozie job is successful, its status will be OK, and the workflow execution path moves to the node you specify in the <ok> element.
- If the Oozie job is unsuccessful, on the other hand, the status will be ERROR, and the job execution moves to the node you specify for the <error> element instead.
- Most commonly, you want the workflow to stop running when it encounters an error, and you do so by specifying the <kill> node when a job receives the ERROR status.

The <kill> node deals with error conditions. Here's an example showing how to configure the <kill> node.

```
<workflow-app ....>
<start to=testMapReduce"/>
<action name="mapReduce">
     ...
     <ok> to="done"/>
     <error to="error"/>
</action>
<kill name="error">
      <message>The 'MapReduce' action has failed</message>
<end name="done"/>
</workflow-app>
```

Note how the <ok> and <error> elements have to="done" or to="error" as their value. The to attribute determines the execution path Oozie must follow in each case. This means that if the job status is OK, go to the element in the workflow file that has the value done, and if the job status is ERROR, go to the element with the value error. In this case, when the status is ERROR, the <error> element says to go to the node with the value error, which happens to be the <kill> node.

Let's learn a bit more about the special <kill> node, which is very helpful when you're trying to handle error scenarios:

- A <kill> node isn't mandatory.
- An action node can use an error transition tag to direct the control flow to a specific (named) <kill> node when an error occurs.
- A control node can also point to a <kill> node based on the outcome of the decision predicates.
- You can define multiple <kill> nodes to handle different types of error conditions.
- A <kill> node results in the ending of the workflow.

You don't have to specify a to attribute when using a <kill> node, unlike in the case of an <end> node, where you do.

When the execution path of a workflow hits the <kill> node, Oozie immediately stops the job execution and sets the final status of the workflow to KILLED. Any running MapReduce jobs will continue to run to completion, but there won't be any further actions following the completion of those jobs, since the workflow itself has been given the completion status of KILLED.

The OK, ERROR and KILLED states are the most useful and common action states that you need to be aware of, although there are several other action states, such as FAILED, PREP, RUNNING, START_MANUAL, END_MANUAL, START_RETRY and END_RETRY, for example.

<decision>

As you learned earlier, using the <fork> node lets you set up parallel execution paths. You can also specify a <decision> control node to specify an if-then-else type of course of action, where the satisfying of a condition will determine whether a subsequent action will be executed.

Here's a simple example that shows how to add if-then-else logic to a workflow execution by specifying the <decision> node.

```
<workflow-app....>
   <start to=decision1"/>
   <decision name=decision1">
      <switch>
        <case to="mapReduce">
         $jobType eq "mapReduce"}
        </case>
        <case to="sqoop">
           $jobType eq "sqoop"}
        </case>
        <case to="pig">
          $jobType eq "pig"}
        </case>
        <default to="hive"/>
      </switch>
    </decision>
<action name="mapReduce">
...
</action>
<action name="sqoop">
...
</action>
<action name="pig">
...
</action>
...
</workflow-app>
```

There are three types of actions in this workflow—a MapReduce action, a Sqoop action and a Pig action. Oozie will execute only one of them. Which one? It depends on what value you specify for the workflow parameter.

The decision node is named decision1 in our example. This decision node includes a case statement (called switch) that will specify the action to be taken based on the value of the workflow parameter `jobType`. Depending on the value of the `jobType` parameter, the control flow will run a MapReduce, Sqoop or Pig job.

> **Note**
>
> A `case` statement is frequently used to specify control flows in a programming language. What the `case` statement means is that in case the first comparison is true, run a specific function, and in case the second or third comparison is true, run a different function.

Note that the decision node named `decision1` uses a switch operation, enabling you to define multiple cases and a mandatory default case as well. The logic inside the case statement itself is written using JSP Expression Language (EL) expressions. Each of these EL expressions evaluates to true or false.

Configuring the Job

When you specify an Oozie workflow action such as MapReduce or Hive, you must also specify the configuration settings for those actions. You can configure the workflow actions in multiple ways. You can specify the action configuration settings inline within the workflow action definition, as shown here.

```
<action name "TestHiveAction">
   <hive>
      <configuraton>
        <property>
          <name>hive.metastore.local</name>
          <value>true</value>
         </property>
         <property>
            ...
         </property>
       </configuration>
     ...
    </hive>
  ...
</action>
```

Any configuration properties that you specify with a `<configuration>` element within the action itself get the highest priority during the Oozie job execution. Alternately, if the action allows it, you can specify the job configuration in an XML format through the `<job-xml>` element in the workflow. If you have multiple actions, you can specify a different job.xml file for each action node, as shown here.

```
<map-reduce>
     ...
     <job-xml>TestJob1.xml</job-xml>
     <job-xml>TestJob2.xml</job-xml>
...
</map-reduce>
```

You must package the job.xml files along with the workflow app and deploy it to HDFS. If you specify the same configuration property in multiple job.xml files, the value you specify in a job.xml file listed later takes precedence over the value you specify in a job.xml file listed before it.

Often, you may be looking at a scenario where you need to run a set of actions where the actions have some common elements. For example, they'll all use the URI for the cluster's NameNode. At times like this, you can cut down on your configuration effort by specifying the `<global>` element.

The `<global>` element, which you always specify at the very beginning of the workflow.xml file, lets you specify a set of configuration parameters that are common to a group of actions. Here's a short example:

```
<workflow-app name=....>
   <global>
     <job-tracker>localhost:8032</job-tracker>
     <namenode>hdfs://localhost:8020</name-node>
     <configuration>
       <property>
         <name>mapred.job.queue.name</name>
         <value>certification</value>
        </property>
     <configuration>
   </global>
   ...
</workflow-app>
```

In this scenario, we specify the `job-tracker` and `namenode` properties inside the `<global>` element, since these two properties have the same value for all our actions. You can override the values you set here for the two properties by specifying different values for them further down in the workflow.xml file.

If you specify any configuration properties inline in the body of the workflow action, they take precedence over values you specify under the `global` section.

Running an Oozie Workflow Job

Okay, you know how to configure the action nodes with the various configuration settings each action type requires, and you also know how to configure the control nodes. You're getting very close to being able to run the Oozie job from the command line, but there's one final step left.

Each time you invoke an Oozie workflow application, you must also let Oozie know the configuration properties for the job itself. You use the properties.xml file (you can name it something else if you so desire) to specify the workflow job properties.

Specifying the Job Properties

Earlier, you learned that you need to package the various files necessary to run a workflow application and place them in HDFS. How does Oozie know where that directory is? You specify this and other job properties in the job.properties file. Unlike the actual workflow files, you don't store this file in HDFS—you save it in the local file system.

Be sure to understand the difference between the job.properties file and the workflow.xml file:

- The job.properties file includes the parameters that you want to pass to Oozie at runtime.
- The workflow.xml file contains the actual instructions for running the Oozie job, whether it be a workflow or a coordinator job. You must store the workflow.xml file in HDFS. This is to make sure that the application running the Oozie job can find the workflow.xml file.

> **Note**
>
> In addition to the workflow.xml file, HDFS must also store the Oozie library directory that contains the JAR files and other files necessary to run the applications that constitute the Oozie job flow.

The job.properties file helps you do two things:

- It enables you to specify key paths. The most important property of all is the location of the application root directory where you stored a workflow's packaged files. Use the `oozie.wf.application` property to specify this directory or the actual workflow.xml file itself. The other property relating to paths is the `oozie.use.system.libpath` property, which tells Oozie where to find the JAR files and libraries in the sharelib path. Several actions such as Hive and DistCp require you to specify this option.
- It helps you parameterize the workflow.xml file. You can use the job.properties file to parameterize the workflow.xml file by specifying variables for some settings in the workflow.xml file, with the actual values listed in the job.properties file. For example, your workflow.xml file can define the NameNode using variables, as in the following:

  ```
  <name-node>${nameNode}</name-node>
  ```

  You can then include the actual value for the `nameNode` variable in the `job.properties` file.

You can create a `job.properties` file in the XML format or in the text format. Here's a simple `job.properties` file in the `name=value` format:

```
nameNode=hdfs://localhost:8020
jobTracker=localhost:8020
oozie.wf.application.path=${namenode}/user/sam/oozie/testJob
oozie.use.system.libpath=true
```

You can specify the same properties in the XML format by using the `<property>`, `<name>` and `<value>` elements, as shown here:

```
<configuration>
  <property>
    <name>nameNode</name>
    <value>hdfs:localhost:8020</value>
```

```
  </property>
  <property>
       ...
  </property>
</configuration>
```

Suppose you parameterize your workflow.xml file by specifying two variables: `NameNode` and `JobTracker`. When you submit the workflow to Oozie, it'll then substitute the actual values for the two parameters by reading the values you specified in the `job.properties` file.

> **Tip**
>
> Remember that you can also configure an Oozie workflow with command-line parameters when you run a workflow. You can use the command line to specify parameters for a specific invocation of a workflow. Any parameter values you specify at the command line will override the parameter's values in the job.properties file.

Deploying Oozie Jobs

In order to run a job, Oozie reads the XML file where you defined the application. Since Oozie requires all of the application files in HDFS, you deploy Oozie applications by copying the directory containing the application files to HDFS.

Every Oozie application consists of a file with the application code and other files such as configuration files, JAR files and scripts. An Oozie workflow, an Oozie coordinator and an Oozie bundle job are each a separate application. Thus, a workflow application is represented by a workflow.xml file together with the supporting files, a coordinator job with a coordinator.xml file and its supporting files, and a bundle job with a bundle.xml file and its supporting files.

Each Oozie application is organized in a directory, with the directory containing all the files required by the application. Since the files of an application often reference each other, it's customary to use relative paths for the files. For example, the JAR files are placed in the lib/ subdirectory of the main application directory (in HDFS). This makes it quite easy for you to move the application to another directory.

Creating Dynamic Workflows

A **dynamic workflow** uses parameterization to save time and effort and avoid unnecessary repetition. In this context, parameterization refers to using parameters instead of hard coded values so you can use the same job for multiple purposes.

For example, you may want to move data into your cluster from a Teradata or Oracle database using Sqoop import jobs. You may want to perform the same job but with slight modifications throughout the day or week. In cases such as these, you can enhance your productivity and cut back on tedious writing of workflow and coordinator configuration files by using dynamic workflows.

Oozie offers support for parameterizing its workflows, coordinators and bundles by letting you use variables, functions and even expressions as the parameters. Using extensive parameterization in your Oozie workflows, for example, makes for a dynamic workflow rather than a static workflow that you need to reconfigure each time you want to run it.

Oozie enables the use of the JSP EL syntax, and the variables, constants, functions and expressions you specify in the EL syntax are called EL variables, EL constants, EL functions and EL expressions, respectively. Most often, you'll be using EL variables to parameterize Oozie workflows and coordinators. Here's one example of an EL variable.

```
<name-node>${nameNode}</name-node>
```

When you submit the workflow for execution, Oozie replaces the variables defined by you with the values you specify for the variable in the job.properties files, as I explained earlier.

Oozie also provides a set of EL constants, such as KB, MB, GB, TB and PB, to represent kilobytes, megabytes and so on. In an Oozie coordinator, Oozie also supports system variables such as `${YEAR}`, `${MONTH}`, `${DAY}` and `${HOUR}`. In a workflow, you can specify system variables to represent Hadoop job counters such as `FILE_BYTES_READ`, `MAP_IN` and `MAP_OUT`. Your workflow can make use of the job counters as shown here:

```
${hadoop:counters("testMRNode")["FileSystemCounters"]["FILE_BYTES_READ"]}
```

You can use the Hadoop counters either to print out information in the log file or to take a specific action based on the values of the mapper and reducer counters following the completion of the mapper/reducer processing.

Oozie offers several EL functions that let you perform useful tasks. For example

- The built-in function `wf:id()` lets you get the ID of the workflow you're executing.
- The `timestamp` function supplies the current UTC time in the format `YYYY-MM-DDThh:mm:ss:sZ`.
- The `fs: fileSize(String path)` function is an HDFS EL function that returns the size of the file you specify, in bytes.

EL expressions are quite powerful, and you've already seen them in action during the discussion of the `<decision>` control node earlier on.

Oozie Coordinators

While the Oozie workflows contain all the job logic, there's something missing in them—workflows don't offer any scheduling capabilities.

Oozie workflows help you run Hadoop applications in a specified sequence. So the workflows are good for manually running the applications. However, in practice, most commonly you'd need to schedule pre-created, stored Oozie workflows. You can schedule

Oozie workflows for execution through an Oozie coordinator, and schedule the jobs either at specific time intervals or base the job execution on the availability of application data. Oozie coordinators are what you use to schedule your Oozie workflows.

The time-interval-based coordinator scheduling works very similar to the familiar Linux `crontab`.

You define an Oozie coordinator with the following entities:

- Start and end time
- Frequency
- Input and output data
- The workflow to run

For example, you can create a coordinator job that runs a workflow at 1 A.M. daily, starting on January 1, 2016 and ending on December 31, 2016.

Once you create an Oozie coordinator, it continues to run workflows automatically until it reaches the end time you define for it. Workflows within a coordinator may or may not be dependent on the availability of input data. If the workflow run depends on input data being available, the workflow won't start until the input data becomes available.

> **Note**
>
> When an Oozie coordinator's workflows don't define any input data, the job is run on a fixed time schedule, just as a Linux `cron` job.

A coordinator, as its name indicates, simply acts as a wrapper around the actual workflow—it doesn't contain any type of job execution logic. A coordinator can start a workflow based on the times you specify or upon the availability of the necessary input data for running a workflow. Coordinators also facilitate the monitoring and controlling of workflow execution. In the following sections, I quickly review the two basic types of Oozie coordinators:

- Time-based coordinators
- Data-based coordinators

Time-Based Coordinators

A time-based coordinator is one where you schedule jobs to execute at a certain time. A time-based coordinator is very similar to how you schedule jobs through the Linux `crontab`.

When do you use a time-based coordinator? Scenarios for using time-based coordinators are easy to come by. In our own clusters, we have several daily and weekly jobs that are designed to produce reports for management and other groups of our companies. We schedule Oozie jobs at night so the reports are completed by the time people log into work early in the morning the next day.

You specify three important items when you create a time-based coordinator:

- Start time: This is not the actual start time of the workflow—it's the first time the workflow is executed (e.g., January 1, 2016).
- End time: This specifies the last time a workflow is run by this coordinator (e.g., December 31, 2016).
- Frequency: This specifies how often the coordinator must run the workflow.

Each time you run a coordinator application, it runs a separate coordinator job. So, you can submit the same coordinator multiple times with different parameters if you wish.

A Simple Time-Based Oozie Coordinator

Oozie coordinators are quite easy to configure when compared to the configuring of an Oozie workflow. Just as you created a workflow.xml file for defining the workflow, you create a coordinator.xml file (you can give it a different name if you wish) to define your Oozie coordinator.

Here's a basic Oozie job coordinator.xml file.

```
<coordinator-app name="test_coord_job"
                 start="2016-01-01T02:00Z "
                 end="2016-12-31T02:00Z"
                 frequency="1440"
                 timezone="UTC"
                 xmlns="uri:oozie:coordinator:0.4">
   <controls>...</controls>
   <action>
      <workflow>
         <app-path>${appBaseDir}/app/</app-path>
         <configuration>
         <property>
            <name>nameNode</name>
            <value>${nameNode}</value>
          </property>
          <property>
            <name>jobTracker</name>
            <value>${jobTracker}</value>
          </property>
          <property>
            <name>testDir</name>
            <value>${appBaseDir}</value>
          </property>
         </configuration>
       </workflow>
   </action>
</coordinator-app>
```

Similar to how you used the `workflow-app` element to start and end an Oozie workflow application, you use a `coordinator-app` element to start and end the Oozie coordinator application. Here are the start time, end time, and frequency for the coordinator.

```
start="2016-01-01T02:00Z"
end="2016-12-31T02:00Z"
frequency="1440"
```

Here's how the `start`, `end` and `frequency` parameters work:

- The start time here specifies when the coordinator should begin executing the workflow by creating a coordinator action. Note that start time isn't the same thing as the scheduled time at which the coordinator runs.
- The end time specifies when the coordinator should stop creating new coordinator actions to run the workflow embedded in the coordinator.
- The frequency parameter species how often the workflow ought to be run, in minutes (every 24 hours, in our example here).

The workflow that this coordinator will run is included between the `<workflow>` and the `</workflow>` elements. The workflow can include any of the action types I discussed in the previous section.

Note that I've parameterized the workflow in this case. The coordinator simply uses these parameters to automate job submission, as in the case of the workflows you saw earlier. The big difference is that whereas in the case of a workflow application I used the `oozie.wf.application.path` property to specify the location of the workflow application files, here I use the `app-path` property to specify the workflow application path.

As with workflows, you can use EL functions that relate to time and frequency in order to provide benefits such as making applications portable across time zones and handling Daylight Saving Time–related changes in time.

> **Tip**
>
> Most of the time, you submit an Oozie coordinator through the Hue interface. Hue makes it very easy to create both Oozie workflows and coordinators and does all the heavy lifting for you. However, you can run a workflow embedded in a coordinator by running the coordinator from the Oozie command line interface or through the Oozie web UI.

Data-Based Coordinators

A data-based coordinator is one which uses the availability of specific data as the trigger for launching a job. Often you need to execute a job only after a specific data file or directory is available, either through another workflow or after an external data ingest.

You use the concept of a dataset to represent data produced by an upstream job or application. Datasets represent data that's generated and sent to Hadoop at fixed intervals. A data-based Oozie coordinator can have one or more datasets. Following are the five attributes of a dataset you need to define:

- `name`: The name of the dataset
- `initial-instance`: The first (time) instance of valid data in a dataset
- `frequency`: How often the data instances occur
- `uri-template`: The template of the data directory defined for the dataset, containing the year, month, day, hour and minute to signify the timestamp when the data was created

- done-flag: The filename that indicates that the data is ready for use by the Oozie workflow

Here's a simple example showing how to define a dataset:

```
<dataset name="test_input1" frequency={coord:hours(4)}"
       <initial-instance="2015-12-31T02:00Z">
   <url-template>
        ${baseDataDir}/data_feed/${YEAR}-${MONTH}-${DAY}-${HOUR}
   <url-template>
   <done-flag>_trigger</done-flag>
</dataset>
```

Okay, so the dataset element in the coordinator.xml file defines the data the workflow is dependent on. How does Oozie know when the data is ready for the workflow? You use yet another element called input-events to handle the dataset dependency. Within the input-events section, of which there is only one in a coordinator.xml file, you can specify one or more data-in sections to let Oozie know about the availability of the data defined in the dataset element(s).

If your job depends on three sets of datasets, you'll need to configure three separate data-in sections under the input-events element. All of this must be quite confusing by now, so here we go with a snippet showing how to define an input-events element in the coordinator.xml file.

```
<input-events>
  <data-in name=testevent_input1" dataset="test_input1">
    <start-instance>${cord:current(-3)}</start-instance>
    <end-instance>${coord:current(-1)}</end-instance>
  </data-in>
</input-events>
```

- The <input-events> section contains the one data-in element present in this example, although it could contain more elements if you wish, each with a unique name of course.
- The data-in element with the name testevent_input1 specifies three instances of the dataset named test_input1 (I used the EL function current() for this).
- The Oozie coordinator for which you define this input-events section will wait to run its workflow until three batches of data arrive from the dataset named test_input1.

> **Note**
>
> Oozie also lets you configure an element analogous to input-events called output-events to specify the data instance produced by the coordinator action. This is mostly for use in cleaning up data during a coordinator reprocessing action.

Suppose you schedule a data-based coordinator to run at a specific time—you can do so because even a data-based coordinator can use the frequency parameter to run at set times. If the necessary data is available at the time you schedule the coordinator to run, say 3 A.M., the workflow is kicked off right away. If the data isn't available at 3 A.M., the coordinator job waits for the input data before starting up the workflow.

What happens if the data isn't available for several days due to a problem with a data ingest flow or something else? No problem so far as the coordinator is concerned—it keeps track of all the missed days and sets off the workflow to process data for each day as it finally arrives into your system. It's helpful that the output data is dated the same as the date of the input data generation.

Time-and-Data-Based Coordinators

Frequently, you want to schedule a coordinator job to execute at a specific time based on whether some data files or directories are available for processing. Following is an Oozie coordinator that is based on both time and the availability of specific data.

```
<coordinator-app name="sampleCoordinator"
                 frequency="${coord:days(1)}"
                 start="${startTime}"
                 end="${endTime}"
                 timezone="${timeZoneDef}"
                 xmlns="uri:oozie:coordinator:0.1">
   <controls>...</controls>
   <datasets>
      <dataset name="input" frequency="${coord:days(1)}" initial-
instance="${startTime}" timezone="${timeZoneDef}">
          <uri-template>${needDataDir}</uri-template>
      </dataset>
   </datasets>
   <input-events>
          <data-in name="sampleInput" dataset="input">
          <instance>${startTime}</instance>
      </data-in>
   </input-events>
   <action>
      <workflow>
          <app-path>${workflowAppPath}</app-path>
      </workflow>
   </action>
</coordinator-app>
```

This coordinator job will run at a specific start time and data and executes once every day—but only if the data set named `needDataDir` is available. It continues to run daily until the end time you specified.

Submitting the Oozie Coordinator from the Command Line

As with the submission of the Oozie workflows, you must upload the coordinator job definition to HDFS. Again, as with the workflow submission, you use a job.properties file (you can name it anything you want) but store it on the local file system.

The job.properties file specifies the values for all the variables you parameterize in the coordinator.xml file. Here are the contents of the job.properties file for our coordinator, which I had named `test-coord-job` in the coordinator.xml file earlier.

```
namenode=hdfs://hadoop01.localhost.com:8020
jobTracker=hadoop01.localhost:8030
```

```
appBaseDir=${nameNode}/user/{user.name}/test-coord-job
oozie.coord.application.path=$appBaseDir}/app
```

The job.properties file is easy to figure out—it does the following:

- Specifies values for the `nameNode` and `jobTracker` parameters that you used in the coordinator.xml file
- Defines the directory pointed to by the `appBaseDir` variable as the HDFS directory where the coordinator job definition files are stored
- Defines the coordinator application path as the directory under the appBaseDir directory in HDFS

Once you're done with configuring the job.properties file, upload the coordinator job definition, which includes the coordinator.xml file, to the HDFS directory you specified with the `oozie.coord.application.path` property in the job.properties file.

Before you upload the job definition, place the coordinator.xml file as well as the workflow.xml file for the workflow in a local directory named test-coord-job.

```
$ hdfs dfs -put test-coord-job/ .
$ hdfs dfs -ls -R test-coord-job/

-rw-r--r--   3 sam hadoop       4314 2016-06-08 21:53 /user/sam/search/
test-coord-job/app
-rw-r--r--   3 sam hadoop       4314 2016-06-08 21:53 /user/sam/search/
test-coord-job/app/coordinator.xml
-rw-r--r--   3 sam hadoop       4314 2016-06-08 21:53 /user/sam/search/
test-coord-job/app oozie-app/workflow.xml
-rw-r--r--   3 sam hadoop       4314 2016-06-08 21:53 /user/sam/search/
test-coord-job/data
-rw-r--r--   3 sam hadoop       4314 2016-06-08 21:53 /user/sam/search/
test-coord-job/data/input
-rw-r--r--   3 sam hadoop       4314 2016-06-08 21:53 /user/sam/search/
test-coord-job/data/input/input1.txt
$
```

Now that your job.properties file is configured and you've also uploaded the coordinator job definition to HDFS, submit the coordinator job as follows:

```
$ export OOZIE_URL=http://hadoop01:11000/oozie
$ oozie job -run -config job.properties
```

This `oozie job -run` command looks similar to the one you used for submitting an Oozie workflow. Oozie will look in the HDFS location you specified with the `oozie.coord.application.path` property and run the coordinator job using the job definition in the coordinator.xml you placed in that location.

Managing and Administering Oozie

In the example shown in the previous section, I exported the `OOZIE_URL` before invoking the Oozie CLI. You need to specify this so the Oozie client can communicate with the Oozie server. The location of the server acts as the end point for contacting the Oozie server's web service.

If you don't want to specify this environment variable each time you invoke the Oozie CLI, you can simply define the `OOZIE_URL` variable on the client machine. You can alternatively pass the location of the Oozie server by adding the `-oozie` option when you invoke the Oozie CLI. So, all of the following ways of invoking the Oozie CLI will work:

```
$ export OOZIE_URL=http://hadoop01:11000/oozie
$ oozie job -run -config job.properties
...
$ oozie job -run -config job.properties
...
```

Here's what I had to do to run an Oozie workflow using the Oozie CLI:

1. I exported the `OOZIE_URL` environment variable.
2. I added the variable to the `.bashrc` file for the user executing the command.

Alternatively, I can specify the location of the Oozie server with the `-oozie` option, as shown here:

```
$ oozie job -run -config job.properties -oozie http://hadoop01.localhost
.com:110000/oozie
```

Note that you use exactly the same command (`oozie job -run ...`) to run an Oozie workflow job or an Oozie coordinator (or bundle job, which I don't show here). Oozie will know whether it's a workflow or a coordinator/bundle from reading the job.properties file you specify at the command line.

Common Oozie Commands and How to Run Them

Oozie comes with several highly useful commands that you can run to manage the Oozie jobs in your cluster. Of course, the `oozie -help` command shows all the available Oozie commands.

You can check the job progress with the `oozie job -info <jobID>` command and kill the coordinator job with the `oozie job -kill <jobId>` command. In both cases, you must supply the Oozie coordinator job ID. You can find the job ID in the Oozie job output following a successful submission of a coordinator job.

You can check the status of an Oozie job with the following command:

```
$ oozie job -info 0000001-00000001234567-oozie-W
```

The output of the `-info` command shows the status as `RUNNING`, `KILLED` or `SUCCEEDED`. Alternatively, you can use Oozie's web UI (`http://localhost:110000/oozie`) to find the same information.

If you want to find the status of *all* the running workflow jobs in your cluster, run the following command:

```
$ oozie jobs -oozie http://localhost:8080/oozie -localtime -len 2 -filter
status=RUNNING
```

In this command, the valid filter names are the name of the workflow application, the user that submitted the job, the group for the job and, finally, the status for the job. We chose the status (RUNNING) filter value in this example.

In order to check the status of multiple coordinators, run the following command:

```
$ oozie jobs -oozie http://localhost:8080/oozie -jobtype coordinator
```

You can check the Oozie system itself with the admin option:

```
$ oozie admin -oozie http://localhost:8080/oozie -status
```

You can validate a workflow.xml file with the following command:

```
$ oozie validate testApp/workflow.xml
```

The validate command will perform an XML schema validation of the workflow.xml file you specify.

You can perform a dry run of a coordinator job with the dryrun option:

```
$ oozie job -oozie http://localhost:8080/oozie job -dryrun -config
job.properties
```

The dryrun option is extremely useful in many scenarios in a production cluster. There are many occasions when you modify one or more attributes of a coordinator and want to see if your changes are going to do what you expect them to do.

You can kill a running Oozie job in the following way:

```
$ oozie job -kill 0000001-00000001234567-oozie-W
```

The suspend command lets you suspend a running Oozie job:

```
$ oozie job -suspend 0000001-00000001234567-oozie-W
```

To resume a suspended job, execute the resume command:

```
$ oozie job -resume 0000001-00000001234567-oozie-W
```

You can get the records of SLA events by issuing the following command:

```
$ oozie sla -oozie http://localhost:8080/oozie -len 1
```

You can run a Pig job through HTTP in the following way:

```
$ oozie ping -oozie http://localhost:8080/oozie -file pigScriptFile -config  job
.properties -X -param_file params
```

Suspending Jobs and Handling Oozie Job Failures

Let's quickly learn how you can suspend Oozie jobs and how to handle Oozie job failures.

Suspending Running Jobs

You may suspend, or pause a running coordinator job. As with workflows, coordinators can finish with a SUCCEEDED or FAILED state, with several other states as well, such as DONE_WITH_ERROR and PAUSED_WITH_ERROR, for example.

Handling Job Failures

If an Oozie workflow should fail for any reason, you can simply rerun the workflow. Oozie is fine with rerunning failed jobs, since it doesn't run the already successful portions of the workflow you're running the second time.

Why is this a big deal? As production system administrators, we're all too familiar with scenarios where a job fails and we would have to re-execute the failed job. Oozie's capability to pick up precisely from the point of failure is a very welcome feature for us administrators who are responsible for efficiently completing all jobs within their assigned SLAs.

> **Note**
>
> You can use the Oozie web UI to run your Oozie workflows and coordinators. Oozie will create the workflow.xml and coordinator.xml files for you once you specify the details of the workflows and coordinators you want to create. You can also view the status of running jobs and find out when the job is scheduled to run again.

Troubleshooting Oozie

In order to troubleshoot the performance of the Oozie server, you should be able to check the Oozie configuration files, as well as the log files generated by Oozie. Here's a summary of the files you may need to check often:

- Oozie configuration files:
  - oozie-site.xml: The Oozie server configuration file
  - oozie-env.sh: Configures the Oozie environment
  - adminusers.txt: Configures the administrative users
  - oozie-log4j.properties: Configures logging
- Oozie log files:
  - oozie-ops.log: Monitoring messages for administrators
  - oozie.log: Log file for web services
  - oozie-instrumentation.log: Instrumentation data
  - oozie-audit.log: Audit data

Oozie Bundles

Oozie bundles are an even higher abstraction than Oozie coordinators. They let you bundle together multiple coordinator applications, with the bundles specifying when a coordinator must run. Thus, an Oozie bundle consists of one or more coordinators, with each of the coordinators in turn consisting of one or more workflow actions.

Oozie bundles are highly useful when handling large data pipelines. They offer a convenient way to group together related coordinators. Since a bundle consists of a related set of coordinators, you can start and stop multiple coordinators in unison.

In smaller environments the use of bundles may not be easily apparent to you, but in large Hadoop environments, especially such as the ones run by Yahoo! and similar large-scale data processors, there are hundreds of thousands of workflows running on a daily basis. Bundles offer a major operational convenience in such environments.

You create a bundle by defining a bundle and using the `bundle-app` element within which you define multiple coordinators. The specification of the `job.properties` file and how you submit an Oozie bundle job is quite similar to how you do so for an Oozie coordinator job.

Oozie cron Scheduling and Oozie Service Level Agreements

Oozie gives you the option to choose a cron-like syntax to schedule your coordinators, and it also lets you specify SLAs for your production jobs. I briefly explain the two concepts in the following sections.

Oozie cron Scheduling

Although time-based coordinators are useful for scheduling jobs at set intervals or frequencies, they're limited in their scheduling capabilities. For example, you can't use time-based scheduling to schedule workflows that need to be run only on specific days of the week or just once every so many days. Luckily, Oozie comes with Linux-like capabilities, which let you schedule operations in a highly flexible fashion.

Here's a time-based coordinator that uses the cron syntax for flexible scheduling.

```
<coordinator-app name="test_app" start="${startTime}" end="{endTime}"
   frequency="0 11-14" * * MON, WED" timezone="UTC"
   xmlns="url:oozie:coordiantor:0.4:>
```

This coordinator runs a workflow only on Monday and Wednesday between the hours of 11 A.M. and 2:00 P.M. The `0` before `11-14` means that the workflow job is kicked off at 0 minutes after the hour.

Oozie SLAs

In production settings, meeting agreed upon SLAs is critical—Oozie lets you set up SLAs for all of your workflows. Just add the `<sla:info>` element to the workflow.xml file for a job, as shown here.

```
</workflow-app>...
...
<sla:info>
 <sla:nominal-time>${nominal_time}</sla:nominal-time>
 <sla:should-start>${10 * MINUTES}</sla:should-start>
 <sla:should-end>${60 * MINUTES}</sla:should-end>
 <sla:max-duration>${60 * MINUTES}</sla:max-duration>
 <sla:alert-events>start_miss,end_miss,duration_miss</sla:alert-events>
 <sla:alert-contact>prod.support@mycompany.com</sla:alert-contact>
 <sla:notification-msg>Data Loading Job has encountered an SLA Event.</
sla:notification-msg>
  </sla:info>
</workflow-app>
```

Once you set the SLA for a workflow or coordinator job as shown here, Oozie will actively track the SLA in the job. You can access the SLA information through the Oozie web console dashboard, REST APIs, JMS messages or email alerts.

Summary

Here's what you learned in this chapter:

- Oozie is a very powerful tool that lets you create sophisticated workflows in a Hadoop cluster.
- While an Oozie workflow lets you configure the actual job you want to run, the coordinator lets you schedule those workflows and the Oozie bundles let you gather together, in one compact place, all related workflows and coordinators.
- You can configure Oozie jobs so that you'll get notifications when SLAs are violated.

15

Securing Hadoop

This chapter covers the following:

- Authentication in Hadoop through Kerberos
- Authorization in Hadoop and the Sentry service
- Auditing in Hadoop
- Securing Hadoop data through encryption

Hadoop, as we know, is an open-source project that includes various modules that were independently developed over time to add various types of functionality to its core capabilities. Security was really an afterthought, and Hadoop lacks a coherent security model. By default, Hadoop assumes a trusted environment. As Hadoop has matured, corporations are of course concerned with the security of sensitive business data that they're increasingly storing in Hadoop-based environments.

Unlike in the case of a regular database, in Hadoop there's no central authentication server or mechanism. If users can manage to access the server running the NameNode and have appropriate permissions on the Hadoop binaries, they can potentially read data they weren't authorized to read and even delete that data. There are no role-based access control (RBAC), object-level or other granular authentication features in Hadoop.

Since you store data in multiple DataNodes, each of them is a potential entry point for an attacker, and you must secure all the nodes in a cluster. In order to encrypt data flowing between clients and the DataNodes, you must use Kerberos or a Simple Authentication and Security Layer (SASL) framework. Communication between the DataNodes and the NameNode also needs to be protected.

Encryption is an important requirement for protecting sensitive data. Lack of encryption at rest and encryption of in-flight data means that internode communications can be intercepted, and private information stored on disk can be accessed.

Hadoop security involves three main concepts—authentication, authorization and auditing.

- The best and accepted way to provide authentication for Hadoop is through Kerberos security. Kerberos provides strong authentication of users and services that work with a Hadoop cluster.
- Authorization, which determines who can access a Hadoop cluster's data, is a key security concern in any environment. You use access control lists (ACLs) to configure authorization. Apache Sentry lets you configure strong, fine-grained authentication for your data.
- Auditing is the tracking of activity within the cluster and can include both user and administrative activity. Encrypting data in transit via the network and data at rest (on disk storage) is extremely important, especially when you're dealing with what's known as personally identifiable information (PII) such as social security numbers.

Hadoop Security—An Overview

With almost daily announcements of major data breaches involving credit card data, social security numbers, medical and other personal data, corporations are extremely concerned about protecting data.

Protecting your data involves securing your networks, web servers, web application servers and database, among other things. Together, the security measures used currently by companies constitute what's known as defense in depth, a concept that has gained tremendous ground over the past several years, with frequent painful reminders provided by sensational and catastrophic corporate security breaches.

Complete security of corporate data is a goal that may never be reached, but defense-in-depth strategies seek to minimize an organization's security vulnerabilities. In order to protect your data, you put in place all the standard corporate security features such as network security, intrusion detection and intrusion prevention systems and so on. On top of this, you add other security layers that control access to the system and limit access to the data.

As Hadoop administrators, you need to learn how to put in place authentication, authorization and accounting policies for accessing and using data stored in the Hadoop clusters, as well as to secure the data in transit and at rest.

Securing Hadoop not only involves securing access to Hadoop and securing the stored data itself (data at rest), but also the whole gamut of security that all IT operations use, such as network security and operating system security. Following are some general principles that underlie enterprise security in a Hadoop environment:

- Ideally, a Hadoop cluster should be in its own network segment, separated from the rest of the IT environment with appropriate firewalls, as well as security measures such as intrusion detection and intrusion protection systems.
- It's common practice to configure a secured VLAN for a Hadoop cluster and limit connections to those initiated from the gateway or edge servers only.

- In general, the network firewalls should permit FTP traffic from a set of FTP servers to the edge nodes. They should also allow the worker nodes to connect to the database servers to send and receive data over specific ports.
- Ingest mechanisms such as Apache Flume should be able to access log events from web servers over specific ports.
- Depending on how clients are allowed to access your cluster—some organizations permit clients to directly access the cluster and some don't—you need to set up the appropriate network firewall policies between the applications and the Hadoop cluster, as well as between the applications and the actual users. In some places, users execute MapReduce and Hive scripts from the command line on one of the cluster's nodes, and in other places users use Hue or a different tool to connect to and work with the cluster.

Hadoop Roles

Each node in a Hadoop cluster hosts different types of services, and the types of services it hosts determines the role the node plays in the Hadoop cluster. You devise security polices for the various nodes based on the type of role they play in the cluster. Clients can be users or third-party tools such as Hue and will access the cluster to perform their work. There are also services such as the Hive metastore, for example, that need to access the cluster.

Let's summarize the various types of roles in a Hadoop cluster as shown here:

- HDFS: NameNode, DataNode, JournalNode, HttpFS, NFS Gateway
- YARN: ResourceManager, NodeManager, JobHistoryServer
- Hive: Hive Metastore Server, HiveServer2, WebHCat Server
- Hue: Hue Server, Beeswax, Kerberos Ticket Renewer
- ZooKeeper: ZooKeeper Server
- Oozie: Oozie Server
- Management Services: Apache Ambari, Ganglia, Nagios, Puppet, Chef

The list shown here isn't by any means exhaustive: There are other roles such as the ones required for HBase, for example. You can classify the cluster nodes into various types based on the type of role they host. Here's one way to do this:

- Master nodes: These nodes run the main Hadoop services.
- Worker nodes: These nodes run the services that store and process data.
- Management nodes: These nodes run the services that help you configure, manage and monitor your cluster and include services such as the Ambari Server, Ganglia, Nagios, Puppet and Chef.
- Gateway nodes: Also known as edge nodes, gateway nodes are where you store the client configuration files and install the client-facing roles such as Hue and Oozie, for example. The following nodes run various types of services that help clients access and work on the cluster:
    - Data gateway nodes: HDFS, HttpFS, NFS Gateway and Flume agents

- SQL gateway nodes: Hive, HiveServer2, WebHCat Server
- User gateway nodes: Client configurations, Hue Server, Oozie Server, Kerberos Ticket Renewer

In the following sections, I review the broad areas of Hadoop security, which include the following concepts:

- Authentication, authorization and accounting
- Securing data at rest
- Securing data in transit

Authentication, Authorization and Accounting

Hadoop (or any other) security involves the three well-known concepts of authentication, authorization and accounting, which I alluded to in previous sections. In the following sections, I discuss how these three essential security concepts are addressed in a Hadoop environment.

Authentication

Authentication is the process through which a server or an application knows exactly who is accessing the server or application. During the authentication process, the burden is on a user accessing the system to provide their **identity**. In a Linux system, for example, when you log in, the system compares your user/password credentials with those in the /etc/password file. When this is successful, you're said to be authenticated with your identity, which is your Linux username.

Kerberos is the most popular security model in today's IT environment. Kerberos is an open-source network authentication protocol that lets the cluster nodes verify their identity with each other. Kerberos is a pure authentication protocol, so it doesn't manage file and directory permissions.

When you implement Kerberos, users wanting access to your cluster will first contact the central Kerberos server named Key Distribution Center (KDC), which contains the credentials database. If the user provided credentials are okay, the KDC grants access to the Hadoop cluster. To summarize, the authentication process through Kerberos has three steps:

- The Authentication Server grants the clients seeking access to the Hadoop cluster a Ticket Granting Ticket (TGT).
- The client decrypts the TGT using their credentials and, using the TGT, gets a service ticket from the Ticket Granting Server (TGS)—the TGS grants access to the Hadoop cluster.
- Clients use the service tickets granted by the TGS to access the Hadoop cluster.

> **Note**
>
> The Kerberos protocol is implemented as a series of negotiations among the clients, the Authorization Server and the Ticket Granting Server.

Authorization

Authorization is the process by which a system determines whether the user has the necessary permissions to use a resource or access specific data. Authorization typically follows successful authentication by the users. The type of authorization varies, and passwords may be required in some cases but not in others.

Authorization is complex in Hadoop. Since Hadoop stores its data in a file system like a Linux system and not in tables like a relational database, it's not possible to restrict users by granting them partial access to the data. There's no central authorization system in Hadoop to help you limit the data access by granting partial access to the data files, but you can do this with Apache Sentry, as I show later in this chapter, or with Apache Ranger.

Services such as Apache Sentry and Apache Ranger enable you to configure fine-grained authorization in Hadoop through a database such as Hive, along with an authorization mechanism. Sentry lets you create rules that specify the possible actions on a table and also create roles, which are sets of rules. Using Sentry, you can specify portions of file data as Hive tables, and Sentry can then help you with the configuration of fine-grained permissions for specific portions of data.

Hadoop's ACL capabilities help you specify fine-grained read and write permissions for specific users without altering the file permissions for all users. The section "HDFS Access Control Lists" in this chapter explains HDFS ACLs, which work quite similarly to Linux (POSIX) ACLs.

Auditing

Auditing privileged actions is the third key component of security. Since even authorized users may at times perform (or try to perform) unauthorized actions, you need to track user activity somehow.

Hadoop's audit log mechanism helps you track specific user actions in the system for security purposes. It's interesting to note here that you can analyze the humongous Hadoop audit logs by storing them in HDFS if you wish and use tools such as Hive to process them. HDFS audit logs help you track all HDFS access activity, and the YARN audit logs enable you to audit job submission activity.

In the following sections, I show you how to set up authorization, authentication and accounting, as well as data security in a Hadoop cluster. Let's start with how you can set up authentication through Kerberos.

Hadoop Authentication with Kerberos

Kerberos is an absolute requirement for user authentication in Hadoop. Kerberos is the most common way of securing a Hadoop cluster, through its robust user authentication mechanism.

Kerberos and How It Works

In Greek mythology, Kerberos (in Greek, Cerberos) is the ferocious multiheaded dog that guards the gates of Hades (Hell) to make sure nobody leaves. In the security world, Kerberos has acquired fame as a strong authentication mechanism, while also intimidating many administrators with its apparent complexity.

Kerberos is an authentication protocol where the hosts are trusted but the network isn't. Kerberos works on the premise that the hosts in a cluster are trusted and its secret key isn't compromised. Kerberos security design involves three key entities:

- Users who want to authenticate themselves.
- The service to which the user is attempting to authenticate.
- Kerberos security server (Key Distribution Center or KDC), trusted by both the user and the service. It's the KDC that stores the secret keys for the users and services.

Kerberos uses a central server. Since a failure of this server means no one can log into your cluster, you are allowed to set up more than one server. Passwords are highly secure, since Kerberos saves them on the central server and doesn't replicate the password information anywhere else.

Once a user logs into a system authenticated by Kerberos (also called a **Kerberized** cluster), that user can continue to access all authorized services without having to authenticate again during that session. In this sense, it's similar to the familiar concept of single sign-on.

In a Kerberized cluster, you can't log in to your cluster with the usual user credentials. In order to log in to any of the cluster nodes, you must use the `kinit` utility. The `kinit` utility isn't present on your server unless your server already has a Kerberos installation. If you try to use the `kinit` utility without installing Kerberos, you'll receive an error. Even if Kerberos is already present on a server, the command will result in an error if you haven't completely configured Kerberos for authorization:

```
# kinit
kinit(v5): Cannot resolve network address for KDC in realm EXAMPLE.COM while
 getting initial credentials
#
```

Kerberos uses a set of unique terms, and to understand how Kerberos authentication works, it's important to grasp what these terms mean. It also employs several unique administrative entities for enforcing security. Understanding these entities is crucial to configuring and managing Kerberos-based security. I briefly explain the key Kerberos terms and administrative entities in the following sections.

Key Distribution Center (KDC)

A KDC is a Kerberos server that contains an encrypted database wherein it stores all the principal entries pertaining to users, hosts and services, including their domain information.

Besides the database, which is stored in the form of a file, a KDC also contains two important components, named the Authentication Service (AS) and the previously discussed TGS. The AS and TGS together handle all of the authentication and access requests made to a Kerberos-secured Hadoop cluster. The Kerberos database stores the principal and realm information.

Authentication Server (AS)

Once a user successfully authenticates to the AS, the AS grants TGTs to clients with which to authenticate to other services in a secure cluster. The tickets are time-limited cryptographic messages that are used by clients to authenticate with the server. The principals will then use the TGT to request authentication and access to a Hadoop service.

Ticket Granting Server (TGS)

The Ticket Granting Server validates a TGT passed along by a client and in turn grants a **service ticket** to the client so they can access a Hadoop service. It's the service ticket that enables the authenticated principal to use the services in the cluster.

Keytab File

A **keytab file** is a secure file that contains the passwords of all the service principals in a domain. Each Hadoop service requires that you place a keytab file on all their hosts. When Kerberos needs to renew the TGT for a service, it looks up the keytab file.

Key Kerberos Terms

Following are the three key Kerberos-related terms you must be familiar with:

- Realm: A realm is the basic administrative domain for authenticating users and serves to establish the boundaries for an administrative server to authenticate users, hosts and services. Each Hadoop user is assigned to a specific domain. It's customary to specify a realm in upper case letters, such as `EXAMPLE.COM`. There can be multiple KDCs and, therefore, multiple realms in a single network.
- Principal: A principal is a user, host or service that's part of a given realm. It's common to refer to users as **user principals** and principals pertaining to services as **service principals**. User principal names (UPNs) denote regular users. Service principal names (SPNs) are logins that are necessary to run Hadoop services or background processes and include Hadoop services such as HDFS and YARN.
- Ticket: When a user wants to authenticate to a Kerberos-supported cluster, the administration server generates a ticket. This ticket contains information such as the username (usually the same as the user's principal), the service's principal, the IP address of the client and a timestamp. A ticket has a configurable maximum lifetime and a session key. Users can also renew their tickets up to a specified time.

The Kerberos Authentication Process

The Kerberos authentication process is pretty straightforward and involves three key steps: the initial client login to a cluster which gets it a TGT from the AS, the granting of service tickets from the TGS and the final step of user authentication to a service. In order to explain the authentication process, I use the following components.

- Realm: `EXAMPLE.COM`
- User principal: `sam@EXAMPLE.COM`
- Service principal: `testservice/host1.example.com@EXAMPLE.COM`
- KDC: `kdc.example.com`

The user named sam, with the UPN of `sam@EXAMPLE.COM`, follows these steps to authenticate to the Kerberized Hadoop cluster and access a service named testservice.

1. When a user logs into a cluster, he or she contacts the AS at `kdc.example.com`, using his or her UPN—for example, `sam@EXAMPLE.COM`.
2. The authentication server grants the user a TGT, which is a token with which the user can authenticate itself. The TGT is encrypted with a key that's the same as the password for user sam. For service principals, the credentials are passed to the authentication server from the keytab file stored on the host.
3. The user decrypts the TGT using the password for the principal `sam@EXAMPLE.COM`. In our example here, user sam presents the TGT to the TGS at `kdc.example.com` to request a service named `testservice/hadoop01.example.com@EXAMPLE.COM`. This service ticket enables the client to access the secure cluster. The client continues to use the same TGT for multiple requests to the TGS until the expiry of the TGT.
4. Once the TGS validates the TGT presented by user sam, it provides sam a service ticket encrypted with the key of the UPN named `testservice/hadoop01.example.com@EXAMPLE.COM`.
5. The user sam authenticates to a specific service in the secure cluster with the service ticket received in step 4. Once user sam presents the service ticket to the service named testservice, the service decrypts it with the key of the UPN `testservice/hadoop01.example.com@EXAMPLE.COM` to validate the service ticket.
6. Now that user sam has been successfully authenticated, the service named testservice will allow user sam to use the service.

Kerberos Trusts

In real life, organizations may use multiple realms to separate different parts of the enterprise or for other reasons. Each of these realms will have their own KDCs, with each KDC aware of principals that are part of its own realm.

If a user from realm A wants to use a service that's in realm B, obviously, one must set up a way for the two realms to work together. **Kerberos trusts** are the way to establish a trusted relationship between two realms, making it possible for principals from one realm to access services from the other.

Suppose you have two different Kerberos realms within your organization. You can name them SALES.EXAMPLE.COM and HR.EXAMPLE.COM. You can configure a trusted relationship between these two realms, which enables a user from SALES.EXAMPLE.COM to trust information coming from the HR.EXAMPLE.COM realm. Of course, setting up this trust enables the second realm to trust information coming from the first realm as well.

> **Note**
>
> Refer to principals in the format username@REALM or username/role@REALM. For a service principal, the naming format is service/hostname@REALM—for example, yarn/hadoop01.localhost@EXAMPLE.COM.

A Special Principal

There's a special principal in each Kerberos database that plays a critical role in establishing a trusted relationship between two realms. This principal has the format krbgt/<REALM>@<REALM>, for internal use by the AS and the TGS.

For our EXAMPLE.COM realm, this'll be krbgt/EXAMPLE.COM@EXAMPLE.COM. Kerberos uses the key for this special principal to encrypt the TGT issued by it. This is to ensure that the TGT issued by an AS can be validated only by the TGS and nobody else.

When you set up a one-way or two-way trust between realms, the special principal I described here must exist in both realms. The password for this principal needs to be the same in both realms as well.

One-Way Trust and Two-Way Trust

A one-way trust allows principals from realm A to access realm B but doesn't allow the users stored in realm B to access realm A. One-way trusts are the most commonly used trust relationship between two realms. Most commonly, organizations want to use the end user information that's stored in the company's Active Directory to access the Hadoop cluster. In such a case you set up a KDC in the Hadoop cluster to hold all the SPN information and the UPN information will be in Active Directory.

In a one-way trust, the user principals exist in a single realm only. Let's say you have two realms that you've named HR.EXAMPLE.COM and SALES.EXAMPLE.COM, between which you want to establish a one-way trust. You must set up the special principal krbtgt in both realms. That is, for the HR realm to trust the SALES realm, you must set up the principal krbtgt/HR.EXAMPLE.COM@SALES.EXAMPLE.COM in both realms.

In a two-way trust, principals in both realms can access the other realm. This requires that the user principals exist in both realms. Therefore, you must create the principal krbtgt/SALES.EXAMPLE.COM@HR.EXAMPLE.COM and the principal krbtgt/HR.EXAMPLE.COM@SALES.EXAMPLE.COM in both realms. This will establish full trust between the realms SALES and HR.

I understand if at this point all this discussion about realms, KDCs, principals, TGTs and so on is probably a bit confusing. Once I explain how you actually set up Kerberos authentication in a Hadoop cluster, however, you'll realize that this isn't really as hard as you might have imagined!

The next section shows how to Kerberize (the configuring of authorization through Kerberos) your Hadoop cluster.

Adding Kerberos Authorization to your Cluster

While there are numerous configuration parameters and settings involved, it's really quite straightforward to Kerberize a Hadoop cluster. You can confidently go about securing your cluster by first making sure you thoroughly understand the Kerberos concepts I explained in the previous sections.

Securing Hadoop through Kerberos involves the following steps.

1. Installing Kerberos in the Hadoop cluster
2. Configuring Kerberos
3. Setting up Kerberos for Hadoop, which involves creating the Kerberos database, the Kerberos Admin user and the service principals and their keytabs
4. Starting up the Kerberos daemons
5. Configuring Hadoop for Kerberos, which involves the mapping of service principals to OS usernames and the addition of several Kerberos-related parameters to Hadoop configuration files such as `hdfs-site.xml` and `yarn-site.xml`
6. Starting up the Hadoop Cluster (such as HDFS and YARN) in the secure mode
7. Testing secure connections to the Hadoop cluster

Let's start with the installation and configuration of Kerberos in your cluster.

Installing Kerberos

In order to configure Kerberos authentication, you must first install and configure Kerberos. This configuration precedes the configuration of the Hadoop cluster with Kerberos.

Installing Kerberos involves the installation of the Kerberos software, of course, but it really means installing the KDC on one of the cluster nodes. You then install the Kerberos client on all the cluster nodes.

Kerberos configuration means you configure various aspects of the KDC pertaining to the administration of the KDC, the lifetime of tickets and so on. Once you do this, you can create the realms, user and service principals and set up your cluster for Kerberos authentication.

Install Kerberos on the master node as shown here:

1. Download the latest release of Kerberos from the MIT website:

```
# wget http://web.mit.edu/kerberos/dist/krb5/1.10/krb5-1.10.6-signed.tar
```

2. Unpack the source code and the encrypted TAR file:

```
# tar -xvf <downloaded release>
```

3. Unpack the krb5-1.11.3.tar.gz file:

```
# tar -xvf krb5-1.11.3.tar.gz
```

4. Move to the installation directory and compile the source code:

```
# cd <installation directory>/src
./configure
```

5. Create the executable with the `make` command:

```
# make
```

Once you install the Kerberos server, install the Kerberos client on all cluster nodes, including the master and the worker nodes, as shown here:

```
# yum install lkrb5-libs krb5-workstation
```

Once you install all the Kerberos packages and install the Kerberos KDC, the next step is to configure the KDC by editing its configuration files. In what follows, I'll use `example.com` as my domain name and `EXAMPLE.COM` as my realm name.

Kerberos uses two main configuration files, named krb5.conf (usually /etc/krb5.conf) and kdc.conf (usually /var/Kerberos/krb5kdc/kdc.conf). There's also a third file called kadm5.acl, usually under the /var/krb5kdc directory.

Configuring Kerberos (krb5.conf)

The krb5.conf file is the Kerberos high-level configuration file that lets you configure the location of the KDC, the admin servers and the mapping of Kerberos realms with hostnames. This file is the Kerberos client configuration file and is read whenever a client attempts to authenticate through the KDC using the `kinit` utility. The default krb5.conf file is usually in the /etc directory, and you can use the default values for most of the configuration parameters in this file.

Configure the krb5.conf file as shown here:

```
[logging]
 default = FILE:/var/log/krb5libs.log
 kdc = FILE:/var/log/krb5kdc.log
 admin_server = FILE:/var/log/kadmind.log

[libdefaults]
 default_realm = EXAMPLE.COM
 dns_lookup_realm = false
 dns_lookup_kdc = false
 ticket_lifetime = 24h
 renew_lifetime = 7d
 forwardable = true

[kdc]
profile = /var/kerberos/krb5kdc/kdc.conf
```

```
[realms]
 EXAMPLE.COM = {
  kdc = kdc.example.com             // the hostname of the KDC
  admin_server = kdc.example.com     // the hostname of the Kerberos Server
(kadmin process)
 }
CERT.EXAMPLE.COM = {
  kdc = kdc.cert.example.com
  admin_server = kdc.cert.example.com
 }

[domain_realm]
 .example.com = EXAMPLE.COM
 example.com = EXAMPLE.COM
 .dev.example.com = EXAMPLE.COM
 dev.example.com = EXAMPLE.COM
```

As you can see here, there are multiple sections in a krb5.conf file. Here's what the sections mean:

- `logging`: Logging method used by Kerberos daemons.
- `lib_defaults`: Default values used by the Kerberos library. The `default_realm` parameter specifies the Kerberos realm to be used if you don't specify one when you authenticate yourself.
- `kdc`: Location of the kdc.conf file.
- `realms`: Realm-specific information such as the location of the Kerberos servers for a realm: there could be several of these, one for each realm. You can specify a port for the KDC and the admin server, and if you don't, it's understood that port 88 will be used for KDC and port 749 for the admin server.
- `domain_realm`: Specifies the mappings between DNS domain names and Kerberos realm names. Given a server's FQDN, the `domain_realm` parameter's value(s) determines the realm to which a host belongs.
- `forwardable`: Tickets can be forwardable if this parameter is set to true, meaning if a user with a TGT logs into a remote system, the KDC can issue a new TGT without the user having to authenticate again.

And here are the key configuration items I edited in the krb5.conf file:

- I edited the `kdc` and `realm` sections to point to my KDC server and my realm, which is `EXAMPLE.COM`.
- I set the `ticket_lifetime` attribute to 24 hours.
- The `renew_lifetime` attribute is set to 7 days. This allows Hadoop components such as Oozie and Hue to renew their Kerberos tickets. Once they're issued, tickets can be renewed for a period of 7 days.

In the krb5.conf file shown here, there are two realms under the `<realms>` section, `EXAMPLE.COM` and `CERT.EXAMPLE.COM`. This helps establish a one-way trust between the two realms. You can include all the UPNs in the EXAMPLE.COM realm and the CERT.EXAMPLE.COM realm can contain all the SPNs for a Hadoop cluster used for testing purposes. This setup helps UPNs in the test cluster to access the EXAMPLE.COM realm by using their credentials in the CERT.EXAMPLE.COM realm.

Once you complete configuring the krb5.conf file, you must copy this to every node in your Hadoop cluster.

Configuring the Key Distribution Center

The next step is to configure the Kerberos server, which you do by configuring the KDC. This involves configuring the database, AS and TGS, all of which are components of the KDC.

In order to configure the KDC, edit the kdc.conf (/var/kerberos/kerb5kdc/kdc.conf) file as shown here:

```
[kdcdefaults]
 kdc_ports = 88
 kdc_tcp_ports = 88

[realms]
 EXAMPLE.COM = {
  profile = /etc/krb5.conf
  supported_enctypes = aes128-cts:normal des3-hmac-sha1:normal
arcfour-hmac:normal des-hmac-sha1:normal des-cbc-md5:normal des-cbc-crc:normal
allow-null-ticket-addresses = true
database_name = /var/Kerberos/krb5kdc/principal
#master_key_type = aes256-cts
  acl_file = /var/kerberos/krb5kdc/kadm5.acl
  admin_keytab = /var/kerberos/krb5kdc/kadm5.keytab
  dict_file = /usr/share/dict/words
  max_life = 2d 0h 0m 0s
  max_renewable_life = 7d 0h 0m 0s
  admin_database_lockfile = /var/kerberos/krb5kdc/kadm5_adb.lock
  key_stash_file = /var/kerberos/krb5kdc/.k5stash
  kdc_ports = 88
  kadmind_port = 749
  default_principle_flags = +renewable
```

In the kdc.conf file configuration, note the following:

- There are two major sections in the kdc.conf file. The kdcdefaults section contains configuration that's common to all realms you list within this file. The section named realms lists the configuration for each realm separately. In our case, we have two realms, but I'm showing the configuration for a single realm named EXAMPLE.COM.
- The kdc_ports and kdc_tcp_ports parameters specify the UDC and TCP ports for the KDC.
- The supported_enctypes parameter specifies the various encryption types supported by this KDC.

- The max_life parameter specifies a value of 2 days. This shows the maximum life for a ticket.
- The max_renewable_life parameter specifies the maximum time within which a ticket can be renewed.
- The master_key_type entry is disabled, but if you need 256-bit encryption, you can download the Java cryptography extension (JCE) to install it. By disabling this parameter, I'm using the default 128-bit encryption.
- The acl_file parameter lets you specify an ACL for UPNs with an admin access to the Kerberos database. For example, if your ACL is of the format */admin@EXAMPLE.COM, all UPNs with the /admin extension have full access to the Kerberos database.
- The dict_file parameter points to the file containing potentially easily guessable or breakable passwords.

The acl_file parameter needs special mention here for administrators. Earlier, you learned about the kadmin utility for Kerberos administrators. Since the kadmin utility itself uses Kerberos to authenticate, you specify the UPNs you want to allow to perform administrative actions in the kadm5.acl file, whose location you specify with the acl_file parameter in the kdc.conf file. Here's an example showing how you specify the UPNs that can perform administrative tasks within the kdc.conf file:

```
*/admin@EXAMPLE.COM    *
```

Note the following:

- The first * means any principal from the EXAMPLE.COM domain can perform administrative actions provided they use the format <user_name>/admin@EXAMPLE.COM
- The second * means that the UPNs can perform any action. If you want to limit the privileges for an administrative user through the kadm5.acl file, you can do so, as shown here:

  ```
  sam/EXAMPLE.COM     *  hdfs/*@EXAMPLE.COM
  ```

  This means that that user sam can perform any action but can do so only on the SPNs starting with hdfs.

Setting Up Kerberos for Hadoop

You have now configured Kerberos, but you aren't there yet! You need to perform the following tasks to prepare Kerberos for authorizing connections to your Hadoop cluster.

1. Create the Kerberos database and the first user principal (root).
2. Start the Kerberos services.

3. Create the service principal (SPN).
4. Create the keytab files.

The following sections show how to perform these tasks.

Creating the Kerberos Database

As you learned earlier, Kerberos consists of three components—a database, the AS and the TGS. By default, there's no database, and you must create it. You can use a flat file or an LDAP directory as the database. Here's how you create the Kerberos database:

```
$ kdb5_util create -r EXAMPLE.COM -s
Loading random data
Initializing database '/var/kerberos/krb5kdc/principal' for realm 'EXAMPLE.COM',
master key name 'K/M@EXAMPLE.COM'
You will be prompted for the database Master Password.
It is important that you NOT FORGET this password.
Enter KDC database master key:
Re-enter KDC database master key to verify:
$
```

The `-s` option stores the master server key for the database in a stash file, which lets you regenerate the master server key automatically each time you start the KDC. Make a note of the master key, as you'll need it later on.

The `kdb5_util create` command creates the following five files under the /usr/local/var/krb5kdc directory:

- Two Kerberos database files named principal and principal.ok
- The Kerberos administrative database file named principal.kadm5
- The administrative database lock file named principal.kadm5.lock
- A stash file named k5.EXAMPLE.COM

The stash file is a copy of the encrypted master key stored on the KDC's local disk. KDC uses this stash file to automatically authenticate itself when it starts the Hadoop daemons.

Creating the Administrator Principal for KDC

You're almost there! Before you can start up the Kerberos services, you must also create the first user principal on the KDC server. This user principal is the root user on the Linux server.

```
$ sudo kadmin.local -q
Authenticating as principal root/admin@EXAMPLE.COM with password.
kadmin.local:  addprinc root/admin
Enter password for principal "root/admin@EXAMPLE.COM":
Re-enter password for principal "root/admin@EXAMPLE.COM":
Principal "root/admin@EXAMPLE.COM.COM" created.
kadmin.local:
```

Starting the Kerberos Services

Now that I've configured Kerberos, I'm ready to start the Kerberos daemons. Start up the Kerberos services as shown here, with the `kadmind` and the `krb5kdc` utilities.

```
# /sbin/service kadmind start
# /sbin/service krb5kdc star
```

The first of the two commands here enables the Kerberos administrator to connect from a remote server to perform Kerberos administration using the `kadmin` client. The second command (`krb5kdc`) starts the KDC server.

Now you're ready to create the set of service principals.

Creating the Service Principals

You must create a service principal to represent each of the Hadoop services such as HDFS and YARN. This enables Hadoop daemons such as hdfs (for the HDFS service), mapred (for MapReduce) and yarn (for YARN) to be authenticated by Kerberos.

You need to create an SPN for every service/daemon pair in your cluster. You must also create service principals for component services such as Hive, Oozie and so on. I show only the creation of the service principals for users hdfs, yarn and mapred here to keep things concise, but you can create the other principals using the same procedure.

In addition to HDFS and YARN, I also create a service principal for HTTP, which is a required web communication protocol implementation for using Kerberos. All three service principals here—hdfs, yarn and mapred—expose HTTP services. By provisioning these principals with an HTTP service name you can enable Kerberos authentication for the web interfaces you use in your day-to-day work.

I use the same `addprinc` command that I had used earlier to create my first user principal (for the root user) to create the following service principals. The command is named `addprinc` (add_principal) since it adds the principals to the Kerberos database.

```
[root@hadoop01]# kadmin
Authenticating as principal root/admin@EXAMPLE.COM with password.
Password for root/admin@EXAMPLE.COM:
kadmin:  addprinc -randkey hdfs/hadoop01@EXAMPLE.COM
Principal "hdfs/hadoop01@EXAMPLE.COM" created.
kadmin:  addprinc -randkey mapred/hadoop01@EXAMPLE.COM
Principal "mapred/hadoop01@EXAMPLE.COM" created.
kadmin:  addprinc -randkey yarn/hadoop01@EXAMPLE.COM
Principal "yarn/hadoop01@EXAMPLE.COM" created.
kadmin:  addprinc -randkey HTTP/hadoop01@EXAMPLE.COM
Principal "HTTP/hadoop01@EXAMPLE.COM" created.
kadmin:
#
```

In this example, the `addprinc` command helped me create a new principal in the Kerberos database. You can display the details of a principal by issuing the `getprinc` command, as shown here:

```
kadmin: getprinc sam@EXAMPLE.COM
```

You can list all principals in the Kerberos database with the `listprinc` command:

```
kadmin: listprinc
```

Finally, you can delete a principal from the Kerberos database with the `delprinc` command:

```
kadmin: delprinc sam@EXAMPLE.COM
```

> **Note**
>
> It's important to understand that in order to implement Kerberos security in a Hadoop cluster, you must provision all the cluster users on all the cluster nodes. Alternatively, you can provision all users in Active Directory and have the Hadoop servers access that directory service. You can restrict the privileges of the provisioned users by restricting them, for example, with a `nologin` shell.

I used the `addprinc` command earlier to create a set of service principals. However, this set of SPNs is by no means comprehensive. You must create an SPN for each service running on each node in the cluster, such as the following:

- NameNode (or NameNodes in a high-availability setup)
- JournalNode
- Secondary NameNode (if not high availability)
- ResourceManager
- NodeManager
- JobHistoryServer

You also need to create user principals for services such as Hue, as shown here:

```
kadmin:  addprinc -randkey hue/hadoop03@EXAMPLE.COM
```

Here, `hue` is the principal the Hue server is running as, and `hadoop03` is the server where the Hue server is running.

Make sure that all directories used by HDFS, such as the NameNode, DataNode and log directories, have hdfs as both the owner and the OS group. Similarly, the directories used exclusively by the MapReduce daemons, such as the MapReduce local and log directories, should have mapred as both the user and the group. And finally, directories used by both hdfs and mapred daemons should be under the group hadoop.

Creating the Keytab File

Each service principal requires a keytab file to store its passwords. A keytab file contains pairs of Kerberos principals and the encrypted key derived from their Kerberos password. It is used for authenticating with the KDC when the services run without any intervention.

A UPN will need to use `kinit` to log into the secure cluster and then provide a password for authentication. However, SPNs can't make an interactive login attempt. The keytab file stores the encryption keys that can be used for a specific SPN, and you can store multiple SPN keys in the same keytab file. In fact, a regular user (UPN) can also use a keytab file in lieu of providing their password during a login, as shown here:

```
$ kinit -kt sam.keytab sam/admin@EXAMPLE.COM
```

Here, the -kt flag indicates that the keytab file should be used instead of a password being entered at the command line.

> **Tip**
>
> You must protect the keytab files carefully, since they hold the keys to the kingdom, especially for administrative principals!

The users yarn, hdfs and mapred all run background Hadoop daemons, so you need to create a keytab file for these service principals. In addition, you need to create a keytab file for the http principal so Kerberos can authenticate Hadoop's web UIs.

Use the kadmin utility to create the keytab files. You really don't need to formally create the keytab files. Using the kadmin utility, you can specify the xst -k options to extract the keytab file for each service principal and place it in the keytab directory for that service principal.

Each service principal's keytab file is uniquely named after the principal, such as yarn.keytab, http.keytab, oozie.keytab and hive.keytab. You must export a separate keytab file for each of the Hadoop daemons running on a Hadoop node.

For example, to create the keytab file for the service YARN, do the following:

```
root@hadoop01]# kadmin
Authenticating as principal root/admin@EXAMPLE.COM with password.
Password for root/admin@EXAMPLE.COM:
kadmin: xst -k yarn.keytab hdfs/hadoop01@EXAMPLE.COM HTTP/hadoop01@EXAMPLE.COM
Entry for principal hdfs/hadoop01@EXAMPLE.COM with kvno 5, encryption type
aes128-cts-
Entry for principal HTTP/hadoop01@EXAMPLE.COM with kvno 4, encryption type
des-cbc-md5 added to keytab WRFILE:yarn.keytab
...
root@hadoop01]#
```

In a similar fashion, create keytab files for all the other service principals.

You may want to verify that the service principals are associated correctly by issuing the klist command as shown here, from the NameNode server in your cluster:

```
$ kinit
Enter password for sam@EXAMPLE.COM:
$ klist
Ticket Cache: FILE:/tmp/krb5cc_5000
If the service principal name's first component (hdfs in this example) is the
same as its username, there's no need to create any further rules, since the
DEFAULT rule Default principal:  sam@EXAMPLE.COM
...
$
```

Similarly, you can issue the following command to ensure that the hue service principal's keytab file was created correctly:

```
$ kinit -k -t /etc/hue/hue.keytab hue/hue.server.fully.qualified.domain.name@
YOUR-REALM.COM
```

If the user hasn't authenticated first, there will be no credentials in the cache, and they'll receive the "No credentials cache found" message when they issue the klist command.

Once you create the keytab files for the service principals, move the files to the /et/hadoop/conf directory and secure the files, as shown here:

```
# mv hdfs.keytab yarn.keytab mapred.keytab /etc/hadoop/conf
# chown hdfs:hadoop /etc/hadoop/conf/hdfs.keytab
# chown yarn:hadoop /etc/hadoop/conf/yarn.keytab
# chown mapred:hadoop /etc/hadoop/conf/mapred.keytab
# chmod 400 /etc/hadoop/conf/hdfs.keytab /etc/hadoop/conf/yarn.keytab
```

As mentioned earlier, you must do this on every node where the service represented by the service principal is running. Use an automated deployment tool to move the keytab files to all the cluster nodes. You can store the keytab files in the `$HADOOP_CONF_DIR` directory, such as /etc/hadoop/conf, for example.

Now that I've configured Kerberos and set it up to work with Hadoop by creating all the necessary service principals and their keytab files, it's time to configure Kerberos to work with my Hadoop cluster.

Securing a Hadoop Cluster with Kerberos

So far, I've configured Kerberos and prepared it for authorizing Hadoop users. To secure my cluster with Kerberos, I need to link this Kerberos configuration with Hadoop, by adding the Kerberos information to the relevant Hadoop configuration files. These are the same Hadoop configuration files you're familiar with, such as the `core-site.xml` and the `hdfs-site.xml` files.

I need to do the following to complete authorization through Kerberos:

- Map the service principals to their operating system usernames
- Add the Kerberos information to the Hadoop configuration files

The following sections show how to map service principals to their OS usernames and configure the Hadoop configuration files with Kerberos-related information.

Mapping Service Principals

Kerberos uses rules configured in the core-site.xml file, by specifying the `hadoop.security.auth_to_local` parameter, to map service principals to their operating system usernames.

The default rule, named `DEFAULT`, simply translates a service principal's name to the first component of their name. Remember that a service principal's name has either two components, such as `sam@EXAMPLE.COM`, or can use a three-part string such as `hdfs/namenode.example.com@EXAMPLE.COM`. Hadoop maps Kerberos principal names to their local usernames.

If the service principal name's first component (*hdfs* in this example) is the same as its username, there's no need to create any further rules since the `DEFAULT` rule is sufficient in this case. Note that alternatively, you can also map principals to usernames in the krb5.conf file by configuring the `auth_to_local` parameter there.

If your service principal's name is different from its OS username, you must configure the `hadoop.security.auth_to_local` parameter to specify **rules** for translating the principal names to the operating system names. As explained earlier, the default value of this parameter is simply `DEFAULT`. A rule provides the mechanism to translate the service principal names and consists of the following three parts or components:

- Base: The base specifies the number of components in the service principal's name, followed by a colon and a pattern for building the username from the service principal's name. In the pattern, `$0` means the realm, `$1` refers to the first component in the service principal's name and `$2` refers to the second component. The format is specified as `[<number>:<string>]` and is applied to the principal's name to arrive at the translated principal name, also called the initial local name. Here are a couple of examples:
  - If the base format is `[1:$1:$0]`, then the UPN of `sam@EXAMPLE.COM` is given the initial local name of `sam.EXAMPLE.COM`.
  - If the base format is `[2:&1@$0]`, then the SPN `hdfs/namenode.example.com @EXAMPLE.COM` is given the initial local name of `hdfs@EXAMPLE.COM`.
- Filter: The filter (or **acceptance filter**) is the component that uses a regular expression that matches the generated string in order to apply the rules. For example, the filter `(.*EXAMPLE\.COM)` matches all strings ending in `@EXAMPLE.COM`, such as `sam.EXAMPLE.COM` and `hdfs.EXAMPLE.COM`.
- Substitution: This is a command that uses sed-like substitution to translate a regular expression pattern with a fixed replacement string. The full specification of the rule is `RULE:[<number>:<string>](<regular expression>)s/<pattern>/<replacement>/`.

  You can surround a part of the regular expression with parentheses and reference this in the replacement string by a number, such as `\1`. The substitution command, `s/<pattern>/<replacement>/g`, works just like a regular Linux substitution command, with the `g` specifying a global substitution. Here are some examples of how the substitution command translates the expression `sam@EXAMPLE.COM` under various rules:

  ```
  s/(.*)\.MYCOMPANY.COM/\1/:      sam
  s/.MYCOMPANY.COM//        :     sam
  s/M/E                     :     sam.EXAMPLE.COM
  ```

  You can provide multiple rules, and once a principal matches a rule, the rest of the rules are skipped. You can include a `DEFAULT` rule at the end, so it'll match if none of the earlier rules do.

You can map users to groups through the `hadoop.security.group.mapping` parameter. The default mapping implementation looks up the user and group mappings through local shell commands.

Since this default implementation uses the Linux interfaces to establish a user's group membership, you must provision the group on all servers that run the services involved in authentication decisions, such as the NameNode, ResourceManager and DataNodes—essentially, your group information must be consistent throughout the cluster.

In cases where you need to use groups that are provisioned on an LDAP server such as Active Directory and not on the Hadoop cluster itself, you can use the `LDAPGroupsMapping` implementation.

Adding Kerberos information to Hadoop Configuration Files

In order to enable Kerberos authentication in a Hadoop cluster, you must add the Kerberos-related information to the following configuration files:

- core-site.xml
- hdfs-site.xml
- yarn-site xml

Each of these files will configure various aspects of HDFS and YARN to work together with Kerberos. Let's take these configuration files one by one.

core-site.xml File Additions

You need to add the following configuration parameters to the core-site.xml file.

- `hadoop.security.authentication`: This parameter sets the authentication type for the cluster. The default value is `simple`. For Kerberos authentication, specify the value `kerberos`.
- `hadoop.security.authorization`: This parameter enables authorization for the security protocols to check for file permissions.
- `hadoop.security.auth_to_local`: This parameter determines how to map Kerberos principal names to OS usernames with mapping rules.
- `hadoop.rpc.protection`: This parameter determines the protection level. Following are the three possible values for this parameter:
  - `authentication`: Client/server mutual authentication only
  - `integrity`: Guarantees the integrity of data in addition to authentication
  - `privacy`: Provides authentication and integrity of data, and also encrypts the data flowing between clients and server

Once you configure all of the parameters in the `core-site.xml` file, the additions will look like the following:

```
<property>
  <name>hadoop.security.authentication</name>
  <value>kerberos</value>
</property>
<property>
  <name>hadoop.security.authorization</name>
  <value>true</value>
  </property>
<property>
  <name>hadoop.security.auth_to_local</name>
  <value>[2:$1]kerberos</value>
```

```
</property>
<property>
  <name>hadoop.rpc.protection</name>
  <value>privacy</value>
</property>
```

YARN-Related Configuration Changes

You need to edit the yarn-site.xml file to add both keytab locations and principal information for YARN-related services such as the users who start the ResourceManager and the NodeManager daemons. Here are the parameters you add to the yarn-site.xml file:

- `yarn.resourcemanager.principal`: This is the name of the principal (yarn) that starts the ResourceManager in the cluster (suggested value: `yarn/_HOST@EXAMPLE.COM`).
- `yarn.resourcemanager.keytab`: This is the location on the local file system where the yarn user's keytab file is stored. (suggested value: `/etc/hadoop/conf/yarn.keytab`).
- `yarn.nodemanager.principal`: This is the yarn principal that starts the NodeManager (suggested value: `yarn/_HOST@EXAMPLE.COM`).
- `yarn.nodemanager.keytab`: This is the location of the keytab file for the yarn user.
- `yarn.nodemanager.container-executor.class`: This specifies the class for launching applications in yarn (suggested value: `org.apache.hadoop.yarn.server.nodemanager.LinuxContainerExecutor`).
- `yarn.nodemanager.linux-container-executor.group`: This is the group to which the Linux container belongs (suggested value: `yarn`).

The last two parameters help the NodeManager use the `LinuxContainerExecutor`, which enables YARN to run containers using the same UID as that of the user that submitted the job. After editing the yarn-site.xml file, you must configure the `LinuxContainerExecutor` by creating a file named container.executor.cfg and adding the following parameters to it:

- `yarn.nodemanager.log-dirs`: Specifies the Hadoop log directories. The reason you specify this parameter is to ensure that log file permissions are correctly set. Suggested value: /var/log/yarn (same as the values you specify in the yarn-site.xml file for the log directories).
- `yarn-manager.local-dirs`: The list of paths to the local NodeManager directories. These should be the same as the values you specify for local directories in the yarn-site.xml file.
- `yarn.nodemanager.linux-container-executor.group`: The value should be `yarn`.
- `banned.users`: This list of users prevents jobs from being submitted to the cluster via these accounts. Default values: hdfs, yarn, mapred and bin.
- `min.user.id`: Specifies the value of the user ID above which jobs are allowed to be submitted to the cluster. (suggested value: 1000). By convention, Linux super users have a user ID less than 1000, so this prevents jobs from being submitted with those IDs.

HDFS-Related Configuration Changes

You need to configure the keytab locations and principal names for the HDFS daemons in the hdfs-site.xml file. How do you manually configure a potentially large number of DataNodes? You don't! Hadoop offers a variable named `_HOST` that you can use instead of having to separately configure each HDFS daemon on every node in the cluster.

The `HOST` variable resolves to the FQDN of the server when a user or service connects to the cluster. Do remember that ZooKeeper and Hive don't support the specification of the `HOST` variable.

You must add three types of Kerberos-related configuration parameters to the hdfs-site.xml file:

- Kerberos principal information
- Keytab file location information
- Addresses and ports of the http/https services.

Configure the Kerberos service principals with the following set of configuration parameters:

- `dfs.namenode.kerberos.principal`: Specifies the Kerberos principal name for the NameNode. (value: `hdfs/_HOST@EXAMPLE.COM`)
- `dfs.secondary.namenode.kerberos.principal`: Specifies the principal for the secondary NameNode web server (value: `hdfs/_HOST@EXAMPLE.COM`).
- `dfs.web.authentication.kerberos.principal`: HTTP principal name (value: `HTTP/_HOST@EXAMPLE.COM`)
- `dfs.namenode.kerberos.internal.spnego.principal`: The http principal for the HTTP service (value: `HTTP/_HOST@EXAMPLE.COM`)
- `dfs.secondary.namenode.kerberos.internal.spnego.principal`: The http principal for the HTTP service (value: `HTTP/_HOST@EXAMPLE.COM`)
- `dfs.datanode.kerberos.principal`: Principal for the DataNode service (value: `hdfs/_HOST@EXAMPLE.COM`)

You specify the keytab file locations with the following parameters:

- `dfs.web.authentication.kerberos.keytab`: Kerberos keytab file location for the http service principal (value: `/etc/hadoop/conf/spnego.service.keytab`)
- `dfs.datanode.kerberos.principal`: Kerberos principal for the user that starts and stops the DataNode (value: hdfs, specified as `hdfs/_HOST@EXAMPLE.COM`)
- `dfs.namenode.keytab.file`: Keytab file with the credentials of the NameNode service and host principals
- `dfs.journalnode.kerberos.keytab.file`: Keytab file for the JournalNode (value: `hdfs.keytab`)

- `dfs.secondary.namenode.keytab.file`: Keytab file with the credentials of the NameNode service and host principals
- `dfs.datanode.keytab.file`: Location of the keytab file for the DataNode

In order to configure WebHDFS for a Kerberized cluster, you need to add the following two parameters to the hdfs-site.xml file on the NameNode and all the DataNodes.

```
dfs.web.authentication.kerberos.keytab (value=hdfs.keytab)
dfs.web.authentication.kerberos.principal (value=HTTP/_HOST@EXAMPLE.COM)
```

Securing the DataNodes

Before you can fire up the cluster in the secure mode, there's one last thing you must do—secure the DataNode. You must set the following environment variables for Jsvc, a set of libraries and applications that help Java applications run easily on Linux, so the DataNode can run in the secure mode.

```
$ export HADOOP_SECURE_DN=hdfs
$ export HADOOP_SECURE_DN_PID_DIR=/var/lib/hadoop-hdfs
$ export HADOOP_SECURE_DN_LOG_DIR=/var/log/hadoop-hdfs
$ export JSVC_HOME=/usr/lib/bigtop-utils  // if this directory doesn't
exist, use /usr/libexec/bigtop-utils
```

Make sure you set the environment variables on all DataNodes in your cluster.

Finally, you're ready to start cluster operations in the secure mode, with Kerberos authentication.

Starting the Cluster in the Secure Mode

We've finally reached the fun part! Now you can start your cluster in the Kerberized or secure mode. Start the NameNode as shown here after logging in as root:

```
# /usr/lib/hadoop/sbin/hadoop-daemon.sh start namenode
```

You should see the following Kerberos-related messages, which confirm that Kerberos is successfully authenticating the principals hdfs and http using their keytab files:

```
2016-06-08 18:48:11,405 INFO  security.UserGroupInformation
(UserGroupInformation.java:loginUserFromKeytab(844)) - Login successful for user
hdfs/hadoop01.localhost@EXAMPLE.COM using keytab file /etc/hadoop/conf/hdfs.keytab
2016-06-8 18:48:11,506 INFO  server.KerberosAuthenticationHandler
(KerberosAuthenticationHandler.java:init(185)) - Login using keytab /etc/hadoop/
conf/hdfs.keytab, for principal http/hadoop01.localhost@EXAMPLE.COM
```

Start the DataNodes and NodeManagers on all servers as shown here:

```
#/usr/lib/hadoop/sbin/hadoop-daemon.sh start datanode
#/usr/lib/hadoop/sbin/hadoop-daemon.sh start nodemanager
```

Start the Secondary NameNode, ResourceManager and JobHistoryServer services.

```
#/usr/lib/hadoop/sbin/hadoop-daemon.sh start secondarynamenode
#/usr/lib/hadoop/sbin/hadoop-daemon.sh start historyserver
```

You have successfully implemented Kerberos for secure authentication if you've come this far!

How Kerberos Authenticates Users and Services

Once you configure authentication through Kerberos, all Hadoop services will use it. That is, all Hadoop services will authenticate themselves through Kerberos and the clients will, of course, need to authenticate as well with the KDC.

Users authenticate to the NameNode and the ResourceManager services through Hadoop's RPC calls using the Simple Authentication and Security layer (SASL) framework. Within SASL, Kerberos will act as the authentication protocol to authenticate users that need access to a Hadoop service. Three types of authorization tokens help this process—delegation tokens, job tokens and the Block Access Token. I will explain these tokens in the following sections.

Delegation Token

Delegation tokens are used to authenticate users to the NameNode. The NameNode provides the delegation token to the user once the user authenticates to the NameNode through Kerberos. After the user authenticates, the delegation token is shared with the ResourceManager, which will use this token to access HDFS resources on behalf of the user, and which also renews the token for long-running jobs.

Job Token

When a user submits a job to the ResourceManager, it creates a secret key that it shares with all the DataNodes that run this MapReduce job. The job token ensures that authenticated users can access only authorized jobs and authorized directories in the local file system of the DataNodes. DataNodes also use the job token for securely communicating with each other.

Block Access Token

The Block Access Token ensures that only authorized users access HDFS data on the DataNodes. As explained in Chapter 8, "The Role of the NameNode and How HDFS Works," clients retrieve data from the DataNodes once they receive the block IDs from the NameNode. The NameNode also issues a Block Access Token that the client sends to the DataNode along with the request for the data blocks, to show that they're authenticated for the data access.

Managing a Kerberized Hadoop Cluster

Now that you have a Kerberized cluster, it's useful to learn more about some of the key administrative utilities that you'll need for administering Kerberos. I briefly describe the most important administrative tools in the following sections.

Kerberos Utilities and Daemons

Kerberos provides several utilities to help you work with the KDC, as listed here.

- `kdb5_util`: This is the maintenance utility for the Kerberos database, and it helps you create a Kerberos realm and perform other tasks such as updating and viewing the keytab files.
- `kpasswd`: This utility helps you change user passwords.
- `klist`: This utility helps you view Kerberos tickets currently in the client's local credential cache.
- `kadmin.local`: This administrative utility is for directly accessing the Kerberos database. This utility enables the root user of the server where the Kerberos database is stored to update the Kerberos database.
- `kadmin`: This administrative utility is used for remote administration.
- `kinit`: This Kerberos client authenticates with Kerberos and retrieves the TGT.

There are two key Kerberos daemons with which you should be familiar:

- The `kdadmind` daemon is the Kerberos admin server daemon and performs operations such as adding new principals and changing passwords.
- The `krb5kdc` daemon represents the Kerberos AS and is responsible for authenticating users and granting tickets.

Key Administration Commands

Once you Kerberize your Hadoop cluster, users can't just issue commands such as the following after logging into a cluster node:

```
[sam@hadoop01 ~] $ hdfs dfs -cat test.txt
```

The user receives an error message stating that the system "failed to find any kerberos tgt." This means that the user didn't obtain a TGT before issuing the HDFS command. The user needs to first obtain his or her TGT by issuing the `kinit` command. Once users obtain the ticket by successfully authenticating themselves, they can issue all the HDFS commands as usual.

```
[sam@hadoop01 ~] $ kinit
Password for sam@EXAMPLE.COM:
[sam@hadoop01 ~] hdfs dfs -cat test.txt
```

It may seem cumbersome to have to issue the `kinit` command to perform HDFS operations in a secure cluster, but don't despair! There are multiple ways in which you can reduce your burden:

- Once a user authenticates successfully with the `kinit` command, the user can continue to use various services without having to authenticate again in that session.

- Alternatively, you can configure the Linux system to obtain the Kerberos TGT and run all subsequent HDFS commands without having to issue the `kinit` command again in that session.
- Finally, you can also configure the Linux system so you can obtain your TGT during the login to the Linux server itself.

As you've seen, users need to issue the `kinit` command to authorize themselves with Kerberos. There are three other useful Kerberos commands users need to be familiar with, as explained here.

- `klist`: This command lists a user's ticket cache, which includes the TGT and both current and expired tickets. The default location and name of the cache file is /tmp/krb5cc_<uid>, with uid being the user's numeric ID on the local server.
- `kpasswd`: This command allows users to change their Kerberos password.
- `kdestroy`: This command allows users to clear their ticket cache. As time goes by, users accumulate expired tickets in their ticket caches and the `kdestroy` command cleans those tickets out. Once a user clears the ticket cache, the user is expected to authenticate again with the `kinit` command. You can also use the `kdestroy` command when you're making up a new configuration.

The `kinit` command isn't just a command you use when you authenticate with Kerberos. Typically, a ticket's lifetime is 24 hours, but you can request a renewable ticket that can be renewed for up to 7 days. A user can ask for a renewable ticket by executing the following command:

```
[sam@hadoop01 ~] $ kinit -r7d
```

This `kinit` command asks for a renewable ticket good for 7 days.

Setting Up One-Way Trust with Active Directory

Once you Kerberize a Hadoop cluster, all users must be provisioned through Kerberos as user principals (UPNs). What do you do if you have potentially hundreds or thousands of users?

Users are already centrally managed in a corporate LDAP directory such as Active Directory (AD). You simply set up a one-way trust between the AD realm and the KDC realm in your Hadoop cluster.

Service principals (SPNs) such as yarn, hdfs and mapred can be defined in the Hadoop cluster within its local KDC. Since server principals can generate large amounts of traffic, especially when all the DataNodes start up at once, it's a good idea not to set them on the corporate AD to avoid potential service denial issues.

Normally, Hadoop utilizes the user groups defined in the Linux (or other OS) system to authorize users within the Hadoop cluster. However, Active Directory also uses security groups to manage user credentials and roles. You can set up user and role management in Active Directory for this reason.

When users want to connect with the Hadoop cluster, they contact AD first, and it issues a Kerberos ticket for the user. Using mapping rules defined in the KDC stored in the Hadoop cluster, the user IDs are mapped to the appropriate user groups.

User and group information is synchronized between AD and the Hadoop KDC to enable the Hadoop daemons to retrieve group information from the local KDC without having to contact AD. Here's a summary of how all of this works:

1. The user provides credentials and authenticates with AD.
2. AD authenticates the user and issues a Kerberos ticket to the user.
3. The user presents the Kerberos ticket to the Hadoop cluster.
4. Hadoop daemons retrieve the user group information from AD to authorize the user access. In cases where the user ID and the Kerberos principal are different, Hadoop looks up the mapping of user IDs to user principals from the core-site.xml file.

The important thing to note here is step 2. How does Hadoop accept a ticket that was issued by AD? This is where the concept of trust, which we discussed earlier, comes in. If you set up a one-way cross-realm trust between AD and the local Hadoop KDC, all Hadoop daemons will trust all tickets issued by AD.

Integrating AD with Hadoop to Set Up a One-Way Trust

Following is a brief description of how to integrate AD with Hadoop and set up a one-way trust between AD and the local Hadoop KDC. Note that some of these tasks are performed by the AD administrator. Before you perform these steps, make sure you add the AD Kerberos realm (corporate realm) to the krb5.conf file, under the `<realms>` section.

1. Add your Hadoop KDC to AD by executing the following command on the AD server:

   ```
   ksetup /addkdc TESTREALM.COM kdc-server TESTCORPORATEDOMAIN.COM
   ```

2. Enable trust between the KDCs in Hadoop and AD by running the following on the AD server:

   ```
   netdom trust TESTREALM.COM /Domain:TESTCORPORATEDOMAIN.COM /add /realm
   /passwordt: <password>
   ```

3. Configure the encryption protocol for communications between AD and the local KDC:

   ```
   ksetup /SetEncTypeAttr TESTREALM.COM <enc_type>
   ```

4. Add the necessary user principals in AD:

   ```
   kadmin:   addprinc -e "rc4-hmac:normal des3-hmac-sha1:normal"
   krbgt/testcorporatedomain.com@TESTCORPORATEDOMAIN.COM
   ```

5. Add the Hadoop service principals on the Hadoop local KDC server:

   ```
   kadmin:  addprinc -e "rc4-hmac:normal des3-hmac-sha1:normal" krbgt/
   testdomain.com@TESTREALM.COM
   ```

6. Use the LDAP Synchronization Connector (LSC) to enable the synchronization of the user groups between AD and the Hadoop local KDC.

A final step remains: To correctly translate the usernames in the corporate directory, add the following parameter to all nodes in the cluster:

```
<property>
  <name>hadoop.security.auth_to_local</name>
  <value>
    RULE:[1:$1@$0](^.*@AD-REALM\.CORP\.FOO\.COM$)s/^(.*)@AD-REALM\.CORP\.FOO\
.COM$/$1/g
    RULE:[2:$1@$0](^.*@AD-REALM\.CORP\.FOO\.COM$)s/^(.*)@AD-REALM\.CORP\.FOO\
.COM$/$1/g
    DEFAULT
  </value>
</property>
```

The configuration shown here translates the UPNs in the corporate realm to just the first part of the UPN.

Hadoop Authorization

Authenticating yourself to the cluster doesn't guarantee access to the cluster resources. While authentication ensures that users and services are *who* they claim to be, authorization ensures *what* users can actually do once they gain access to your system. You can deny or grant access to Hadoop data and services through the configuration of authorization policies.

In a Hadoop cluster, you have several services such as HDFS and YARN, and each of these services may support a different authorization model. Let's start with authorization at the HDFS level, which constitutes the permissions users need to access files stored in HDFS.

HDFS Permissions

HDFS file permissions serve as an authorization check for every attempt to access an HDFS file or directory. HDFS file permissions are quite similar to those you normally use in a Linux or UNIX file system.

There are several similarities; however, there are also significant differences between the HDFS and the POSIX model used by Linux and other operating systems. In Linux, for example, every file and directory has a user and a group. There's really no concept of a user or group in HDFS itself—HDFS simply derives the user and group from the underlying operating system entities, such as the users and groups you create in a Linux file system.

In a Kerberized cluster, a user's Kerberos credentials determine the identity of the client process. In the default mode of operation called **simple** security mode, the user's identity is determined by the host operating system.

As with a Linux file system, you assign separate file permissions for the owner of a file or directory, the members of a group and the rest of the world. You use the familiar r, w and x permissions as in Linux, and this is how they work:

- r: Lets a user read a file and list a directory's contents
- w: Lets a user create or delete a file or directory
- x: Lets you access a child of a directory

As with a Linux file system, you can use the octal representation (numbers) to set the mode of a file, such as 755 or 777, for example. In Linux the x denotes a permission to execute a file, but there's no such concept in HDFS.

Also similar to the Linux file system is the concept of a umask, which you can specify for files and directories. The default umask is 22, but you can set a lower value, such as 18, for key configuration files in the hdfs-site.xml file in the following way:

```
<property>
  <name>dfs.permissions.umask-mode</name>
  <value>0018</value>
</property>
```

Configuring HDFS Permissions

You can configure HDFS permissions by setting the parameter dfs.permissions.enabled to true in the hdfs-site.xml file. Since the default value for this parameter is true, and thus permission checking is already turned on, you don't need to really do anything else for HDFS to use its permission checks as explained in this section.

Configuring HDFS Super Users

Unlike in the Linux file system, the host root user isn't the super user of HDFS. The super user is simply the username under which you started the NameNode, which is usually the operating system user hdfs—hence the user hdfs is commonly the super user for HDFS.

You can configure a super user group by setting the dfs.permissions.superusergroup parameter in the hdfs-site.xml file, as shown here:

```
<property>
  <name>dfs.permissions.supergroup</name>
  <value>supergroup</value>
</property>
```

I used the name supergroup as the group for super users. However, you can specify any name you wish to denote the super user group. Any users you assign to this group will be an HDFS super user.

> **Tip**
>
> Be careful about adding users to a super user group. Any member of this group, as well as the user named hdfs (typically the username under which the NameNode runs in a cluster) can read and write to any file as well as delete any file or directory in HDFS.

How HDFS Performs a Permissions Check

A client's identity consists of the client (user) name and a list of groups that it's a member of. HDFS performs a file permissions check to ensure that the user is the owner or a member of the groups list with appropriate group permissions. If neither checks out, HDFS checks the "other" file permissions of the user and if that check also fails, it denies the client's request for access to HDFS.

As mentioned earlier, in the default *simple* operation mode, it is the client process ID identified by its operating system username and in the Kerberos mode, it is the Kerberos credentials that determine the client identity.

Depending on the mode you are running your cluster in, once HDFS determines a user's identity, it determines the list of groups the user belongs to using the `hadoop.security.group.mapping` property from the core-site.xml file. The NameNode performs the mapping of users to groups.

If your groups don't exist on the Linux servers but are provisioned only on a corporate LDAP server, you must configure an alternate group mapping service called `org.apache.hadoop.security.LdapGroupsMapping`, not the default group mapping implementation.

Changing HDFS File Permissions

You can use the following commands to change file modes in your cluster.

```
code  chmod [-R] mode file ...          // you must be the owner of the file or a
super owner
chgrp [-R] group file ...               // the user must be a member of the group
and own the file, or be the super user
chown [-R] [owner][:[group]] file ...   // only the super user can do this
```

You can issue the command `lsr <file_name>` to view the owner, group and mode of a file.

HDFS Access Control Lists

HDFS supports the use of ACLs to set finer-grained permissions for specific users and groups. ACLs are a good way to go when dealing with complex file permission and access requirements and you want to grant privileges in a fine-grained manner.

By default, ACLs are disabled in HDFS. In order to use HDFS ACLs, enable them on the NameNode by adding the following property to the hdfs-site.xml file:

```
<property>
  <name>dfs.namenode.acls.enabled</true>
  <value>true</value>
</property>
```

An ACL includes a set of ACL entries, and you can use the entries to grant or deny read and write (or execute) permission to specific users or groups. Each ACL entry has a type and a permission string as well as an optional name. Here's a sample ACL showing the permissions:

```
user  :rw-
user:sam:rwx
group::r-x
group:sales:rwx
mask:r–
other::r–
```

It's much easier to understand how HDFS ACLs work by using some examples:

1. Check the file permissions on a directory owned by a user named sam, as follows:

```
bash-3.2$ hdfs dfs -ls /data/sam
Found 3 items
drwxr-xr-x   - hdfs supergroup          0 2015-05-20 11:27 /data/sam
drwxr-xr-x   - hdfs supergroup          0 2015-05-20 11:27 /data/sam/test
drwxr-xr-x   - hdfs supergroup          0 2015-05-24 15:44 /data/sam/test2
bash-3.2$
```

2. Check the current ACLs, if any, on the directory with the `getfacl` command, which enables you to view permissions:

```
$ bash-3.2$ hdfs dfs -getfacl /user/sam
# file: /user/sam
# owner: hdfs
# group: supergroup
user::rwx
group::r-x
other::r-x
bash-3.2$
```

   The `getfacl` command displays ACLs of files and directories.

3. Issue the `-setfacl` command to grant the user sam read and write permissions on the directory /data/sam. In addition, grant `rwx` permissions to the analysts group on the same directory:

```
[sam@hadoop01 ~]$ hdfs dfs -setfacl -m user:data:r-x /data/sam
[sam@hadoop01 ~]$ hdfs dfs -setfacl -m group:developers:rwx /data/sam
```

   The `setfacl` command lets you set ACLs for files and directories.

4. Check the new file permissions that have changed as a result of the new ACL you created:

```
[sam@hadoop01 ~]$ hdfs dfs -ls /data
Found 1 items
drwxr-xr-x+   - sam analysts          0 2016-06-06 16:04 /data/sam
```

   The file permission list has a plus (+) sign added at the end, to denote an ACL entry for this file's permissions.

5. Check the new ACL you just created with the `-getfacl` command:

```
[sam@hadoop01 ~]$ hdfs dfs -getfacl /data/sam
# file: /data/sam
# owner: sam
# group: analysts
user::rwx
user:sam:r-x
group::r-x
group:developers:rwx
mask::rwx
other::r-x
```

   Even though you may grant user-specific permissions on a file or a directory with an ACL, those permissions must be within the ambit of the file mask. In the output of the -getfacl command, there's a new entry named mask, and its value is rwx in this case, meaning that the user sam will indeed have rwx permissions on this directory. The mask property defines the most restrictive permissions on a file. If the mask were to be r-x instead, although user sam has rwx permissions, the effective permissions will be just r-x.

6. Change the file permissions with the chmod command as shown here, and then check the ACL with the -getfacl command again to see what it does to the new ACL's mask:

```
[sam@hadoop01 ~]$ hdfs dfs -chmod 750 /data/sam
[sam@hadoop01 ~]$ hdfs dfs -getfacl /data/sam
# file: /data/sam
# owner: sam
# group: analysts
user::rwx
group::r-x
group:developers:rwx     #effective:r-x
mask::r-x
other::---
```

7. Remove all the ACLs you created on a directory with the -setfacl command with the -b option, as shown here:

```
[sam@hadoop01 ~]$ hdfs dfs -setfacl -b /data/sam
[sam@hadoop01 ~]$ hdfs dfs -getfacl /data/sam
# file: /data/sam
# owner: sam
# group: analysts
user::rwx
group::r-x
other::---
```

Up until now, I discussed how you can set up ACLs that are enforced during permission checks. You can also apply a default ACL to a directory. A default ACL doesn't have any impact on permission checking for currently existing files and directories. Instead, the default ACL you create for a directory determines the ACL that new files (and directories) will receive when you create them under the parent directory.

HDFS Extended Attributes

HDFS enables you to add additional metadata with files and directories called extended HDFS attributes, so applications can store additional information in an inode. For example, extended HDFS attributes help an application specify the character encoding for a document. HDFS extended attributes can be seen as an extension to the traditional HDFS file system permissions.

Although there are five types of namespaces with different access restrictions, only the **user** namespace is used by client applications. There are three other types of namespaces—**system**, **security** and **raw**—for internal HDFS and other system use. The **trusted** namespace is reserved for the HDFS super user. HDFS extended attributes in the user namespace are managed through HDFS file permissions.

By default the HDFS extended attributes are enabled, and the parameter `dfs.namenode.xattrs.enabled` in the hdfs-site.xml file is what you'd need to set to true/false to enable/disable the feature. Use the `setfattr` command to associate a name and value for an extended attribute with a file or directory:

```
hdfs dfs -setfattr -n name [-v value] | -x name <path>
```

You can view the name and values of the extended attributes for a file or directory thus:

```
hdfs dfs -getfattr [-R] -n name -d [-e en] <path>
```

Service Level Authorization

When a client connects to a Hadoop service, access is granted based on whether the user has the necessary permissions and is authorized to access the service. For example, a user may have the necessary permissions to submit a YARN job to the cluster. Service level authorization is the first access control check and comes before checking file permissions.

Enabling Service Level Authorization

You can enable service level authorization by setting the `hadoop.security.authorization` property in the core-site.xml file, as shown here:

```
<property>
  <name>hadoop.security.authorization</name>
  <value>true</value>
</property>
```

Once you turn on service level authorization in your cluster, you need to configure the various Hadoop services through an ACL for each of the services.

Using ACLs for Configuring Server Level Authorization

In order to configure service level authorization, you configure an ACL for each of the Hadoop services in the $HADOOP_CONF_DIR/hadoop-policy.xml file. In each ACL for a service, you list the users and groups to whom you wish to grant access in a comma separated list as shown here:

```
user1,user2,user3 group1,group2,group3
```

Note that the user and group lists in the ACL definition for a service are separated by a space. You can also specify just a set of users or a set of groups, as shown here:

```
user1,user2,user2
group1,group2,group3
```

Here's how the users and groups are allowed to access a Hadoop service based on the ACL you list for that service:

- A value of `*` means that all users can access the Hadoop service and a value of `" "` means no users have access.

- If you don't specify an ACL for a service, the default value you specify with the optional property `security.service.authorization.default.acl` is used to determine access.
- If you don't specify the `security.service.authorization.default.acl` property, all users are allowed to access that service (this is the same as specifying a value of `*` for the ACL).

Note the following about how you can control group access:

- If you specify `user1,user2  salesgrp`, user1, user2, all users in the group named salesgrp are allowed access.
- If you specify `user1,user2 ` , with a space at the end, no groups are allowed access.
- If you specify `salesgrp` with a leading space, only users from this group are allowed access.

Configuring Service Level Authorization

As mentioned in the previous section, you configure service level authorization through the ACLs you specify in the hadoop-policy.xml file. You can configure ACLs for DataNode and NameNode protocols, as well as client protocols that specify whether users can communicate with a Hadoop service. You can classify the protocols into two types: administrative and client protocols.

The following example shows how you can set the client protocol ACL to allow users to submit YARN jobs to the cluster.

```
<property>
  <name>seccurity.job.client.protocol.acl</name>
  <value>sam,nick,nina mapreduce/value>
</property>
```

The `security.job.client.protocol.acl` property allows you to create a whitelist of users and groups allowed to run jobs in the cluster. The configuration shown in the example here specifies that only the users sam, nick and nina from the MapReduce group are allowed to submit YARN jobs to the Hadoop cluster.

Note how I separate the user and group lists with a space. Clients use this value to communicate with the ApplicationMaster service for a job, and the recommended values are `yarn`, `mapred` and `hadoop-users`, for example, where `hadoop-users` is a group you create for users that run Hadoop jobs.

The configuration property `security.job.task.protocol.acl` specifies the protocol used by YARN jobs to report the progress of tasks (map and reduce tasks can speak to the NodeManager using this protocol). Since the ID of the user using this protocol is set to the ID of the YARN job, you must always set this property to the value `"*"/`. The reason is that, by doing so, the user and the job ID are linked together. Jobs will fail if you set a different value for this parameter.

Blocking Access to Specific Users and Groups

You can specify a **blocked ACL control list** for a Hadoop service to specify a list of users/groups that are not allowed to access the service. You may specify both an access control list and a blocked access control list for the same user or group. In such a case, the user must be listed in the ACL but not in the blocked ACL. The following example shows how to block the user jim from submitting YARN jobs to the cluster.

```
<property>
  <name>.blocked.hadoop.job.client.protocol.acl</name>
  <value>jim/value>
</property>
```

As you can see, all you need to do is add the term `.blocked` to the configuration of the ACL.

Controlling HDFS Administrative Access

Although you configure ACLs in the hadoop-policy.xml file as explained earlier, Hadoop can limit some administrative actions, such as performing a manual failover of the NameNode in an HA setup to just HDFS cluster administrators. This could be the HDFS super user but need not be. You can configure HDFS cluster administrators by setting the `dfs.cluster.administrators` property in the hdfs-site.xml file, as shown here:

```
<property>
  <name>dfs.cluster.administrators</name>
  <value>hdfs admin_group</value>
</property
```

The default value for this parameter is an empty space, meaning no users have administrative access.

Refreshing a Service Level Authorization Configuration

You can dynamically modify the service level configuration for the NameNode and the ResourceManager without restarting those daemons. You can refresh the authorization configuration for the NameNode and the ResourceManager by issuing the `dfsadmin -refreshServiceAcl` commands, as shown here:

```
$ bin/hdfs dfsadmin -refreshServiceAcl
$ bin/yarn dfsadmin -refreshServiceAcl
```

Role-Based Authorization with Apache Sentry

There are many services in a Hadoop cluster, and the list only grows with time. In the long run, you simply can't keep up with the configuration and management of service level authorization by configuring at the component level. Fortunately, there's Apache Sentry to the rescue! Apache Sentry provides fine-grained role-based authorization for data you store in HDFS. Sentry provides role-based authorization control (RBAC) for HDFS data. Sentry currently works with Hive and Impala.

While HDFS authorization schemes and the usage of ACLs to provide service level authorization do serve a vital role in authorizing Hadoop users, there's really no overarching authorization system in Hadoop.

Apache Sentry is an attempt to provide a unified and consistent means of authorization across the Hadoop environment, so Hadoop administrators can specify exactly what a user is allowed to do in a Hadoop system.

Sentry's role-based access system enables the administrator to control user access at a granular level. In order to set up fine-grained authorization in your cluster, you must classify the data for access and determine the users who need access to specific sets of data and also the levels of access that are required. You can specify granular authorization by using Hive and Sentry together.

Key Sentry Concepts

Sentry uses several types of **privilege models** to make its authorization decisions. It applies the SQL model, for example, to Hive and the Bigtable model to HBase and Accumulo. Hadoop components such as Hive and HBase use a Sentry **binding** to delegate authorization decisions to Sentry. The Sentry binding applies the appropriate model for determining authorization.

When users wish to perform an action such as reading a file, Sentry relies on **users**, **groups** and **privileges** to authorize the user requests:

- A user is any user that has access to a Hadoop component such as Hive or HBase.
- A group is a set of users with similar needs and privileges.
- A privilege in the context of Sentry consists of two components: an **object** and the **action** the user wants to perform on that object. For example, an object could be a database and the action could be a read or write operation.

> **Note**
>
> By default, Sentry denies access to all objects.

Once you define the logical groups that require access to specific parts of data, you can design roles to define fine-grained authorization policies, with each role specifying a set of permissions. You then assign the roles to the groups.

Sentry Policies

Sentry determines authorization based on authorization policies that you configure. Two entities—a policy providers and a policy engine—work together in making authorization decisions:

- Policy providers store the authorization policies in a text file or in a database.
- Sentry uses its policy engine to check the policy provider to determine whether an action requested by a user is authorized.

Sentry Roles

Sentry doesn't grant privileges directly to users. Rather, it groups a set of privileges in a role. Thus, a role can be seen as a set of privileges, such as an "administrator" or "analyst" role, for example. Users are assigned to groups and a role is always assigned to a group, not to a user. Here's what you need to know with regard to Sentry roles, privileges and groups:

- A role is granted privileges.
- Users belong to a group.
- Roles are assigned to a group, never to a user.
- Privileges can't be granted directly to a group.
- Users can belong to multiple groups.
- The same role can be assigned to multiple groups.

Sentry Privilege Models

Sentry uses specific privilege models for each service for which it provides authorization. Each privilege model specifies a set of privileges and a set of object types to which the privileges can be applied.

The available privileges in each privilege model determine the granularity of the Sentry authorization controls. You can select the appropriate Sentry authorization policies for your environment by understanding the privilege models Sentry uses.

In this section, I focus on Sentry's SQL privilege model, since that's what Sentry uses for Hive authorization.

Sentry provides the `SELECT`, `INSERT` and `ALL` privileges for SQL access. The SQL privilege mode is hierarchical, meaning, for example, if you grant `SELECT` privileges on a table, implicitly you're also granting privileges on any view based on that table.

The Sentry Service

Hive and Impala can utilize the **Sentry service**, which uses a database for storing Sentry policies rather than using a text file. Although you can continue to use the older way of configuring a **Sentry policy file** (without a Sentry service), the best approach is to use the Sentry service.

The Sentry service is a daemon process that lets the various Hadoop ecosystem components perform policy lookups. You can configure the components in Sentry so they can delegate authorization decisions based on Sentry policies.

When a client accesses HiveServer2, it connects to the Sentry service using the Sentry binding inside HiveServer2. The Sentry service will consult the Sentry policy database to determine whether the clients are authorized to perform the actions they are trying to perform in Hive. This is so because the Sentry policy database stores all authorization policies.

You use the sentry-site.xml file for configuring the Sentry service.

Sentry and Hive Authorization

When clients access Hive tables, the only controls in place are the HDFS file permissions, which aren't very strong. A user can easily make changes to the Hive metastore. There are no restrictions on a user's ability to create tables, insert data into tables or run queries based on any Hive tables. Hive authorization through Sentry allows you to install fine-grained authorization policies.

Although Hive uses familiar database terminology such as tables, rows and partitions, Hive tables are in fact HDFS directories, and the partitions for a Hive table are subdirectories under the main HDFS Hive directory. You can assign various Hive privileges such as select, update and alter to users, groups or roles, at the database or table level.

However, Hive has serious deficiencies when it comes to permissions:

- Hive doesn't have a built-in capability to prevent a mismatch between the metadata stored in the Hive metastore and the HDFS file permissions, since you can change the HDFS permissions directly.
- Hive can't limit permissions to parts of a table's data, and it also can't provide column-level permissions or define server-level roles.

Sentry enables you to create roles at the server, database and table level. You can use these roles to provide partial access to a table's data to users, if you so wish.

A key security concern is the protection of the Hive metastore database from arbitrary changes made by clients.

The purpose of HiveServer2 is to support requests coming from clients through JDBC and ODBC user interfaces. HiveServer2 accesses the Hive metastore to get the metadata information and also performs the necessary Hive actions for clients. Using Sentry, you can ensure that all HiveServer2 contacts are authorized and also that users *must* use HiveServer2 to work with Hive databases.

In summary, when configuring Sentry authorization for Hive, you must secure both HiveServer2 and the Hive metastore.

In this chapter, I show you how to set up Sentry authorization for Hive. If you're using Impala, you must set up appropriate configuration for enabling Impala authorization through Sentry.

Configuring the Sentry Server for Hive Authorization

In order for Hive to use Sentry authorization, both the Hive metastore and HiveServer 2 should be able to use the Sentry service. You must enable the Sentry service for Hive in the sentry-site.xml file, using the configuration properties I explained earlier. Later, I'll point to the location of this sentry-site.xml file in the hive-site.xml configuration file, which I also need to configure so Hive can work with Sentry.

A couple of important properties of the sentry-site.xml file merit an explanation:

- The `hive.sentry.provider` property specifies how Sentry determines the group information. The value I specified here, `HadoopGroupResourceAuthorizationProvider`, means that Sentry will use the method you configured the Hadoop cluster with. For example, Sentry can read the groups from the local operating system or get the group information from LDAP if you've configured Kerberos security.

- The sentry.metastore.service.users configuration property specifies the users can directly connect to the Hive metastore, bypassing Sentry authorization. Thus, users hive, hue and hdfs, all service users, can bypass Sentry in our example here.

Configuring Hive for Sentry

As mentioned earlier, you need to configure both HiveServer2 and the Hive metastore to work with the Sentry service if you want to use Sentry authorization. The configuration of the necessary properties to enable HiveServer2 communication with the Sentry service will look like the following in the hive-site.xml file:

```
<configuration>
...
  <property>
    <name>hive.server2.enable.doAs</name>
    <value>false</value>
  </property>
  <property>
    <name>hive.server2.session.hook</name>
    <value>org.apache.sentry.binding.hive.HiveAuthzBindingSessionHook</value>
  </property>
  <property>
    <name>hive.sentry.conf.url</name>
    <value>file:///etc/hive/conf/sentry-site.xml</value>
  </property>
  <property>
    <name>hive.security.authorization.task.factory</name>
    <value>org.apache.sentry.binding.hive.SentryHiveAuthorizationTaskFactoryImpl
</value>
  </property>
</configuration>
```

Note the following:

- The hive.server2.enable.doAs configuration property disables impersonation. This means that queries are executed as the user that runs the HiveServer2 service.
- The hive.sentry.conf.url configuration property points to the location of the Sentry configuration file.
- The hive.server2.session.hook configuration property specifies the binding that passes along the authorization decisions to Sentry.

While impersonation is disabled with this configuration, the HDFS permissions on the Hive warehouse are still open. In order for Sentry to authorize a client's data access, you must also tighten HDFS permissions, as shown here:

```
$ hdfs dfs -chown -R hive:hive  /user/hive/warehouse
$ hdfs dfs -chmod -R 771        /user/hive/warehouse
```

The Hive warehouse directory is usually /user/hive/warehouse. In the example shown here, I set the permissions on the warehouse directory to 771 (-rwxrwx--x). This means that users who don't belong to the group hive have no permissions on this directory.

Once you change the HDFS file permissions as shown here, only the user hive can access the Hive tables (HDFS files) when end users run their queries.

Two more things:

- In order to let the Hive user submit YARN jobs, you must add the following property to the container-executor.cfg file:

  ```
  allowed.system.users = nobody, hive
  ```

- Next, you must configure the Hive metastore so it can work with the Sentry service, as shown here (in the hive-site.xml file):

```
<configuration>
...
  <property>
    <name>hive.metastore.client.impl</name>
    <value> org.apache.sentry.binding.metastore.SentryHiveMetaStoreClient</value>
  </property>
  <property>
    <name>hive.metastore.pre.event.listeners</name>
    <value>org.apache.sentry.binding.metastore.MetastoreAuthzBinding</value>
  </property>
  <property>
    <name>hive.metastore.event.listeners</name>
    <value>org.apache.sentry.binding.metastore.SentryMetastorePostEventListener
</value>
  </property>
</configuration>
```

Administering Sentry Policies

Sentry roles and how you assign permissions to them play a crucial role in Sentry policy administration. You can configure Sentry permissions by issuing the Sentry policy commands interactively from the Sentry server. You can also do so through Beeline, the HiveServer2 SQL command line interface. Note that once you enable Sentry, you can only use Beeline for executing Hive queries (not Hive CLI). A couple of examples:

- `GRANT privilege on object TO ROLE role_name`: Grants a specific privilege on an object to a role
- `REVOKE privilege ON object FROM ROLE role_name`: Revokes a granted privilege on an object from a role

Sentry Policy Administration Examples

In the previous section I listed several Sentry authorization policies. Following are some examples showing how to set those policies. Perform these operations as the user hive from the `beeline` CLI.

1. Create a role for the hive administrators:

   ```
   0: jdbc:hive2://hadoop01.localhost:10000> CREATE ROLE hive_admin;
   ```

   The `CREATE ROLE` command creates a role with the name that you specify. You can remove a role from the Sentry database with the `DROP ROLE` command.

2. Grant the newly created role to the sqladmin group:

   ```
   0: jdbc:hive2:// hadoop01.localhost10000> GRANT ROLE hive_admin TO GROUP
   sqladmin;
   ```

   The `GRANT ROLE` command grants a role to a group.
3. Grant the role `hive_admin` permissions on the server:

   ```
   0: jdbc:hive2:// hadoop01.localhost:10000> GRANT ALL ON SERVER hadoop01 TO
   ROLE hive_admin;
   ```

4. Show all roles in the database:

   ```
   0: jdbc:hive2:// hadoop01.localhost:10000> SHOW ROLES;
   ```

   The `SHOW ROLES` command shows all roles in the database for the Sentry admin user.
5. Show all the privileges for the `hive-admin` role:

   ```
   0: jdbc:hive2:// hadoop01.localhost:10000> SHOW GRANT ROLE hive_admin;
   ```

6. Set current role to the `hive_admin` role:

   ```
   0: jdbc:hive2:// hadoop01.localhost:10000> SET ROLE hive_admin;
   ```

7. List the roles in the current session:

   ```
   0: jdbc:hive2:// hadoop01.localhost:10000> SHOW CURRENT ROLES;
   ```

   The `SHOW CURRENT ROLES` command shows the roles in effect in the current session.
8. List all tables:

   ```
   0: jdbc:hive2:// hadoop01.localhost:10000> SHOW TABLES;
   ```

9. Remove all roles in the current session:

   ```
   0: jdbc:hive2:// hadoop01.localhost:10000> SET ROLE NONE;
   ```

   The `SET ROLE NONE` command disables all roles for a specific user. The `SET ROLE` command enables a specific role for a user for the current session, and the `SET ROLE ALL` command enables all roles for a specific user.

Auditing Hadoop

While Kerberos authentication ensures that only authorized users and services can log in and perform actions inside the Hadoop cluster, and authorization policies control what these users and services can actually do in the cluster, you must also ensure that you can track user and service actions through appropriate **auditing**. Auditing is also referred to as accounting and is a key component of IT security.

In a Hadoop cluster, you can track actions performed in HDFS, HBase, MapReduce, Hive, Impala and so on. For example, HDFS audits will cover actions that read and write data to HDFS. Hadoop lets you configure audit logging of all of its components separately.

Auditing HDFS Operations

You can configure two separate audit logs for HDFS actions. User activity such as creating files and changing their permissions is tracked by the hds-audit.log file, and the SecurityAuth-hdfs.audit file tracks server-level authorization actions.

Hadoop uses Log4j for logging. You configure Log4j for Hadoop by specifying the logging attributes in the log4j.properties file, located in the /etc/hadoop/config directory.

When you set up Log4j logging, Hadoop records all HDFS operations in the hdfs-audit.log file. Here are the partial contents of an hdfs-audit.log file, showing how it tracks HDFS operations performed by the user sam.

```
...
...INFO FSNamesystem.audit: allowed=true  ugi=sam@EXAMPLE.COM
 (auth:KERBEROS) ip=/192.168.56.1 cmd=listStatus src=/user/sam dst=null r-----
...INFO FSNamesystem.audit: allowed=true  ugi=sam@EXAMPLE.COM
 (auth:KERBEROS) ip=/192.168.56.1  cmd=setPermission src=/user/sam/test
dst=null
```

This log reveals that the user sam was successfully authorized by Kerberos (`auth:KERBEROS`). It also shows that the following HDFS operations performed by user sam were allowed:

- `listStatus`: Directory listing of the directory /user/sam
- `create`: Creating a file named test in the /user/sam directory (I deleted some output)
- `setPermission`: Changing permissions on the file /user/sam/test to `rw-r-----`

Auditing YARN Operations

Hadoop logs YARN operations by users in two different log files. The ResourceManager log file includes activities performed by the ResourceManager such as submitting application requests and allocating containers. The NodeManager log files track events performed by each NodeManager involved in the YARN application, such as container requests, for example.

You configure YARN audit event tracking by specifying the configuration properties in the YARN log4j.properties file.

Let's say user sam submits a MapReduce application through YARN. Here's what the ResourceManager log file shows (partial output):

```
... INFO USER=sam IP=192.168.56.1  OPERATION=Submit Application Request
  TARGET=ClientRMService  RESULT=SUCCESS  APPID=...
... INFO USER=sam OPERATION=AM Released Container
  TARGET=SchedulerApp RESULT=SUCCESS APPID=...
...INFO USER=sam OPERATION=Application Finished - Succeeded
  TARGET=RMAppManager RESULT=SUCCESS  ...
```

You can see that YARN successfully authorized the following types of YARN applications for the user sam:

- Application request
- Allocated container
- Released container
- Application finished—successful

> **Note**
>
> As with HDFS and YARN operations, you can also audit Hive and Oozie operations

Securing Hadoop Data

Data encryption is the most common way to protect key corporate data stored in a database or in HDFS. Protecting data stored in devices such as the hard drives that form the basis for HDFS storage is called the encryption of **data at rest**.

However, data isn't always stationary—Hadoop operations continually move data around over the internal networks as well as on the Internet. Protecting data on the move is called encrypting **data in transit** (also called over-the-wire encryption).

Whether it's on disk or in transit data encryption, you choose among several well-known encryption algorithms and standards such as AES, DES and Tripe DES.

Hadoop offers native HDFS encryption. You can encrypt data at the application, database and the file system or disk level. Each of these encryption levels involves a tradeoff between performance and data protection. HDFS native encryption, also called HDFS Transparent Encryption, is somewhere in between a database-level and a file system-level encryption. It offers good performance and transparent encryption of data without having to configure application-level encryption, which involves code changes to support encryption.

HDFS encryption protects you from attacks aimed at both the file system and OS levels, since HDFS encrypts data stored on the disk system.

In order to fully protect your data, in addition to encrypting data stored in HDFS, you must also think about how to encrypt data in motion, the intermediate data stored in the local file system, MapReduce shuffle data, and external data ingested by Hadoop through data ingestion tools such as Sqoop and Flume.

HDFS Transparent Encryption

HDFS native encryption is both transparent and end to end. It's transparent because users don't need to make any changes to their code to encrypt data—Hadoop takes care of all the encryption and decryption work. It's also end-to-end encryption because only the client encrypts (and decrypts) data, without HDFS ever having to store the unencrypted data or the unencrypted data encryption keys.

Architecture

HDFS uses a new concept termed **encryption zones** to encrypt its data. Each encryption zone is an HDFS directory (could also be multiple directories) designed for automatic encryption and decryption of data stored in that directory. Encryption keys are stored and managed by a dedicated server called the Hadoop Key Management Server (KMS).

Here's what you need to know about encryption zones and how they work with encryption keys:

- Each encryption zone you create has a unique encryption zone key (EZK).
- Each file within an encryption zone has a unique data encryption key (DEK).
- HDFS only handles an encrypted data encryption key (EDEK) and not the DEK.
- In order to read or write data, HDFS clients need to decrypt the EDEK to get the DEK for that file to read from or write data to that file.

How Encryption Works

The NameNode, the KMS and the DFS client interact to encrypt and decrypt HDFS data. When you create a file in HDFS, the NameNode requests the KMS to generate a new EDK, which the NameNode will then store as part of the file's metadata.

The Hadoop client uses both the EDEK and the DEK to finally decrypt an encrypted HDFS file stored in an encryption zone (EZ).

Figure 15.1 shows Hadoop's TDE architecture.

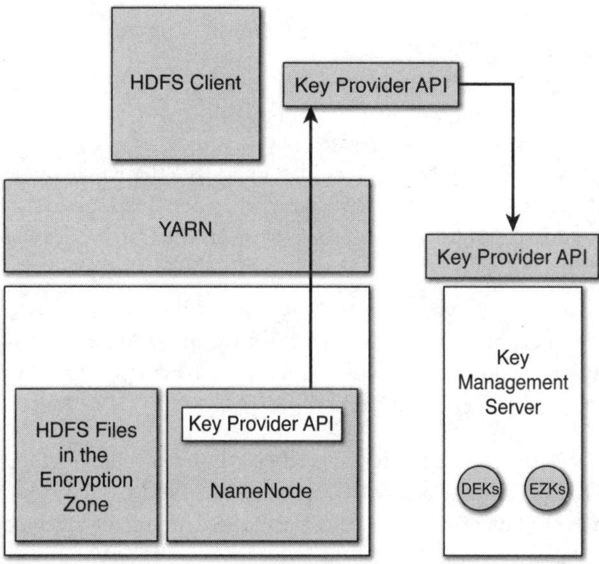

Figure 15.1 Architecture of Hadoop's transparent data encryption

Even if an unauthorized user tries to access an HDFS encrypted file, the user can get the encrypted keys but not the encryption zone keys, which are managed separately by the KMS, thus keeping your data secure.

Configuring KMS

Hadoop KMS is a cryptographic key management server and is a Java web application that runs on the Tomcat web application server that's bundled with Hadoop. KMS acts as the mediator between HDFS and its clients and the key server. KMS generates both EZKs and DEKs and decrypts the EDEKs as well. It communicates with the key server through the `KeyProvider` Java API.

Due to the key role (no pun intended) the KMS plays in HDFS encryption, you must run this server on a host that's separate from all the other Hadoop components. KMS lets you configure multiple instances for scalability and for high availability. In order to work with KMS for encrypting HDFS, you must configure the KMS backing KeyProvider properties.

In addition, it's advisable to set up KMS with Transport Layer Security (TLS) wire encryption. You can do this by adding the environment variables `KMS_SSL_KEYSTORE_FILE` and `KMS_SSL_KEYSTORE_PASS` to the kms-env.sh file. These two properties specify the location of the KeyStore file and its password, respectively.

Once you set up these configuration properties, start up the KMS server as shown here:

```
$ sbin/kms.sh start
```

Now that you've configured and started up the KMS Server, it's time to configure the KeyProvider.

Configuring Encryption

After configuring KMS, you must also configure the KeyProvider. Following are the two key configuration parameters for the KeyProvider:

- `hadoop.encryption.key.provider.url`: The URI the KeyProvider uses when dealing with encryption zones; for example, `kms://https@kms.example.com:16000/kms`. You must set this property on all the DataNodes and NameNodes in the core-site.xml file.
- `hadoop.security.key.provider.path`: The URI for the KeyProvider to use when dealing with encryption keys as a client; for example, `kms:/https@kms.example.com:16000/kms`. You must set this property in the core-site.xml file on all the DataNodes and the client node as well.

There are also several cryptography-related configuration parameters you can set in the core-site.xml file on all the DataNodes and the NameNodes, such as `hadoop.security.crypto.cipher.site`. For now, you can just use the defaults for all the cryptography-related parameters.

Encrypting HDFS

With the configuration of the KMS and the NameNode and HDFS clients behind us, you're ready to create the HDFS encryption zones. Use the `hadoop key` command first to create the encryption keys and the `hdfs crypto` command to create the encryption zones, as shown here:

```
# hadoop key create testkey     // do this as a regular user, not the super user
```

Log in as the super user (hdfs) and create an encryption zone, which involves creating a new directory first and then making it an encryption zone, with the help of the `-createZone` command option.

```
# hdfs dfs -mkdir /testzone
# hdfs crypto -createZone -keyName testkey -path /testzone
```

You can check that the new encryption zone has been created with the `-listzones` option:

```
# hdfs crypto -listZones
/testzone
#
```

Note that the directory you're making into an encryption zone must be empty. Finally, as the super user again, change the ownership of the zone to that of a regular user.

```
# hdfs dfs -chown testuser:testuser  /testzone
```

Once you create an encryption zone as shown here, all files created in that zone will be encrypted. If a client needs to read a file in the encryption zone, the file needs to be decrypted. If you want to encrypt currently existing data, you can do so by moving that data into a new encryption zone with DistCp or by other means.

If you're interested in encrypting data produced by the various Hadoop components that aren't stored in HDFS itself, you can do so either by using full disk encryption with a tool such as the open source LUKS, or by encrypting at the file system level with a tool such as ecryptFS, Dataguise for Hadoop (DG) or Gazzang zNcrypt, all of which are open-source encryption solutions.

Encrypting Data in Transition

Hadoop moves around quite a bit of data, so encrypting data in transit is a key security concern. In earlier days, it was common to use the Secure Socket Layer (SSL) for encrypting data in transit, but now, TLS is the established cryptographic protocol for encrypting data in transit.

You need to configure the encryption of data in transit differently based on the method of communication (RPC, TCP/IP, etc.) used by YARN, HDFS and other clients. You can configure Hadoop's RPC encryption by setting the `hadoop-rpc.protection` property in the core-site.xml file, as shown here:

```
<property>
   <name>hadoop.rpc.protection</name>
```

```
    <value>privacy</value>
</property>
```

By setting the value privacy for the hadoop.rpc.protection parameter, I'm putting the Java SSL implementation used by Hadoop in the auth-conf mode, which provides authentication, integrity and confidentiality. Two other modes, authentication and integrity, provide only authentication and integrity respectively.

When DataNodes exchange data between them or send it to a client, they use the **HDFS data transfer protocol** and use a direct TCP/IP socket for the communication. You can configure HDFS data transfer encryption by configuring the following two properties in the hdfs-site.xml file:

```
<property>
  <name>hadoop.encrypt.data.transfer</name>
  <value>true</value>
</property>

<property>
  <name>dfs.encrypt.data.transfer.cipher.suites</name>
  <value>AES/CTR/NoPadding</value>
</property>
```

The second configuration parameter sets AES as your encryption algorithm. Make sure you configure the hadoop.rpc.protection property as shown earlier (value=privacy) first, to enable RPC encryption for the encryption keys.

For encrypting data in transit that uses the HTTP protocol, you can use the HTTPS protocol, which is HTTP with either SSL or TLS, to encrypt the HTTP endpoints. HTTPS configuration involves several steps such as creating the private keys, security certificates and so on and saving them in a Java KeyStore.

Other Hadoop-Related Security Initiatives

Providing security for Hadoop is vital, and there's a lot of work going on in this area, with new security projects coming on board all the time. In this section, I briefly describe the most useful of the new security projects.

Securing a Hadoop Infrastructure with Apache Knox Gateway

Apache Knox Gateway, usually referred to as Knox, provides perimeter security for controlling Hadoop access while adhering to your corporate security policies. Knox provides server-level authorization at the perimeter. It provides authentication and token verification at the perimeter and integrates its authentication with corporate identity management and SSO systems, letting you use identities you provision in the corporate systems to securely access the Hadoop cluster.

Knox isn't a substitute for Kerberos. Knox encapsulates Kerberos and simplifies the Kerberos security model by doing away with the complex client-side configuration usually required for Kerberos. Knox is a stateless reverse-proxy framework that aggregates the REST/HTTP calls to the Hadoop components. Knox allows enterprise users to securely use REST APIs without having to deal with Kerberos. However, implementers still have to deploy and manage the SSL certificates, which isn't much easier than managing Kerberos.) Knox provides authentication, authorization, auditing and other security services.

Apache Ranger for Security Administration

Apache Ranger provides centralized administration of security policies and also provides centralized access control and auditing services. It integrates with various Hadoop components such as HBase, HDFS, Hive, Knox and Storm and ensures consistent coverage across the stack.

Ranger consists of a Policy Admin Server and a User/Group Synchronization Server. The admin server serves as the main interface for security administration. The synchronization server helps pull users and groups from an LDAP server such as Active Directory and stores it within the Ranger administration policy database for defining security policies for them. Ranger plugins help it secure various Hadoop components.

Once you define polices on files and directories, the Ranger Plugin evaluates all HDFS requests and grants appropriate access. Similarly, when you integrate with Hive, the Ranger Plugin acts as the authorization provider for HiveServer2 and evaluates all requests for Hive access based on the specific ranger policies you create.

As with authorization, Ranger also lets you configure auditing through security policies. It provides for the auditing of both resource access and administrative operations.

Finally, you can integrate Ranger with Knox—the Ranger Knox Plugin enforces server-level authorization through Ranger policies by acting as the authorization provider inside the Knox Gateway.

Summary

Here's what you learned in this chapter:

- In order to secure your Hadoop environment, you must take care of authentication, authorization and auditing.
- Kerberos is the accepted authentication solution for Hadoop, and this chapter explained how you can go about setting up Kerberos authentication in your environment.
- While you can use HDFS ACLs for authorization, in order to set up a policy-based authorization system, you must use something like the Sentry service.
- Auditing events is quite critical, and you can audit all events for YARN and HDFS.
- Encryption of data is essential for securing data at rest, and Hadoop comes with built-in encryption capabilities.
- To complete the circle of security, you must also secure data in transit.

V

Monitoring, Optimization and Troubleshooting

16

Managing Jobs, Using Hue and Performing Routine Tasks

This chapter covers the following:

- Using YARN commands to manage Hadoop jobs
- Decommissioning and recommisssioning nodes
- Setting up a high-availability ResourceManager
- Performing common management tasks
- Implementing specialized HDFS features
- Managing the MySQL database
- Backing up key data
- Using Hue to manage your cluster

This chapter is kind of a grab bag, in the sense that it discusses several Hadoop administration tasks that an administrator is frequently called upon to perform. I start off with an explanation of the set of YARN commands that help you manage Hadoop jobs. Chapter 17, "Monitoring, Metrics, and Hadoop Logging," explains how to use Hadoop's web UI to manage jobs, but it's good to learn how to work with the `yarn` command as well.

I next explain typical administrative tasks such as decommissioning and recommissioning nodes. I didn't get a chance earlier on to show how to set up high availability for the ResourceManager, so I stuck it in this chapter!

Although I've devoted several chapters to managing HDFS, there are some important HDFS features that you may want to set up in your cluster, such as short-circuit local reads and mountable HDFS. This chapter introduces these useful features.

Hue is a wonderful interface, highly useful to Hadoop users and to you, the administrator, for creating, scheduling and managing jobs through the Oozie job scheduler. I show how to install, configure and use Hue to help manage your cluster.

Although you don't (and really, can't, due to the size of the data) perform HDFS backups as you do for the data in a relational database, you do need to back up the NameNode metadata. Similarly, you must back up the metadata for several common components such as Hue, Hive, Sqoop, Oozie and Sentry. I show you how to back up data from the MySQL database, which happens to be the most commonly used relational database in Hadoop environments.

Let's start with a review of the Hadoop `yarn` command and learn how to use it to manage jobs.

Using the YARN Commands to Manage Hadoop Jobs

Hadoop's `yarn` command is very helpful in managing various aspects of YARN. Although the ResourceManager web UI is quite useful, when things break down, you need the command line to fix things. The command has a wide operational scope, in the sense that it helps you manage a large range of Hadoop tasks with it, such as reporting and killing running applications, obtaining job and daemon logs and even managing the ResourceManager.

You can find out all the available options for the `yarn` command by issuing the `yarn` command without any parameters, as shown here.

```
# yarn
Usage: yarn [--config confdir] COMMAND
where COMMAND is one of:
  resourcemanager -format-state-store   deletes the RMStateStore
  resourcemanager                       run the ResourceManager
...
Most commands print help when invoked w/o parameters.
#
```

You can use `yarn` commands to monitor and manage your applications from the command line. For example, you can view the status of running jobs with the `yarn application` command. Similarly, you can kill a running application gracefully from the command line with the `yarn administration -kill` command, instead of hacking the process to death with the Linux `kill` command.

One of the handiest `yarn` commands is the `yarn top` command, which lets you quickly see the cluster usage at a point in time. As Figure 16.1 shows, the `yarn top` command provides summary information about the number of submitted, running and completed jobs. It also shows you the amount of memory and CPU cores allocated for all jobs in the cluster.

In this chapter, our focus is on monitoring and managing the cluster, so let's learn how you can monitor YARN using the `yarn` command. You can view basic job information and perform other tasks such as kill a running job by issuing the `yarn application` command. The `yarn application` command is helpful in performing the following administrative tasks:

- Listing the applications that are running in the cluster
- Killing running applications
- Getting the status of running applications

The following sections show how to use the key application-related `yarn` commands.

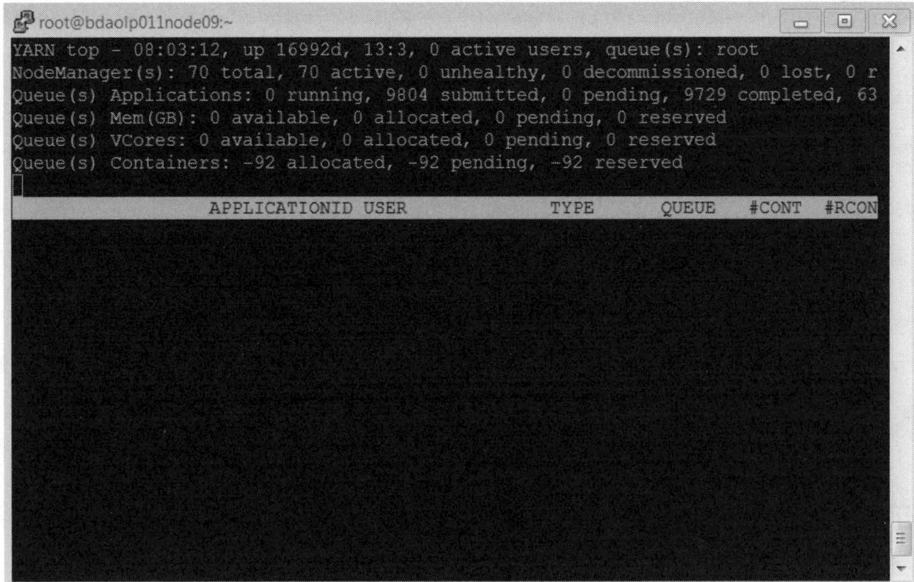

Figure 16.1 The `yarn top` utility

Viewing YARN Applications

You can issue the command `yarn application` with the `-list` option to view all the applications (what you call a job, YARN calls an application) in the cluster right now, as shown here:

```
# yarn application -list
15/12/23 05:11:37 INFO client.ConfiguredRMFailoverProxyProvider:
Failing over to rm219
Total number of applications (application-types: [] and states:
[SUBMITTED, ACCEPTED, RUNNING]):2
                Application-Id      Application-Name        Application-Type
User            Queue                   State           Final-State
Progress                         Tracking-URL
application_1448106546957_4368    PriceAggregatorJob               MAPREDUCE
salesuser       root.produser           RUNNING             UNDEFINED
55.07%   http://hadoop02:40417
application_1448106546957_4369  DataSorter-Xml2AvroTransformerJob
MAPREDUCE        produser       root.produserproduser                RUNNING
UNDEFINED                    5% http://hadoop03:27264
#
```

The `application -list` command retrieves the list of all jobs regardless of their state. A job can have the following states: `ALL`, `NEW`, `NEW_SAVING`, `SUBMITTED`, `ACCEPTED`, `RUNNING`, `FINISHED`, `FAILED` and `KILLED`.

You can filter the list of applications by specifying its state, (or a comma-separated list of application states, with the `-appStates` option). For example, you can limit the list of jobs to a specific state, such as RUNNING or FAILED, by specifying the -appStates option with the yarn application -list command, as shown here:

```
# yarn application -list -appStates running
15/12/23 05:12:10 INFO client.ConfiguredRMFailoverProxyProvider:
Failing over to rm219
Total number of applications (application-types: [] and states: [RUNNING]):2
...
#
```

The output for this command shows just those YARN jobs that are in the RUNNING state.

Similarly, the output from issuing the following command shows all failed jobs:

```
# yarn application -list -appStates FAILED
16/07/10 08:12:05 INFO client.ConfiguredRMFailoverProxyProvider:
Failing over to rm219
Total number of applications (application-types: [] and states: [FAILED]):12
                Application-Id      Application-Name        Application-Type
User            Queue                   State                 Final-State
Progress                         Tracking-URL
application_1462081872415_4296  MY_POS Spark Data Exploration
SPARK        bdaldr       root.bdaldr                 FAILED
FAILED                  100% http://hadoop:8088/cluster/app/
application_1462081872415_4296
...
```

You can view all applications, including those that have completed, by adding the all option to the -list command, as shown here:

```
$ yarn application -list -appTypes all
```

Note that YARN shows the application ID for an application when you issue the yarn application -list command. This application ID is very useful for running other yarn commands, such as those that retrieve the status of a specific job or a command that kills a job.

Checking the Status of an Application

You can view the status of a specific application by specifying its application ID, along with the -status option.

```
$ yarn application -status <application ID>
```

You can also check the status of an application attempt by issuing the yarn applicationattempt command, which has the following syntax:

```
$ yarn applicationattempt  -list <Application Id> -status <Application Attempt Id>
```

Killing a Running Application

When you start a YARN application from the command line, you can't terminate it by hitting CTRL-C on your terminal. You'll get the prompt back, but the job continues to run in the cluster! You can kill the JVM for the application from the Linux command line, but the right way to terminate a job is to issue the application -kill command as shown here.

```
$ yarn application -kill application_1389385968629_0025
16/07/10 16:53:30 INFO client.YarnClientImpl: Killing application application_
1389385968629_0025
16/07/10 16:53:30 INFO service.AbstractService: Service:org.apache.hadoop.yarn
.client.YarnClientImpl is stopped.
```

When you issue the `yarn application -kill` command, you'll get back the prompt immediately, with no messages of any kind to let you know that your bidding was done! The job will have been killed, and you can confirm this by checking the ResourceManager web UI or by simply issuing the following `yarn` command:

```
$ yarn application -list -appTypes running
```

Checking the Status of the Nodes

The `yarn node` command lets you list all the cluster's nodes and check their status, as shown here:

```
# yarn node -all  -list
16/06/30 10:26:25 INFO client.ConfiguredRMFailoverProxyProvider:
Failing over to rm219
Total Nodes:70
         Node-Id                     Node-State    Node-Http-Address
Number-of-Running-Containers

hadoop01.localhost:8041             RUNNING       hadoop02.localhost:8042    17
hadoop03.localhost:8042             RUNNING       hadoop02.localhost:8042    20
hadoop02.localhost:8041             RUNNING       hadoop03.localhost:8042    18
hadoop04.localhost:8042             RUNNING       hadoop04.localhost:8042    24
...
#
```

Checking YARN Queues

You can check the status of a job queue with the `yarn queue` command:

```
# yarn queue -status produser
16/06/30 21:20:16 INFO client.ConfiguredRMFailoverProxyProvider:
Failing over to rm219
Queue Information :
Queue Name : root.produser
        State : RUNNING
        Capacity : 50.0%
        Current Capacity : 15.9%
        Maximum Capacity : -100.0%
        Default Node Label expression :
        Accessible Node Labels :
#
```

Getting the Application Logs

The `logs` option for the `yarn` command helps you access logs for completed YARN applications. Here's the syntax of the `yarn logs` command:

```
$ yarn logs
Retrieve logs for completed YARN applications.
usage: yarn logs -applicationId <application ID> [OPTIONS]
```

```
general options are:
 -appOwner <Application Owner>   AppOwner (assumed to be current user if
                                 not specified)
 -containerId <Container ID>     ContainerId (must be specified if node
                                 address is specified)
 -nodeAddress <Node Address>     NodeAddress in the format nodename:port
                                 (must be specified if container id is
                                 specified)
$
```

You can get the logs only for jobs that have finished running. You can first list all the completed jobs with the following command:

```
# yarn application -list -appStates finished
```

From the output of this command, retrieve the application ID for the job you're interested in, and get the logs for that application by issuing the `yarn logs -applicationId` command as shown here:

```
$ yarn logs -applicationId application_1462081872415_7661 sg224323
```

Hadoop assumes that the user issuing this command is the application owner as well. If that's not the case, you must specify the application owner with the `-appOwner` option, as shown here:

```
$ yarn logs -applicationId application_1462081872415_7661 sg224323 -appOwner alapati
```

Alternatively, you can specify a container ID (`-containerId`) and a node address (`-nodeAdress`). Note that you must specify both of these parameters together, as shown here:

```
$ yarn logs -containerId 123456 -nodeAddress hadoop01.localhost:port
```

If you haven't enabled **log aggregation**, you'll see a message similar to the following when you try to retrieve application logs through the `yarn logs` command.

```
# yarn logs -applicationId application_1447271764045_0377
16/072/09 07:54:59 INFO client.ConfiguredRMFailoverProxyProvider:
Failing over to rm219
/tmp/logs/root/logs/application_1447271764045_0377does not exist.
Log aggregation has not completed or is not enabled.
#
```

Hadoop 2's log aggregation feature is explained in Chapter 17, in the section titled "Understanding Hadoop Logging."

Yarn Administrative Commands

The commands you've learned about in the previous section are termed YARN user commands by Hadoop. In addition to these commands that let you check the application status and get the application logs and so on, there's a set of important yarn administrative commands that help you manage the ResourceManager in a high availability configuration. You can perform several ResourceManager-related tasks with the `yarn rmadmin` command.

The key yarn administrative commands are the following:

- `yarn rmadmin refreshNodes`
- `yarn rmadmin -transitionToActive`
- `yarn rmadmin -transitionToStandby`
- `yarn rmadmin -failover`
- `yarn rmadmin -getServiceState`
- `yarn rmadmin -checkHealth`

Later in this chapter, in the section "Setting Up ResourceManager High Availability," I show you how to use the yarn administrative commands.

Decommissioning and Recommissioning Nodes

Once in a while you may need to take a non-master node—that is, a node running a DataNode and/or a NodeManager service—out of the cluster, because you're shrinking the cluster size, or you want to remove a failed node or for general maintenance.

You can add or remove nodes while the cluster is running. Instead of just yanking a node out of the cluster, which could lead to potential data loss issues (if the removed node happens to hold the only copy of a file block), it's wise to decommission them first before taking the server out of the cluster. Decommissioning DataNodes allows the cluster to gracefully recover. If you're decommissioning several nodes, it allows the replication to be preserved and not disrupt running jobs.

When you decommission a node, Hadoop ensures that the node doesn't contain any blocks that aren't replicated on the other nodes. When you decommission a node, Hadoop automatically replicates the data blocks stored in the retired node to ensure that it satisfies the data replication level you chose (the default, as you know by now, is three replicas).

> **Note**
>
> If you're running a test cluster with just three nodes and the replication factor for the cluster is at the default level of three replicas, you can't decommission the DataNode.

If the NodeManager is decommissioned, the ResourceManager is made aware of it and it won't schedule any new tasks on that node. It also reschedules any tasks that it has already assigned to this NodeManager.

Let's say a node runs both a DataNode and a NodeManager service, as is common in a Hadoop environment. It's normal to decommission and recommission both the DataNode and the NodeManager together in this case.

You can decommission a DataNode or a NodeManager even when the server on which the DataNode or the NodeManager runs doesn't have any issues. For example, there may be situations where you want a NodeManager to stop accepting new tasks; decommissioning the NodeManager is the way to do this.

Including and Excluding Hosts

Before you can decommission our example node that runs both a DataNode and a NodeManager, let's review the concept of excluding and including nodes in a cluster.

While it's not mandatory, you can choose to include or exclude either the DataNode or the NodeManager services that usually run on each worker node. You specify all eligible nodes with the /etc/hadoop/conf/dfs.include file and all ineligible nodes with the /etc/hadoop/conf/dfs.exclude file. Using the include and exclude files is optional—if you don't use a dfs.include file, all DataNodes are included in the cluster unless you explicitly exclude the nodes by specifying them in the dfs.exclude file.

You specify the location of the include and exclude files by providing the file names as the value for the `dfs.hosts.include` and `dfs.hosts.exclude` properties in the hdfs-site.xml file.

By default, all NodeManagers running on every node in the cluster are included in the cluster, if you don't specify a yarn.include file. This is true unless you specifically exclude a node by adding it to the yarn.exclude file. As is the case with HDFS, you can point to your yarn.include and yarn.exclude files by specifying the `yarn.resourcemanager.nodes.include-path` and the `yarn.resourcemanager.nodes.exclude-path` properties in the yarn-site.xml file. Here's what the two parameters enable you to do:

- `yarn.resourcemanager.nodes.include-path` shows the path to the nodes you wish to include.
- `yarn.resourcemanager.nodes.exclude-path` shows the path to the nodes you wish to exclude.

Once you specify the include/exclude files in the yarn-site.xml file, run the following command on the server where the ResourceManager is running:

```
# yarn rmadmin -refreshNodes
```

Before you can decommission either a DataNode or a NodeManager service, you must set or modify a couple of properties by editing the hdfs-site.xml file (for the DataNode) and the yarn-site.xml file (for the NodeManager), as explained here:

1. For the DataNode, edit the hadoop-site.xml file, ensuring that there's a reference to the exclude file wherein you'll list the soon-to-be-decommissioned node. You can do this by adding the parameter `dfs.hosts.exclude` in the hdfs-site.xml file:

```
<property>
   <name>dfs.hosts.exclude</name>
    <value>$HADOOP_CONF_DIR/dfs.exclude</value>
</property>
```

2. For the NodeManager, edit the yarn-site.xml file, as shown here:

```
<property>
  <name>yarn.resourcemanager.nodes.exclude-path</name>
  <value>$HADOOP_CONF_DIR/yarn.exclude</value>
 </property>
```

Decommissioning DataNodes and NodeManagers

You follow basically the same procedures for decommissioning both a DataNode and a NodeManager, as explained in the following sections.

Decommissioning a DataNode

Follow these steps to decommission a DataNode.

1. On the node running the NameNode service, edit the $HADOOP_CONF_DIR/dfs.exclude file and add the name of the node you wish to decommission. If you wish to decommission multiple nodes at the same time, you can do so by listing each node on a separate line in this file.
2. From the same node, reload the NameNode configuration so it's made aware of the excluded DataNodes by running the following command:

   ```
   $ su $HDFS_USER
   $ hdfs dfsadmin -refreshNodes
   ```

   In this case, HDFS_USER is the user that owns HDFS, which is normally the user named hdfs.

   The NameNode will read all of its configuration when you run this command, including the contents of the exclude file. It'll then start decommissioning the nodes you specified in the exclude file.

   The decommissioning process can take some time, with the time depending on the size of the disk drives. As part of the decommissioning, Hadoop needs to replicate the HDFS data blocks on the soon-to-be-decommissioned node to other nodes in the cluster. You can check the progress of the decommissioning by issuing the `dfsadmin -report` command at intervals. This command will show you the nodes that are connected to the cluster. At the bottom of the dfsadmin report, you'll see the status of the node you are currently decommissioning:

   - Before starting the decommissioning:

     ```
     Name: 10.192.2.37:50010 (hadoop011node17.example.com)
     Hostname: hadoop011node17.example.com
     Rack: /prod011
     Decommission Status : Normal
     Configured Capacity: 34892832342016 (31.73 TB)
     ```

   - After starting the decommissioning:

     ```
     Decommissioning datanodes (1):

     Name: 10.192.2.37:50010 (hadoop011node17.example.com)
     Hostname: hadoop011node17.example.com
     Rack: /prod011
     Decommission Status : Decommission in progress
     Configured Capacity: 34892832342016 (31.73 TB)
     DFS Used: 22083549471327 (20.08 TB)
     Non DFS Used: 18905551136 (17.61 GB)
     DFS Remaining: 12790377319553 (11.63 TB)
     ```

```
DFS Used%: 63.29%
DFS Remaining%: 36.66%
Configured Cache Capacity: 25391267840 (23.65 GB)
Cache Used: 0 (0 B)
Cache Remaining: 25391267840 (23.65 GB)
Cache Used%: 0.00%
Cache Remaining%: 100.00%
Last contact: Sun Jul 10Dec 31 13:26:27 CST 2016
```

- After the completion of the Decommissioning:

```
$
Name: 10.192.2.38:50010 (hadoop011node18.example.com)
Hostname: hadoop011node18.example.com
Rack: /prod011
Decommission Status : Decommissioned
Configured Capacity: 0 (0 B)
DFS Used: 0 (0 B)
Non DFS Used: 0 (0 B)
DFS Remaining: 0 (0 B)
DFS Used%: 100.00%DFS Remaining%: 0.00%
S
```

You can also check the DataNode web UI for the DataNode that's being decommissioned (`http://<DataNodehost:50070`) and check its admin state. The admin state should be changed to "Decommission in progress" at this point.

When you see that the decommissioning of the DataNode is completed, all of its blocks have been replicated to other nodes. The DataNode web UI at this point should report the state of the DataNode as "Decommissioned," as well.

3. If you're using a dfs.include file for your cluster, delete the decommissioned node information from that file and refresh the nodes again, as shown here:

```
$ su $HDFS_USER
$ hdfs dfsadmin -refreshNodes
```

4. Once the DataNode decommissioning is completed you can shut down the node on which the DataNode was running.

Decommissioning a NodeManager

Follow these steps to decommission a NodeManager:

1. Add the name of the NodeManager host to the $HADOOP_CONF_DIR/yarn .exclude file on the server where the NameNode is running. Make sure you specify the FQDN of the hostname(s).
2. Remove the decommissioned node information from the $HADOOP_CONF_DIR/yarn.include file, if you're using the yarn.include file.
3. Refresh the ResourceManager by executing the following command:

```
# su $YARN_USER
$ yarn rmadmin -refreshNodes
```

In this command, the user YARN_USER is the user that owns YARN, which usually is the user named yarn.

4. As with the DataNode decommissioning, once the NodeManager decommissioning is completed, you are free to shut down the node on which the NodeManager was running.

Recommissioning Nodes

Recommissioning a node means you want to add it back to the cluster. Recommissioning, as you can tell, is the opposite of decommissioning, and hence, requires you to trace your steps back.

Let's assume that the node you want to recommission runs both a DataNode and a NodeManager service. Start up the host first. In order to recommission it, remove the host name from the exclude file in both HDFS and YARN (dfs.exclude and yarn.exclude). Then run the following two commands, and you're good to go:

```
$ hdfs dfsadmin -refreshNodes
$ yarn rmadmin -refreshNodes
```

In a high-availability HDFS environment where you have two NameNodes, you must run the `dfsadmin -refreshNodes` command on both NameNodes, as shown here:

```
sudo -u hdfs hdfs dfsadmin -fs hdfs://hadoop01.localhost:8020 -refreshNodes
sudo -u hdfs hdfs dfsadmin -fs hdfs://hadoop02.localhost:8020 -refreshNodes
```

Similarly, in a high-availability ResourceManager environment, explained later in this chapter, you must run the following command on both nodes:

```
sudo -u hdfs yarn rmadmin -refreshNodes
```

Things to Remember about Decommissioning and Recommissioning

While the procedures for decommissioning and recommisssioning nodes are pretty straightforward, there are a couple of things you ought to keep in mind to make these processes more efficient.

Decommissioning a NodeManager is pretty straightforward and is usually completed virtually immediately. However, as alluded to earlier, decommissioning a DataNode could be a time-consuming affair. Recall that when you decommission a DataNode, the NameNode makes sure that all the blocks on that DataNode are going to be available in the other nodes, up to the number of replicas you configured (or the default replication factor, which is three). To do this, the NameNode copies the DataNode's data blocks in small batches, and if the DataNode has a substantial number of data blocks, it could take several hours for the decommissioning process to complete. Meanwhile, you'll be wondering if the decommissioning process has failed (you can monitor the decommissioning process via the DataNode's web UI). In order to avoid this, it's a good idea to tune HDFS first by doing the following:

- Raising the DataNode Java heap size using the Java option `-Xmx`.
- Setting or raising the DataNode balancing bandwidth with the `dfs.balance.bandwidthPerSec` parameter, which determines the maximum amount of network bandwidth (in bytes per second) a DataNode can use for balancing HDFS data.

- Raising the replication maximum threads and maximum replication thread hard limits by setting the `dfs.datanode.max.transfer.threads` property in the hdfs-site.xml file. This parameter controls the maximum number of threads to be used for transferring data into and out of a DataNode. The default value is 4,096.
- Raising the replication work multiplier per iteration (the default value is 2, but you can raise it to 10 or more) by setting the `dfs.namenode.replication.work.multiplier.per.iteration` parameter, which is deemed an *advanced* parameter by Hadoop, meaning you ought to exercise care when setting this parameter. This parameter determines the total block transfers that can begin in parallel at any DataNode. The number of blocks is determined by multiplying the value of this parameter by the total number of active nodes in the cluster. The resulting number is the number of data blocks to be transferred immediately, per DataNode heartbeat.

Adding a New DataNode and/or a NodeManager

You can add new DataNodes to increase the storage capacity of your cluster. Adding NodeManagers, on the other hand, will increase your cluster's processing capacity. In most cases, you run both a DataNode and a NodeManager service on all worker nodes (except the master nodes), so let's learn how to perform this task, which is probably going to be a common task as most Hadoop clusters grow over time by adding more nodes to the cluster.

Here are the basic steps in adding new nodes to a cluster:

1. Install Hadoop software on the new node(s). Copy the Hadoop configuration files to the new node, using a tool such as `rsync` or `scp`, as shown here:

   ```
   $ rsync -a <master_node_IP>:$HADOOP_HOME/etc/hadoop/$HADOOP_HOME/etc/hadoop
   ```

2. Setting up passwordless SSH between the master nodes and the new nodes is optional, but you can go ahead and do it.
3. Add the IP address of the node to the $HADOOP_HOME/etc/hadoop/slaves file on the master node.

Once you perform these steps, Hadoop will add the node to your cluster, but you can't yet store data on that server or run jobs on it. In order to do the former, you must start the DataNode service, and to do the latter, you must start up the NodeManager service, as shown here:

```
$ $HADOOP_HOME/sbin/hadoop-deamons.sh start datanode
$ $HADOOP_HOME/sbin/yarn-daemons.sh start nodemanager
```

When it comes to recommissioning, the NodeManager doesn't need any special attention, with the ResourceManager immediately starting the scheduling of new tasks on this NodeManager. As for the newly recommissioned DataNode, while Hadoop immediately starts storing new HDFS data on the DFS directories of this DataNode, it won't move any existing HDFS data over to this node. Therefore, especially when you're adding a bunch of DataNodes to the cluster, it's a good idea to start the HDFS balancer after the node addition, to ensure that the HDFS data is spread evenly across your cluster.

ResourceManager High Availability

While setting up high availability for the NameNode ensures that clients will always be able to access HDFS data, that's only half the battle as far as high availability goes. As you know, in a Hadoop cluster, in addition to HDFS, you also need the ResourceManager (RM) to be running for clients be able to do anything. If the node on which the ResourceManager is running crashes, YARN is inaccessible and your clients can't run anything on the cluster. Thus, configuring high availability for the ResourceManager is highly recommended in a production setting, and the following sections show how to set it up.

ResourceManager High-Availability Architecture

As with NameNode high availability, you configure a pair of active/passive ResourceManagers to avoid the single point of failure risk in running a single ResourceManager. The active ResourceManager writes its state to a ZooKeeper instance in the ZooKeeper ensemble. If the active ResourceManager fails for any reason, Hadoop uses the state stored in ZooKeeper, enabling the standby ResourceManager to start with the correct state.

You can move an RM from the standby to the active state manually or configure the failover to happen automatically with Hadoop's automatic failover feature. If you want to manually transition the states, you must use the `yarn rmadmin` command and transition the active ResourceManager to the standby status and the standby ResourceManager to the active status.

If you enable automatic failover between the active and standby ResourceManagers, Hadoop uses the ZooKeeper-based ActiveStandbyElector to help decide which of the two RMs should be active at any time by detecting RM failures and selecting another ResourceManager as the active ResourceManager. Unlike in the case of NameNode HA, you don't use a daemon such as ZFKC, since the ActiveStandbyElector is embedded in the two ResourceManagers.

You list both the active and the standby RM in the yarn-site.xml file. When ApplicationMasters and NodeManagers can't connect to the active RM, they will keep trying the connection until they hit the new active RM. When the standby RM receives any web requests, it redirects them to the active RM.

Assuming you've enabled RM restart, when a failover occurs the new active RM continues its work from where the previous active RM stopped functioning, using the state of the active RM that's stored in ZooKeeper. All applications that were submitted to the previous RM will have a new attempt automatically spawned. The state of the RMs is persisted to a state-store that's accessible by both ResourceManagers. You can use either a file-based store or a ZooKeeper-maintained store called the `ZKRMStateStore`.

Unlike in the case of NameNode high availability, you don't need to set up a fencing mechanism, because the state-store saves the state of the RMs in the ZKRMStateStore, preventing any split-brain situations where multiple ResourceManagers may try to assume the active role.

Setting Up ResourceManager High Availability

You can set up ResourceManager high availability by configuring several high-availability related parameters in the yarn-site.xml file. There are other parameters, as well, but these are the minimal set of parameters you'll need to configure.

```
<property>
  <name>yarn.resourcemanager.ha.enabled</name>
  <value>true</value>
</property>
<property>
  <name>yarn.resourcemanager.cluster-id</name>
  <value>prodcluster1</value>
</property>
<property>
  <name>yarn.resourcemanager.ha.rm-ids</name>
  <value>rm100,rm140</value>
</property>
<property>
  <name>yarn.resourcemanager.hostname.rm1</name>
  <value>master1</value>
</property>
<property>
  <name>yarn.resourcemanager.hostname.rm2</name>
  <value>master2</value>
</property>
<property>
  <name>yarn.resourcemanager.zk-address</name>
  <value>zk1:2181,zk2:2181,zk3:2181</value>
</property>
</property>
<property>
  <name>yarn.resourcemanager.recovery.enabled</name>
  <value>true</value>
</property>
```

The following property is mandatory when you enable ResourceManager recovery.

```
<property>
    <name>yarn.resourcemanager.store.class</name>      <value>org.apache.hadoop
.yarn.server.resourcemanager.recovery.ZKRMStateStore</value>
 </property>
<property>
   <name>yarn.client.failover-proxy-provider</name>
   <value>org.apache.hadoop.yarn.client.ConfiguredRMFailoverProxyProvider</value>
 </property>
```

The very first parameter in the list, yarn.resourcemanager.ha.enabled, lets you enable ResourceManager high availability in your cluster. For the property yarn .resourcemanager.ha.rm-ids, I used rm100 and rm140 as the ResourceManager IDs, but you can specify any pair of numbers. The `yarn.resourcemanager.recovery.enabled` parameter enables job recovery on a restart or failover of the ResourceManager.

ResourceManager Failover

Automatic failover of the ResourceManager is enabled by default. If you prefer manual failovers and want to prevent automatic failovers from happening, you can do so by setting the value of the `yarn.resourcemanager.ha.automatic-failover.enabled` parameter to `false` in the yarn-site.xml file. Note that although automatic failover is *enabled* by default, you must *configure* it, as shown in the following section.

Configuring Automatic RM Failover

You can configure the automatic ResourceManager failover process by setting the parameters `yarn.resourcemanager.ha.automatic-failover.zk-base-path` and `yarn.resourcemanager.cluster-id` in the yarn-site.xml file.

```
<property>
  <name>yarn.resourcemanager.ha.automatic-failover.zk-base-path</name>
  <value>/yarn-leader-election</value>
<description>Optional setting. The default value is /yarn-leader-election
</description>
</property>

<property>
   <name>yarn.resourcemanager.cluster-id</name>
   <value>yarn-cluster</value>
</property>
```

The ResourceManager Restart Feature

The ResourceManager restart feature is unrelated to the ResourceManager high-availability feature, although it does sound like it has something to do with it. The restart feature ensures that the ResourceManager performs seamlessly between restarts, without affecting applications running in the cluster. The application state is persisted, and upon recovery, the ResourceManager reloads the state. The ResourceManager doesn't need to kill the ApplicationMaster and start running the applications from the beginning again.

When you restart the ResourceManager, it won't kill any of the applications running in the YARN cluster. The ResourceManager recovers its running state that existed at the time it was stopped by using the container statuses it receives from the NodeManagers in the cluster. When a NodeManager resynchronizes with the ResourceManager, it doesn't kill the running containers. It sends the status of all containers to the ResourceManager after registering with it again following a restart of the ResourceManager. The ApplicationMaster will resend outstanding resource requests to the ResourceManager, as well, so that those requests aren't lost.

The configuration property yarn.resourcemanager.recovery.enabled enables the ResourceManager restart feature, as shown here.

```
<property>
  <name>yarn.resourcemanager.recovery.enabled</name>
  <value>true</value>
</property>
```

Deploying a High-Availability ResourceManager Cluster

Earlier, I showed the configuration properties you must use to set up RM high availability. There are a few things you must do to activate your high-availability ResourceManager configuration. Here are the steps:

1. Make sure both of the nodes where the ResourceManager runs have identical yarn-site.xml files.
2. The value you've set for the clientPort parameter in the ZooKeeper configuration file (zoo.cfg) must match the port value in the yarn-site.xml files.

   ```
   <property>
      <name>yarn.resourcemanager.zk-state-store.address</name>
      <value>localhost:2181</value>
   </property>
   ```

3. Start the ZooKeeper service with the following command:

   ```
   /usr/lib/zookeeper/bin/zkServer.sh start
   ```

4. Start all HDFS services, including the NameNodes (in an HA environment there are two NameNodes), the Standby NameNode (if you haven't set up an HA NameNode service) and all DataNodes, in that order.
5. Start all YARN services, including the primary and secondary ResourceManagers on the two nodes where they run, as well as the JobHistoryServer and the NodeManager services.

   ```
   $ yarn start resourcemanager   // on primary RM server
   $ yarn start resourcemanager   // on secondary RM server

   $ yarn start historyserver     // on server where JobHistoryServer runs
   $ yarn start nodemanager     // on all servers where NodeManager service runs
   ```

6. If you've chosen the default feature of automatic ResourceManager failover, you're all set, as Hadoop will select the active ResourceManager by itself. If you've instead disabled automatic failover, both RMs will now be in the standby state. You must transition one of them to the active mode with the following command:

   ```
   $ yarn rmadmin -transitionToActive rm100
   ```

   The ResourceManager identified by the ID rm100 (in our example) will transition into the active state, and the other ResourceManager, identified by the ID rm140 (in our example), will run in the standby mode.

Using the ResourceManager High-Availability Commands

In addition to configuring automatic failover, you can also perform a manual transition of a ResourceManager to a different status (from active to standby and vice versa). Use the `yarn rmadmin` command for administering RM high availability. Use the ResourceManager IDs you set earlier with the `yarn.resourcemanager.ha.rm-ids` parameter to distinguish between the two ResourceManagers.

You can get the current state of the two ResourceManagers in an HA architecture by issuing the `getServiceState` command:

```
# yarn rmadmin -getServiceState rm100
active
# yarn rmadmin -getServiceState rm140
standby
#
```

Provided you haven't enabled automatic failover, you can manually transition an RM from one state to another with the following commands:

```
$ yarn rmadmin -transitionToStandby <serviceId> [--forceactive]

$ yarn rmadmin -transitionToStandby <serviceId>

$ yarn rmadmin -failover [--forcefence] [--forceactive] <serviceId> <serviceId>
```

Performing Common Management Tasks

As a Hadoop administrator, there are several routine tasks you need to perform in your cluster. The earlier chapters have explained the key areas of Hadoop administration. Here, we provide several common administrative tasks which weren't part of the earlier discussion of various topics.

Moving the NameNode to a Different Host

Let's say the server on which the NameNode is running is experiencing hardware problems and you want to move the NameNode to a healthy host. Here are the steps you must follow to move the NameNode over to a new host:

1. If the server on which you want to run the NameNode service already has all the Hadoop and other software installed, you can proceed to the next step. Otherwise, you must first install all the necessary software packages such as Apache Hadoop and the rest that are on the current host.
2. Shut down the NameNode and all the DataNodes, if they are not already down.
3. Make a backup of the directories specified by the `dfs.name.dir` parameter on the current NameNode host.
4. Using an OS utility such as `scp`, copy the directories over to the new host.
5. Start the NameNode service and the DataNodes.

Managing High-Availability NameNodes

Chapter 11, "NameNode Operations, High Availability and Federation", explained NameNode high availability in detail, so we aren't going to explain that again here. However, from the point of view of managing high-availability NameNodes, it is important to understand how to transition a NameNode to the active state, should you find both of your NameNodes in the standby state, and you haven't configured automatic failover.

If both NameNodes are in the standby state, you can transition one of the NameNodes to the active state by doing the following:

```
$ sudo -u hdfs haadmin -transitionToActive nn1
```

You can force a manual failover by doing the following:

```
$ sudo -u hdfs haadmin -failover nn1 nn2
```

When you run this command, the currently active NameNode nn1 will become the new standby and the current standby, nn2, will take over as the new active NameNode.

Using a Shutdown/Startup Script to Manage your Cluster

When you have a test cluster with a handful of clusters, it's not really a big deal how you go about starting and shutting down the Hadoop daemons. However, when you're dealing with real-life Hadoop clusters with many nodes, it's good to automate everything, including the starting and stopping of the Hadoop services. The following code shows how to automate the starting of the Hadoop daemons in a cluster. It's very easy to add the corresponding code for shutting down the cluster on your own!

```
start_service() {
    test -f /etc/init.d/$1 && echo "Starting $1" && service $1 start
}

start_hadoop() {
    start_service hue
    start_service oozie
    start_service hive-server2
    start_service hive-metastore
    start_service hadoop-yarn-resourcemanager
    start_service hadoop-hdfs-namenode
    start_service hadoop-hdfs-httpfs
    start_service hadoop-mapreduce-historyserver
    start_service hadoop-hdfs-journalnode
    start_service hadoop-yarn-nodemanager
    start_service hadoop-hdfs-datanode
}
```

In order to automate the cluster startup, you should run this code on every node of your cluster. This script will start up all the Hadoop daemons, plus all the third party tools such as Hive and Oozie as well.

Balancing HDFS

Chapter 9, "HDFS Commands, HDFS Permissions and HDFS Storage," explained the importance of periodically balancing HDFS and also demonstrated how to use the hdfs balancer utility to balance the HDFS data. It's a good idea to set up a simple cron job to run the balancer job on a regular basis. You can run the hdfs balancer every day, but there's no hard and fast rule as to the best frequency for the balancing job. The best way to figure out whether the frequency of balancing is okay is to issue the hdfs dfsadmin -report command and check how closely the nodes are balanced in terms of HDFS data. The following example shows how to check how balanced the HDFS data is in a cluster:

```
# sudo -u hdfs hdfs dfsadmin -report | cat <(echo "Name: Total") - | grep '^\
(Name\|Total\|DFS
 Used\)' | tr '\n' '\t' | sed -e 's/\(Name\)/\n\1/g' | sort --field-separator=:
--key=5,5n

Name: Total      DFS Used: 2141803616206687 (1.90 PB)     DFS Used%: 59.08%
Name: 10.192.0.106:50010 (hadoop03.example.com)    DFS Used: 46065068713731 (41.90
TB)      DFS Used%: 50.25%
Name: 10.192.0.108:50010 (hadoop05.example.com)    DFS Used: 46077744360551 (41.91
TB)      DFS Used%: 50.26%
Name: 10.192.0.110:50010 (hadoop07.example.com)    DFS Used: 46176056279144 (42.00
TB)      DFS Used%: 50.37%
...
#
```

In this case, the DFS Used percentage is pretty much the same on most nodes, so no balancing is required. If you run the balancer now, there's no harm—it wraps up very quickly since there's not much for it to do.

Sometimes a balancer job gets stuck, or is just too slow. You can restart the balancer in such a situation. First find out the process ID (PID) of the running balancer process with the following command:

```
# ps aux | grep '\-Dproc_balancer' | grep -v grep
```

Once you find the PID of the balancer job, kill it, and also remove the balancer lock file, as shown here:

```
# rm /tmp/hdfs-balancer.lock
```

Balancing the Storage on the DataNodes

By default, a DataNode writes new block replicas to disk in a round robin fashion. However, at times you may want the DataNodes to consider the available free space on each of the disk drives when deciding where to write new replicas. In order to do this, you configure a policy that lets the DataNodes choose the disk volumes according to specific policies.

Ordinarily you want to configure HDFS so the DataNodes distribute their writes in a way that balances the available storage among the DataNode's disk drives.

You can configure the following two aspects of HDFS to accomplish this:

- The amount of bytes of free space by which DataNode disks can differ before they're considered imbalanced
- The percentage of new block allocations that will be sent to disk drives with more free space than other drives

The following configuration properties enable you to set up storage balancing in your cluster.

- `dfs.datanode.fsdataset.volume.choosing.policy`: This property enables storage balancing among the volumes of a DataNode. The default value is `org.apache.hadoop.hdfs.server.datanode.fsdataset.availableSpaceVolumeChoosingPolicy`.
- `dfs.datanode.available-space-volume-choosing-policy.balanced-space-threshold`: The value you set for this property determines the amount by which volumes can differ from each other in terms of free disk space before they're considered imbalanced. The default value is 10,737,418,240 (10GB). If the free space on each of the disk drives in a DataNode is within this range compared to the other disk volumes, the block assignments are done on the default basis of a pure round-robin policy.
- `dfs.datanode.available-space-volume-choosing-policy.balanced-space-preference-fraction`: This property determines the proportion of new block allocations that'll be sent to volumes with more free disk space than others. The default value is 0.75, and you can set this property in the range of 0.0–1.0.

Managing the MySQL Database

You'll need to use a relational database for storing various types of data, including the metadata for Hue, Hive, Oozie and other Hadoop components. While you can use any relational database, such as Oracle, Postgres, or MySQL, it appears that MySQL is a popular choice. I therefore briefly show how to manage the MySQL database in your cluster.

This section covers the following topics:

- Configuring a MySQL database
- Configuring MySQL high availability

Configuring a MySQL Database

Since the component metadata stored in the relational database is highly critical, it's a best practice to set up high availability for the database service. Let's configure a simple MySQL server database by following the steps listed here:

1. Download the MySQL binaries from here:

   `http://dev.mysql.com/downloads/`

2. Create a mysql user and group:

   ```
   # groupadd mysql
   # useradd -r -g mysql mysql
   ```

   I chose to use mysql for the group as well as the owner, but you can specify other names if you wish. Since this user is required for ownership purposes only and not for logging into MySQL, I specified the `-r` option when creating the user, meaning this user won't have any login permissions to the server hosting MySQL.

3. Unzip the downloaded MySQL binaries zip file. Here, I unzip the file into the /usr/local directory:

```
# cd /usr/local
# tar xzvf /path/to/mysql-VERSION-OS.tar.gz
# ln -s full-path-to-mysql-VERSION-OS-mysql
```

   Unpacking the distribution will create the installation directory named mysql-VERSION-g. You must create a symbolic link to that directory. You can then access the installation directory as /usr/local/mysql.

4. Change the owner and group. If you don't have the root privileges, you must prefix the following commands with sudo:

```
# cd mysql
# chown -R mysql .
# chgrp -R mysql .
# scripts/mysql_install_db  --user-mysql
# chown -R root .
# chown -R mysql data
```

5. Start the MySQL server:

```
# bin/mysqld_safe  --user=mysql &
```

   When running this command as the root user, in order to ensure that MySQL runs as an unprivileged non-root user, include the -user option. If you run this command as the mysql user, you don't need to specify the -user option when starting the server.

6. Run a few simple tests to ensure that MySQL is performing correctly:

```
# bin/mysqladmin version
# bin/mysqladmin variables
```

7. Shut down the MySQL server to make sure it shuts down correctly, and then start it back up again so you can start using it:

```
# bin/mysqladmin -u root shutdown
# bin/mysqld_safe  --user=mysql &
```

Now that we have MySQL configured to run in your cluster, it's time to set up high availability for it, in light of its importance as a metadata repository for critical components such as Hive.

Configuring MySQL High Availability

You can set up a replicated MySQL environment using one of two modes: master-slave or master-master in active-passive mode. The master-slave model is simple and lets you create a cold standby that you can use to replace the master server when the master goes down for any reason. You must manually switch the slave to a master mode when the master fails. The master-master replication is also referred to as multimaster replication.

You're mostly likely to use the MySQL database as a backend to the Hive metastore. It's recommended that you configure the master-master replication mode where one service is active and the other server passive. In this mode, transactions are written to any one server at a given time, avoiding any inconsistences in transaction updates if you update both the databases at the same time. Although you can set up things such that transactions are written to both databases simultaneously, it's advisable to use the active master server for transaction writes and the passive master server for reading data, as well as for use as an active master if the original master server fails. It's easy to turn the passive server into an active master very quickly, using appropriate monitoring scripts. In the following section, let's learn how to set up a master-master replication in the active-passive mode.

Setting Up a Master-Master MySQL Replication

Follow these steps to configure your master-master replication for MySQL:

1. On both the master servers, which I refer to as Master1 and Master2, create an account for the replication user that you'll use for replicating data.

```
> Grant replication slave, replication client on *.* to 'replicat'@'
<server_name>'
   identified by 'replpasswd';
```

2. Edit the /etc/my.cnf file on the Master1 server, as shown here:

```
[mysqld]
server-id=1
replicate-same-server-id = 0
auto-increment-increment = 2
auto-increment-offset =1
master-connect-retry =1
master-connect-retry = 60
log-bin = /var/log/mysql/mysql-bin
log-bin-index = /var/log/mysql/bin-log.index
log-error = /var/log/mysql/relay.log
relay-log-index = /var/log/mysql/relay-log.index
expire-log-days=14
```

3. Edit the /etc/my.cnf file on the Master2 server. Specify the same attributes as you did for Master1 with two changes (server-id and auto-increment-offset), and a new attribute, `read-only`.

```
server-id=1
auto-increment-offset=2
read-only = 1
```

> **Note**
>
> The commands to start the MySQL database assume a Red Hat Enterprise Linux server. If you're using other Linux distributions, the commands may be slightly different.

4. Start the MySQL service on the active master, Master1, as shown here, and run the following commands:

```
# service mysql start
# mysql -user=root -p
```

```
> change master to master_host='master2.mydomain';
> master_user='replicat',
> master_password='replicatpass',
> master_log_file='mysql-bin.000001',
> master_log_pos=0;
> start slave;
```

5. On the passive server, Master2, start the MySQL daemon and run the same set of commands as you did in step 4, modifying the set of commands as follows.

```
# service mysql start
# mysql -user=root -p
> change master to master_host='master1.mydomain';
```

You've now configured a master-master MySQL replication setup, with server Master1 as the active server and server Master2 as the passive server, ready to take over from Master1 at a moment's notice.

Switching the Active and Passive Roles

It's easy to switch a passive master to the role of an active master server. Assuming that Master1 is the active master and Master2 is the passive master, here are the steps to follow to switch the active and passive roles between the two servers.

1. Make sure any services using the MySQL database in your cluster, such as the Hive's Metastore server, are shut down. This way, you keep new transaction writes from coming in to be written to the active master database.
2. In the active master (Master1) configuration file, add the line `read-only = 1`.
3. After waiting for a sufficient amount of time for the previously passive master, Master2, to catch up with the replication of changes from the active master, switch its read-only flag off by removing the line `read-only = 1` from its configuration file.
4. In all the applications, such as the Hive metastore, that use the MySQL database, point to the new active master server and restart those applications.

Backing Up Important Cluster Data

HDFS data is almost invariably not backed up—Hadoop's built in redundancy through replication of data should take care of most data-protection requirements. If you do want to ensure that some small portion of the cluster's data is backed up to a different cluster or offsite, you can do that with the help of a utility such as DistCp, as explained in Chapter 8, "The Role of the NameNode and How HDFS Works."

What you must back up, however, are two things: the HDFS metadata and the metastores for components such as Oozie, Sqoop, Hive, Sentry and Hue (and Ambari, as well, if you happen to use it). The following sections explain how to handle these backups.

Backing Up HDFS Metadata

HDFS metadata is serious business—if you lose it for any reason and your NameNode happens to go down, the NameNode can't find the HDFS data when you restart it. You must therefore periodically (at least once a day) back up the HDFS metadata.

You can back up the HDFS metadata using Hadoop's commands and/or by backing up the relevant directories using an OS utility. I show both strategies in the following sections.

Backing Up the HDFS Metadata on the NameNode

In order to back up the HDFS metadata from the NameNode server, go to the directory listed in the NameNode data directories property (`dfs.datanode.data.dir`) on the server running the active NameNode. If you have multiple directories listed, you need to back up only one directory, since it'll be an exact copy of the other directories.

Assuming your NameNode data directory is named /data/dfs/nn, here are the steps to back up the HDFS metadata.

1. Log in as the root user and shut down the active NameNode.
2. Change the directory to /data/dfs/nn.

```
# cd /data/dfs/nn
```

3. Back up all the folders in this directory using the following command.

```
# tar -cvf /backup/nn_backup data.tar .
./
./current/
./current/fstime
./current/VERSION
./current/edits
. /image/
./image/fsimage
```

Backing Up the Metadata Using the -fetchImage Command

You can also use the Hadoop-provided `-fetchImage` command to back up the HDFS metadata. Follow these steps to back up the HDFS metadata:

1. Place the active NameNode in safe mode so HDFS is in a read-only state when you back up its metadata. Also verify that the cluster is in safe mode.

```
# su hdfs
bash-3.2$ hdfs dfsadmin -fs hdfs://hadoop011node01.example.com -safemode enter
Safe mode is ON
$

$ hdfs dfsadmin -fs hdfs://hadoop11node01.example.com -safemode get
Safe mode is ON
$
```

2. Run the `-saveNamespace` command, which will save the current in-memory image file to a new fsimage file and reset the edits file, as well:

```
$ hdfs dfsadmin -fs hdfs://hadoop011node01.example.com -saveNamespace
Save namespace successful
$
```

3. Issue the -fetchImage command to back up the HDFS metadata to disk.

```
$ mkdir /tmp/Backups_node01
$ hdfs dfsadmin -fs hdfs://hadoop011node01.example.com -fetchImage /tmp/
Backups_node01
16/08/26 11:41:01 INFO namenode.TransferFsImage: Opening connection to
http://bdaolc011node01.sabre.com:50070/imagetransfer?getimage=1&txid=latest
16/08/26 11:41:01 INFO namenode.TransferFsImage: Image Transfer timeout
configured to 60000 milliseconds
16/08/26 11:41:04 INFO namenode.TransferFsImage: Transfer took 3.45s at
72463.81 KB/s
$
```

4. Verify the metadata backup.

```
$  ls -altr /tmp/Backups_node01
total 250552
drwxrwxrwt 22 root root        4096 Aug 26 11:40 ..
-rw-r--r--  1 hdfs hadoop 256297032 Aug 26 11:41 fsimage_0000000000490831699
drwxr-xr-x  2 hdfs hadoop      4096 Aug 26 11:41 .
$
```

5. Take the active NameNode out of safe mode.

```
$ hdfs dfsadmin -fs hdfs://hadoop011node01.example.com -safemode leave
Safe mode is OFF
$
```

Backing Up the Metastore Databases

Although you can set up a separate metastore database for each Hadoop component that requires it, you don't need to do so as it makes for more complex management. Simply use a single database such as MySQL as the repository for storing the metastore data for all of Hadoop's components that need a metastore.

The metastore for Sqoop, Hive and Sentry is relatively small, and that for Hue depends on the number of users and the activity of the users in Hue. The Oozie server metastore can grow very large over time. To back up the metadata for all the components, you must first stop all the services and then back up the database.

Assuming you're using the MySQL database as the repository for the metastores of the Hadoop components, issue the mysqldump command to back up the MySQL database. Here's the syntax:

```
$ mysqldump -hhostname -uusername -ppassword database > /backup/mysql/mysql_backup.sql
```

Using Hue to Administer Your Cluster

Hue (which stands for "Hadoop user experience") is a web application that lets users access the Hadoop cluster components, such as Hive, Pig and Sqoop, through the web. It's also a platform for building custom applications. Hue acts as a sort of a container application that hosts a suite of applications and communicates with the servers that represent the various Hadoop components. As an administrator, probably the single biggest use for Hue is to manage your Oozie jobs through Hue's excellent interface to

Oozie. In Chapter 14, "Working with Oozie to Manage Job Workflows," you learned how you can create Oozie workflows and coordinators. After looking at the Oozie workflow and coordinator XML files, you're probably thinking: "I love this Oozie thingy, but I don't like all the manual configuration and the messing around with yucky-looking XML configuration files!" Well, with Hue, you don't need to worry. You can create powerful Oozie workflows and coordinators through Hue without ever editing a single configuration file.

Figure 16.2 shows how useful Hue is to an administrator in tracking running Oozie jobs and identifying the status of jobs. You can check the start and end times for completed jobs to ascertain whether they ran within their expected time windows. For running jobs, you can figure out from this page approximately when a job will complete its execution. If a job failed, you can click on that job on this page and check its configuration as well as its job logs. Now, that's an awesome productivity improvement for a busy Hadoop cluster admin, who doesn't usually have the time to log into various servers and check the logs manually and pore over Oozie XML workflow (and coordinator) configuration files to troubleshoot job failures! Similarly, the Oozie Editor makes it mere child's play to create complex workflows, coordinators and bundles.

Hue is of great use to both regular users and Hadoop administrators. Hue is commonly used by analysts and others to run Hive and Pig jobs in the Hadoop cluster—not only can users see the job progress but they can access their past queries and applications, too. From the administrator's point of view, you can not only run Hadoop jobs but also schedule them as well as monitor their progress and status through Oozie. Hue provides a comprehensive interface through which to schedule your Oozie workflow and coordinator jobs and view the status of those jobs.

The big thing about Hue is that it'll let users access Hadoop's HDFS data directly from a browser without ever having to log into the command line.

Allowing Your Users to Use Hue

You must create Hue accounts for any users that you want to grant the ability to use the various applications hosted by Hue. Typically, users will want a Hue login to work with the Hive, Impala or Pig interfaces to Hadoop to perform data-analysis tasks. Many such users in a real-life cluster use Hue as their only tool to work with a Hadoop cluster. To create a user login, do the following:

1. Log into Hue as an administrator.
2. Select the Manage Users dropdown in the upper right hand side, under the administrator's username.
3. Select Add User to create a new user. Navigate through three screens to create a user by supplying information such as the user name and password and the group to which you want to assign the user.

As a cluster administrator, you'll have super user status. Super users can launch any of the Hue applications, such as Oozie and Sqoop, as well as manage users and their

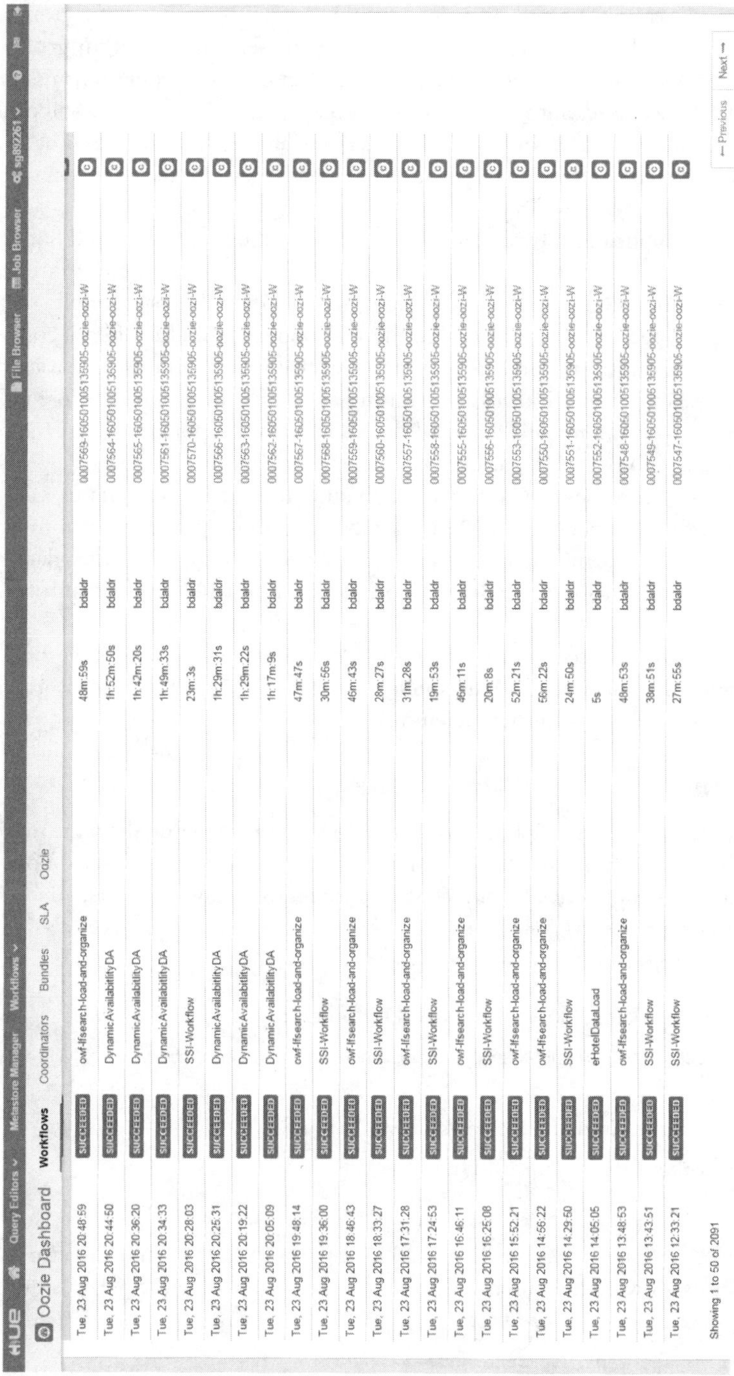

HUE | Query Editors | Metastore Manager | Workflows | File Browser | Job Browser | sg892261

Oozie Dashboard | Workflows | Coordinators | Bundles | SLA | Oozie

Tue, 23 Aug 2016 20:48:59	SUCCEEDED	owf-lfsearch-load-and-organize	48m:59s	bdaldr	0007569-160501005135905-oozie-oozi-W
Tue, 23 Aug 2016 20:44:50	SUCCEEDED	DynamicAvailabitlityDA	1h:52m:50s	bdaldr	0007564-160501005135905-oozie-oozi-W
Tue, 23 Aug 2016 20:36:20	SUCCEEDED	DynamicAvailabitlityDA	1h:42m:20s	bdaldr	0007565-160501005135905-oozie-oozi-W
Tue, 23 Aug 2016 20:34:33	SUCCEEDED	DynamicAvailabitlityDA	1h:49m:33s	bdaldr	0007561-160501005135905-oozie-oozi-W
Tue, 23 Aug 2016 20:28:03	SUCCEEDED	SSI-Workflow	23m:3s	bdaldr	0007570-160501005135905-oozie-oozi-W
Tue, 23 Aug 2016 20:25:31	SUCCEEDED	DynamicAvailabitlityDA	1h:29m:31s	bdaldr	0007566-160501005135905-oozie-oozi-W
Tue, 23 Aug 2016 20:19:22	SUCCEEDED	DynamicAvailabitlityDA	1h:29m:22s	bdaldr	0007563-160501005135905-oozie-oozi-W
Tue, 23 Aug 2016 20:05:09	SUCCEEDED	DynamicAvailabitlityDA	1h:17m:9s	bdaldr	0007562-160501005135905-oozie-oozi-W
Tue, 23 Aug 2016 19:48:14	SUCCEEDED	owf-lfsearch-load-and-organize	47m:47s	bdaldr	0007567-160501005135905-oozie-oozi-W
Tue, 23 Aug 2016 19:36:00	SUCCEEDED	SSI-Workflow	30m:56s	bdaldr	0007568-160501005135905-oozie-oozi-W
Tue, 23 Aug 2016 18:46:43	SUCCEEDED	owf-lfsearch-load-and-organize	46m:43s	bdaldr	0007559-160501005135905-oozie-oozi-W
Tue, 23 Aug 2016 18:33:27	SUCCEEDED	SSI-Workflow	28m:27s	bdaldr	0007560-160501005135905-oozie-oozi-W
Tue, 23 Aug 2016 17:31:28	SUCCEEDED	owf-lfsearch-load-and-organize	31m:28s	bdaldr	0007557-160501005135905-oozie-oozi-W
Tue, 23 Aug 2016 17:24:53	SUCCEEDED	SSI-Workflow	19m:53s	bdaldr	0007558-160501005135905-oozie-oozi-W
Tue, 23 Aug 2016 16:46:11	SUCCEEDED	owf-lfsearch-load-and-organize	46m:11s	bdaldr	0007555-160501005135905-oozie-oozi-W
Tue, 23 Aug 2016 16:25:08	SUCCEEDED	SSI-Workflow	20m:8s	bdaldr	0007556-160501005135905-oozie-oozi-W
Tue, 23 Aug 2016 15:52:21	SUCCEEDED	owf-lfsearch-load-and-organize	52m:21s	bdaldr	0007553-160501005135905-oozie-oozi-W
Tue, 23 Aug 2016 14:56:22	SUCCEEDED	owf-lfsearch-load-and-organize	56m:22s	bdaldr	0007550-160501005135905-oozie-oozi-W
Tue, 23 Aug 2016 14:29:50	SUCCEEDED	SSI-Workflow	24m:50s	bdaldr	0007551-160501005135905-oozie-oozi-W
Tue, 23 Aug 2016 14:05:05	SUCCEEDED	eHotelDataLoad	5s	bdaldr	0007552-160501005135905-oozie-oozi-W
Tue, 23 Aug 2016 13:48:53	SUCCEEDED	owf-lfsearch-load-and-organize	48m:53s	bdaldr	0007548-160501005135905-oozie-oozi-W
Tue, 23 Aug 2016 13:43:51	SUCCEEDED	SSI-Workflow	38m:51s	bdaldr	0007549-160501005135905-oozie-oozi-W
Tue, 23 Aug 2016 12:33:21	SUCCEEDED	SSI-Workflow	27m:55s	bdaldr	0007547-160501005135905-oozie-oozi-W

Showing 1 to 50 of 2091

← Previous | Next →

Figure 16.2 The Oozie Dashboard

privileges. For non-administrative users, you need to assign them to specific groups that you create beforehand. A typical scenario is where you create three or four groups, such as developers, analysts and data scientists, and give each of those groups permission to launch specific Hue applications. Each user you create will be assigned to one of these groups and thus inherit that group's permissions. For example, you can allow the analyst group to invoke the Hue, Hive and Impala Editors. These users can then connect to Hive, Pig and Impala to analyze HDFS data.

The Hue shell application, by default, lets you access the Pig, HBase and Sqoop 2 command-line shells and is similar to a Linux terminal. You can also configure other applications that offer a CLI as part of the Hue shell application. For example, you can configure access to the Flume shell through the shell application. Hue offers a convenient way to run extract, transform and load (ETL) chains that involve multistage processing, such as pulling data from an RDBMS and running a Pig script on that data before moving it to a Hive table. You can manually run all the ETL chain components from Hue or just schedule an Oozie job from Hue to do all the work for you.

The Hue server stores session, authentication and Hue application data in a database, which by default is the open-source Derby database. In a production environment, as with the other Hadoop components that require a database to store their metadata, you should use a professional-grade database such as MySQL instead of the default Derby database.

Hue applications can also run Hue-specific daemon processes, such as the Beeswax server, that track the query states. Hue applications use Thrift or the states stored in this database to communicate with these daemons.

Installing Hue

In a pseudo-distributed Hadoop cluster, you can run the Hue server on the same machine as the Hadoop cluster. You can install the Hue server on a remote node or on one of the nodes that are part of your Hadoop cluster. In small to medium clusters, you can use one of your master nodes to run the Hue server.

Follow these steps to install Hue.

1. Download the latest Hue binaries as shown here:

   ```
   # wget https://dl.dropboxusercontent.com/u/730827/hue/releases/3.8.1/
   hue-3.8.1.tgz
   ```

2. Untar the tarball and change to the installation directory.
3. Use the `make` utility to install Hue:

   ```
   # make install
   ```

4. The `make` command will usually install Hue in the /usr/local/hue directory. Since the root user owns the Hue installation directories, change the permissions to an appropriate user if you need to.

   ```
   # chown -R sam:sam /usr/local/hue
   ```

Hue is usually deployed in a gateway node in the Hadoop cluster, so you don't need to have any core Hadoop services or clients running on the Hue host. Hue provides a "view on top of Hadoop" and you can install it on any server. You install Hue and then configure it so it points to a Hadoop cluster. By default, Hue is aware of only a single local machine. In order for it to work with a Hadoop cluster, you need to let Hue know where the Hadoop services are running in your cluster.

Configuring Your Cluster to Work with Hue

You configure Hue in the hue.ini file, so it knows about your Hadoop cluster and how to connect to the various components. Before you can configure the hue.ini file, however, you must first configure your Hadoop cluster so it is ready to accept connections from Hue. Once you do this, you can specify your cluster configuration in the hue.ini file.

Configuring Hadoop for Hue

In order for HDFS to work with Hue, you must do the following:

- Enable WebHDFS or HttpFS
- Add the necessary proxy user hosts and groups for Hue
- Optionally, enable HDFS ACLs (I discuss ACLs in Chapter 15, "Securing Hadoop"

In order to configure WebHDFS and HttpFS and add the required proxy users, you must add a few properties to multiple Hadoop configuration files. You must configure Hue to work either with WebHDFS or HttpFS. In a high-availability NameNode architecture, you must use HttpFS. For Hue to work with WebHDFS and HttpFS, you need to configure WebHDFS and also configure Hue as a Proxy user, as shown here:

- Configuring WebHDFS: Make sure the property `dfs.webhdfs.enabled` is set to `true` in the hdfs-site.xml file. This will enable the WebHDFS REST API on the NameNode as well as the DataNodes. You need to do this in order to list or create HDFS files.
- Configuring Hue as a proxy user: It's important to configure Hue as a proxy user for all users and groups, so it can submit requests to the cluster on behalf of any of the users. What you need to configure to ensure that Hue acts a proxy user varies, depending on whether you're going to let Hue use WebHDFS or HttpFS.

If you want to let Hue use WebHDFS, add the following to the core-site.xml file.

```
<property>
  <name>hadoop.proxyuser.hue.hosts</name>
  <value>*</value>
</property>
```

Specifying * as the value means that users from any host can submit work to the Hadoop cluster through Hue.

In the same file, configure Hue as a proxy user for all users and groups—this allows Hue to impersonate all end users and submit requests on behalf of them. Here's how to set this up:

```
<property>
  <name>hadoop.proxyuser.hue.groups</name>
  <value>*</value>
</property>
```

These two parameters ensure that Hue can act as a proxy user for any user or group (this is also called **user impersonation**) and submit work on behalf of those users and groups.

If Hue is using HttpFS instead, add the same two configuration parameters shown above to the /etc/hadoop-httpfs/conf/httpfs-site.xml file. You must restart the HttpFS daemon after making the two changes. Regardless of whether Hue is going to use WebHDFS or HttpFS, make sure you also add these two configuration properties to the core-site.xml file, as well, also making sure to restart the cluster services once you edit the file.

In order to allow user impersonation in Oozie through Hue, add the following two parameters to the oozie-site.xml file.

```
<property>
 <name>oozie.service.ProxyUserService.proxyuser.<default_user>.hosts</name>
  <value>*</value>
</property>

<property>
<name>oozie.service.ProxyUserService.proxyuser.<default_user>.groups</name>
  <value>*</value>
</property>
```

Finally, if you're using HCatalog, you also need to add the following two parameters to the core-site.xml file:

```
<property>
  <name>hadoop.proxyuser.hcat.hosts</name>
  <value>*</value>
</property>

<property>
  <name> hadoop.proxyuser.hcat.groups</name>
  <value>hadoop</value>
</property>
```

These two parameters specify the host and group access for HCatalog.

Configuring Hue

So far, I've just configured the Hadoop cluster for Hue. In order for Hue to function properly with your cluster components, you must configure the Hue configuration file, named hue.ini (/usr/share/desktop/conf/hue.ini). This file consists of several sections, such as Desktop, Hadoop, YARN, Beeswax, Pig Editor, Oozie Editor/Dashboard, Job Browser and so on, and you specify the configuration parameters pertaining to each component under the appropriate section. Essentially what the Hue configuration file contains are the addresses and ports of crucial Hadoop services such as HDFS, YARN, Oozie and Hive.

As you can see, the hue.ini file contains a separate section for each Hadoop component. Let's review the main configuration parameters you must set in each of these sections.

Configuring Desktop Features

Under the <desktop> section, the secret_key parameter is for enabling security for Internet browser cookie sessions and could be any random string between 30-60 characters long. In the <desktop> section, you must also define the web host and its port as follows:

```
http_host:=hadoop01.localhost
http_port=8888
```

You must also set up the URL for the web services to access Hue:

```
webhdfs_url=http://hadoop01.localhost:50070/v1/
```

You can optionally blacklist an application, preventing it from running in the cluster through Hue, by adding the following under the [desktop] section:

```
# Comma-separated list of apps not to load at server startup.
# Note that rdbms is the name used for dbquery.
app_blacklist=spark,impala,sqoop,rdbms
```

It's easy to re-enable a blacklisted application—simply remove the application name from the list of blacklisted applications specified by the attribute app_blacklist and restart the Hue Server.

Configuring the Hadoop Cluster (Hadoop and YARN)

The Hadoop cluster configuration is under two sections—hadoop for configuring HDFS and the yarn_clusters section for configuring YARN. Here are parts of the hadoop and yarn_clusters portions of a typical hue.ini file.

```
[hadoop]
# Configuration for the HDFS Namenode
[[hdfs-clusters]]
   [[[default]]]
     # Enter the filesystem uri
     fs_defaultfs=hdfs://hadoop01.localdomain:8020
    # Use WebHdfs/HttpFs as the communication mechanism.
    # Domain should be the NameNode or HttpFs host.
      webhdfs_url=http://localhost:50070/webhdfs/v1
#   Configuration for YARN  (MR2)
  [[yarn_clusters]]
   [[[default]]]
     # Enter the host on which you are running the ResourceManager
     resourcemanager_host=hadoop02.localdomain
     # The port where the ResourceManager IPC listens
     resourcemanager_port=8030
     # Whether to submit jobs to this cluster
      submit_to=True

     # URL of the ResourceManager API
     resourcemanager_api_url=http://hadoop02.localdomain:8088
```

```
# URL of the HistoryServer API
history_server_api_url=http://hadoop02.localdomain:19888
 # URL of the ProxyServer API
proxy_api_url=http://hadoop02.localdomain:8088
```

Note the following:

- The `submit_to=True` configuration under the `yarn_clusters` section allows Oozie to submit YARN jobs to the Hadoop cluster.
- The ResourceManager often runs on `http://localhost:8088` by default.
- You must specify the ProxyServer- and the JobHistoryServer-related information, so you can later list and kill running YARN applications and retrieve their logs through Hue's Job Browser.

Configuring Oozie

The `liboozie` section is where you configure Oozie within Hue by specifying the URL where the Oozie service runs. To submit and monitor workflows, the Oozie server should be running, of course.

```
[liboozie]
# The URL where the Oozie service runs. This is required in order for
# users to submit jobs. Empty value disables the config check.
oozie_url=http://hadoop02.localdomain:11000/oozie
```

Configuring Beeswax

You'll need a running HiveServer2 instance to access Hive through Hue. If the HiveServer2 is running on a different server, it's a good idea to copy the hive-site.xml from that server to the server where Hue is running. This is to ensure that Hue knows about the security and other custom HiveServer2 configuration properties. Within the beeswax section of the hue.ini file, you need to set two important properties:

- `hive_server_host=hadoop01.localdomain`: The server where HiveServer2 is running
- `hive_server_port=10000`: The port where the HiveServer2 Thrift server is running

Configuring ZooKeeper

Specify the following settings to configure the ZooKeeper ensemble.

```
[zookeeper]
 [[clusters]]
   [[[default]]]
     # Zookeeper ensemble. Comma separated list of Host/Port.
     # e.g. localhost:2181,localhost:2182,localhost:2183
     host_ports=hadoop02.localdomain:2181
     # The URL of the REST contrib service (required for znode browsing)
     rest_url=http://hadoop02.localdomain:9998
```

Now that you've configured Hue to work with various components, you're ready to start working with it.

Managing Hue

A running Hue server usually needs very little in terms of regular management. Once you complete the configuration of Hue as explained in the previous sections, you need to know how to start and stop the Hue server. In this section, I will show you how to start and stop the Hue server.

You can start the Hue server with the supervisor command, as shown here:

```
$ /usr/local/hue/build/env/bin/supervisor
[INFO] Not running as root, skipping privilege drop
Starting server with options {'ssl_certificate':None, 'workdir':None,...
$
```

You can also specify the -d switch to start the Hue supervisor in the daemon mode.

You can start and stop the Hue server as follows:

```
$ sudo /etc/init.d/service hue start
$ sudo /etc/init.d/service hue stop
```

Whenever you modify Hue configuration through the hue.ini file, restart the Hue server as shown here:

```
$ sudo /etc/init.d/service hue restart
```

Working with Hue

Working with Hue is a breeze! You can set up non-administrative users in Hue so they can run their Hive, Impala and Pig jobs from there without requiring a login to the cluster nodes. You can access HBase tables as well as move data around with Sqoop (and Sqoop 2) directly from Hue. In addition, you can manage HDFS data. There are various scenarios for which you can put Hue to good use. One of the most important of these is the use of the Oozie Editor/Dashboard application. You can use this application to perform the following administrative tasks:

- Check the running and completed workflow and coordinator jobs.
- Check the configuration of the Oozie workflows and coordinators.
- See which workflows are available.
- Create and import workflows, coordinators and bundles.

You can access various Hadoop components through Hue. For example, you can access HDFS through the File Browser and Hive and Pig through the Query Editors tab and Oozie workflows through the Workflows tab. Let's take a scenario where you want to create an Oozie job by creating Oozie workflows and coordinators for the job. If you aren't using Hue, you'll really have to get your hands dirty! You'll have to muck with umpteen XML (ugh!) configuration files and job property files and so on, as explained in Chapter 14. Using Hue, you can set up a job in a few short minutes—Hue, through its excellent Oozie interface, takes care of the creation of all the XML files, job properties and other files and even lets you quickly configure a service level agreement (SLA) for your job.

Or, take a different scenario where you want to monitor running Oozie jobs and restart any jobs that failed. Hue makes it a breeze to do this through the Oozie interface—you can check the status of both running and finished jobs, review the logs for failed jobs to find the root cause for the failure and fix the issues and restart the job. In real life situations, quick troubleshooting is the key to maintaining your critical SLAs, and Hue makes it very easy to troubleshoot jobs.

From the administrator's point of view, probably the biggest benefit of using Hue is that you can schedule and manage all your Oozie workflows, coordinators and bundles from the Hue interface—without having to deal with complicated XML files. You don't even need to use the Oozie web UI to manage the Oozie jobs. In addition to creating workflows and scheduling them, you can also monitor the progress of running jobs and suspend or kill those jobs from the Hue Oozie interface. The Oozie Editor and the Oozie Dashboard in Hue are true blessings for any Hadoop administrator since they make your life so easy when it comes to managing Hadoop jobs!

Implementing Specialized HDFS Features

Although you can use HDFS straight out of the box, so to speak, you can also avail yourself of several special features provided by Hadoop to enhance the performance and ease of use of HDFS. In the following sections, I discuss these additional capabilities of HDFS:

- Deploying HDFS and YARN in a multihomed network
- Short-circuit local reads
- Mountable HDFS
- Using NFS Gateway to mount HDFS to a local file system

Deploying HDFS and YARN in a Multihomed Network

By default, you specify HDFS endpoints as specific IP addresses or hostnames, meaning HDFS daemons will bind to a single IP address. You can set up things so that the cluster nodes are connected to multiple network interfaces, for security or performance reasons. Security is enhanced because you can restrict the traffic between the nodes to a separate network from that used for the cluster's network traffic. High-bandwidth interconnects like InfiniBand or Fibre Channel enhance network performance. Support for more than one network interface is called a **multihomed network**. You can also do this to provide redundancy by letting a node use multiple network adapters to connect to a single network, to protect against a network adapter failure.

You mustn't confuse a multihomed network with the use of NIC bonding, which presents only a single logical network to the clients. With a multihomed network, you can connect to the HDFS daemons from more than one network. HDFS endpoints, by default, are specified as hostnames or IP addresses, and this means that the HDFS daemons always bind to a single IP address. In order to make the daemons reachable from other networks you must force the bonding of the server endpoints to the wildcard IP address `INADDR_ANY`, which is 0.0.0.0. You don't need a port number with this specification. You need to configure the following parameters in the hdfs-site.xml file, so they all have a value of 0.0.0.0.:

- `dfs.namenode.rpc.bind-host`
- `dfs.namenode.servicerpc-bind.host`
- `dfs.namenode.http-bind-host`
- `dfs.namenode.https-bind.host`

You can configure YARN for a multihomed environment. You control the binding argument passed to the Java socket listener so it can be forced to listen on interfaces other than the interface pointed to by the client-facing endpoint address. You can force YARN services to listen on all of a multihomed host's interfaces by setting the `bind-host` parameter to the all-wildcard value 0.0.0.0. You don't specify a port number because the port is either based on the port configured for the service or falls back to the in-code default. For example, if you set the value of the `yarn.resourcemanager.bind.host` parameter to 0.0.0.0, and the `yarn.resourcemanager.address` is configured as `rm.prodcluster.internal:9999`, the ResourceManager will listen on all host addresses on the port 9999.

By configuring the `bind-host` parameter (in the yarn-site.xml file) in the following way, you ensure that all ResourceManager services and web applications listen on all the interfaces in a multihomed network.

```
<property>
    <name>yarn.resourcemanager.bind-host</name>
    <value>0.0.0.0.</value>
</property>
```

Similarly, you configure the `yarn.nodemanager.bind-host`, also in the yarn-site.xml file, and the `mapreduce.jobhistory.bind-host` parameter (mapred-site.xml file) to the value 0.0.0.0 to ensure that the main YARN and MapReduce daemons listen on all addresses and interfaces of a multihomed cluster.

Configuring the `bind-host` parameter is transparent to users, and they just connect to a service based on the address you configured for it. They may connect to different interfaces based on their network locations and on name resolution.

Short-Circuit Local Reads

If the client reading HDFS data is located on the same server as the DataNode, it can directly read the files, which is quicker than the DataNode transmitting the data to the client. Short-circuit reads are reads made by clients directly from the local file system while bypassing the DataNode using UNIX domain sockets, which offer a pathway for communication between clients and DataNodes.

Short-circuit reads aren't enabled by default. In order to use short-circuit reads, you need to configure the following properties on the client as well as on the DataNode:

```
<property>
  <name>dfs.client.read.shortcircuit</name>
  <value>true</value>
</property>
<property>
  <name>dfs.domain.socket.path</name>
  <value>/var/lib/hadoop-hdfs/dn_socket</value>
</property>
```

Short-circuit local reads offer both improved performance and enhanced security. A key principle of Hadoop is data locality, whereby HDFS attempts to handle most reads as local reads by reading data where the client (reader) is located on the same node as the data they're reading.

When a client performs a local read, clients transfer data by connecting to the DataNode through a TCP socket. For each client reading a block, the DataNode needs to keep a thread around the TCP socket, leading to overhead in the kernel. Short-circuit reads optimize data transfer and speed up applications. Since the client and data are located on the same node, this optimization bypasses the DataNode in the data path and enables the client to read local data directly from disk.

The short-circuit local read mechanism is made secure because it uses Linux's "file descriptor passing" mechanism. This allows the DataNode to open the block and metadata files and pass them to the client directly. The client can't modify the files it receives from the DataNode, since the file descriptors are read-only. The client is never passed the block directories, so it can't read data it doesn't have access to.

Short-circuit reads make use of a file descriptor cache (name `FileInputStreamCache`) to avoid reopening files to read the same blocks again. You can tune the cache with the following parameters:

- `dfs.client.read.shortcircuit.streams.cache.size`: This controls the cache size. If you set this to 0 you turn off the cache.
- `dfs.client.read.shortcircuit.streams.cache.expiry.ms`: This controls cache timeout.

You can stick to the defaults for both parameters, unless you have a large amount of active data and a high file-descriptor count, in which case you can increase the parameter values.

Mountable HDFS

Often, you'll need to merge several MapReduce job output files and send them to external teams. Ideally, it'll be nice to have these files on the local system. You could set up a special mount point called `mountableHDFS` or Filesystem in Userspace (FUSE), in such scenarios. FUSE lets you implement mountable file systems in user space. You can use the hadoop-hdfs-fuse package to set up mountable HDFS, which lets you use your HDFS file system as if it were a regular Linux file system. FUSE allows several basic file operations but won't turn HDFS into a POSIX-compliant file system.

Using Mountable HDFS

Once you set up FUSE, you can view the HDFS directories from a local mount point, as seen in the following example.

```
[machine1] ~ > df -kh /export/hdfs/
Filesystem           Size  Used Avail Use% Mounted on
fuse                 4.1P  642T  3.5P  21% /export/hdfs
[machine1] ~ > ls /export/hdfs/
home  tmp  Trash  user  usr  va
```

You can mount HDFS on most Linux systems as a standard file system, using the Linux `mount` command. Once you mount the HDFS directories, you can use regular Linux file system commands, such as `ls`, `cp`, `cd`, `find` and `grep`. Although you can export FUSE mounts using NFS, meaning you can mount HDFS on one machine and then export it using NFS, for performance reasons, you are better off auto-mounting FUSE on all machines from which you want to access HDFS.

Configuring Mountable HDFS

In this example, I show how to install hadoop-hdfs-fuse on a Red Hat compatible system.

1. Use `yum` to install the hadoop-hdfs-fuse package, as shown here:

   ```
   $ sudo yum install hadoop-hdfs-fuse
   ```

2. You can now start mounting your HDFS directories on the local Linux file system. First, create a directory where you want to mount HDFS on the Linux file system.

   ```
   $ mkdir -p /export/hdfs
   ```

3. You can test that your mount point works by issuing the following command:

   ```
   $ hadoop-fuse-dfs dfs://hadoop01.localhost:5500 /export/hdfs
   ```

   The server name and port numbers are for the NameNode address. If you're running a HA NameNode service, you must specify just the nameservice ID—you don't need to provide the port number.

4. Make the following changes to the /etc/fstab file:

   ```
   hadoop-fuse-dfs#dfs://hadoop01.localhost:5500 /export/hdfs fuse -
   allow_other,rw,usetrash, 2 0
   ```

   Adding the mount information to the /etc/fstab file makes the new mount points persist through server reboots.

5. Mount the directory using the following command:

   ```
   $ mount /export/hdfs
   ```

   You can mount multiple HDFS instances by changing the directory mount point in the previous command.

6. If you run the following command from a different terminal, you'll see your HDFS directories on the local Linux file system:

   ```
   $ ls /export/hdfs
   ```

You're now viewing your HDFS mount point as if it were a local Linux directory. You can get help for the FUSE feature by typing in `hadoop-fuse-dfs -help` at the command line. Note that both reads and writes will be slower than usual when using FUSE. Although the recommended approach to mounting a FUSE system is through adding the mount-point information to the /etc/fstab directory, you can also manually mount it with the following command:

```
$ hdfs -o server=namenodee,port=9000,allow_other,rdbuffer=131072, /mnt/hadoop
```

If you receive a message stating that the "Transport endpoint is not connected" on the node(s) where you mounted FUSE, the FUSE mount has apparently died. You must connect to that node (s) and remount the file system:

```
umount /mnt/hadoop
mount /mnt/hadoop
```

It's a good idea to run the FUSE mount in the debug mode to spot errors and problems with the mount, as shown here:

```
$ hdfs -o server=namenode,port=9000,allow_other,rdbuffer=131072,-d /mnt/hadoop
```

Using an NFS Gateway for Mounting HDFS to a Local File System

A client can mount HDFS as part of their own Linux file system by configuring an NFSv3 Gateway. The client uses a gateway machine, which can be any host in your cluster or any other HDFS client. Once a client mounts HDFS to their local file system, they can work with HDFS just as if it were another Linux local file system.

Configuring an NFSv3 Gateway

In order to use the NFSv3 Gateway, you must configure it by following these steps:

1. On a Red Hat Linux compatible server, install the following three required packages on the NFSv3 Gateway Machine.

   ```
   # yum install nf-utils nfs-utils-lib hadoop-hdfs-nfs3
   ```

   Add the following property to the hdfs-site.xml file on the server acting as the NFSv3 Gateway machine.

   ```
   <property>
     <name>dfs.nfs3.dump.dir</name>
     <value>/tmp/.hdfs-nfs</value>
   </property>
   ```

   The NFS Gateway server uses the directory specified by the `dfs.nfs3.dump.dir` parameter to save writes from the client, which can be in random order until it can correctly reorder them.

2. On the server hosting the NameNode, add the following to the hdfs-site.xml file.

   ```
   <property>
     <name>dfs.namenode.accesstime.precision</name>
     <value>3600000</value>
   </property>
   ```

The `dfs.namenode.accesstime.precision` parameter ensures that the access time for HDFS files is precise up to the value you specify for this parameter. The default value for the parameter is one hour (3,600,000 milliseconds). If you set a value of 0, it disables the access times for HDFS.

3. Finally, you need to configure the user, such as hdfs, that will be running the gateway, so the user can serve as a proxy for all users. By setting * as the value for the following two parameters in the core-site.xml file on the NameNode server, you allow the gateway user to proxy any group and also allow requests from any hosts to be proxied.

```
<property>
   <name>hadoop.proxyuser.hdfs.groups</name>
   <value>*</value>
</property>

<property>
    <name>hadoop.proxyuser.hdfs.hosts</name>
    <value>*</value>
 </property>
```

You can now restart the NameNode to let the configuration changes take effect.

Using the NFSv3 Gateway

Now that you've configured the gateway, you must start the NFS server. To start your newly configured NFSv3 Gateway, first shut down any NFS servers that are running, and start the new HDFS-related NFS services:

```
$ sudo service nfs stop
$ sudo service hadoop-hdfs-nfs3 start
```

You can verify that the HDFS namespace is ready to be mounted with the following `showmount` command:

```
$ showmount -e <nfs_server_ip_address>
```

The NFS client can import the HDFS file system with the `mount` command as shown here.

```
$ mount -t nfs -o vers=3,proto=tcp,nolock <nfs_server_hostname>:/ /hdfs_nfs_mount
```

Summary

Here's what you learned in this chapter:

- Although you may use Hadoop's web UIs and a vendor-provided administrative tool such as Cloudera Manager for routine administration, it's good to learn how to use the YARN command line tools (such as the `yarn` command) to work with Hadoop jobs. When troubleshooting clusters, sometimes the command line tools are all you have.

- Decommissioning and recommisssioning DataNodes (and NodeManagers) is always going to be a common chore for Hadoop administrators, as you're dealing with large numbers of commodity servers that could fail at any time, due to the well-known MTTF factor. The key thing here is to learn how to minimize the time it takes to move a DataNode back into the cluster, and this chapter explains several things you can do in this regard.
- Managing and backing up the relational database that stores all the metadata for Hadoop's components is a more critical task than it might appear. If you lose the component metadata, you'll lose access to the data the components such as Hive and Oozie need to function. Backups are boring, but they are life savers.
- Hue can be of great help in monitoring jobs, creating Oozie jobs and managing them, besides being a great tool for users who work with HDFS, Hive, Impala, Spark and other tools.
- You may or may not be currently implementing any of the "specialized" HDFS features I discussed in this chapter, but it's good to know that they're there for you to implement if the need arises.

17

Monitoring, Metrics and Hadoop Logging

This chapter covers the following:

- Monitoring Linux servers
- Hadoop metrics
- Monitoring with Ganglia
- Hadoop logging
- Using Hadoop's web UIs for monitoring

This chapter deals with monitoring your cluster health. Along with Chapter 16, "Managing Jobs, Using Hue and Performing Routine Tasks," Chapter 18, "Tuning the Cluster Resources, Optimizing MapReduce Jobs and Benchmarking," Chapter 19, "Configuring and Tuning Apache Spark on YARN," Chapter 20, "Optimizing Spark Applications," and Chapter 21, "Troubleshooting Hadoop—A Sampler," this chapter is part of the core set of chapters that describes the day-to-day work of a Hadoop administrator, which involves monitoring, managing, tuning and troubleshooting the cluster and the jobs that run in that cluster.

I start off with a quick review of how to effectively monitor the Linux servers on which most Hadoop clusters run. Monitoring Hadoop includes the tracking of system resource utilization and identifying performance bottlenecks. In order to do this, you must track things such as the levels of I/O bandwidth, data transfer rates, network latency, swap space utilization and the number of disk I/O operations per second. Linux has several easy-to-use, yet very powerful, system performance monitoring tools, and I provide an introduction to those tools.

Once your cluster gets to a meaningful size, start thinking about using centralized configuration management tools to manage your cluster. Tools such as Puppet and Chef are a must for performing various tasks, such as copying files and generally keeping the cluster configuration in sync. Similarly, tools such as Nagios and Ganglia help you monitor the performance and health of your cluster and also put in place an alerting system for administrators (and, more and more, for developers as well). If you're using a third-party cluster management tool such as Cloudera's Cloudera Manager, or Hortonworks's Ambari, you don't need to use these other tools as much, since the management tools provide most of the functionality you need to perform all the cluster-wide operations. This chapter explains how to set up Ganglia to monitor your cluster.

Logging is extremely important in managing Hadoop environments. Administrators should be able to take full advantage of the many types of logs emitted by the Hadoop daemons and the YARN jobs that run in your cluster. Understanding Hadoop's logging framework is critical to your success as an administrator, so this chapter dedicates substantial space to the discussion of logging.

In addition to Hadoop logging, you also need to understand where all the Hadoop components such as ZooKeeper, Hive, Pig and Impala store their logs, so you can troubleshoot failed or poorly performing jobs.

In addition to tracking system resource usage, you must also use Hadoop's performance counters to estimate whether the task response times are acceptable. For example, if the shuffle time is slow, the reduce tasks will take longer. Hadoop has a rich set of built-in metrics, and this chapter explains Hadoop's metrics.

Monitoring Linux Servers

Most Hadoop installations run on Linux systems and thus it is imperative that you understand the key aspects of Linux monitoring and also become familiar with useful Linux system-monitoring tools. A slow system could be the result of a bottleneck in processing (CPU), memory, disk or bandwidth.

System-monitoring tools help you to clearly identify the bottlenecks causing poor performance. Monitoring Linux involves tracking key system resources such as the storage subsystem, CPU, memory and network. In the following sections, I explain what you ought to monitor and how to use various monitoring tools to get the job done.

Basics of Linux System Monitoring

Monitoring a Linux system from a performance point of view mainly involves monitoring the following:

- CPU
- Memory
- Disk storage
- Bandwidth

I'll address each of these areas and explore exactly what monitoring these entities involves.

Monitoring CPU Usage

As long as you aren't utilizing 100 percent of the CPU capacity, you still have juice left in the system to support more activity. Spikes in CPU usage are common, but your goal when checking out excessive CPU usage is to track down which processes are causing excessive usage of the CPU. Following are the key factors to remember while examining CPU usage:

- User versus system usage: You can identify the percentage of time CPU is being used for user applications as compared with time spent servicing the operating system's overhead. Obviously, if the system overhead accounts for an overwhelming proportion of CPU usage, you may have to examine it further.
- Runnable processes: At any given time, a process is either running or waiting for resources to be freed up. A process that is waiting for the allocation of resources is called a **runnable process**. The presence of a large number of runnable processes indicates that your system may be facing a power crunch—it's CPU-bound.
- Context switches and interrupts: When the operating system switches between processes, it incurs some overhead due to the so-called **context switches**. If you have too many context switches, you'll see a deterioration in CPU usage. You'll incur similar overhead when you have too many interrupts caused by the operating system when it finishes certain hardware- or software-related tasks.

Monitoring Memory Usage

Memory is one of the first places you should look when you have performance problems. If you have inadequate memory (RAM) on the server, your system may slow down due to excessive swapping of memory. Memory swapping means that the system is transferring memory pages to disk devices to free up memory for other processes.

Here are some of the main factors to focus on when you are checking system memory usage:

- Page ins and page outs: If you see a high number of **page ins** and **page outs** in your memory-usage statistics, it means that your system is doing an excessive amount of paging, which involves the moving of pages from memory to disk due to inadequate available memory. Excessive paging could lead to a condition called **thrashing**, which means you are using critical system resources to move pages back and forth between memory and disk.
- Swap ins and swap outs: The swapping statistics also indicate how adequate your current memory allocation is for your system.
- Active and inactive pages: If you have too few inactive memory pages, it may mean that your physical memory is inadequate.

Monitoring Disk Storage

When it comes to monitoring disks, you should look for two things. First, check to make sure you aren't running out of room—applications add more data on a continuous basis, and it is inevitable that you will have to constantly add more storage space. Second, watch your disk performance—are there any bottlenecks due to slow disk input/output performance?

Here are the basic things to look for:

- Checking for free space: Using simple commands, a system administrator or a DBA can check the amount of free space left on the system. It's good, of course, to do this on a regular basis so you can head off a resource crunch before it's too late. You can use the `df` and the `du` commands to check the free space on your system.
- Reads and writes: The read/write figures give you a good picture of how "hot" your disks are running. By examining the read/write numbers, you can tell whether your system is handling its workload well or whether it's experiencing an extraordinary I/O load at any given time.

Monitoring Bandwidth

By measuring the network bandwidth usage, you can measure the efficiency of the transfer of data between devices. Bandwidth is harder to measure than simple I/O or memory usage patterns, but it's very useful to collect bandwidth-related statistics.

Your network is an important component of your system—if the network connections are slow, everything appears to run slowly. Simple network statistics like the number of bytes received and sent will help you identify network problems.

High network packet collision rates, as well as excessive data transmission errors, will lead to bottlenecks. You need to examine the network using tools like `netstat` (discussed later) to see if the network has any bottlenecks.

Monitoring Tools for Linux Systems

In order to find out what processes are running, you'll most commonly use the well-known Linux process command, `ps`. Of course, to monitor system performance, you'll need more sophisticated tools than the elementary `ps` command. The following sections cover some of the important tools available for monitoring your system's performance.

Monitoring Memory Use with `vmstat`

The `vmstat` utility helps you monitor memory usage, page faults, processes and CPU activity. Here is some sample output from the `vmstat` command. The `S` parameter indicates the setting of the unit size, `M` indicates the unit size (1048576) and the integer `1` is the inteval between updates (in this case, every second).

```
# vmstat -S M 1
procs ---------memory------------swap-------io------system-------cpu-------
r  b   swpd free    buff  cache   si   so   bi    bo    in   cs    us sy  id  wa st
0  0     0  11601   3980  72370   0    0   781  1016    0     0  15 1    83 1  0
0  0     0  11601   3980  72370   0    0     0     0  795 1470   0 0   100 0  0
0  0     0  11601   3980  72370   0    0     0    28  818 1543   0 0   100 0  0
0  0     0  11601   3980  72370   0    0     0     0  867 1558   0 0   100 0  0
#
```

Under the `procs` subheading in the CPU part of the output, the first column, `r` refers to the run queue. If your system has 24 CPUs and your run queue shows 20, that means 20 processes are waiting in the queue for a turn on the CPUs, and it's definitely not a bad thing. If the same `r` value of 24 occurs on a machine with 2 CPUs, it indicates the system is CPU-bound—a large number of processes are waiting for CPU time.

In the CPU part of vmstat's output, us stands for the amount of CPU usage attributable to the users of the system, including your database processes. The sy part shows the system usage of the CPU, and id stands for the amount of CPU that is idle. In our example, most or all of the CPU is idle for each of the four processors.

In the vmstat output, the CPU statistic cs stands for the number of context switches, and the column in indicates the number of interrupts (per second).

The vmstat utility can help you identify performance bottlenecks. For example, if the vmstat output shows that memory is being swapped to disk (column so) or swapped from disk (column si) then you may need to either add more physical memory to the node or lower the number of mappers and reducers running on that node.

Viewing Memory Usage with meminfo and free

An easy way to check memory usage on a server is through the /proc/meminfo command. Many Linux tools such as top, ps and free use the data in the meminfo file as their source. The following example gets you the first five pieces of information from the file, but there are a large number of other statistics in this file.

```
# head -5 /proc/meminfo
MemTotal:         98934060 kB
MemFree:           2954400 kB
Buffers:           3695172 kB
Cached:           46993320 kB
SwapCached:              0 kB
#
```

The free command, which uses the data in the /prc/meminfo file, is a quick way to get memory usage information:

```
# free
             total       used       free     shared    buffers     cached
Mem:      98934052   74366552   24567500          0    4652432   52999412
-/+ buffers/cache:   16714708   82219344
Swap:            0          0          0
#
```

Viewing I/O Statistics with iostat

The iostat utility gives you input/output statistics for all the disks on your system. The iostat command takes two parameters: the number of seconds before the information should be updated on the screen and the number of times the information should be updated. The output is displayed in four columns.

Here's an example of the iostat output:

```
# iostat 4 5
Linux 2.6.39-400.249.3.el5uek (hadoop09.examplecom)        12/06/2016

avg-cpu:  %user   %nice %system %iowait  %steal   %idle
          15.15    0.00    1.09    0.53    0.00   83.22

Device:            tps   Blk_read/s   Blk_wrtn/s   Blk_read   Blk_wrtn
sda              23.30      3580.03      3900.79 10756271178 11720007348
sda1              0.01         0.69         0.00    2064167       1036
```

```
sda2              8.51        608.52        130.81 1828323145  393030664
sda3              0.00          0.00          0.00      11879          0
sda4             14.78       2970.81       3769.98 8925860707 11326975648
sdb              20.13       2709.73       2908.45 8141441164 8738485276
#
```

Disk I/O issues can affect Hadoop processes negatively since Hadoop uses disk I/O during multiple phases during the MapReduce pipeline process. It's a good idea to use the TestDFSIO benchmark (explained in Chapter 18) to understand the throughput capabilities of the storage system. Often, a CPU or RAM issue may masquerade as a storage bottleneck. It's therefore a good idea to first rule out a CPU or memory bottleneck before investigating the storage subsystem.

Analyzing Read/Write Operations with `sar`

The Linux `sar` (system activity reporter) utility offers a very powerful way to analyze how the read/write operations are occurring from disk to buffer cache and from buffer cache to disk. By using the various options of the `sar` command, you can monitor disk and CPU activity, in addition to buffer cache activity.

The output for the `sar -b` command (buffer activity) has the following columns:

- bread/s: The number of read operations per second from disk to the buffer cache
- lread/s: The number of read operations per second from the buffer cache
- %rcache: The cache hit ratio for read requests
- bwrit/s: The number of write operations per second from disk to the buffer cache
- lwrit/s: The number of write operations per second to the buffer cache
- %wcache: The cache hit ratio for write requests

Here's the output of a typical `sar` command, which monitors your server's CPU activity, using the `-u` option (the `1 10` tells `sar` to refresh the output on the screen every second for a total of ten times):

```
# sar -u 1 10
Linux 2.6.39-400.249.3.el5uek (hadoop01.localhost)        12/06/2016

08:59:10 AM       CPU     %user     %nice   %system   %iowait    %steal     %idle
08:59:11 AM       all      0.00      0.00      0.04      0.00      0.00     99.96
08:59:12 AM       all      0.04      0.00      0.04      0.00      0.00     99.92
08:59:13 AM       all      0.04      0.00      0.04      0.00      0.00     99.92
08:59:14 AM       all      0.04      0.00      0.04      0.00      0.00     99.92
08:59:15 AM       all      0.00      0.00      0.04      0.00      0.00     99.96
...
#
```

Using the `top` Command for Monitoring Resource Usage

`top` is a great tool for finding out which user/processes are using the most resources on a server. Here's an example:

```
# top
top - 08:59:52 up 34 days, 18:37,  1 user,  load average: 0.44, 0.26, 0.29
Tasks: 323 total,   2 running, 320 sleeping,   0 stopped,   1 zombie
Cpu(s): 15.2%us,  1.0%sy,  0.0%ni, 83.2%id,  0.5%wa,  0.0%hi,  0.1%si,  0.0%st
Mem:  98934060k total, 87217948k used, 11716112k free,  4076468k buffers
Swap:        0k total,        0k used,        0k free, 74271600k cached

  PID USER      PR  NI  VIRT  RES  SHR S %CPU %MEM    TIME+  COMMAND
15827 hdfs      20   0 59132  716  480 R 45.1  0.0   0:00.23 du
   59 root      20   0     0    0    0 S  2.0  0.0   3:37.10 ksoftirqd/13
11223 root      39  19     0    0    0 S  2.0  0.0  86:26.51 kipmi0
11536 flume     20   0 1902m 115m 5276 S  2.0  0.1  27:06.52 java
    1 root      20   0 10416   96    0 S  0.0  0.0   1:14.33 init
    2 root      20   0     0    0    0 S  0.0  0.0   0:00.43 kthreaddtop

...
#
```

CPU bottlenecks are easy to recognize—you'll see very high processor load times, such as 80 or 90 percent, or even higher. You are also likely to see a total processer load time that's more than 50 or 60 percent across the cluster. It's possible for a single process to grab too much CPU due to a poorly designed Hadoop job. Tuning the map or reduce tasks will lower the CPU usage in such cases. Of course, switching to faster processors or adding more processors will also help relieve CPU contention.

You can check for CPU contention by looking at the numbers for context switches and interrupts. The Linux operating system is a multitasking system with multicore CPUs. The OS stores the CPU state, called the **context**, when it switches between processes, so it can resume execution from the point where it left off. Restoring the context is called a context switch. If the number of context switches is high, it's an indication that the CPU is busy and is spending a lot of time storing/restoring the process states. Often this is due to assigning too many map or reduce tasks per node.

Network Monitoring with dstat

Hadoop uses the network heavily when the reduce tasks get the map task outputs during the shuffle phase. Network utilization is also higher when the reduce jobs output the results to HDFS. Monitoring the network helps identify potential network bottlenecks. A good network monitoring tool such as `dstat` can reveal the workload of the network. A couple of useful rules of thumb:

- If the network data rate is about 20 percent of the network bandwidth or higher, it indicates an overloaded network.
- A high rate of **interrupts** indicates that the network traffic is overloading the network.

The `dstat` tool reveals both the network data rates and the number of interrupts, as shown in the following example:

```
# dstat
----total-cpu-usage---- -dsk/total- -net/total- ---paging-- ---system--
usr sys idl wai hiq siq| read  writ| recv  send|  in   out | int   csw
 15   1  83   1   0   0|  38M   48M|   0     0 |   0     0 |7263  7142
  0   0 100   0   0   0|   0   48k|2829k 2067k|   0     0 |1040  1680
```

```
  0   0 100   0   0   0|   0    24k|2828k 1932k|   0     0 | 929  1473
  0   0 100   0   0   0|   0  9576k|2829k 1808k|   0     0 |1047  1685
  0   0 100   0   0   0|   0   176k|2571k 1679k|   0     0 |1000  1585
  0   0 100   0   0   0|   0    16k|2957k 2061k|   0     0 | 993  1620
#
```

Hadoop Metrics

Hadoop metrics are collections of information about various Hadoop daemons. For example, the ResourceManager daemon produces metrics about the job queues. Hadoop Metrics (formally called Metrics 2) are vital when you are analyzing the performance of Hadoop's services. Hadoop provides extremely useful metrics, which help you monitor, tune and debug MapReduce and other jobs. Each of the Hadoop daemons emits metrics.

Hadoop 2's metrics and its logging system are highly useful during performance investigations and tuning exercises. Hadoop's distributed architecture makes it inherently difficult to monitor the cluster and diagnose the problems, compared to how you monitor and troubleshoot a database running on a single server. Hadoop's application logs and job metrics provide insights about various aspects of a job, but they lack metrics regarding disk and network utilization per job or per task. Similarly, cluster-level resource utilization by task or application isn't available either. Thus, raw logs and metrics aren't highly useful in their original state.

There are several open-source monitoring systems that help you consolidate the metrics and logs provided by Hadoop into useful service-related performance summaries and graphs, as well as alerts. In addition to Ganglia, you may also want to consider tools such as Chukwa, which is a data-collection system for monitoring large distributed systems, and Apache Ambari, which helps you deploy and manage Hadoop clusters.

Hadoop's web UIs for its various services, such as the NameNode web UI and the DataNode web UI, rely on the internal metrics that Hadoop automatically collects to help you understand how those services are performing.

Hadoop conveniently groups its metrics into several named contexts, such as the `jvm` context for the Java Virtual Machine metrics and `rpc` for debugging RPC calls.

Hadoop metrics are a veritable treasure-trove of useful real-time and historical information that'll help you troubleshoot the performance of your cluster and debug issues pertaining to both Hadoop services and the applications they support. In this context, it's important to distinguish between Hadoop metrics and the well-known MapReduce job counters:

- MapReduce job counters provide information such as the total bytes read and written by an application, while Hadoop metrics have a much broader range of focus and show you information about all the Hadoop services, such as the NameNode, JournalNode and DataNode, as well as user- and group-related information.
- As an administrator, you review MapReduce counters to help understand issues such as a slow-running MapReduce job. Hadoop metrics have a much broader domain, so to speak—they help you troubleshoot and tune the entire range of administrative issues, such as the NameNode startup duration, authentication failures, number of current connections, file creation and deletion operations, current space used free space left and so on.

Hadoop Metric Types

Hadoop's daemon metrics fall into various groups, based on the context in which they're emitted, as explained here:

- JVM metrics: These metrics are emitted by the JVMs running in the cluster and include JVM heap size and garbage collection related metrics, such as the current heap memory used (`MemHeapUsedM`) and the total GC count (`GcCount`).
- RPC metrics: Metrics in the `rpc` context contain metrics such as host name and ports and include metrics such as the number of sent bytes (`SentBytes`), current number of open connections (`NumOpenConnections`) and number of authentication failures (`RpcAuthenticationFailures`).
- DFS metrics: Metrics in the `dfs` context include the metrics that pertain to the NameNode, the HDFS file system, the DataNodes and the JournalNodes.
  - The NameNode-related `dfs` metrics show the total number of files created (`CreateFileOps`) and the time it takes to load the fsimage file after a startup of the NameNode (`FsImageLoadTime`).
  - The `FSNameSystem` metrics show various things related to the HDFS blocks and HDFS capacity, such as the current number of missing blocks (`MissingBlocks`), the current number of corrupt blocks (`CorruptBlocks`) and the current used capacity in all the DataNodes (`CapacityUsedGB`).
  - JournalNode-related metrics include sync-latency-related information as well as metrics related to the number of transactions and bytes written.
  - DataNode metrics show metrics relating to the number of data blocks read and written, average times for each operation and the total number of volume failures.
- YARN metrics: Metrics in the YARN context include cluster metrics, such as the current number of active and unhealthy NodeManagers, and queue metrics relating to the ResourceManager application queues, such as the current number of running applications (`AppsRunnning`) and the current number of active users (`ActiveUsers`). Metrics in the YARN context also include NodeManager-specific metrics, such as the total number of launched, killed and failed containers, as well as the current allocated and available memory.
- User and group metrics: The user- and group-related metrics context shows information such as the total number of successful and failed Kerberos logins and the times for group resolution.
- Default context: These are metrics that reveal the statistics for the NameNode startup and show the precise time it took for the various phases of the NameNode startup process, such as loading the fsimage and edits files, the checkpoint saving phase and the time it takes for the NameNode to get out of safe mode.

Using the Hadoop Metrics

The previous section provided a glimpse into the wide variety of metrics that can be generated by Hadoop daemons. What do you do with all these metrics? You can use these metrics to find out how your cluster is performing. For example, JVM metrics such as `GcCount` and `GcTimeMillis` indicate high JVM memory activity, and a high `ThreadsWaiting` counter means the JVM may require additional memory. DFS-related metrics can tell you if there are a high number of file creations and deletions in the cluster. RPC authentication failure metrics show if there are any suspicious attempts to authenticate to the cluster. Similarly, other metrics can point out an unusually high usage of system memory, CPU or local and HDFS storage.

Capturing Metrics to a File System

To collect the metrics and use them for tuning and troubleshooting purposes, you must configure the various Hadoop daemons to gather the metrics at specified intervals and output the metrics. You output the metrics using a plug-in. The metrics emitted by the Hadoop daemons are called **sources** and the plug-ins are called **sinks**. So, sources produce data, and sinks consume the data or output it.

There are various types of plug-ins available, with the default plug-in being `FileContext`, which writes the metrics to a file. A `NullContext` will discard the metrics and the `GangliaContext` will send the metrics to the Ganglia monitoring system (explained in the section titled "Using Ganglia for Monitoring").

In order to capture the metrics generated by Hadoop, you need to configure the hadoop-metrics2.properties file, which is normally located in a directory such as /etc/hadoop/conf. The following example shows how to store metrics pertaining to the NameNode and the DataNodes in this file. You can add other metrics, such as JVM metrics, for example, to the same file.

```
# The following entries show how to capture metrics from the NameNode and
# DataNodes to a sink named "tfile" (output to file).
# Defining sink for file output
*.sink.tfile.class=org.apache.hadoop.metrics2.sink.FileSink
# Filename for NameNode metrics capture
namenode.sink.tfile.filename = namenode-metrics.log
# Filename for DataNode metrics
datanode.sink.tfile.filename = datanode-metrics.log
```

In this example, I'm using a local file to capture metrics from the NameNode and the DataNode. When I show how to send metrics to a Ganglia sink later, I show the entries you should add to this file for capturing data to a Ganglia sink.

In order to focus on key metrics and to avoid getting lost in a sea of metrics, you can filter the Hadoop metrics on the basis of source, context, record and metrics. Within a source, you can filter on the basis of a pattern such as `include` or `exclude`, with the `include` pattern being accorded precedence over the `exclude` pattern. Filters let you manage metrics efficiently by limiting the output to the metrics file you configured in the hadoop-metrics2-properties file. Following are some examples showing how to limit metric output through various custom filters.

Before you can set up custom filters, add the following parameters to the hadoop-metrics2-properties file:

```
# Syntax: <prefix>.(source|sink).<instance>.<option>

*.sink.file.class=org.apache.hadoop.metrics2.sink.FileSink
*.source.filter.class=org.apache.hadoop.metrics2.filter.GlobFilter
*.record.filter.class=${*.source.filter.class}
*.metric.filter.class=${*.source.filter.class}

# The following limits metrics to just those from the dfs context.
bcl.sink.file0.class=org.apache.hadoop.metrics2.sink.FileSink
bcl.sink.file0.context=dfs
# The following will filter out metrics from the specified host.
jobtracker.source.dfs.record.filter.exclude=hadoop01.localhost*
# The following will filter out metrics matching the pattern cpu*.
jobtracker.sink.file.metric.filter.exclude=cpu*
```

It isn't realistic to hope to manually review the numerous files in all the cluster nodes to examine the performance of the Hadoop daemons. There are a couple of ways you can go about this. You can store the data in a Hive external table or in HBase tables. You can then set up an alert mechanism to send appropriate alerts. However, the best way to access Hadoop metrics is by sending the alerts to a Ganglia sink. Sending metrics to a Ganglia sink involves no extra work (after configuring Ganglia, of course) and is very similar to how you direct the alerts to a file as shown earlier. Ganglia is a popular tool for monitoring the state of a system. Nagios, an open-source product like Ganglia, is good for setting up alerts. In the next section, I explain the basics of using Ganglia to monitor your system and also how to integrate Ganglia with Hadoop to configure critical alerts based on various Hadoop daemon metrics.

Using Ganglia for Monitoring

The open-source software Ganglia is a great tool that's widely used by enterprises for metric collection and tracking, as well as for the aggregation of metrics. You can set up Ganglia to run on your cluster nodes, so Hadoop can send its metrics data to the Ganglia sinks. You can then set up Nagios to use these metrics as the basis for sending out critical alerts to you.

Ganglia can monitor very large clusters. Ganglia collects metrics such as CPU usage and free disk space and can also help monitor failed nodes. Ganglia provides useful graphical information about the state of the cluster and its nodes. The Ganglia collector runs the monitoring daemons and collects the metrics. The collector presents a real-time view of memory and disk and network usage through a web user interface, along with metrics pertaining to running processes. The following sections explain:

- The architecture of Ganglia
- How to integrate Ganglia with a Hadoop cluster

Ganglia Architecture

There are four main components in a Ganglia monitoring system: gmond, `gmetad`, `rrdtool` and `gweb`. Here's what these four key components do.

- `gmond`: Each host in your cluster will run the `gmond` daemon, whose job it is to collect the metrics data from all the cluster nodes. Every node runs the `gmond` daemon, and the node will receive metrics from the rest of the cluster nodes. This means that the polling process (`gmetad`, which is explained next) needs to poll just a single node to get the cluster metrics and also that node failures won't affect the polling process.
- `gmetad`: This is the daemon that polls the nodes for metric data. It can get a metric dump for the entire cluster from any one node in the cluster. The `gmetad` daemon creates RRD tables to store the metric data.
- `RRDtool`: This component stores the metric data polled by the `gmetad` daemon. You can configure `rrdtool` to aggregate metric data values so that you can easily access not only current data but also historical data, using very little storage space.
- `gweb`: This is the web interface to the metrics collected by the Ganglia monitoring system through the data stored in the RRD databases. You can view specific metrics using graphs and also create custom graphs by drilling down into the details for a specific metric or host. You can also extract metric data using CSV, JSON and other formats through the `gweb` visualization interface. The `gweb` process is actually a PHP program that runs on the Apache web server.

Setting Up the Ganglia and Hadoop Integration

In order to get going with Ganglia in your Hadoop cluster, you need to do the following:

- Install Ganglia (server and clients)
- Extract the Ganglia configuration files
- Configure the Ganglia components (`gmond`, `gmetad`, etc.)
- Set up the Hadoop metrics

Let's start by learning how to install and work with Ganglia so you can direct the Hadoop alerts to a Ganglia sink instead of to a file on the local system (but you can send the metrics to both a file and to the Ganglia sink, if you need to).

Installing Ganglia

In order to install Ganglia, select a node in your Hadoop cluster as the node to host the Ganglia server. It's on this server node that the `gmetad`, `gweb` and `rrdtool` daemons will run.

1. Install the server RPMs on the Ganglia server as shown here (for a RHEL/CentOS system):

```
# yum install ganglia-gmond-3.2.0-99 ganglia-gmetad-3.2.0-99 gweb-2.2.0-99
```

2. Install the client RPMs to run the gmond process on all the cluster nodes as shown here.

```
# yum install ganglia-gmond-3.2.0-99
```

Extracting the Configuration Files

Once you install the Ganglia software, extract the configuration files in the configuration_files.zip folder and copy the files in the ganglia folder to a temporary directory such as /tmp/ganglia.

On the node serving as your Ganglia server host, create a directory named objects and copy the Ganglia object files to that directory:

```
# mkdir-p /usr/libexec/ganglia
# cp /tmp/ganglia/ganglia/objects/*.*  /usr/libexec/ganglia
# cp /tmp/ganglia/scripts/*  /etc/init.d
```

Configuring the gmetad and gmond Daemons

The gmond.conf file consists of several sections such as `global`, `cluster`, `host`, `upd_receive_channel`, `tcp_receive_channel` and `modules`. Most of these are self-explanatory, and you can use the default values for them. You can set up custom metric collection *groups* for the metrics you consider critical, such as free memory (`mem_free`), system load (`load_five`—load averaged every 5 minutes) and total free disk space (`disk_free`). You can set up metric-collection groups as shown in the following example, which sets up a group for the amount of free memory:

```
collection_group {
  collect_every = 40
  time_threshold = 300
  metric {
    name = "mem_free"
    value_threshold = 1024
    title = "Free Memory"
   metric {
    name = "bytes_out"
    value_threshold = 4096
    title = "Sent Bytes"

 }
}
```

As mentioned earlier, the `gmetad` daemon, which polls the metric data, runs only on a single server (the Ganglia server). Set up the data sources from which `gmetad` should poll the metric data in the gmetad.conf file, as shown here:

```
# Format:
# data_source "service name" [polling interval] address1:port addreses2:port ...
data_source "NameNode" 50 ahdoop01.localhost:8658
data_source "ResourceManager" 50 hadoop03.localhost:8664
data_source "JobHistoryServer" 50 hadoop02.localhost:8659
data_source "DataNode" 50 hadoop02.localhost:8662
```

With the Ganglia infrastructure all configured and ready to go, it's time to add the Hadoop metrics to the mix.

Setting Up the Hadoop Metrics

In order to set up your Hadoop cluster for working with Ganglia, you need to perform the following tasks on each node in the cluster:

1. Stop all Hadoop services.
2. Copy the Ganglia metrics file to the Hadoop configuration directory:

```
$ cd $HADOOP_CONF_DIR
$ mv hadoop-metrics2.properties-GANGLIA  hadoop-metrics2.properties
```

3. Edit the metrics properties file to configure the hostname of the Ganglia server:

```
namenode.sink.ganglia.servers=test.ganglia.server.hostname:8661
datanode.sink.ganglia.servers=test.ganglia.server.hostname:8660
jobtracker.sink.ganglia.servers=test.ganglia.server.hostname:8662
tasktracker.sink.ganglia.servers=test.ganglia.server.hostname:8660
maptask.sink.ganglia.servers=test.ganglia.server.hostname:8660reducetask
.sink.ganglia.servers=test.ganglia.server.hostname:8660
```

4. Restart all the Hadoop services.

Using Nagios for Alerting

Nagios is an open-source monitoring system that helps you check the health of your system and is a very good alerting and monitoring tool. You can use Nagios to monitor the cluster resources and the status of applications as well as system resources such as CPU, disk and memory. While Ganglia is more about gathering and tracking metrics, Nagios relies on its built-in notification system to focus on alerts. Nagios can help you with the following:

- Getting up-to-date information about the cluster infrastructure
- Raising failure alerts
- Detecting potential issues
- Monitoring resource availability

Understanding Hadoop Logging

Hadoop logs are of great help when troubleshooting failed jobs. Jobs may fail due to issues within the applications, or due to hardware and platform bugs. Hadoop daemon logs reveal the sources of any issues within the daemon processes that affected a job. You can analyze the application logs to pinpoint the root cause of performance issues such as a slow-running job.

Unlike an Oracle database, for example, which has but a single alert log that tracks changes and logs issues, Hadoop has a complex logging structure. This complex logging structure does appear bewildering when you first start dealing with it. Not to fear, however, as once you understand the Hadoop logging structure, you'll find it a breeze to navigate through the logging framework and learn how to mine the logs to your best advantage.

Troubleshooting issues in your cluster may require you to review both application logs and Hadoop daemon logs—I discuss both types of logs in the following sections. But first, a note about the different types of application logs and how to view logs.

Hadoop Log Messages

You can access Hadoop log messages for your Spark, Hive and other jobs through perusing the individual log files or through Hadoop's excellent built-in web interfaces. It's easier to access the logs through the web interfaces most of the times since they save you time and help you to quickly get to the root cause of a performance issue or job failure. Once I explain the Hadoop logging infrastructure, I explain how to use Hadoop's various web UIs to track jobs and analyze their performance.

Types of Logs

There are three types of logs produced by each task in a Spark or MapReduce job:

- stdout: All `system.out.println()` messages are directed to the log file named stdout. You can use custom messages for the stdout log.
- stderr: All `system.err.println()` messages are directed to the log file named stderr. You can use custom messages for the stderr log.
- syslog: All Log4j (standard logging library) logs are sent to the log file named syslog. You can have your custom messages sent here. This is the most significant log for understanding how a task has fared and why it's slow, has failed to start or has stopped running in the middle of the job. Any unhandled exceptions during job execution are trapped by syslog, so it's where to go to understand map and reduce task failures.

> **Note**
>
> The syslog file always contains logging information—the stdout and stderr files are empty unless your code specifies stdout- and stderr-type logging.

Let's say a mapper program contains the following code:

```
logger.info("Mapper Key =" + key);
```

In this case, the mapper uses only Log4j logging and doesn't log to the standard output streams. So, you expect to see logging messages from this job recorded only in the syslog file—this file will always contain information, regardless of whether you have custom Log4j logging code or not, since it's the log for all Log4j messages from the system. In this case, you won't see any logging information in the stdout and stderr files—they'll be there but will be empty.

The reducer code has the following logging-related code:

```
logger.info("Reducer Key =" + key);
System.out.println("Reducer system.out >>> " + key);
System.err.println("Reducer system.err >>> " + key);
```

Since the reducer has specified all three types of logs, you may find logging information in all three log files (stdout, stderr and syslog) for the reducer tasks.

You can learn how to review logs through Hadoop's web UIs in the section titled "Using Hadoop's web UIs for Monitoring." You can learn how to review the logs manually in the section titled "Multiple Ways of Viewing the Application Logs."

> **Note**
>
> Configure Log4j logging by editing the log4j.properties file. This file is, by default, located in the directory specified by the `$HADOOP_CONF_DIR` variable. When you change the logging properties, the changes take place immediately without requiring a cluster restart.

Daemon and Application Logs and How to View Them

Application developers and administrators who are relatively new to Hadoop are sometimes confused when it comes to the reviewing of daemon and application logs. If you're using Cloudera or Hortonworks and use their management interfaces such as Cloudera Manager or Ambari, you can get to the logs with the click of a button. Otherwise, you're often left scratching your head as to exactly where the various logs are stored and which of the many logs that are available to you are really significant.

Hadoop generates two main types of logs:

- It generates logs for all of its daemons such as the NameNode and DataNode. The daemon logs are useful mostly for administrators, since they help troubleshoot issues such as unexpected failures of key Hadoop services like the DataNodes and the NameNode.
- Hadoop also generates logs for every application you run in the cluster. Hadoop application logs are very important to application developers as well as administrators, since they help you understand the root causes of a job failure and a performance slowdown, among other things.

You can view Hadoop application logs in multiple ways:

- From the Hadoop web UIs (specifically the ResourceManager web UI). The ResourceManager web UI saves you the bother of going to where the logs are stored and viewing the log files. You can also view the logs through the JobHistory web UI.
- By examining the log information directly from the log files.
- For some application logs, from HDFS, where they're stored if you enable *log aggregation*, which I highly recommend.
- Via the `yarn` command (explained in Chapter 16).

So, there are two major types of logs that you need to focus on as a Hadoop administrator—application logs and the Hadoop daemon logs. The following sections explain application logging first, and then I discuss how to manage the Hadoop daemon logs.

How Application Logging Works

Application logs are critical in analyzing the performance of Hadoop jobs and in troubleshooting issues with job execution. In order to understand how to use Hadoop application logs, it's useful to understand how exactly the logs are generated in the first place. So, we start by explaining the steps involved in the processing of a MapReduce job, which culminate in the generation and storing of the log files for each job processed by Hadoop.

Where Hadoop Stores Its Logs

In order to efficiently analyze Hadoop logs, it's important to understand that Hadoop uses several locations in your system to store job-related information and logs, both while the job is running and after the job is completed. The three locations are the following:

- HDFS: This is the location where Hadoop creates a staging directory for storing job execution files such as the job.xml file that contains the Hadoop parameters used in running a job. If you configure Hadoop's **log aggregation** feature, (which is explained later in this chapter), Hadoop also uses HDFS for long term (the actual duration being configurable by you) storage of the Hadoop job logs.
- NodeManager local directories: These are directories you create on the local file system where Hadoop stores the shell scripts generated by the NodeManager service to execute the ApplicationMaster container. You can create the NodeManager local directories anywhere in the local Linux file system. It's not uncommon to create them under the same file system as the Hadoop HDFS file system, as shown here:

  ```
  /u05/hadoop/dfs              //create HDFS files under this directory
  /u05/hadoop/nm               //create local directories for NodeManager
                               //under this directory
  ```

  You specify the location of the NodeManager local directories with the `yarn.nodemanager.local.dirs` parameter in the `yarn-site.xml` file.
- NodeManager log directories: These are the local directories on Linux where the NodeManager stores the actual log files for the applications a user runs. All the containers (for Spark, MapReduce and other job tasks) that a job is executing on the NodeManager for this node store their application logs in this directory. The default value for this parameter is `${yarn.log.dir}/userlogs`. It's important to understand that `yarn.log.dir` is really not an OS environment variable (like the `JAVA_HOME` variable, for example). This is a Java system property that you configure through the yarn-env.sh file. By default, the `yarn.log.dir` property is set to the same value as the OS environment variable `YARN_LOG_DIR`.

Specify the location of the NodeManager log directories with the yarn .nodemanager.log-dirs parameter in the yarn-site.xml file. For example, take a look at the following:

```
<property>
   <name>yarn.nodemanager.log-dirs</name>
   <value>/var/log/hadoop-yarn </value>
</property>
```

The HDFS staging directories and the NodeManager local directories contain fields with the job parameters and the shell scripts that execute the ApplicationMaster. It is the NodeManager log directories that are of much more importance to you on a day-to-day basis, since these directories contain the actual application log files.

What the NodeManager Log Directories Contain

Log files for an application actually mean the container logs. Each application's localized log directory will have the following directory structure:

```
${yarn.nodemanager.log-dirs}/application_${appid}/
```

The appid variable stands for the application ID of the MapReduce job. Each container's log directories will be underneath this directory and will use the following directory naming convention:

```
container_{$contid}
```

Each of a container's directories will contain the actual log files that we're interested in—these are the three types of Hadoop logs generated by this container, which we described earlier in this chapter: stderr, stdin and syslog. The individual container log directories will be placed under the ${yarn.nodemanager.log-dirs}/application_${appid} directory, in directories that are named container_{$containerId}. Each container directory will contain files named stderr, stdout and syslog. This is where you find out information about the container's errors during its run.

As mentioned earlier, the default value for the yarn.nodemanager.log-dirs property is ${yarn.log.dir}/userlogs. Let's say you want to examine the log files for an application with the application ID of 1423588006739_0015. Here's the directory structure you'll need to traverse to get to the container log files for this application.

```
${yarn.nodemanager.log-dirs}=/var/log/hadoop-yarn
${appid}= 1423588006739_0015
{contid}= 1423588006739_0015_01_001667
```

The full name of this container will be container_1423588006739_0015_01_001667, and you can access its syslog, stderr and stdout log files by going to the following directory:

```
/var/log/hadoop-
yarn/container/application_1423588006739_0015/container_1423588006739_0015_01_001667
```

How Hadoop Uses HDFS Staging Directories and Local Directories During a Job Run

When you launch a Yarn job, Hadoop makes use of both HDFS (we're not talking about using the data stored in HDFS—here we're discussing how Hadoop uses HDFS for logging and storing job-related information) and the local directories on various nodes in the cluster. Hadoop uses HDFS for staging the job and the local directories for storing various scripts that are generated to start up the job's containers (which will run the map and reduce tasks). The following sections explain how Hadoop uses HDFS and the local directories during job execution.

How HDFS Is Used for Staging a Job

When users execute a MapReduce job, they usually invoke a Job Client to configure the job and to launch it. As part of the job execution, the Job Client does the following things:

- It first checks to see if there's a staging directory under the user's name in HDFS. If not, it creates it. The staging directory has the format /user/<username>/ .staging.
- The Job Client creates a file named job_<jobID>_conf.xml under the .staging directory, within a directory named after the job (such as ./staging/ job_ 1437150959773_3620) and a file named just job.xml. These files include the Hadoop parameters used in executing this job.
- In addition to the job-related files, a file from the Hadoop JAR (Java archive) file named hadoop-mapreduce-client-jobclient.jar is also placed in the .staging directory, after renaming it to job.jar.

In the following example, a user named produser has the following contents inside the user's staging directory after submitting a new job:

```
bash-3.2$ hdfs dfs -ls /user/produser/.staging/job_1437150959773_3620/
Found 7 items
-rw-r--r--   10 produser produser    7781304 2016-01-0207:19 /user/produser/.
staging/job_1437150959773_3620/job.jar
-rw-r--r--   10 produser produser       1767 2016-01-0207:19 /user/produser/.
staging/job_1437150959773_3620/job.split
-rw-r--r--    3 produser produser        145 2016-01-0207:19 /user/produser/.
staging/job_1437150959773_3620/job.splitmetainfo
-rw-r--r--    3 produser produser     430268 2016-01-0207:19 /user/produser/.
staging/job_1437150959773_3620/job.xml
-rw-r--r--    3 produser produser        310 2016-01-0207:19 /user/produser/.
staging/job_1437150959773_3620/job_1437150959773_3620.summary
-rw-r--r--    3 produser produser      10242 2016-01-0207:20 /user/produser/.
staging/job_1437150959773_3620/job_1437150959773_3620_1.jhist
-rw-r--r--    3 produser produser     451071 2016-01-0207:19 /user/produser/.
staging/job_1437150959773_3620/job_1437150959773_3620_1_conf.xml
bash-3.2$
```

Once the staging directory is set up, the Job Client submits the job to the ResourceManager. The Job Client also sends back to the console the status of the job progression, by showing the percentages of completion for the map and reduce phases of the job (map 5%, reduce 0%, etc.).

Note that all of this is happening in the HDFS file system and not on the local directories of the Linux server. Once the job is launched by the Job Client, the ApplicationManager for this job swings into action.

How the NodeManager Uses the Local Directories

The ResourceManager's ApplicationsManager (not to be confused with the ApplicationMaster for the job!) service selects a NodeManager on one of the cluster's nodes to launch the ApplicationMaster process, which is always Container #1 (the very first container to be created) in a YARN job. Which NodeManager the ResourceManager chooses will depend on the available resources at the time of launching the job—you can't specify the node on which to start the job.

The NodeManager service starts up and generates various scripts in the local application cache (the appCache directory) to execute the ApplicationMaster container. The ApplicationMaster's directories are stored in the locations that you've specified for the NodeManager's local directories with the `yarn.nodemanager.local-dirs` configuration property in the yarn-site.xml file. In our case, this property is configured in the following way:

```
<property>
  <name> yarn.nodemanager.local-dirs</name>
  <value> /u01/hadoop/yarn/nm, /u02/yarn/hadoop/nm, /uo3/hadoop/yarn/hadoop/nm</value>
</property>
```

The `yarn.nodemanager.local-dirs` property lets you provide a list of directories wherein the NodeManager can store its localized files. Underneath these directories, you'll find the actual application's localized file directory with the following directory structure:

```
${yarn.nodemanager.local-dirs}/usercache/${user}/appcache/application_${appid}
```

To get to the individual container work directories, you must drill down a level further. The container work directories will be subdirectories under the application's root directory and will be named after the container, as shown here:

```
container_${contid}
```

The default value for this parameter is `${hadoop.tmp.dir}/nm-local-dir`.

The following output shows the contents of the ApplicationMaster container's directory (note the container's number, xxxx_000001):

```
#cd
/u07/hadoop/yarn/nm/usercache/produserproduser/appcache/application_1448106546957_
4813/container_e158_1448106546957_4813_01_000001
# ls -altr
total 60
```

```
drwx--x--- 2 yarn yarn 4096 Dec 27 12:09 tmp
-rw-r--r-- 1 yarn yarn   12 Dec 27 12:09 .container_tokens.crc
-rw-r--r-- 1 yarn yarn   99 Dec 27 12:09 container_tokens
-rw-r--r-- 1 yarn yarn   48 Dec 27 12:09 .launch_container.sh.crc
-rwx------ 1 yarn yarn 4721 Dec 27 12:09 launch_container.sh
-rw-r--r-- 1 yarn yarn   16 Dec 27 12:09 .default_container_executor.sh.crc
-rwx------ 1 yarn yarn  720 Dec 27 12:09 default_container_executor.sh
-rw-r--r-- 1 yarn yarn   16 Dec 27 12:09 .default_container_executor_session
.sh.crc
-rwx------ 1 yarn yarn  666 Dec 27 12:09 default_container_executor_session.sh
lrwxrwxrwx 1 yarn yarn   97 Dec 27 12:09 job.xml -> /u04/hadoop/yarn/nm/usercache/
produser/appcache/application_1448106546957_4813/filecache/13/job.xml
lrwxrwxrwx 1 yarn yarn   97 Dec 27 12:09 job.jar -> /u06/hadoop/yarn/nm/usercache/
produser/appcache/application_1448106546957_4813/filecache/11/job.jar
drwx--x--- 4 yarn yarn 4096 Dec 27 12:09 .
drwxr-xr-x 2 yarn yarn 4096 Dec 27 12:09 jobSubmitDir
drwx--x--- 7 yarn yarn 4096 Dec 27 12:09 ..
#
```

Two files in this directory are worth noting:

- The job.xml file contains the configuration properties that this job will use for YARN, MapReduce and HDFS. For each of Hadoop's configuration properties, the file lists the property's name, value and source. The source of the configuration properties could be one of the following:
  - One of the *-default.xml files
  - One of the *-site.xml files
  - Programmatically set by the user

  Here's some sample output from a job.xml file:

  ```
  <property><name>mapreduce.output.fileoutputformat.compress.codec
  </name><value>org.apache.had
  oop.io.compress.DefaultCodec</value><source>programatically</source>
  </property><property><na
  me>map.sort.class</name><value>org.apache.hadoop.util.QuickSort
  </value><source>prgramaticall
  y</source></property><property><name>mapreduce.job.classloader.system
  .classes</name><value>j
  ava.,javax.,org.apache.ommons.logging.,org.apache.log4j.,
  org.apache.hadoop.,core-
  default.xml,hdfs-default.xml,          mapred-default.xml,yarn-
  efault.xml</value><source>programatically</source></property>
  ```

- The launch_container.sh script is used by the NodeManager to launch a container, in this case the ApplicationMaster container (the container that's always numbered *-000001).

The NodeManager will execute the launch_container.sh script to execute the ApplicationMaster class and run the ApplicationMaster container. The ApplicationMaster starts up and sends requests to the ResourceManager for the allocation of containers for hosting the necessary number of mappers and reducers needed for this application.

Launching the NodeManager and Creating the Map/Reduce Containers

The ResourceManager replies to the requests made by the ApplicationMaster for container allocation with a list of available NodeManagers. The ApplicationMaster will contact those NodeManagers running on various cluster nodes to launch the mapper/reducer containers it needs to complete the job.

Each NodeManager will generate various scripts in the local application cache under the NodeManager local directory (as explained earlier, this is set with the `yarn.nodemanager.local-dirs` property), and these scripts are very similar to the ones created for the ApplicationMaster service, as explained in the previous section. That is, the application cache directory for each container will contain files named job.xml, launch_container.sh and so on. The appCache directory will be named after the map or reduce containers, as shown here:

```
# pwd
/u01/hadoop/yarn/nm/usercache/produser/appcache/application_1437683566204_0050/
container_e103_1437683566204_0050_01_000922
```

You don't need to worry about the nm-local-dir directory filling up with the job files under the appCache subdirectory—the files are removed automatically when the job completes. However, some jobs do contain large files, and when the appCache directory doesn't have sufficient room to accommodate them, the job fails.

The configuration property `yarn.nodemanager.delete.debug-delay-sec` determines for how long (in seconds) the local log directories are retained after an application completes. Once the configured time elapses, the NodeManager's DeletionService process deletes the application's local file directory structure, including its log directory. You must set the value of this parameter high enough (such as at least 30 minutes = 1,800 seconds), so you have sufficient time to review the application's logs.

This concludes our explanation of the use of an HDFS staging directory when you execute a job and how the local directories (NodeManager local directories) are used for storing the various scripts generated by the NodeManager during job execution, for both the ApplicationMaster container and the map and reduce containers. The next step is learning where the actual job logs go and how to access them for troubleshooting a job.

Application Logs

As the application runs, it generates logs and stores them under the directory you specified with the `yarn.nodemanager.log-dirs` parameter (in the yarn-site.xml file), as explained earlier. In my case, this is the directory named /var/log/hadoop-yarn. Here's a typical list of files found under this directory:

```
# pwd
/var/log/hadoop-yarn/container
# ls
application_1421391094042_1789  application_1423526287495_0063
application_1421391094042_1790  application_1423526287495_0101
...
#
```

To get to the containers belonging to an application that ran on a node, here's what I need to do:

```
# cd application_1424873694018_2360
# ls
# [root@bdaolp013node03 application_1424873694018_2360]# ls
container_1424873694018_2360_01_000063  container_1424873694018_2360_01_011880
container_1424873694018_2360_01_000074  container_1424873694018_2360_01_012775
...
#
```

Under the directory that belongs to each container, you'll find the stderr, stdout and syslog files pertaining to that container, as shown here:

```
# cd container_1424873694018_2360_01_021986
# ls -altr
total 13840
-rw-r--r-- 1 yarn yarn        0 Feb  8  2015 stdout
drwx--x--- 9 yarn yarn     4096 Feb  8  2015 ..
drwx--x--- 2 yarn yarn     4096 Feb  8  2015 .
-rw-r--r-- 1 yarn yarn 14137434 Feb  8  2015 syslog
-rw-r--r-- 1 yarn yarn        0 Feb  8  2015 stderr
#
```

In this case (and this is fairly common) the stdout and stderr logs are empty since the application's code didn't use them. However, as I mentioned earlier, the all-important syslog file will always log the job execution details, as well as any custom logging messages that the developers configured through custom Log4j loggers. Here are the partial contents of a typical syslog file:

```
2016-06-28 22:39:36,403 INFO [main] org.apache.hadoop.mapred.Task:
Task:attempt_1421391094042_1789_m_000002_0 is done. And is in the process of committing
2016-06-28 22:39:36,431 INFO [main] org.apache.hadoop.mapred.Task: Task attempt_
1421391094042_1789_m_000002_0 is allowed to commit now
2016-06-28 22:39:36,437 INFO [main] org.apache.hadoop.mapreduce.lib.output
.FileOutputCommitter: Saved output of task 'attempt_1421391094042_1789_m_000002_
0' to hdfs://bdaolp01-ns/data/lfsearch/work/batch_00002/output/transformer/_
temporary/1/task_1421391094042_1789_m_000002
2016-06-28 22:39:36,464 INFO [main] org.apache.hadoop.mapred.Task: Task 'attempt_
1421391094042_1789_m_000002_0' done.
~
```

Remember that a typical job runs on several nodes, each with a separate NodeManager. On each of the nodes, you'll find the logs pertaining to just those containers (maps/reducers) from the job that ran on that node.

Logging Levels for Map and Reduce Tasks

The standard logging levels you set for the entire cluster may not be appropriate for all jobs and tasks. You can set custom logging levels for both map and reduce tasks, with the help of the following properties:

- `mapreduce.map.log.level`: Sets the logging level for the map task. The allowed levels are `OFF`, `FATAL`, `ERROR`, `WARN`, `INFO`, `DEBUG`, `TRACE` and `ALL`.

- `mapreduce.reduce.log.level`: Sets the logging level for the reduce task. The allowed levels are `OFF`, FATAL, `ERROR`, WARN, `INFO`, `DEBUG`, `TRACE` and `ALL`.

The default logging level for both map and reduce tasks is `INFO`. You can override both logging level settings at the cluster level by setting a different value in the `mapreduce.job.log4j-properties-file`.

Retention Duration for the Application Logs (without Log Aggregation)

As the application continues to run, the NodeManager will append log data to the log files for each container running on that node. Once the job completes, the NodeManager retains the application logs for 3 hours (10,800 seconds) and then deletes them. You can change the retention period by setting the `yarn.nodemanager.log.retain-seconds` parameter in the yarn-site.xml file, as shown here:

```
<property>
   <name>yarn.nodemanager.log.retain-seconds</name>
   <value>86400<value>
<property>
```

This configuration saves the logs for 24 hours after job completion and deletes them after that. Often you need to examine logs for a job that completed several hours, or even days, ago. You can ensure access to older logs by configuring log aggregation, as explained in the next section. If your log retention time is over or if you've set up log aggregation in your cluster, you may encounter the following error when you try to access a log:

```
# cd application_1448106546957_5313
-bash: cd: application_1448106546957_5313: No such file or directory
#
```

Log aggregation saves the log files by moving them from the local file system to HDFS and retaining them there for the duration of the interval you configured. Retaining the job logs for a longer term in this fashion significantly aids you in understanding job performance as well as during troubleshooting exercises. The following section shows how to set up log aggregation in your cluster.

> **Note**
>
> Log aggregation is disabled by default—this means that unless you explicitly configure log aggregation, all of an application's logs are automatically deleted after three hours by default!

Storing Job Logs in HDFS through Log Aggregation

By default, Hadoop stores all logs on the nodes where a job's tasks have run. You learned in the previous section that the application logs are deleted automatically after a specific time period. You can configure log aggregation to ensure that you can retain the logs by storing them in HDFS. Log aggregation means that once a job completes, Hadoop will automatically aggregate the job logs from all the nodes where tasks for a job have run and move them to HDFS. Logging is a YARN-related property. Log aggregation is disabled by default, and you can enable it by setting the yarn.log-aggregation-enable parameter in the yarn-site.xml file:

```
<property>
   <name>yarn.log-aggregation-enable</name>
   <value>true</value>
</property>
```

Since log aggregation is disabled by default, the default value for the yarn.log-aggregation-enable parameter is false. Once you enable log aggregation, there are a few other things for you to take care of to ensure that log aggregation works correctly, as explained in the following sections.

Where (in HDFS) Hadoop Stores the Aggregated Logs

Once you enable log aggregation, the NodeManager concatenates all the container logs into a single file and saves them in HDFS. It also deletes the logs immediately from the local directory (specified by the yarn.nodemanager.log-dirs parameter). You configure where in HDFS Hadoop stores the logs it aggregates with the yarn.nodemanager.remote-app-log-dir parameter, as shown here:

```
<property>
  <name>yarn.nodemanager.remote-app-log-dir</name>
  <value>/tmp/hadoop/logs</value>
</property>
```

The yarn.nodemanager.remote-app-log-dir parameter specifies where exactly in HDFS the NodeManagers should store the aggregated logs. The default location is /tmp/logs in HDFS. If you store the aggregated logs in the local file system, the JobHistoryServer and other Hadoop daemons won't be able to access and serve these logs. This is the reason for storing them in HDFS.

While the yarn.nodemanager.remote-app-log-dir parameter sets the location of the *root HDFS directory* that stores the aggregated log files, the actual log files are stored one directory deeper, under subdirectories named for the user executing the job. Each user will have their aggregated logs stored in HDFS in the following folder:

```
${yarn.nodemanager.remote-app-log-dir parameter}/${user.name}/
```

And here's an example:

```
$ hdfs dfs -ls /tmp/logs/produser
Found 1 items
drwxrwx---   - produser hadoop          0 2016-07-10 09:00 /tmp/logs/produser/logs
$
```

The related logging configuration property yarn.nodemanager.remote-app-log-dir-suffix (default value is logs) obviously is helpful in setting the name of the remote log directory in HDFS. Hadoop creates the remote log directory in HDFS at the location arrived at by this formulation:

```
{yarn.nodemanager.remote-app-log-dir}/${user}/{thisParam}
```

Again, the default value for the suffix is `logs`. The actual HDFS location for a specific application is `${yarn.nodemanager.remote-app-log-dir}/${user.name}/logs/<application ID>`. Here's an example showing the log files in HDFS for a user named produser:

```
$ hdfs dfs -ls /tmp/logs/produser/logs/
[hdfs@hadoop013node03 ~]$ hdfs dfs -ls /tmp/logs/produser/logs/
Found 293 items
drwxrwx---   - produser hadoop          0 2015-12-19 23:22 /tmp/logs/produser/
logs/application_1448106546957_4016
drwxrwx---   - produser hadoop          0 2015-12-20 00:22 /tmp/logs/produser/
logs/application_1448106546957_4018
...
$
```

I next drill down to the log directory for a single application (application_1448106546957_4016) and see what's under that directory:

```
$ hdfs dfs -ls /tmp/logs/produser/logs/application_1448106546957_4016
Found 60 items
-rw-r-----   3 produser hadoop   12739972 2015-12-19 23:22 /tmp/logs/produser/
logs/application_1448106546957_4016/hadoop01.example.com_8041
...
-rw-r-----   3 produser hadoop   13532113 2015-12-19 23:22 /tmp/logs/produser/
logs/application_1448106546957_4016/hadoop08.example.com_8041
$
```

I'm trying to get the aggregated application logs for a single application run by the user produser, but I'm seeing 60 files. What gives? This is correct, since Hadoop aggregates the job logs into per-node log files consisting of the logs for all containers that were executed on each node that was part of the application execution. There simply isn't a single aggregated log file for the entire application.

Configuring Log Retention

As mentioned earlier, by default, log aggregation isn't enabled. Under this configuration, the following two parameters determine the log retention and log deletion behavior.

- `yarn.nodemanager.log.retain-seconds`: The time in seconds to retain user logs on the individual nodes. Note that this parameter comes into play only when log aggregation isn't in force. When you enable log aggregation, Hadoop removes the user logs stored in the local directories immediately after it bundles them and moves them to HDFS. The default value for this parameter is 10,800 seconds (3 hours).
- `yarn.nodemanager.log.deletion-threads-count`: The number of threads used by the NodeManagers to clean-up logs once the log-retention time is up.

As explained earlier, if you enable log aggregation by setting the parameter `yarn.log-aggregation-enable` to `true`, the files are aggregated and stored in HDFS after the application completes. The following additional log retention configuration parameters come into play if you enable log aggregation:

- `yarn.log-aggregation.retain-seconds`: The value you set for this property determines the length of time (in seconds) for which the aggregated logs must be retained, after which they're automatically deleted. Any negative number, such as -1, will disable log deletion. You can set the value to 604,800 for this parameter to retain the aggregated application logs for 7 days. If you set a very high retention period, you'll be using up valuable HDFS storage for retaining the logs.
- `yarn.log.server.url`: The URL where aggregated logs can be accessed after the application completes. NameNodes redirect the web UI users to this URL, and it currently points to the MapReduce Job History. Here's an example showing how to set this property:

```
<property>
 <name>yarn.log.server.url</name>
 <value>http://hadoop03.localhost:19888/jobhistory/logs/</value>
</property>
```

> **Note**
>
> Job history files older than the value you configure for the `mapreduce.jobhistory.max-age-ms` property (in milliseconds) will be deleted when the job history cleaner runs. The default value for this property is 604,800,000 (1 week).

Accessing the Log Files Stored in HDFS

Finally, it's time to get to an actual log file in HDFS! You can do this by accessing the aggregated logs from a specific node, as shown here.

```
[hdfs@hadoop03 ~]$ hdfs dfs -ls /tmp/logs/produser/logs/
application_1448106546957_4791/hadoop01.localhost_8041
-rw-r-----   3 produser hadoop   20022565 2015-12-27 10:41 /tmp/logs/produser/
logs/application_1448106546957_4791/hadoop01.localhost_8041
[hdfs@bdaolp013node03 ~]$
```

To examine the contents of the log stored in HDFS, you can issue a command such as the following, which saves the file in a local directory:

```
[hdfs@hadoop03 ~]$ hdfs dfs -get
/tmp/logs/produser/logs/application_1448106546957_4791/hadoop03.localhost._
8041 test.log

15/12/27 14:16:56 WARN hdfs.DFSClient: DFSInputStream has been closed already

[hdfs@hadoop03 ~]$ ls
test.log
[hdfs@hadoop03 ~]$
```

Following are the sample contents from a typical aggregated log file from a specific node for a job:

```
2015-12-27 10:33:32,117 INFO [main] org.apache.hadoop.mapred.Task:
Task:attempt_1448106546957_4791_m_000056_0 is done. And is in the process of committing
```

```
2015-12-27 10:33:32,162 INFO [main] org.apache.hadoop.mapred.Task: Task attempt_
1448106546957_4791_m_000056_0 is allowed to commit now
2015-12-27 10:33:32,168 INFO [main] org.apache.hadoop.mapreduce.lib.output
.FileOutputCommitter: Saved output of task 'attempt_1448106546957_4791_m_000056_
0' to hdfs://bdaolp01-ns/data/ /work/batch_00001/output/transformer/_temporary/
1/task_1448106546957_4791_m_000056
2015-12-27 10:33:32,214 INFO [main] org.apache.hadoop.mapred.Task: Task 'attempt_
1448106546957_4791_m_000056_0' done.
```

Log aggregation serves many useful purposes, and it's a best practice to configure it. Users and administrators often need to perform a historical analysis of job logs. Rather than trying to set up a custom log-collection process, you simply enable log aggregation so you can automate the storing of the job logs for the length of time that you desire, in HDFS.

Multiple Ways of Viewing the Application Logs

You can view the application logs in three different ways:

- View the aggregated logs by getting them from HDFS (as shown in the previous section titled "Accessing the Log Files Stored in HDFS")
- View them through the Hadoop web UIs
- Once the job completes, view them from the JobHistoryServer UI

Once the (aggregated) application logs are in HDFS, it's a simple matter of copying them to a local directory to review them, as shown here:

```
$ hdfs dfs -copyToLocal ........... application_123456789/*    ./tmp
```

You can also view the logs while the application is still running, by going to the ResourceManager UI.

After the application completes, the logs are managed by the JobHistoryServer, so you can go to the JobHistoryServer UI to view the logs of completed applications.

As I explained in Chapter 16, you can also issue the `yarn logs` command to get at the logs. The `yarn logs` command helps retrieve logs for completed applications:

```
$ $HADOOP_YARN_HOME/bin/yarn logs
Retrieve logs for completed YARN applications.
usage: yarn logs -applicationId <application ID> [OPTIONS]

general options are:
-appOwner <Application Owner>   AppOwner (assumed to be current user if
                                not specified)
-containerId <Container ID>     ContainerId (must be specified if node
                                address is specified)
-nodeAddress <Node Address>     NodeAddress in the format nodename:port
                                (must be specified if container id is
                                specified)
```

You can print the logs for a completed application by providing its application ID:

```
$ yarn logs -applicationId <application ID>
```

You can view the application logs for a specific container by doing this:

```
$ yarn logs -applicationId <application ID> -containerId <Container ID>
-nodeAddress <Node Address>
```

Working with the Hadoop Daemon Logs

Hadoop daemons such as the ResourceManager, the NodeManager and the DataNodes all produce log files that are highly useful during the troubleshooting of a cluster issue.

Setting the Location for the Daemon Logs

You specify the log file location in the yarn-env.sh and hadoop-env.sh files with the `YARN_LOG_DIR` and the `HADOOP_LOG_DIR` parameters, respectively.

I specify the two parameters as follows:

- In yarn-env.sh, `export YARN_LOG_DIR=/var/log/hadoop-yarn`
- In hadoop-env.sh, `export HADOOP_LOG_DIR=/var/log/hadoop-mapred`

The various Hadoop daemons will use the following log directories after this:

- JobHistoryServer: /var/log/hadoop-mapred on the server where the JobHistoryServer runs
- NameNode: /var/log/hadoop-mapred on the server where the NameNode(s) run
- Secondary NameNode—/var/log/hadoop-mapred on the server where the NameNode(s) run
- DataNodes: /var/log/hadoop-mapred on all servers where the DataNodes run
- ResourceManager: /var/log/hadoop-yarn on the node(s) where the Resource-Manager runs
- NodeManager: /var/log/hadoop-yarn on all nodes where the DataNodes run

`hadoop.job.history.location` specifies the location to store the job history files of running jobs. This path is on the host where the NodeManager runs. For each of the Hadoop daemons in the respective log directory, there's a log file with the .out extension, as shown here:

- hadoop-mapred-historyserver-<HistoryServer_Host>.out
- yarn-yarn-yarn-nodemanager-<nodemanager_host>.out
- yarn-yarn-resourcemanager-<resourcemanager_host>.out

The log files with the .out extension are written to during the startup of a daemon. If you have trouble starting up any of the Hadoop daemons, here's where you ought to be looking. Once the daemon starts up, there's no more information about the daemons written to these .out log files.

For each of the Hadoop daemons, in the log directory you've configured for them, there's also a log file with the `.log` extension, as shown here:

- hadoop-mapred-historyserver-<HistoryServer_Host>.log
- yarn-yarn-yarn-nodemanager-<nodemanager_host>.log
- yarn-yarn-resourcemanager-<resourcemanager_host>.log

It's the .log files that are crucial for troubleshooting any errors with the Hadoop daemons, such as a daemon crashing unexpectedly. Chapter 21 shows examples of log files with typical errors. You can get the actual stack trace of the error encountered by the daemons by going through these log files.

Rotation and Deletion of Log Files

You control the rotation of the log files through the /etc/hadoop/conf/.log4j.properties file. Older rotated log files can be appended with a data stamp or a number such as 1 through 10, for example.

Hadoop's default `DailyRollingFileAppender` doesn't have a `maxbackupIndex` to limit the logs, as is the case with the `RollingFileAppender`. If you decide to stick with the default, you need to set up a script to clean up the logs regularly. You can schedule a `cron` job such as the following for this purpose:

```
find /var/log/hadoop/ -type f -mtime +14 -name "hadoop-hadoop-*" -delete
```

This script will delete all log files older than 14 days.

> **Note**
>
> You can set the `mapreduce.job.tags` property to configure tags for a YARN job. At job-submission time, the tag is passed to YARN, and your queries to YARN for applications can be filtered using these tags.

Setting the Log Level for Hadoop Daemons

You can view the current log level of Hadoop daemons or change them with the `yarn daemonlog` command. The command has the following basic syntax:

```
# yarn daemonlog

Usage: General options are:
        [-getlevel <host:httpPort> <name>]
        [-setlevel <host:httpPort> <name> <level>]
#
```

The `-getlevel` command option prints off the log level of the daemon running at the host and port you specify. Here's an example:

```
# yarn daemonlog -getlevel hadoop03:8042 NodeManager
Connecting to http://hadoop03:8042/logLevel?log=NodeManager
Submitted Log Name: NodeManager
```

```
Log Class: org.apache.commons.logging.impl.Log4JLogger
Effective level: INFO
[root@hadoop03 ~]#
```

You can modify the current log level with the `-setlevel` command option for the daemon running on the host and port you specify, as shown here:

```
# yarn daemonlog -setlevel hadoop02:8042 NodeManager ERROR
Connecting to http://hadoop02:8042/logLevel?log=NodeManager&level=ERROR
Submitted Log Name: NodeManager
Log Class: org.apache.commons.logging.impl.Log4JLogger
Submitted Level: ERROR
Setting Level to ERROR ...
Effective level: ERROR

#
# yarn daemonlog -getlevel hadoop02:8042 NodeManager
Connecting to http://hadoop02:8042/logLevel?log=NodeManager
Submitted Log Name: NodeManager
Log Class: org.apache.commons.logging.impl.Log4JLogger
Effective level: ERROR
#
```

Using Hadoop's Web UIs for Monitoring

Hadoop provides several very useful web UIs that help you monitor various aspects of your cluster. Both YARN and HDFS come with web UIs for monitoring the status of the daemons as well as the jobs. For example, the ResourceManager web UI shows you the status of all running jobs and their progress, as well as the history of completed jobs. In this section, you'll learn how to monitor your cluster, including the jobs running within it, with the help of Hadoop's web UIs.

The Hadoop web UIs most useful to you are the following:

- The ResourceManager web UI
- The Job History web UI
- NameNode web UI

In the following sections, you'll learn how to use the Hadoop web UIs to monitor and manage your cluster.

Monitoring Jobs with the ResourceManager Web UI

The ResourceManager web UI is a great tool for monitoring YARN jobs. Using this UI, you can view the status of the running jobs, as well as the history of completed jobs. The UI helps you locate the failed Hadoop jobs and lets you easily access the Hadoop daemon logs directly through the UI, helping you quickly troubleshoot job errors.

The URI for the ResourceManager web UI is `http://<RM_Host_Server>:8088/`.

Of course 8088 is the default port but you can change it if you need to. Figure 17.1 shows the ResourceManager web UI.

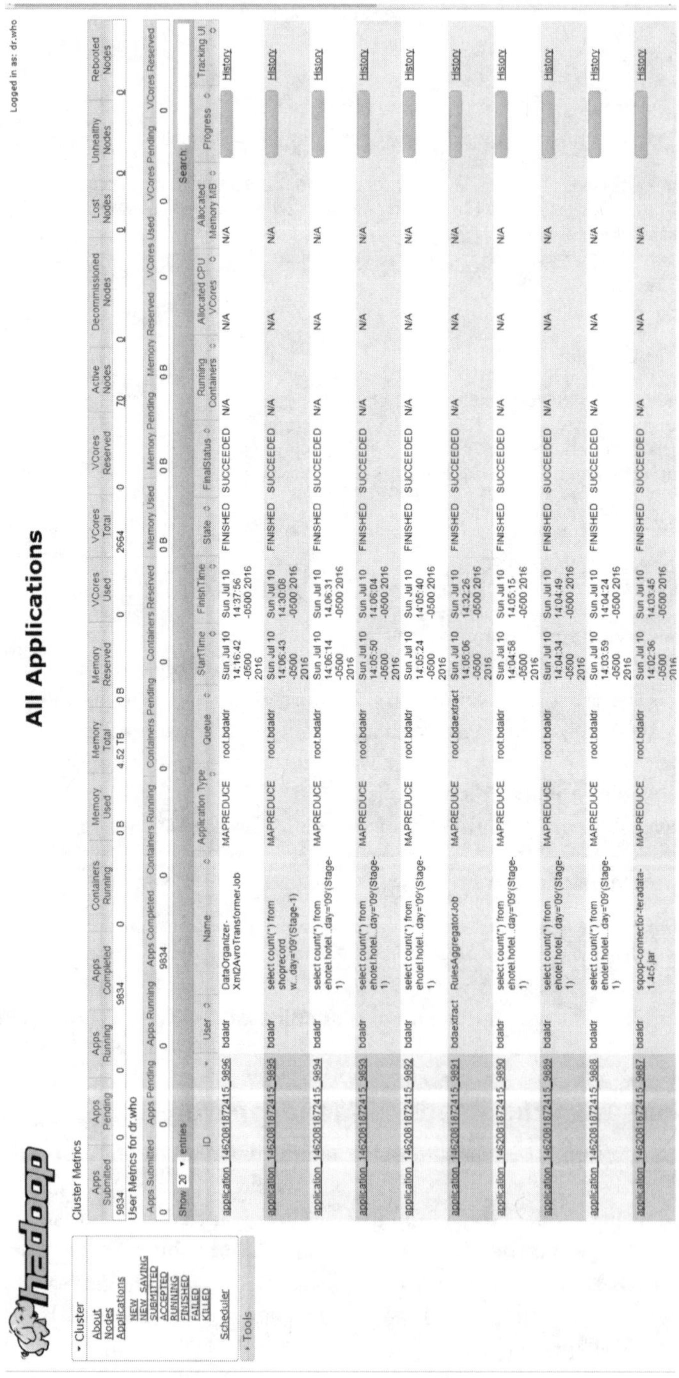

Logged in as: dr.who

hadoop

All Applications

- Cluster
  - About
  - Nodes
  - Applications
    - NEW
    - NEW_SAVING
    - SUBMITTED
    - ACCEPTED
    - RUNNING
    - FINISHED
    - FAILED
    - KILLED
  - Scheduler
- Tools

Cluster Metrics

Apps Submitted	Apps Pending	Apps Running	Apps Completed	Containers Running	Memory Used	Memory Total	Memory Reserved	VCores Used	VCores Total	VCores Reserved	Active Nodes	Decommissioned Nodes	Lost Nodes	Unhealthy Nodes	Rebooted Nodes
9834	0	0	9834	0	0 B	4.52 TB	0 B	0	2664	0	70	0	0	0	0

User Metrics for dr.who

Apps Submitted	Apps Pending	Apps Running	Apps Completed	Containers Running	Containers Pending	Containers Reserved	Memory Used	Memory Pending	Memory Reserved	VCores Used	VCores Pending	VCores Reserved
0	0	0	9834	0	0	0	0 B	0 B	0 B	0	0	0

Show 20 entries Search:

ID	User	Name	Application Type	Queue	StartTime	FinishTime	State	FinalStatus	Running Containers	Allocated CPU VCores	Allocated Memory MB	Progress	Tracking UI
application_1462081872415_9896	bdaldr	DataOrganizer-Xml2AvroTransformerJob	MAPREDUCE	root.bdaldr	Sun Jul 10 14:16:42 -0500 2016	Sun Jul 10 14:37:56 -0500 2016	FINISHED	SUCCEEDED	N/A	N/A	N/A		History
application_1462081872415_9895	bdaldr	select count(*) from shoprecord w...day='09'(Stage-1)	MAPREDUCE	root.bdaldr	Sun Jul 10 14:06:43 -0500 2016	Sun Jul 10 14:30:08 -0500 2016	FINISHED	SUCCEEDED	N/A	N/A	N/A		History
application_1462081872415_9894	bdaldr	select count(*) from ehotel.hotel...day='09'(Stage-1)	MAPREDUCE	root.bdaldr	Sun Jul 10 14:06:14 -0500 2016	Sun Jul 10 14:06:31 -0500 2016	FINISHED	SUCCEEDED	N/A	N/A	N/A		History
application_1462081872415_9893	bdaldr	select count(*) from ehotel.hotel...day='09'(Stage-1)	MAPREDUCE	root.bdaldr	Sun Jul 10 14:05:50 -0500 2016	Sun Jul 10 14:06:04 -0500 2016	FINISHED	SUCCEEDED	N/A	N/A	N/A		History
application_1462081872415_9892	bdaldr	select count(*) from ehotel.hotel.. day='09'(Stage-1)	MAPREDUCE	root.bdaldr	Sun Jul 10 14:05:24 -0500 2016	Sun Jul 10 14:05:40 -0500 2016	FINISHED	SUCCEEDED	N/A	N/A	N/A		History
application_1462081872415_9891	bdaextract	RulesAggregatorJob	MAPREDUCE	root.bdaextract	Sun Jul 10 14:05:06 -0500 2016	Sun Jul 10 14:32:26 -0500 2016	FINISHED	SUCCEEDED	N/A	N/A	N/A		History
application_1462081872415_9890	bdaldr	select count(*) from ehotel.hotel...day='09'(Stage-1)	MAPREDUCE	root.bdaldr	Sun Jul 10 14:04:58 -0500 2016	Sun Jul 10 14:05:15 -0500 2016	FINISHED	SUCCEEDED	N/A	N/A	N/A		History
application_1462081872415_9889	bdaldr	select count(*) from ehotel.hotel...day='09'(Stage-1)	MAPREDUCE	root.bdaldr	Sun Jul 10 14:04:34 -0500 2016	Sun Jul 10 14:04:49 -0500 2016	FINISHED	SUCCEEDED	N/A	N/A	N/A		History
application_1462081872415_9888	bdaldr	select count(*) from ehotel.hotel.. day='09'(Stage-1)	MAPREDUCE	root.bdaldr	Sun Jul 10 14:03:59 -0500 2016	Sun Jul 10 14:04:24 -0500 2016	FINISHED	SUCCEEDED	N/A	N/A	N/A		History
application_1462081872415_9887	bdaldr	sqoop-connector-teradata-1.4c5.jar	MAPREDUCE	root.bdaldr	Sun Jul 10 14:02:36 -0500 2016	Sun Jul 10 14:03:45 -0500 2016	FINISHED	SUCCEEDED	N/A	N/A	N/A		History

Figure 17.1 The ResourceManager web UI

Here are the things that the ResourceManager shows:

- On the landing page (All Applications), you can see key facts such as the following:
  - Number of containers in use
  - Total amount of available memory and number of virtual cores (vcores)
  - Amount of memory and number of vcores currently being used
  - The amount of virtual memory in use
  - The number of active, decommissioned and lost nodes

  This overall view is something I always take a quick look at before plunging into the details of the jobs. You can get a bird's eye view of the cluster health status right from here. You can immediately, within seconds, ascertain whether your cluster is healthy and has enough resources to handle the current workload. It also tells you right away whether the nodes are healthy and gainfully employed or whether they have been decommissioned or have been made "unusable nodes" for whatever reason by Hadoop.
- All jobs, whether they're running or have completed, have the following information listed in the All Applications page:
  - Start time
  - Finish time (if it has completed running)
  - State—RUNNING or FINISHED
  - Final Status—SUCCEEDED or FAILED for completed jobs (for currently running jobs, this column has the value UNDEFINED)

You can use the ResourceManager web UI to perform various tasks, such as the following:

- Finding failed and killed jobs
- Reviewing the YARN job logs
- Drilling into both failed and completed jobs to review the job details (mappers, reducers, etc.)

The following sections show how to perform these tasks with the ResourceManager web UI.

Finding Failed and Killed Jobs

In order to find all the jobs that failed, you need to look in a couple of different places in the ResourceManager web UI, as explained here.

- First, sort on the State column to find all jobs with the State and Final Status showing the value FAILED. (You can do the same thing by clicking on the FAILED link on the left hand side of the ResourceManager web UI, shown in Figure 17.2.) This takes you to the FAILED applications page, which lists all the failed jobs. A failed job in this context is really a job that failed to launch for whatever reason—the job

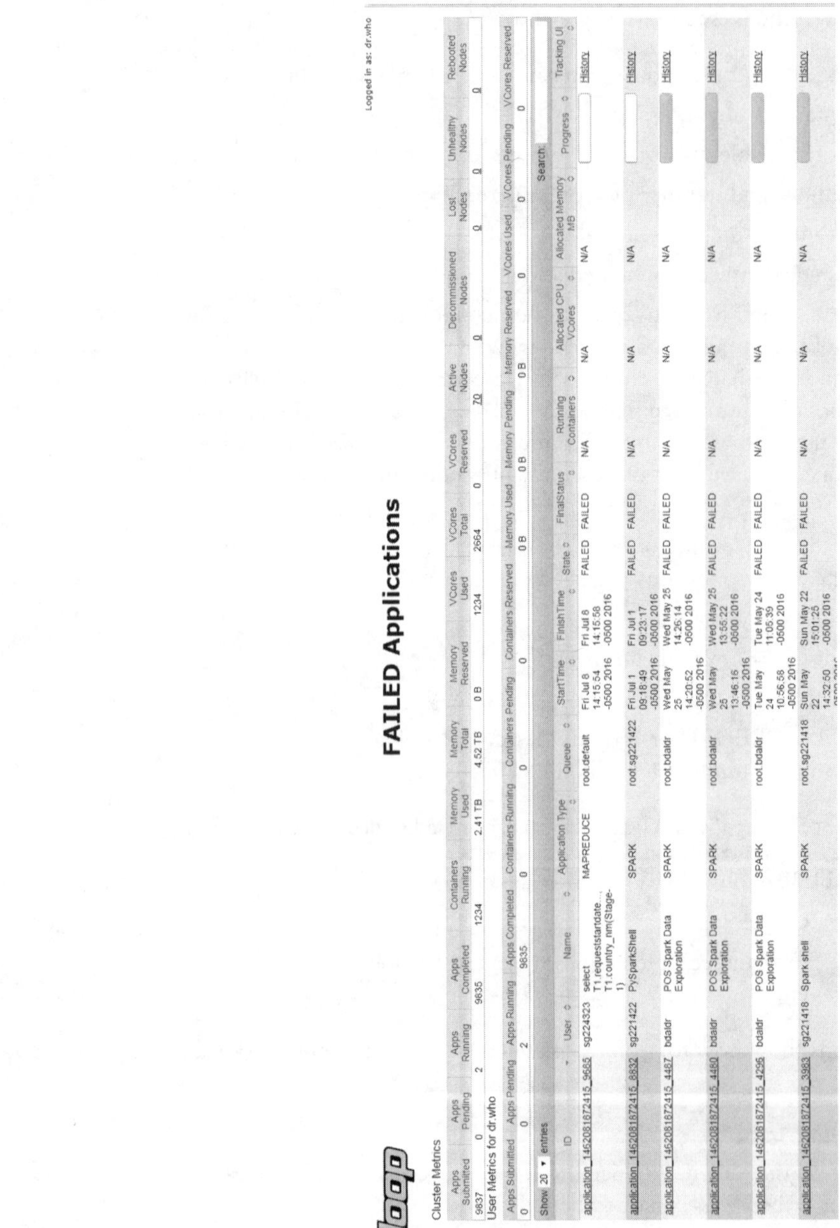

Logged in as: dr.who

hadoop

FAILED Applications

Cluster
About
Nodes
Applications
NEW
NEW_SAVING
SUBMITTED
ACCEPTED
RUNNING
FINISHED
FAILED
KILLED
Scheduler
Tools

Cluster Metrics

Apps Submitted	Apps Pending	Apps Running	Apps Completed	Containers Running	Memory Used	Memory Total	Memory Reserved	VCores Used	VCores Total	VCores Reserved	Active Nodes	Decommissioned Nodes	Lost Nodes	Unhealthy Nodes	Rebooted Nodes
9837	0	2	9835	1234	2.41 TB	4.52 TB	0 B	1234	2664	0	70	0	0	0	0

User Metrics for dr.who

Apps Submitted	Apps Pending	Apps Running	Apps Completed	Containers Running	Containers Pending	Containers Reserved	Memory Used	Memory Pending	Memory Reserved	VCores Used	VCores Pending	VCores Reserved
0	0	2	9835	0	0	0	0 B	0 B	0 B	0	0	0

Show 20 entries Search:

ID	User	Name	Application Type	Queue	StartTime	FinishTime	State	FinalStatus	Running Containers	Allocated CPU VCores	Allocated Memory MB	Progress	Tracking UI
application_1462081872415_9685	sg224323	select T1.requeststartdate..., T1.country_nm(Stage-1)	MAPREDUCE	root.default	Fri Jul 8 14:15:54 -0500 2016	Fri Jul 8 14:15:58 -0500 2016	FAILED	FAILED	N/A	N/A	N/A		History
application_1462081872415_8832	sg221422	PySparkShell	SPARK	root.sg221422	Fri Jul 1 09:18:49 -0500 2016	Fri Jul 1 09:23:17 -0500 2016	FAILED	FAILED	N/A	N/A	N/A		History
application_1462081872415_4487	bdaldr	POS Spark Data Exploration	SPARK	root.bdaldr	Wed May 25 14:20:52 -0500 2016	Wed May 25 14:26:14 -0500 2016	FAILED	FAILED	N/A	N/A	N/A		History
application_1462081872415_4480	bdaldr	POS Spark Data Exploration	SPARK	root.bdaldr	Wed May 25 13:46:16 -0500 2016	Wed May 25 13:55:22 -0500 2016	FAILED	FAILED	N/A	N/A	N/A		History
application_1462081872415_4296	bdaldr	POS Spark Data Exploration	SPARK	root.bdaldr	Tue May 24 10:56:58 -0500 2016	Tue May 24 11:05:39 -0500 2016	FAILED	FAILED	N/A	N/A	N/A		History
application_1462081872415_3983	sg221418	Spark shell	SPARK	root.sg221418	Sun May 22 14:32:50	Sun May 22 15:01:25 -0500 2016	FAILED	FAILED	N/A	N/A	N/A		History

Figure 17.2 Identifying Failed Jobs in the ResourceManager web UI

was initiated, but it never got to the processing stage. You can find the reason for the failure by clicking the application ID under the ID column. In the application page that appears, you can see a summary of the reason for the job failure, as shown here:

```
             Application application_1447271764045_0096 failed 2 times due
             to AM Container

             for appattempt_1447271764045_0096_000002 exited with exitCode:
             -1000

             For more detailed output, check application tracking page:
Diagnostics:
             http://hadoop04.localhost.com:8088/proxy/application

             _1447271764045_0096/Then, click on links to logs of each attempt.

             Diagnostics: No space available in any of the local directories.

             Failing this attempt. Failing the application.
```

- Next, on the All Applications page, again sort the State column, but this time, check for those jobs whose Status column shows FINISHED, but whose Final Status column shows FAILED. When you click on the Job ID of this type of job, you'll see a generic statement stating that the job is considered failed since one or more of the job's tasks have failed:

```
             Task failed task_1448106546957_3947_r_000088
Diagnostics:
             Job failed as tasks failed. failedMaps:0 failedReduces:1
```

- Unlike in the previous case, where the jobs never launched, jobs with the FINISHED/FAILED status have actually launched and run to completion but encountered one or more task failures (usually a handful, but sometimes it could be a large number of tasks). You can click on the logs link on the application page to review the reasons for the task failures. Chapter 21, which deals with troubleshooting your cluster, explains how to fix various types of job and task failures.

In addition to the failed jobs and tasks, you may also view jobs that show the State and Final Status values of KILLED. These are usually jobs that were terminated midway by users but not necessarily always so.

Reviewing the Job Logs

The job logs for a job are kept in the YARN logs on the servers where a job launches. Instead of logging into that server and viewing the log files, you can do so with the help of a couple of clicks from the ResourceManager web UI.

For a running job (a job whose Final Status columns has the value UNDEFINED), click on the job's ID, such as Application_1448106546957_3979 in the ID column, which is the very first column in Figure 17.2. This will take you to the application page, where you click on the link named "logs" at the bottom right of the page. This will take you to a web page that shows the three types of logs—stderr, stderr and syslog—as shown here:

```
Log Type: stderr
Log Upload Time: Thu Dec 31 07:23:34 -0600 2015
Log Length: 243
log4j:WARN No appenders could be found for logger (org.apache.hadoop.metrics2
.impl.MetricsSystemImpl).
log4j:WARN Please initialize the log4j system properly.
log4j:WARN See http://logging.apache.org/log4j/1.2/faq.html#noconfig for more info.

Log Type: stdout
Log Upload Time: Thu Dec 31 07:23:34 -0600 2015
Log Length: 0

Log Type: syslog
Log Upload Time: Thu Dec 31 07:23:34  -0600 2015
Log Length: 25542
Showing 4096 bytes of 25542 total. Click here for the full log.
 In stop, writing event JOB_FINISHED
2015-12-19 07:45:29,909 INFO [Thread-77] org.apache.hadoop.mapreduce.jobhistory
.JobHistoryEventHandler: Copying hdfs://hadoop01--ns:8020/user/produser/.staging/
job_1448106546957_3982/job_1448106546957_3982_1.
...
org.apache.hadoop.mapreduce.v2.app.TaskHeartbeatHandler: TaskHeartbeatHandler thread
interrupted
```

Note that in this case the stderr and stdout log files are empty since the code hasn't used any custom stdout and stderr logging. You can click on the "here" link to get the complete syslog file for this job. This is where you normally find the root cause for a job slowdown or failure.

For a completed job (a job whose State shows FINISHED), the process to get to the log files is pretty similar. Instead of clicking on the job ID link, however, you click on the history link at the far end of the ResourceManager web UI page that corresponds to the Job ID of the job you're troubleshooting.

Finding Details about Running and Completed Jobs

The ResourceManager web UI offers several means of checking the status of running jobs. By clicking on a Job ID on the All Applications page, you can get to the Job page of the application, shown in Figure 17.3.

Actually, you can get the Job page for an application in a couple of ways. Here's one way:

1. On the left side menu of the All Applications page, click RUNNING JOBS.
2. Click the Job ID under the ID column for the job you want to drill into.
3. On the next page, click the ApplicationMaster link in the Application Overview section.
4. On the next page, click the Job ID link (there's only one since this is the page for the job you're interested in).

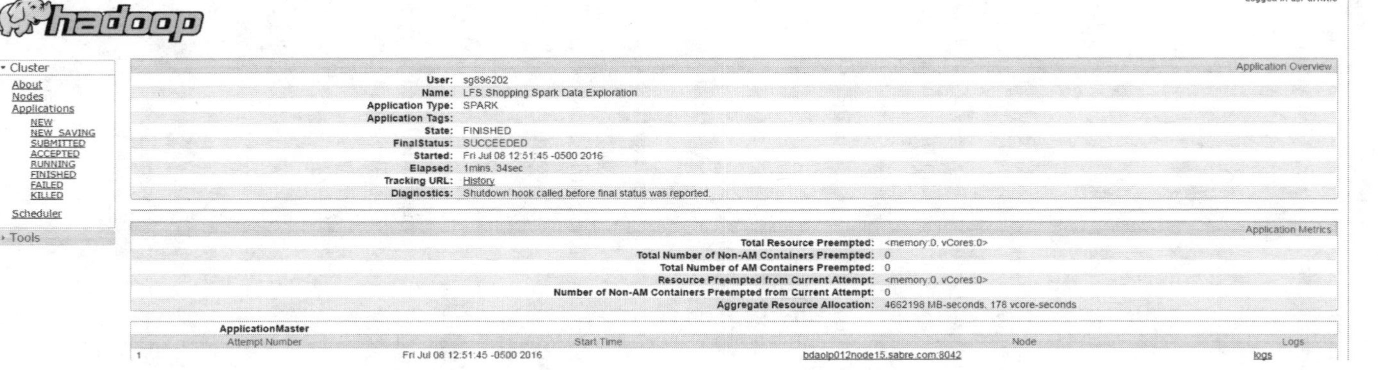

Figure 17.3 The Job page in the ResourceManager web UI

The Job page of a YARN application allows you to click on the Logs link to quickly check the job's logs. More importantly in some ways, it lets you check how a currently running job is progressing. Here's a summary of the information you can get from this page:

- The start time and the length of time the job has been running
- The total number of map and reduce tasks in the job
- The number of completed maps/reducers
- The number of successful map/reduce tasks
- The number of failed map/reduce tasks
- The number of killed map/reduce tasks

On the Job page, for both map and reduce tasks under the RUNNING link, you can click the link to check the progress of the map or reduce job. You can get some highly useful information from here, such as

- The progress of the task in terms of the percentage of work completed.
- The elapsed time thus far for the map/reduce task.
- The status of the map or reduce task. For a map task, the status is map. For a reduce task, there are three states: copy, merge and reduce.

The capability to drill down into the tasks and see what they're actually doing right now lets you gain a pretty good picture of where exactly a slow-running job is stuck. For MapReduce jobs, it's not uncommon for all the map or reduce tasks to complete except for a single straggler process. This is usually due to issues pertaining to a data skew, as explained in Chapter 18, "Tuning the Cluster Resources, Optimizing MapReduce Jobs and Benchmarking."

The JobHistoryServer Web UI

You can access the logs of completed jobs through the JobHistory Server. You do this by entering the following URL in your browser's address bar:

```
http://hadoop03.localdomain:19888/jobhistory
```

Make sure you replace the server name with the name of the server that runs the JobHistory service in your cluster. You can access details about completed jobs from the JobHistoryServer web UI, shown in Figure 17.4. The JobHistoryServer contains information only pertaining to completed jobs. The time period for which you can go back depends on the value you've configured for the `yarn.log-aggregation.retain-seconds` parameter. If you've configured 7 days as the value for this parameter, the JobHistoryServer stores history for the past 7 days. Note that you can also access the JobHistoryServer from the ResourceManager web UI by clicking the History link on the All Applications page.

By clicking on the application's Job ID, you can view the same details for a completed job that I listed in the previous section for a running job.

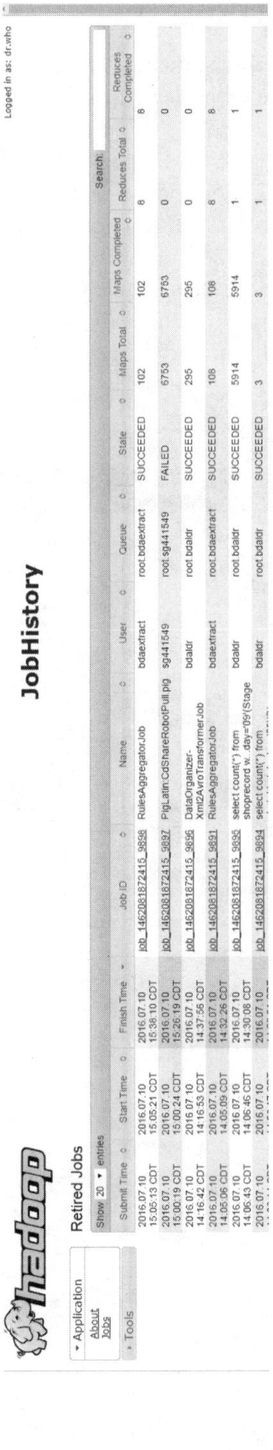

hadoop

Logged in as: dr.who

JobHistory

- Application
  - About
  - Jobs
- Tools

Retired Jobs

Show 20 entries Search:

Submit Time	Start Time	Finish Time	Job ID	Name	User	Queue	State	Maps Total	Maps Completed	Reduces Total	Reduces Completed
2016.07.10 15:05:13 CDT	2016.07.10 15:05:21 CDT	2016.07.10 15:38:10 CDT	job_1462081872415_9898	RulesAggregatorJob	bdaextract	root.bdaextract	SUCCEEDED	102	102	8	8
2016.07.10 15:00:19 CDT	2016.07.10 15:00:24 CDT	2016.07.10 15:26:19 CDT	job_1462081872415_9897	PigLatin:CdShareRobotPull.pig	sg441549	root.sg441549	FAILED	6753	6753	0	0
2016.07.10 14:16:42 CDT	2016.07.10 14:16:53 CDT	2016.07.10 14:37:56 CDT	job_1462081872415_9896	DataOrganizer-Xml2AvroTransformerJob	bdaldr	root.bdaldr	SUCCEEDED	295	295	0	0
2016.07.10 14:05:06 CDT	2016.07.10 14:05:09 CDT	2016.07.10 14:32:26 CDT	job_1462081872415_9891	RulesAggregatorJob	bdaextract	root.bdaextract	SUCCEEDED	108	108	8	8
2016.07.10 14:06:43 CDT	2016.07.10 14:06:46 CDT	2016.07.10 14:30:08 CDT	job_1462081872415_9895	select count(*) from shoprecord w...day='09'(Stage	bdaldr	root.bdaldr	SUCCEEDED	5914	5914	1	1
2016.07.10	2016.07.10	2016.07.10	job_1462081872415_9894	select count(*) from	bdaldr	root.bdaldr	SUCCEEDED	3	3	1	1

Figure 17.4 The JobHistoryServer showing information about completed YARN jobs

Monitoring with the NameNode Web UI

You can monitor a lot of things with the NameNode web UI, which you can access at `http://<namenode_host>:50070`. The Overview page shows a summary of the storage space and the health of the DataNodes.

There are two very useful pages you can view in the NameNode web UI. The DataNode Information page, shown in Figure 17.5, provides a useful summary of the current used and free HDFS storage. It also shows a bit of information that's hard to come by—the number of failed volumes, if any, for each of the DataNodes.

The other page I find quite useful in the NameNode web UI is the Browse Directory page, which you can access by clicking on Utilities in the main page. The Browse Directory page offers as good a visual summary of HDFS storage as any. Figure 17.6 shows the Browse Directory page.

Hadoop Overview Datanodes Datanode Volume Failures Snapshot Startup Progress Utilities

Datanode Information

In operation

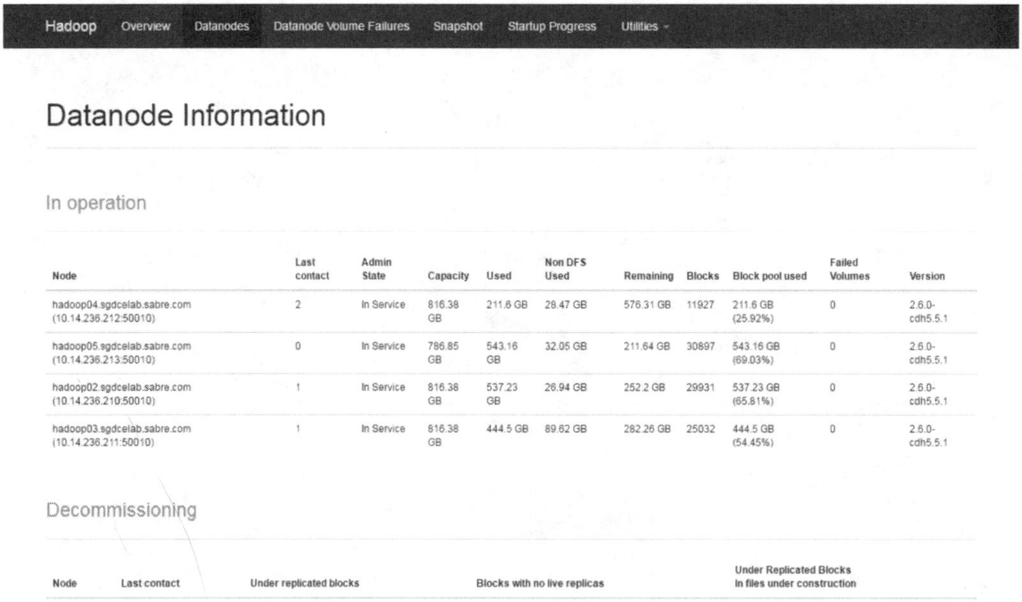

Node	Last contact	Admin State	Capacity	Used	Non DFS Used	Remaining	Blocks	Block pool used	Failed Volumes	Version
hadoop04.sgdcelab.sabre.com (10.14.236.212:50010)	2	In Service	816.38 GB	211.6 GB	28.47 GB	576.31 GB	11927	211.6 GB (25.92%)	0	2.6.0-cdh5.5.1
hadoop05.sgdcelab.sabre.com (10.14.236.213:50010)	0	In Service	786.85 GB	543.16 GB	32.05 GB	211.64 GB	30897	543.16 GB (69.03%)	0	2.6.0-cdh5.5.1
hadoop02.sgdcelab.sabre.com (10.14.236.210:50010)	1	In Service	816.38 GB	537.23 GB	26.94 GB	252.2 GB	29931	537.23 GB (65.81%)	0	2.6.0-cdh5.5.1
hadoop03.sgdcelab.sabre.com (10.14.236.211:50010)	1	In Service	816.38 GB	444.5 GB	89.62 GB	282.26 GB	25032	444.5 GB (54.45%)	0	2.6.0-cdh5.5.1

Decommissioning

Node	Last contact	Under replicated blocks	Blocks with no live replicas	Under Replicated Blocks In files under construction

Figure 17.5 The DataNode Information page in the NameNode web UI

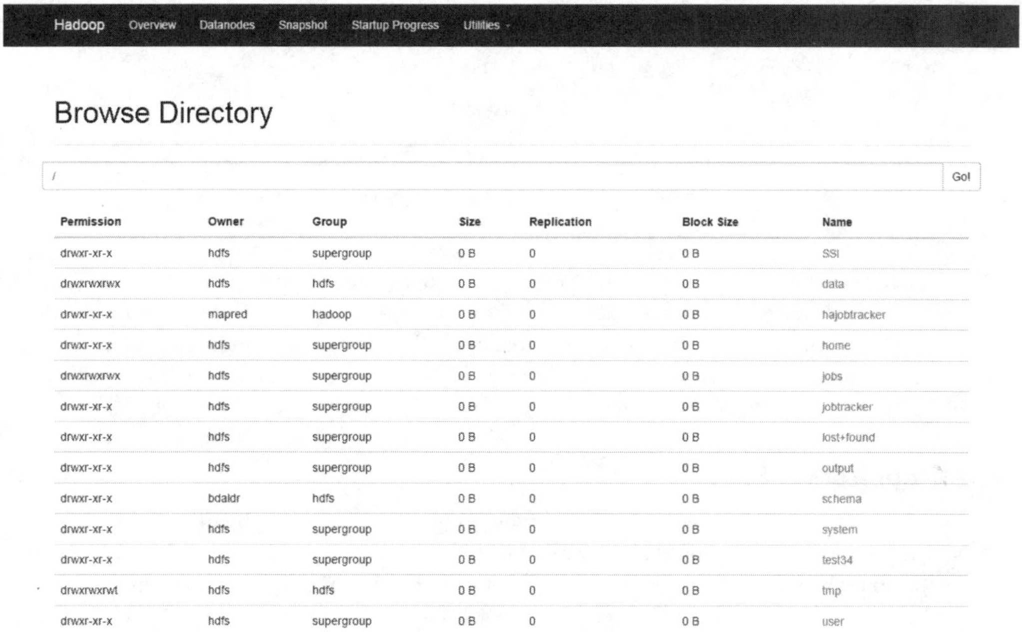

Hadoop Overview Datanodes Snapshot Startup Progress Utilities

Browse Directory

/ Go!

Permission	Owner	Group	Size	Replication	Block Size	Name
drwxr-xr-x	hdfs	supergroup	0 B	0	0 B	SSI
drwxrwxrwx	hdfs	hdfs	0 B	0	0 B	data
drwxr-xr-x	mapred	hadoop	0 B	0	0 B	hajobtracker
drwxr-xr-x	hdfs	supergroup	0 B	0	0 B	home
drwxrwxrwx	hdfs	supergroup	0 B	0	0 B	jobs
drwxr-xr-x	hdfs	supergroup	0 B	0	0 B	jobtracker
drwxr-xr-x	hdfs	supergroup	0 B	0	0 B	lost+found
drwxr-xr-x	hdfs	supergroup	0 B	0	0 B	output
drwxr-xr-x	bdaldr	hdfs	0 B	0	0 B	schema
drwxr-xr-x	hdfs	supergroup	0 B	0	0 B	system
drwxr-xr-x	hdfs	supergroup	0 B	0	0 B	test34
drwxrwxrwt	hdfs	hdfs	0 B	0	0 B	tmp
drwxr-xr-x	hdfs	supergroup	0 B	0	0 B	user

Figure 17.6 The Browse Directory page in the NameNode web UI

Monitoring Other Hadoop Components

As a Hadoop administrator, you'll need to monitor many components of Hadoop. I touch on a couple of them here. Chapter 19 will review Spark monitoring in depth.

Monitoring Hive

Chapter 16 showed you why you need to use an external database such as MySQL for storing the Hive metastore data, so multiple users can connect to Hive through the Hive prompt. As a Hadoop administrator, you'll be supporting a large number of Hive users often, so it's important for you to monitor the health of the Hive metastore.

In order to stay on top of things with Hive monitoring, it's a good idea to regularly check the following:

- Checking client connectivity to the metastore
- Testing basic Hive operations, such as creating and dropping databases and tables
- Monitoring the Hive logs for errors and issues

The Hive temporary space, called the Hive scratch free space, can fill up often due to the saving of large amounts of intermediate data during Hive job executions. That,

Figure 17.7 The Spark web UI

of course, will result in the failure of all subsequent and currently running Hive jobs that need to use the scratch space. If you're using a tool such as Nagios, be sure to add the hosts running both the Hive metastore and Hive clients to Nagios's list of host checks. In addition, Nagios can check database health, so you can add the Hive metastore database health check to Nagios, as well.

Monitoring Spark

The best way to monitor Spark jobs in your cluster is through the Spark web UI. When you run a Spark job, you'll also get the URL for the Spark web UI from the job's output. I'll explain the Spark web UI in detail in Chapter 19, which is devoted entirely to the tuning and monitoring of Spark applications. Figure 17.7 shows the Spark web UI.

Summary

Here's what you learned in this chapter:

- Monitoring a Hadoop cluster is quite important—after all, you set up the cluster only once but monitor it every day! Fortunately, you can employ a wide array of tools to monitor a Hadoop environment, and I explained the most important of these tools.
- Although I haven't discussed them in this chapter, tools such as Cloudera Manager and Ambari help you effectively manage a Hadoop cluster. Even if you're using one of these tools in your cluster, it's worth investing the effort to set up monitoring with a third-party tool such as Ganglia or Zabbix.
- Lots of Hadoop users get confused about Hadoop logs, but in reality it's quite straightforward to access all the logs you need for your troubleshooting exercises. Configuring log aggregation is a best practice as it provides several benefits when compared with the default logging. Understanding how Hadoop metrics work and integrating them with a tool such as Nagios goes a long way in troubleshooting various issues.
- Last, but definitely not the least, make good use of the amazing web UIs offered by Hadoop. The most useful of these web UIs may be the ResourceManager web UI, which helps track the status of running jobs and identify failed jobs, and also helps you drill down to the logs of the failed jobs without having to log into the servers or look in HDFS.

18

Tuning the Cluster Resources, Optimizing MapReduce Jobs and Benchmarking

This chapter covers the following:

- Allocating memory and CPU in your cluster
- Optimizing MapReduce
- Optimizing Hive and Pig
- Understanding Hadoop counters
- Benchmarking your cluster

As Chapter 2, "An Introduction to the Architecture of Hadoop 2," points out, administering Hadoop 2 involves configuring a dizzying array of configuration parameters at the cluster, storage and processing levels. Consequently, this and the next two chapters explain a large number of Hadoop 2 performance configuration properties and show you how to effectively set them. It's a known fact that misconfiguration of a cluster is at the heart of an overwhelming majority of performance and other issues.

While you can run a development or test cluster by setting a mere handful of configuration parameters and letting all other parameters take their default values, production clusters need more diligence as well as trial and error to figure out the optimal settings for these parameters. Therefore, learning how to effectively set the configuration parameters will significantly help you in managing, tuning and troubleshooting your cluster in a production setting.

Benchmarking a cluster performance helps you evaluate the performance of a new or existing cluster compared to that of other clusters or of the same cluster running with a different configuration or with different hardware specifications. This chapter discusses two commonly used benchmarking tools—TestDFSIO and TeraSort.

Broadly speaking, you can group Hadoop performance-related issues into two main areas: the first is the way you configure memory, CPU and other resources in the cluster. The second group is application tuning, wherein you focus on how you can write code in a specific way or specify some configuration parameters to make jobs run faster. In this chapter, I discuss the optimization of MapReduce, Hive and Pig applications—Chapter 19, "Configuring and Tuning Apache Spark on YARN," is dedicated to a discussion of Spark performance tuning and monitoring.

Both Pig and Hive use MapReduce underneath—therefore, when you're seeking to enhance Pig and Hive performance, you must pay heed to all the standard MapReduce performance-related principles that are discussed in this chapter. In addition, both Pig and Hive have their own performance-related configuration parameters (these are completely apart from the Hadoop performance-related parameters), and you must also take advantage of those parameters to get the most of your Pig and Hive jobs. The sections "Optimizing Pig Jobs" and "Optimizing Hive Jobs" in this chapter outline the optimal performance settings for Pig and Hive.

Handling memory allocation is a critical part of a Hadoop administrator's job. All YARN job tasks run in containers, which are logical entities that consist of a set amount of RAM and some processors (CPU). The number of containers your cluster can run determines its processing capacity. Hadoop provides several configuration parameters that enable you to set apart memory for YARN jobs at the aggregate level and also let you configure the size of the containers you want allocated to map and reduce jobs. The chapter shows you how to optimize memory allocation for your cluster.

How to Allocate YARN Memory and CPU

Allocating hard-to-get memory and CPU resources among competing users and applications is probably the single biggest performance-related task for an administrator. How you allocate RAM and CPU determines whether applications run fast and whether you are using all available memory optimally rather than wasting scarce resources.

Memory allocation is more configurable and has a bigger impact on jobs, so I spend quite a bit more time discussing it, compared to the allocation of CPUs. Once the servers are bought and paid for (or, contracted for, if you're running operations in the cloud), there is little you can do to configure CPUs. When it comes to memory, however, you can configure various properties to make the most of the amount of memory you've got.

Allocating Memory

In Chapter 3, "Creating and Configuring a Simple Hadoop Cluster," I explained how to allocate memory to the map and reduce containers by setting appropriate parameters. Let's expand on that topic a bit here, in light of the crucial role memory allocation plays in the performance of your cluster.

You configure all the YARN memory allocations in the yarn-site.xml file. Let's say your cluster has 12 nodes, each with 48GB RAM and 12 disks. Each node has dual

6-core CPUs, making a total of 12 cores on each node. You don't allocate YARN memory with cluster-wide settings—you do so by configuring memory settings on each node. In addition to supporting YARN jobs, don't forget that the nodes must also run the Linux (or other) operating system and probably some other non-Hadoop applications as well. Let's assume that you allocate roughly 10 percent of the total memory on each node to take care of these non-Hadoop uses. The rest of the memory on each node is available for the use of Hadoop. From this memory, first you need to allocate memory for the Hadoop daemons running on each of the nodes. You can now use the remaining memory for allocating to YARN containers.

In YARN, the container is the fundamental unit of processing capacity. As you know by now, a container is a logical entity that contains specific amounts of memory and CPU. When you run an application in YARN, it allocates processing capacity to that application by assigning a specific number of containers to it. For a MapReduce application, the total number of containers assigned is the sum of the mappers and the reducers required to complete the job (the number of mappers depends on the size of the dataset, and you need to specify the number of reducers).

The processing capacity of a Hadoop cluster is the sum of the processing capacities of all of its nodes. And the processing capacity of a node is the maximum number of containers that can be created in that node. The amount of memory you make available for processing YARN applications on each node sets the maximum limit on the memory available for YARN on each node. In our example, I assumed 10 percent memory allocation for non-Hadoop use. How many containers Hadoop can create depends on how you size the containers. Note that the 10 percent I assumed is a very liberal estimate—a more conservative estimate would also take into account the memory requirements for services such as the Impala daemon, which may require as much as 16GB RAM, and the HBase Region Server process, which may need an additional 12-16GB RAM. So, everything depends on the type of services you are running on a certain node.

Once you determine the size of RAM you can allocate to YARN, you need to figure out the following:

- Sizing the map and reduce containers
- Sizing the ApplicationMaster
- Sizing the memory for the JVMs

The following sections explain how to allocate memory among all these entities. Hadoop memory allocation for MapReduce jobs is best understood by looking at the allocation as consisting of two different parts: configuring the memory available for YARN, and configuring the memory available for MapReduce (which runs on YARN and utilizes its memory to execute its map and reduce tasks). Let's start with how you configure the YARN memory allocation.

Configuring YARN Memory

Let's say you have 64GB of RAM available on each node where you're running YARN's NodeManager service, allowing each of these nodes to run map and reduce jobs.

You're supposed to leave around 10 percent of the total memory for the operating system's use, so we need to allocate at least 6.4GB of RAM for the OS. Following this, let's assign the round figure of 40GB out of the total RAM of 64GB to YARN.

You must provide YARN this information by configuring the `yarn.nodemanager.resource.memory-mb` parameter in the yarn-site.xml file on this node. The default value of this parameter is only 8GB, so if you don't configure this parameter, regardless of how much memory you have available on a node, YARN can only use 8GB of it for itself! In this case, I configure YARN to use 40GB of RAM as follows:

```
<property>
  <name>yarn.nodemanager.resource.memory-mb</value>
  <value>40960</value>
</property>
```

> **Note**
>
> The total memory available in a cluster for processing YARN jobs is the sum of the value of the `yarn.nodemanager.resource.memory-mb` parameter on all the nodes. It's important to understand that the value you set for this parameter need not be the same on all the nodes. If you want to assign less memory on certain nodes, you can do so.

The `yarn.nodemanager.resource.memory-mb` parameter sets the amount of physical memory (in MB) that Hadoop can allocate for containers. After configuring the total amount of a node's memory available for YARN processing with the `yarn.nodemanager.resource.memory-mb` parameter, you must also tell YARN how to allocate this memory (in our case, 40GB) among the containers that you want YARN to run on a node. In general, it's a good idea to run 1-2 containers per disk and per core.

Since our nodes have 12 disks and 12 cores each, let's allow for a maximum of 20 containers per node. Since we've allocated a total of 40GB of RAM for YARN, you would need approximately 2GB as the minimum size of a container. I arrived at this number by dividing 40GB of RAM by the number of total containers I want to allocate per node, which is 20. The result is 40GB of RAM/20 containers = 2GB of RAM per container. You then need to configure this minimum size by setting the `yarn.scheduler.minimum-allocation-mb` parameter in the yarn-site.xml file, as shown here:

```
<property>
  <name>yarn.scheduler.minimum-allocation-mb</value>
  <value>2048</value>
</property>
```

This configuration means that YARN can create a total of 20 containers by default on this node, since the minimum size of a container is configured as 2GB (2,048MB). There are no specific rules for sizing the minimum size of a container—as a rule of thumb, you can set the minimum container size at 1GB if your total memory on each node available for YARN is less than 24GB and to 2GB if it's above 24GB. Again, this is just a rough way of figuring out the minimum size of a container.

Once you set the minimum allocatable memory, YARN will allocate memory to containers in increments of the value you set for the yarn.scheduler.miminum.allocation-mb parameter. YARN always allocates containers that are sized the same or larger than the configured value of the `yarn.scheduler.minimum-allocation-mb` parameter (that is, >=2GB of RAM).

As a counterpart to the minimum specification for a YARN container, there's a parameter named `yarn.scheduler.maximum-allocation-mb` that enables you to configure the maximum allowable memory for YARN, including other YARN services beyond the NodeManager. The value you set for the `yarn.nodemanager.resource.memory-mb` parameter can't exceed the value for the `yarn.scheduler.maximum-allocation-mb` parameter.

Now that you've configured the maximum memory YARN can use on the node and also the minimum size of the containers, it's time to configure memory allocation for MapReduce's map and reduce tasks.

> **Note**
>
> Hortonworks provides a handy script named yarn-util.py to calculate YARN and MapReduce memory allocation settings based on the memory and CPU specifications of the nodes in your cluster. Please see `https://docs.hortonworks.com/HDPDocuments/HDP2/HDP-2.3.0/bk_installing_manually_book/content/determine-hdp-memory-config.html` for details.

Configuring MapReduce Memory

Assigning memory to the map and reduce tasks involves configuring three separate entities:

- The physical memory allocation for both map and reduce tasks
- The Java Virtual Memory (JVM) heap size for the map and reduce tasks
- The virtual memory allocation for each map/reduce task

The following sections explain how to configure these three memory components.

Allocating Memory for a Map and a Reduce Task

You must tell YARN the memory to request from the ResourceManager for each map and reduce task with the `mapreduce.map.memory.mb` and the `mapreduce.reduce.memory.mb` parameters, as shown here:

```
<property>
  <name>mapreduce.map.memory.mb</value>
  <value>2048</value>
</property>

<property>
  <name>mapreduce.reduce.memory.mb</value>
  <value>4096</value>
</property>
```

Both these parameters are related to MapReduce processing, so you should set these parameters in the mapred-site.xml file. The default value for both parameters is the same—1GB. Since we've allocated 40GB of total RAM for YARN, the configuration shown here means that you could have anywhere between 20 map tasks (40/2) and 10 reduce tasks (40/4) running at any given time on this node. Usually it's a combination somewhere within these maximum ranges. Note that there are certain MapReduce tasks that may not have any reduce tasks.

There's no hard and fast rule as to the size of the containers for the map and reduce tasks, except that the size has to be at least equal to the minimum size of a YARN container. Note how the size of both the map and reduce containers is the same, or higher than the YARN minimum container size configured in the previous section through the `yarn.scheduler.minimum-allocation-mb` parameter. In this example, the container for the map task is sized at 2GB, and the container for a reduce task is sized at 4GB. However, a map or reduce task can't really use all the memory you assign to the container for its processing, as the following section explains.

Configuring the JVM Heap Size

Hadoop performs each map or reduce task in a dedicated Java Virtual Machine (JVM). The JVM uses a portion of the memory you allocate to a map or reduce task with the parameters `mapreduce.map.memory.mb` and `mapreduce.reduce.memory.mb`, respectively. However, the JVM can't take all of the container's memory, since there's some overhead for non-JVM purposes, such as stack, PermGen and so on. So, you configure the JVM heap size for both a map and a reduce task with the following settings.

```
<property>
  <name>mapreduce.map.java.opts</value>
  <value>-Xmx1576m</value>
</property>

<property>
  <name>mapreduce.reduce.java.opts</value>
  <value>-Xmx3072m</value>
</property>
```

The two Java-related parameters shown here set the maximum Java heap size for each map/reduce task on this node. This is the same as the upper limit of the physical RAM that a map or reduce task can consume. If the Java heap size is set too low, it could lead to Java Out of Memory (OOM) errors. If you set it too high, you run the risk of wasting precious RAM and thus limiting the maximum number of tasks your cluster can support. Therefore, it's important that you figure out the right size for these parameters with some initial trial and error in your cluster with actual workloads. It's important to remember here that the default values for both these parameters is just 200MB (-Xmx200m), so you must in all likely likelihood bump this value up by a significant amount, depending on the size of the RAM you assign for the `mapreduce.map.memory.mb` and the `mapreduce.reduce.memory.mb` configuration properties in the mapred-site.xml file.

To execute a map or reduce task, YARN runs a JVM within the container for the map or reduce task. You use the `mapreduce.map.java.opts` and the `mapreduce.reduce.java.opts` parameters to pass options to the JVM. For example, the `Xmx` option sets the maximum heap size of the JVM.

To pass the memory allocation parameters as Hadoop job options, you can do the following:

```
hadoop jar <jarName> <youClassName> -Dmapreduce.reduce.memory.mb=5120 -
Dmapreduce.reduce.java.opts=-Xmx4608m <otherArgs>
```

The configuration of the `java.opts` parameters for the map and reduce containers sets an upper limit for the physical memory (RAM) that a map and reduce task can actually use to process data. In the previous example, I used 1,576MB for the map task and 3,072MB for the reduce task, which is roughly 75 percent of the container size for the map and reduce tasks. There's no hard and fast rule for sizing the JVM heap size—in general, an allocation of two-thirds or three-fourths of the container size for the JVM will do the trick.

Configuring the Virtual Memory for Map and Reduce Tasks

The Java heap size settings shown in the previous section configure the maximum size of the physical RAM that map and reduce tasks can use. You can also set the maximum virtual memory (physical memory + paged memory) that a map or a reduce task can use. The `yarn.nodemanager.vmem-pmem-ratio` parameter (in the yarn-site.xml file) lets you configure the ratio of the physical to virtual memory, as shown here:

```
<property>
    <name>yarn.nodemanager.vmem-pmem-ratio</name>
    <value>3.1</value>
</property>
```

The default value of the `yarn.nodemanager.vmem-pmem-ratio` is 2.1, meaning that both the map and reduce containers can be allocated virtual memory that's up to 2.1 times the size of the physical memory you allocate for these two tasks. For example, since we set the value of the `mapreduce.map.memory.mb` parameter to 2048, the total virtual memory allowed for a map task will be 2.1x2,048=4,300MB. Similarly, the maximum virtual memory allowed for a reduce job will be 2.1 X 3,072=6,451MB.

If a map or reduce task exceeds its physical memory, the NodeManager will kill the task due to memory oversubscription, and you'll see a message similar to the following n the log file:

```
Current usage: 2.1gb of 2.0gb physical memory used; 1.6gb of 3.15gb virtual memory
used. Killing
container.
```

The two YARN parameters `yarn.nodemanager.pmem-check-enabled` and `yarn.nodemanager.vmem-check-enabled` determine whether physical memory and virtual memory limits are enforced for containers. By default, the value for both of these parameters is `true`, meaning that both limits are enforced.

Configuring Memory for the ApplicationMaster and the NodeManager

Now that you know how to configure the container size for map and reduce tasks, there's one more configuration item left—it's the sizing of the ApplicationMaster container. It's extremely important that you configure the ApplicationMaster memory carefully to suit your cluster's processing requirements.

Each application requires the spawning of a single ApplicationMaster container. Applications with smaller amounts of data can get by with sizing the ApplicationMaster container at 1 or 2GB. For larger applications, it's wise to configure this container with a larger size, as shown here:

```
<property>
  <name>yarn.app.mapreduce.am.resource.mb</value>
  <value>3072</value>
</property>

<property>
  <name>yarn.app.mapreduce.am.command-opts</value>
  <value>-Xmx2364m</value>
</property>
```

The first parameter, `yarn.app.mapreduce.am.resource.mb`, sets the size of the ApplicationMaster container—it's the amount of memory the ApplicationMaster needs. The second parameter, `yarn.app.mapreduce.am.command-opts`, sets the size of the JVM that runs the ApplicationMaster code. The default size of the JVM is 1GB, so the parameter's default value appears as `-Xmx1024m`. If you want to enable verbose garbage collection (GC) logging to a file under the /tmp directory and set the maximum size of the Java heap to 1GB, here's how you set this parameter:

```
-Xmx1024m-verbose:gc -Xloggc:/tmp@taskid@gc
```

In this example, `@taskid` is replaced by the current TaskID and the logging is done to a file named for the task under the /tmp directory.

You can also optionally set the `yarn.app.mapreduce.am.admin-command-opts` parameter to configure the Java opts for the MapReduce ApplicationMaster process for administrative purposes, and the default value is 0, meaning that it isn't set by default.

As with the map and reduce containers, you can also configure the number of virtual CPU cores for the ApplicationMaster process. The parameter you need to set for this is `yarn.app.mapreduce.am.resource.cpu-vcores`, and its default value is 1.

> **Note**
>
> As with all Hadoop parameters, if you don't explicitly include a parameter in the corresponding site.xml file, the values from the default configuration file will apply (yarn-default.xml in this case).

A Summary of the Memory-Related Configuration Properties

So many memory-related parameters, so much to remember! I think it's a good idea to capture all our memory related configuration parameters in one place, so you can refer to it during your cluster configuration exercises. Table 18.1 shows each of the configuration options that allow you to tweak Hadoop memory, the configuration file in which you set them, and the default values for each of the memory parameters.

Figure 18.1 shows the relationship between the total memory you allocate for all containers on a node through the `yarn.nodemanager.resource.memory-mb` parameter and how the map and reduce JVMs derive their memory from the map and reduce container's memory. The difference between the map or reduce container memory size and the size of the map or reduce JVM is allocated to handling the container's overhead.

Table 18.1 **Hadoop Memory-Related Configuration Priorities**

Configuration Option	Default Value	Configuration file
mapreduce.map.java.opts	-Xmx768m	mapred-site.xml
mapreduce.reduce.java.opts	-Xmx768m	mapred-site.xm
mapreduce.map.memory.mb	1024m	mapred-site.xml
mapreduce.reduce.memory.mb	1024m	mapred-site.xml
yarn.app.mapreduce.am.resource.mb	1536m	mapred-site.xml
yarn.scheduler.minimum-allocation-mb	1024m	yarn-site.xml
yarn.scheduler.maximum-allocation-mb	8192m	yarn-site.xml
yarn.nodemanager.resource.memory-mb	8192m	yarn-site.xml

Suppose you set the value of the `mapred.map.memory.mb` parameter to 1024 (actually the default value). Let's say you set the `mapreduce.map.java.opts` parameter to `-Xmx800m`. The NodeManager allocates a container sized 1,024MB to the map task and launches a JVM for the map task with the maximum heap size of 800MB. The difference between the container size of 1GB and the JVM size of 800MB, which is 224MB, is used for overhead, for things such as native libraries, permanent generation space and so on.

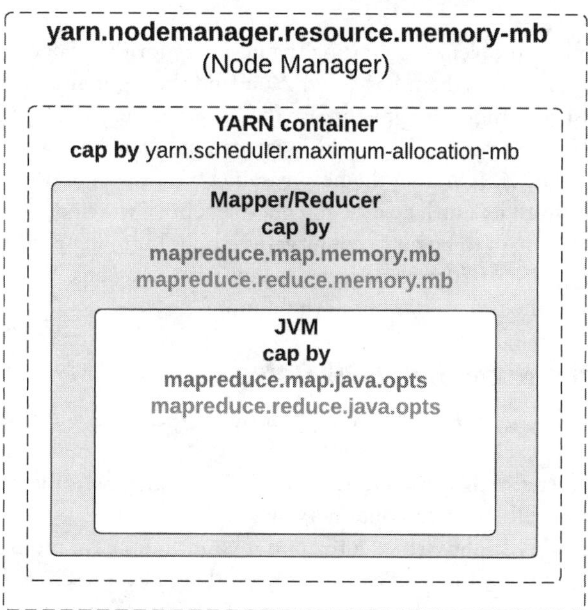

Figure 18.1 Relationship between the map and reduce container memory and the map and reduce JVM memory

You can monitor the actual memory usage of a map or reduce task during a job run with the MapReduce task counters explained in the section "Hadoop Counters" in this chapter. The following counters provide a snapshot of the memory usage that helps you understand memory utilization during the task execution:

- PHYSICAL_MEMORY_BYTES
- VIRTUAL_MEMORY_BYTES
- COMMITTED_HEAP_BYTES

Once a MapReduce job completes executing, it'll dump a bunch of job counters. You can view the counters on the screen or in the job's log or view them in the Resource-Manager web UI. The following memory-related counters show the physical and virtual memory allocation for the job:

```
Physical memory (bytes) snapshot=21850116096
Virtual memory (bytes) snapshot=40047247360
Total committed heap usage (bytes)=22630105088
```

When a YARN container grows beyond the heap size you've configured with the `mapreduce.map.java.opts` or the `mapreduce.reduce.java.opts` paraameter, the map or reduce task will fail with the following error message:

```
"Container [pid=12878, containerID=container_1840146564231_0002_01_001809]
 is running beyond physical memory limits. Current usage: 2.0 GB of 2.0 GB
physical memory used; 3.1 GB of 12.5 GB virtual memory used. Killing
container."
```

The way to fix this problem is by raising the heap size for the map or reduce container, depending on which one of them has failed. You find the right amount to increase by trial and error. Just remember that if you raise the heap size very high, of course it'll help the task succeed but at great cost to you since you can now launch fewer map and reduce containers in your cluster. If you set the heap parameters at the cluster level, every change is magnified in terms of its impact, since all containers in all the nodes will use the same settings. Therefore, it pays to be quite conservative about bumping up the heap memory. Keep incrementing it by 10-20 percent each time until the task runs. You want to allocate enough memory for the task to run but nothing more.

Configuring the Number of CPU Cores

As with the memory configuration, you can configure the node-wide limit for the allocation of virtual cores. That setting is configured with the `yarn.nodemanager.resource.cpu-vcores` parameter in the yarn-site.xml file. This parameter sets the maximum number of vcores that can be allocated to containers on a node.

The default setting is eight virtual cores, and if your nodes have more cores, you need to bump the value of this parameter accordingly—otherwise, YARN will use only eight virtual cores at any time, regardless of how many CPU cores the node has! Once you configure the maximum vcores per node, you can configure the following two parameters, which set the minimum and maximum allocation of virtual cores for each container request made to the ResourceManager:

- `yarn.scheduler.minimum-allocation-vcores`
- `yarn.scheduler.maximum-allocation-vcores`

The `yarn.nodemanager.resource.cpu-vcores` parameter configures the maximum virtual cores per node. In addition, you can also configure (or accept the default values) of the number of virtual cores to request for each map and reduce task. The following parameters allow you to set the number of virtual cores allotted to each map and reduce task:

- `mapreduce.map.cpu.vcores`
- `mapreduce.reduce.cpu.vcores`

The default value for both parameters is one.

Relationship between Memory and CPU Vcores

If you have plenty of free memory and thus have the ability to create many more containers, do remember that each of the containers needs a CPU to run. So, the cluster's real ceiling for running containers may be limited to the sum of the CPUs on all the nodes. This is why it's important to ensure that you not only acquire servers with plenty of RAM, but also enough CPUs to run the tasks.

You might also be wondering at this point what would happen if a user runs a job that requires thousands of map and reduce containers. That user may keep other jobs from running until the user finishes processing his or her job. Fortunately, that's not the case in a real life cluster, where users routinely submit jobs requiring tens of thousands and even hundreds of thousands of containers when the cluster's capacity is capped at only a thousand or so containers.

Both of Hadoop's schedulers, the Fair Scheduler and the Capacity Scheduler, ensure that multiple jobs can share the cluster and hence its containers simultaneously through a judicious allocation of available resources among competing applications. Refer to Chapter 13, "Resource Allocation in a Hadoop Cluster," for the details of how each of the two available Hadoop resource schedulers achieves this goal.

Configuring Efficient Performance

You can improve performance through appropriate configuration of several Hadoop properties that pertain to various areas such as speculative execution. Let's review the most important ways in which you can improve performance, from the cluster point of view.

Speculative Execution

It's not uncommon to experience failing or slow hardware, software misconfiguration and random delays on specific nodes in a cluster that lead to a general slowdown in the entire cluster, also called the stragglers problem. Hadoop attempts to take care of this problem with its **speculative execution** feature, which lets the same task be executed simultaneously on different nodes, by tagging the task that completes first as the successful task and killing the other task.

In general, since MapReduce task processing is designed to be idempotent, it's safe to use speculative execution and by default speculative execution is enabled. However, in cases such as where a job calls on external resources, you may need to disable speculative execution. You can enable/disable speculative execution independently for map and reduce processes with the following parameters:

- `mapreduce.map.speculative`: The default value of this parameter is `true`, which means that Hadoop may execute multiple instances of some map tasks in parallel.
- `mapreduce.reduce.speculative`: The default value of this parameter is `true`, which means that Hadoop may execute multiple instances of some reduce tasks in parallel.

So, speculative execution for both map and reduce tasks is enabled by default and you can disable it by setting the two parameters shown here to the value `false`.

The causes for slow execution on a task are hard to determine, since the tasks do complete successfully after taking a long time to finish. Under speculative execution of tasks, Hadoop simply determines that a task is running much slower than what it expects and launches a copy of the same task as a backup. This happens in cases such as when one of the disks is performing poorly due to a faulty disk controller. The job has 50 reducers and 49 of them have completed fast, but the entire job waits on the last reducer, which is working with data stored on the slow disk.

You can fine tune speculative execution by setting the maximum and minimum number of tasks that can be executed at any time. Here are the parameters that you can configure to fine tune speculative execution:

- `mapreduce.job.speculative.speculative-cap-running-tasks`: Sets the maximum percentage of running jobs that can be simultaneously executed at any given time. The default is 0.1.
- `mapreduce.job.speculative.speculative-cap-total-tasks`: Limits the maximum percentage of all tasks that you can simultaneously execute at any time. The default is 0.01.
- `mapreduce.job.speculative.minimum-allowed-tasks`: Sets the minimum number of tasks that can be speculatively executed at any time. The default value is 10 (tasks).
- `mapreduce.job.speculative.slowtaskthreshold`: Sets the number of standard deviations by which a task's average progress rates must be below the average progress of all other running tasks for deeming the task as "too slow" and thus eligible for speculative execution.

Individual tasks run in isolation from each other and trust Hadoop to deliver the correct inputs. Therefore, the system can process the same input multiple times to take care of slow-running tasks. As the number of tasks in a job dwindles down, Hadoop schedules copies of the remaining map tasks across nodes that have plenty of processing capacity—this is the essence of speculative execution. When each task completes, it reports to the ResourceManager, and the copy of the task finishing first becomes the definitive copy for that task. Hadoop then instructs the ResourceManager to kill the other tasks and abandon their output. The reducers receive their input from the map process that completes successfully first.

Here's a snippet from a task log when speculative execution is in force. Hadoop kills the job attempt attempt_1432039974837_0172_r_000002_1 because another job for the same task, attempt_1432039974837_0172_r_000002_0, succeeded first:

```
attempt_1432039974837_0172_r_000002_1   0.00  KILLED  NEW  N/A N/A
     N/A N/A
     0sec   Speculation: attempt_1432039974837_0172_r_000002_0 succeeded first!
```

Deprecated Configuration Parameters

As Hadoop goes through revisions, and with newer releases coming out regularly, many configuration properties are modified or dropped. It's therefore a good idea both during the initial configuration of your cluster and later during performance tuning to keep the list of all deprecated configuration parameters in front of you as you ponder which parameters to use or modify. You can review all the currently deprecated parameters by going to the following site in the Hadoop 2 documentation:

`http://hadoop.apache.org/docs/r2.7.1/hadoop-project-dist/hadoop-common/DeprecatedProperties.html`

Sometimes you can get away with using a deprecated parameter in a new release, but it's a good practice not to do so. After all, there are good reasons for putting a parameter in the deprecated parameter list! Often the deprecated properties have been replaced with new and improved parameters, or they just have become obsolete in a new release. Many parameters well known to Hadoop users such as `mapred.reuse.jvm.num.tasks` and `mapred.hosts.exclude` are now in the list of deprecated parameters.

Configuring JVM Reuse

Each map and reduce task runs inside a single JVM. If you have a larger number of map/reduce tasks running, the initialization of the JVMs for all those tasks could prove expensive to the cluster in terms of both the time it takes to initiate the JVMs and higher resource usage. Each MapReduce job is executed inside a separate JVM process, which is forked by the ResourceManager. Creating JVMs is expensive in terms of the overhead. By default, each task uses a dedicated JVM, and when the task completes, its JVM is killed by the ResourceManager. Thus, the number of JVMs spawned for a job is equal to the number of tasks.

You can tell Hadoop to reuse the JVMs by not killing them after a map or reduce task completes. Use the parameter `mapreduce.job.jvm.numtasks` to specify how many tasks can reuse the same JVM. You configure the parameter `mapreduce.job.jvm.numtasks` in the mapred-site.xml file, as shown here:

```
<property>
  <name>mapreduce.job.jvm.numtasks</name>
  <value>2</value>
</property>
```

Initializing new JVMs is resource intensive, especially when you have a large number of tasks running in your cluster. You can optimize by reusing JVMs so they can run multiple tasks sequentially.

The `mapreduce.job.jvm.numtasks` parameter applies to tasks in general, regardless of whether they're map or reduce tasks. In this example, the value of the `mapreduce.job.jvm.numtasks` parameter is 2, meaning that the JVM can run two tasks instead of the default single task. The default value for this parameter is 1, meaning a dedicated JVM is required for reach map/reduce task, and there's no JVM reuse. Note that if you set the value to -1, the JVM can run an unlimited number of tasks. Obviously you don't want to do this, since that means all tasks will run in the same JVM!

Hadoop runs the JVMs for all the map and reduce tasks in isolation. If your map or reduce method takes just a few seconds, spawning a fresh JVM for each map/reduce task is overkill, due to the long initialization process for the JVM to kick in.

JVM Reuse and HotSpot

Hotspot can find the sections of the code where it can convert the Java byte code into native machine code. Hotspot can do this if you can run your code on JVM for a long time. When you reuse JVMs, Hotspot builds the mission-critical sections into native machine code to improve its performance. Long-running tasks benefit from this optimization.

JVM reuse can lead to significant improvements in performance—try it out!

Reducing the I/O Load on the System

Operations performed in memory are many times faster than those performed on disk. During MR processing, intermediate data needs to be sorted. Ideally, sorting is done in the memory buffer for the map/reduce task, which is contained within its JVM heap, as configured in the parameters `mapred.map.java.opts` and `mapred.reduce.java.opts`. If the buffer size is too small, there'll be intermediate spills to disk which will have to be read and merged later on. Here are the configuration parameters you can set to reduce, or even eliminate, the amount of spillage to disk, and thus reduce the I/O load in your cluster.

- `mapreduce.task.io.sort.mb`: You can configure the total amount of buffer memory to use while sorting files (in MB), with this parameter. The default value is 100MB. Each merge stream is given 1MB by default, to minimize seeks. You can raise the default setting of 100MB to up to a quarter or half of the map/reduce Java heap size.

- `mapreduce.task.io.sort.factor`: This parameter determines how many streams to merge at the same time during the sorting of files by either a map or a reduce task. The default value is 10. Higher values mean Hadoop requires fewer passes to merge the map spills, which of course means lower disk I/O.

You may think that raising the value of the `mapreduce.task.io.sort.factor` parameter will always be a good strategy since the more input files that are merged at once, the fewer will be the passes that are required to merge the map spills. However, the merged data is placed in the memory buffer that you configure with the `mapreduce.task.io.sort.mb` parameter. If you keep increasing the sort factor, the size of the I/O chunk will keep getting smaller, meaning the cluster will perform more small I/O requests to read the data. This isn't good for performance, so the general recommendation is to leave the sort factor at its default value of 10MB.

Tuning Map and Reduce Tasks—What the Administrator Can Do

Developers are in charge of coding applications, and I do have a list of things they can try to do to improve the performance of MapReduce jobs. However, administrators can also help in improving performance of these jobs by doing several things, as summarized in the following sections.

The performances of any Hadoop tasks, including MapReduce tasks, are impacted by various sources, such as

- The storage, CPU, memory and network configuration and their status
- The code of the map and reduce tasks
- Settings of Hadoop's performance-related configuration properties

Chapter 17, "Monitoring, Metrics and Hadoop Logging," discusses monitoring and evaluating the resources available to Hadoop. In this chapter, we'll discuss more efficient coding strategies for map and reduce tasks, as well as configuring Hadoop's performance-related properties.

Before we can actually get to the brass tacks of performance tuning of MapReduce processing, we need to understand how to measure Hadoop's performance. Benchmarks, which we explain later in this chapter, are one way to figure out how efficiently the cluster is processing a set of test data that you generate. However, benchmarks are limited—TeraSort, after all, benchmarks only sort performance. As we'll discuss later, Hadoop's job counters are a significant source of performance tuning and troubleshooting information. In our discussion of the tuning of map and reduce tasks, we'll make liberal use of these job counters.

An easy way to get to all the Hadoop job counters is by using the ResourceManager Job UI. Click on Counters in the job's main page to view the Hadoop job counters.

Both map and reduce tasks consist of clear steps or phases. In order to tune the map and reduce tasks, you need to understand how Hadoop steps through these phases.

In the following sections, you'll learn how to tune map and reduce tasks separately, paying attention to the individual steps of both tasks.

Tuning the Map Tasks

There are several phases to a map task. In order to understand why a job is running slowly, you need to understand the phases of a map task execution. Here's a summary of the successive phases of a map task.

1. The **read** phase: In this phase, the map task reads the input data, with the read size being the same as the Hadoop block size you've configured, such as 256MB, for example. For this phase, you need to look at the total duration of the read phase and also how much data each map task reads.
2. The **map** phase: During this phase, Hadoop maps the data. In this phase, you need to look at the total number of processed records and the average execution time per record. Checking input record sizes across the map tasks will reveal the presence of skewed data, which could delay the final job.
3. The **spill** phase: In this phase, Hadoop sorts the intermediate data and partitions it for the various reduce tasks and writes the intermediate data to disk. You need to look at the total time taken by the spill phase.
4. The **merge** phase: The different spill files are merged into a single spill file for each reduce task. You need to review the time taken for the merge step.

Before we start discussing the key factors affecting map and reduce tasks, first let's understand the importance of task locality.

Data Locality

Data locality is critical to a MapReduce job and its map/reduce tasks. In the listing of the job counters shown in the "Job Counters" section in this chapter, you can find key locality-related counters. For example, a MapReduce job may have a total of 64 map tasks and 8 reduce tasks. Here's how the tasks break down in terms of their locality:

- Launched map tasks: 64
- Launched reduce tasks: 8
- Rack-local map tasks: 10
- Data-local map tasks: 54

Hadoop likes to assign tasks to the NodeManagers on nodes where the required input data is located. If the data needs to be transferred from other nodes to the computing node, Hadoop incurs an extra network cost to stream the data over. Ideally, all your jobs will be data-local map tasks, where the data is available right on the same node where the processing occurs. The next best thing of course is rack-local map tasks, which get the data from other nodes in the same rack. Tasks that aren't local to either the data or the rack involve the most cost in terms of network transfers of data.

Tuning map tasks means tuning the various phases of a map task, paying attention to the phases that are consuming a lot of time. You can tune some aspects of the map tasks by tuning various map-programming techniques. You can also tune the maps by tweaking the Hadoop map-related configuration parameters. We'll discuss the programming techniques later in this chapter. Let's first look at what you, as an administrator, can manage to do to improve the performance of the map tasks.

Input and Output

Configuring appropriate input and output strategies goes a long way toward making jobs run faster. You can, for example, configure compression at multiple levels for a MapReduce job—during the input stage, the intermediate stages and, finally, in how the output is presented. Any steps you take to perform more efficient input and output will reduce both disk and network I/O and speed up jobs.

The Input Split Size

Input splits govern MapReduce data processing. The number of mapper tasks is based on how many input splits Hadoop calculates for a job. Each map task thus determined is assigned to a DataNode where the input split is stored. Hadoop (through the ResourceManager) does its best to process the input splits locally where possible.

The MapReduce counters reveal the average number of input bytes for a map task. You can also find the size of the HDFS input files by going to the HDFS DFS Home at this location: `http://machinename:50070/dfshealth.jsp`. Click Browse the File System to view the file sizes and their replication factor, as well as the HDFS block size of the files. If you've configured a block size of 512MB for HDFS, and the files are all sized 1MB, obviously you have input data made up of numerous small files.

Hadoop is meant, basically, for batch processing vast amounts of data. Therefore, ideally, you should be running mostly large and medium MR jobs in your cluster, rather than a large number of tiny MR jobs. Instead of running thousands of small jobs, you should consolidate them into a few large jobs and process more data at a time, thus increasing performance. A key goal here should be to designate each MR job to process at least several gigabytes of data.

As I explained in Chapter 10, "Data Protection, File Formats and Accessing HDFS," Hadoop doesn't work very well with very small files, as it leads to inefficiencies in processing. You need a large number of processes to process the small files, which takes up a lot of resources, besides slowing down your job. Of course, small files also have a deleterious impact on the efficiency of the NameNode, as explained in Chapter 9. Again, you can use several strategies to fix the "small files problem":

- Consolidate several small files into a large file.
- Use Hadoop archive (HAR) files.
- Create container files with something like Avro, to serialize the input data.

If, on the other hand, the input bytes for each map task are much larger than the HDFS block size, it means that Hadoop is unable to split the input file. As you can recall from Chapter 10, compression codecs such as gzip aren't splittable.

Output

Using compression for MapReduce output, as described in Chapter 5, "Running Applications in a Cluster—The MapReduce Framework (and Hive and Pig)," will enhance the write performance of HDFS. As Chapter 10 explains, choosing the proper file format is very important, especially for the output of the reduce tasks. Since zlib/gzip/lzo files can't be split, MapReduce is forced to use a single map to process an entire file. File formats such as SequenceFiles are more efficient since they are compressible and splittable.

When dealing with large individual output files, it's a good idea to use larger block sizes (`dfs.block.size`). The output goal should be to emit a few large files, with each file covering several HDFS blocks and compressed as well. Note that the number of output files is the same as the number of reduces.

Compression

Compressing intermediate map output (see Shuffle) improves performance by reducing network traffic between the map and reduce processes. A compression codec such as lzo provides decent compression ratios while consuming a low amount of CPU.

Compressing the final reduce output means applications can benefit. Both zlib and Gzip are good choices in most cases due to the high compression ratio they offer at a decent speed. Compressing your data leads to significant performance enhancements. Remember that MR jobs typically deal with data multiple times—they load data from external storage into memory and also write the results of reduce tasks to disk. Data is also sometimes copied over the network from remote nodes. Both disk I/O and network I/O are expensive operations, and compressing your data leads to significant improvements in performance, as explained in Chapter 10. You can set various configuration parameters such as `mapred.compress.map.output` (for configuring the map output) to efficiently process data.

Tuning the Map Phase

During the map phase, the map tasks write data to the local file system. The tasks generate intermediate data, which they first store inside a memory buffer before spilling it to disk. The following configuration parameters (to be set in the mapred-site.xml file) have a bearing on the spill size and how many times the map task may spill data to disk:

- `mapreduce.task.io.sort.mb`: The amount of memory (in MB) to use (determines the size of the memory buffer) during the sorting of files. The default value is 100MB.
- `mapreduce.task.io.sort.factor`: The number of merge threads to merge at once during file sorting. The default value is 10 streams.

- `mapreduce.map.sort.spill.percent`: The extent to which the buffer can fill before its contents are spilled to disk. The default threshold is 0.80.

The memory buffer for the intermediate data output is part of the map task's memory allocation, set by the `mapreduce.map.memory.mb` parameter. As you will recall, the RAM you allocate for the map task contains both JVM and overhead, with the JVM's size based on the value of the configuration parameter `mapreduce.map.java.opts`. The memory buffer is part of the map's JVM heap space.

Once the size of the contents inside the map's memory buffer reach the threshold set by the `mapreduce.map.sort.spill.percent` parameter (default is 80 percent), the map task flushes the buffer's contents to the local disk system, a process also referred to as spilling.

Ideally, the map intermediate records should be spilt to disk just one time. If the spill is occurring more than once, it indicates inefficient processing, since reading from disk is much slower than reading from memory. You can check the number of spills by looking at the following two counters under the MapReduce Framework counter group:

- Spilled Records
- Map Record Outputs

In one of our completed jobs in my cluster, both of these counters have the same value—65,526,585. This is good as it means the data was spilt only once to disk.

> **Note**
>
> If there are no reduce tasks in a job, the map tasks won't have any output they need to spill to disk. In this case, the counters for all the map tasks will show a value of 0.

In another one of my jobs, the following is how the map output and spilled record counters stack up:

```
Spilled Records        : 19988312
Map Record Outputs     :  9994156
```

I can confirm that there were multiple spills to disk during this task by reviewing the task's logs, also viewable through the ResourceManager web UI (I tell you—this is your best friend for troubleshooting and tuning Hadoop jobs!):

```
2016-07-12:06:56,353 INFO [main] org.apache.hadoop.mapred.MapTask: Spilling map output
2016-07-12:06:56,353 INFO [main] org.apache.hadoop.mapred.MapTask: kvstart =
95251456(381005824); kvend = 79076168(316304672); length = 16175289/33554432
2016-07-12:08:22,675 INFO [SpillThread] org.apache.hadoop.mapred.MapTask:
Finished spill 1
2016-07-12:08:25,184 INFO [main] com.sabre.bigdata.ssi.mapper.CsvToAvroMapper:
Closing mapper...
2016-07-12:08:25,191 INFO [main] org.apache.hadoop.mapred.MapTask: Starting flush
of map output
2016-07-12:08:25,191 INFO [main] org.apache.hadoop.mapred.MapTask: Spilling map output
2016-07-12:08:25,191 INFO [main] org.apache.hadoop.mapred.MapTask: bufstart =
225137891; bufend = 397124345; bufvoid = 536870912
```

```
2016-07-12:08:25,191 INFO [main] org.apache.hadoop.mapred.MapTask: kvstart =
56284468(225137872); kvend = 48657712(194630848); length = 7626757/33554432
2016-07-12:09:07,150 INFO [main] org.apache.hadoop.mapred.MapTask:
Finished spill 2
...
```

The log file for the map task reveals that there were indeed two separate spills—this job is a good candidate for tweaking the size of the Hadoop sort-related parameters that I listed earlier in this section. Spilling to disk more than once is suboptimal, and you can avoid this in two different ways: You can raise the value of the `mapreduce.map.sort.spill.percent` parameter if it's too low (in my case it's already high at 80 percent, so not much there) or you can bump up the value of the parameter `mapreduce.task.io.sort.mb`. In this example, I can raise it to a value of 200MB or 400MB, to get rid of the extra disk spill.

When you raise this parameter's value, it's a good idea to also raise the related parameter `mapreduce.task.io.sort.factor`. If you're doubling the value of the `mapreduce.task.io.sort.mb` parameter, also double the value of the `mapreduce.task.io.sort.factor` parameter. In general, try to keep the latter parameter's value to about a tenth of the first parameter's value, which is what it is when you use the default values for the two parameters.

Tuning the Reduce Tasks

As with the map tasks, reduce tasks involve multiple phases, with the length of each phase depending on the configuration settings as well as the amount of data the tasks need to process. Following are the three major phases of a reduce task.

- The **shuffle** (and merge) phase: The shuffle process fetches the intermediate data generated by the map phase. You need to be concerned with the total time it takes to transfer intermediate data from the map tasks to the reduce tasks and also to merge and sort the data.
- The **reduce** phase: This is the phase that uses a custom reduce function that's applied to the input key and its values. During this phase, each reduce task is assigned a part of the map task's intermediate output data. The reduce task fetches from each map task the content of this part of the output. You need to measure the total time for the reduce phase to evaluate the efficacy of this phase.
- The **write** phase: The final phase of a reduce task is writing the reduce output to HDFS.

In the ResourceManager web UI, drill down to the page that lists all the reduce tasks for a job, as shown in Figure 18.2. A reduce task has three components—shuffle, sort (merge) and the reduce function itself.

For example, if you take the first reduce task, its elapsed time is shown as 5 minutes, 36 seconds. (You can identify a reduce task by the "r" in a task's name, which is task_1448106546957_4596_**r**_000001 in this example. A map task will have a "m" inside its

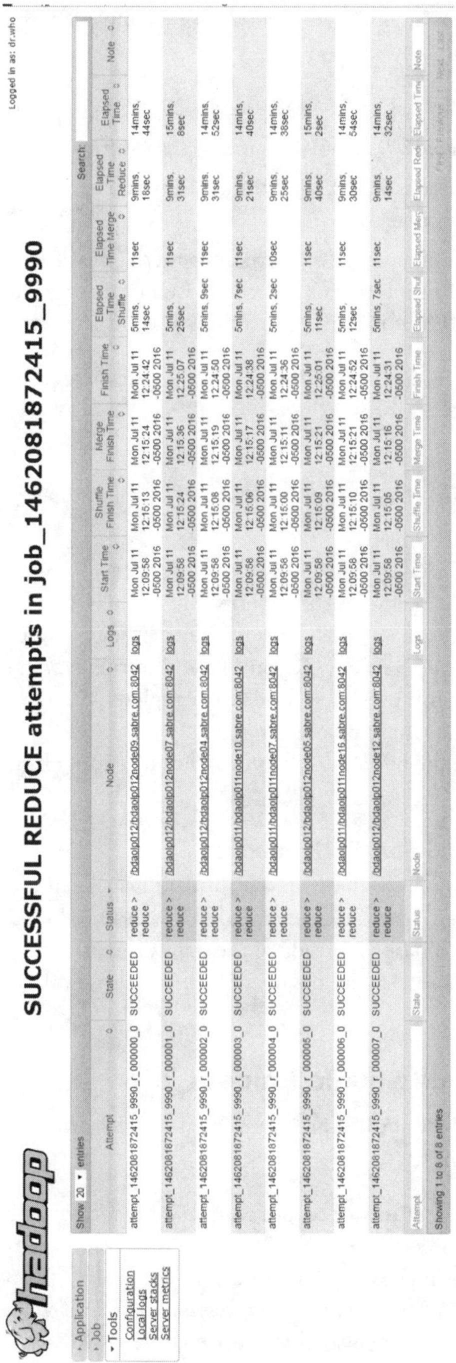

Attempt	State	Status	Node	Logs	Start Time	Shuffle Finish Time	Merge Finish Time	Finish Time	Elapsed Time Shuffle	Elapsed Time Merge	Elapsed Time Reduce	Elapsed Time	Note
attempt_1462081872415_9990_r_000000_0	SUCCEEDED	reduce > reduce	/bdaolp012/bdaolp012node09.sabre.com:8042	logs	Mon Jul 11 12:09:58 -0500 2016	Mon Jul 11 12:15:13 -0500 2016	Mon Jul 11 12:15:24 -0500 2016	Mon Jul 11 12:24:42 -0500 2016	5mins, 14sec	11sec	9mins, 18sec	14mins, 44sec	
attempt_1462081872415_9990_r_000001_0	SUCCEEDED	reduce > reduce	/bdaolp012/bdaolp012node07.sabre.com:8042	logs	Mon Jul 11 12:09:58 -0500 2016	Mon Jul 11 12:15:24 -0500 2016	Mon Jul 11 12:15:36 -0500 2016	Mon Jul 11 12:25:07 -0500 2016	5mins, 25sec	11sec	9mins, 31sec	15mins, 8sec	
attempt_1462081872415_9990_r_000002_0	SUCCEEDED	reduce > reduce	/bdaolp012/bdaolp012node04.sabre.com:8042	logs	Mon Jul 11 12:09:58 -0500 2016	Mon Jul 11 12:15:08 -0500 2016	Mon Jul 11 12:15:19 -0500 2016	Mon Jul 11 12:24:50 -0500 2016	5mins, 9sec	11sec	9mins, 31sec	14mins, 52sec	
attempt_1462081872415_9990_r_000003_0	SUCCEEDED	reduce > reduce	/bdaolp011/bdaolp011node10.sabre.com:8042	logs	Mon Jul 11 12:09:58 -0500 2016	Mon Jul 11 12:15:06 -0500 2016	Mon Jul 11 12:15:17 -0500 2016	Mon Jul 11 12:24:38 -0500 2016	5mins, 7sec	11sec	9mins, 21sec	14mins, 40sec	
attempt_1462081872415_9990_r_000004_0	SUCCEEDED	reduce > reduce	/bdaolp011/bdaolp011node07.sabre.com:8042	logs	Mon Jul 11 12:09:58 -0500 2016	Mon Jul 11 12:15:00 -0500 2016	Mon Jul 11 12:15:11 -0500 2016	Mon Jul 11 12:24:36 -0500 2016	5mins, 2sec	10sec	9mins, 25sec	14mins, 38sec	
attempt_1462081872415_9990_r_000005_0	SUCCEEDED	reduce > reduce	/bdaolp012/bdaolp012node05.sabre.com:8042	logs	Mon Jul 11 12:09:58 -0500 2016	Mon Jul 11 12:15:09 -0500 2016	Mon Jul 11 12:15:21 -0500 2016	Mon Jul 11 12:25:01 -0500 2016	5mins, 11sec	11sec	9mins, 40sec	15mins, 2sec	
attempt_1462081872415_9990_r_000006_0	SUCCEEDED	reduce > reduce	/bdaolp011/bdaolp011node16.sabre.com:8042	logs	Mon Jul 11 12:09:58 -0500 2016	Mon Jul 11 12:15:10 -0500 2016	Mon Jul 11 12:15:21 -0500 2016	Mon Jul 11 12:24:52 -0500 2016	5mins, 12sec	11sec	9mins, 30sec	14mins, 54sec	
attempt_1462081872415_9990_r_000007_0	SUCCEEDED	reduce > reduce	/bdaolp012/bdaolp012node12.sabre.com:8042	logs	Mon Jul 11 12:09:58 -0500 2016	Mon Jul 11 12:15:05 -0500 2016	Mon Jul 11 12:15:16 -0500 2016	Mon Jul 11 12:24:31 -0500 2016	5mins, 7sec	11sec	9mins, 14sec	14mins, 32sec	

Figure 18.2 The reduce tasks for a job, showing the time elapsed for the various stages

name, as in task_1448106546957_4596_**m**_000001, for example.) In this case, here's how the total elapsed time breaks down:

- The Start Time for the task task_1448106546957_4596_r_000001 is 10.10.50.
- The Shuffle Finish Time is 10.12.46. This means the shuffle took 1 minute, 56 seconds.
- The Merge Finish Time is 10.12.59. This means that the merge (sort) part of the reduce task took 13 seconds.
- The Finish Time for the task is 10.16.25. This means that the third and final part of the Reduce task (running the actual reduce function as well as writing the final reduce output to HDFS) consumed 3 minutes and 26 seconds.

As mentioned earlier, the total elapsed time for this map task is 5 minutes and 35 seconds (335 seconds), which is broken into:

- Shuffle: 116 seconds
- Merge: 13 seconds
- Reduce: 206 seconds

Breaking down the reduce tasks in the manner shown here and being familiar with the benchmark numbers for the various states of the task helps you evaluate the performance of a job's tasks on any given day. If you know that the average shuffle and reduce phase usually take so many minutes or seconds to complete, you can see if the tasks are unusually slow during one of these phases.

Let's see how to improve the reduce task performance by tuning how the task performs during its various phases.

Enhancing the Shuffle and Sort Performance

During the shuffle and sort phase, the map output data is merged into a single reduce input file and sorted by a key, and becomes the input for the reducer task. A good way to tune the shuffle and sort phase is to reduce the data on which the reduce tasks needs to perform a sort merge. Compressing data, using combiners, and filtering data also helps with this.

Tuning the MapReduce Shuffle Process

You can tune the MapReduce shuffle process with the following configuration parameters in the mapred-site.xml file:

- `mapreduce.reduce.shuffle.merge.percent`: The usage threshold at which an in-memory merge will be initiated, expressed as a percentage of the total memory allocated to storing in-memory map outputs (as defined by the `mapreduce.reduce.shuffle.input.buffer.percent` parameter). The default value is 0.66. When this threshold is reached, the available shuffle contents in memory are merged into a single file.

- `mapreduce.reduce.shuffle.input.buffer.percent`: The percentage of memory to be allocated from the reducer's heap memory to storing intermediate outputs copied from multiple mappers during the shuffle. The default value is 0.70.
- `mapreduce.reduce.input.buffer.percent`: The percentage of memory (relative to the maximum heap size) to retain map outputs during the reduce stage. When the shuffle is concluded, any remaining map outputs in memory must consume less than this threshold before the reduce task can begin. The default value is 0.0.
- `mapreduce.reduce.shuffle.memory.limit.percent`: Maximum percentage of the in-memory limit (set by the `mapreduce.reduce.shuffle.input.buffer.percent` parameter) that a single shuffle (that is, the output copied from a single map task) can consume. The default value is 0.25. If the shuffle size is above this, it'll be written to disk on the server where the reduce task runs.
- `mapreduce.map.sort.spill`: Controls the spill process. Once this limit is reached in the buffer, its contents will be spilled to disk. The default value is 0.8.

Tuning the Sort

Ensure there's sufficient memory for the sort buffer, so the map-side sorts are fast. You can see dramatic performance improvements by making sure most of the map output is stored in the map's sort buffer. Remember that you must have sufficient heap memory in the map's JVM for this. You must ensure that the JVM heap size is large enough to hold the map task's input and output records in memory.

Enhancing the Performance of the Reduce Phase

The reduce phase involves a lot of data transfers between the map and reduce tasks and hence a high volume of network traffic. Hadoop offers several configuration properties to help tune the reduce process, as explained here:

- `mapreduce.reduce.shuffle.parallelcopies`: Sets the number of parallel transfers run by the reduce task during the copy (shuffle) phase. The default value is 5.
- `mapreduce.reduce.shuffle.input.buffer.percent`: Sets the percentage of memory to be allocated from the maximum heap size to the storing of map outputs during the shuffle process. The default value is 0.70.
- `mapreduce.reduce.input.buffer.percent`: Determines the percentage of memory (relative to the Java heap size) to use for retaining map outputs during the reduce process. Once the shuffle completes, any remaining map outputs in memory must consume memory under this threshold before the reduce process can begin.
- `mapreduce.shuffle.transfer.buffer.size`: Comes into play if you set the property `mapreduce.shuffle.transferTo.allowed` to `false`. This property sets the size of the buffer used in the buffer copy code for the shuffle phase. The size of this buffer will determine the size of the I/O requests. The default value for this parameter is 131072.

- mapreduce.reduce.shuffle.memory.limit.percent: Sets the maximum percentage of the in-memory limit that a single shuffle can consume. Default value is 0.25.
- mapreduce.reduce.shuffle.merge.percent: Sets the threshold for the initiation of an in-memory merge. The threshold is a percentage of the total memory allocated to the storing of in-memory map outputs by setting the mapreduce.reduce.shuffle.input.buffer.percent parameter. The default value for this parameter is 0.66.

Configuring the Reducer Initialization Time

Often, there's plenty of processing capacity in terms of the containers that YARN can launch, but the reducers don't start until almost all the map jobs have completed. You can configure the reduce tasks to start once a certain percentage of map tasks have completed. The parameter mapred.reduce.limit.completed lets you configure how soon the reduce jobs can start. The parameter mapred.reduce.slowstart.completed can range from 0 to 1 and is specified as a percentage of completed map tasks.

The default value of the mapred.reduce.slowstart.completed parameter is 0.05 (5 percent), meaning that when 5 percent of all map tasks in a job have completed, the reduce task can start. It might seem at first that a very low percentage (such as the default value of 0.05) is what you must use, since that means the reduce tasks can start early. However, there's a catch! The reduce tasks will actually ramp up by getting ready for the copy and shuffle of the intermediate output—they actually won't start. The reducers can start only after all mappers have completed, so this means that the reducers will be taking up all the containers and actually will be doing quite a bit of waiting before they can start.

By setting this property to a low value such as 0.1, for example, you make the reduce tasks start earlier. If you set a higher value than the default of 0.05, you can decrease the overlap between the mappers and reducers and let the reducers wait less time before they can start. If you set the value for this parameter very high—that is, close to 1—you're going to make the reduce tasks wait for a majority of the map tasks to complete, meaning the job takes longer to complete. Ideally you should set this parameter higher than the default, but you can arrive at the optimal value only after some experimentation, as is true of many Hadoop configuration parameters, especially those related to performance.

You set the mapred.reduce.slowstart.completed parameter in the mapred-site.xml file, as shown here:

```
<property>
   <name>mapred.reduce.slowstart.completed.maps</name>
   <value>0.05</value>
</property>
```

The parameter shown here determines the number of map tasks that should be complete before any reduce tasks are attempted. If the reduce tasks don't wait long enough you run the risk of causing the "Too many fetch-failure" errors during task attempts.

Optimizing Pig and Hive Jobs

Pig and Hive are popular processing tools, although newer tools such as Impala and Spark are gaining in prominence. Often developers are befuddled as to why their Pig or Hive job takes forever to finish, although they spent a lot of time and effort on configuring several well-known Hadoop performance-related configuration parameters, such as those relating to sorting, which you learned about earlier in this chapter. The reason for their befuddlement is that Pig and Hive have their own built in optimizations, and you need to learn how to take advantage of those optimizations to get the most out of these tools. In the following sections, I discuss:

- Optimizing Hive jobs
- Optimizing Pig jobs

Optimizing Hive Jobs

The following section discuss some strategies that enhance Hive query performance.

Use Partitioning and Bucketing

Always try to organize data into partitions so Hive can prune the data and get at the required information with far fewer seeks than when it has to read all the data in a table. Specifying the `PARTITION_BY` clause in a `CREATE TABLE` statement will partition the data.

Bucketing is another strategy that can help lower the number of processing steps and reduce the data used in join operations. You can bucket data by specifying the `CLUSTERED BY` clause when creating a table. Once you do this, each time you insert data in the bucketed table, you must set the bucketing flag, as shown here:

```
SET hive.enforce.bucketing = true;
```

To further optimize some types of queries, you can specify bucket sampling by processing only some of the data in a data set, especially when testing complex queries or during the data exploration phase. The `TABLESAMPLE` clause inside a SQL query will help you use the bucket-sampling feature.

> **Note**
>
> Hortonworks has made available a test bench for experimenting with Apache Hive at any data scale. Please see `https://github.com/hortonworks/hive-testbench` for details.

Use Parallel Execution

Often, complex Hive jobs that contain large numbers of map and reduce tasks are executed serially. You can have Hadoop run the tasks simultaneously to reduce the query execution time. Here's the parameter you set to configure parallel execution for Hive jobs:

```
SET hive.exec.parallel=true;
```

Use the ORCFILE Format

Use the ORCFILE format for the Hive tables. The ORCFILE format is much faster due to its use of optimization techniques such as predicate push down and compression of data. The following example shows how to store a table in the ORCFILE format and use compressed storage with Snappy.

```
CREATE TABLE A_ORC (customerID int, name string, age int, address string)
STORED AS ORC tblproperties ("orc.compress" = "SNAPPY");
INSERT INTO TABLE A_ORC SELECT * FROM A;
CREATE TABLE B_ORC (customerID int, role string, salary float, department string)
STORED AS ORC tblproperties ("orc.compress" = "SNAPPY");
INSERT INTO TABLE B_ORC SELECT * FROM B;
SELECT A_ORC.customerID, A_ORC.name, A_ORC.age, A_ORC.address join B_ORC
.role, B_ORC.department, B_ORC.salary ON A_ORC.customerID=B_ORC.customerID;
```

Joins that involve multiple ORCFILE-based Hive tables are much faster than joins of tables that store data as text.

Choose Hive's Cost-Based Optimization

Before executing a query, Hive optimizes the query's logical and physical execution plans. Hive can consider multiple plans before choosing the "best" one among those plans for the execution. Each potential execution plan involves different join orders, different join types and, in essence, different ways of accessing the data you're interested in.

Hive can use cost-based optimization to select the query plan with the least cost (cost being evaluated in terms of resource usage). However, you must explicitly ask Hive to use cost-based optimization by setting the following parameters at the very beginning of your Hive queries:

```
set hive.cbo.enable=true;
set hive.compute.query.using.stats=true;
set hive.stats.fetch.column.stats=true;
set hive.stats.fetch.patition.stats=true;
```

Use the `PARALLEL` keyword when processing large data sets.

Use Hive's Built-In Capabilities

Hive has several built-in features that help run queries much faster than when you use straight SQL. For example, the following query uses Hive's `OVER` and `RANK` OLAP analytical functions to get the job done without the usual subquery and inner joins.

```
SELECT * FROM
SELECT *, RANK() over (partition by sessionID,
order by timestamp desc) as rank
FROM clicks) ranked_clicks
WHERE ranked_clicks.rank=1;
```

Use Vectorization

If your queries involve aggregations, scans, filters and joins, you can gain a significant performance benefit by performing the work in batches of rows (1,024 at a time), instead of working on one row at a time.

You can enable vectorization by setting the following two parameters:

```
set hive.vectorized.execution.enabled = true;
set hive.vectorized.execution.reduce.enabled = true;
```

Optimizing Pig Jobs

Following are some strategies to make your Pig jobs run faster.

Use Pig Optimization Rules

Pig has numerous optimization rules that speed up queries. These optimization rules are turned off by default, so you must selectively enable the rules. I'll list a few of them here, but you can check all the optimization rules by viewing Pig's performance documentation at `https://pig.apache.org/docs/r0.9.1/perf.html`.

- Project early and often
- Filter early and often
- Prefer `DISTINCT` over `GROUP BY`
- Compress results of intermediate jobs

Set Parallelism

You can use the `SET default_parallel` or the `parallel` option to hard code a set number of reducers for a Pig job. However, it's better to specify the degree of parallelism by calculating it yourself. You can do this by first finding the number of mappers by using the split size of the input data, which should be a multiple of the default split size and usually in the 256-512MB range. Using our handy rule of thumb of a ratio of 5:1 between mappers and reducers, you can then figure out the number of reducers.

Let's say your mappers use an input data split of 512MB. The reducers should then take about 2.5GB of data (512MB x 5), using our 5:1 ratio.

Another way to figure out if you need more or fewer reducers is to look at the completion time for reducers. If the reducers are finishing up in just a minute or so, you have too many reducers and you should reduce them—ideally reducers should take anywhere between 5 to 15 minutes on average.

If you aren't using the `SET default_parallel` clause in the Pig script or the `parallel` keyword in the code, you can use two other Pig properties to configure the parallelism of the reduce tasks.

- The `reducers.bytes.per.reducer` property, which determines the input size of the reducer, has a default value of 1GB, and you can raise it to 2GB.
- The `reducers.max` property, which determines the maximum number of reducers, defaults to 999 reducers. You can set this property to a lower value to reduce the maximum number of reduce jobs for a Pig job.

If you set both the properties listed here, the value that's smaller takes precedence. For example, if the input size is 100GB, you can employ the following settings:

```
-Dpig.exec.reducers.bytes/per.reducer=${1024 * 1024 * 1024 *2} \
-Dpig.exec.reducers.max=50 \
```

Use Pig's Specialized Joins

Pig offers several specialized joins. Use one of these when your data and the queries seem to meet the requirements.

- Replicated joins: Use this when one or more relations in a join is small enough to fit into main memory.
- Skewed joins: These joins are helpful when the underlying data is skewed and you need to counteract the skew.
- Merge joins: A merge join is the same as a sort-merge join. This type of join is helpful when both inputs in the join are already sorted on the join key, since the data avoids going through unnecessary sort and shuffle phases.

Benchmarking Your Cluster

As you've figured out by now, Hadoop has many dials and knobs that enable you to configure and fine tune its performance. In fact, you're faced with a bewildering array of choices regarding the configuration parameter settings. One of the ways you can check potential configuration changes is by running benchmark tests for the cluster performance. Benchmark test results help you compare different settings and even the performance of different clusters.

When putting a new Hadoop cluster into the production mode or when upgrading a cluster, it is a good idea to stress test the cluster. Stress tests tell you if the cluster can deliver acceptable response times under heavy loads and also let you understand the scalability limits of your cluster. When stress testing web applications or databases, it's normal to hit them with a heavy load to see how they fare. However, in the case of Hadoop, we're more interested in benchmarking—measuring the performance of specific jobs such as querying, machine learning, indexing and so on.

Apache Hadoop comes with several useful benchmarking tools. By running these tools, you can check the performance of your cluster and be able to compare it with the performance of other clusters. This section introduces you to the most useful benchmarking tools that are part of the Apache Hadoop distribution.

Hadoop's built-in benchmarks are provided under two key directories: hadoop-mapreduce-client-jobclient-*-tests.jar and hadoop-*examples*.jar. Both of these are located in your Hadoop installation directory.

In the following sections, we'll review the most commonly used benchmarking tools:

- TestDFSIO
- TeraGen/TeraSort/TeraValidate

Using TestDFSIO for Testing I/O Performance

Often, you'd like to check how well the storage subsystem is performing. Other times, you may want to get to the root causes of performance issues. Hadoop's TestDFSIO benchmarking tool helps you perform read and write tests for HDFS data. As mentioned previously, when you are going to production with a new cluster or right after an upgrade to a new version of Hadoop, it's a good idea to run a quick stress test to check out HDFS, and TestDFSIO is a great tool for that.

> **Note**
>
> There's no mention of TestDFSIO in Hadoop's documentation, so if you're interested in more details check out its source code at: $HADOOP_HOME/src/test/org/apache/hadoop/fs/TestDFSIO.java.

TestDFSIO relies on MapReduce jobs to benchmark HDFS and is an I/O bound test. In the following sections, we'll run read and write tests of HDFS with TestDFSIO's help.

A Write Test

Run a write test with TestDFSIO by specifying the `-write` option, as shown here:

```
$hadoopjar /usr/lib/gphd/hadoop-mapreduce/hadoop-mapreduce-client-jobclient-2.0.2-alpha-
gphd-2.0.1.0-tests.jar TestDFSIO -write nrFiles 20 -filesize 250GB
```

By default, TestDFSIO creates one map task for each file you specify. The `nrFiles` option specifies the number of files to generate within HDFS. This is the same as the number of map tasks that will be executed. Since the `nrFiles` attribute specifies 20 as its value, Hadoop creates, or writes, 20 files in HDFS, each sized 1GB. When you run this command, Hadoop writes the files to the /benchmarks/TestDFSIO/io_data directory in HDFS. The `filesize` option generates a file for each map task with this size. Since our file size is specified as 250GB and the number of files (`nrFiles`) as 20, the example generates 5000GB of data in HDFS.

The output you're really after, the benchmark results, is written to a Linux directory, from where you run the benchmark, as well as to the screen. You can specify the filename with the `-resFile` parameter.

> **Note**
>
> You can view all the options available for the TestDFSIO command by executing the command with the `-help` option.

Here's the output of a TestDFSIO write test on our cluster:

```
16/07/12 10:56:45 INFO fs.TestDFSIO: ----- TestDFSIO ----- : write
16/07/12 10:56:45 INFO fs.TestDFSIO:            Date & time: Tue Jul 12 0:48:48 2016
16/07/12 10:56:45 INFO fs.TestDFSIO:        Number of files: 64
16/07/12 10:56:45 INFO fs.TestDFSIO: Total MBytes processed: 1048576.0
16/07/12 10:56:45 INFO fs.TestDFSIO:      Throughput mb/sec: 23.046824301966463
16/07/12 10:56:45 INFO fs.TestDFSIO: Average IO rate mb/sec: 23.143465042114258
16/07/12 10:56:45 INFO fs.TestDFSIO:  IO rate std deviation: 1.5490700854356283
16/07/12 10:56:45 INFO fs.TestDFSIO:     Test exec time sec: 796.676
16/07/12 10:56:45 INFO fs.TestDFSIO:
```

A Read Test

You can use the output files generated by the write test you performed earlier as inputs for your read test. The following command runs the read test using the 20 input files generated by the write test.

```
$hadoopjar/usr/lib/gphd/hadoop-mapreduce/hadoop-mapreduce-client-jobclient-2.0.2-alpha-
gphd-2.0.1.0-tests.jar TestDFSIO
-read -nrFiles 20 -fileSize 250GB
```

And here's the output of the TestDFSIO read test:

```
16/07/12 11:03:45 INFO fs.TestDFSIO: ----- TestDFSIO ----- : read
16/07/12 11:03:45 INFO fs.TestDFSIO:            Date & time: Tue Jul 12 0:58:24 2016
16/07/12 11:03:45 INFO fs.TestDFSIO:        Number of files: 64
16/07/12 11:03:45 INFO fs.TestDFSIO: Total MBytes processed: 1048576.0
16/07/12 11:03:45 INFO fs.TestDFSIO:      Throughput mb/sec: 46.94650035960607
16/07/12 11:03:45 INFO fs.TestDFSIO: Average IO rate mb/sec: 47.33715057373047
16/07/12 11:03:45 INFO fs.TestDFSIO:  IO rate std deviation: 4.734873712739776
16/07/12 11:03:45 INFO fs.TestDFSIO:     Test exec time sec: 414.219
16/07/12 11:03:45 INFO fs.TestDFSIO:
```

You can remove all the test data generated by TestDFSIO by running the following command:

```
$ hadoop jar hadoop-mapreduce-client-jobclient-*-tests.jar TestDFSIO -clean
```

This command will delete the HDFS directory /benchmarks/TestDFSIO/io_data.

Interpreting the Results

One of the first things you want to look at is the throughput, both for the read and the write tests. The test execution time (last counter) shows the time it takes for the `hadoop jar` command to complete; the lower the value the better the test performance.

Using the output of the TestDFSIO command, you can calculate the throughput of storage using the following formula:

Total read throughput and total write throughput =
number of files * throughput (MB/sec)

Benchmarking with TeraSort

TeraSort is a popular benchmark for Hadoop workloads and is used as an industry-standard tool to evaluate Hadoop performance. The tool basically sorts 1TB of data to benchmark performance. TeraSort uses HDFS and MapReduce to sort data. You can use TeraSort in various situations, such as when you've adjusted several performance-related configuration parameters and you would like to compare the "before and after" performance.

You can create effective performance baselines by using the TeraSort benchmarking suite.

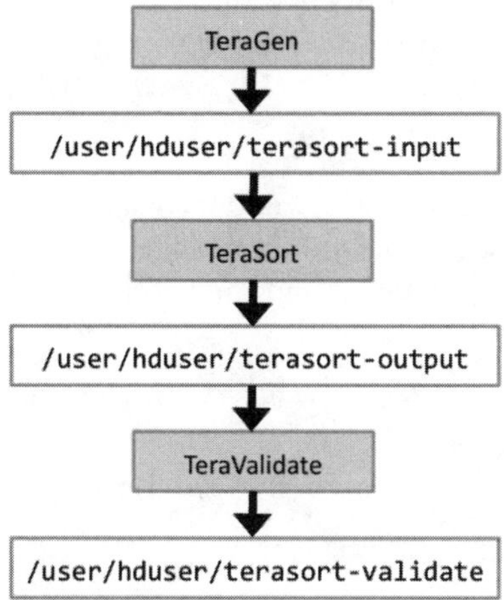

Figure 18.3 Workflow of a TeraSort benchmark run

The TeraSort Suite

TeraSort is actually a suite of utilities, consisting of TeraGen, TeraSort and TeraValidate. A TeraSort benchmark exercise requires you to perform the following steps.

1. Run the TeraGen utility to generate the input data. This will create an input file that can be used by the TeraSort utility to perform the actual sort operation.
2. Run the TeraSort test on the input data. The job of this tool is to sort the input file by using the Hadoop cluster and its HDFS and MapReduce components. The goal is to stress cluster resources such as network bandwidth and I/O.
3. Run the TeraValidate utility. This utility checks the sorted data for accuracy.

Figure 18.3 shows the workflow involved in a TeraSort run.

Running TeraGen

Run TeraGen first because this tool generates the necessary data that you need for the TeraSort test run. Here's an example showing how to run the TeraGen utility.

```
$ hadoop jar $HADOOP_PREFIX/hadoop-*examples*.jar teragen 10000000000 /user/data/
terasortinput
```

This command generates an input with 1TB of data in the /user/data/terasort-input directory.

Note that you specify the size of the input file in the number of 100-byte rows, and not bytes. Thus "10000000000" refers to the number of rows, each of which has a size of 10 bytes, thus generating an input of 1TB of data. You must ensure that the HDFS directory /user/data is empty before you run this command.

During the test, the TeraGen utility uses the configured block size for HDFS. However, you may experiment with different block sizes by adding the `dfs.block-size` parameter to the `teragen` command, as in `fs.block-size=536870912 (512MB)`, for example.

Running TeraSort

TeraSort, as its name indicates, is the actual MapReduce sorting job that's the heart of the TeraSort benchmark. There are two stages to the TeraSort test—a map stage and a reduce stage. The map stage is CPU bound and the reduce stage is I/O bound.

Here's our TeraSort example:

```
$ hadoop jar $HADOOP-PREFIX/hadoop-*examples*.jar terasort /user/data/terasort-input
/user/data/terasort-output
```

Note that you specify the output generated by the TeraGen utility as the input for the TeraSort command.

Running TeraValidate

The job of TeraValidate is to verify that the output data generated by the TeraSort utility is correct—that is, it's sorted properly. If the data is correctly sorted, the TeraValidate run doesn't generate any output. If it does detect issues with the sorted output, it outputs the keys that are out of order in the output file.

Here's our example showing how to run the TeraValidate test using the output from the TeraSort command:

```
$ hadoop jar hadoop-*examples*.jar teravalidate /user/data/terasort-output
/user/data/terasort-validate</pre>
```

How to Use the Benchmarks

The TeraSort job tells you how long it took to process the input data that you generated. You can get a performance baseline by initially running the TeraSort job with something close to the default Hadoop parameter settings. Following this, you must perform the TeraSort test iteratively, each time modifying a certain set of configuration parameters. For example, you can play with different values for key configuration properties such as the following:

- Replication factor
- HDFS block size
- Memory settings for the map and reduce tasks (such as the `mapreduce.map.memory.mb` and `mapreduce.map.java.opts` parameters)

Using Intel's HiBench Tool

Intel offers a tool named HiBench, which helps perform several benchmarks. HiBench is a collection of shell scripts that you can get from GitHub (`https://github.com/intel-hadoop/HiBench`). The file hibench-config.sh contains several options that let you select the source and output files and so on. Once you select the configuration for the test, run this shell script first. Next, run the command `bin/run-all.sh`. The output is written to HDFS in the file hibench.report. Note that since HiBench was originally written for Hadoop 1.0, you'd need to make changes to the configuration before you run it in Hadoop 2.0 clusters.

HiBench is pretty comprehensive—besides TestDFSIO and TeraSort, it also lets you benchmark machine learning tasks such as the naïve Bayes classifier and k-means clustering, as well as benchmark tests for page rank and Nutch indexing jobs.

Using Hadoop's Rumen and GridMix for Benchmarking

Hadoop offers GridMix, a benchmarking tool, to model the resource profiles of production jobs using a mix of synthetic jobs. GridMix uses MapReduce job traces that profile a description of the job mix. The Rumen tool is used to build a job trace in JSON format, and GridMix uses this job trace to benchmark the cluster. Since Rumen is a prerequisite for running GridMix benchmarks, the following sections first explain how to use Rumen to analyze the job history and then show you how to benchmark your cluster with GridMix.

Using Rumen to Generate Job Traces

Data from MapReduce logs is critical to simulation and benchmarking. However, the data inside the logs needs to be parsed at times to provide specific inputs to simulators (such as GridMix, for example). Rumen is a built-in data extraction and analysis tool that can extract useful data by parsing MapReduce JobHistory logs and storing the data as a condensed digest. The resulting data after you run Rumen is "enhanced data," since Rumen performs statistical analysis of its digest to estimate variables the original log files don't have, such as the cumulative distribution functions for map/reduce runtimes, which is very useful in extrapolating the task runtime of incomplete jobs as well as synthetic tasks.

Rumen consists of two components, the trace builder and folder, as described here:

- Trace builder: Converts the JobHistory log into the JSON format so it can be easily read.
- Folder: Used for scaling the runtime of a trace. You can increase and decrease the trace run time by adding dummy jobs to the trace or dropping some jobs from the input trace.

The trace builder converts MapReduce JobHistory files into JSON objects and writes them to the trace file. Following is the general syntax of the `TraceBuilder` command:

```
java org.apache.hadoop.tools.rumen.TraceBuilder [options] <jobtrace-output>
<topology-output>
<inputs>
```

By default, trace builder reads only the files directly placed under the input folder to generate the trace. You can use the option -recursive to make trace builder recursively scan the input folder for all job history files.

Before you start running the Rumen commands (TraceBuilder and Folder), ascertain where the job history files are stored in your cluster by checking the value of the configuration parameter mapreduce.jobhistory.done-dir or mapreduce.jobhistory.intermediate-done-dir in the mapred-site.xml file.

Since Rumen requires specific libraries to be present in the class path, it's a good idea to execute the TraceBuilder command as shown here, by specifying the $HADOOP_HOME/bin/hadoop jar command to run the command:

```
$HADOOP_HOME/bin/hadoop jar \
  $HADOOP_HOME/share/hadoop/tools/lib/hadoop-rumen-2.5.1.jar \
  org.apache.hadoop.tools.rumen.TraceBuilder \
  file:///tmp/job-trace.json \
  file:///tmp/job-topology.json \
  hdfs:///tmp/hadoop-yarn/staging/history/done_intermediate/testuser
```

This command does the following:

- Analyzes the jobs in the HDFS directory /tmp/hadoop-yarn/staging/history/done_intermediate/testuser
- Outputs the job trace on the file /tmp/job-trace.json
- Captures the rack topology information in the Linux /tmp directory, in the file /tmp/job-topology.json

The folder utility, the other component of Rumen, performs *folding*, which is the fixing of the output duration of the trace and adjusting the job timelines to respect the final output duration. Here's an example that shows how to run the Folder command.

```
java org.apache.hadoop.tools.rumen.Folder \
  -output-duration 1h \
  -input-cycle 20m \
  file:///tmp/job-trace.json \
  file:///tmp/job-trace-1hr.json
```

This command folds an input trace with 10 hours of runtime and produces an output trace with 1 hour of runtime.

Once you use Rumen to build the job trace in the JSON format for the jobs you want to benchmark, it's time to get going with the GridMix tool, which helps you perform the benchmarks.

Using GridMix for Benchmarking

GridMix uses the job trace generated by Rumen to get the original job submission times, and it also retrieves the read and write counts (both byte and record counts) for all tasks in a job. Using the data it obtains from the job trace, GridMix creates a synthetic job that matches the byte/record pattern of the original job whose run was captured by the Rumen trace.

Tip

GridMix makes several simplifying assumptions, an important one being that it assumes that the records consumed or emitted from a task are evenly distributed, without the skew that's generally observed in real life. Each map will generate an identical percentage of data as input to the reducers, which isn't always true.

MapReduce tasks use various resources such as CPU, RAM and the JVM heap. GridMix captures the resource usage information stored in MapReduce task counters to emulate the actual resource usage during the simulated tasks that it runs. The goal is to create the identical load during the test that was experienced when the job originally ran in your cluster.

Once you have the trace file ready from Rumen, you can run GridMix to benchmark the cluster. Here's an example that shows how to execute the `gridmix` command (as with Rumen, it's a good idea to use the Hadoop `jar` command to run GridMix to make sure the necessary library JAR files are present in the class path.

```
HADOOP_CLASSPATH=$HADOOP_HOME/share/hadoop/tools/lib/hadoop-rumen-2.5.1.jar \
  $HADOOP_HOME/bin/hadoop jar $HADOOP_HOME/share/hadoop/tools/lib/hadoop-
gridmix-2.5.1.jar \
    -libjars $HADOOP_HOME/share/hadoop/tools/lib/hadoop-rumen-2.5.1.jar \
    [-generate <size>] [-users <users-list>] <iopath> <trace>
```

In this command, here's what the various options mean:

- `generate`: Generates the input data for the synthetic jobs.
- `users`: Points to the user list file (through the `users-list` attribute).
- `iopath`: The working directory for GridMix—can be either the Linux file system or HDFS. Hadoop recommends that you use the same file system as that used by the original set of jobs.
- `trace`: Specifies the path to the job trace that you generated with Rumen earlier.

There are numerous other configuration options you can specify, and the Hadoop GridMix documentation explains them.

An interesting thing about GridMix is that it's highly configurable. Besides routine parameters such as `gridmix.output.directory` (specifies the directory for the GridMix benchmark output) and the maximum size of the input files (default is 100MB), there are several parameters that let you control various aspects of the jobs. Here's a brief summary of some of the most useful of these parameters:

- `gridmix.job.type`: Lets you specify the job type for the synthetic job run by GridMix. There are two possible values: `LOADJOB` and `SLEEPJOB`. The default value is `LOADJOB`, which emulates the workload in the Rumen trace. The value `SLEEPJOB` lets you specify synthetic jobs where the tasks simply sleep for a specific time, as observed in the job trace from Rumen.

- `gridmix.job-submission.policy`: You can control the rate of job submission with this parameter, using different algorithms. You can choose among the following types of job submission policies:
  - `STRESS`: This policy submits jobs to keep the cluster under a stable stress level of workload, preventing an overloading or an underloading situation. GridMix uses internal thresholds to determine whether the cluster is overloaded or underloaded.
  - `REPLAY`: This job policy submits the synthetic jobs exactly according to the time intervals in the job trace captured by Rumen.
  - `SERIAL`: This policy submits jobs in a serial fashion, by submitting a new job only after the currently running job completes.
- `gridmix.compression-emulation.enable`: Enables compression emulation in the GridMix simulated jobs. The default value of this parameter is `TRUE` for jobs of the `LOADJOB` type. When compression emulation is turned on, GridMix generates compressible input data and uses a decompressor to read the data, provided the original job's input files were compressed. Similarly, GridMix enables map output compression and job output compression for the simulated job, if the original job used compression for these entities (map output and job output).

Uberized Jobs

If a YARN job is very small, the ApplicationMaster for the job can execute the map and the reduce tasks for the job within a single JVM. The principle here is that for these tiny jobs the management overhead and the cost of distributed task allocation outweigh any potential benefits of executing the tasks in parallel. Hadoop can "uberize" a job if all the following conditions are satisfied:

- There are less than 10 mappers (configurable with the `mapreduce.job.ubertask.maxmaps` property).
- There's only a single reducer (configurable with the `mapreduce.job.ubertask.maxreduces` property).
- The total input size is less than 1 HDFS block (configurable with the `mapreduce.job.ubertask.maxbytes` property).

By default Hadoop disables the capability of a job to run as an uber job by using the default value for the uberization parameter `mapreduce.job.ubertask.enable`.

Here's part of a job log showing how Hadoop chooses not to uberize a job:

```
org.apache.hadoop.mapreduce.v2.app.job.impl.JobImpl: Not uberizing job_
1438373860823_0024 because: not enabled; too many maps; too many reduces;
too much input; too much RAM;
```

Hadoop Counters

One of the most useful ways to examine job performance and try to isolate problems is to take advantage of Hadoop's counters. Hadoop provides several built-in counters, and you can set up custom counters as well. In general, a counter helps you find out the number of times a particular event occurred during the execution of a job.

You can access the Hadoop counters for an application through the ResourceManager web UI, as explained in Chapter 17.

Counters help you verify the following types of things:

- The correct number of mappers and reducers were launched and completed.
- The correct number of input bytes were read, and the expected number of output bytes were written.
- The correct number of records were read and written (to the local file system and to HDFS).
- The CPU usage and memory consumption were appropriate for the job.

Hadoop's built-in counters fall into several counter groups, of which the most important are the following:

- File system counters
- Job counters
- MapReduce framework counters

In addition to these three counter groups, Hadoop also shows you counters from three other counter groups by default: shuffle error counters, file input format counters and file output format counters.

Custom counters are those you configure for your application.

Figure 18.4 shows the Counters page for a completed MapReduce job (you can view counters for a failed job as well). Note that you can get the Hadoop counters not only at the aggregate job level, but also at the individual map or reduce task level—this helps greatly when trying to figure out why one of the map or reduce tasks is taking significantly longer to complete compared to the rest of the tasks.

In the following sections, we'll take a quick look at the key Hadoop counters you can use to understand job execution.

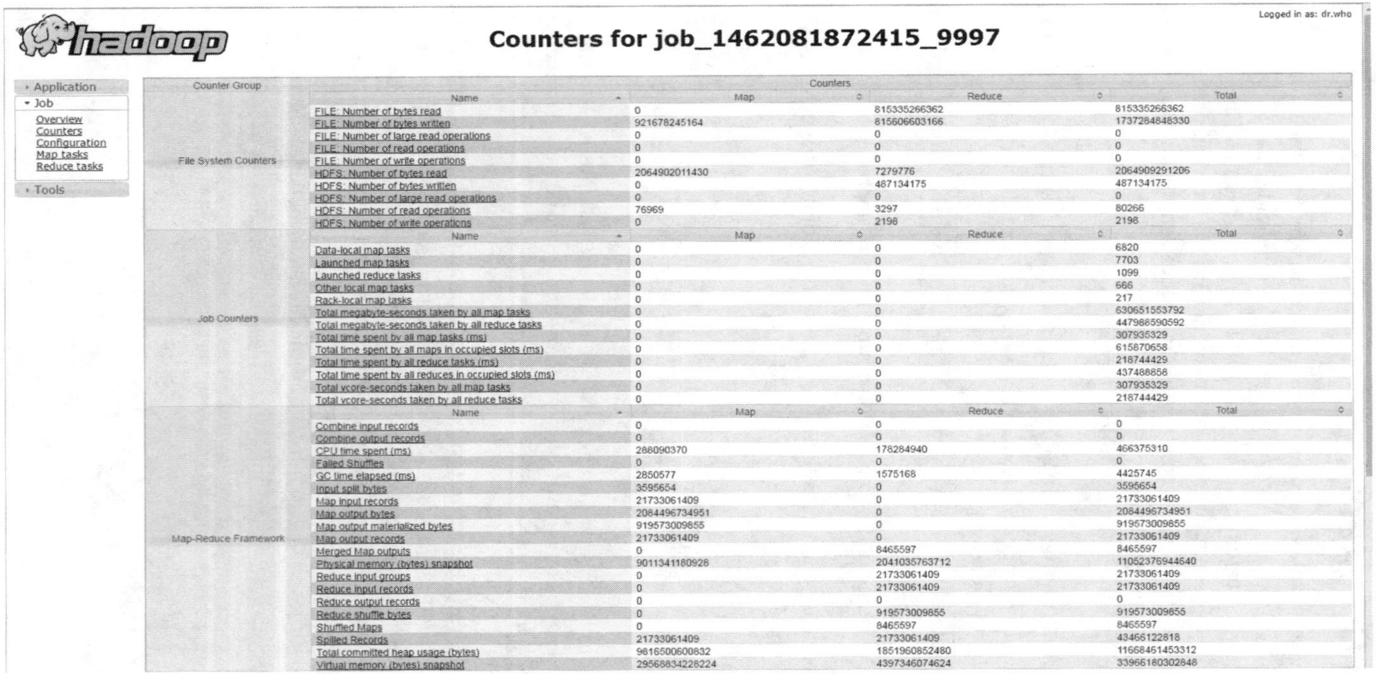

Logged in as: dr.who

hadoop

Counters for job_1462081872415_9997

- Application
- Job
  - Overview
  - Counters
  - Configuration
  - Map tasks
  - Reduce tasks
- Tools

Counter Group	Name	Map	Reduce	Total
File System Counters	FILE: Number of bytes read	0	815335266362	815335266362
	FILE: Number of bytes written	921678245164	815606603166	1737284848330
	FILE: Number of large read operations	0	0	0
	FILE: Number of read operations	0	0	0
	FILE: Number of write operations	0	0	0
	HDFS: Number of bytes read	2064902011430	7279776	2064909291206
	HDFS: Number of bytes written	0	487134175	487134175
	HDFS: Number of large read operations	0	0	0
	HDFS: Number of read operations	76969	3297	80266
	HDFS: Number of write operations	0	2198	2198
Job Counters	Data-local map tasks	0	0	6820
	Launched map tasks	0	0	7703
	Launched reduce tasks	0	0	1099
	Other local map tasks	0	0	666
	Rack-local map tasks	0	0	217
	Total megabyte-seconds taken by all map tasks	0	0	630651553792
	Total megabyte-seconds taken by all reduce tasks	0	0	447988590592
	Total time spent by all map tasks (ms)	0	0	307935329
	Total time spent by all maps in occupied slots (ms)	0	0	615870658
	Total time spent by all reduce tasks (ms)	0	0	218744429
	Total time spent by all reduces in occupied slots (ms)	0	0	437488858
	Total vcore-seconds taken by all map tasks	0	0	307935329
	Total vcore-seconds taken by all reduce tasks	0	0	218744429
Map-Reduce Framework	Combine input records	0	0	0
	Combine output records	0	0	0
	CPU time spent (ms)	288090370	178284940	466375310
	Failed Shuffles	0	0	0
	GC time elapsed (ms)	2850577	1575168	4425745
	Input split bytes	3595654	0	3595654
	Map input records	21733061409	0	21733061409
	Map output bytes	2084496734951	0	2084496734951
	Map output materialized bytes	919573009855	0	919573009855
	Map output records	21733061409	0	21733061409
	Merged Map outputs	0	8465597	8465597
	Physical memory (bytes) snapshot	9011341180928	2041035763712	11052376944640
	Reduce input groups	0	21733061409	21733061409
	Reduce input records	0	21733061409	21733061409
	Reduce output records	0	0	0
	Reduce shuffle bytes	0	919573009855	919573009855
	Shuffled Maps	0	8465597	8465597
	Spilled Records	21733061409	21733061409	43466122818
	Total committed heap usage (bytes)	9816500600832	1851960852480	11668461453312
	Virtual memory (bytes) snapshot	29568834228224	4397346074624	33966180302848

Figure 18.4 The counters page for a job showing the various counter groups

File System Counters

File system counters show valuable information regarding read and write operations in both the local file system and HDFS. Here are the key counters you should understand.

- FILE_BYTES_READ: The total numbers of bytes read from the local file system by the map and reduce tasks.
- FILE_BYTES_WRITTEN: Total number of bytes written to the local file system. These writes include the writes during the map phase when mapper tasks write intermediate results to the local file system. Reducer tasks also write to the local file system during the shuffle phase when they spill intermediate results to the local file system during sorting.
- HDFS_BYTES_READ: Total bytes read from HDFS.
- HDFS_BYTES_WRITTEN: Total bytes written to HDFS.

Note that the total amount of bytes read and written will depend on the compression algorithms the application uses.

Here's an example that shows the file system counters from a job:

```
File System Counters
        FILE: Number of bytes read=8229940
        FILE: Number of bytes written=16873548
        FILE: Number of read operations=0
        FILE: Number of large read operations=0
        FILE: Number of write operations=0
        HDFS: Number of bytes read=548134850
        HDFS: Number of bytes written=3294726
        HDFS: Number of read operations=18
        HDFS: Number of large read operations=0
        HDFS: Number of write operations=2
```

Job Counters

Job counters are counters relating to the Hadoop jobs and don't change while a job is running. Following are the key job counters.

- DATA_LOCAL_MAPS: Number of map tasks executed on local data (HDFS). Ideally, all map tasks should execute on a local rack.
- TOTAL_LAUNCHED_MAPS: Shows the number of map tasks launched for a job and includes failed tasks. This number is, in general, the same as the number of input splits for the job.
- TOTAL_LAUNCHED_REDUCES: Shows the total number of reducer tasks launched for a job.
- NUM_KILLED_MAPS: The number of killed map tasks.
- NUM_KILLED_REDUCES: The number of killed reduce tasks.

- MILLIS_MAPS: Total time taken for running map tasks, including tasks that were started speculatively.
- MILLIS_REDUCES: Total time taken for running reduce tasks, including tasks that were started speculatively.

Here's' the output from a job showing the job counters:

```
Job Counters
                Launched map tasks=2
                Launched reduce tasks=1
                Data-local map tasks=1
                Rack-local map tasks=1
                Total time spent by all maps in occupied slots (ms)=0
                Total time spent by all reduces in occupied slots (ms)=0
                Total time spent by all map tasks (ms)=186047
                Total time spent by all reduce tasks (ms)=5628
                Total vcore-seconds taken by all map tasks=186047
                Total vcore-seconds taken by all reduce tasks=5628
                Total megabyte-seconds taken by all map tasks=381024256
                Total megabyte-seconds taken by all reduce tasks=11526144
```

MapReduce Framework Counters

Counters in the MapReduce framework group show aggregated information for all tasks in a job.

- MAP_INPUT_RECORDS: Total number of input records read for the job during the map phase
- MAP_OUTPUT_RECORDS: Total number of records written for the job during the map phase
- CPU_MILLISECONDS: Total time spent by all tasks on CPU
- GC_TIME_MILLIS: Total time spent during garbage collection of the JVMs
- PHYSICAL_MEMORY_BYTES: Physical memory consumed by all tasks
- REDUCE_SHUFFLE_BYTES: Total number of output bytes from map tasks copied to reducers during the shuffle phase
- SPILLED_RECORDS: Total number of records spilled to disk for all the map and reduce tasks

Learning how to spot job performance inefficiencies through analyzing counters is important. For example, when the REDUCE_SHUFFLE_BYTES counter, which shows the total bytes in the intermediate results transferred from the mappers to the reducers, is very high, job performance slows down. The reason for this is that shuffle processes tend to be heavy network resource consumers.

Values for job counters such as TOTAL_LAUNCHED_MAPS don't change over the course of the job execution. However, the values for counters such as PHYSCIAL_MEMORY_BYTES do change over the course of the job and let you see how the memory usage varies over the course of the job execution or during a specific task attempt.

Following is the output from a MapReduce job showing the MapReduce framework counters:

```
Map-Reduce Framework
        Map input records=35558
        Map output records=35558
        Map output bytes=36910848
        Map output materialized bytes=8234020
        Input split bytes=1343
        Combine input records=0
        Combine output records=0
        Reduce input groups=35328
        Reduce shuffle bytes=8234020
        Reduce input records=35558
        Reduce output records=35328
        Spilled Records=71116
        Shuffled Maps =2
        Failed Shuffles=0
        Merged Map outputs=2
        GC time elapsed (ms)=2521
        CPU time spent (ms)=233390
        Physical memory (bytes) snapshot=3263873024
        Virtual memory (bytes) snapshot=11202859008
        Total committed heap usage (bytes)=3947888640
```

Custom Java Counters

Developers can define custom counters for both mappers and reducers, for counting various things such as the number of missing, malformed or bad records, for example, or the minimum and maximum values for specific entities. Custom counters are usually defined by a Java `enum`, or by an equivalent method using strings. The string interface lets you create counters dynamically, and `enums` are easier to configure and are good enough for most Hadoop jobs.

> **Note**
>
> It's possible to retrieve job counter values using Java APIs, without using the web UI. You can do this while the job is still running, but it's advisable to wait until the job completes, so your counters are accurate and stable.

Limiting the Number of Counters

Regardless of whether it's a Hadoop built-in counter or a custom counter, each of the counters occupies space in the ResourceManager's JVM. Also, the ResourceManager must keep track of every single counter for both the map and reduce tasks until the entire job completes, which adds to the processing overhead of the job. Therefore, you must be careful not to specify too many counters in a job. Typically, about 100-200 counters (including both built-in and custom) is all you'll need.

The configuration property `mapreduce.job.counters.max` in the mapreduce-site.xml file sets the limit on the number of user counters allowed per job. The default value for this parameter is 120. If you exceed this value, you'll receive an error.

An application can define custom counters and update them in the map or reduce methods. The MapReduce framework aggregates these counters on a global basis. You can use custom counters to track a few key global entities. Custom counters aren't designed for application developers to aggregate all the fine-grained application statistics!

Optimizing MapReduce

There are several well-known optimization techniques for making a MapReduce job run faster—compressing data is probably the best known of these. There are several other optimizations available to speed up MapReduce, and this section outlines the most important of these techniques.

Map-Only versus Map and Reduce Jobs

Usually a MapReduce job has both a map and a reduce phase. The map phase processes the input data in key/value format and produces key/value pairs as the output. The reduce phase accepts the map output for each key and iterates through each value for a key and produces zero or more key-value pairs. Sometimes you don't need the reduce phase, as when you use a `SELECT` or `WHERE` clause in a SQL statement. In such cases you use a map-only job to process the input data.

Map-only jobs don't need to go through the expensive sort/shuffle phase, so they run very fast. By default, Hadoop always configures a single reducer for a MapReduce job even when the developer doesn't specify a reducer class because he or she is running a map-only job. Hadoop will move the mapper output from the map nodes to the reducer node, incurring needless network overhead. Developers can make the map-only jobs run much faster by explicitly specifying the `job.setNumReduceTasks(0)` method as part of their map-only jobs.

MapReduce jobs that require aggregation such as `SUM`, `MAX` and `GROUP BY` clauses require both map and reduce phases. Developers can make the jobs more efficient by using the map phase to perform partial computations. This reduces the output that the mappers need to send to the reducers. If you don't perform the partial computations during the map, the mappers need to send all of their data to the reducers and have them perform the computations, which is much more expensive. The reduce step in this case is used to perform the aggregations.

The following sections show how developers can take advantage of several optimizations that are part of the MapReduce API to enhance MapReduce job performance.

How Combiners Improve MapReduce Performance

A combiner is a MapReduce optimization that minimizes the number of key/value pairs that need to be sent from the mappers to the reducers. A combiner, in essence, performs some of the reduce task's job using map operations, by processing the intermediate results of the key/value pairs emitted by the mappers. The map phase performs partial aggregations and sends this data over to the reducers.

Combiners provide the benefit of map-side aggregation—they cut down on the amount of data that's shuffled from maps to the reduce tasks. Combiners make the shuffle process more efficient by reducing network traffic. However, you need to ensure that the combiner does actually provide enough aggregation to warrant its use, since combiners do involve extra serialization and deserialization of the map output records. If your application doesn't aggregate the map output by 20 or 30percent, it doesn't really benefit from using a combiner.

You can use the MapReduce counters pertaining to the input and output records to check the efficiency of the combiner.

This book isn't about MapReduce programming, so we aren't going to delve into the programming aspects of implementing combiners, except to say that in order to implement a combiner, the developer can simply use the existing reduce function as the combiner. The combine class implements the reducer interface, is called with multiple values of the map output and overrides the `reduce ()` method with its code.

Tip

Custom combiners can reduce the I/O between mappers and reducers.

You can check the impact of the combiner by reviewing the counters named Combine Input Records and Combine Output Records in the MapReduce Framework group of counters. If a job isn't using any combiners, both of these counters show a zero value. In this case, without the combiner class, the number of the reduce input records matches the map record records. So, I have the following counters with no combiners:

```
Combine Input records:                    0
Combine output records:                   0
Map output records:             27684496984
Reduce input records:           27684496984
```

If the job does use combiners, you'll see values for the combine-related counters, as shown here for one of our Hadoop jobs:

```
Combine Input records:      27684496984  (Map)
Combine output records:      6986214761 (Map)
Map output records:          27684496984
Reduce input records:         6986214761
```

In addition, when the combiner is in place, the reduce input records aren't the same as the map output records, as they were in the case when we had no combiners. The number of reduce input records is way lower than the number of map output records! The reduce input records are just a quarter of the total map output records in our example. The use of the combiner has lowered the reduce input data to 6,986,214,761 from the original number of records, which was 27,684,496,984. A sharp reduction such as this in the number of the reducer input records enhances the reduce performance since you need to transfer a much smaller volume of data to the reduce function.

Tip

A custom combiner is designed to reduce the I/O between the mappers and reducers. It does this by sending smaller outputs from the mapper nodes to the reducers. However, running the combiner isn't free—there's overhead involved in it. Sometimes, a combiner may actually slow the MapReduce job down due to its own overhead!

Using a Partitioner to Improve Performance

Reducers process the key/value pairs received by them from the mappers. While this data is sorted by the key, by default, those keys are randomly allocated to the reducers. Hadoop sends the same key to the same reducer, irrespective of which mapper emanates those keys. It's much more efficient to customize the mapper process to determine which key goes to which reducer. Developers can do this by coding the partitioner class, which can specify which key is sent to which reducer.

If you're testing the custom partitioner in a test cluster, make sure it's not running in the local mode, where you can only use a single reducer, leading to the bypassing of the partitioner. A partitioner comes into play only when multiple reducers are in play, so test the job in a regular cluster or at least in a pseudo-distributed cluster.

Compressing Data During the MapReduce Process

You can lower MapReduce processing time as well as the I/O and network traffic significantly by taking advantage of compression during all the phases of a MapReduce job. Chapter 10 explains Hadoop compression and how to enable and configure it, so I won't go into the details here, except to mention that you can enable compression at the following phases of a MapReduce job:

- Map input: During the map phase, you can compress the input data to the map tasks. Not only will the compressing of the input data save storage, it'll also speed up the transfer of the input data. Use splittable algorithms such as bzip2 or a SequenceFile format with zlib compression.
- Map output (shuffle and sort): During this phase, you can compress the intermediate (map) output. The shuffle is usually the most expensive processing step due to the large amounts of network traffic that it generates, and when dealing with large sets of intermediate data, it's a good strategy to compress it. Compressing the map output files lowers the number of bytes that the reduce function needs to read. Use fast codecs such as Snappy or lzo (or lz4) to compress the intermediate map output. For example, while the lzo codec generates much larger compressed files than the gzip codec, it makes the map phase complete about four times faster on average, since it's much faster in reading data off the disk. Speed (and not compressed file size) is the hallmark of this compression codec. After enabling the compression of the map output, change the value of the `mapred.output.compression.type` parameter to `BLOCK`, from its default value of `RECORD`, to increase the compression ratio.
- Reduce: You can compress the final reduce output.

> **Note**
>
> Compressing the map outputs will reduce the network traffic between the map and reduce tasks.

Minimizing the Output of the Mappers

Map processes "spill" their output to disk; thus, limiting the mapper output is crucial to performance, since it involves not only disk I/O, but network I/O and the use of memory. You can improve performance significantly by keeping mapper output as low as possible. You can reduce the mapper output through all the following strategies:

- Configure compression for mapper output, as explained in Chapter 10. This is probably the easiest to configure and offers the biggest bang for the buck, so to speak.
- Filter out records not on the reducer side, but on the mapper side.
- Extend the BinaryComparable interface or use text for the key of the map output.
- Use the least amount of data for creating the map output key and the map output value.

Balancing Work among the Reducers

It's not uncommon to see a MapReduce job almost finish, except that one last reducer task is still running. This happens when there's a data skew and one of the reducers is processing most of the mapper output (or at least, a much larger amount of output than the other mappers). Since the data is unevenly distributed among the reducers, the reducers with the most data will take the longest, thus delaying the job.

Two common solutions to the data skew problem are the following:

- If you can identify the keys that are causing the skew, the developers can create a preprocessing job using `MultipleOutputs` to separate the keys. A separate MR job is then used to process the separated keys that are slowing down the job.
- The developers can implement a better hash function in the `partitioner` class.

Too Many Mappers or Reducers?

Applications that process large data sets with just one or a small number of reducers can improve performance by raising the number of reducers. Multiple reducers can process a large number of output records faster than a single reducer can. It's definitely not good when you have the following:

- A large number of maps that run for a very short time, such as 5 or 10 seconds each
- Large data sets with small block sizes (HDFS) such as 64 or 128MB, leading to tens of thousands of mappers
- Processing too many small files that are smaller than the HDFS block size, each mapper processing one of the small files
- Straightforward aggregations without using the combiner

Using too high a number of reducers isn't smart either. If the job involves numerous reducers, each processing less than 1 or 2GB of data, it's not running very efficiently.

Applications running with hundreds of thousands of maps need to evaluate and see if they can reduce the number of maps.

If an application uses tens or hundreds of counters for each map/reduce task, it's going to overwhelm the ResourceManager with the higher memory usage it entails.

When Is It Too Many?

The number of mappers should generally have a 10:1 ratio to the number of reducers—this is just a rule of thumb, nothing more than that. Using optimizations such as combiners helps keep the number of reducers much smaller in comparison with the number of mappers.

Here are some guidelines that help you determine whether you're running way too many mappers or reducers.

- If the number of reducers is the same or even more than the number of mappers, you most likely have too many reducers.
- If most of the mappers and reducers are finishing in a few seconds, and the reducers are running faster than the mappers, you're very likely running too many mappers.
- If the number of part files in HDFS is greater than the number of reducers, there are too many reducers.
- If several output part-* files in HDFS are empty after the job completes, you chose had too many reducers.
- You may be running too many mappers if the number of mappers is equal to the number of input files, but the input files are sized smaller than the default Hadoop split size.

Configuring the Number of Map/Reduce Tasks in a Job

You can let Hadoop determine the number of map/reduce tasks in a job, and you can also programmatically set them. The following configuration parameters let you limit the number of map and reduce tasks per a single MapReduce job:

- `mapreduce.job.maps`: Sets the default number of map tasks per job. The default is 2.
- `mapreduce.job.reduces`: Determines the default number of reduce tasks per job. This parameter is usually set to 99 percent of the cluster's reduce capacity, so the reduce tasks can still be executed in a single wave, even if a node fails. The default value is 1.

You can limit the number of map and reduce tasks in a job that can run *simultaneously* with the help of the following two parameters:

- `mapreduce.job.running.map.limit`: Determines the maximum number of map tasks per job that can run simultaneously
- `mapreduce.job.running.reduce.limit`: Determines the maximum number of reduce tasks per job that can run simultaneously

The default value for both of these parameters is 0, which means there's no limit on the number of map/reduce tasks from a job that can run simultaneously.

> **Note**
>
> MapReduce is designed to process large chunks of data. Since the MapReduce framework processes one HDFS file per map task by default, if you have a large number of input files, it's more efficient to use special input formats such as `MultiIFileInputFormat` to process multiple files per each map task. Also, it's a good idea to process larger chunks of data per map. A good strategy then would be to coalesce multiple small input files into fewer maps and use a larger HDFS block size for processing very large data sets, which helps process more input data per map.

Number of Maps

The number of maps depends on the total size of the input. If your input is 10TB and your block size is 256MB, the job is going to need about 41,000 maps. There's a startup cost to every map—it takes some time to set up the map tasks, so ideally the maps should run for at least a couple of minutes to execute, for large jobs.

Running a large number of map tasks, each running for a brief time, isn't an efficient processing method. If a job is taking more than 100,000 maps, regardless of the size of the input, take a close look at the input and your block size to see if you can reduce the number of tasks.

You must strive to size your map tasks such that all the map task outputs can be sorted in a single pass, by storing the outputs in the sort buffer.

Limiting the number of maps means the following:

- Lower scheduling overhead.
- More available containers for new tasks.
- More efficient map-side sorting (in memory).
- Fewer seeks required to shuffle the map output to the reducers (each map produces output for the reducers).
- Larger shuffled segments, which means the overhead of connections is lower—you need the connections to move the data across the network.
- Reduced side merging of sorted map outputs is more efficient since there are fewer merges required due to the lower number of sorted segments of the map outputs.

Note that too few map tasks isn't great, either, since they affect your ability to recover from a failed map task, with a single failure of a large map slowing the application down.

Number of Reduces

The performance of the shuffle process determines the efficiency of the reduce tasks for the most part.

You can't have too many or too few reduces for the following reasons:

- If you have too few reduces, the node on which the reduce tasks are running will be carrying a heavy load. Reducers processing a large set of data (such as 100GB, for example) aren't advisable for this reason. Also, when each reducer is processing a huge chunk of data, any reducer failures have an adverse impact on your recovery from the failure.
- Too many reducers aren't good because it has an adverse impact on the shuffle process. It also ends up creating too many small files as the job's final output. The NameNode has to track all these files, which affects its ability to efficiently service other applications that may need to use that data.

Ideally each of the reducers in a job should process around 1-2GB of data but not more than around 10GB of data in general.

Summary

Here's what you learned in this chapter:

- Allocating memory wisely to YARN jobs is a big part of optimizing the use of your cluster resources. If you allocate too much memory for your containers, you waste your cluster's resources—in effect you shrink the capability of the cluster. Too little memory means tasks will run longer and even fail sometimes. Nowhere is it more important to learn and understand Hadoop's configuration parameters than when configuring memory in your cluster.
- You can use various strategies to optimize MapReduce jobs—some of these strategies require the set up of cluster-wide configuration properties by the administrator, and others require changes on the development side, including the writing of more efficient code and use of advanced concepts such as combiners and partitioners.
- You can take advantage of several optimization techniques for improving the performance of Hive and Pig jobs.
- It's a good idea to perform benchmarking exercises at important times such as adding more servers or changing important configuration parameters. Benchmarking also enables you to compare the performance of different clusters.
- Understanding Hadoop's built-in counters is beneficial in troubleshooting jobs and tuning the performance of jobs.

19

Configuring and Tuning Apache Spark on YARN

This chapter covers the following:

- Allocating resources for Apache Spark on YARN
- Dynamic resource allocation
- Storage formats and compressing data
- Using the Spark UI to understand performance
- Tuning garbage collection
- Performance tuning of Spark Streaming applications

This chapter and the one that follows are all about how to make Spark applications run fast! As you have learned, you can run Spark in the standalone mode on Mesos or on YARN. Since this is a book on Hadoop administration, I show how to configure and tune Spark so it works well with Hadoop, especially YARN, Hadoop's processing framework. Tuning Spark applications running on YARN involves focusing on two broad areas:

- Tuning the resource allocation in a YARN/Hadoop cluster for the Spark applications
- Tuning the Spark applications to make sure they're efficient

In this chapter, I discuss how to optimize resource allocation for Spark running in a YARN/Hadoop cluster. Following this, in Chapter 20, "Optimizing Spark Applications," I explain how you can optimize Spark applications so you can get the best performance out of them.

Configuring Resource Allocation for Spark on YARN

Processing capacity in the form of CPU cores and memory in the form of RAM are the two key system resources you allocate to Spark. You'll learn how to allocate CPU and memory in the following sections.

Allocating CPU

The key to Spark's computations is the resilient distributed dataset (RDD), an abstraction that consists of multiple partitions. One Spark task will process a single RDD partition on a single CPU core.

The parallelism of a Spark job depends on the number of partitions in an RDD and the number of available CPU cores. By default, Spark uses just two cores with a single executor.

Allocating Memory

Spark utilizes memory for two purposes: executing jobs and storing data. Execution memory is what Spark uses for performing shuffles, joins, sorts and aggregations. Storage memory is for caching data and for propagating internal data within the cluster. A job can use all the available memory for storage when it isn't using any execution memory. Execution can evict storage from memory, but only until the memory used by storage hits a threshold. Spark provides a subregion within its memory where cached blocks can live for long without being evicted for the use of execution. However, the converse isn't true, since storage can never evict execution.

Spark's dynamic automatic memory allocation feature lets it automatically adjust the fraction of memory it needs to allocate for shuffle and caching.

The memory Spark can commandeer determines the maximum size of shuffle data structures it uses for grouping, joins and aggregations. Finally, Spark needs some memory for off-heap storage as well. Spark makes tradeoffs among the memory it needs to allocate for storing the RDDS, for running the shuffle processes and for the off-heap storage.

Jobs consist of tasks. Tasks execute the Spark code. The driver is the boss—it assigns tasks to the worker nodes. The worker processes run the executors, which can include multiple tasks. The driver program is responsible for running the application and managing all necessary operations when the application performs an action.

How Resources are Allocated to Spark

When you run Spark on YARN, Hadoop doesn't see anything special, so to speak, about YARN—it's just another application, just as MapReduce is an application that runs on YARN. This is wonderful, since all the things that you've learned about the YARN architecture, resource allocation and tuning remain fully valid when running Spark on YARN.

As you learned earlier in this book, YARN relies on two key entities: the ResourceManager, which manages the resources available in a Hadoop cluster, and the ApplicationMaster, which is in charge of requesting resources from the ResourceManager and allocating them to the NodeManagers running on each of the nodes so the cluster can execute individual tasks. The ApplicationMaster is application specific—when discussing MapReduce execution earlier, I was referring to a MapReduce-framework-specific ApplicationMaster. When running Spark jobs, YARN uses the Spark-specific ApplicationMaster.

YARN allocates resources through the logical abstraction called containers, which refer to a set of resources such as memory and CPU. For example, a container may consist of 2 CPU cores and 4GB of RAM. When Spark's ApplicationMaster requests resources from the ResourceManager, it does so by estimating the resource requirements of the job and requesting a specific number of containers to complete the job. Based on the availability of resources in the cluster, the ApplicationMaster will ask the NodeManagers on the worker nodes to each launch a specific number of containers.

When you run Spark on YARN, Spark sits right on top of the YARN architecture and uses the same procedures to request resources as all other frameworks and applications. Thus, YARN containers are the way YARN allocates resources to Spark jobs. Regardless of the fact that Spark uses entities such as a driver and executors for each job, when it comes to the actual allocation of resources, all Spark sees is a bunch of YARN resource containers. All the executors and the driver run inside these containers. The ApplicationMaster handles all the inter-container communications.

The ApplicationMaster itself will run in a single container. Executors, the workhorses of Spark, run inside a YARN container as well (1 executor per container). When I discussed MapReduce resource allocation in Chapter 18, "Tuning the Cluster Resources, Optimizing MapReduce Jobs and Benchmarking," I referred to map and reduce containers. But that's where we stopped, in the sense that each map or reduce task was assumed to be run inside its own container and that was that. When it comes to Spark executors, there's a more fine-grained entity within the executor container—tasks. Each executor container will have a set of tasks that actually performs a chunk of the work.

Spark uses two key resources managed by YARN: CPU and memory. While disk I/O and network performance have a bearing on application performance, YARN doesn't really focus on those resources.

Limits on the Resource Allocation to Spark Applications

In Chapter 3, "Creating and Configuring a Simple Hadoop 2 Cluster," you learned how you can set YARN properties to control the maximum amounts of memory and virtual CPU cores that YARN can use. Spark's resource usage (RAM and CPU) is limited by the same properties, so let me summarize them here for you:

> **Note**
>
> You can set the configuration properties in different ways. Take the property that sets the number of executor cores (discussed in the next section). You can set the `spark.executor.cores` property inside the spark-defaults.conf file, or in a `SparkConf` object. Alternatively, you can specify the `-executor-cores` flag when you invoke `spark-submit`, `spark-shell`, or `pyspark` from the command line.

- The `yarn.nodemanager.resource.memory-mb` parameter sets the ceiling on the memory that you can allocate to all containers running on a cluster node where the NodeManager runs. This memory can be used for Spark as well as for non-Spark applications (MapReduce and other programs).

- The yarn.nodemanager.resource.cpu-vcores property determines the maximum number of cores used by all the containers on a node.

As you can recall from my discussion of how YARN allocates memory (see Chapter 6, "Running Applications in a Cluster—The Spark Framework"), memory allocation is done in chunks, with the chunk size based on the value of the yarn.scheduler.minimum-allocation-mb property—the minimum chunk of memory that YARN can assign for every container request.

How to Set the Spark Configuration Properties

You set the Spark resource configuration in the spark-defaults.conf file, and the resource allocation parameters are named spark.xx.xx, as in spark.driver.cores.

You can set the Spark properties in three ways:

- Set them in the code via SparkConf (in a Cloudera setup it's the /etc/spark/conf/spark-defaults.conf file).
- Set the switches in the spark-submit tool.
- Store the configuration property values in the spark-defaults.conf file.

A typical Spark defaults.conf file looks like the following:

```
executor.memory    8G
spark.driver.memory      16G
spark.driver.maxResultSize 8G
spark.akka.frameSize     512
```

The **precedence order** is in the same order as I've listed the alternatives, with the configuration properties you set in the code getting the highest precedence.

In Chapter 6, I explained how you can launch a Spark application in two different modes in YARN:

- In the **yarn-client** mode, the Spark driver runs inside the client process. The YARN ApplicationMaster process requests resources from YARN on behalf of the application.
- In the **yarn-cluster** mode, the Spark driver runs within the YARN-managed ApplicationMaster process—the client goes away after initiating the application. The cluster mode isn't appropriate for using Spark in an interactive fashion. Spark applications that need user input need to use spark-shell or pyspark (client mode).

Spark resource allocation in a Hadoop/YARN cluster depends on Spark's run mode, so let's discuss the allocation in the client and the cluster mode separately.

Remember that everything you learned about configuring resource allocation for YARN (in Chapter 3, and in more detail in Chapter 18) remains very much valid when dealing with allocating resources for Spark.

YARN needs to allocate resources to the following key Spark entities:

- The Spark driver
- The executors

Let's start by looking at how you allocate resources to the Spark driver.

Allocating Resources to the Driver

Before I start discussing how you can allocate resources to the Spark driver, let me summarize the role played by the driver.

The Driver's Duties

The driver process, as its name indicates, is the boss—it assigns tasks to the worker nodes. It also maintains the Spark context that stores all the application settings and helps track the resources available to the application. The Spark context also lets the driver perform other tasks besides handing tasks to the workers, such as storing the accumulator and broadcast variables.

The application driver process does the following:

- Breaks the application into jobs, stages and tasks by working with the Spark execution engine
- Services the library dependencies to the executor process that performs tasks on behalf of the Spark application
- Works with the YARN ResourceManager to get resources assigned on various nodes to perform the tasks that comprise the Spark application

> **Note**
>
> In the Spark runtime, the driver is in charge of
>
> - Defining and invoking actions on the RDDs
> - Tracking the RDD's lineage
>
> The workers (executors) do the following:
>
> - Store the RDD partitions
> - Perform the RDD transformations

Once the driver gets the resources it requests from YARN to execute a Spark application, it creates an execution plan, which is a directed acyclic graph (DAG) of actions and transformations for the application code, and sends it to the worker nodes to which it assigns resources.

Spark will then optimize the DAG, such as minimizing the shuffles, for example, and decomposing it into stages and finally individual tasks that actually execute the application's code. Stages are sets of transformations that Spark performs on the RDDs. Figure 19.1 shows the basic Spark workflow. The worker processes run the code as well as store the cached data.

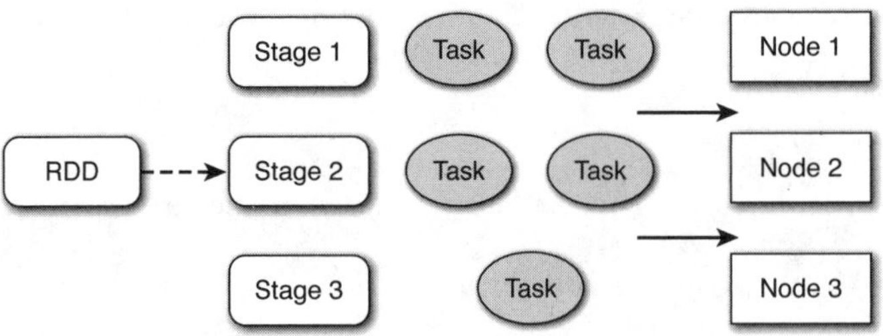

Figure 19.1 The Spark workflow

The driver process contains two components that handle the assignment of tasks:

- The DAG scheduler process divides the DAG into tasks.
- The task scheduler, which knows about the availability of resources, schedules the tasks on various nodes in the cluster. Once the task scheduler does its task assignment, the complete DAG is sent over to the worker nodes where executors carry out the DAG's operations. If any tasks fail or are lagging behind, the task scheduler will restart the failed jobs or create additional tasks to pick up the load of the stragglers.

Since you can run YARN in both the client mode and the cluster mode, let's learn how to allocate resources to the Spark driver in both of these modes in the following sections.

Resource Allocation for the Driver in the Client Mode

In the client mode, Spark resource allocation depends on the following two configuration properties.

- `spark.yarn.am.memory`: Use this property to assign the memory used by the YARN ApplicationMaster in the client mode. The default value is `512m`. Here is an example:

  ```
  spark.yarn.am.memory 777m
  ```

  You can assign memory in kilobytes (k), megabytes (m), gigabytes (g), terabytes (t) and even petabytes (p) if you have it!
- `spark.yarn.am.cores`: This property lets you specify the number of CPU cores the YARN ApplicationMaster can use in the client mode. Here is an example:

  ```
  spark.yarn.am.cores 4
  ```

  The default value for this parameter is 1.

Since YARN assigns all resources in the form of containers, what would be the size of the containers? The fact that I've set the memory allocation (through the `spark.yarn.am.memory` parameter) at `777m` doesn't mean that YARN will assign containers sized 777MB.

Spark allocates a certain amount of off-heap memory to the AM process in the client mode. The property `spark.yarn.am.memoryOverhead` determines the size of this off-heap memory allocation. The default value is the following:

```
AM Memory*0.10, with a minimum of 384M.
```

In this case, I assigned 777MB for the AM, and 10 percent of that is 77.7MB, which is lower than the minimum of 384MB for overhead. The YARN container size for the AM will be 777MB + 384MB, which is 1,161MB.

The default value of this property is 1,024MB, so to allocate 1,161MB in our case, YARN needs to round up things and allocate a container that's 2,048MB (2GB) in size for the AM. So, our AM container will have 2GB RAM (with a Java heap size of `-Xmx777M`) and 4 CPU cores per our configuration.

> **Note**
>
> In Spark on YARN, executors run inside "containers."

Resource Allocation for the Driver in the Cluster Mode

In the yarn-cluster mode of operation, the Spark driver runs inside the YARN ApplicationMaster process. So, the resources you allocate for the job's ApplicationMaster are what determines the resources available to the driver. Following is how you configure the driver-related resource configuration properties that control the resource allocation for the ApplicationMaster.

- `spark.driver.cores`: This is how you specify the number of cores used by the driver in the YARN cluster mode. Since in the cluster mode the driver runs inside the same JVM as the YARN ApplicationMaster, this property controls the CPU cores allocated to the YARN ApplicationMaster process. For example:

  ```
  spark.driver.cores 2 (default is 1)
  ```

  In a production setting, raise the value of this parameter to something like 8 or 16.
- `spark.yarn.driver.memory`: Specifies the amount of memory for the driver in the cluster mode. For example:

  ```
  spark.yarn.driver.memory 1024m (default is 512m)
  ```

  The default is only 0.5GB, and in a production setting, just as you do for the `spark.driver.cores` property, you must raise the value of this property to something like 8 or 16GB.

If you were to set these parameters at the command line when submitting your Spark application, you'd do it like so:

```
$ yarn-cluster /opt/test/spark/spark-1.3.1/bin/spark-submit
--class org.apache.spark.examples.SparkPi  \
--driver-memory 1665m \
--driver-cores 2 \
/opt/test/spark/spark-1.3.1/lib/spark-examples*.jar 1000
```

Note that, as with the client mode, there's an analogous property named `spark.yarn.driver.memoryOverhead` for specifying the off-heap memory in the cluster mode. This property is by default 10 percent of the memory you assign to the ApplicationMaster, with a minimum value of `384m`.

As with the extra memory you allocate for the individual executors, the off-heap storage memory for the driver is a dynamic entity. Thus, although you assign 10 percent for the off-heap storage, the actual usage will be between 6-10 percent over the life of the application.

> **Tip**
>
> In the yarn-cluster mode, when you configure the Spark driver resources, you are indirectly configuring the YARN ApplicationMaster service since the driver runs inside the ApplicationMaster.

Now that you've learned how to configure resources for the Spark driver, it's time to find out how to allocate resources for the executors.

Configuring Resources for the Executors

All Spark work is performed on the worker nodes—that is, all the tasks run on the worker nodes. You assign almost all of the resources for a Spark job to the executors, which run within JVMs. The only entity other than the executors for which you assign memory is the driver, and compared to the total amount of resources you allocate to the executors, the driver's resources aren't that high. Figure 19.2 shows the architectures of the executor and task.

There are two aspects to managing the executors:

- Configuring the number of executors
- Allocating resources (RAM, etc.) to the executors

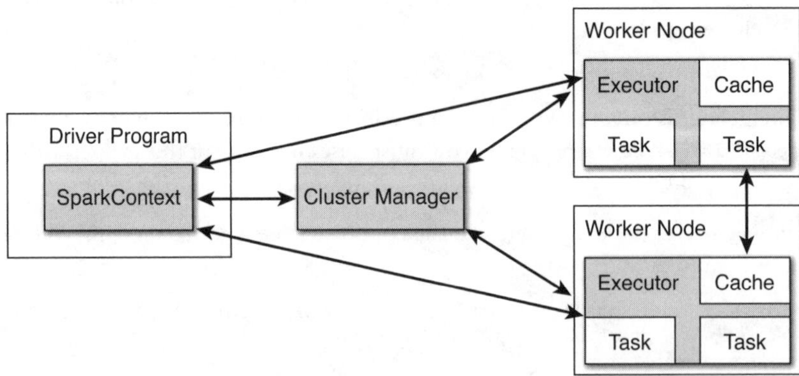

Figure 19.2 The architecture of the executors and workers running on a worker node

> **Tip**
>
> The `spark.executor.memory` property is specific to the JVM. When using pySpark, make sure there's enough memory left for running Python itself.

Configuring the Number of Executors

Regardless of the mode of operation (client or cluster), there's only a single driver. However, you can control the number of executors with the `spark.executor.instances` property (or the `--num-executors` command-line flag).

The default value for the `spark.executor.instances` property is 2.

If you choose to configure dynamic allocation (`spark.dynamicAllocation.enabled`) and set the `spark.executor.instances` property, dynamic allocation is turned off. Spark uses the number of executors you specify instead. This means that the `spark.executor.instances` property overrides the `spark.dynamicAllocation` property.

If you turn on dynamic allocation (explained in the following section), you must ensure that you don't set the `spark.executor.instances` property, since Spark applications automatically increase or decrease their requests for executors based on the workload of pending tasks.

> **Tip**
>
> When dynamic allocation is turned on, you can override it by setting the `-num-executors` flag or the `spark.executor.instances` configuration property.

In Spark an executor is synonymous with a container so far as resource allocation is concerned—one executor, one container. Therefore, allocation of executors for Spark turns into the allocation of containers by YARN. When Spark calculates the number of executors it needs, it communicates with the ApplicationMaster, which in turn contacts the YARN ResourceManager to request the containers.

Allocating Resources for the Executors

Unlike in the case of the resource allocation for the driver process, when it comes to allocating resources for the executors, you do the same thing in both the client and the cluster modes.

Use the following two parameters to set the memory and CPU allocations for the Spark executors that perform the grunt work for the Spark applications.

- `spark.executor.memory`: Configures the Java heap memory for the executors. You can also configure this by setting the `-executor-memory` flag. The `spark.executor.memory` property configures the size of the Java heap for the executors. You influence the following two key areas of Spark execution by setting the executor memory:
  - The amount of data Spark can cache
  - The maximum size of the shuffle used for aggregations, joins and grouping
- `spark.executor.cores`: Sets the number of cores for an executor. You can also add the `--executor-cores` flag to set this property.

JVMs use some Java heap memory for things such as internal strings and direct byte buffers (this is also called **off heap** usage). Spark adds the value you set for the `spark.yarn.executor.memoryOverhead` property to the executor memory when making its full memory request to YARN for allocating the executor memory. The default for this memory overhead is max (384MB, 0.10*`spark.executor.memory`) and is determined by the parameter `spark.yarn.executor.memoryOverhead`. This parameter thus determines the amount of off-heap memory to be allocated per executor. This memory is used by the executor for storing entities such as internal strings, other native overheads and so on. Note that this tends to grow with the size of the executor size and ranges between 6-10 percent on average.

When YARN assigns the memory to the executors, some rounding up is involved. The YARN properties `yarn.scheduler.minimum.allocation-mb` and `yarn.scheduler.increment-allocation-mb` determine the actual size of the minimum and incremental requests for RAM.

The default value of 1GB is too low for many Spark applications. In a production setting, you can raise the value to a much higher value such as 3, 8 or 16GB per executor.

When you configure multiple tasks per executor, the memory you assign for the executor (`spark.yarn.executor.memory`) is divided equally among the tasks.

Figure 19.3 shows where the Spark executor memory allocation sits relative to the total memory you allocate to YARN through the `yarn.nodemanager.resource.memory-mb` parameter.

> **Tip**
>
> The number of CPU cores you assign per executor determines the number of concurrent tasks per executor.

About 5-6 tasks per executor usually will achieve full write throughput. If you allocate more CPU cores than this, the HDFS client will find it hard to process all the concurrent threads. So, too many executor threads aren't advisable. The executors you

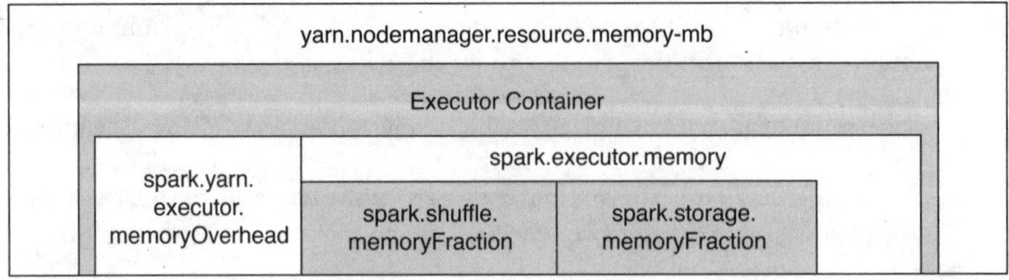

Figure 19.3 How the executor memory fits into the YARN memory and the components of an executor container

assign for a job won't be released until the job finishes, even though you may not be using them. Thus, keeping the number of executors low will keep you from wasting the cluster resources.

Tasks and Executors

By setting the number of cores an executor can run, you're really configuring the number of concurrent tasks an executor can run. Each processing core runs a single process, in this case a task, at a time. So the number of tasks that can be run by an executor is hard limited by the number of processor cores you configure for that executor.

The amount of memory that's available to any single Spark operation is limited to the memory you give to an executor divided by the number of tasks running inside that executor.

As with the driver memory allocation, there's a way to specify off-heap memory for overhead. The `spark.yarn.executor.memoryOverhead` parameter helps set the overhead, and it works the same way as its counterparts for the driver memory allocation. That is, it is 10 percent of the value you set for the `spark.executor.memory` parameter:

```
spark.yarn.executor.memoryOverhead = executorMemory*0.10 (minimum of 384m)
```

The following example shows how to set all the properties I've discussed thus far when submitting your Spark application:

```
$ ./bin/spark-submit --class org.apache.spark.examples.SparkPi \
    --master yarn \
    --deploy-mode cluster \
    --driver-memory 4g \
    --executor-memory 2g \
    --executor-cores 1 \
    --queue thequeue \
    lib/spark-examples*.jar \
    10
```

Table 19.1 summarizes the way you allocate containers for Spark executors.

Table 19.1 **A Summary of the Resource Allocation for a Spark Executor**

Configuration	Description	Default Value
`spark.executor.instances` (`--num-executors`)	Number of executors	2
`spark.executor.cores` (`--executor-cores`)	Number of CPU cores per executor	1
`spark.executor.memory` (`--executor-memory`)	Java heap size per executor	512MB
`spark.yarn.executor.memory` (overhead minimum is 384MB)	off-heap memory	executorMemory * 0.10

How Spark Uses its Memory

In the previous sections, I explained how you allocate memory to Spark by allocating memory to the driver and executors. How exactly does Spark use this memory you allocate to it? Spark uses the memory allocated to it for two purposes: executing code and storing data. Memory Spark uses for execution includes the memory required by operations such as shuffles, joins and sorts. Storage memory is what Spark uses for caching and moving internal data across the cluster.

Storage and computation use the same pool of memory—when no memory is being used for execution, storage can use all the available memory and, similarly, execution can use all the memory when no data is being cached in memory.

The need for more execution memory can lead to eviction of objects occupying memory, until memory used for storage falls under a threshold. The threshold means that applications that cache RDDs can in effect guarantee or reserve a minimum storage space in which to store RDDs without the fear of those RDDs being evicted.

> **Note**
>
> The default values for `spark.memory.fraction` (0.75) and `spark.memory.storageFraction` (0.5) are true for Spark 1.6. For Spark 2.0, the values are 0.6, and 0.5, respectively.

Configuring Memory Usage

In order to understand how Spark assigns memory for execution and storage, I use the following symbols to represent various components of memory (see Figure 19.3 for a graphical representation of Spark memory allocation):

- M: Represents the unified memory for storage and execution
- R: Minimum storage space (the threshold) below which you can't evict RDDs from storage

Use the following two configuration properties to adjust the memory available for storage and execution:

- `spark.memory.fraction`: This fraction expresses M as a fraction of the JVM heap space. The default value is 0.75. What this means is that 25 percent of the memory you allocate to the executor is used for storing entities such as user data structures and internal Spark metadata. In reality, this fraction shows M as a fraction of the JVM. Apache Spark recommends that you leave this property at its default value.
- `spark.memory.storageFraction`: This parameter helps configure the size of reserved memory (R) for storage as a fraction of total memory—that is, R as a fraction of M. The default is 0.5. Note that in Spark 2.0, the spark.memory.fraction property defaults to 0.6 and this property (spark.memory.storageFraction) has a default value of 0.5. This means that any RDDs cached by an application are

protected against eviction until they cross the threshold of 50 percent of the memory allocated for storage. Note that the higher you make this value, the less working memory there is for execution, and tasks may spill to disk more often. Apache Spark recommends that you leave this property at its default value.

The default value of 0.5 for this property means that Spark uses 50 percent of the executor's memory to cache RDDs and the other 50 percent for storing regular objects during the execution of tasks. If you're beset by excessive garbage collection, you may decide that you don't need 50 percent for the RDDs and reduce it to say 40 percent so 60 percent is available for object creation, thus lessening the need for garbage collection. Here is how to change the memory fraction going to RDD storage:

```
$ spark-shell --conf spark.storage.memoryFraction=0.4
```

If Spark is spending too much time performing garbage collection, you can reduce the fraction of memory devoted to RDD caching by lowering the value of the `spark.memory.storageFraction` property.

So, How Much Memory Can an Executor Really Use?

The memory you allocate to the executors is key to how a Spark application performs. Let's say you set the value of the `spark.executor.memory` property at 4GB. How much of this do the tasks running inside an executor get to actually use for executing code? The following analysis shows how much memory the executor can actually use for executing code.

1. Before it does anything, Spark subtracts about 300MB as "reserved memory" from the Java heap, which is 4GB in this example. So, you're now left with 4,096 – 300 = 3,796MB in the Java heap.
2. The `spark.memory.fraction` parameter, whose default value is 0.75, will shrink the available memory to 0.75 * 3,796MB = 2,847MB or 2.78GB.
3. The `spark.memory.storageFraction` property (default value 0.5) will ensure that 50 percent of the memory left for the executor in step 2 is reserved for storage where it can cache data. The storage fraction in our example then is 0.5 * 2,847MB = 1,423.5MB. This is the initial storage memory region size.
4. The executor can use the other 50 percent—that is, 1,423.5MB—for executing the application code.

I've done this little exercise for a good reason. Take a good look at your application and figure out approximate ratios for storage and execution. Based on this, adjust the values of the `spark.memory.fraction` and the `spark.memory.storageFraction` properties. Spark recommends that you leave the default settings on since they apply to most use cases. However, each Spark application is different, so in some cases you may pay no heed to the recommendation and feel free to adjust the values of these two critical memory-related parameters.

Finding Current Memory Usage

If you want to figure out how much memory an RDD needs, the best thing to do is to go ahead and create the RDD and cache it. You can then review the Spark web UI's Storage page statistics to figure out current memory usage by the RDD.

You can use the SizeEstimator's `estimate` method to estimate the memory used by a specific object. You can find details about the SizeEstimator here:

```
https://spark.apache.org/docs/1.4.0/api/java/org/apache/spark/util/SizeEstimator.html
```

You can try out various storage/execution memory settings to optimize memory usage.

Things to Remember

Following are some of the important things you may want to think about when configuring resources for the Spark driver and the executors.

Use Trial and Error for Sizing the Executor Memory

If you run the executors with an excessive amount of memory, garbage collection (GC) could get lengthier and bite you. However, in many cases you need to set a higher memory allocation for the executors since the default is only 1,024MB. You can try different higher settings during your tuning exercises to find the appropriate number for a specific application. In most cases you don't need to size the memory for an executor larger than 6GB. Around 40GB seems to be a good size for high memory allocation to a single executor. Any higher, and garbage collection could end up adversely affecting application performance, although this is mitigated if you're using newer GC methods such as G1GC.

> **Note**
>
> A task will process a single RDD partition on a single CPU core.

Limit the Number of Tasks per Executor

In general, a small number of large executors yields better results than having a large number of small executors, which requires moving data around through the network. You don't gain much by increasing the number of cores per executor beyond 4 or 5. This number of cores means there will be 4 or 5 tasks running concurrently per executor, and together, they can get you a pretty high write throughput.

If you have too many threads running at the same time, the HDFS client may have trouble keeping up. You're likely to see HDFS I/O issues in this scenario.

Executors with just one task negate the benefits of running multiple tasks per container (JVM). You'll learn in Chapter 20 that **broadcast variables** are replicated on each executor. If you have too many tiny executors (a single core and just enough memory to run one task), you're holding too many copies of the same data. If you were to use larger executors you could reap the benefits of running multiple tasks within the same JVM—in this case, all the tasks inside an executor can use the same copy of the broadcast variable.

There's also a tradeoff you need to consider between a large number of executors (`num-executors`) and large memory (`executor-memory`) for an executor. Larger amounts of memory for an executor does not always translate into better performance. Excessive memory for executors is not advisable since it may lead to too many garbage collection delays. Thus, it may be better to configure a larger number of smaller executors, rather than a few executors running with large JVMs.

Here's a simple example (influenced by Sandy Ryza's excellent article on tuning Spark jobs, available at `http://blog.cloudera.com/blog/2015/03/how-to-tune-your-apache-spark-jobs-part-2/`).

Let's assume you have 6 nodes, each with 72GB of memory, and 16 processor cores. Leaving a good amount for general overhead, you can allocate 64GB of memory for YARN by setting the `yarn.nodemanager.resource.memory-mb` parameter to 64GB on each node.

You can create a very small number of executors and assign each of them a large number of resources, as shown here:

```
--num-executors 6 (1 executor per node)
--executor-cores 15
--executor-memory 60 g (don't forget that you'll need to account for some memory
for executor memory overhead as well)
```

Using 15 cores per executor is overkill and will lead to a poor HDFS I/O throughput. You can alternatively do the following, where you create a very large number of executors, each with the minimum amount of cores (1):

```
--num-executors 90 (15 executors per node)
--executor-cores 1
--executor-memory 4g
```

This isn't great either, since you're using too fine-grained a resource allocation, with numerous tiny executors running around. Running too many small executors means that you can't benefit from running multiple tasks within a single JVM. When you want to use the broadest variables for optimal performance, for example, you'll need to replicate them on each executor. Too many executors mean that there'll be a lot of copies of the data. A much better strategy would be to configure things in the following way:

```
--num-executors 17 (3 executors per node for 5 nodes and 2 executors for the
sixth node)
--executor-cores 5
--executor-memory 19g
```

In this configuration, you'll end up with three executors running on five of the six nodes, with the last node running just two executors, since it also runs the ApplicationMaster. The executor memory of 19GB per executor was arrived at by using the following simple set of computations:

```
Total memory YARN can use on a server = 64g
```

Initial executor memory is calculated as 64/3 = approximately 21GB. You subtract 0.07 of this to account for the executor memory overhead. The remaining amount of memory is what you can allocate to each of the executors, as shown here:

```
21*0.07 = 1.47
21 - 1.47 = 19
```

Type of Workloads and Resource Allocation

In practice, your resource allocation for the executors will depend on your workloads. Here are some guidelines:

- In ETL jobs, you often have map-only jobs, or just a few reduces. Since ETL jobs don't often cache their data, you don't need to specify a storage fraction for these types of jobs. In other words, you can set the value of `spark.memory.storageFraction` to zero for these types of jobs. You can start out with executors sized at 2-4GB (`--executor-memory 4g`, for example) and two cores (`--executor-cores 2`).
- Data analysis jobs benefit immensely from caching, since Spark often repeatedly queries the same datasets. How high the executor memory ought to be will depend on the size of the dataset. If you assume it's going to take around 2GB of memory per gigabyte of data, and your dataset is 40GB in size, executor memory will be 40GB (`--executor-memory 40g`). If you are working with a machine-learning job, where the application driver does heavy work during the building of the model, you can bump up the memory to the driver, say by specifying a value such as `spark.driver.memory=3g`.

Probably the best way to figure out how to optimally allocate memory to your Spark jobs is to check the memory usage by jobs in the Spark UI. Under the Executors tab, you need to focus on the following two columns to check memory usage:

- The **Storage Memory** column shows the current storage memory allocation to the executors and the driver. This column shows both the amount of memory available and the memory that's being actually used on each executor for caching data. If you notice that the executors are using all of the memory under Storage Memory, you may want to increase the size of the executor.
- The **Shuffle Write** column reflects the amount of data that was spilled to disk before performing a shuffle operation. If you see a large amount of shuffle writes, increase the memory for execution to reduce the intermediate disk writes because of the shuffle operations.

Cluster or Client Mode?

In the client deployment, your `spark-submit` script creates the driver in the same process as submit-script. You can easily track and debug the application since the output messages are printed right on the screen. If you issue the `spark-submit` command from your laptop and then shut down the laptop to go home or something, the job is going to die, whereas in the cluster mode it doesn't matter—once you launch the job, it'll continue to run on the cluster's nodes. When you run in the cluster mode it is the ResourceManager that determines on which specific node the driver process will run—you can't specify it. Therefore, it's important that you set up all the dependent libraries, such as the JAR files and Python .py files, on all the nodes of your cluster.

While the client mode is mainly meant for REPL (read-evaluate-print-loop) based experimentation and development (you can get results immediately), and not considered suitable for running long-lived Spark applications, there are some good reasons to use this mode in a production setting. I show a good example later in this section.

The `spark.driver.maxResultSize` configuration property determines the total size of all the partitions in each Spark action, such as `collect()`. The default value of this property is 1GB, and you may want to bump it up when dealing with large datasets since the job will be killed if the total size of the partitions is beyond the limit you set for this property. If you're going to raise the value of this parameter, make sure you also bump up the value of the configuration property `spark.driver.memory`.

> **Tip**
>
> A value of 0 for the `spark.driver.maxResultSize` configuration property makes its value unlimited.

When dealing with a long-running Spark application, it's useful to know that Spark stores all metadata, such as stages and tasks, that it has generated during the course of the application run. By default, Spark retains this information throughout the length of the application run. When you run Spark for days on end, such as in a Spark Streaming application, you can tell Spark to periodically get rid of metadata older than a threshold. You do this by setting the `spark.cleaner.ttl` parameter to a positive number (in seconds). The default value is `infinite:` and could prove to be a drain on the driver's memory. Remember that when you do this, Spark will also remove all RDDs that have been in memory for longer than the duration you've set.

It's important to understand that the driver isn't merely in charge of telling executors and tasks which operations to perform. Often it also centralizes data that its gets from all the executors running as part of a job. For example, the `collect()` method on an RDD will end with all executors sending their data to the driver. When an application is crunching through very large data files that are in the terabytes range, especially, the application may crash since the driver often doesn't have the amount of memory to store these large data sets.

> **Tip**
>
> If your job aggregates large amounts of data (for example with a `collect()` action), allocate more memory to the driver. Otherwise, driver memory can be quite small.

Let's say you want to join two 1TB data sets. Your Hadoop/YARN cluster nodes all have 256GB of RAM. The two files need to be joined in memory but none of the nodes in your cluster can handle it if you run the job in the yarn-cluster mode. A better strategy here would be to run the job from a client that you've built with a very large amount of RAM, such as 3TB, and run the job in the client mode. The driver will run from that special node, and Spark can now perform the join in its memory. You can launch all other Spark applications in the yarn-cluster mode.

Frequently, applications are submitted from a gateway machine that's physically co-located with the worker nodes. Client mode works well in this case. If you're going to submit applications from machines not co-located with the worker nodes (say from your laptop), cluster mode will be better since it'll minimize the network latency between the driver and the executors.

Configuring Spark-Related Network Parameters

Spark uses the Akka framework for its network communications. There are two important network configuration properties you may need to adjust in a production environment:

- `spark.akka.framesize`: This property, whose default value is 128 (MB), sets the maximum message size for messages sent between the driver and the executors concerning the map output size. You may want to change this if a job is running a very large number of map and reduce tasks and you notice references to the frame size.
- `spark.akka.threads`: This property sets the number of akka actor threads to use for communication. If you've configured the driver with many CPU cores, you may need to raise this from its default value of 4.

Dynamic Resource Allocation when Running Spark on YARN

Under dynamic execution, a Spark job doesn't reserve executors in advance. It simply acquires executors and relinquishes them as the jobs progress. When the first job finishes, Spark releases the executors that were assigned to this job back to the cluster, so other applications can use those resources. The Spark application will acquire a new set of executors only when a new jobs starts. As you can tell, this increases the rate of utilization of the cluster.

You can set the number of Spark executors with the `spark.executor.instances` property as explained in the following section.

However, Spark allows you to dynamically adjust the resources an application consumes based on its workload. This means that the application won't run with a fixed number of executor processes—the number of executors will go up and down based on the application's workload.

Dynamic and Static Resource Allocation

In order to understand how dynamic resource allocation helps you, you need to delve deeper into how Spark handles the executors. Executors tend to be long running—once a job finishes, the executors aren't immediately killed with the job. Rather, they remain after the current job finishes and are reused by future jobs. This lets the future jobs access the intermediate data cached in memory.

Spark's execution model is quite different from that of MapReduce and similar systems. Whereas MapReduce launches short-lived containers for each map and reduce task (containers are killed after the map or reduce task completes), Spark reuses long-running executors for speed. Long-lived executors mean that when you're running jobs from spark-shell, the spark-shell may become idle, but it continues to hang on to the cluster resources for a long time, which means other applications can't use those resources. This is a static resource model then and results in more resources being allocated than are used.

Note

Dynamic allocation lets you take advantage of Spark's speed due to its reuse of cluster resources, without getting hurt by Spark's tendency to hold onto resources for a long time.

Dynamic allocation is intended to more efficiently utilize a cluster's resources. It allows Spark applications to scale the executors up and down based on your workload. It removes executors if they're idle (for N seconds) and if it needs more executors, it requests them. Additional executors are requested when there are pending tasks. The scaling up of executors is done in multiple rounds, with an exponential increase in the number of executors over time, as long as Spark sees that there are pending tasks. Spark uses the exponential growth strategy in case it needs many executors.

Long running ETL jobs, interactive applications using the Spark shell and any applications with large shuffles are all good use cases for dynamic allocation of resources.

How Spark Manages Dynamic Resource Allocation

Spark monitors the number of pending tasks periodically, to determine if it should increase or decrease the number of executors. If there is a large backlog of pending tasks, Spark applications will add executors in a progressively increasing fashion, by adding 1, 2, 4 and 8 executors or more.

You can configure dynamic resource allocation at a fine-grained level by using the following configuration properties:

- `spark.dynamicAllocation.schedulerbacklogTimeout`: This is the duration (in seconds) for which there have been pending tasks waiting for resources.
- `spark.dynamicAllocation.sustainedSchedulerBacklogTimeout`: This is the same as the previous parameter, but it is used for subsequent executor requests.
- `spark.dynamicAllocation.executorIdleTimeout`: If the executors have been idle for the duration specified by this property (in seconds), Spark de-allocates the idle executors.

Enabling Dynamic Resource Allocation

By default, dynamic allocation is disabled. In order to set up your applications for dynamic resource allocation, make the following configuration changes:

1. Set the `spark.dynamicAllocation.enabled` property to `true` in Spark's configuration file (spark.default.conf) or in the application.
2. Set up an external shuffle service in the worker nodes. You do this by adding the spark-<version>-yarn-shuffle.jar file to the class path of the NodeManagers running on each of the nodes in the Hadoop cluster. The location of this JAR file varies. If you build Spark yourself, it'll be under $SPARK_HOME/network/yarn/target/scala-<version>.

3. On each of the cluster's nodes, add spark-shuffle to the yarn.nodemanager .aux-services property (yarn-site.xml file).

```
<property>
<name>yarn.nodemanager.aux-services</name>
<value>spark_shuffle</value>
</property>
```

4. Set the yarn.nodemanger.aux-services.spark-shuffle.class to org.apache .spark.network.yarn.YarnShuffleService. (in the yarn-site.xml file).

```
<property>
<name>yarn.nodemanager.aux-services.spark_shuffle.class</name>
<value>org.apache.spark.network.yarn.YarnShuffleService</value>
</property>
```

5. Set the spark.shuffle.service.enabled property to true.
6. Restart the NodeManagers on all nodes.

Enabling dynamic resource allocation obviates the need for specifying the number of executors each time you run a job with the -num-executors property. Spark and YARN together will take the responsibility of adjusting the number of executors based on the workload.

Dynamic resource allocation is a truly useful feature—long-running Spark jobs that are resource intensive won't hog critical resources, instead releasing them back to YARN so it can use them for other jobs.

Strategy—Use Higher-Level APIs

Using a higher-level rather than a lower-level API is in most cases a smart way to improve performance. This means that you use

- DataFrame APIs for core processing instead of RDDs
- Spark ML instead of Spark MLib for machine learning applications
- Spark SQL for structured query processing

Storage Formats and Compressing Data

The way you store the input data for Spark processing is crucial to the performance of Spark applications. You consider the same variables when evaluating the appropriate file format for Spark processing as you do when dealing with MapReduce processing, as explained in Chapter 10, "Data Protection, File Formats and Accessing HDFS." The key considerations for the file format then, are

- Splittability of the file
- Can the file splits be processed in parallel?
- Size of the files
- Compression possibilities and available compression codecs

Storage Formats

You can store data in various storage formats. Spark can handle both structured and unstructured storage formats, such as text files, SequenceFiles and Hadoop file formats. CSV files, JSON files and XML files are special, structured text files.

As I explained in Chapter 7, "Running Spark Applications," you can use the `textFile` method to let Spark read a text file. Spark can also read a set of text files from a folder in a single move using the `wholeTextFiles` method.

Let's see how to best handle the specialized text files when working with Spark.

CSV Files

In order to analyze data sorted in the CSV format, you need to create a DataFrame on top of it. While you can use the default `textFile` method and specify a schema yourself, there's a better alternative. Use the Databrick's `spark-csv` package to make things easier. Here's an example showing how to use the `spark-csv` package:

```
val df = sql.Context.read
.format("com.databricks.spark.csv")
.option("header", "true"),
.option("inferSchema", "true").load("mydata.csv")
```

JSON Files

You can provide the schema programmatically or let Spark infer the schema from the data. There are two benefits to providing the data yourself:

- It saves time since Spark doesn't have to read the whole dataset to infer the schema.
- You can make Spark ignore the fields you don't need by specifying only the fields you want.

XML files do not work well as a file format because of their verbosity and their not having an XML object for each line. Due to these reasons, these files can't be read in parallel. You can use the `textFile` method to read an XML file, but then you'll be reading it line by line. Although it's not great performance-wise, you can use the `wholeTextfile` method (explained in Chapter 7) to read files when the XML files are small enough to fit in memory. The key of the resulting pair RDD will have the file's path, and the text file will be the value.

SequenceFiles

SequenceFiles are a popular Hadoop storage format, since you can efficiently process them compressed and uncompressed. The sync markers of SequenceFiles make it easy to identify record boundaries. You can parallelize any work you do with SequenceFiles.

Avro Files

Avro is a binary data format where the schema is stored together with the data, making it easy for any application to read the data.

The Spark package spark-avro reads and writes Avro files and converts the same from Avro to the spark SQL schema. Here's how to load an Avro file:

```
import com.databricks.spark.avro._
val avroDF = sqlContext.read.avro("pathToAvroFile")
```

Parquet Files

Parquet is recommended as a storage file format for Spark SQL. Parquet is a columnar file format, which means that you read only the required columns when performing aggregation queries. Parquet file format is efficient storagewise, and is also very efficient compressionwise.

Spark SQL lets you process Parquet files both while preserving the schema and when the schema evolves as when you add new columns to data over time. **Schema evolution** is a feature that can detect and merge the schema changes.

Here's an example that shows how you read a Parquet file with schema merging in effect:

```
val parquetDF = sqlContext.read
                .option("mergeSchema", "true")
                .parquet("parquetFolder")
```

Parquet storage format is great when the source data is partitioned. Let's say the data is partitioned into multiple files such as file1.parquet, file2.parquet and file3.parquet. When you issue a Spark SQL query, Spark will read only those file folders that are required by the `WHERE` clause of the query.

File Sizes

HDFS stores data in blocks, and each HDFS block is mapped to a single partition, which processes all the data in that partition. So, the number of tasks is proportional to the number of blocks and thus the size of your dataset.

HDFS uses a separate block for each file, regardless of the size of the file. So, if you have a large number of small files, you'll be running too many tasks, stressing the driver for the application, which needs to track all these file paths. This results in memory pressure on the driver.

If you're using large files and the files aren't splittable, each of them has to be handled by a single task, which leads to very large partitions—which leads to inefficient data processing.

Compression

You use compression to reduce storage requirements. Here, the compression codec (defined and explained in Chapter 10) plays a key role in determining how efficiently your data is processed. Suppose you have a file that's 10GB in size and your HDFS data block size is 256MB. You'll thus need 40 blocks to store the data and, therefore, 40 tasks to process the data in that file. If this file were to be stored in the gzip format, however, Spark can't run these 40 tasks in parallel to decompress the data, as the gzip format won't allow the decompressing of a single block apart from the rest of the blocks. You end up with just a single task having to process the entire large file, which makes for very slow processing, of course.

As I explained in Chapter 10, when working with compressed data you're engaging in a tradeoff between the compression ratio and speed. Here's a summary:

- gzip offers a good compression ratio. This compression codec is not splittable.
- bizp2 offers an even better compression ratio than gzip and is splittable.
- lzo and lz4 don't offer great compression ratios, but they are very fast. lzo is not splittable unless indexed.
- Snappy is very fast and is splittable.

The Snappy compression codec deserves special mention since it's blazingly fast and is splittable. Since it offers great decompression speeds, if you're planning to read the same dataset often, Snappy makes for a good choice.

You must be careful in how you evaluate the splittability of a file. You need to consider the file format as well here. Let's say you compress a file in the text format with a non-splittable compression codec. When Spark compresses the file, it does so by compressing the entire thing into a single block, using just a single task to do so. However, if you were to use a format such as SequenceFiles or optimized row columnar (ORC) files that support a block structure, Spark can compress the file in parallel using multiple tasks, since the compression can be applied to each block.

Unsplittable files should be small enough that they can be handled by a single Spark task.

Setting the Local Directories for Spark

The `spark.local.dir` property sets the directory you want to use as a scratch space for Spark—this will serve to store both the map output files and the RDDs that Spark stores on disk.

Since I'm discussing Spark on YARN, in the cluster mode, the value you set for the `yarn.nodemanager.local-dirs` parameter (or the `LOCAL_DIRS` environment variable) for YARN will override the value you've set for the `spark.local.dir` property. That is, both the Spark executors and the Spark driver will use the local directories you've configured for YARN with the `yarn.nodemanager.local-dirs` parameter.

In the client mode, however, the Spark executor will use the local directories you configured with the `yarn.nodemanager.local-dirs` parameter, but the Spark driver, since it doesn't run on the YARN cluster in the client mode, uses the directories you specify with the `spark.local.dir` parameter.

Monitoring Spark Applications

The best way to monitor Spark applications and get detailed job statistics is to simply go to the Spark web UI. You can track Spark jobs just as you would a MapReduce job through the `yarn` command as well.

Using the Spark Web UI to Understand Performance

The Spark UI is extremely useful in helping monitor running jobs as well as analyzing jobs that have competed execution.

Here's the URL for accessing the Spark UI:

```
http://<driver_node-ip>:allocatedPort-default4040>
```

The default port is 4040, so when you launch a new application, the web UI is launched on port 4040. If multiple Spark drivers are running, Spark will go down the list of ports, like 4041, 4042 and so on until it finds a free port to launch a web UI for the application.

The Spark UI has several useful tabs, as I explain in the following sections.

The Environment Tab

When you're troubleshooting performance, it's important to know the configuration in place when Spark ran a job. The Environment tab shows all the configuration parameters when a job launched a Spark context, as well as all the JAR files used. Figure 19.4 shows the Environment page in the web UI.

The Jobs Tab

The Jobs tab shows the currently executing jobs and compiled jobs. It shows the number of tasks and stages that were successful and the duration of the job itself. Figure 19.5 shows the Jobs page in the Spark web UI.

The Stages Tab

The Stages tab shows all the stages both completed and running for all jobs. It also shows the amount of input processed as well as the amount of output created by the stages. The

Spark 1.5.0-cdh5.5.1 Jobs Stages Storage Environment Executors SQL Spark shell application UI

Environment

Runtime Information

Name	Value
Java Home	/usr/java/jdk1.8.0_66/jre
Java Version	1.8.0_66 (Oracle Corporation)
Scala Version	version 2.10.4

Spark Properties

Name	Value
spark.app.id	application_1467289669067_5853
spark.app.name	Spark shell
spark.authenticate	false
spark.driver.appUIAddress	http://10.192.2.24:4040
spark.driver.extraLibraryPath	/opt/cloudera/parcels/CDH-5.5.1-1.cdh5.5.1.p1168.923/lib/hadoop/lib/native
spark.driver.host	10.192.2.24
spark.driver.port	26895
spark.dynamicAllocation.enabled	true

Figure 19.4 The Environment page showing the configuration parameters for a Spark job

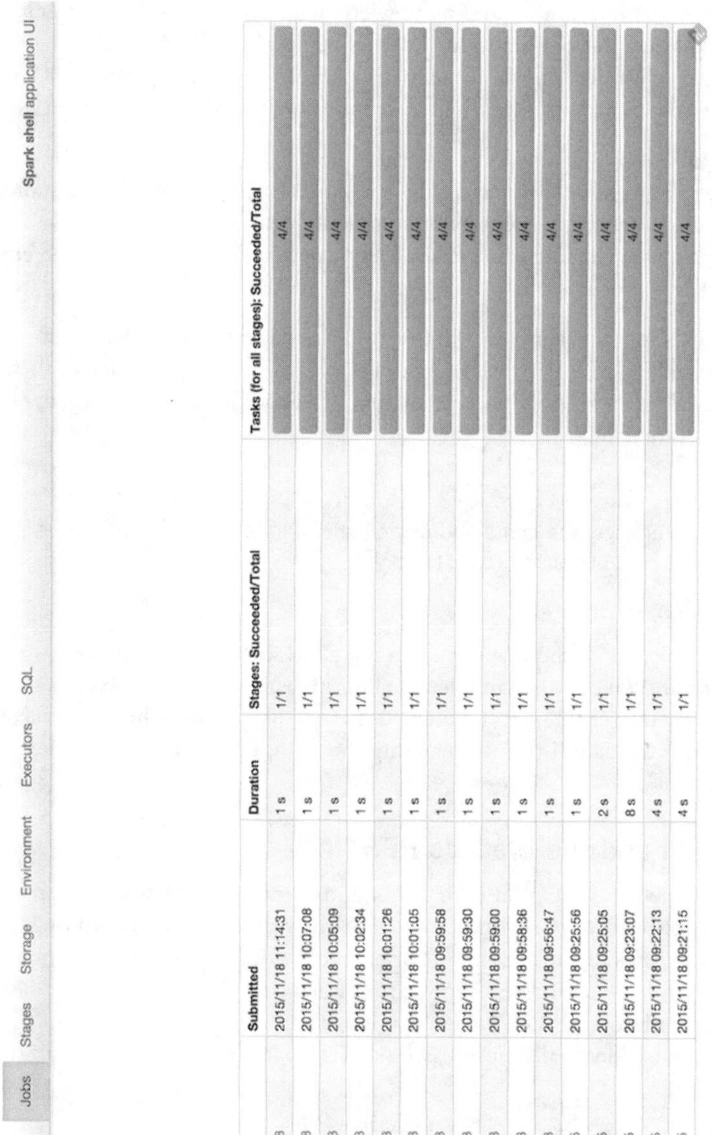

Spark 1.6.0-SNAPSHOT Jobs Stages Storage Environment Executors SQL **Spark shell** application UI

Spark Jobs (?)

Total Uptime: 3.2 h
Scheduling Mode: FIFO
Completed Jobs: 16

▸ Event Timeline

Completed Jobs (16)

Job Id	Description	Submitted	Duration	Stages: Succeeded/Total	Tasks (for all stages): Succeeded/Total
15	count at <console>:28	2015/11/18 11:14:31	1 s	1/1	4/4
14	count at <console>:28	2015/11/18 10:07:08	1 s	1/1	4/4
13	count at <console>:28	2015/11/18 10:05:09	1 s	1/1	4/4
12	count at <console>:28	2015/11/18 10:02:34	1 s	1/1	4/4
11	count at <console>:28	2015/11/18 10:01:26	1 s	1/1	4/4
10	count at <console>:28	2015/11/18 10:01:05	1 s	1/1	4/4
9	count at <console>:28	2015/11/18 09:59:58	1 s	1/1	4/4
8	count at <console>:28	2015/11/18 09:59:30	1 s	1/1	4/4
7	count at <console>:28	2015/11/18 09:59:00	1 s	1/1	4/4
6	count at <console>:28	2015/11/18 09:58:36	1 s	1/1	4/4
5	count at <console>:28	2015/11/18 09:56:47	1 s	1/1	4/4
4	count at <console>:25	2015/11/18 09:25:56	1 s	1/1	4/4
3	count at <console>:25	2015/11/18 09:25:05	2 s	1/1	4/4
2	count at <console>:25	2015/11/18 09:23:07	8 s	1/1	4/4
1	count at <console>:25	2015/11/18 09:22:13	4 s	1/1	4/4
0	count at <console>:25	2015/11/18 09:21:15	4 s	1/1	4/4

Figure 19.5 The Jobs page showing execution details of Spark jobs

Stages tab is very useful in understanding how efficiently Spark is processing jobs, because this is where you can find out how much data is being handled by the shuffle process. Too much time performing shuffles usually means that you haven't partitioned your data very well, that you aren't using the right operations or a combination of the two.

The DAG Page

The DAG page shows how Spark schedules the stages in a Spark job. Understanding the DAG for key jobs is crucial, since it helps you identify the stage boundaries as well as the specific operations that are causing shuffles to occur and new stages to be created.

The Storage Tab

The Storage tab is useful when you want to find the status of the cache. It shows you the RDD storage level, the percentage of an RDD that's cached, the size of the cache in memory, as well as the size of the cache on disk. If a Spark job doesn't cache any RDDs, you won't see a Storage page.

> **Note**
>
> Developers can also get the same information shown here by using the method `SparkContext.getRDDStorageInfo()`.

The Task Metrics Tab

The Task Metrics page is where you find all the good stuff about memory usage and garbage collection. You can also find details about the duration of all the tasks in a job. If one task runs way longer than all the other tasks in a job, it's an indication of data skew and hence an uneven load distribution among the tasks. Figure 19.6 shows the Task Metrics page.

Spark System and the Metrics REST API

Spark incudes a metrics system on each driver and executor that lets you get metrics sent by the master process, the worker processes, the driver and the executors. You can send the Spark metrics to various sinks. For example, you can use Spark's Graphite Sink to send application metrics to the Graphite monitoring system.

Spark comes with several REST APIs that let you get application metrics in a JSON format so you can build visualizations based on them. Here are the endpoints of the APIs:

```
http://server-url:18060/api/v1
http://<driver-node-ip>i<allocatedPort-default4040>/api/v1
```

The Spark History Server on YARN

The Spark job UI is useful to you only while a job is running. When a job completes, you won't find any information in the job UI. Use the Spark history server for historical information about jobs that completed running. You can view details about older applications that were executed a while ago by going to `http://<server-url> 18080`.

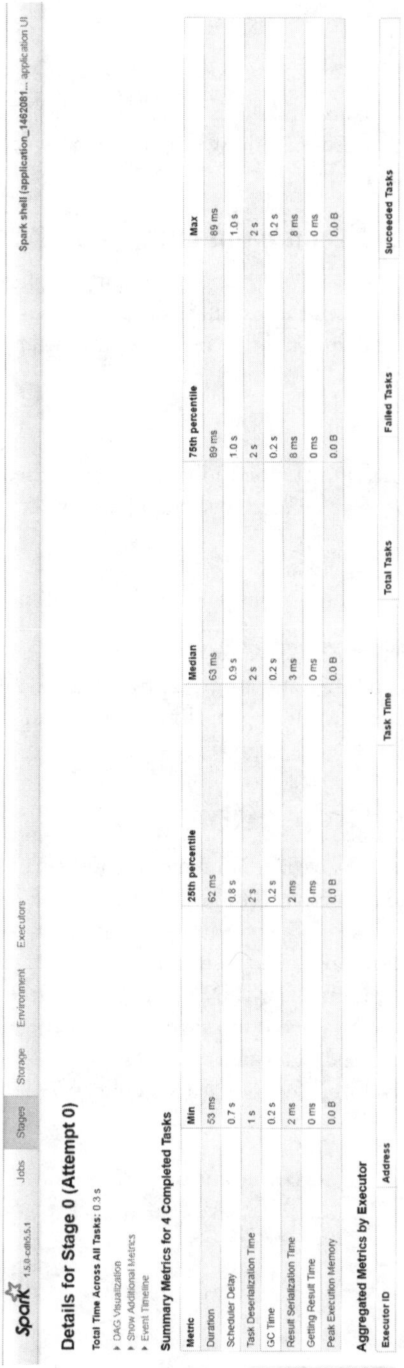

Spark 1.5.0-cdh5.5.1
Jobs Stages Storage Environment Executors
Spark shell (application_1462081... application UI
Details for Stage 0 (Attempt 0)
Total Time Across All Tasks: 0.3 s
DAG Visualization
Show Additional Metrics
Event Timeline
Summary Metrics for 4 Completed Tasks

Metric	Min	25th percentile	Median	75th percentile	Max
Duration	53 ms	62 ms	63 ms	89 ms	89 ms
Scheduler Delay	0.7 s	0.8 s	0.9 s	1.0 s	1.0 s
Task Deserialization Time	1 s	2 s	2 s	2 s	2 s
GC Time	0.2 s	0.2 s	0.2 s	0.2 s	0.2 s
Result Serialization Time	2 ms	2 ms	3 ms	8 ms	8 ms
Getting Result Time	0 ms	0 ms	0 ms	0 ms	0 ms
Peak Execution Memory	0.0 B	0.0 B	0.0 B	0.0 B	0.0 B

Aggregated Metrics by Executor

Executor ID	Address	Task Time	Total Tasks	Failed Tasks	Succeeded Tasks

Figure 19.6 The Task Metrics page of the Spark web UI

But first, you must start the history server as shown here:

```
$ ./sbin/start-history-server.sh
```

The address of the Spark History Server is provided to the YARN ResourceManager when the Spark application finishes. This creates a link between the ResourceManager UI and the Spark History Server UI.

Tracking Jobs from the Command Line

In Chapter 17, "Monitoring, Metrics and Hadoop Logging," I showed how to use Hadoop's `yarn` commands to track jobs. You can use all those commands to track your Spark jobs as well, such as the following command that lists the running applications:

```
$ yarn application -list
```

Getting the Logs

Once you retrieve the application ID for a job, you can list the contents of all log files from all the containers that were created for an application like so:

```
$ yarn logs -applicationId <app_id>
```

And you can view aggregated logs for the job via the HDFS shell.

Debugging and Query Plans

You can get a description of an RDD and its lineage by using the `toDebugString()` method on the RDD. You can check the query plan through the DataFrame API by using `DataFrame#explain()`.

Tuning Garbage Collection

Spark tends to store large chunks of data in memory; thus, Java memory management and how Java performs garbage collection (GC) of objects plays a big role in Spark performance. Improving GC is critical to improving performance.

Ideally, a Spark application should be reusing the same RDDs for multiple operations. If an application uses a large number of RDDs, there's going to be a higher amount of Java garbage collection. Since Java needs to make room for the new objects by removing older objects, finding the unused older objects takes effort. The more Java objects you have laying around, the larger the cost of garbage collection. Therefore, ideally, you should do the following:

- Cache the objects in their serialized form—this ought to be your first strategy.
- Use data structures with fewer objects, such as arrays of `Ints` rather than a `LinkedList`.

The Mechanics of Garbage Collection

In order to tune GC, one must understand the basics of how a JVM manages its memory. Here's how the Java heap space is divided:

- Old generation: Stores the objects with long lifetimes.
- Young generation: Stores objects that are short-lived, such as temporary objects created during the execution of a task. The young generation has three regions: Eden, Survivor1 and Survivor2.

There are two types of garbage collections in a JVM:

- Minor GC: Minor garbage collections are run on the Eden component of the young generation, when Eden gets full. Objects in Eden that are still in use are copied to Survivor2. If the objects are old or if Survivor2 is full, the objects are moved to the old generation.
- Full GC: A full garbage collection is invoked when the old generation is full.

GC is often an issue since there's an inherent conflict (or tradeoff) between the working memory that tasks need to perform their work and the need to cache RDDs.

> **Note**
>
> Each JVM (executor) must contain enough memory to support 2-3 tasks.

Your objective is to make sure that all the older (long-lived) objects are stored in the old generation and you have enough room in the young generation for storing new, temporary objects that have a short life. This will keep garbage collection activity to a minimum.

> **Note**
>
> The key to efficient management of the JVM memory is to keep full garbage collections to a minimum.

Full GCs adversely affect performance. So, if your GC status show that the old generation is near capacity, reduce the fraction of the memory devoted to caching RDDs (`spark.memory.storageFraction`). This will keep task execution from being slowed down. Any time you see multiple full GCs during a task execution, it's a sign that the memory for execution has been under-configured—raise it.

If you notice too many minor GCs in the GC logs, raise the memory allocation for the Eden component of the young generation.

How to Collect GC Statistics

You can find out the frequency of garbage collection and the amount of time spent performing GC by specifying certain Java options at runtime, as shown here:

```
./bin/spark-submit --name "My app" --master local[4]
  --conf "spark.executor.extraJavaOptions=
-XX:+PrintGCDetails
-XX:+PrintGCTimeStamps" myApp.jar
```

The two GC parameters shown here will write diagnostic information about garbage collection to stdout, so you can analyze GC behavior. Once you add these GC-related options, the worker logs will show the GC-related messages when a GC occurs.

You can analyze the heap dumps of running processes to check which structures are increasing the garbage collection. Often it's code that creates objects for each row. This means the code needs to be modified.

Tuning Spark Streaming Applications

Our discussion of tuning the performance of applications using Spark Core applies to Spark Streaming applications as well. However, there are additional tuning parameters and configurations you can employ to improve streaming application performance.

The three main things so far as tuning Spark applications are concerned (other than the standard Spark tuning and configuration), are the following:

- Reduce batch processing times
- Set the right batch size so data processing keeps up with the rate of data ingestion
- Tune memory usage and garbage collection (GC) overhead

Reducing Batch Processing Time

You can adopt various strategies to reduce the batch processing times, as summarized in the following sections.

Parallelize Data Ingestion

In order to keep data ingestion from being a bottleneck, you can parallelize the data you receive over the network from entities such as Kafka, Flume, and sockets.

By default, each input DStream receives a single stream of data via the single receiver it creates. In order to parallelize the receiving of data, developers can create multiple input DStreams. Each input DStream will receive a different partition of the source data stream. For example, you could have two Kafka input DStreams, each receiving a different Kafka input stream. More receivers means a higher throughput.

Instead of configuring multiple input streams and receivers to receive data, you can also repartition the input data streams with the following:

```
inputStream.repartition(<number of partitions>)
```

There are two parameters that determine the number of tasks per receiver for every batch—batch interval and block interval. The parameter `spark.streaming.blockInterval` lets you configure the block interval. Data that's being ingested is consolidated into blocks of data before Spark can store it in memory. The number of tasks that are needed to process the received data is dependent on the number of blocks in each batch. You can increase the number of tasks to take advantage of available processing power by reducing the block interval. The recommended minimum value for this parameter is 50 ms.

Parallelize the Data Processing

On the data-processing side, you should be always on the lookout to increase the degree of parallelism if you have sufficient processing power available. The Spark configuration parameter `spark.default.parallelism` helps you set the default number of parallel tasks.

Setting the Right Batch Interval

In order to handle production data, your system should be able to keep up with the rate at which data is flowing into the system. If the batch processing times are greater than the batch interval, you've got a problem, as you can't sustain the data flows.

The batch interval for a streaming application is quite critical. You can check the delay being experienced by a processing batch by looking for "Total delay" in the Spark driver Log4j logs. Experiment with various batch intervals, starting from a fairly high interval such as 5-10 seconds, and work your way down. Your goal should be to get to where the delay is steady and is comparable to the batch size.

Tuning Memory and Garbage Collection

All the memory tuning and configuration I've explained earlier in this chapter also applies to Spark Streaming. However, there are a few additional tuning parameters that apply to Spark Streaming applications.

Regarding memory, make sure you have allocated sufficient memory for streaming applications, as the data from receivers is stored with the storage level `MEMORY_AND_DISK_SER_2`, which means data will be spilled to disk when it doesn't fit in memory.

So far as GC goes, streaming applications demand low latency, and thus it's imperative that you avoid major GC pauses. As explained in Chapter 20, using Kryo serialization instead of the default Java serialization reduces serialized sizes and memory requirements. The concurrent mark-and-sweep (CMS) GC is highly recommended to keep GC pauses low and keep batch processing times consistent. You must set the CMS GC on both the driver and the executor. On the driver you do it through the `-driver-java-options` flag and for the executors by configuring the property `spark.executor.extraJavaOptions`.

Summary

Here's what you learned in this chapter:

- Choosing the number of executors, as well as the memory and CPU cores you allocate to executors, is critical to Spark job performance.
- Dynamic resource allocation lets Spark automatically adjust the number of executors based on the workflow and thus uses resources effectively.

- The storage format of your input data and the compression strategy you adopt can make a considerable difference in the performance of Spark applications.
- Make extensive use of the Spark web UI, not only to troubleshoot failed jobs, but also to understand the nature of a Spark application, such as the number of partitions, the number of executions and the stages, as well as the amount of storage used and the locality of the processing.

20

Optimizing Spark Applications

This chapter covers the following:

- Understanding the Spark execution model
- Shuffle operations and how to minimize them
- Selecting appropriate operators
- Partitioning and parallelism
- Understanding Spark's query optimizer
- Caching data

In the previous chapter, I focused on those aspects of Spark configuration that an administrator can control. I discussed how you allocate memory and CPU to a YARN-based Spark system. More specifically, I focused on how to allocate resources to the all-important work horses of a Spark job—the executors—as well as how to choose an efficient file storage format. In this chapter, I review how one can tune Spark applications to improve performance. The focus here is more on how you can use Spark's built-in features to write more effective application code.

There are two areas you need to focus on to optimize Spark applications. The first area focuses on writing optimal code and using appropriate operators to efficiently process your data. Properly parallelizing your Spark jobs so you aren't running too many or too few tasks is easier said than done, especially in the beginning, but it's definitely something you should set your sights on doing, since it's probably the single biggest determinant of performance for Spark applications. Also, you must learn the significance of shuffle operations and learn the best strategies to avoid or minimize data shuffling, which could adversely affect performance.

The second broad area that you need to learn about is how to use Spark's built-in capabilities to your best advantage. This means using features such as partitioning and caching of data.

To optimize Spark applications, it's important that you get a good handle on how Spark executes an application. So I kick off this chapter with an overview of the Spark execution model.

Revisiting the Spark Execution Model

Understanding the Spark execution model is the key to optimizing the performance of Spark applications, regardless of whether they're run in a standalone Spark cluster or on YARN (or Mesos). Developers and administrators both will benefit from understanding the Spark execution model.

The Spark Execution Model

Spark applications contain a single driver process and a bunch of executor processes running on various cluster nodes. The driver manages the workflow, and the executors perform the work through multiple tasks. In a YARN-managed Spark setup, the ResourceManager determines on which nodes the tasks can run.

Spark Applications

A Spark application consists of operations (transformations and actions) involving RDDs. RDDs are the heart of all Spark programming. A DataFrame is the core abstraction of the RDD and helps transform data into what appears to be a single object, masking the fact that it sits on top of data that's potentially distributed across a large number of machines.

When you launch a Spark application, a Spark job is created to perform the work. Spark first creates an **execution plan** based on the RDDs the action uses.

Jobs

An application gets its results by launching one or a set of jobs. A job involves the set of computations that Spark performs to return the results of actions on the RDDs back to the driver program that launches the application.

> **Note**
>
> A job is triggered by an action, such as `count()` or `saveAsTextFile()`.

An application launches a job by calling an RDD's `action` method. When the `action` method is invoked, the job starts. Depending on whether the RDD is cached, the action, and hence the job, starts by either retrieving the cached RDD data or reading the data from storage.

Spark will then apply the necessary transformations to create the RDD required by the `action` method. It also performs any computations that the action requires. Once all the transformations and computations are completed and the result is delivered to the driver program, the job completes.

A Quick Summary of Spark Execution Terms

- Task: A unit of execution that runs on a single node—there are one or more tasks per each executor.
- Stage: A group of tasks, based on partitions of the input data, that perform the same computations on their chunk of the data in parallel.
- Job: Same as an application. May have one or more stages.
- Pipelining: The collapsing of RDDs into a single stage, when RDD transformations can be performed without moving data.
- Directed acyclic graph (DAG): A logical graph of RDD operations.
- Resilient distributed dataset (RDD): Parallel, read-only dataset (contains one or more partitions).

The Execution Plan

The execution plan starts with the RDDs that reference cached data or that aren't dependent on other RDDs. The goal of the execution plan is to get to the final RDD that is required to get the action's results.

Stages

The execution plan puts together the job's transformations into different stages. Each stage of a job comprises a set of similarly coded tasks, with each task working on a subset of the data. The key here is that each stage's transformations can be completed without **shuffling** all of the data.

A shuffle is an expensive operation that redistributes data among the nodes of a cluster. Each chunk of data becomes a partition of an RDD. The distribution of data across the nodes isn't random but based on specific criteria.

A **job** consists of several stages, each of which consists of one or a set of **tasks**. A job is split into a DAG of stages. The way Spark groups tasks into stages is by using **shuffle boundaries**. A set of tasks that can be performed without having to perform a shuffle are put in the same stage. If a subsequent task requires the data to be shuffled, that marks the beginning of a different stage.

Tasks

Tasks are the entities that actually do the real work. Spark submits tasks to the executors. The scheduling of the tasks on a cluster's nodes has a lot to do with data locality, which I explain in the section titled "The Importance of Data Locality" later in this chapter.

If there's a node failure during task execution, Spark automatically resubmits the task to a different node.

In order to understand how Spark decomposes a computation into tasks, let's use the following example, which defines three RDDs—`lines`, `lineLengths` and `totalLength`.

```
val lines = sc.textFile("data.txt")
val lineLengths = lines.map(s => s.length)
val totalLength = lineLengths.reduce((a, b) => a + b)
```

Here's what Spark does with our three RDDs:

- `lines`: This is the base RDD, to be created from an external file. Right now it just points to the external file data.txt.
- `lineLengths`: This RDD is also not computed right away due to Spark's lazy execution model, because it's an RDD defined as a result of a transformation (map) and not an action.
- `totalLength`: This is the RDD that we're really after, and the `reduce` action sets off the computations needed to create this RDD.

When Spark sees the `reduce` operation, which is an action on an RDD, it creates the tasks to be run on the cluster's nodes to perform the computations, starting from the creation of the first RDD (`lines`) from the text file. Each node in the cluster runs a part of the `map` operation required to create the RDD `lineLengths`. The nodes also perform a local `reduce` before returning their portion of the answer (which is the RDD `totalLength`) to the driver program that launched the application and the tasks.

All Spark programs follow the same procedures as shown in our example in this section, namely:

1. Create an input RDD from external data.
2. Transform the base RDD with operations such as `filter` to define new, more pertinent RDDs.
3. Persist any intermediate RDDs that the application may need to use later, using the `persist()` or `cache()` methods.
4. Launch RDD actions such as `count()` or `first()` to start parallel computations on the cluster's nodes.

> **Note**
>
> Specifying the `cache` method is equivalent to specifying the `persist` method with the default storage level.

Shuffle Operations and How to Minimize Them

A shuffle is how Spark redistributes data so it's grouped differently across all partitions. Let's take the case of `reduceByKey` operation, which when called on a dataset of (K, V) pairs returns a dataset of (K, V) pairs where the values for each key are aggregated using the given reduce function *func*.

The `reduceByKey` operation generates a new RDD that contains all the values for a single key combined in a tuple. In order to compute this single key, all the values for the key must be located together on the same partition. So, in order to perform its `reduceByKey` reduce task, Spark performs what it calls an **all-to-all operation**—it reads from all the partitions and retrieves all the values for all the keys and places them in a single partition so it can compute the result for each key—this is the shuffle operation.

Both the `reduceByKey` and the `groupByKey` operations, as well as join operations such as `cogroup` and `join`, lead to a shuffle. In addition, the repartition operations `repartition` and `coalesce` also cause a shuffle.

A WordCount Example to Our Rescue Again

I'll invoke that old standby, WordCount, to illustrate how shuffling works. Let's say you're running the following simple WordCount program in Spark:

```
rdd = sc.textFile("input.txt")\
flatMap(lambda line: line.split())\
map(lambda word: (word, 1))\
reduceByKey(lambda x, y: x + y, 3)\
collect()
```

Spark compiles the necessary operations on the RDDs into a DAG. In a DAG, an RDD points to its lineage or the parent it is derived from or dependent on. Figure 20.1 shows how the different RDDs in our program point to their ancestors.

We know that a Spark job is always broken up into stages, each of which consists of tasks, with each task working on a different partition. Each of the stages is executed sequentially. How does Spark decide how to split the job into different stages? As long as the data in the RDDs is being transformed so that it's grouped the same way as its parent, the data doesn't need to be redistributed, and hence they remain in the same stage. In our example, flatmap and map don't need to redistribute data, so they belong in the same stage—stage 1. Figure 20.2 shows how the job is broken up into stages.

The `reduceByKey` transformation requires redistributing data, so it marks a shuffle boundary, and the `reduceByKey` operation is performed in stage 2. The shuffle moves data across the cluster so it's grouped differently across the partitions. Shuffle is inherently an expensive operation since it involves copying data across nodes.

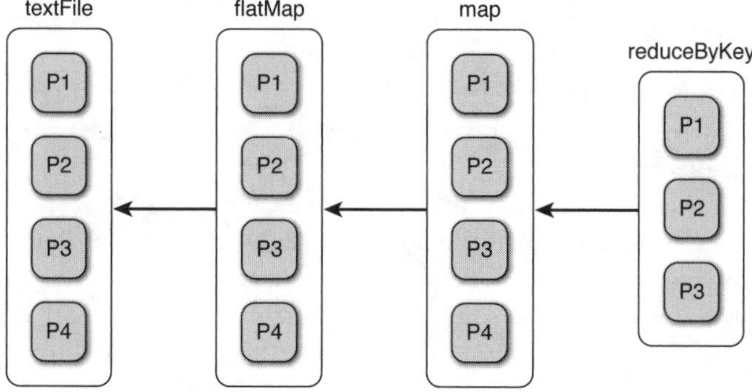

Figure 20.1 How RDDs are derived from their parents

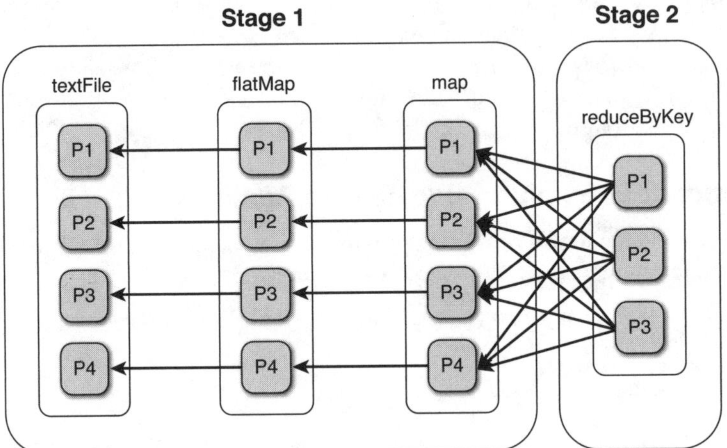

Figure 20.2 Shuffle boundaries and multiple stages

Spark creates tasks to perform all the operations necessary to complete the jobs. Map tasks help organize the data, and reduce tasks aggregate the data. Within each stage, similar operations are "pipelined" into tasks and executed in parallel, as shown in Figure 20.2. Both `reduceByKey` and `groupByKey` are common examples of a distributed shuffle. While both of these functions will produce the correct answer, the `reduceByKey` operator works much better on large datasets. That's because Spark knows it can combine output with a common key on each partition before shuffling the data.

Impact of a Shuffle Operation

Since a shuffle involves the copying of data across servers via the network and data serialization, it's a costly operation in terms of both network and disk I/O. Shuffle is an expensive operation that involves sorting the data, repartitioning it and serializing/deserializing when you send it over the network. It also involves the compression of data to reduce the disk I/O.

Increased Use of Memory

Spark uses map and reduce (not to be confused with the MapReduce map/reduce tasks) tasks to organize the shuffle data. It uses map tasks to organize the data and reduce tasks to aggregate the key to get the final result for each key.

Operations such as `reduceByKey` and `aggregateByKey` use high amounts of the Java heap memory to support the data structures they create in memory to organize (before the shuffle) and aggregate (after the shuffle) the shuffle data.

High Disk I/O

Since the operations such as `reduceByKey` spill their data structures to disk when they can't be contained in memory, you incur the overhead of high disk I/O.

> **Note**
>
> You specify the location of Spark's temporary storage directory with the `spark.local.dir` configuration property (default value is `/tmp`) when you configure the Spark context.

Spark generates intermediate files on disk and retains them until the RDDs they reference go out of use and are garbage collected. This is so that Spark can use the intermediate files if it ever needs to recompute the lineage of the RDDs. So, a long-running Spark job may end up using a lot of disk space in the temporary storage directory.

More Garbage Collection

As mentioned in the previous section, a high amount of shuffling could lead to higher amounts of garbage collection (GC) activity, with all the negative things associated with a high amount of GC.

Configuring the Shuffle Parameters

As with the rest of Spark's configuration, you have a lot of knobs to play with when it comes to configuring shuffle behavior. The key shuffle-related configuration parameters can be summarized as follows:

- In order to limit the fixed memory overhead for fetching the map output simultaneously from each reduce task, set the `spark.reducer.maxSizeInFlight` property. The default is 48MB, and the recommendation here is to keep it small when your Spark memory is limited.
- You can optimize the number of disk seeks and system calls during the creation of the intermediate shuffle files by setting the `spark.shuffle.file.buffer` property. The default value for this parameter is 32KB, and it represents the size of the in-memory buffer for a shuffle file output stream.
- There are two compression-related properties in the context of shuffling, both of which are set to `true` by default:
  - `spark.shuffle.compress`: Determines whether Spark should compress the map output files
  - `spark.shuffle.spill.compress`: Specifies whether to compress data that's spilled during a shuffle

Compression and Shuffle Operations

Spark's map jobs write their shuffle out to a shuffle file. The number of shuffle files is the same as the total number of mappers times the number of reducers. You can reduce the number of shuffle files by setting the `spark.shuffle.compress` property to `true`.

Once the map phase completes, Spark's reduce phase begins, with the reducers pulling the shuffled data. You can configure the `spark.reducer.maxSizeInFlight` parameter to control the network buffer size for getting the map output to the reducers.

You can add an intermediate merge phase between the map and reduce phases to reduce both the output and the number of shuffle files. By setting the `spark.shuffleconsolidateFiles` property to `true`, you can introduce shuffle file consolidation. Once you do this, the number of shuffle files will be fewer—since they will equal the number of reducers per core rather than the number of reducers per mapper.

What Determines Whether There Is a Shuffle?

Earlier, I explained how the DAG scheduler creates an execution plan for each action that is triggered within a Spark application. The execution plan consists of various transformations with dependencies among them. The nature of the dependencies is quite crucial, and there are two basic types of dependencies among the RDDs:

- A narrow dependency between RDDs exists when each partition from a parent RDD maps to a single partition in a child RDD. This means there's a one-to-one relationship between a parent RDD partition and a child RDD partition.
- A wide dependency between RDDs exists when a parent's RDD is used by several child RDD partitions—that is, there's a one-to-many mapping between the parent and child RDD partitions.

Spark assembles all transformations with narrow dependencies into a separate stage. When Spark encounters a wide dependency it creates a new stage.

Figure 20.3 illustrates narrow and wide RDD dependencies.

The key to understanding whether there's going to be a shuffle is to learn the difference between **narrow** and **wide transformations**. An RDD contains a fixed set of partitions, with each partition containing records. In the case of narrow transformations,

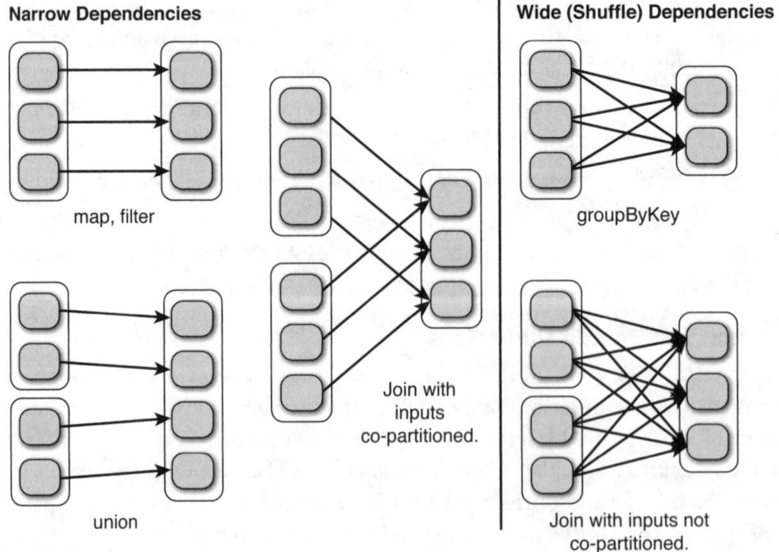

Figure 20.3 Narrow and wide RDD dependencies

such as a map or a filter, the records needed to create a single partition are also in a single partition in the parent RDD. Here's an example that shows a narrow RDD:

```
sc.textFile("someFile.txt").
  map(mapFunc).
  flatMap(flatMapFunc).
  filter(filterFunc).
  count()
```

There's only one action in this case, and it depends on the transformations of the original RDD that you created from a text file. This action will execute entirely in a single stage.

To illustrate the difference between narrow and wide dependencies, let's take an example such as the following:

```
val numbers = sc.parallelize(nrCollection)
val multiplied - numbers.filter(_2% == 0).map(_ * 3).collect()
```

All the transformations in this code snippet are narrow, since none of them require the input partition data to be distributed in multiple output partitions. Hence, Spark can execute all the RDD transformations within the same stage. None of the outputs of the transformations in this case require data to come from partitions other than their inputs.

Transformations such as groupByKey and reduceByKey involve wide dependencies. The data required to compute the records in a single partition often live in multiple partitions of the parent RDD. In order to get all tuples with identical keys into the same partition, Spark must execute a shuffle. A shuffle moves data across the Hadoop cluster, and this results in a new stage, with a new set of partitions.

Code such as the following involves multiple stages (three in this case), due to transformations with multiple dependencies.

```
val tokenized = sc.textFile(args(0)).flatMap(_.split(' '))
val wordCounts = tokenized.map((_, 1)).reduceByKey(_ + _)
val filtered = wordCounts.filter(_._2 >= 1000)
val charCounts = filtered.flatMap(_._1.toCharArray).map((_, 1)).
  reduceByKey(_ + _)
charCounts.collect()
```

This code counts the number of words and filters those words that occur more than 1,000 times in the input text file and then counts the number of times a character appears within those words. The collect action sets off the job.

Since the reduceByKey operation (same as a transformation) requires repartitioning the data by keys, it's a wide transformation and hence triggers a **stage boundary**. A stage boundary marks a point where the tasks in the parent stage(s) write data to disk, which is fetched by tasks in the child stage. Since they require heavy disk I/O and network I/O, stage boundaries are expensive, and you should try and avoid them. In this example, there are two transformations that are stage boundaries since they have wide dependencies. Due to these two reduceByKey operations, the code ends up being processed in three separate stages. Once the stages are delineated, Spark launches tasks to compute the partitions that will form the final RDD. Each stage will consist of a set of tasks that perform the identical transformation on a different chunk of the data.

> **Note**
>
> Tasks are assigned to executors based on the locality and the availability of resources. If the partition a task wants to perform exists already in memory on a node, the task execution will occur on that node since it's faster than reading data from disk.

You can usually specify the `numPartitions` argument for a transformation that results in a stage boundary. This argument determines how many partitions Spark must split the data into during the child stage.

Selecting Appropriate Transformations (Operators)

Shuffles are expensive in terms of both disk and network I/O—no two ways about it. You should select an arrangement of operators that minimizes the number of shuffles and the amount of data that is moved around by any shuffles that you can't avoid.

Often you can choose among multiple actions and transformations to get the results you're looking for. Not all operators are equal, however, and the choice of the operators could have a significant bearing on performance.

Telling Spark to Clean Up After Itself

In a cluster where Spark runs for long periods of time, a huge amount of metadata is created over time. Spark needs to keep all this metadata, such as the stages and tasks it creates for various applications, somewhere. Therefore, this is overhead. You can specify that Spark periodically cleans its metadata, to reduce the overhead of managing the metadata. The configuration property `spark.cleaner.ttl` determines how long (in seconds) Spark will retain its metadata. The default value is infinite, so Spark never cleans up its metadata on its own! Set this property to a reasonable interval so Spark periodically cleans up after itself.

A common mistake is to use some transformations to get the results you're after but ignore the behind-the-scenes operations, often adversely affecting the performance of the applications. A good example is the choice between the two Spark operators `reduceByKey` and `groupByKey`, both of which let you apply functions on top of all the values of specific keys.

Let's take a simple example that illustrates the difference between using the two common operations `reduceByKey` and `groupByKey`. Let's say you are running a word count program and that it consists of an RDD with the list of words you are going to count. When you use the `groupByKey` operator, all values of a key must be processed by a single task. This requires Spark to shuffle the complete data set and send all the work pairs of a key to a single node for processing. Not only is the shuffle going to cost you in terms of all the usual resource usage, the job might even fail when one key has too many values and fails with an OOM error. Figure 20.4 shows the impact of performing the word count with the `groupByKey` operators.

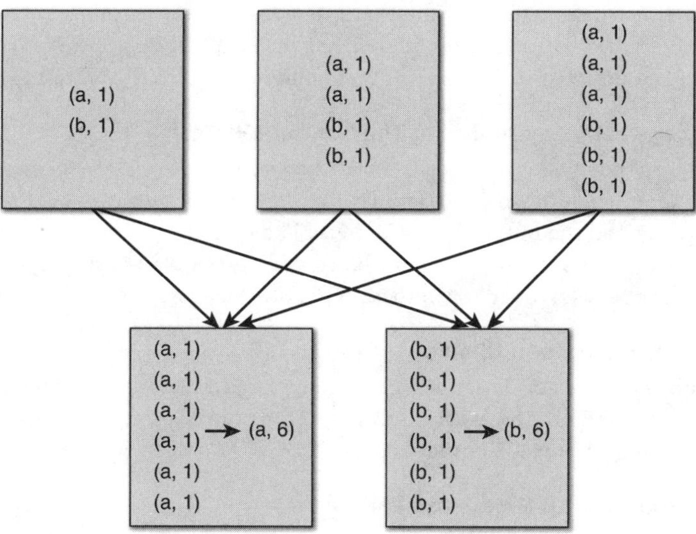

Figure 20.4 How the `groupByKey` operator performs the word count

The `reduceByKey` operator does things much better. The function you pass to the `reduceByKey` operator is applied to all the values of a key locally and Spark just sends these intermediate results across the cluster. Figure 20.5 shows how the `reduceByKey` operation tackles the word count job.

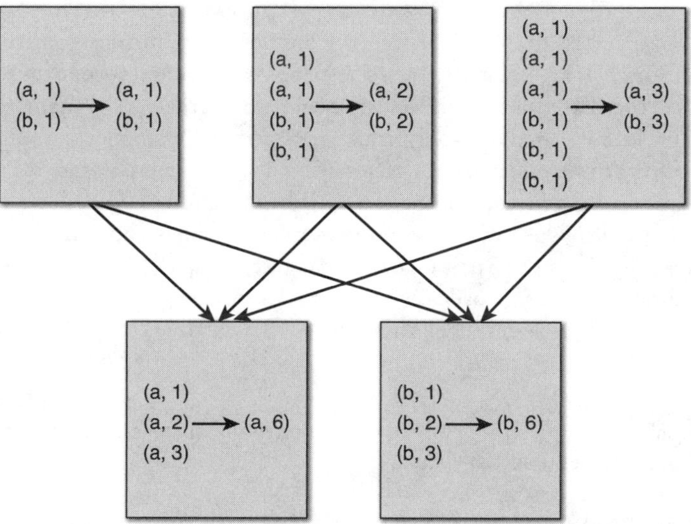

Figure 20.5 How the `reduceByKey` operator performs the word count

For associative and reductive operations such as the one in this example, it's a good idea to stay away from the `groupByKey` operator. Using the `reduceByKey` operator results in a vastly smaller amount of data that needs to be compressed and shuffled across the cluster.

When `aggregateByKey` Is Better Than `reduceByKey`

Although the `reduceByKey` operator is better than `groupByKey` in most cases, when the input values are different in an operation, you must avoid this operator. Let's say the input values are strings and the output values are sets. The map operation in this case results in too many temporary small objects in the process of creating a set of strings for each key. Use the `aggregateByKey` operator in these types of scenarios.

When `cogroup` Is a Good Choice

If you are joining two datasets already grouped by key and retain the grouping, use a `cogroup` operator and not the usual `flatMap-join-groupBy` pattern to avoid the overhead of unpacking and repacking the groups.

Avoiding a Shuffle with Broadcast Variables

When you're joining two datasets, you can avoid a shuffle by using **broadcast variables**. In Spark, broadcasting values means that all the cluster nodes will have their own copy of that value. If you're dealing with small lookup tables or maps required by each executor, broadcasting makes for efficient processing and is a good practice to follow.

A small lookup table can fit entirely in memory on an executor and Spark can load it into a hash table (on the driver) and broadcast it to all executors in the cluster. Transformations being run on the executors can reference this hash table for their lookups—you thus avoid the expensive shuffle operation.

Spark uses two types of shared variables: broadcast variables and accumulators. Each of them serves a different purpose. When an application consists of a large number of tasks that need to access the same variable(s), consider using broadcast variables.

Broadcast variables are what you use to distribute large amounts of data across your cluster so tasks can share those variables and avoid the overhead of copying the data. Broadcast variables are shared read-only values that Spark caches in memory on all nodes. Instead of copying these values within each task, Spark lets the tasks share the values that it stores only once on each node of the cluster. The number of copies doesn't depend on the number of partitions—it depends on the number of nodes. Since the node count is usually way smaller than the partition count, Spark ends up copying items fewer times, improving its performance. Broadcast variables are read-only, so Spark doesn't have to change the copies on all nodes when the value of that variable changes on a machine.

> **Tip**
>
> If a job's tasks use large objects from the driver program, such as lookup tables that don't change, turn it into a broadcast variable.

If local executors have a copy of the variable, the tasks read the data from there. Otherwise they need to get it from the driver. Spark has a couple of different ways it can broadcast data. The HTTP broadcast uses an HTTP server on the driver's machine to get the data from the driver. If the driver needs to send copies of a variable to all the cluster nodes, it might affect the network. The alternative broadcast implementation is the Torrent broadcast, which chunks the data into small blocks. Once an executor fetches a set of blocks, it acts as a seeder and sends those blocks over to the other executors. In order to set the block size under the Torrent broadcast implementation you need to set the `spark.broadcast.blocksize` property to the value you want. Here's an example:

```
val configuration = new SparkConf()
configuration.set("spark.broadcast.factory",
"org.apache.spark.broadcast.TorrentBroadcastFactory")
configuration.set("spark.broadcast.blockSize", "3m")
```

Besides broadcast variables, Spark lets you use another type of shared variable named *accumulators*. Accumulators aggregate information from the executors on their way back to the driver. Accumulators let you safely update shared variables. The values are computed within each task and added on the driver. Therefore, operations you apply on the accumulator variables must be associative.

Partitioning and Parallelism (Number of Tasks)

Parallelism is the heart of Spark's execution model. The Spark driver executes parallel operations in a cluster. It is Spark's RDDs, which are in essence distributed datasets, that make parallel processing possible. Data in an RDD is partitioned across a cluster's nodes so it can be worked on in a parallel fashion.

Parallelism is the number of tasks in a job. When the Spark DAG transforms a job into stages, each partition is going to be processed by a separate task. Therefore, the parallelism of a Spark application is directly related to the RDD's partitions. Spark breaks up the dataset processing into stages, with multiple tasks in each stage. The number of tasks in a stage is equal to the number of partitions in the last data set in a stage. And, the number of partitions in any dataset is equal to the number of partitions in that dataset's parent datasets.

Since parallel processing is the key to crunching through large sets of data efficiently, the number of partitions is probably the most significant variable affecting the performance of a Spark application.

When using HDFS for your storage, the number of partitions is the same as the number of `InputSplits`, which is usually the same as the number of HDFS blocks.

Spark never works on the entire data set as a whole when you offer the data to it in the form of an RDD. When Spark runs an application, it breaks the data (that is, the RDD) into partitions. It's this partitioning strategy that lets Spark parallelize its work. Spark runs as a separate task for each partition of the cluster. All tasks within any given stage are identical—that is, each of them performs the same operation, but on a different chunk of data. After all tasks are completed, the results of all tasks are combined into a single RDD.

How many partitions should Spark slice the distributed dataset into? Ideally you want to have 2-4 partitions per CPU in your cluster. Spark sets the number of partitions automatically based on the size of the input file. You can also set it yourself by passing the number of partitions as the second parameter to the `parallelize` method, as shown here:

```
sc.parallelize (mydata, 20)
```

This creates 20 partitions out of the RDD named `mydata`.

You can also specify the number of partitions when loading data into an RDD from a file. Here's an example that shows how to load an RDD with a custom number of partitions as the second parameter:

```
scala> sc.textFile("hdfs://localhost:9000/user/sam/words",10)
```

Level of Parallelism

To fully utilize your cluster resources, you must set the level of parallelism for an operation high enough. Spark automatically sets the level of parallelism (number of tasks) for operations such as a map transformation on an RDD based on the size of the input data. For operations such as the distributed reduce operations (`groupByKey`, `reduceByKey`), Spark determines the level of parallelism based on the number of partitions in the parent RDD.

You can also specify the degree of parallelism as an argument or configure the `spark.default.parallelism` property to change it from its default value. When you create an RDD by parallelizing a collection, the `spark.default.parallelism` property determines the default number of partitions.

In a YARN-based Spark case, the default number of partitions is the higher of two and the total number of cores on all executors. You can override the default number of partitions in both cases—when creating an RDD over a file and when you create an RDD by parallelizing a collection, as shown here:

```
sc.textFile(<inputPath>, <minPartitions>)
sc.parallelize(<sequence>, <numSlices>)
```

> **Note**
>
> Aim for running 2-3 tasks per CPU core on each node.

How Spark creates an RDD has a direct bearing on the number of partitions. When Spark creates an RDD over an HDFS file, the number of partitions will be equal to the number of blocks in that file. That is, there'll be one partition per file. You can therefore control the number of partitions in this case by using a smaller or larger block size. You can also configure the `InputFormat` to specify the number of splits.

Most frequently Spark creates an RDD by applying transformations to existing RDDs. In many cases, the number of partitions in the RDD is the same as the number of partitions in the parent RDD. Transformations that involve wide dependencies will have a partition number that is based on the largest number of partitions from the dependent RDDs.

> **Note**
>
> One of the most important determinants of performance is the **degree of parallelism** employed by a job.

A Spark job, as you've learned, consists of separate stages, with each stage decomposed into multiple tasks.

Since Spark groups RDDs into stages, the number of tasks in a stage is the same as the number of partitions in the last RDD of a stage. This is true in general, although there are exceptions in the case of the `coalesce` and `union` transformations, for example, where the transformation can create an RDD with fewer or more partitions than its parent RDD.

You can check the number of partitions in an RDD by calling `rdd.partitions().size`. You can also find the number of partitions by checking the Spark web UI. You'll see the number of partitions in the Spark Stages page under the Completed Stages section of the Spark web UI. For example, the following example creates an RDD:

```
scala> val someRDD = sc.parallelize(1 to 100, 4)
someRDD: org.apache.spark.rdd.RDD[Int] = ParallelCollectionRDD[0] at parallelize
at <console>:21

scala> someRDD.map(x => x).collect
16/07/19 13:46:10 INFO SparkContext: Starting job: collect at <console>:24
```

Spark creates a total of 4 partitions, just as I've asked it to:

```
16/07/19 13:46:15 INFO TaskSetManager: Starting task 0.0 in stage 0.0
(TID 0, hadoop07.example.com, partition 0, PROCESS_LOCAL, 1973 bytes)
...
16/07/19 13:46:16 INFO TaskSetManager: Finished task 3.0 in stage 0.0 (TID 3)
 in 25 ms on hadoop07.example.com (4/4)
```

You can see on the Spark Stages page of the Spark web UI, as shown in Figure 20.6, that the Tasks: Succeeded/Total column reveals that 4 out of 4 tasks were successfully completed. So, total tasks represent the total number of partitions for a Spark job.

Some RDDs have no parents, such as those you create with the help of the `parallelize` method. In this case, you can specify the degree of parallelism, or it defaults to the value of `spark.default.parallelism`.

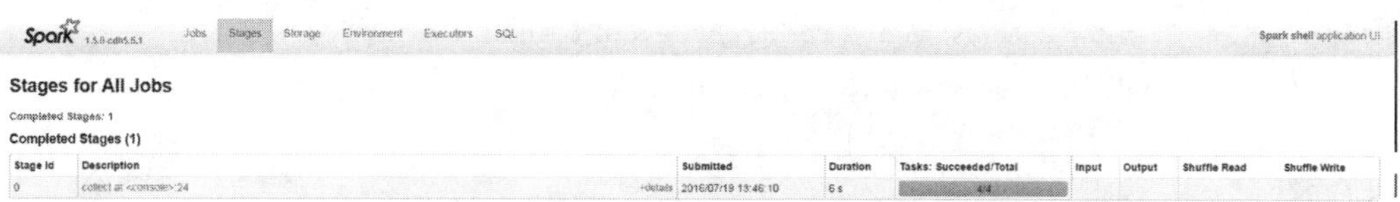

Figure 20.6 The Spark Stages page in the Spark web UI, showing the number of partitions processed by a Spark job

Problems with Too Few Tasks

Too few tasks per executor can mean trouble due to the demand for memory from aggregation operations such as a join operation. Large aggregation operations that require large shuffles have a detrimental effect on job performance. These operations have a large number of records that need to be held in memory, and too few tasks may lead to the following issues:

- GC-induced pauses that result in slower execution times.
- More disk I/O and sorting since Spark spills the records to disk when they all don't fit in memory. Fewer partitions means data in some partitions may be too large to fit in memory and needs to be spilled to disk to keep from running into out-of-memory exceptions.

Tasks should take a minimum of 100 ms to complete (the web UI for Spark shows these details). If they are not, there probably are too many tasks—you have a higher degree of parallelism than you need. If the tasks are taking much longer than 100 ms each to complete, you may want to gradually increase the degree of parallelism by a factor of the original number of tasks.

If the size of your working set is too high, say because one of the reduce tasks in a `groupByKey` operation is too large, the job performance may take a dive, owing to spills from memory to disk and increased overhead of garbage collection. Just go ahead and raise the degree of parallelism so the average input set shrinks to a manageable size.

Setting the Default Number of Partitions

You can set the default number of partitions in an RDD with the `spark.default.parallelism` configuration property, as shown here:

```
$ spark-shell --conf spark.default.parallelism=10
```

You can check the default parallelism value like this:

```
scala> sc.defaultParallelism
```

The `spark.default.parallelism` property determines the default number of partitions retuned by the following operations:

- Transformations such as `reduceByKey` and join
- Parallelize operations (when you don't set the number of partitions)

There's also a default value for the `spark.default.parallelisms` property, confusing as it sounds! This is how the default number of partitions is determined:

- For operations such as join and `reduceByKey` that involve a distributed shuffle, the default is the largest number of partitions in a parent RDD.

- If an operation has no parent RDD (such as when you use the `parallelize` command) it depends on the cluster manager you're using. In the case of YARN, it's the larger of two, or the total number of cores on all the executor nodes in the cluster.

Ideally, the number of partitions should be set the same as the number of CPUs you assign to the application. Unless you have a really large data set, this will result in correctly dimensioned partitions.

While too few partitions limit the concurrency of Spark operations, too many partitions can also be a problem since you may have to deal with excessive overhead caused by launching too many tasks. You'll know you have too many partitions when you have tasks that finish right away (in a few seconds) or don't perform any reads or writes. The degree of parallelism is probably too high in these cases. However, too many tasks, while they increase the overhead, are not as bad as too few tasks, which will take you into the dreaded area of spilling data to disk.

The ideal number of partitions depends on the size of the dataset, the amount of RAM you assign to each task and the type of partitioner you use for partitioning. A good rule of thumb is to set the number of partitions per RDD to the number of CPUs in the cluster multiplied by about 2-4.

How to Increase the Number of Partitions

O.K., now that we've established that a higher number of partitions is beneficial for performance, how exactly do you go about raising the number of partitions? The strategy will depend on where the stage is getting its data from.

If the stage is getting (reading) data from HDFS, here's what you can do:

- Use a smaller block size when writing the input data to HDFS. Since there's usually a separate partition for each HDFS block read by the Spark job, you'll naturally get more partitions this way.
- Set the `InputFormat` parameter so more splits are created. RDDs that use the `textFile` format for example will have the number of partitions dependent on the MapReduce InputFormat.
- Use the `repartition` transformation.

Alternatively, if a stage is receiving input from another stage, you can set the `numPartitions` argument for the transformation that triggers the stage boundary, as shown here:

```
val rdd2 = rdd1.reduceByKey(_ + _, numPartitions = X)
```

Setting the number of partitions is usually a trial-and-error based procedure and there are no hard and fast rules. You should aim at running sufficient tasks so the data for each task fits in the memory that task has.

A big advantage of Spark over MapReduce is that for Spark there is minimal startup overhead for a task, unlike in the case of MapReduce. So, go for a large number of partitions and thus, a greater number of tasks where possible, for faster performance.

Using the Repartition and Coalesce Operators to Change the Number of Partitions in an RDD

You can change the number of partitions in an RDD with the help of two operators: `repartition` and `coalesce`. You need to understand when to use each of these operators.

> **Note**
>
> If you see that you have thousands of mostly idle tasks, it's a good idea to coalesce and reduce the number of partitions. On the other hand, if you aren't really using all the available processing capacity in your cluster, it's a good idea to increase the parallelism by repartitioning.

Repartition

The `repartition` operator reshuffles data and distributes it into a large or smaller number of partitions compared to an RDD's current partition count. The `repartition` function, which shuffles data across the network to create a new set of partitions, enables you to change the partitioning of an RDD outside the context of operations such as grouping and aggregation. Just remember that repartitioning is usually a pretty expensive operation.

You must in general seek to minimize the number of shuffles that occur in your cluster. However, a shuffle that increases parallelism is actually quite a good thing at times. Let's say your data is composed of large files that can't be split. The `InputFormat` may create a few very large partitions. By repartitioning the data into a larger number of partitions, you allow later transformations of the RDDs to take advantage of your cluster's full processing power. The repartitioning, of course, involves a shuffle, but it's for a good cause this time around!

A second example where repartitioning and the consequent triggering of a shuffle may be good for you is when you aggregate data in the driver through a `reduce` or `aggregate` action. In this case, the single driver thread trying to merge all the data that has been aggregated over a large number of partitions can become a bottleneck. You can perform a shuffle transformation such as a `reduceByKey` or `aggregateByKey` first to consolidate the data into a few partitions. The values of each partition are merged together and sent to the driver for the final aggregation, thus lowering the stress on the driver.

Coalesce

The `coalesce` method is an optimized version of `repartition`. The `coalesce` method avoids the data movement inherent in repartitioning, but only if you're decreasing the number of partitions in an RDD.

Use the `coalesce` method to pack the RDDs after operations such as a `filter`, where the data is smaller than before the action.

When you invoke the coalesce method, you can specify either the values shuffle=true or shuffle=false. Set shuffle=false if the number of partitions to be created is greater than the current number of partitions. Otherwise, set shuffle=true.

Here is an example that shows how the coalesce method can reduce the number of partitions.

```
> input = sc.textFile("s3n://mylog-files/2016/*.log.gz") # this will match a large
number of files
> input.getNumPartitions()
42148
> lines = input.filter(lambda line: line.startswith("2016-08-16 08:")) # selective
> lines.getNumPartitions()
42148
> lines = lines.coalesce(5) # Coalesce the lines RDD into 5 partitions
> lines.getNumPartitions()
5
>>> lines.count() # occurs on coalesced RDD
```

> **Note**
>
> The spark.default.parallelism property controls the default number of partitions for a new RDD, and it also determines the number of tasks to be used by operations such as groupByKey that require shuffling the data.

In order to find out if you can safely call coalesce, you can use the functions rdd.partitions.size (Java and Scala) and rdd.getNumPartitions (Python) to get the current size and number of the RDD's partitions. This helps you ensure that you are indeed going to coalesce the RDD into fewer partitions than its current number of partitions.

Two Types of Partitioners

Spark can use two types of partitioners when it needs to partition data—the HashPartitioner or the RangePartitioner (you can also write custom partitioners)—to determine how to distribute the data across the partitions inside an RDD. Here is how the two partitioners distribute the values in an RDD across partitions:

- The HashPartitioner uses the key code as the basis of the distribution of the values.
- The RangePartitioner partitions data by range, with the ranges approximately equal in size.

For pair RDDs, the HashPartitioner is the default partitioner. If any of the input RDDs has a partitioner, the output RDD will use the same partitioner.

Data Partitioning and How It Can Avoid a Shuffle

You can improve the performance of jobs that involve transformations that result in data shuffling (join, reduceByKey, groupByKey) by partitioning the RDDs ahead of time. If you partition the RDDs, you can completely bypass the shuffle process.

Anytime you can partition an RDD, the values for specific keys will be in the same partition and, therefore, can be locally processed without having to shuffle data across the network.

Shuffling data across the network becomes even more of an issue when you join RDDs. However, when you join a partitioned RDD with an unpartitioned RDD, the partitioned RDD will be processed locally. Only the unpartitioned RDD will need to be sorted and its data sent over the network to the necessary nodes. The final RDD you end up with will preserve the partitioner of the partitioned RDD.

Even better is the case where both the RDDs in a join are partitioned with the same partitioner. This means that Spark won't have to shuffle the data from either of the RDDs across the network. Some transformations, such as the join in the following example, don't result in a shuffle at all. Spark skips a shuffle when a prior transformation partitions data according to the *same* partitioner. First, here's our example:

```
rdd1 = myRdd.reduceByKey(...)
rdd2 = otherRdd.reduceByKey(...)
rdd3 = rdd1.join(rdd2)
```

In this case, the two `reduceByKey` transformations cause two shuffles of the data. However, to perform the final `join` operation, no shuffle is required if the datasets happen to have an identical number of partitions. This is so because both partitions use the default hash partitioning. Identical partitioning means that the set of keys for any single partition in `rdd1` will occur in a single partition of `rdd2`. Since the contents of any one output partition of the child RDD (`rdd3`) depend on the contents of just a single partition in both the parent RDDs `rdd1` and `rdd2`, there's no need for a third shuffle for performing the `join` operation.

Optimizing Data Serialization and Compression

Two data-related concepts—data serialization and compression—play a crucial role in Spark application performance. Let's learn the basic ideas pertaining to data serialization and data formats.

Data Serialization

Serialization is a critical area in optimizing Spark performance since Spark often transfers data across the cluster over the network, stores it in memory or spills it to disk. So the way Spark serializes the objects that represent the data is of great significance.

Spark uses deserialized Java object representation for records it keeps in its memory and a serialized binary representation for records it stores on disk or transfers via the network.

You can reduce the memory requirements for large objects by storing them in a serialized form, using a serialized storage level such as `MEMORY_ONLY_SER`, which will make Spark store RDD partitions as a single large byte array. When reading the data, you pay the piper though, since Spark has to deserialize the objects.

The following two persistence levels support the serialization of RDDs:

- `MEMORY_ONLY_SER`: Serializes RDDs before storing them and creates a one-byte array for each partition
- `MEMORY_AND_DISK_SER`: Same as the `MEMORY_ONLY_SER` storage level, but will store partitions that don't fit in memory on disk.

Choosing the appropriate serializer can make a huge difference. An improper choice of the serializer means that serialization of objects takes longer or uses up a large number of bytes. Spark uses the `spark.serializer` property to determine the serializer that converts between the serialized and deserialized representations. The default Java serializer is slow, and the objects of most classes that are serialized are in large formats. The recommended serializer is the Kryo serializer (`org.apache.sparkserializer.kryoserializer`). In order to use Kryo serialization, start the Spark shell and set Kryo as the serializer:

```
$ spark-shell --conf spark.serializer=org.apache.spark.serializer.KryoSerializer
```

> **Note**
>
> The reason Spark uses the Java serializer by default is due to the overhead of registering the custom classes.

The choice between different serialization mechanisms is a choice among speed, space usage and support of Java objects. The default serializer is Java serialization. The Kryo serializer is much faster and its output a more compact binary representation of the objects. Kryo is strongly recommended by Apache Spark, as it uses only a small fraction of the memory used by the Java serializer.

Configuring Compression

Spark can compress the following types of data:

- RDD partitions
- Broadcast variables
- Shuffle output

Apache Spark recommends that you compress broadcast variables before sending them across to all the nodes in the cluster. The default value for the `spark.broadcast.compress` parameter is `true`, so this is already configured for you.

You can choose to configure the compression of serialized RDD partitions (say, when you specify the `StorageLevel.MEMORY_ONLY_SER` storage level). This strategy can drastically reduce the storage space used by the RDD.

You can specify lzf compression to improve shuffle performance when dealing with large shuffles. You can specify the `lzf` codec as shown here:

```
conf.set("spark.io.compression.codec", "lzf")
```

> **Note**
>
> Spark uses the `snappy` compression codec by default, and you can also specify the `lz4` and `lzf` codecs.

The way you store data on disk is determined by the data format you choose. Extensible binary formats such as Avro, Parquet, Thrift and Protocol Buffers are ideal for Spark. Whatever you do, stay away from JSON files!

Understanding Spark's SQL Query Optimizer

Spark SQL uses a cost-based query optimizer to select optimal access paths to data. Cost-based optimization is the generation of multiple alternative plans and then figuring out the cost of the plans. The goal is to use the plan with the least cost in terms of computing resources.

When you use a SQL statement against a DataFrame, Spark SQL executes a query plan that consists of the following:

- The parsed logical plan
- The analyzed logical plan
- The optimized logical plan
- The physical plan

The query plan uses Spark SQL's **catalyst optimizer**, with the optimizer running through the plan parsing and optimization phases, followed by a physical plan evaluation and cost optimization–based optimal access-path selection.

Understanding the Optimizer Steps

In the following sections, I explain the basics of the Catalyst optimizer's transformation framework which involves four key phases.

> **Note**
>
> Use the `explain` function on the Spark SQL query you're interested in to see the full details of the steps followed by the Catalyst optimizer to assess and optimize the logical and physical plans to get the RDD result back.

Analyzing the Logical Plan

During the analysis of the logical execution plan, the optimizer reviews the SQL query and does the following:

- Creates a logical plan that's at first unresolved (the columns may not exist, for example)
- Resolves the logical plan using the catalog object
- Creates the logical plan

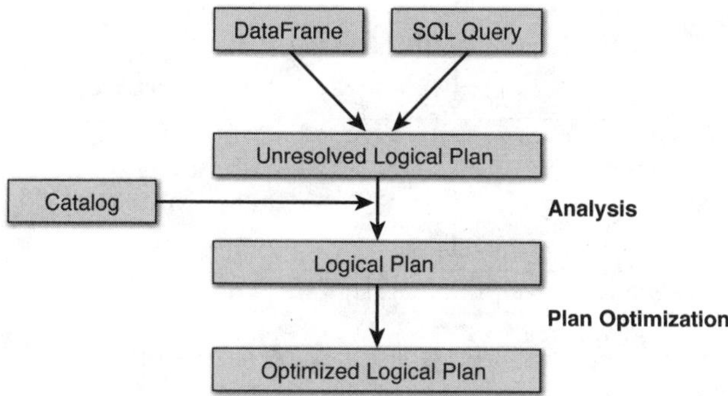

Figure 20.7 The optimized logical plan

Optimizing the Logical Plan

Optimizing the logical plan involves applying standard optimization techniques to the logical plan. For example, the predicate pushdown optimization pushes part of the query to where the data is located, thus filtering most of the data out. Obviously this cuts back on the network traffic in a cluster. Figure 20.7 shows how the optimizer arrives at the optimized logical query plan.

Physical Plan

During this phase, Spark generates multiple physical access plans from the logical plan and estimates the cost for each physical plan. It chooses the physical plan with the least cost for implementation.

> **Note**
>
> The Catalyst optimizer uses advanced programming language features such as Scala's pattern matching and quasiquotes.

Figure 20.8 shows how the optimizer generates one or more physical plans and selects the "best" plan for implementation.

Code Generation

In the final phase of query optimization, the Catalyst optimizer uses Scala's quasiquotes feature to compile parts of the query to Java byte code at runtime.

Viewing Spark Properties

Often, when you are running a Spark application, you wonder which configuration properties the app is actually using. Well, you don't need to wonder. Just go to the application web UI at `http://<driver>:4040` and view the Spark properties in the Environment tab. If you've specified a configuration property in the spark-default.conf file, through spark-conf or the command line, you'll see it there. If you haven't set a configuration property, Spark uses the default value for it.

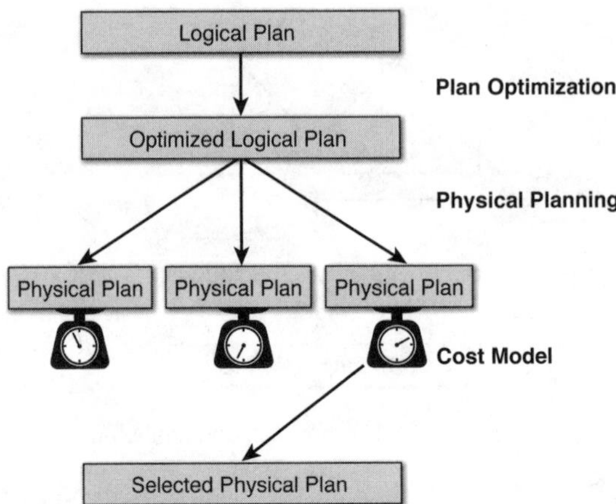

Figure 20.8 How the optimizer selects the best physical plan for implementation

> **Note**
>
> The Catalyst optimizer uses the operations that built the DataFrame into a physical plan for execution. Python users will notice that their performance will match that of the Scala users, since the optimizer generates JVM byte code for execution.

Spark's Speculative Execution Feature

In Chapter 18, "Tuning the Cluster Resources, Optimizing MapReduce Jobs and Benchmarking," you learned about how YARN uses speculative execution when running MapReduce jobs. Spark lets you configure speculative execution for its jobs as well. Speculative execution means that if one or more tasks in a stage are lagging behind the other tasks, Spark relaunches these tasks.

By default, speculative execution is turned off, and you can turn it on by setting the `spark.speculation` configuration property to `true`. When you set this parameter to `true`, Spark will perform speculative execution of tasks. If one or more tasks are running slowly in a stage, Spark will relaunch those tasks. The `spark.speculation.interval` property determines how often Spark checks for tasks to speculate (default is 100 ms).

The reasons for stragglers depend on the workload. For example, in an in-memory workload, you're likely to see more GC-related stragglers when compared with workloads that mostly use disk. Reading and writing massive amounts of data to disk often results in stragglers as well.

Spark uses the `spark.speculation.multiplier` property (default value is 1.5) to determine whether a task is deemed slow enough for speculative execution. The default value of 1.5 means that a task should be running 1.5 times slower than the median task duration for it to be considered a candidate for speculative execution.

Spark waits until a percentage of tasks in a stage are completed before it enables speculative execution for the tasks running in that stage. You can configure this percentage by setting the `spark.speculation.quantile` configuration property, whose default value is 0.75.

The Importance of Data Locality

Spark relies on the principle of data locality, which is a term that indicates how close the data you want to process is to the code that processes the data. It's far more efficient to ship code around rather than moving data, since code is much smaller than data.

In our case, since I'm interested in running Spark and YARN together on a Hadoop cluster, Hadoop's principles of rack-based data locality are very much in play here. Based on the data's location, there are several levels of data locality in a Hadoop/YARN cluster:

- `PROCESS_LOCAL`: This is the ideal data locality, as the data is co-located with the code inside the same JVM.
- `NODE_LOCAL`: This is the second best locality, with data located on the same node where the processing occurs.
- `NO_PREF`: This is data that has no preference for locality and that can be accessed with the same speed from anywhere.
- `RACK_LOCAL`: Data is on the same rack but on a different server.
- `ANY`: Data is located on other racks in the Hadoop cluster.

Figure 20.9 shows how to quickly find out if a job ran locally by inspecting a given stage in the Spark web UI. In the Stages tab, the "Locality Level" column shows the locality of the data the job used. In this example, all the data was collocated with the code (`PROCESS_LOCAL`).

Although Spark ideally likes to perform all its work on the most proximate (most local) locations, it's not possible to do this all the time. In cases where Spark realizes that there's no idle executor to process data locally (`PROCESS_LOCAL` or `NODE_LOCAL`), it has two options:

- Wait until an executor frees up so it can start the task on locally available data on the same server
- Start a new task immediately in a location that has idle executors but not data, and move data there for processing

Often Spark waits for a free executor until a timeout expires and then it starts moving data to nodes with free executors. If you're seeing that Spark is choosing poor locations, you can configure the timeouts to move between the various locality levels. Following is a summary of the locality-related configuration parameters.

- `spark.locality.wait`: This parameter specifies the duration of time for which Spark waits to launch a task in a more local location before it decides to launch it in a more remote node. The default is 3 seconds. As Spark searches for a more local locality (process_ local to node_local to rack_local), it waits for the same duration as specified by this parameter.
- `spark.locality.wait.node`: This parameter lets you customize the locality wait for node locality. You can skip node locality and go straight to rack locality by setting the value of this parameter to 0.

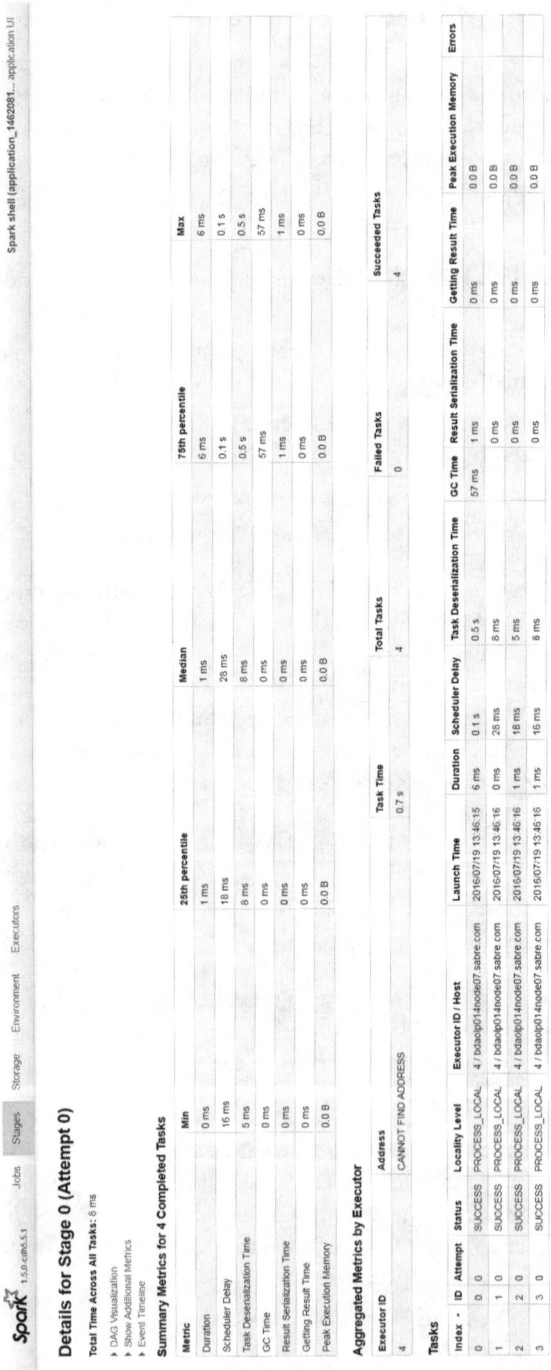

Details for Stage 0 (Attempt 0)

Total Time Across All Tasks: 8 ms

- DAG Visualization
- Show Additional Metrics
- Event Timeline

Summary Metrics for 4 Completed Tasks

Metric	Min	25th percentile	Median	75th percentile	Max
Duration	0 ms	1 ms	1 ms	6 ms	6 ms
Scheduler Delay	16 ms	18 ms	28 ms	0.1 s	0.1 s
Task Deserialization Time	5 ms	8 ms	8 ms	0.5 s	0.5 s
GC Time	0 ms	0 ms	0 ms	57 ms	57 ms
Result Serialization Time	0 ms	0 ms	0 ms	1 ms	1 ms
Getting Result Time	0 ms	0 ms	0 ms	0 ms	0 ms
Peak Execution Memory	0.0 B	0.0 B	0.0 B	0.0 B	0.0 B

Aggregated Metrics by Executor

Executor ID	Address	Task Time	Total Tasks	Failed Tasks	Succeeded Tasks
4	CANNOT FIND ADDRESS	0.7 s	4	0	4

Tasks

Index ▲	ID	Attempt	Status	Locality Level	Executor ID / Host	Launch Time	Duration	Scheduler Delay	Task Deserialization Time	GC Time	Result Serialization Time	Getting Result Time	Peak Execution Memory	Errors
0	0	0	SUCCESS	PROCESS_LOCAL	4 / bdaolp014node07.sabre.com	2016/07/19 13:46:15	6 ms	0.1 s	0.5 s	57 ms	1 ms	0 ms	0.0 B	
1	1	0	SUCCESS	PROCESS_LOCAL	4 / bdaolp014node07.sabre.com	2016/07/19 13:46:16	0 ms	28 ms	8 ms		0 ms	0 ms	0.0 B	
2	2	0	SUCCESS	PROCESS_LOCAL	4 / bdaolp014node07.sabre.com	2016/07/19 13:46:16	1 ms	18 ms	5 ms		0 ms	0 ms	0.0 B	
3	3	0	SUCCESS	PROCESS_LOCAL	4 / bdaolp014node07.sabre.com	2016/07/19 13:46:16	1 ms	16 ms	8 ms		0 ms	0 ms	0.0 B	

Figure 20.9 How to check the data locality for a Spark job

Caching Data

An RDD is created either by reading the data from a text file or a database or by transforming another RDD. Under Spark's lazy execution strategy, it creates an RDD only when an action method of the RDD is invoked, at which point it creates the RDD from its parents. Spark will perform all the necessary transformations all the way up the lineage tree of the RDD to get you the RDD required by the invoked action.

Caching is a big deal in Spark computations—once an RDD is cached, future actions that use the RDD can be many times (usually ten times or more) faster than creating the RDD from scratch. By saving intermediate results of computations or table data in memory, Spark can save time it would need to spend recomputing RDDs or loading data from disk.

When caching an RDD, Spark partitions are stored in memory or on disk on the node that computes the partitions. Subsequently, any actions that are performed on top of these partitions won't need Spark to recompute the partitions.

The lazy evaluation model of Spark means that when you use the same RDD the second (and third) time, Spark recomputes the RDD by default when you call an action on the RDD. Iterative algorithms often go over the same data multiple times, so this is an inefficient way to read the same data over and over.

By default, every time you run an action on a transformed RDD, it is recomputed. Persisting an RDD in memory through the `cache` or `persist` method lets Spark access the RDD way faster when it needs it again. Here's a simple example that computes the RDD named *result* twice, first for the `count` action and next for the `collect` action:

```
val result = input.map(x => x*x)
println(result.count())
println(result.collect().mkString(","))
```

Here's another example that helps understand the way Spark performs an action.

```
val logs = sc.textFile("path/to/log-files")
val errorLogs = logs filter { l => l.contains("ERROR")}
val warningLogs = logs filter { l => l.contains("WARN")}
val errorCount = errorLogs.count
val warningCount =  warningLogs.count
```

The `count` action is called twice, and each time it's invoked, it reads the source text file from disk. Spark reads the data from text, both when `errorLogs.count` and when `warningLogs.count` are called.

Spark lets applications cache RDDs in memory. When you choose to cache an RDD, Spark stores it in the executor's memory and not in the driver's memory. An RDD represents a distributed dataset and an executor performs computations on some of the partitions of an RDD. So, each executor will store the RDD partitions it's working with.

When you cache an RDD, Spark doesn't do anything right away to compute the RDD and store it in memory, since it follows a lazy execution model. But the very first time you call an action on a cached RDD, Spark saves the RDD in memory. Any following actions in the application benefit from this caching, since they don't need to recompute the RDD, say from reading data all over from the text file as in our example, or by generating the RDD from the RDDs parent RDDs. This means that applications that reuse the same data multiple times benefit from caching the RDDs.

Fault-Tolerance Due to Caching

While the main purpose behind caching is to speed up repeated computations that use the same RDDs, they also provide fault tolerance. Should any partition of an RDD be lost, Spark can automatically recompute it.

When a node with cached partitions of RDDs crashes, the Spark application continues to run without any problem. Once Spark recomputes the lost partition, it caches the recreated partition on a different node. How does Spark recreate the lost partitions(s)? Spark uses the RDD **lineage information** to recreate the lost partitions. It uses the same transformations that were used in creating it initially.

How to Specify Caching

An application can specify either the `cache` or the `persist` method to cache an RDD.

Specifying the cache Method

The `cache` method lets you cache the RDD in memory, as shown in the following example:

```
val logs = sc.textFile("path/to/log-files")
val errorsAndWarnings = logs filter { l => l.contains("ERROR") ||
l.contains("WARN")}
errorsAndWarnings.cache()
val errorLogs = errorsAndWarnings filter { l => l.contains("ERROR")}
val warningLogs = errorsAndWarnings filter { l => l.contains("WARN")}
val errorCount = errorLogs.count
val warningCount =  warningLogs.count
```

When exactly is an RDD cached? Let's say I have the following:

```
testRdd.cache()
testRdd.count()
testRdd.collect()
```

Since an RDD is cached when you perform the first action and not before, just the `collect` action can use the cached values.

> **Tip**
>
> If your application isn't going to read a dataset multiple times, caching is actually going to make the job slower. You do pay a price for caching. If the cost of the memory pressure due to caching is higher than the benefit of avoiding a recomputation of an RDD, caching is not good. If the dataset can be easily recomputed and the app isn't going to access it too many times, recomputation may actually be faster.

Specifying the `persist` Method

The second way to store an RDD in memory to benefit future computations is by invoking the `persist` method. You can look at `persist` as a more general way of caching RDDs, since it lets you specify storage formats other than memory for storing RDDs.

If you call the `persist` method without any parameters, it works the same as the `cache` method—it stores the RDD in memory. Here's an example:

```
val lines = sc.textFile (/data/examples/data1.txt)
lines.persist()
```

Bothe `cache` and `persist` do the same thing for you—they store the RDD temporarily, and the default location for both methods is memory. The difference between the two methods is that the `persist` method lets you specify alternate storage levels for storing the data inside the RDDs.

If you are concerned about Spark's memory usage and you think you're using too much memory, there are alternatives beyond having to use just memory for storage. If you decide to store the RDDs and they don't fit into the JVM memory, you can specify multiple storage-level options, such as the following:

- `MEMORY_ONLY`: This is the default storage level and stores the RDD as a deserialized Java object. If there isn't enough room in memory for the RDD, the partitions that can't be cached will be recomputed when they're needed. Here's an example:

  ```
  val lines = sc.textFile (/data/examples/data1.txt)
  lines.persist (MEMORY_ONLY)
  ```

  All of the following will use the `MEMORY_ONLY` storage level:

  ```
  testRdd.cache()
  testRdd.persist()
  testRdd.persist(StorageLevel.MEMORY_ONLY_)
  ```

- `MEMORY_AND_DISK`: Stores the RDDs in memory as deserialized Java objects, and if there isn't enough room, will store the partitions on disk for future reads. Here's an example:

  ```
  testRdd.persist(StorageLevel.MEMORY_AND_DISK)
  ```

- `MEMORY_ONLY_SER`: Stores the RDD in memory only as serialized Java objects (storing them in the deserialized form is the default), which are more space efficient. However, you expend greater amounts of CPU power to read the serialized data later on, as the serialized form requires more parsing. Here's how you specify this storage level:

  ```
  testRdd.persist(StorageLevel.MEMORY_ONLY_SER)
  ```

- `MEMORY_AND_DISK_SER`: Similar to the `MEMORY_ONLY_SER` level but uses disk to store the partitions that don't fit in memory. Here's an example:

  ```
  testRdd.persist(StorageLevel.MEMORY_AND_DISK_SER)
  ```

- `DISK_ONLY`: Skips memory and stores all the partitions of the RDD on disk. Here's an example:

  ```
  testRdd.persist(StorageLevel.DISK_ONLY)
  ```

- MEMORY_ONLY_2, MEMORY_AND_DISK_2 and so on: These storage levels work the same as the corresponding storage levels described earlier, with the difference that each partition is stored on two nodes for resilience purposes. Here's how you set this storage level:

```
testRdd.persist(StorageLevel.MEMORY_ONLY_2)
testRdd.persist(StorageLevel.MEMORY_ONLY_SER_2)
testRdd.persist(StorageLevel.MEMORY_AND_DISK_2)
testRdd.persist(StorageLevel.MEMORY_AND_DISK_SER_2
testRdd.persist(StorageLevel.DISK_ONLY_2)
```

Note

Serialization saves on memory usage, but its counterpart, deserialization, increases CPU usage.

Here's an example that shows how to set the storage level inside a Spark program. In this example, I specify the DISK_ONLY storage level to store all the partitions on disk, bypassing memory altogether.

```
import org.apache.spark.storage.StorageLevel
val result = input.map(x => x * x)
result.persist(StorageLevel.DISK_ONLY)
println(result.count())
println(result.collect().mkString(","))
```

Tip

A collect() operation on an RDD results in the dataset being copied to the driver. If you're collecting a large RDD and the driver's memory allocation isn't big enough to handle it, guess what happens? You'll see the dreaded OOM exception. I suggested a strategy in Chapter 19, "Configuring and Tuning Apache Spark on YARN," to get around it, which involves running such operations in the Client mode (and not in the cluster mode) and allocating plenty of memory to the driver to handle the huge dataset. If you can't do this, the other strategy to keep your job from failing is to simply use take or takeSample to select a limited number of elements from the dataset.

Here's how you set the storage level when running something from the Spark shell:

1. Start the Spark shell:

   ```
   $ spark-shell
   ```

2. Import the StorageLevel you want to specify:

   ```
   scala> import org.apache.spark.storage.StorageLevel._
   ```

3. Create your RDD:

   ```
   scala> val words = sc.textFile("words")
   ```

4. Cache the new RDD:

   ```
   scala> words.persist(MEMORY_ONLY_SER)
   ```

Once the `persist` method is called on the RDD before the first action (`count`), the second action (`collect`) benefits from not having to recompute the RDD (`result`).

In both Scala and Java, the default persistence level will store the RDD data as unserialized objects. Python always stores objects as serialized data, so it stores the data in the Java heap as pickled objects. Python also stores the data it writes to disk in the serialized form.

> **Note**
>
> The choice of a storage level is irrelevant when using Python-based applications, since all stored objects are serialized with the Pickle library.

Checking the Cache

When caching RDDs, often you want to know how many partitions Spark has stored. In the following simple example, I specify the cache procedure to make Spark cache the RDD before it processes it.

```
scala> val someRDD = sc.parallelize(1 to 100, 4)
someRDD: org.apache.spark.rdd.RDD[Int] = ParallelCollectionRDD[0] at parallelize
at <console>:21

scala> someRDD.setName("toy").cache
res0: someRDD.type = toy ParallelCollectionRDD[0] at parallelize at <console>:21
scala> someRDD.map(x => x).collect
```

Once the job completes, I can use the Spark web UI's Storage page, as shown in Figure 20.10, to understand what exactly Spark has stored from this operation.

Figure 20.10 shows how the Storage page reveals the various useful details about caching, such as the storage level, cached partitions, the fraction cached and, finally, the size of the cache in memory and on disk.

Choosing among the Storage Levels

As you can tell, choice of a storage level implies choosing a specific tradeoff between speedy performance (in memory storage) and CPU usage. If the partitions fit all in memory, then the default storage level of `MEMORY_ONLY` (`StorageLevel.MEMORY_ONLY`—store deserialized objects in memory) is the best strategy—this speeds up the RDD computations while using CPU in an efficient manner.

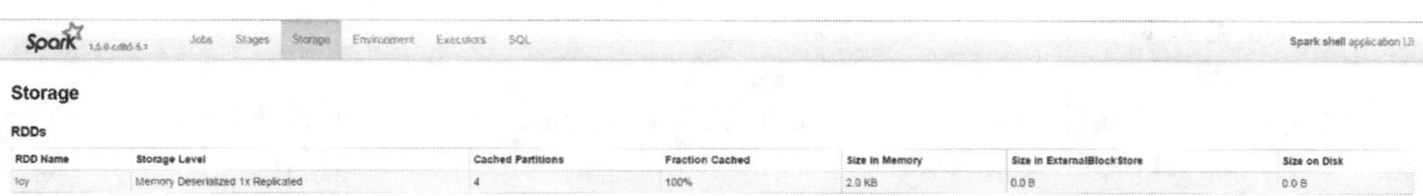

Figure 20.10 Spark web UI's Storage page showing the caching information

If you're going to perform frequent operations on an RDD, or you need to access an RDD quickly, `MEMORY_ONLY` is a good storage level to use. However, you do pay a price—you're going to use a lot memory. Also, when caching a large number of small objects, the application is going to keep the garbage collector busy.

If you can't fit the partitions entirely in memory, follow these Spark guidelines:

- Avoid spilling to disk unless the application is filtering a huge amount of data, since recomputing the partitions is going to be slow, as compared to in-memory computations.
- The next best strategy to using `MEMORY_ONLY` is to use `MEMORY_ONLY_SER` with a fast serialization library such as Kryo serialization, which I discussed earlier. `MEMORY_ONLY_SER` helps cut down on garbage collection.
- For faster fault recovery, choose the replicated storage levels (such as `MEMORY_ONLY_2`).

In a production setting, `MEMORY_AND_DISK` may be critical in helping you avoid data loss. Serializing the state to disk means that if an application fails, you're ensuring that the state is captured and persisted on disk. This is especially critical for long-running applications. If there are unexpected spikes in the size of the data, a disk-backed RDD can handle it while memory-only RDDs will result in an out-of-memory exception. The `MEMORY_AND_DISK` storage level can help avoid expensive recomputations.

For Spark Streaming applications, as I explained in Chapter 19, it's a good strategy to run with the `MEMORY_ONLY_2` option to minimize the possibility of being unable to recover the state by storing everything in memory twice.

> **Note**
>
> Spark automatically removes older RDD partitions from cache using the well-known least-recently-used algorithm. You can manually remove an RDD using the `RDD.unpersist` method. You need to be careful about not caching unnecessary data. If you try to cache too many RDDs relative to the memory you have, Spark evicts the older partitions. If the partitions belong to memory-only storage levels, it has to recompute them when they are required the next time. If you've configured a memory and disk storage level upon evicting the partitions from memory, Spark writes them to disk (way slower than memory). So, regardless of the storage level, eviction of RDDs that may need to be read multiple times means more time to read (from disk), or recompute those partitions.

Using Tachyon

In addition to the storage levels I described, you can also choose to store an RDD in a serialized format in Tachyon, using the experimental `OFF_HEAP` storage level. There's less garbage collection overhead with the `OFF_HEAP` storage level. If you have a bunch of Spark applications running, the `OFF_HEAP` storage level may help, as it lets executors share a memory pool. You also have the further advantage that if individual executors crash, you don't lose any cached RDDs, since the RDDs don't live in the executors—they're stored in Tachyon. Here's how you set this storage level:

```
testRdd.persist(StorageLevel, OFF_HEAP)
```

Finding the RDD Cache Information

You can view the RDD cache information in the Spark UI's Storage page. This page shows the storage level, the number of partitions that are cached and the cached fraction and its size.

Caching Spark Tables

Up until now, I explained how you can cache RDDs in memory (and/or on disk). You can also cache tables that you plan on querying often. Spark SQL uses a special way to cache tables and I explain that in this section.

When the Spark SQL cache stores cached tables in memory, it does so in a columnar format. Since queries based on this columnar format will be using only the required columns, performance is going to be better. Spark SQL automatically chooses the appropriate or best compression codec for all the columns to minimize the memory usage and garbage collection.

Unlike in the case of the Spark RDD cache, when you cache a table, it doesn't have to await an action so it can be cached. The table already exists, so when you say "Cache this table," the table is immediately cached in the Spark SQL cache. You can however, change this behavior by making it a "lazy operation":

```
sparkSqlContext.sql("cache lazy table myTableName")
```

You can use one of the following ways to remove a table from the Spark SQL:

```
dataFrame.unpersist()

sparkSqlContext.uncacheTable("myTableName")

sparksqlContext.sql("uncache table myTableName")
```

Summary

Here's what you learned in this chapter:

- To be able to tune the performance of Spark applications, you must get a good handle on the basic Spark execution model.
- Minimizing expensive shuffle operations is at the heart of Spark performance tuning, and selecting appropriate aggregation operators is a key strategy in achieving this goal.
- You can't have too few or too many partitions. You need to know when to use the repartition and coalesce operations to change the number of partitions in an RDD.
- Caching data is beneficial and knowing the storage levels you can specify for caching helps optimize caching strategies to suit the requirements of your applications.

21

Troubleshooting Hadoop—A Sampler

This chapter covers

- Troubleshooting space-related issues
- Troubleshooting memory issues
- Handling different types of failures
- Troubleshooting Spark job execution

I'm going to keep this, the last chapter of the book, short and sweet. Troubleshooting is a vast area and I want to give you a flavor of some of the more interesting issues you might run into in your Hadoop cluster. Hadoop has many configuration properties, and a mastery of those properties is essential to getting the most out of your investments in a Hadoop cluster. However, only some of the errors you run into every day can be fixed by reconfiguring Hadoop's various components.

I don't consider the performance analysis of poorly running Hive, Spark or other jobs running in a cluster as troubleshooting. The reasons for a "hanging" or long-running job may be due to poor code or improper choice of operators, inefficient join strategies, or a zillion other things. Similarly, I don't attempt to discuss the reasons for a process (such as Hive or Hue) not starting up or crashing—these again are usually due to configuration errors/changes on either the host server or in the component, and there could be numerous reasons for these type of failures—they all come under routine systems administration of any type and aren't really special to Hadoop administration.

Space-Related Issues

Hadoop uses several types of storage. Besides HDFS itself, Hadoop stores logs in the host's /var directory, as well as in the local directories. Space-related issues in any of these areas can cause job failures, so it's a good idea to keep an eye on the local directories used by Hadoop.

As you learned in Chapter 17, "Monitoring, Metrics and Hadoop Logging," the NodeManager always stores the application log files in the local directories. This is true even when you enable log aggregation where Hadoop stores job logs in HDFS, since all logs are first stored on local storage. If the mount point on which the log directory is located fills up, the NodeManager won't be able to write its log files on that node. The same is the case if the directories where the Hadoop daemons are logging are full.

To avoid task and potential job failures, you must proactively check the available free space under these mount points and get rid of all unnecessary files. If you can't remove enough space, you may want to expand the size of the mount point itself.

You can determine which files to remove from these directories by running commands such as the following on the nodes with a problem space situation:

```
# find ./ -size +100000 -type f -ls | sort -n  // lists files larger than 25MB
# du -a /var | sort -n -r | head -n 10  //lists the top 10 files in size,
in a sorted order
```

If you set the location of the Hadoop daemon logs and application local directories used by the NodeManager to the /var directory, understand that this directory shares the root file system (the "/" partition) with other directories such as tmp. You are likely to use the /var directory for logging output from several Hadoop-related components, such as ZooKeeper, Hive and Hue, in addition to the Hadoop daemons and NodeManager application logs. So, it pays to work up a simple shell script that alerts you to a low space condition on this mount point.

If the NodeManager local directories specified by the `yarn.nodemanager.local-dirs` parameter fill up on a node, an application may fail because it tried to launch more than the configured number of task attempts on that node. You'll receive an error similar to the following in the application's log file:

```
Application application_1437683566204_0394 failed 2 times due to AM Container for
 appattempt_1437683566204_0394_000002 exited with exitCode: -1000 due to:
No space available
in any of the local directories.

.Failing this attempt.. Failing the application.
```

Dealing with a 100 Percent Full Linux File System

Once in a while a file system might report that it is 100 percent full. If this happens to be a mount point such as the root file system, it spells immediate trouble, as that's where most files store their Hadoop-related local logs (under /var/log). Obviously some user generated a large dump file, or a huge temporary file was stored in the directory that became full. Use the following procedures to free up space in the directory that's fully used up.

Use the `find` command to determine the largest files under a mount point. Here's one such command:

```
# du -a /var | sort -n -r | head -n 10
```

Once you identify the largest files, remove all the files that aren't critical for the cluster operation.

HDFS Space Issues

HDFS space issues could be of two types: The first is when you're low on HDFS free space in your cluster. The second is when individual users bump up against the HDFS quotas you've allocated to them. These users could also be what you may call **functional accounts**, which are generic usernames under which you submit jobs, such as an HDFS user named produser, for example.

If HDFS free space is getting low in your cluster, there are two basic solutions for increasing the space: adding more nodes or adding more drives to the existing nodes.

Another way you can increase the free HDFS space is by deleing data you no longer need, as well as by reducing the replication factor for historical data that isn't deemed quite as important as newer data.

If jobs issued by users are failing due to their hitting their maximum configured HDFS space quota, you need to increase the space quotas for the users with the `dfsadmin setSpaceQuota` command, as explained in Chapter 9, "HDFS Commands, HDFS Permissions and HDFS Storage."

Once way to stay a step ahead of HDFS quota–related problems is by periodically running a command such as the following, which shows the current usage of HDFS space by all my users, as well as the extent of the HDFS space quota each user still has available:

```
$ hdfs dfs -count -q -h /user/*

        none             inf            30 G            20 G            1
.0                 0 /user/alapati
        none             inf            30 G            5 G             2
0                  0 /user/analyst
...
```

This partial output from the `hdfs dfs -count q -h` command shows that the user alapati has used 10GB out of that user's allocated space quota of 30GB. Thus the user has 20GB still left under that user's space quota. If users are bumping up against their assigned space quotas, increase the space quotas with the `dfsadmin -setSpaceQuota` command.

Local and Log Directories Out of Free Space

Earlier in this chapter you learned that you can specify the local directories for the NodeManager with the `yarn.nodemanager.local-dirs` parameter and the log directories for the NodeManager with the `yarn.nodemanager.log-dirs` parameter. Hadoop performs a disk health check at frequent intervals. If the free space falls below a threshold value, no new containers will be launched by the NodeManager on the node where it runs.

Two key parameters—`yarn.nodemanager.disk-health-checker.min-healthy-disks` and `yarn.nodemanager.disk-health-checker.max-disk-utilization-per-disk-percentage`—play a critical role in how the NodeManager behaves in the face of a low space issue on either the local directories or the log directories. Here's how the two parameters determine the percentage of space Hadoop uses on each storage disk and how it considers a node to have a sufficient number of healthy storage drives:

- `yarn.nodemanager.disk-health-checker.max-disk-utilization-per-disk-percentage`: Once a disk reaches a space-utilization threshold set by this parameter, it's marked bad (or unhealthy). You can set a value between 0.0 and 100.0 for this parameter, and the default value is 90.0. Once a disk exceeds 90 percent usage, it can still be used, but it is marked bad or unhealthy internally. Remember that this applies to the directories you specify as values for both the `yarn-nodemanager.local-dirs` and `yarn.nodemanager.log-dirs` parameters.
- `yarn.nodemanager.disk-health-checker.min-healthy-disks`: This parameter determines the minimum fraction of the total disks on a node that must be healthy. If the number of healthy drives (local-dir or log-dir) on a node falls below this threshold, the NodeManager will not launch new containers on this node. In effect, this node gets taken out of the cluster so far as processing goes. The default value for this parameter is 0.25. If you have twelve disks on a node, this means that at least a quarter of them—that is, three drives—must be healthy in order for the NodeManager to start new containers on the node.

Let's say you're using the default values for both the `yarn.nodemanager.disk-health-checker.max-disk-utilization-per-disk-percentage` and the `yarn.nodemanager.disk-health-checker.min-healthy-disks` parameters. If you are tight on space and more than 10 drives on a 12-drive node reach the 90 percent threshold, the NodeManager will keep containers from being started on these nodes—meaning, the job's new tasks on that node will fail and you'll see an error such as the following:

```
Application Type:     MAPREDUCE
Application Tags:
State: FAILED
FinalStatus: FAILED
Started:        Sat Jul 16 04:01:10 -0500 2016
Elapsed:        13sec
Tracking URL:   History
Diagnostics:
Application application_1437683566204_0350 failed 2 times due to AM Container for
appattempt_1437683566204_0350_000002 exited with exitCode: -1000 due to: No space
available in any of the local directories.
.Failing this attempt.. Failing the application.
```

This error shows that the NodeManager refuses to start the task with ID 000002 because more than the minimum number of disks are "unhealthy." On a 3TB drive, 90 percent used space means there's still 300GB free—and most likely you can continue to use the drives. You can do one of two things (or both) under the circumstances:

- Lower the threshold for marking a disk as bad by setting a lower value for the `yarn.nodemanager.disk-health-checker.max-disk-utilization-per-disk-percentage` parameter.
- Lower the minimum number of healthy drives by setting the `yarn.nodemanager.disk-health-checker.min-healthy-disks` parameter.

The best long term solution, obviously, is to acquire more nodes for the cluster.

The parameter `yarn.nodemanager.disk-health-checker.min-free-space-per-disk-mb` determines how much free space there ought to be in the local-dirs and the log-dirs for the directories to be used by the NodeManager. The default is 0.

Disk Volume Failure Toleration

If a very small percentage of a cluster's DataNodes are dead, no need to fret about it, trying to bring up those nodes—you have better and more critical things to attend to in a Hadoop cluster! However, do track the number of dead nodes and when the number reaches a significant amount, work on bringing the nodes back. Unlike traditional databases, where losing a disk could have a catastrophic impact, Hadoop will merrily chug along even when storage failures occur. Your cluster will operate the same, but with a smaller total storage capacity. Unlike in traditional RAID systems, you can fix the failed disks when it's convenient to do so. You can configure how many disk failures a node can tolerate by setting the following parameter:

```
<property>
   <name>dfs.datanode.failed.volumes.tolerated</name>
   <value>4</value>
</property>
```

In this case, Hadoop will tolerate the failure of four disk volumes on a DataNode before it blacklists it. It's important to understand that by default a DataNode will shut down following the failure of a single volume (disk drive). So, the default value for the `dfs.datanode.failed.volumes.tolerated` parameter is zero. Make sure you set it to a positive number such as 2, 3 or 4 to make sure that DataNodes don't shut down following a single volume failure. Once the number of failures reaches the number you set, the DataNode will be marked a "dead node."

The easiest way to find out whether you have any failed volumes in your Hadoop cluster is by reviewing the NameNode UI's Datanode Volume Failures page, as shown in Figure 21.1.

Hot Swapping a Disk Drive

You can add or replace a disk drive without bringing down the DataNode, since Hadoop supports hot swappable drives for DataNodes. You need to use the new command `dfsadmin -reconfig datanode` to perform the hot swap. Following is a high-level description of the procedures for a hot swap of disk drives.

1. Format and mount the new disk drive.
2. Update the `dfs.datanode.data.dir` config property in the hdfs-site.xml file. Remove the failed data volumes you are replacing and add the new data volumes.
3. Execute the `dfsadmin -reconfig datanode HOST:PORT start` command to start the reconfiguration.
4. Unmount the removed data volume directories and remove the disks from the server once the reconfiguration task completes.

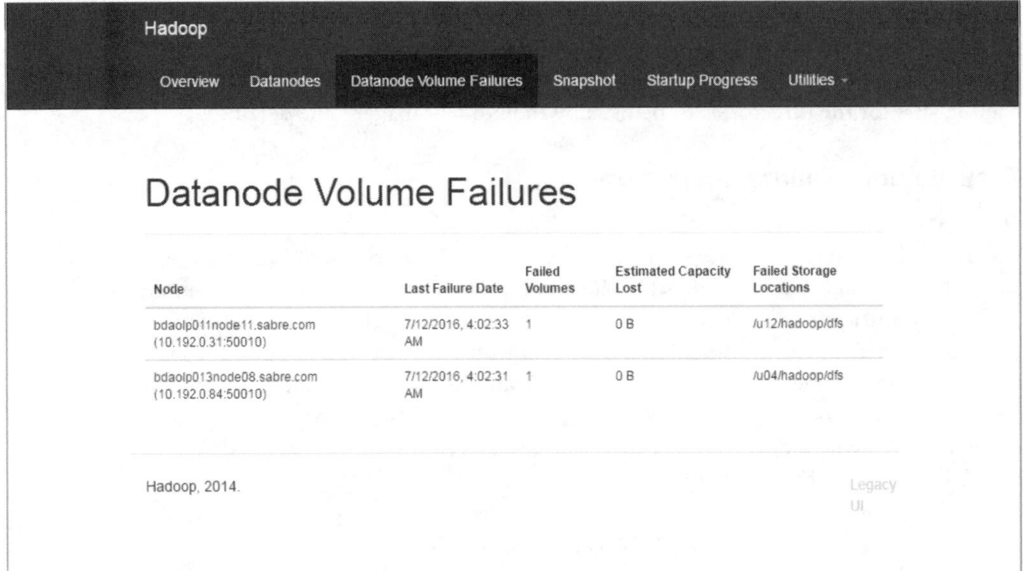

Figure 21.1 The NameNode UI's DataNode Volume Failures page, showing the number of failed volumes

Setting the `dfs.datanode.du.reserved` Parameter

In Chapter 3, "Creating and Configuring a Simple Hadoop 2 Cluster," you learned how the `dfs.datanode.du.reserved` parameter in the hdfs-site.xml file lets you set the amount of the reserved space (in bytes per volume) for non-HDFS use. Although the directories on which you store HDFS files are mostly designed for HDFS usage, they aren't entirely for HDFS usage. The directories also hold the temporary data for Hadoop jobs. Make sure to leave enough space free for holding the temporary data of the largest Hadoop jobs you expect to run.

Using Replication Well

Hadoop uses a default replication level of three as explained in Chapter 3 and repeated elsewhere. While a higher replication factor, of course, means higher usage of disk space, there are advantages to a higher level of replication. A high replication level has two clear benefits:

- Faster performance, especially when dealing with "hot" data required by multiple applications.
- Higher reliability—the higher the replication level, the more reliable the data is from a storage point of view.

Handling YARN Jobs That Are Stuck

Once in a while you may run into a situation where Spark (or MapReduce) applications are initiated in YARN but never make it to the RUNNING state. The jobs just remain stuck in the ACCEPTED state. The same thing can happen when Oozie launches the job or you run it manually. The jobs remain stuck in the ACCEPTED state and don't transition to the RUNNING state. If you check the ResourceManager web UI, you'll see the job status as ACCEPTED as well. If you check the application log, you'll see messages such as the following:

```
2016-09-01 00:48:14,121 INFO
org.apache.hadoop.yarn.server.resourcemanager.scheduler.fair.FairScheduler:
Added Application Attempt appattempt_1420073214126_0002_000001 to
scheduler from user: admin
2015-09-01 00:48:14,121 INFO
org.apache.hadoop.yarn.server.resourcemanager.rmapp.attempt.RMAppAttemptImpl:
appattempt_1420073214126_0002_000001 State change from
SUBMITTED to SCHEDULED
```

You have no recourse but to kill these jobs (`yarn application -kill <appid>`) in most cases and run them anew, either manually or by letting the next scheduled Oozie job start a new job. Diagnosing and fixing the stalled job issue is often quite easy. I explain how to fix this in two common scenarios.

A major cause of jobs that are stuck and don't start running (possibly forever), is lack of sufficient resources to launch the job. If a job makes a request for a high amount of RAM for a container such as, say, 64GB, but there's no node in the cluster with 64GB free memory, YARN won't start the job. There isn't much you can do in this case but wait until sufficient memory is freed up over the course of time to enable the launching of the job. You'll need to relaunch the job, as it won't transition out of the ACCEPTED state on its own. In the long run, you may want to explore increasing the RAM for the cluster nodes.

The other reason why jobs may hang and languish in the ACCEPTED state forever is because you've limited the maximum number of jobs through the Fair Scheduler or the Capacity Scheduler. To ensure that you haven't set the maximum simultaneously runnable jobs too low, if you're using the Fair Scheduler to allocate resources in your cluster, check the value of the maxRunningApps queue element (this sets the limit on the number of apps from the queue to run at once) in the fair-scheduler.xml file. The maxRunningApps attribute sets the limit on the maximum number of applications that can be run by a user at any time. If you're using the Capacity Scheduler, check the value of the following properties in the capacity-scheduler.xml file (the properties set the maximum number of applications that can be concurrently active in both running and pending states):

```
yarn.scheduler.capacity.maximum-
applications / yarn.scheduler.capacity.<queue-
path>.maximum-applications
```

If you're using a tool such as Cloudera Manager, of course, you'll need to make the changes through the tool. For example, if you're using Cloudera Manager, you can do this by going to Clusters > Dynamic Resource pools > Configuration. At this point, you can click first on Default Settings and check the value of the Max Running Apps per Resource Pool attribute. Next, you need to edit the configuration of the specific resource pool from within which this application was launched and bump up the value of the Max Running Apps configuration property.

JVM Memory-Allocation and Garbage-Collection Strategies

Everything runs in a Java Virtual Machine (JVM) in Hadoop. To troubleshoot well, you must understand how JVMs allocate memory and how they perform garbage collection, which is how a JVM reclaims older and unused memory so it can allocate it for other uses. Different garbage-collection strategies have a different impact on the performance of applications in your cluster.

Chapter 17, "Monitoring, Metrics and Hadoop Logging," showed how to monitor your cluster through Ganglia or by reviewing the various Hadoop logs. When everything fails, it's time to review a Java heap dump to get at the root cause of issues in the YARN containers!

Understanding JVM Garbage Collection

A Java **heap** is where the objects of a Java program are stored. When you allocate memory to a map or reduce container's JVM, as explained in Chapter 3 and Chapter 18 "Tuning the Cluster Resources, Optimizing MapReduce Jobs and Benchmarking," it is these parameters that determine the size of the Java heap for a YARN container. The heap can contain live objects, dead objects, and free unassigned memory. When no running program can reach a specific object in a heap, it's considered "garbage" and the JVM gets ready to remove it from the heap. Garbage collection is how a JVM releases unused Java objects in the Java heap.

Each JVM's heap comprises three separate parts, called generations. The three generations are named young (new generation), old and permanent. The JVM allocates initial size to both the young and old generations with the `-Xms` option, and the maximum size of the segment is set by the `-Xmx` option. You can also initialize the size of the young generation with the `-XX:NewSize` option and specify the size of the old generation with the `-XX:Newratio` option. If you set the `-XX:NewRatio` parameter to 3, it means that the old generation's size is three times as large that of the new generation.

Figure 21.2 shows the generations in the Java heap.

The new generation consists of three segments—Eden, Survivor Space I and Survivor Space II. Objects are created in the Eden component first and traverse through the Survivor Space I segment before ending up in the Survivor Space II segment. Finally the objects are moved to the old generation component. In a minor garbage collection,

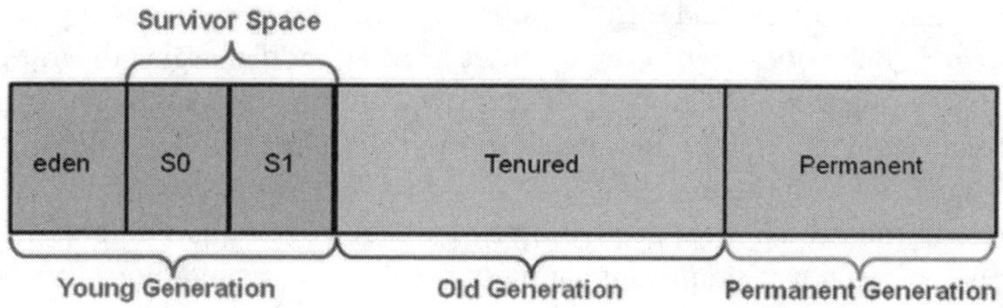

Figure 21.2 The structure of a JVM's generations

the JVM moves objects within the young generation. When the JVM can't move any objects into the old generation space, it triggers a major garbage collection process, which isn't good for any running applications such as your YARN applications.

The size of the Java heap plays a crucial role in how often and how much time the JVM spends collecting garbage. Time spent collecting garbage is waiting time, not processing time, so applications take longer to complete if the JVMs are spending an inordinate amount of time collecting garbage. By assigning a very high amount of memory to the JVM heap, you can of course reduce garbage collection and even eliminate it completely. However, that means your cluster can support fewer containers overall, as each container uses up a very large chunk of memory for its JVM memory. This means that the cluster can support fewer simultaneously running applications. The trick here is to minimize the time spent by the JVMs in garbage collection, while supporting as many containers (and thus, applications) overall as you can.

If your JVMs run out of heap space, you'll see the following out of memory (OOM) errors:

```
java.lang.OutofMemoryError
Exception in thread "main"
```

Specifying the Java Heap Size Values

When you configure the size of a container, internally, YARN will start the Java process as follows:

```
java -XX:NewSize=128m  -XX:MaxNewSize=128m  -XX:SurviviorRatio=8  -Xms512m   -Xmx512m
```

The `m` in the parameter settings means megabytes. `-Xms` and `-Xmx` refer to the minimum and maximum sizes of the Java heap.

Regardless of what heap sizes you set for the child JVMs, you should ensure that you don't end up swapping pages to disk because of too high an allocation for the JVMs for map and reduce tasks.

Optimizing Garbage Collection

You can choose a specific garbage collection schema or strategy to tune the JVM memory usage. You can optimize the garbage collection process by choosing the appropriate garbage-collection strategy for your applications.

For applications with short and infrequent garbage-collection processes, a garbage-collection strategy isn't critical. However, for those applications that deal with large amounts of data, it may be important to fine tune the garbage collection process by picking the appropriate collection strategy. In these applications, throughput suffers significantly due to high garbage collection times.

If you add up the time lost for processing by garbage collecting hundreds and thousands of objects it could be a significant chunk of the total processing time taken by an application.

Analyzing Memory Usage

You can obtain so-called **heap dumps** from a YARN container to analyze how an application is using its memory. A common tool for obtaining heap dumps is the `jmap` tool, which requires the process ID to attach itself to the running Java process and dumps the heap contents to a file, as shown here:

```
# jmap -dump:format=b,file=~/mr-container.hprof -F 2345
Attaching to process ID 12345, please wait...
Debugger attached successfully.
Server compiler detected.
JVM version is 20.6-b01
Dumping heap to /opt/rm.hprof ...
Finding object size using Printezis bits and skipping over...
Finding object size using Printezis bits and skipping over...
Heap dump file created
#
```

You can read the heap dumps generated by the `jmap` utility with either the `jhat` utility or visually through the Eclipse Memory Analyzer. The Eclipse Memory Analyzer reveals the objects using the most heap space in the JVM process.

Out of Memory Errors

Once in a while, you may encounter an OOM error when trying to list files in HDFS using `hdfs dfs -ls` on a directory:

```
java.lang.OutOfMemoryError:
Java heap space
```

Or you may see the following error:

```
Exception in thread "main" java.lang.OutOfMemoryError: Java heap space
at java.util.Arrays.copyOf(Arrays.java:2367)
at
java.lang.AbstractStringBuilder.expandCapacity(AbstractStringBuilder.java:130)
at
java.lang.AbstractStringBuilder.ensureCapacityInternal(AbstractStringBuilder.java:114)
at...
```

This happens because the HDFS client's default heap size of 246MB is too low when you're attempting to list a directory with a large number of objects. Increase the heap size of the Hadoop client by specifying a higher value for the heap size, as shown here:

```
$ HADOOP_HEAPSIZE=1024 hdfs dfs -ls /user/sam
```

The Hadoop client will now have a greater Java heap size to perform the lookup of the HDFS directory contents.

Following is another example where a Spark job crashes with an OOM error:

```
ERROR Executor: Exception in task 25.0 in stage 16.0 (TID 999)
java.lang.OutOfMemoryError: GC overhead limit exceeded
    Resolution:
spark.executor.memory : Amount of memory to use per executor process, in the same
format as JVM memory strings.
```

In this case the problem and the solution are given to you! You need to increase the memory for the executor by bumping up the value of the `spark.executor.memory` configuration property, as I explained in Chapter 19, "Configuring and Tuning Apache Spark on YARN."

Spark and JVM Garbage Collection

It's not uncommon for Spark applications to use 100GB and even higher amounts of memory for the heap space. Garbage-collection-induced delays and crashes are a common concern in many Spark environments.

The standard garbage-collection strategies used by Java applications are the Concurrent Mark Sweep (CMS) and the ParallelOld garbage-collection strategies. The first strategy aims at lower latency and the second, a higher throughput. Both strategies could prove to be performance bottlenecks—the CMS GC because it doesn't do any compaction, and the ParallelOld GC, which performs only whole-heap compactions, because it can induce long pauses in application performance. If your application needs real-time response, in general, the CMS GC works best, and if your applications are mostly analytical in nature, you can use ParallelOld GC.

Since Spark has both streaming and batch-processing capabilities you might want to consider the newer Garbage-First GC (G1GC) introduced by the Hotspot JVM version 2.6. This collector is going to eventually replace CMS GC, and its goal is to simultaneously provide low latency and high throughput.

Whichever GC strategies you might pursue, the fact remains that the most critical tuning aspects are those that optimize the use of memory by reducing intermediate object creation or replication, storing long-lived objects off heap and limiting the creation of very large objects.

Out of the memory you allocated to an executor, Spark allots 75 percent to storage and execution. If you don't need a lot of memory for storing RDDs, you can lower the memory fraction allocated to RDD caching by setting the `spark.storage.memoryFraction` property, as shown here:

```
$ spark-shell --conf spark.storage.memoryFraction=0.2
```

ApplicationMaster Memory Issues

When a client launches an application, a single ApplicationMaster (AM) container is launched first, with the ID 000001 for the container. For jobs that are crunching through large amounts of data, the AM container needs to be sized adequately. The default size of 1GB is usually enough, but it is not going to be so for every application.

When the ApplicationMaster reaches the limits of its memory, the application will fail, as shown here:

```
Application application_1424873694018_3023 failed 2 times due to AM Container for
appattempt_1424873694018_3023_000002 exited with exitCode: 143 due to: Container
[pid=25108,containerID=container_1424873694018_3023_02_000001] is running beyond
physical memory limits. Current usage: 1.0 GB of 1 GB physical memory used; 1.5 GB
of 2.1 GB virtual memory used. Killing container.

Container killed on request. Exit code is 143

Container exited with a non-zero exit code 143

.Failing this attempt.. Failing the application.
```

You need to raise the ApplicationMaster memory allocation to keep this error from recurring.

Job and Task IDs

The ResourceManager creates an application ID for each new application that's launched in the cluster. The format of the application ID is composed of the time when the ResourceManager started and an incrementing counter to uniquely identify the application, as shown here:

```
application_1410450250506_0003
```

In this case the ResourceManager started at the time specified by the timestamp 1410450250506. This application naming format means that all applications started after the startup of the ResourceManager will have a common first part and are differentiated by the incrementing counter at the end, such as _0003, _0004 and so on.

The job ID corresponds to the application ID and is generated by replacing the `application` prefix with the `job` prefix, as shown here:

```
job_1410450250506_0003
```

Each job contains multiple mapper and reducer tasks. Each of those tasks gets its own ID, which follows the same pattern as the job ID, with `task` replacing `job` at the beginning and a unique number for the specified task at the end (`m` represents mappers and `r` represents reducer tasks). Here are two examples, one for a mapper task and the other for a reducer task.

```
task_1410450250506_0003_m_000003
task_1410450250506_0003_r_000001
```

Since a task may be executed more than once due to a task failure or because the task was preempted, each task attempt gets its own ID, as shown here:

```
attempt_1410450250506_0003_m_000003_0
```

Handling Different Types of Failures

It's not uncommon for various cluster services to fail on occasion. Following is a quick review of how Hadoop handles failures pertaining to various components in the Hadoop architecture.

Handling Daemon Failures

Key services such as the NameNode or the ResourceManager are liable to crash at times. Hadoop contains excellent failure-handling capabilities to deal with any type of failure in the system. The key thing to remember is that Hadoop is highly fault reliant—both YARN and HDFS will continue their processing unimpeded when one or more disks go bad, or even one or more servers go down. This is the beauty of the built-in data replication capability of Hadoop.

Starting Failures for Hadoop Daemons

Once in a while you may run into a problem where you are unable to start up a DataNode or the NameNode(s). You can check whether the DataNodes and the NameNodes are running with the Linux jps command, as shown here:

```
$ jps
10561 Jps
20605 NameNode
17176 DataNode
18521 ResourceManager
19625 NodeManager
18424 JobHistoryServer
```

On confirming that the DataNode (or NameNode) isn't running, check whether any other programs are using the ports that were assigned to the DataNodes or NameNodes.

```
sudo netstat -tulpn | grep :8040
sudo netstat -tulpn | grep :8042
sudo netstat -tulpn | grep :50070
sudo netstat -tulpn | grep :50075
```

If you notice any programs grabbing the ports that the DataNodes need, you must kill those processes. You can get the PID (process ID) with the first command shown here and kill it with the second command:

```
# sudo netstat -tulpn | grep :port
# sudo kill 12345
```

Note that an overwhelming majority of failed DataNodes are due to disk failure. Network issues account for most of the remaining failures.

NameNode Crashes

When the NameNode process crashes or the server hosting the NameNode process becomes unavailable, the cluster also becomes unavailable, unless you've configured

NameNode high availability. Otherwise, you must fix the problem and restart the NameNode on the same server or move the NameNode service to a different node and start it from there.

ResourceManager Crashes

Running applications continue to run even in the absence of the ResourceManager daemon. You can't, however, submit new jobs. Once you restart the ResourceManager, there's no need to resubmit all your jobs. YARN provides built-in fault tolerance.

Since you can't run any applications in your cluster without the ResourceManager, you must configure high availability for it by running a pair of ResourceManagers per cluster, one in the active and the other in the standby mode.

ApplicationMaster Crashes

When the ApplicationMaster for an application crashes, the ResourceManager will start it from the point where it had stopped functioning. The ResourceManager will reattempt the application two times by default. You have the option of setting job recovery for the ApplicationMaster, whereby it only reruns the incomplete tasks after it restarts, following a failure. If job recovery is set to false, the ApplicationMaster reruns all tasks upon its restart.

NodeManager Failures

If the NodeManager fails, the ResourceManager removes it from the list of active NodeManagers. The ApplicationMaster will mark all jobs running on that node as failed tasks. The job itself isn't considered a failure—tasks that are declared as failed on a specific node are scheduled to run on other nodes in the cluster.

Task and Job Failures

If a container running a map or reduce task fails, by default the ApplicationMaster will reattempt the task four times before marking the task as a failed task.

Configuring the Number of Retries for Failed Map Tasks

Unlike a regular Java or SQL program, a failed map task doesn't mean that the task remains in the failed state; Hadoop likes to retry a failed map task. Let's say a map task fails due to a node exhausting all of its local directories. When the ResourceManager retries the job, more than likely, the task will be assigned to a different node, and it's very likely to succeed.

You can configure the maximum number of times the ResourceManager should retry a failed map task by setting the `mapred.map.max.attempts` parameter, as shown here:

```
<property>
  <name>mapred.map.max.attempts</name>
  <value>4</value>
</property>
```

If the task fails even after four retries, the ResourceManager will finally declare the task as failed. In this case the value for the `mapred.map.max.attempts` parameter is set to 4, and its default value is 2.

Retrying Jobs After a Failure

You can configure multiple attempts to run an application following a job failure. The parameter mapreduce.am.max-attempts lets you set the maximum number of application settings. Note that this is an application-specific setting and thus must be set at the application level and not at the cluster level.

The default value for the mapreduce.am.max-attempts parameter is 2, meaning the ResourceManager will retry the start of the ApplicationMaster at least once for every application.

Configuring Work Preserving Recovery for YARN Components

When a ResourceManager or a NodeManager restarts, you could potentially lose in-flight work. To prevent this, you use the **work preserving recovery** feature for both the ResourceManager and the NodeManager. ResourceManager high availability is a prerequisite for enabling the work preserving recovery feature.

In order to enable work preserving recovery, set the value of the yarn-resourcemanager .work-preserving-recovery.enabled parameter and the yarn.nodemanager.recovery .enabled parameter to true in the yarn-site.xml file.

```
<property>
   <name>yarn.resourcemanager.work-preserving-recovery.enabled</true>
    <value>true</value>
</property>

<property>
   <name>yarn.nodemanager.recovery.enabled</true>
    <value>true</value>
</property>
```

In addition, for the NodeManager recovery enablement, you must configure a directory on the local file system for storing the state information. You do this with the yarn. nodemanager.recovery.dir parameter, whose default value is ${hadoop.tmp.dir}/ yarn-nm-recovery. Since you don't want to store things on the /tmp directory, assign a different location for this directory. Finally, you must also set the yarn.nodemanager .address parameter to an address with a specific port number, such as 0.0.0.0:12345 instead of using an ephemeral port. By default, the NodeManager RPC server uses the ephemeral port 0, which means it can use a different port after a restart, thus keeping clients from connecting to it after a NodeManager restart.

Troubleshooting Spark Jobs

Spark has become the preeminent processing framework in the Hadoop environment. Therefore, it's appropriate that I spend a bit of time going over some important Spark job troubleshooting issues.

Spark can automatically handle failed tasks, and you can also kill Spark jobs. You can also specify the maximum number of attempts and the maximum number of failures for a job.

Spark's Fault Tolerance Mechanism

Spark automatically reexecutes failed tasks and even slow-running tasks. If one of the worker machines goes down while working on transforming an RDD, Spark will relaunch the task on a different server. The same goes when a task is taking way too long to complete. Spark also recomputes any partitions that were removed from the cache during memory pressure by relying on the RDD's lineage.

Killing Spark Jobs

You can kill jobs from Spark's web UI. The `spark.ui.killEnabled` property determines whether you can kill a job from the UI—the default is `true`.

If you're running a job in the yarn-cluster mode, YARN restarts the driver after a failure without killing the executors. In the client mode, however, YARN will automatically kill all the executors when the driver is killed.

Maximum Attempts for a Job

You can specify the maximum number of attempts that'll be made to submit an application through the `spark.yarn.maxAppAttempts` property. However, since you're running Spark on YARN, make sure that the value for this property doesn't exceed the maximum number of attempts in YARN, which is configured by the `yarn.nodemanager.am.max-attempts` property in the yarn-site.xml file.

You can configure the maximum number of executor failures before the Spark application is failed for good by setting the `spark.yarn.max.executor.failures` property. The default value for this parameter is `numExecutors` *2, with a minimum of three failures.

Maximum Failures per Job

You can configure the number of individual task failures before Spark gives up on a job through the `spark.taskmaxFailures` configuration property. The default value for this parameter is 4.

Debugging Spark Applications

As with MapReduce jobs, how you access the Spark logs depends on whether you've configured log aggregation.

Viewing Logs with Log Aggregation

If you've enabled log aggregation (through the `yarn.log-aggregation-enable`), the logs generated by all the executor containers are copied to HDFS—they're also deleted immediately from the local servers. There are several ways in which you can access Spark logs, as I explain here.

You can view the job logs from the command line with the yarn command, which I explained in Chapter 17, as shown here:

```
yarn logs -applicationId <app_ID>
```

This command will print the contents of all the log files from all the containers for a Spark job.

Viewing the Logs from HDFS

Alternatively, you can view the container logs in HDFS, either through the HDFS shell or the API. You can find the directory where the logs are stored by checking the configuration settings for the following two parameters:

```
yarn.nodemanager.remote-app-log-dir
yarn.nodemanager.remote-app-log-dir-suffix
```

Viewing the Logs from the Spark Web UI

You can also view Spark job logs from the Executors tab in the Spark web UI. For this to work, you must run the Spark History Server and the MapReduce History Server. In addition, you must configure the `yarn.log.server.url` property in the yarn-site.xml file.

When you reach for the Spark job logs from the Spark web UI, the URL for the Spark History Server UI redirects you to the MapReduce History Server and shows the aggregated logs.

Viewing Logs When Log Aggregation Is Not Enabled

When you haven't turned on log aggregation, YARN stores the Spark job logs locally in each machine. The exact location is specified by the `yarn-app-logs-dir` parameter in the yarn-site.xml file.

In order to view the logs for an executor, you must go to the server that stores the container's logs for that executor under the directory specified by the `yarn-app-logs-dir` parameter. As with MapReduce logs, the log files are organized into subdirectories named after the application ID and the container ID.

You can also view the unaggregated Spark logs on the Spark web UI (Executors tab), but you don't need to run the MapReduce History Server in that case.

Reviewing the Launch Environment

When dealing with certain problems, such as the debugging of class path problems, you can access the application cache on the directories specified by the `yarn.nodemanager.local-dirs` property on the nodes where the containers were launched. The application cache includes the launch script, the JAR files and the environment variables used during the container launch.

Summary

Here's what you learned in this chapter:

- Space-related problems could be alleviated by knowing how to configure key configuration parameters such as `yarn.nodemanager.disk-health-checker.min-healthy-disks` and `yarn.nodemanager.disk-health-checker.max-disk-utilization-per-disk-percentage`.
- You can configure YARN's work preserving recovery feature for both the ResourceManager and the NodeManager to save in-flight work following the restart of the ResourceManager or a NodeManager.
- Understanding JVM garbage collection is critical to good application performance. Consider using the newer garbage collection strategies such as G1GC.

A

Installing VirtualBox and Linux and Cloning the Virtual Machines

You can install the test cluster discussed in Chapter 4, "Planning for and Creating a Fully Distributed Cluster," on a laptop, a desktop or a server. The steps are the same regardless of the machine you use. As I mentioned in Chapter 4, I used Oracle Enterprise Linux for running my three-node cluster. However, you can use Red Hat Linux, CentOS, Fedora, Ubuntu, or any other Linux distribution you wish. Everything works either exactly the same way or with very minor differences.

Please note that while the installation steps are for a specific version of Linux and VirtualBox, you don't have to use the same release I show here. A more recent release should work pretty much the same way as shown here, as the procedures don't change from release to release. You can search the Internet for full-blown examples of the installation of both VirtualBox and Linux, and there are several of those, with screenshots for every step.

You can break down the installation process into the following steps:

1. Install Oracle VirtualBox.
2. Install Oracle Enterprise Linux on a virtual server.
3. Install Hadoop 2.6.0 on the virtual server.
4. Configure Hadoop 2.6.0 on the virtual server.
5. Clone the initial virtual server to create the other two virtual servers.

I describe steps 1, 2 and 5 in this appendix. Steps 3 and 4 deal with the installation and configuration of Hadoop, which is covered in detail in Chapter 3, "Creating and Configuring a Simple Hadoop 2 Cluster," and Chapter 4. (Chapter 3 shows the installation and preliminary configuration, and Chapter 4 shows more configuration details. The following sections then, describe how to do the following:

- Install Oracle VirtualBox
- Install Oracle Enterprise Linux
- Clone the Linux server (after finishing the installation and configuration of Hadoop on this server)

Installing Oracle VirtualBox

You can install VirtualBox by first downloading the software from `https://www.virtualbox.org/wiki/Downloads`.

From the list of available VirtualBox binaries, select the latest version, which may or may not be the one I used in this case. Note that I'm setting up VirtualBox on a machine running Windows with 16GB of RAM.

1. Run the following command to install VirtualBox.

   ```
   # rpm -Uvh VirtualBox-4.2-4.2.6_82870_fedora17-1.x86_64.rpm
   ```

2. Start VirtualBox and click New on the toolbar. Enter a name for your new VM, and select Linux for Type and Oracle (64 bit) for Version. Click Next.
3. In the Memory Size page, select 4096 as the RAM size. Click Next.
4. In the Hard Drive page, choose the default action of Create a virtual hard drive now, and click Create.
5. In the Hard Drive Type page, accept the default hard drive type (VDI), and click Next.
6. In the Storage on Physical Hard Drive page, accept the Dynamically allocated option for storage, and click Next.
7. In the File location and Size page, select the size of the hard drive. You can set it at 20GB, but if you have tons of free space on your hard drive, set it at a much higher value so you can play with huge datasets! Click Create.
8. Click the Network link in the new VM's main page, which will appear at this point. Click Next.
9. In the Network page, make sure Adapter 1 is enabled and is set to Bridged Adapter. Click OK.
10. In the System page, move Hard Disk to the top of the boot order, and also uncheck the Floppy option. Click OK.

At this point, your VM is ready and functional. Start up the VM, so you can install Linux on it.

Installing Oracle Enterprise Linux

In this example, I show how to download and install Oracle Enterprise Linux (OEL). OEL is essentially the same as Red Hat Enterprise Linux (RHEL) and is also similar to CentOS and Fedora. You can install any of these distributions by following the steps I show here.

1. Download Oracle Enterprise Linux from the following location and save the ISO to a directory on the server where VirtualBox is running:

   `https://edelivery.oracle.com/`

   This URL will take you to the Oracle Software Delivery Cloud, where you can download Oracle software products. Please note that you'll need an user ID to log in, and you can create an account at no cost.
2. In VirtualBox, make sure your new VM is highlighted, and click Start.
3. On the Select start-up disk page, select the Oracle Linux OS image that you've downloaded. Click Start.
4. In the Welcome page, select Install or upgrade an existing system.
5. Use a guide from the internet such as the following to complete the installation of Linux:

   `https://oracle-base.com/articles/linux/oracle-linux-6-installation`

Cloning the Linux Server

Once you've created the first Linux server, you need to install and configure Hadoop as explained in Chapters 3 and 4. Once you are finished, clone the first VM to create the other two nodes, which will be part of your three-node Apache Hadoop cluster, similar to what I used in Chapter 4 and onwards in this book.

Follow these steps to clone the Linux server. You need to perform the steps twice to create the hadoop2 and hadoop3 servers.

1. In the VirtualBox Manager window, go to Machine > Clone to start the cloning process.
2. In the Clone a Virtual Machine page, choose a name for the virtual machine (hadoop2 first, and the next time, hadoop3). Click Next.
3. In the Clone Configuration page, select Full Clone, and click Clone.
4. Once the new server is cloned, start it up and log in as the root user. Edit the /etc/sysconfig/network file and set the `HOSTNAME` to the following:

   `HOSTNAME=hadoop2.localdomain` (for the second node)

   `HOSTNAME=hadoop3.localdomain` (for the third node)

5. Start the Network Connections (from System Preferences), and edit the eth0 interfaces to set a new IP address for the cloned server.
6. Reboot the server.
7. Once the cloned server is up, change its MAC address so it's different from the MAC address on the other nodes. Go to the Network Connections again, and edit the MAC address after clicking the Wired tab. All you need to do is change the MAC address of the first server just a little bit. For example, if the last two characters are 00, change them to 01. Make sure you write down the MAC address for this machine somewhere. Click Apply.
8. Shut down the cloned VM.
9. In the VirtualBox Manager, select the hadoop2 (and later, hadoop3) VM, and edit the Network settings. Under Adapter 1, type in the MAC address that you used in step 7.
10. Change the hostname by editing the /etc/hosts file and add the hostname you specified earlier.
11. Start the cloned VM.

As I mentioned earlier, you need to clone the original hadoop1 VM twice to get your three-node Hadoop cluster. Once you finish the cloning, start up all three servers and run a ping test to make sure the three nodes can talk to each other.

At this point, you're ready to perform the cluster configuration I've described in Chapter 4, starting with the section "How the Test Cluster Is Set Up."

Index

D

E

M

N

S

W

X

Y

Z